IT SEEMED LIKE A GOOD IDEA AT THE TIME

Book Ten of the Syndicated Cartoon **Stone Soup**

by
Jan Eliot

For Mary Ann —
Happy Reading!
Jan Eliot

FOUR PANEL PRESS

Eugene, Oregon

Published by Four Panel Press, P.O. Box 50032, Eugene, OR 97405.

Stone Soup® is distributed by Universal Uclick.

It Seemed Like a Good Idea at the Time copyright © 2014 by Jan Eliot. All rights reserved. Printed in China. No part of this book may be used or reproduced in any manner whatsoever without written permission except in the case of reprints in the context of reviews. For reprint permission contact Universal Uclick/Permissions, 1130 Walnut Street, Kansas City, MO 64106-2109.

ISBN-13: 978-0-9674102-9-6

Library of Congress Control Number: 2013955885

First Edition

www.stonesoupcartoons.com

A portion of the profits from this book will go to alleviate hunger through our local food bank, Food for Lane County.

For Ted, who puts up with me.

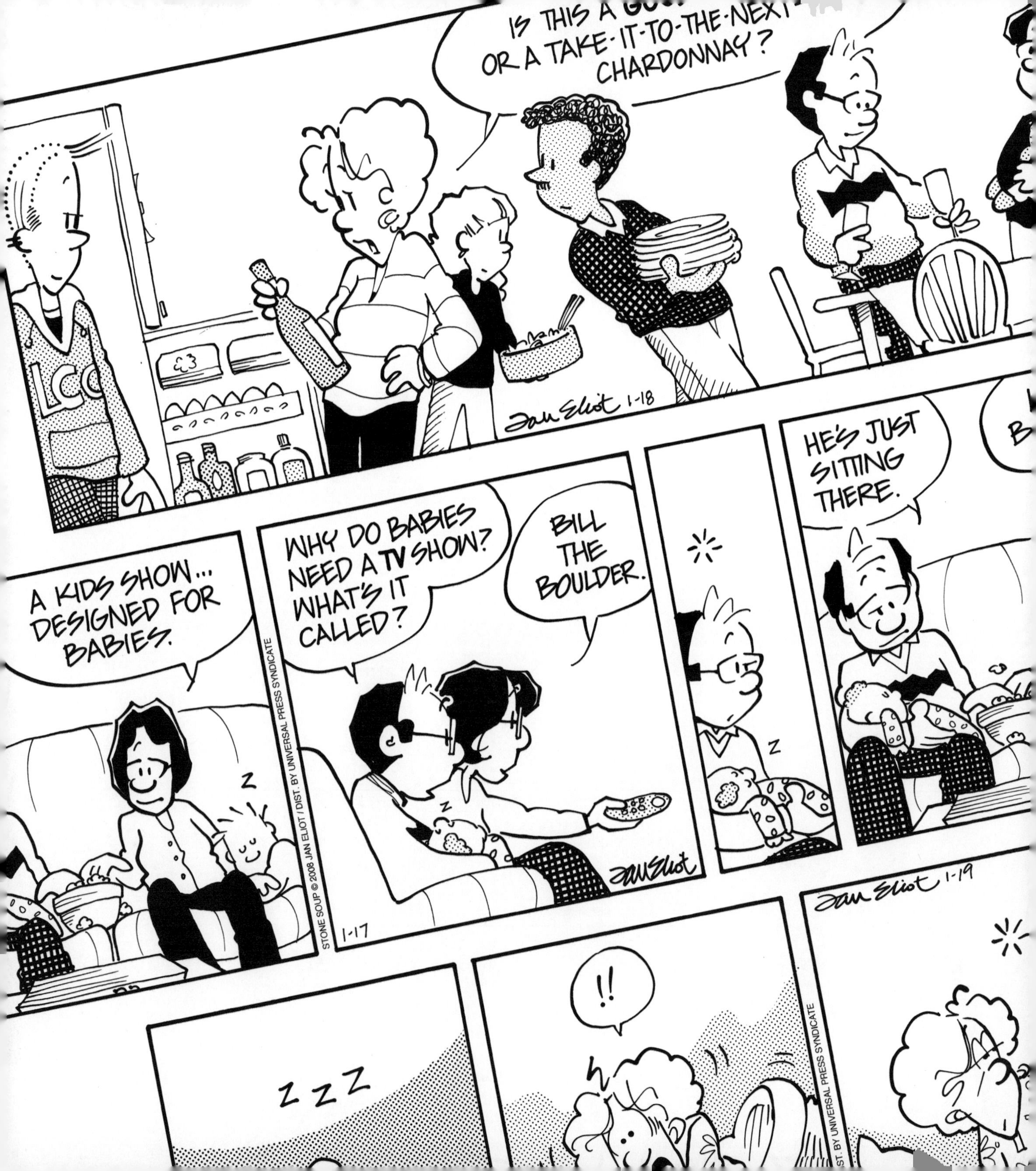
IS THIS A
OR A TAKE-IT-TO-THE-NEXT CHARDONNAY?
LCC
Jan Eliot 1-18
A KIDS SHOW... DESIGNED FOR BABIES.
Z
WHY DO BABIES NEED A TV SHOW? WHAT'S IT CALLED?
BILL THE BOULDER.
Z
Jan Eliot
STONE SOUP © 2008 JAN ELIOT / DIST. BY UNIVERSAL PRESS SYNDICATE
1-17
Z
HE'S JUST SITTING THERE.
Jan Eliot 1-19
Z Z Z
!!
ST. BY UNIVERSAL PRESS SYNDICATE

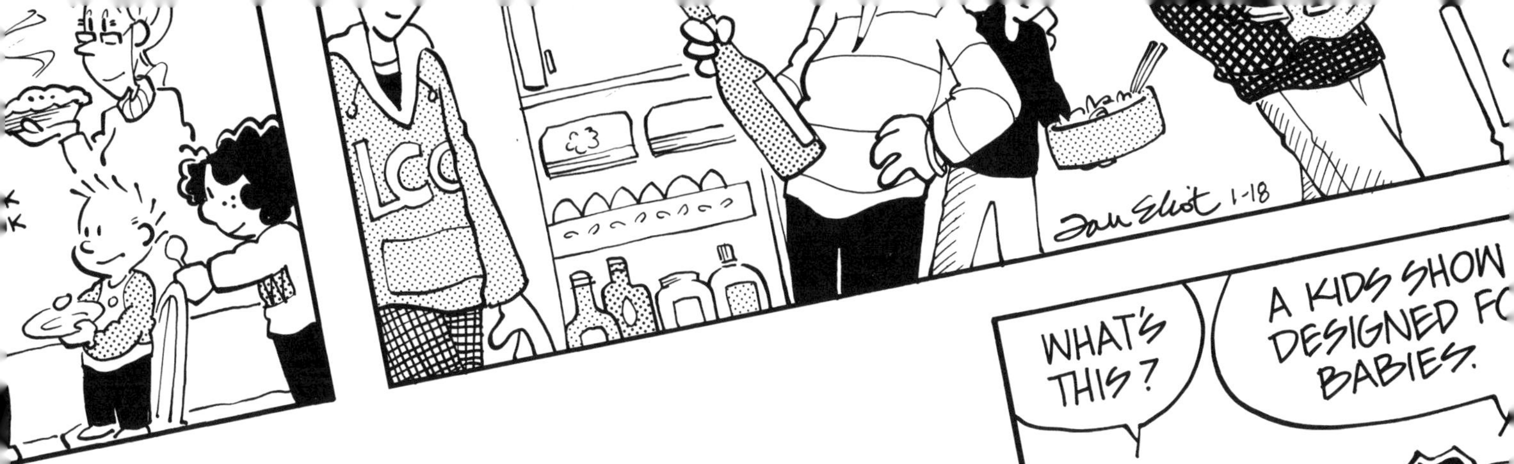

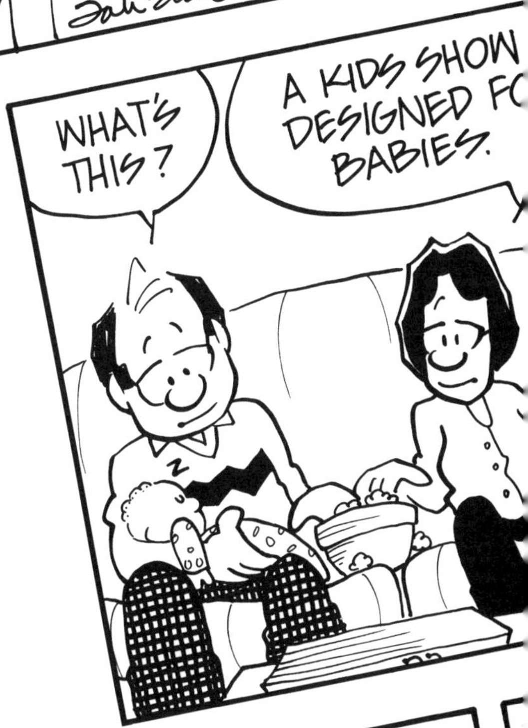
WHAT'S THIS?
A KIDS SHOW DESIGNED FO
BABIES.

Stone Soup is a well-loved comic strip about a big, rowdy, messy family. Maybe one something like yours. It is written with love and empathy for parents and kids everywhere.

Enjoy! Jan Eliot

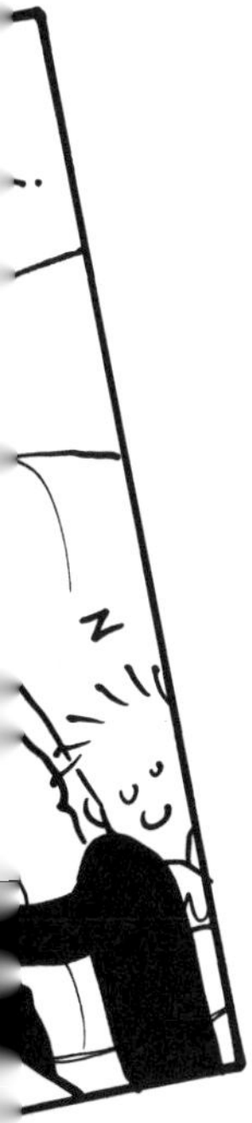

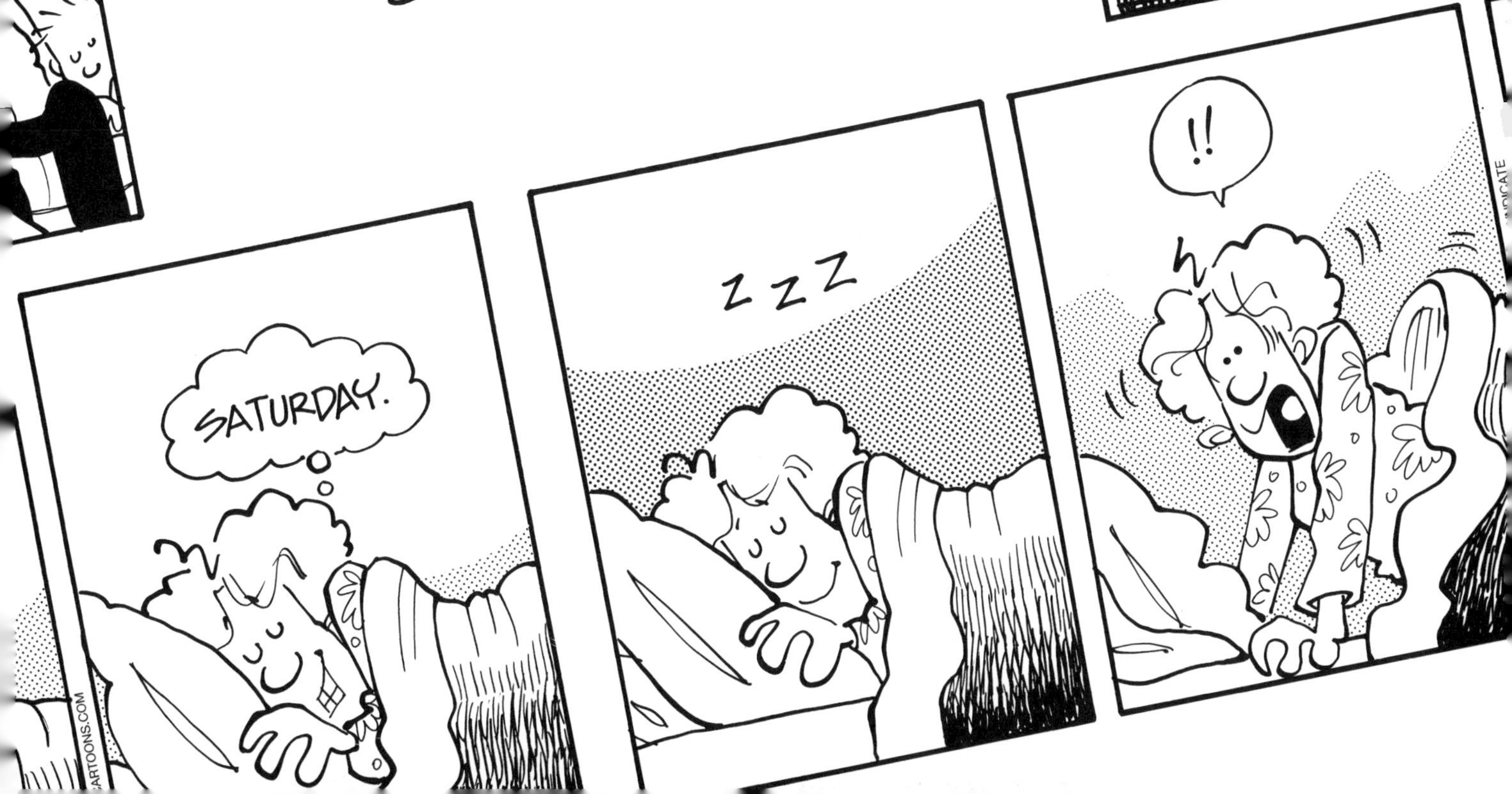
SATURDAY.
Z Z Z
!!

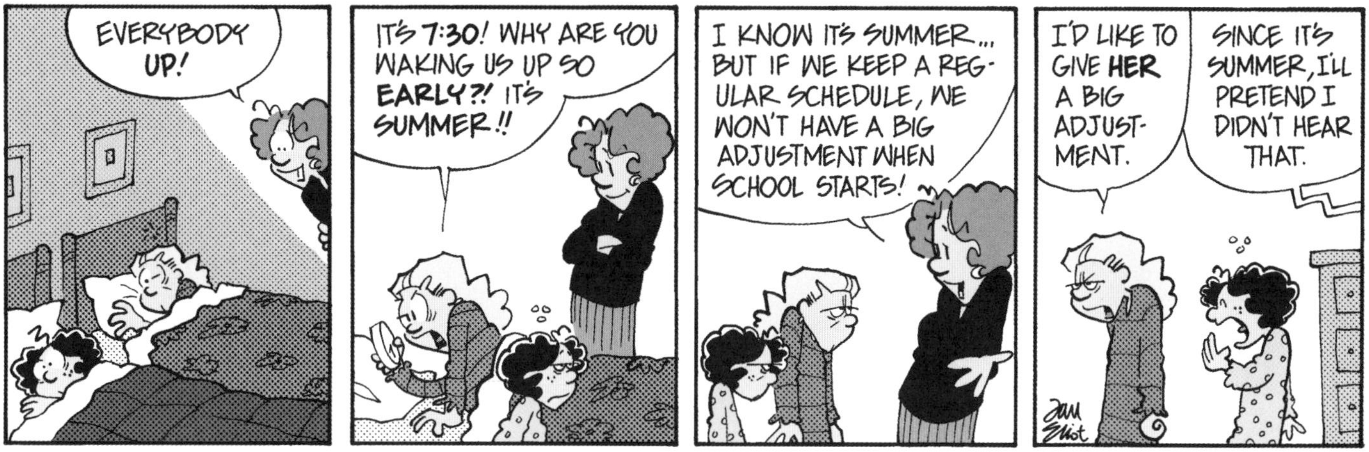
EVERYBODY **UP!**
IT'S **7:30!** WHY ARE YOU WAKING US UP SO **EARLY?!** IT'S **SUMMER!!**
I KNOW IT'S SUMMER... BUT IF WE KEEP A REGULAR SCHEDULE, WE WON'T HAVE A BIG ADJUSTMENT WHEN SCHOOL STARTS!
I'D LIKE TO GIVE **HER** A BIG ADJUSTMENT.
SINCE IT'S SUMMER, I'LL PRETEND I DIDN'T HEAR THAT.
JAN ELIOT

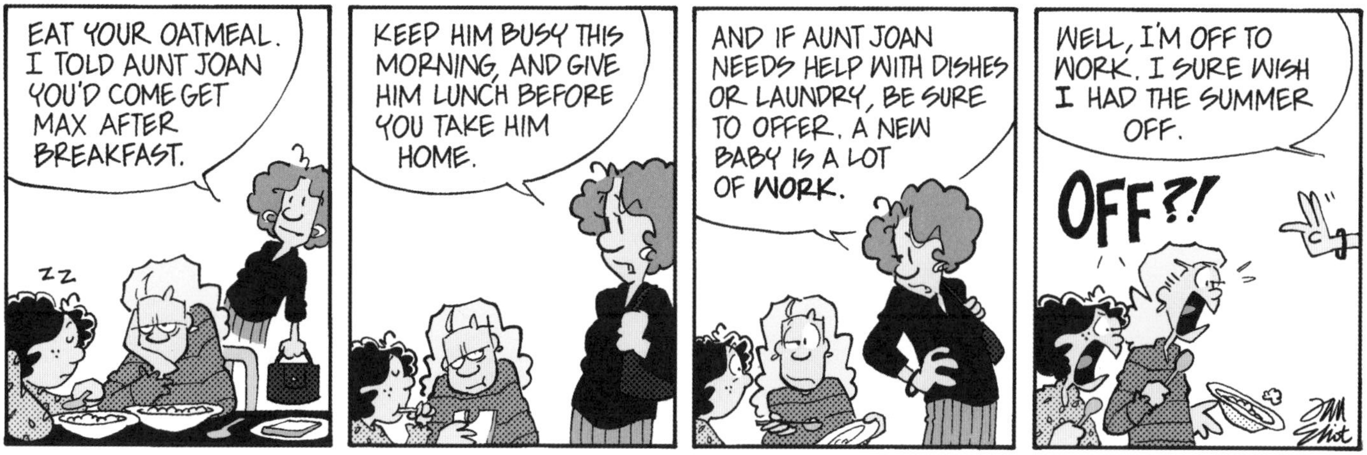
EAT YOUR OATMEAL. I TOLD AUNT JOAN YOU'D COME GET MAX AFTER BREAKFAST.
ZZ
KEEP HIM BUSY THIS MORNING, AND GIVE HIM LUNCH BEFORE YOU TAKE HIM HOME.
AND IF AUNT JOAN NEEDS HELP WITH DISHES OR LAUNDRY, BE SURE TO OFFER. A NEW BABY IS A LOT OF **WORK**.
WELL, I'M OFF TO WORK. I SURE WISH **I** HAD THE SUMMER OFF.
OFF?!
JAN ELIOT

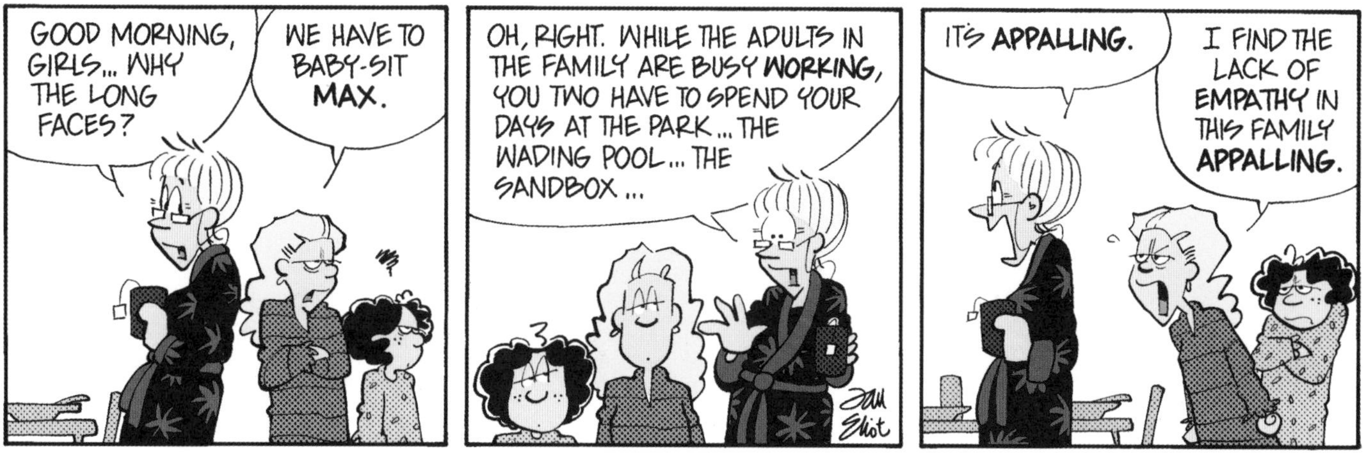
GOOD MORNING, GIRLS... WHY THE LONG FACES?
WE HAVE TO BABY-SIT **MAX**.
OH, RIGHT. WHILE THE ADULTS IN THE FAMILY ARE BUSY **WORKING**, YOU TWO HAVE TO SPEND YOUR DAYS AT THE PARK... THE WADING POOL... THE SANDBOX...
JAN ELIOT
IT'S **APPALLING**.
I FIND THE LACK OF **EMPATHY** IN THIS FAMILY **APPALLING**.

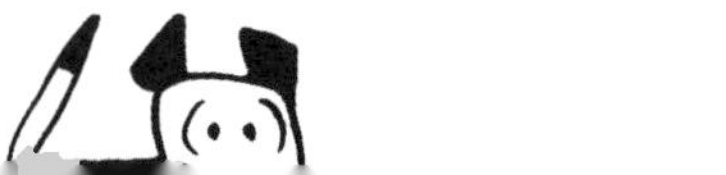

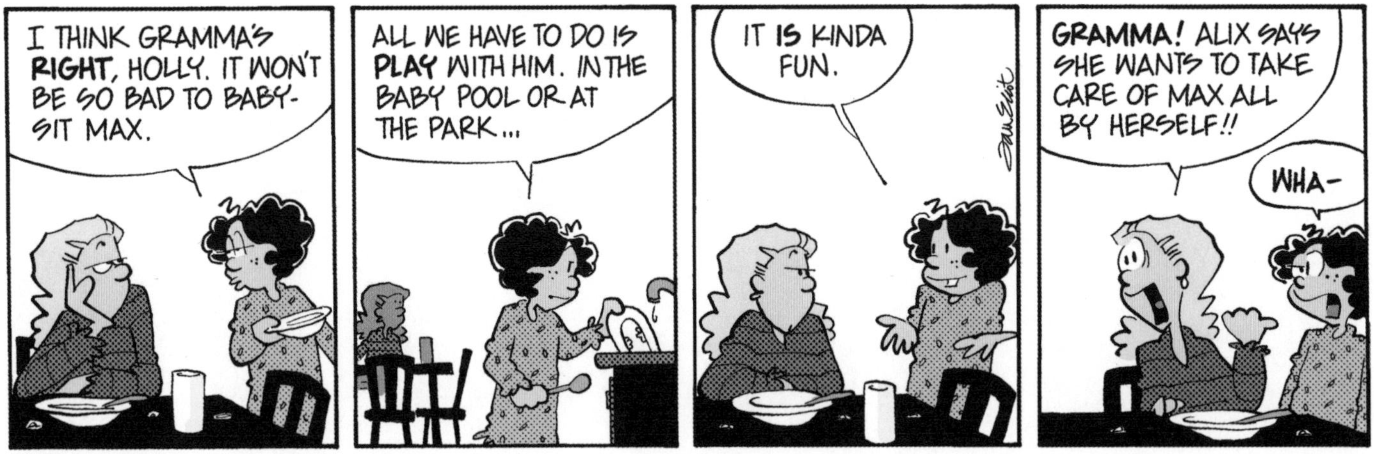
I THINK GRAMMA'S **RIGHT**, HOLLY. IT WON'T BE SO BAD TO BABY-SIT MAX.
ALL WE HAVE TO DO IS **PLAY** WITH HIM. IN THE BABY POOL OR AT THE PARK...
IT **IS** KINDA FUN.
GRAMMA! ALIX SAYS SHE WANTS TO TAKE CARE OF MAX ALL BY HERSELF!!
WHA-

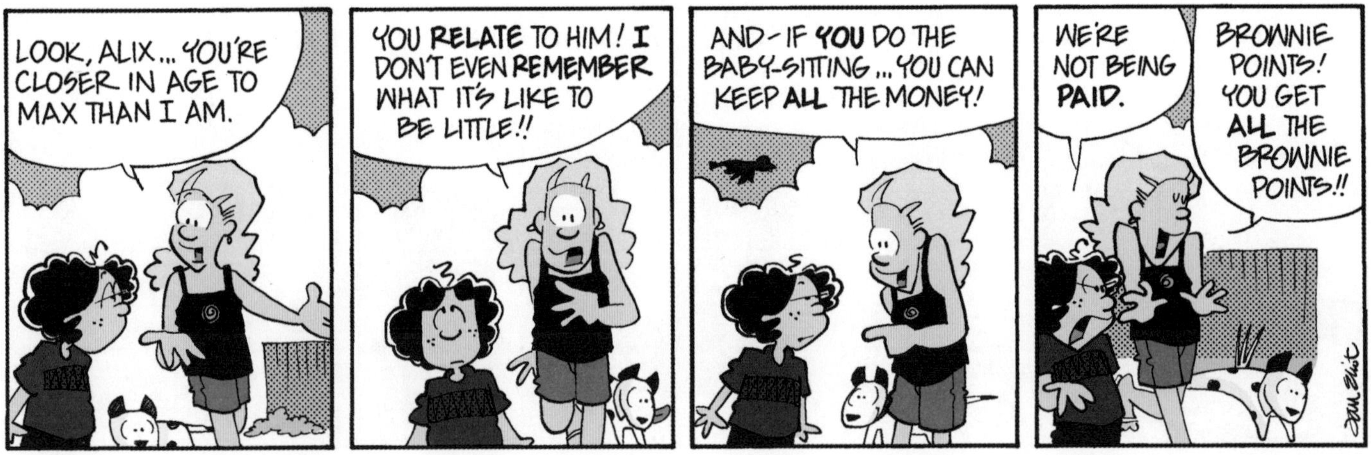
LOOK, ALIX... YOU'RE CLOSER IN AGE TO MAX THAN I AM.
YOU **RELATE** TO HIM! **I** DON'T EVEN **REMEMBER** WHAT IT'S LIKE TO BE LITTLE!!
AND- IF **YOU** DO THE BABY-SITTING... YOU CAN KEEP **ALL** THE MONEY!
WE'RE NOT BEING **PAID**.
BROWNIE POINTS! YOU GET **ALL** THE BROWNIE POINTS!!

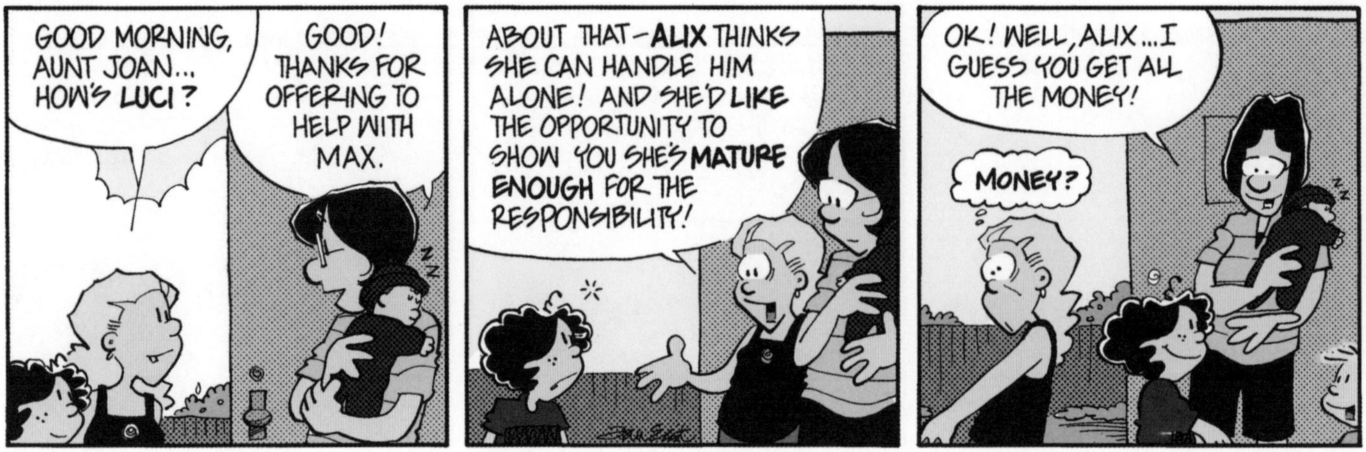
GOOD MORNING, AUNT JOAN... HOW'S **LUCI**?
GOOD! THANKS FOR OFFERING TO HELP WITH MAX.
ABOUT THAT- **ALIX** THINKS SHE CAN HANDLE HIM ALONE! AND SHE'D **LIKE** THE OPPORTUNITY TO SHOW YOU SHE'S **MATURE ENOUGH** FOR THE RESPONSIBILITY!
OK! WELL, ALIX... I GUESS YOU GET ALL THE MONEY!
MONEY?

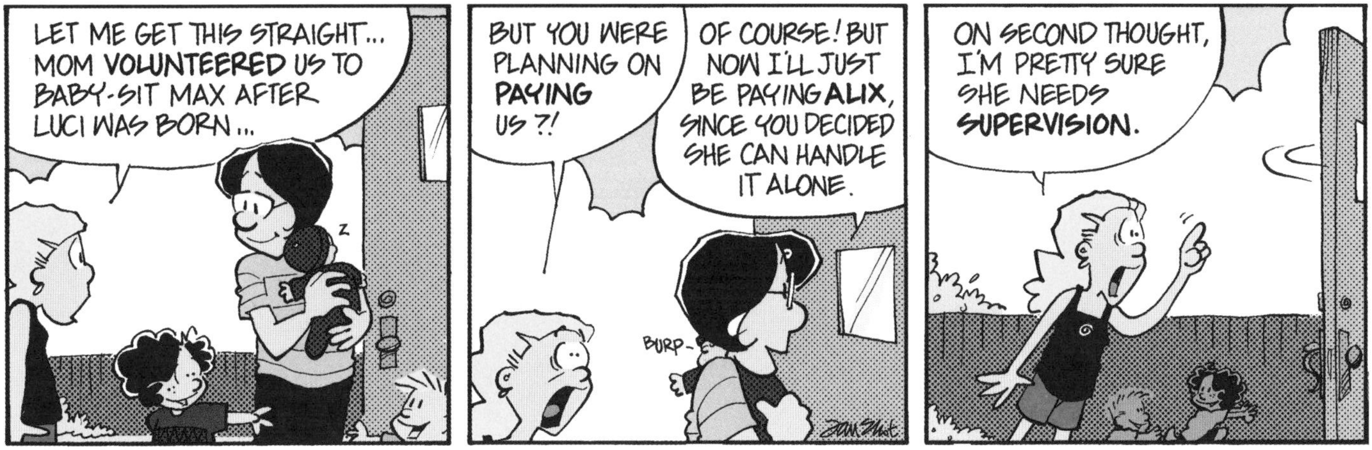
LET ME GET THIS STRAIGHT... MOM **VOLUNTEERED** US TO BABY-SIT MAX AFTER LUCI WAS BORN...
Z
BUT YOU WERE PLANNING ON **PAYING** US ?!
OF COURSE! BUT NOW I'LL JUST BE PAYING **ALIX**, SINCE YOU DECIDED SHE CAN HANDLE IT ALONE.
BURP-
ON SECOND THOUGHT, I'M PRETTY SURE SHE NEEDS **SUPERVISION**.

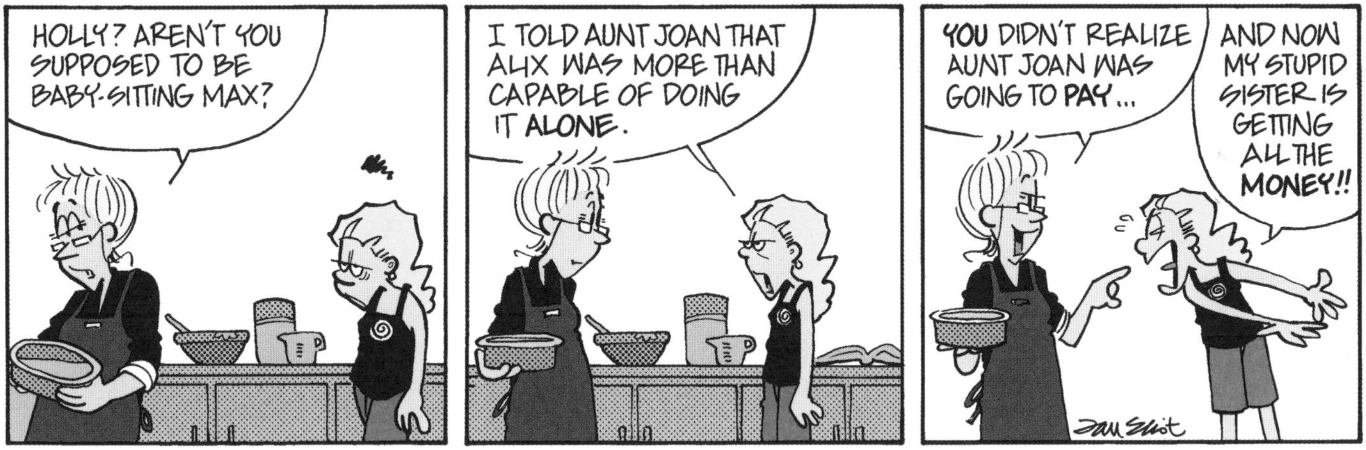
HOLLY? AREN'T YOU SUPPOSED TO BE BABY-SITTING MAX?
I TOLD AUNT JOAN THAT ALIX WAS MORE THAN CAPABLE OF DOING IT **ALONE**.
YOU DIDN'T REALIZE AUNT JOAN WAS GOING TO **PAY**...
AND NOW MY STUPID SISTER IS GETTING ALL THE **MONEY**!!

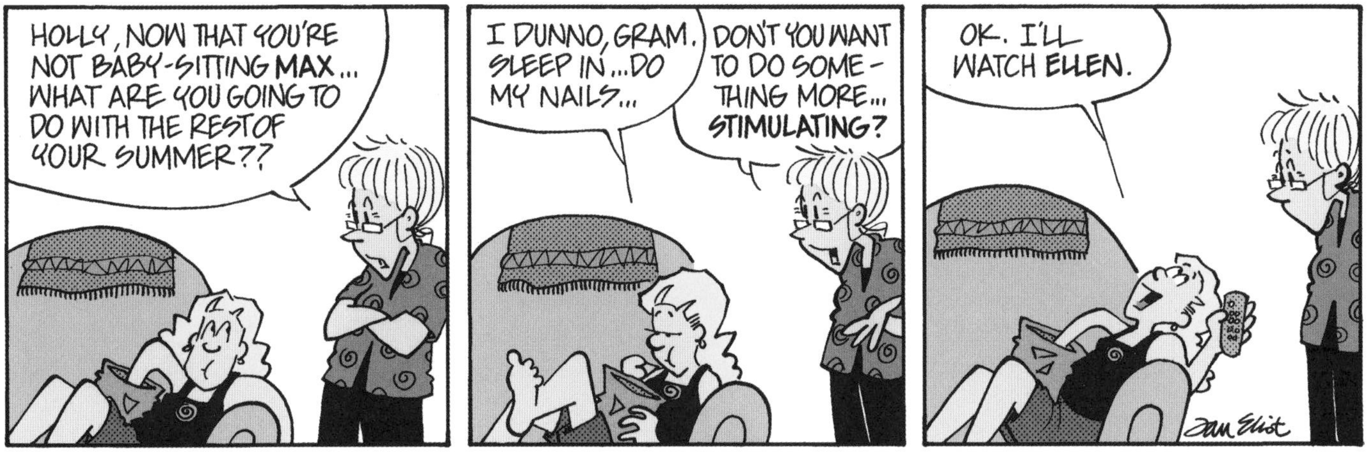
HOLLY, NOW THAT YOU'RE NOT BABY-SITTING **MAX**... WHAT ARE YOU GOING TO DO WITH THE REST OF YOUR SUMMER??
I DUNNO, GRAM. SLEEP IN...DO MY NAILS...
DON'T YOU WANT TO DO SOME-THING MORE... **STIMULATING**?
OK. I'LL WATCH **ELLEN**.

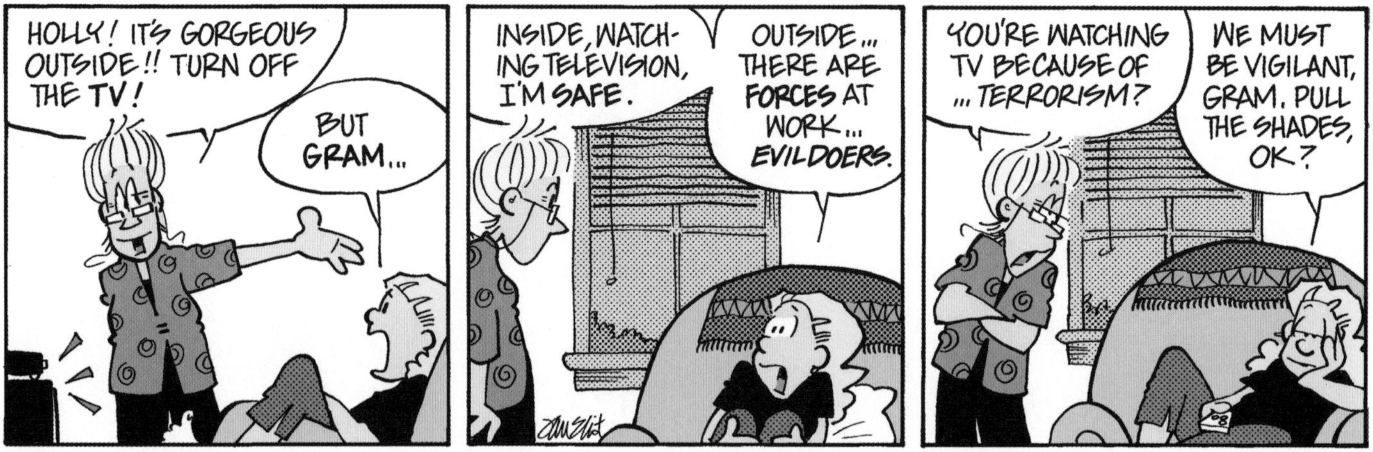
HOLLY! IT'S GORGEOUS OUTSIDE!! TURN OFF THE **TV**!
BUT **GRAM**...
INSIDE, WATCHING TELEVISION, I'M **SAFE**.
OUTSIDE... THERE ARE **FORCES** AT WORK... **EVILDOERS**.
YOU'RE WATCHING TV BECAUSE OF ...TERRORISM?
WE MUST BE VIGILANT, GRAM. PULL THE SHADES, OK?

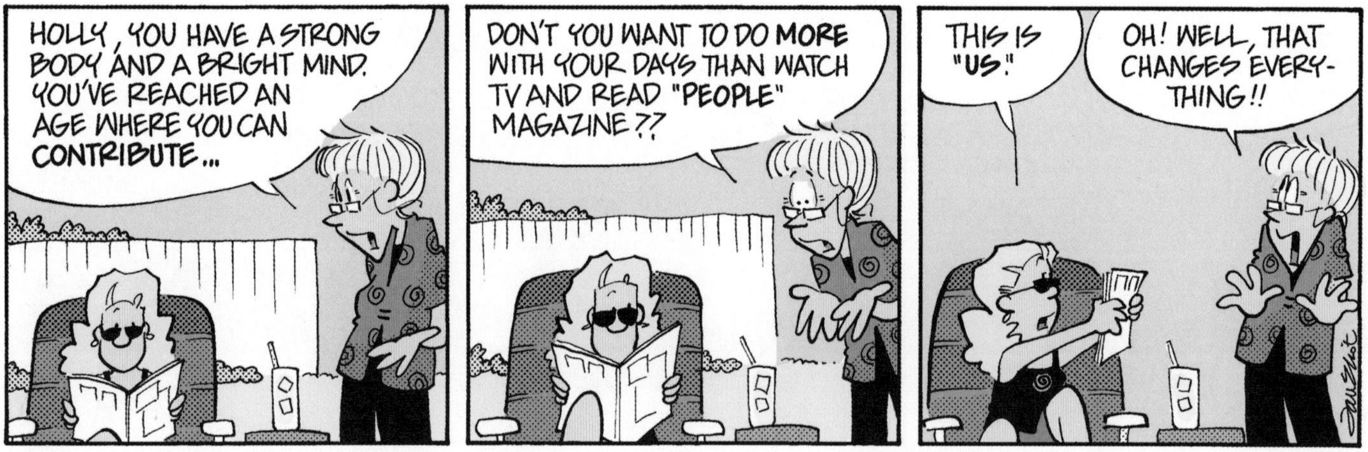
HOLLY, YOU HAVE A STRONG BODY AND A BRIGHT MIND. YOU'VE REACHED AN AGE WHERE YOU CAN **CONTRIBUTE**...
DON'T YOU WANT TO DO **MORE** WITH YOUR DAYS THAN WATCH TV AND READ "**PEOPLE**" MAGAZINE??
THIS IS "**US**."
OH! WELL, THAT CHANGES EVERYTHING!!

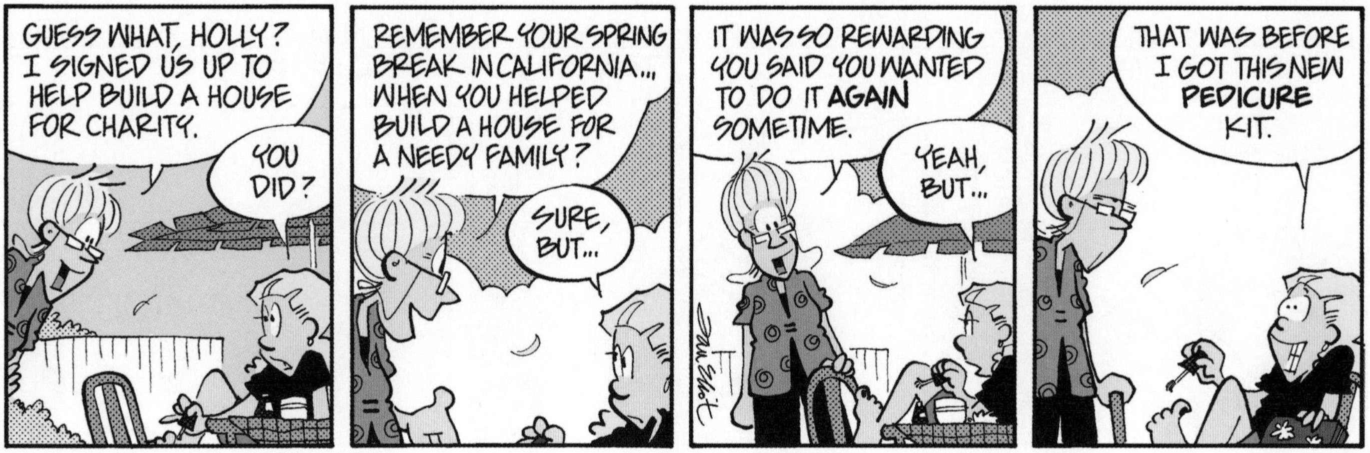
GUESS WHAT, HOLLY? I SIGNED US UP TO HELP BUILD A HOUSE FOR CHARITY.
YOU DID?
REMEMBER YOUR SPRING BREAK IN CALIFORNIA... WHEN YOU HELPED BUILD A HOUSE FOR A NEEDY FAMILY?
SURE, BUT...
IT WAS SO REWARDING YOU SAID YOU WANTED TO DO IT **AGAIN** SOMETIME.
YEAH, BUT...
THAT WAS BEFORE I GOT THIS NEW **PEDICURE** KIT.

Stone Soup

ANDY?
ANDY?
ANDY?!
WHAT?!
YOU'VE BEEN PLAYING THAT VIDEO GAME ALL MORNING! TURN IT OFF AND GO **DO** SOMETHING!
POW
CRASH
CHOOK
CHOOK
RIDE YOUR **SKATEBOARD**! PLAY YOUR **DRUMS**! CALL YOUR **FRIENDS**!!
CONNECT WITH THE **REAL WORLD**!
FINE.
WHAT'S THIS NEW GAME CALLED, ANYWAY?
ALIENATOR 4.
OK, SO... YOU DON'T SEE THE **IRONY** IN THAT??
I DON'T SEE **ANYTHING**. YOU MADE ME TURN IT **OFF**.

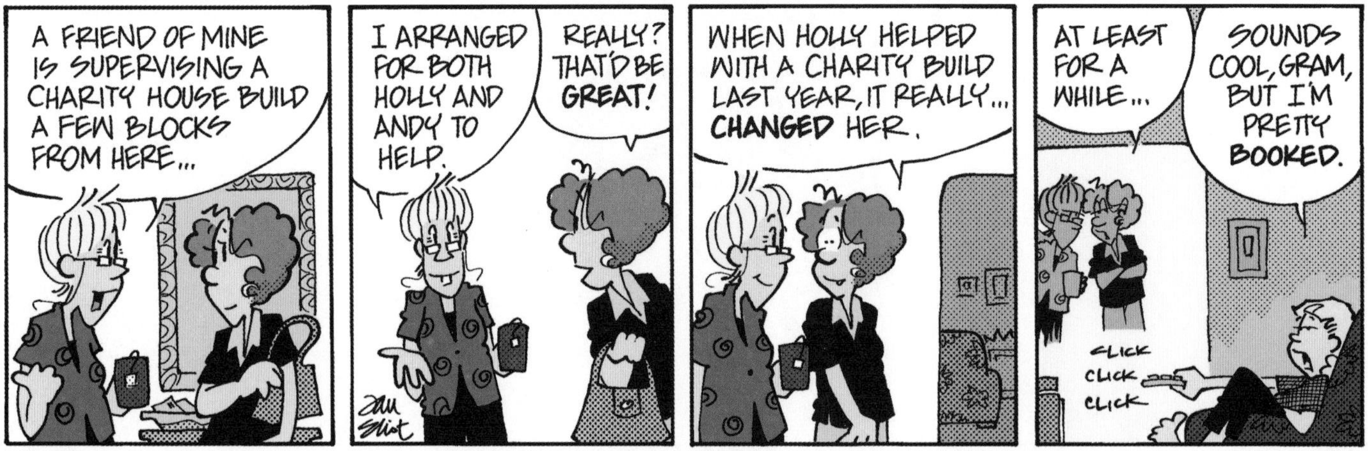
A FRIEND OF MINE IS SUPERVISING A CHARITY HOUSE BUILD A FEW BLOCKS FROM HERE...
I ARRANGED FOR BOTH HOLLY AND ANDY TO HELP.
REALLY? THAT'D BE GREAT!
WHEN HOLLY HELPED WITH A CHARITY BUILD LAST YEAR, IT REALLY... CHANGED HER.
AT LEAST FOR A WHILE...
SOUNDS COOL, GRAM, BUT I'M PRETTY BOOKED.
CLICK
CLICK
CLICK

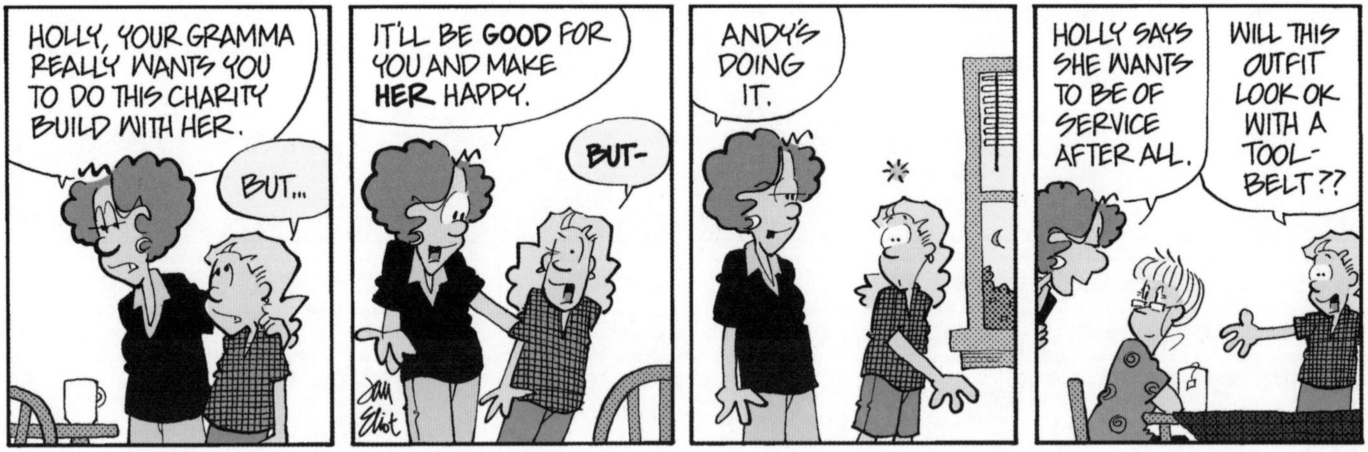
HOLLY, YOUR GRAMMA REALLY WANTS YOU TO DO THIS CHARITY BUILD WITH HER.
BUT...
IT'LL BE GOOD FOR YOU AND MAKE HER HAPPY.
BUT-
ANDY'S DOING IT.
HOLLY SAYS SHE WANTS TO BE OF SERVICE AFTER ALL.
WILL THIS OUTFIT LOOK OK WITH A TOOL-BELT??

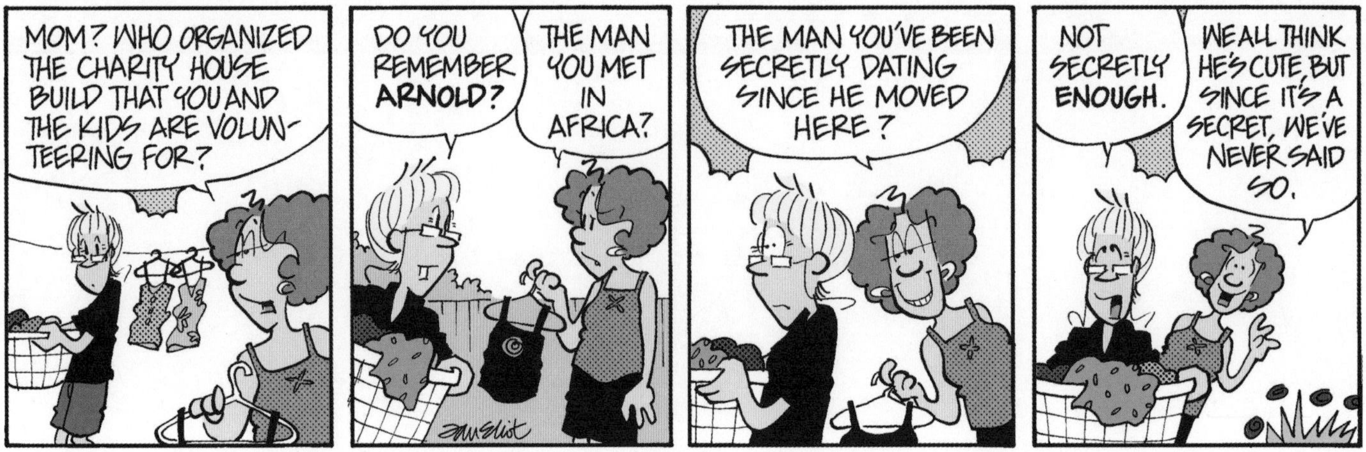
MOM? WHO ORGANIZED THE CHARITY HOUSE BUILD THAT YOU AND THE KIDS ARE VOLUN-TEERING FOR?
DO YOU REMEMBER ARNOLD?
THE MAN YOU MET IN AFRICA?
THE MAN YOU'VE BEEN SECRETLY DATING SINCE HE MOVED HERE?
NOT SECRETLY ENOUGH.
WE ALL THINK HE'S CUTE, BUT SINCE IT'S A SECRET, WE'VE NEVER SAID SO.

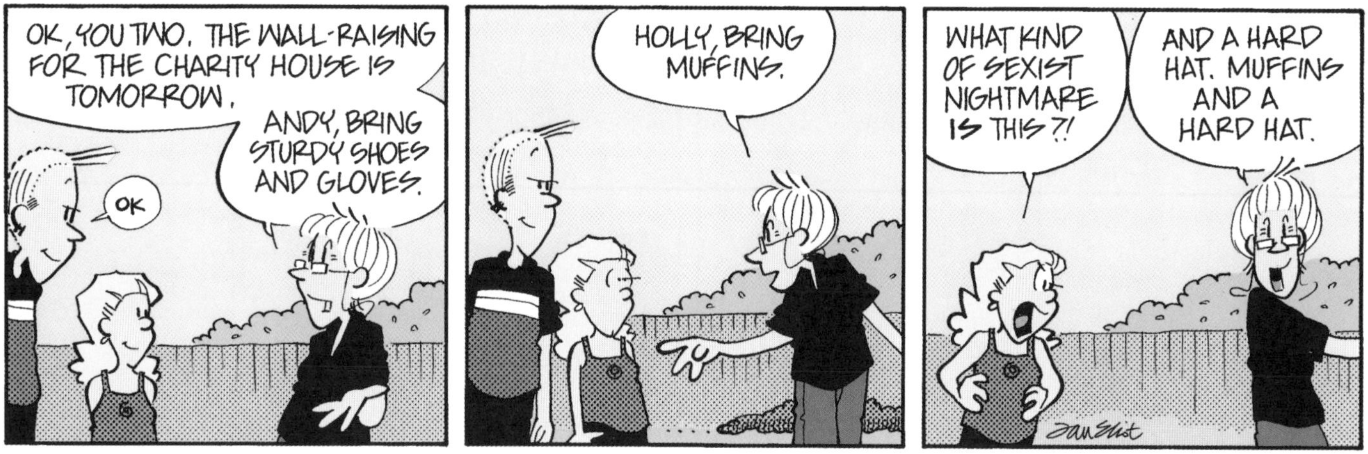
OK, YOU TWO. THE WALL-RAISING FOR THE CHARITY HOUSE IS TOMORROW.
OK
ANDY, BRING STURDY SHOES AND GLOVES.
HOLLY, BRING MUFFINS.
WHAT KIND OF SEXIST NIGHTMARE **IS** THIS?!
AND A HARD HAT. MUFFINS AND A HARD HAT.

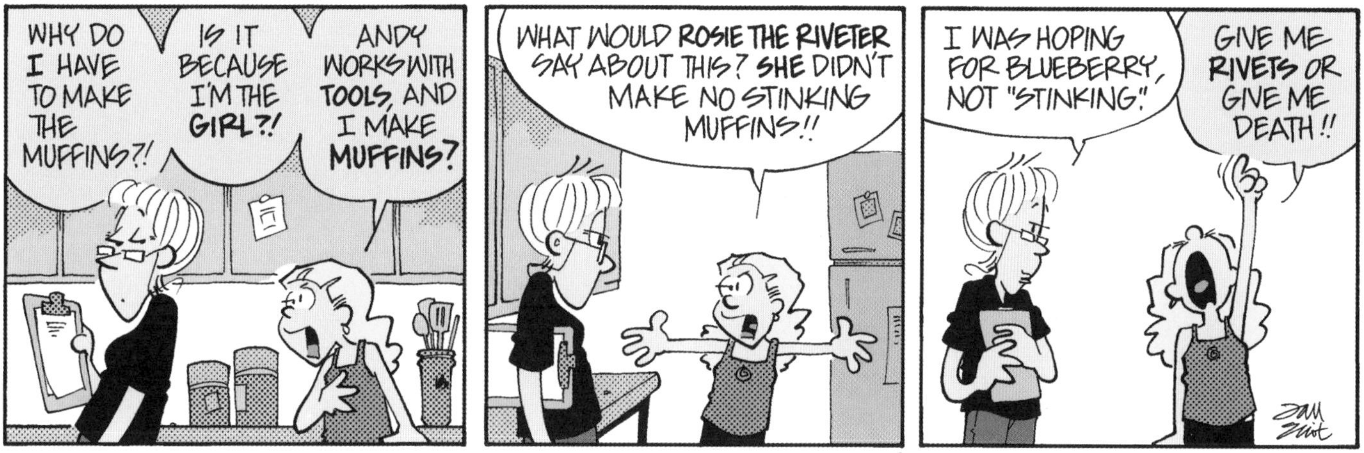
WHY DO **I** HAVE TO MAKE THE MUFFINS?!
IS IT BECAUSE I'M THE **GIRL**?!
ANDY WORKS WITH **TOOLS**, AND I MAKE **MUFFINS**?
WHAT WOULD **ROSIE THE RIVETER** SAY ABOUT THIS? **SHE** DIDN'T MAKE NO STINKING MUFFINS!!
I WAS HOPING FOR BLUEBERRY, NOT "STINKING."
GIVE ME **RIVETS** OR GIVE ME DEATH!!

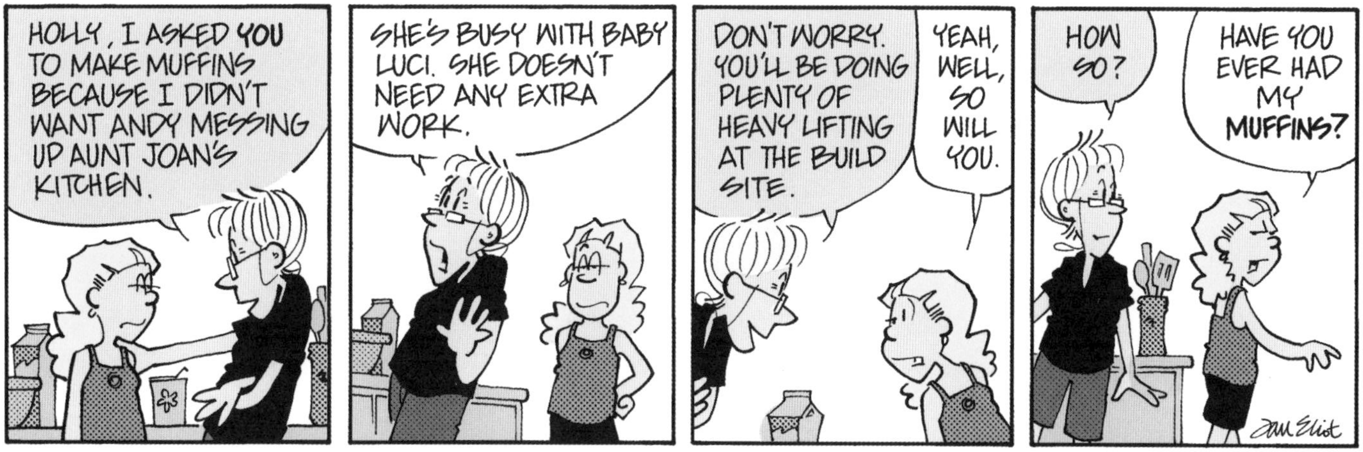
HOLLY, I ASKED **YOU** TO MAKE MUFFINS BECAUSE I DIDN'T WANT ANDY MESSING UP AUNT JOAN'S KITCHEN.
SHE'S BUSY WITH BABY LUCI. SHE DOESN'T NEED ANY EXTRA WORK.
DON'T WORRY. YOU'LL BE DOING PLENTY OF HEAVY LIFTING AT THE BUILD SITE.
YEAH, WELL, SO WILL YOU.
HOW SO?
HAVE YOU EVER HAD MY **MUFFINS**?

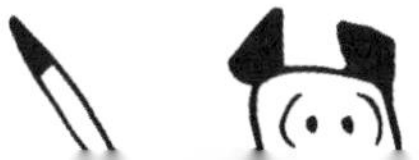

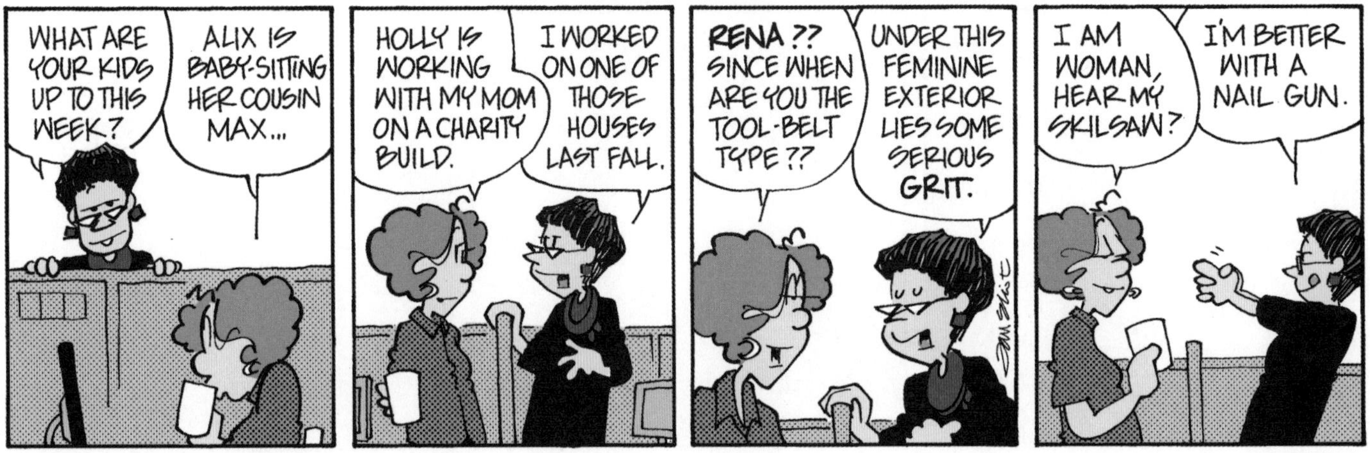
WHAT ARE YOUR KIDS UP TO THIS WEEK?
ALIX IS BABY-SITTING HER COUSIN MAX...
HOLLY IS WORKING WITH MY MOM ON A CHARITY BUILD.
I WORKED ON ONE OF THOSE HOUSES LAST FALL.
RENA?? SINCE WHEN ARE YOU THE TOOL-BELT TYPE??
UNDER THIS FEMININE EXTERIOR LIES SOME SERIOUS GRIT.
I AM WOMAN, HEAR MY SKILSAW?
I'M BETTER WITH A NAIL GUN.

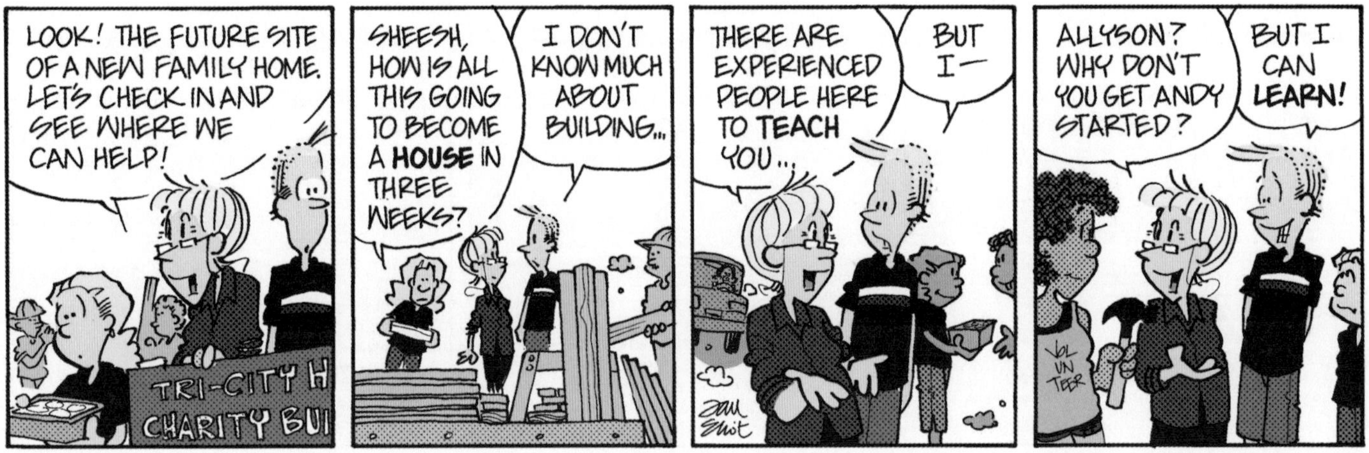
LOOK! THE FUTURE SITE OF A NEW FAMILY HOME. LET'S CHECK IN AND SEE WHERE WE CAN HELP!
TRI-CITY H
CHARITY BUI
SHEESH, HOW IS ALL THIS GOING TO BECOME A HOUSE IN THREE WEEKS?
I DON'T KNOW MUCH ABOUT BUILDING...
THERE ARE EXPERIENCED PEOPLE HERE TO TEACH YOU...
BUT I—
ALLYSON? WHY DON'T YOU GET ANDY STARTED?
BUT I CAN LEARN!
VOL UN TEER

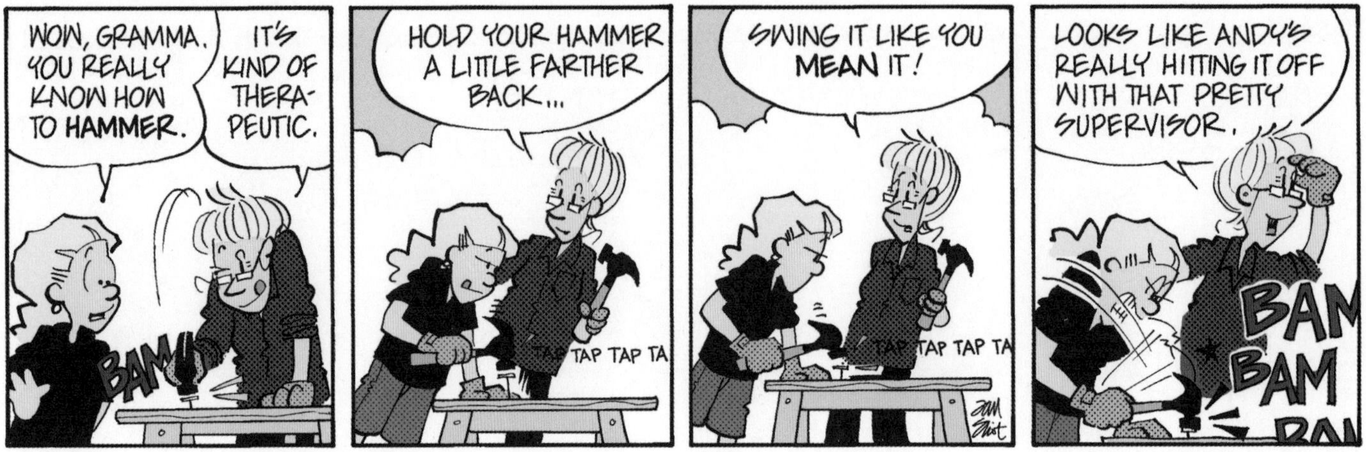
WOW, GRAMMA. YOU REALLY KNOW HOW TO HAMMER.
IT'S KIND OF THERA-PEUTIC.
BAM
HOLD YOUR HAMMER A LITTLE FARTHER BACK...
TAP TAP TAP TA
SWING IT LIKE YOU MEAN IT!
TAP TAP TAP TA
LOOKS LIKE ANDY'S REALLY HITTING IT OFF WITH THAT PRETTY SUPERVISOR.
BAM
BAM

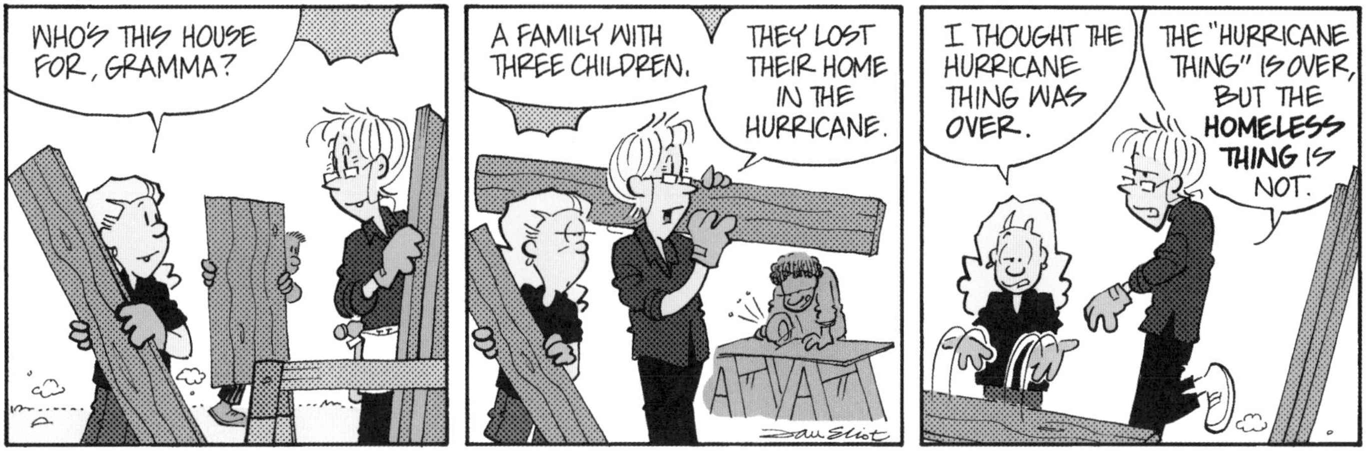
WHO'S THIS HOUSE FOR, GRAMMA?
A FAMILY WITH THREE CHILDREN.
THEY LOST THEIR HOME IN THE HURRICANE.
I THOUGHT THE HURRICANE THING WAS **OVER**.
THE "HURRICANE THING" IS OVER, BUT THE **HOMELESS THING** IS NOT.

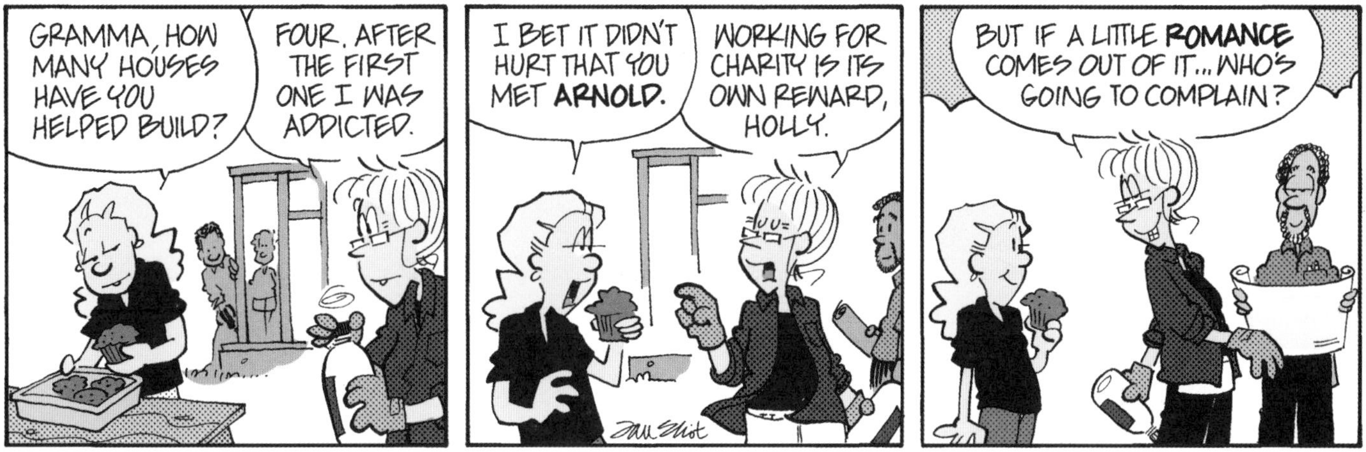
GRAMMA, HOW MANY HOUSES HAVE YOU HELPED BUILD?
FOUR. AFTER THE FIRST ONE I WAS ADDICTED.
I BET IT DIDN'T HURT THAT YOU MET **ARNOLD**.
WORKING FOR CHARITY IS ITS OWN REWARD, HOLLY.
BUT IF A LITTLE **ROMANCE** COMES OUT OF IT... WHO'S GOING TO COMPLAIN?

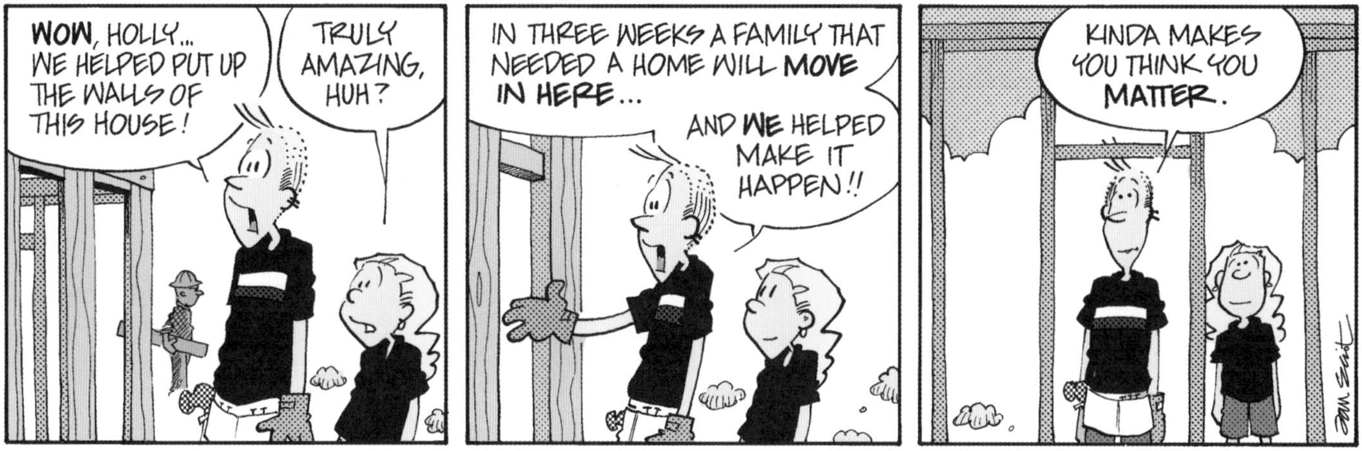
WOW, HOLLY... WE HELPED PUT UP THE WALLS OF THIS HOUSE!
TRULY AMAZING, HUH?
IN THREE WEEKS A FAMILY THAT NEEDED A HOME WILL **MOVE IN HERE**...
AND **WE** HELPED MAKE IT HAPPEN!!
KINDA MAKES YOU THINK YOU **MATTER**.

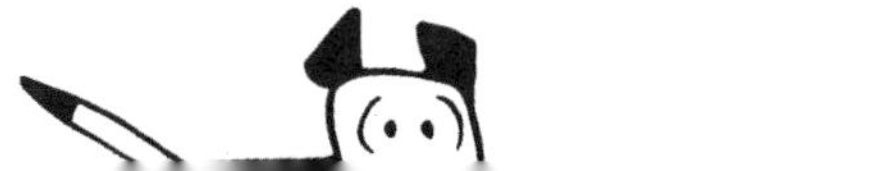

Stone Soup

LOOK AT THIS.
WHAT?
AN INVITATION TO MY 20TH CLASS REUNION.
ARE YOU GOING TO GO?
I DON'T KNOW.
THE 20 IS THE GOOD ONE.
AT THE 10 EVERYONE TRIES TO IMPRESS EACH OTHER. "LOOK! I HAVE A HOT CAR!" "LOOK! I CAN STILL FIT INTO MY CHEERLEADER OUTFIT!!"
BY THE 20, THEY ARE WHAT THEY ARE. NOBODY CARES.
AND THE 30?
DIVORCE, MID-LIFE CRISIS, TEEN-AGERS GONE WILD... THE 30 ISN'T PRETTY.
Jan Eliot
BY THE 40 AND THE 50 — PEOPLE START TO DIE OFF.
YOU MAKE A COMPELLING CASE.
TRUST ME. THE 20 IS IT.

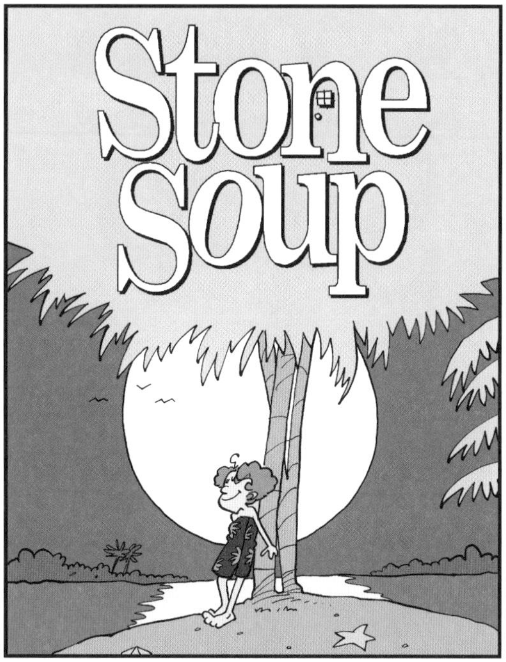
Stone Soup

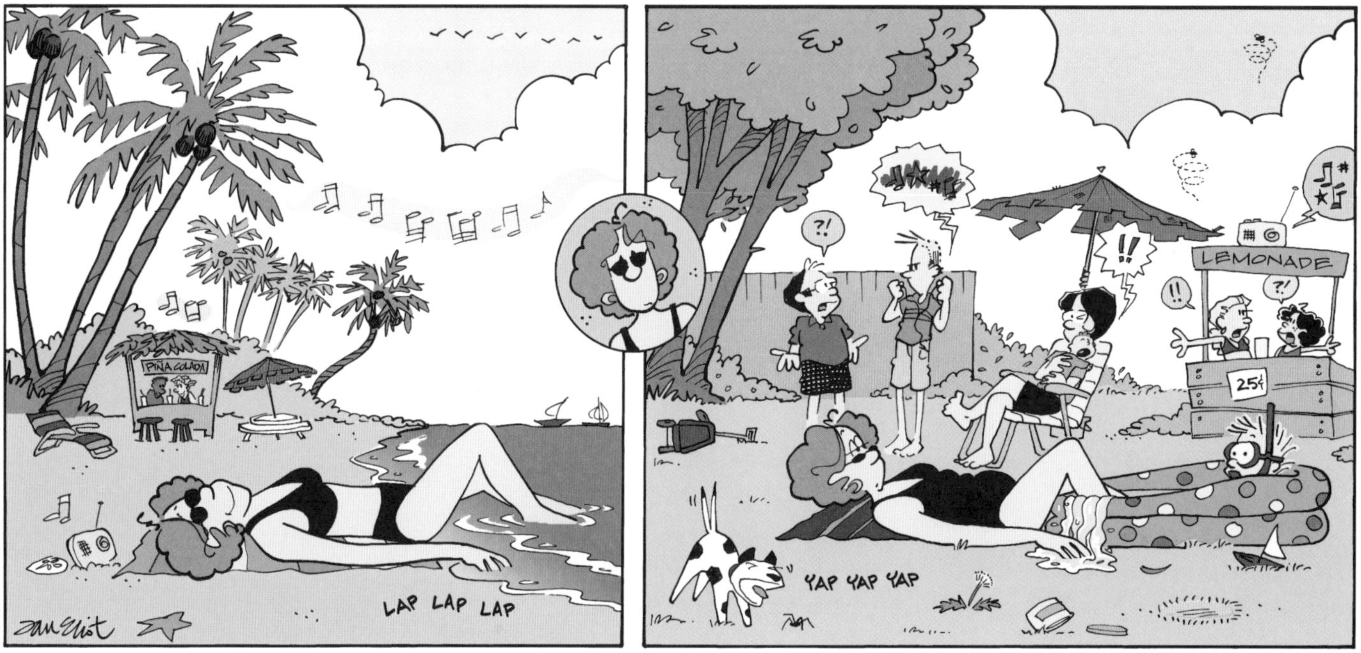
PIÑA COLADA
LAP LAP LAP
Jan Eliot
?!
!!
LEMONADE
!!
?!
25¢
YAP YAP YAP

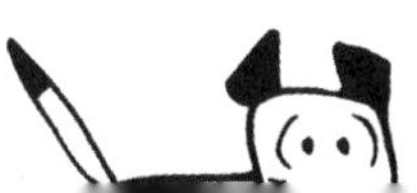

Stone Soup

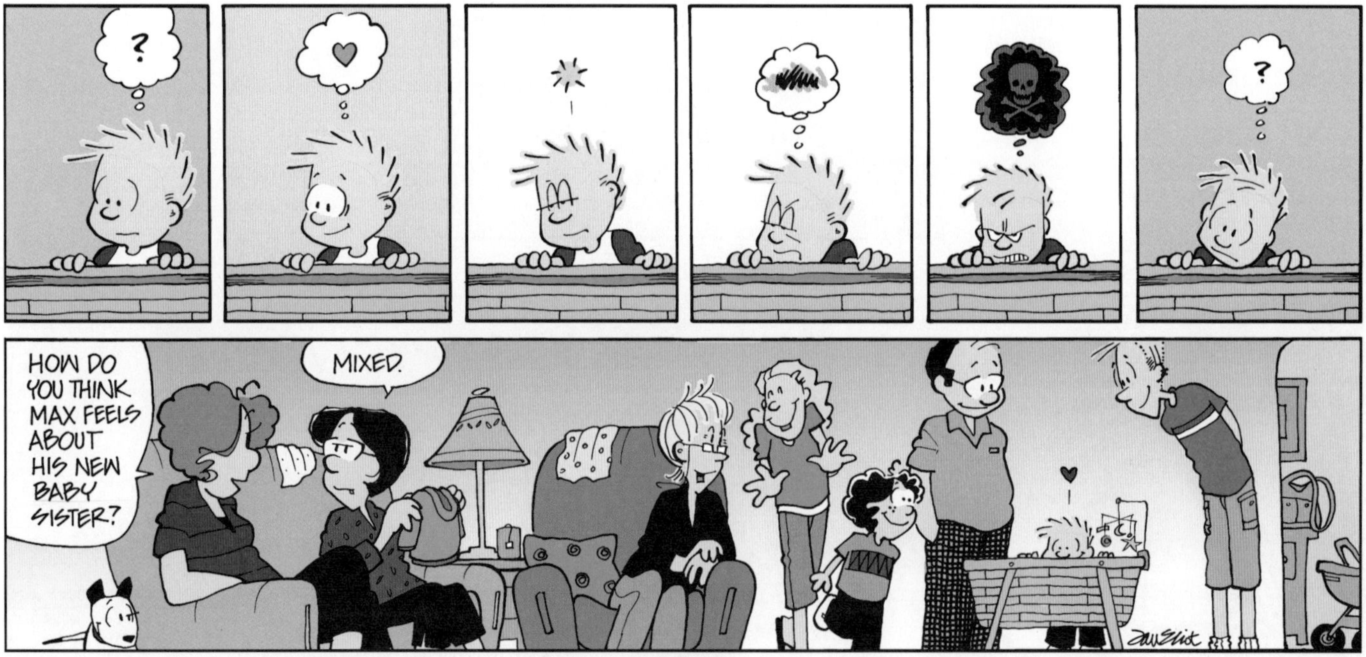
?
HOW DO YOU THINK MAX FEELS ABOUT HIS NEW BABY SISTER?
MIXED.

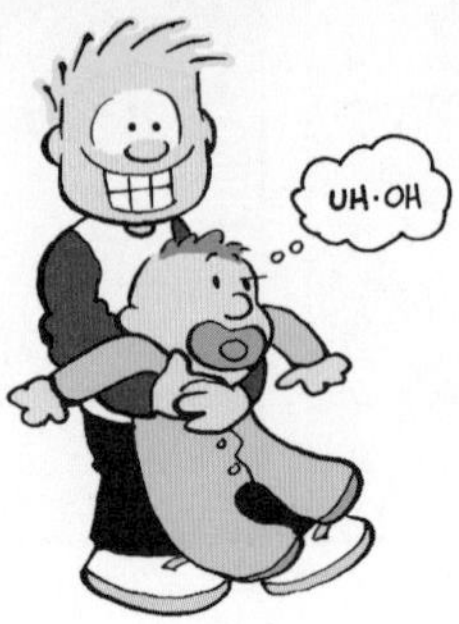
UH-OH

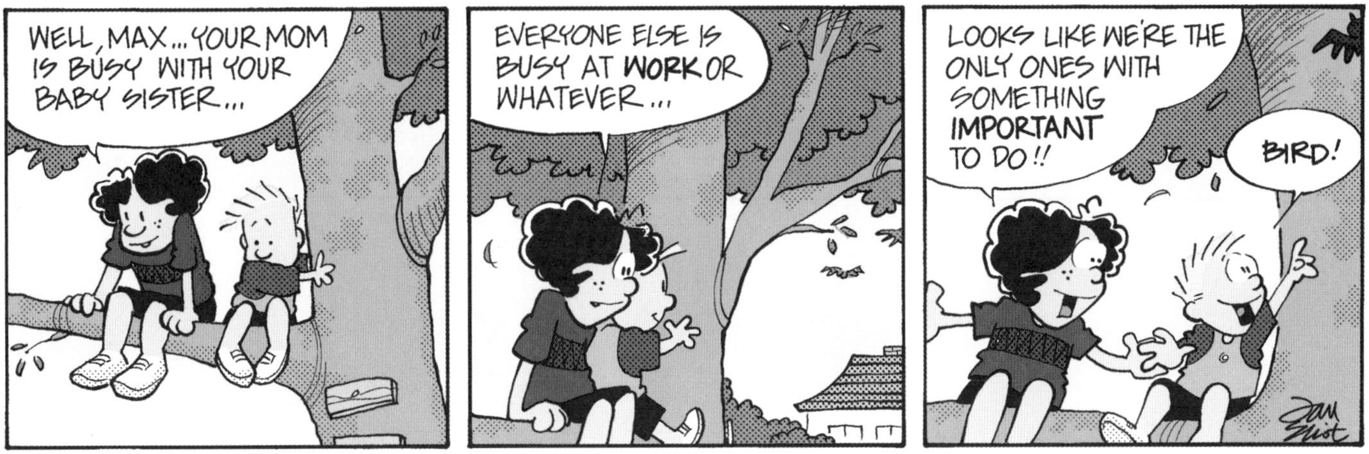
WELL, MAX... YOUR MOM IS BUSY WITH YOUR BABY SISTER...
EVERYONE ELSE IS BUSY AT WORK OR WHATEVER...
LOOKS LIKE WE'RE THE ONLY ONES WITH SOMETHING IMPORTANT TO DO!!
BIRD!

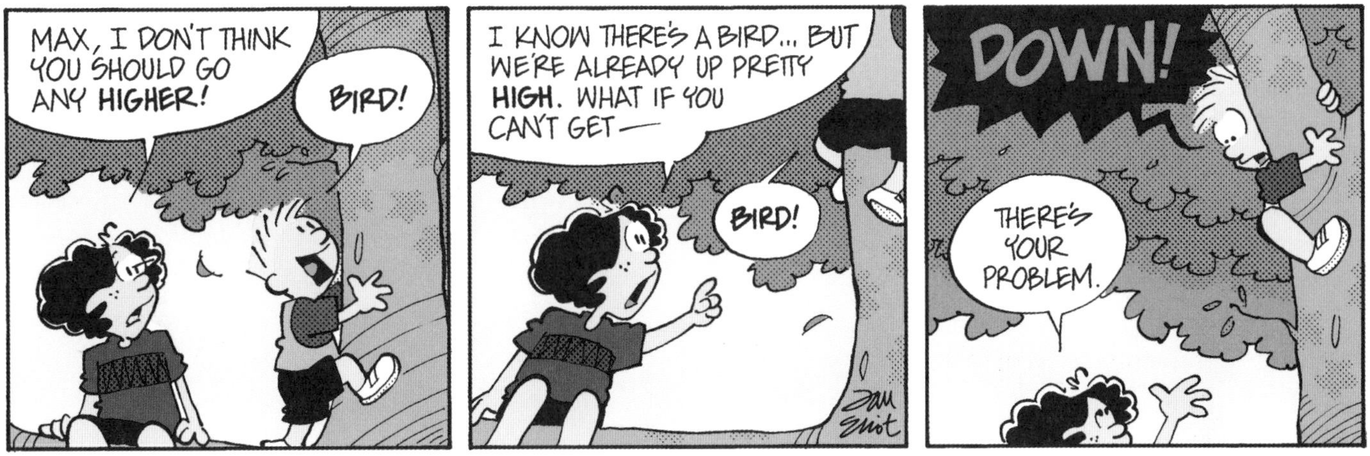
MAX, I DON'T THINK YOU SHOULD GO ANY HIGHER!
BIRD!
I KNOW THERE'S A BIRD... BUT WE'RE ALREADY UP PRETTY HIGH. WHAT IF YOU CAN'T GET—
BIRD!
DOWN!
THERE'S YOUR PROBLEM.

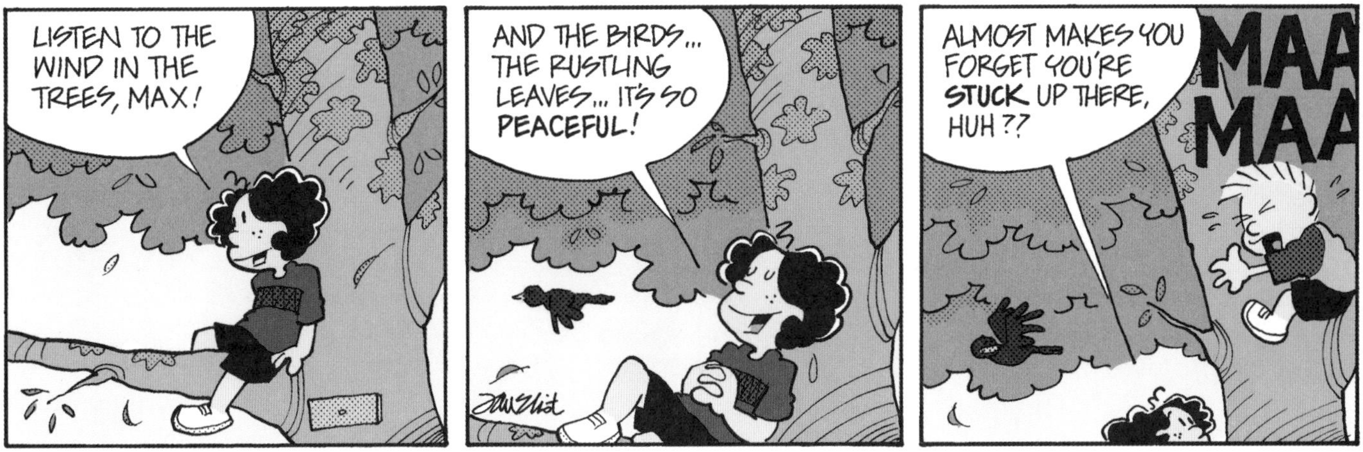
LISTEN TO THE WIND IN THE TREES, MAX!
AND THE BIRDS... THE RUSTLING LEAVES... IT'S SO PEACEFUL!
ALMOST MAKES YOU FORGET YOU'RE STUCK UP THERE, HUH??
MAA
MAA

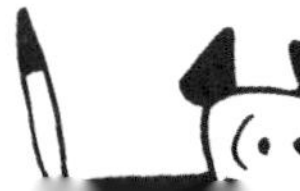

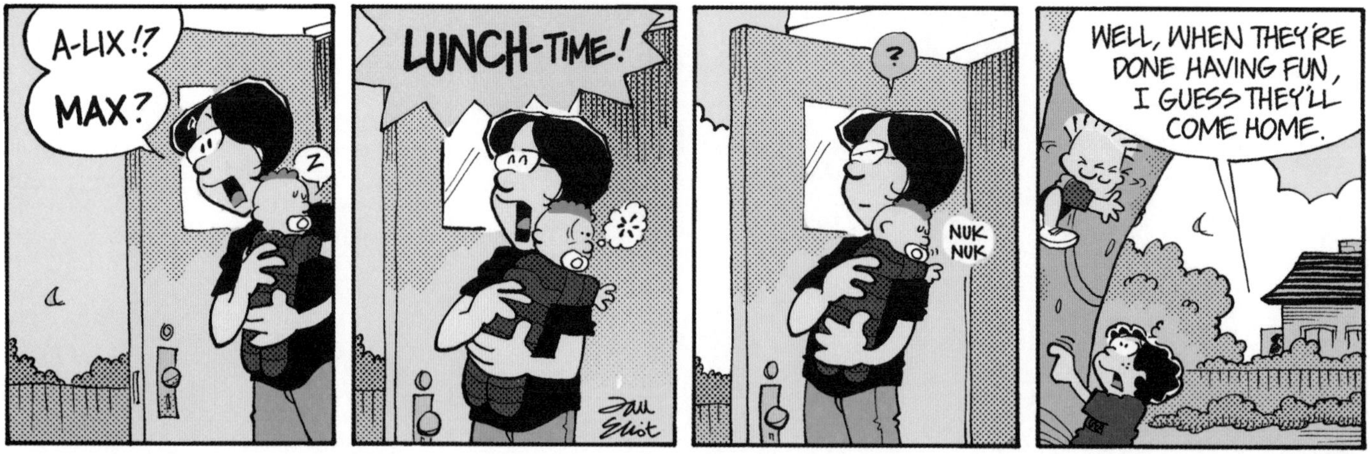
A-LIX!?
MAX?
Z
LUNCH-TIME!
?
NUK NUK
WELL, WHEN THEY'RE DONE HAVING FUN, I GUESS THEY'LL COME HOME.

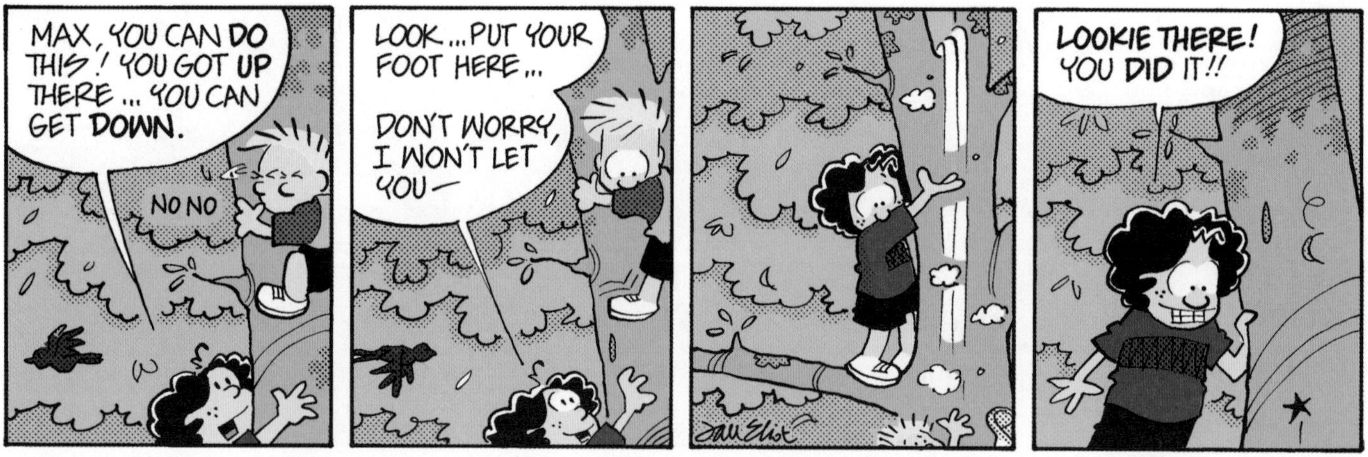
MAX, YOU CAN DO THIS! YOU GOT UP THERE ... YOU CAN GET DOWN.
NO NO
LOOK ... PUT YOUR FOOT HERE ...
DON'T WORRY, I WON'T LET YOU—
LOOKIE THERE! YOU DID IT!!

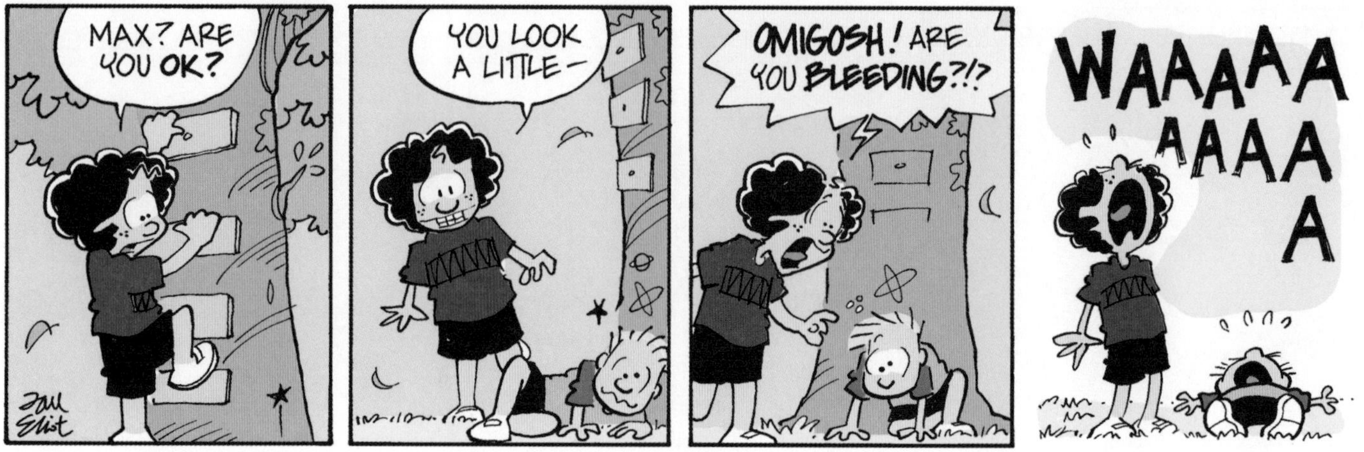
MAX? ARE YOU OK?
YOU LOOK A LITTLE—
OMIGOSH! ARE YOU BLEEDING?!?
WAAAAA AAAA A

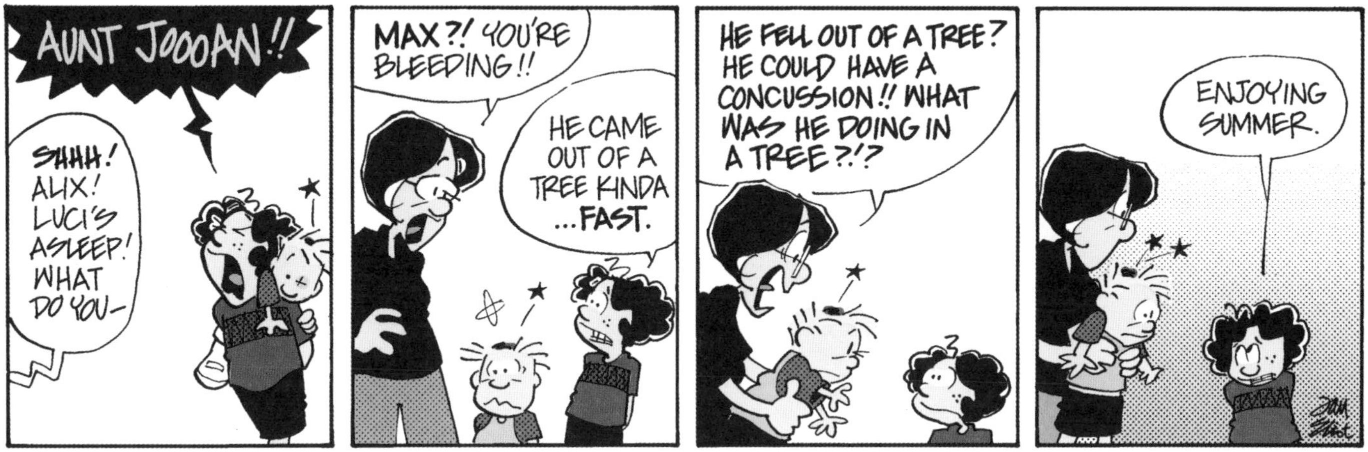
AUNT JOOOAN!!
SHHH! ALIX! LUCI'S ASLEEP! WHAT DO YOU–
MAX?! YOU'RE BLEEDING!!
HE CAME OUT OF A TREE KINDA ...FAST.
HE FELL OUT OF A TREE? HE COULD HAVE A CONCUSSION!! WHAT WAS HE DOING IN A TREE?!?
ENJOYING SUMMER.

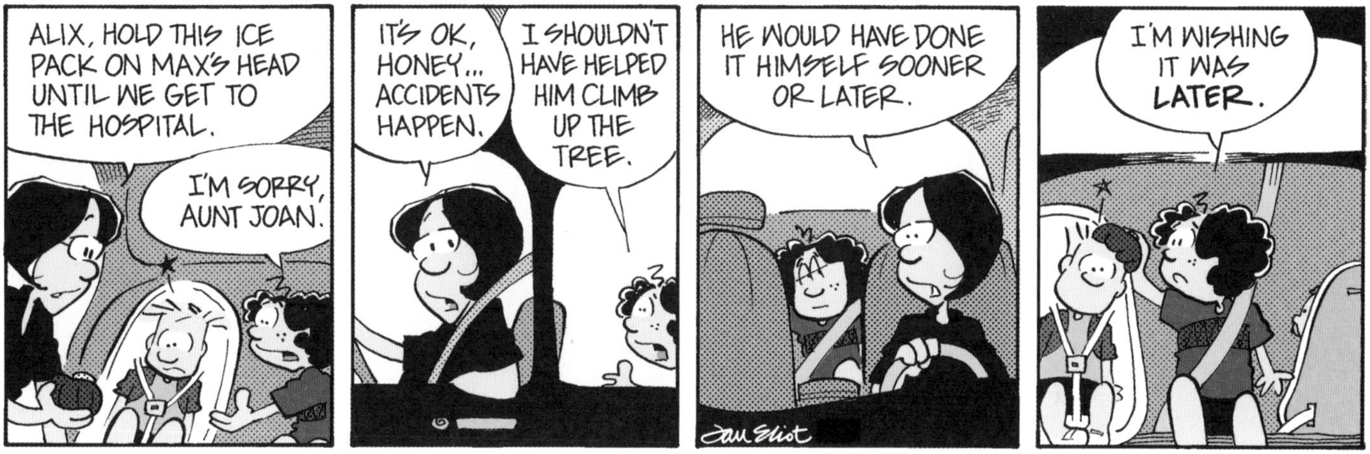
ALIX, HOLD THIS ICE PACK ON MAX'S HEAD UNTIL WE GET TO THE HOSPITAL.
I'M SORRY, AUNT JOAN.
IT'S OK, HONEY... ACCIDENTS HAPPEN.
I SHOULDN'T HAVE HELPED HIM CLIMB UP THE TREE.
HE WOULD HAVE DONE IT HIMSELF SOONER OR LATER.
I'M WISHING IT WAS LATER.

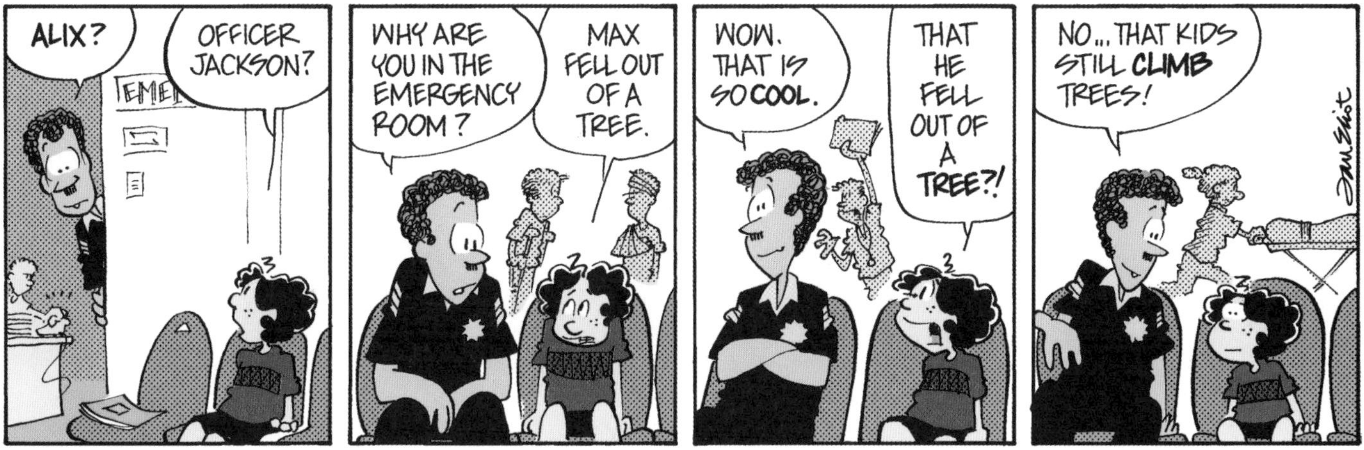
ALIX?
OFFICER JACKSON?
WHY ARE YOU IN THE EMERGENCY ROOM?
MAX FELL OUT OF A TREE.
WOW. THAT IS SO COOL.
THAT HE FELL OUT OF A TREE?!
NO... THAT KIDS STILL CLIMB TREES!

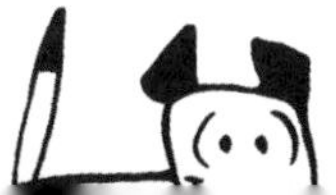

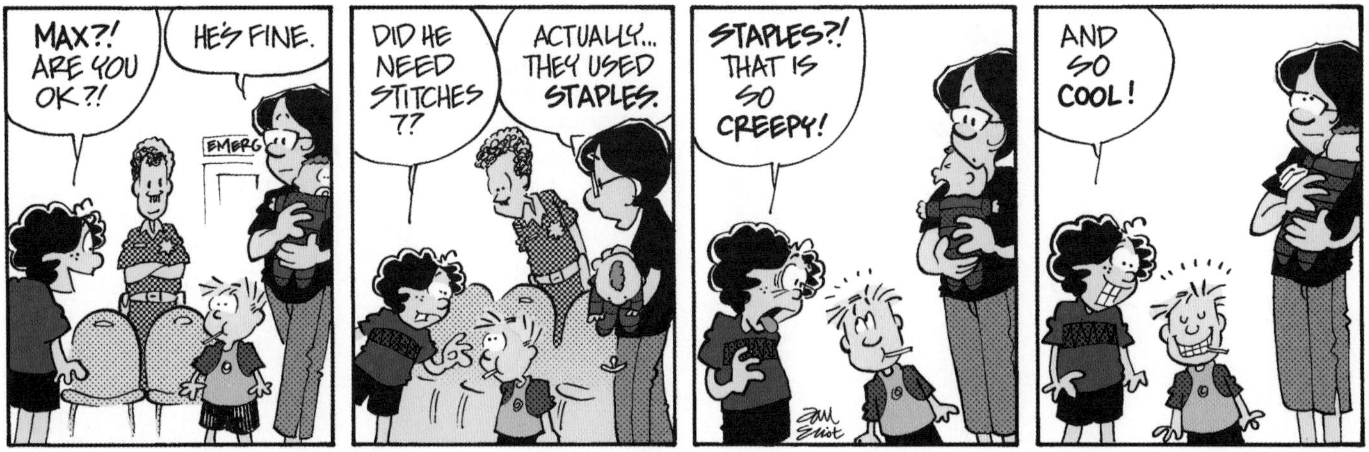
MAX?! ARE YOU OK?!
HE'S FINE.
EMERG
DID HE NEED STITCHES ??
ACTUALLY... THEY USED STAPLES.
STAPLES?! THAT IS SO CREEPY!
AND SO COOL!

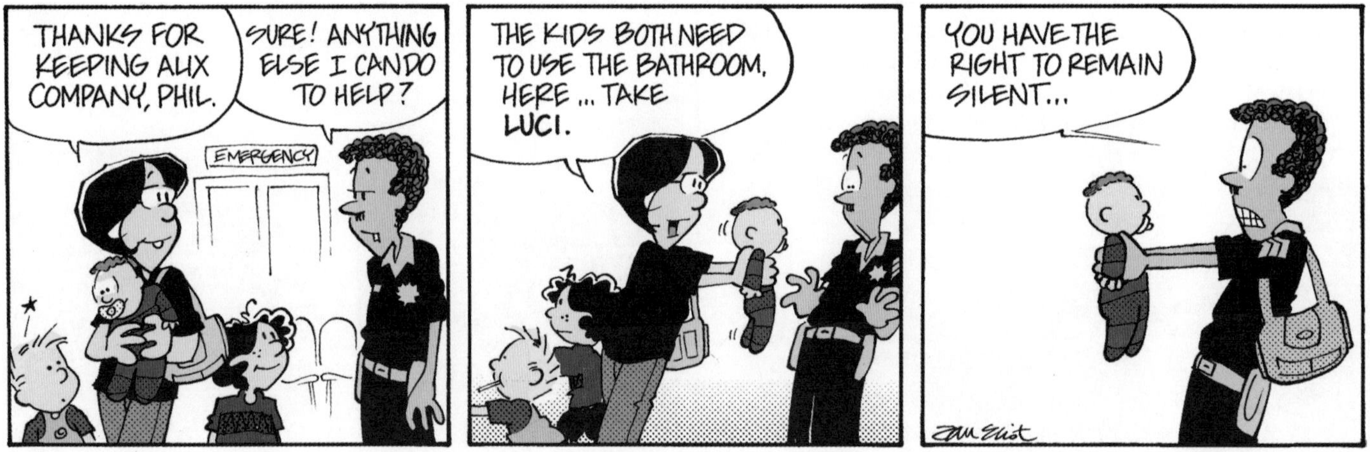
THANKS FOR KEEPING ALIX COMPANY, PHIL.
SURE! ANYTHING ELSE I CAN DO TO HELP?
EMERGENCY
THE KIDS BOTH NEED TO USE THE BATHROOM. HERE ... TAKE LUCI.
YOU HAVE THE RIGHT TO REMAIN SILENT...

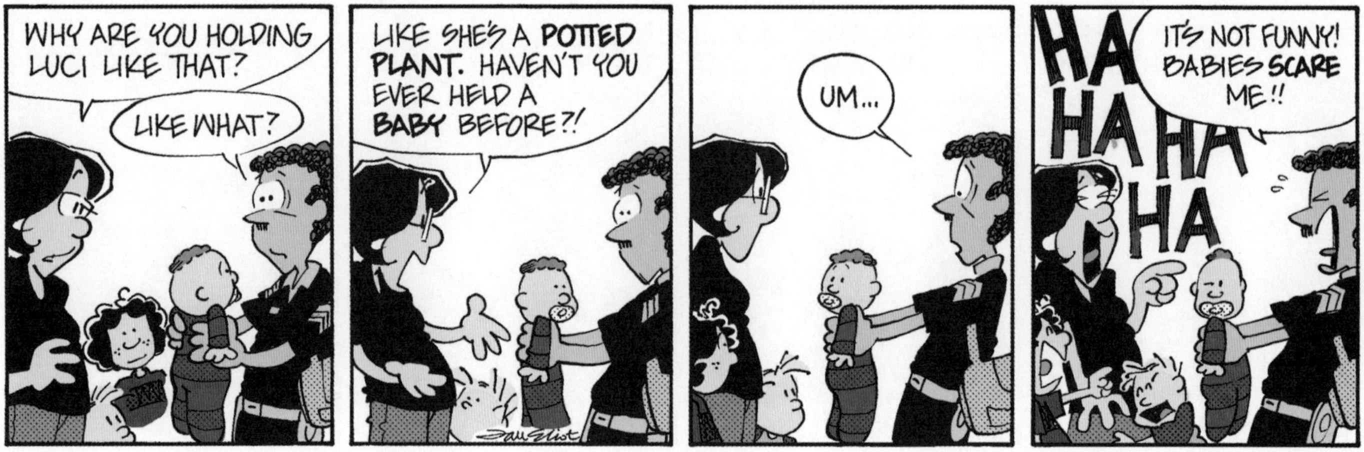
WHY ARE YOU HOLDING LUCI LIKE THAT?
LIKE WHAT?
LIKE SHE'S A POTTED PLANT. HAVEN'T YOU EVER HELD A BABY BEFORE?!
UM...
HA HA HA HA
IT'S NOT FUNNY! BABIES SCARE ME!!

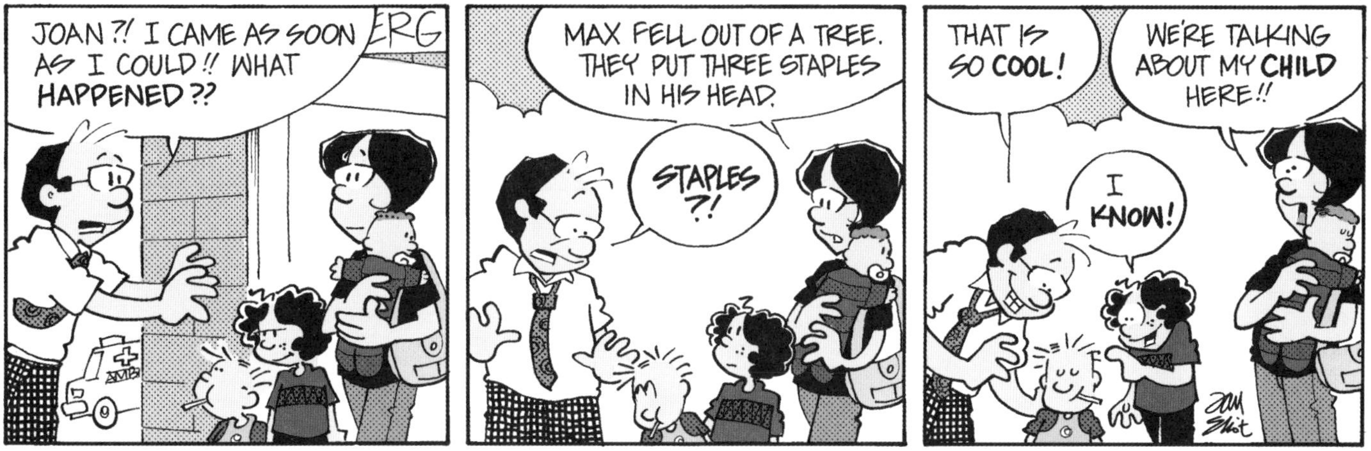
JOAN?! I CAME AS SOON AS I COULD!! WHAT **HAPPENED**??
MAX FELL OUT OF A TREE. THEY PUT THREE STAPLES IN HIS HEAD.
STAPLES?!
THAT IS SO **COOL**!
WE'RE TALKING ABOUT MY **CHILD** HERE!!
I **KNOW**!

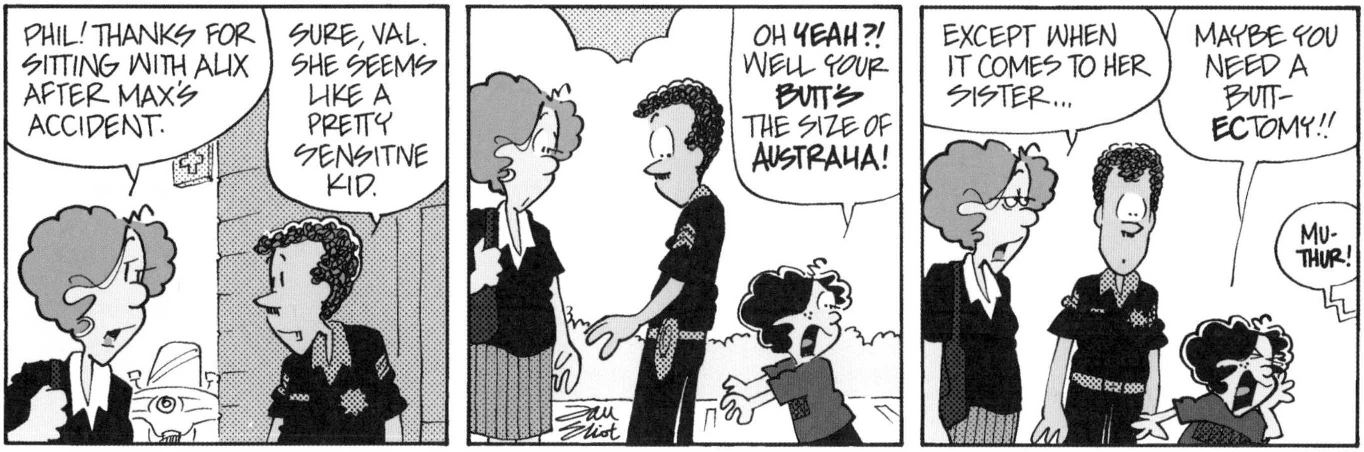
PHIL! THANKS FOR SITTING WITH ALIX AFTER MAX'S ACCIDENT.
SURE, VAL. SHE SEEMS LIKE A PRETTY SENSITIVE KID.
OH **YEAH?!** WELL YOUR **BUTT'S** THE SIZE OF **AUSTRALIA**!
EXCEPT WHEN IT COMES TO HER SISTER...
MAYBE YOU NEED A BUTT-**ECTOMY**!!
MU-**THUR**!

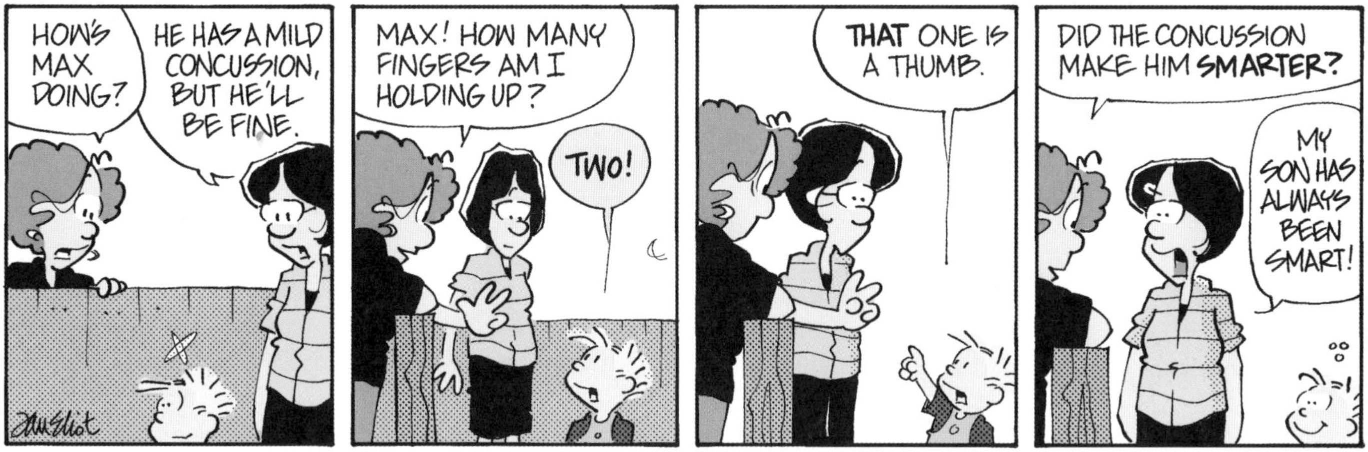
HOW'S MAX DOING?
HE HAS A MILD CONCUSSION, BUT HE'LL BE FINE.
MAX! HOW MANY FINGERS AM I HOLDING UP?
TWO!
THAT ONE IS A THUMB.
DID THE CONCUSSION MAKE HIM **SMARTER?**
MY SON HAS ALWAYS BEEN SMART!

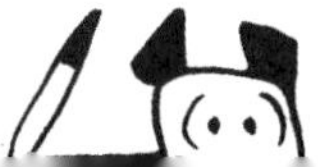

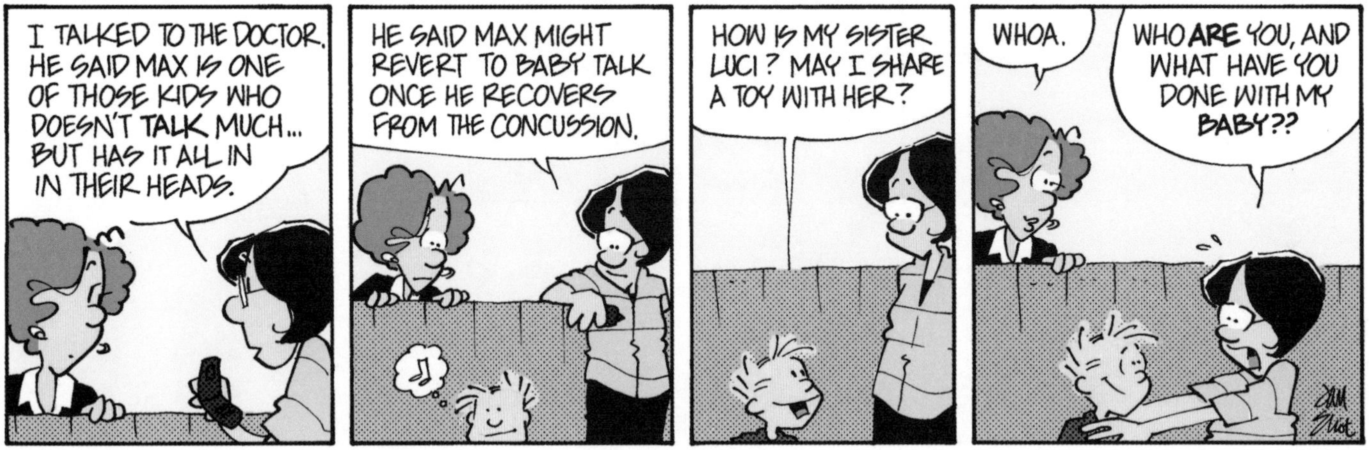
I TALKED TO THE DOCTOR. HE SAID MAX IS ONE OF THOSE KIDS WHO DOESN'T **TALK** MUCH... BUT HAS IT ALL IN IN THEIR HEADS.
HE SAID MAX MIGHT REVERT TO BABY TALK ONCE HE RECOVERS FROM THE CONCUSSION.
HOW IS MY SISTER LUCI? MAY I SHARE A TOY WITH HER?
WHOA.
WHO **ARE** YOU, AND WHAT HAVE YOU DONE WITH MY **BABY**??

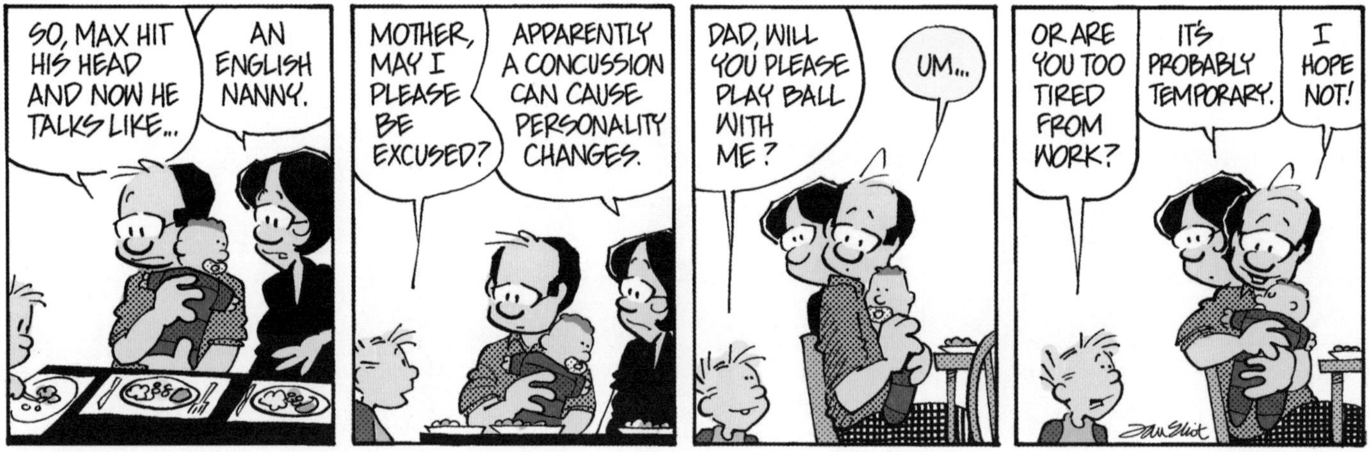
SO, MAX HIT HIS HEAD AND NOW HE TALKS LIKE...
AN ENGLISH NANNY.
MOTHER, MAY I PLEASE BE EXCUSED?
APPARENTLY A CONCUSSION CAN CAUSE PERSONALITY CHANGES.
DAD, WILL YOU PLEASE PLAY BALL WITH ME?
UM...
OR ARE YOU TOO TIRED FROM WORK?
IT'S PROBABLY TEMPORARY.
I HOPE NOT!

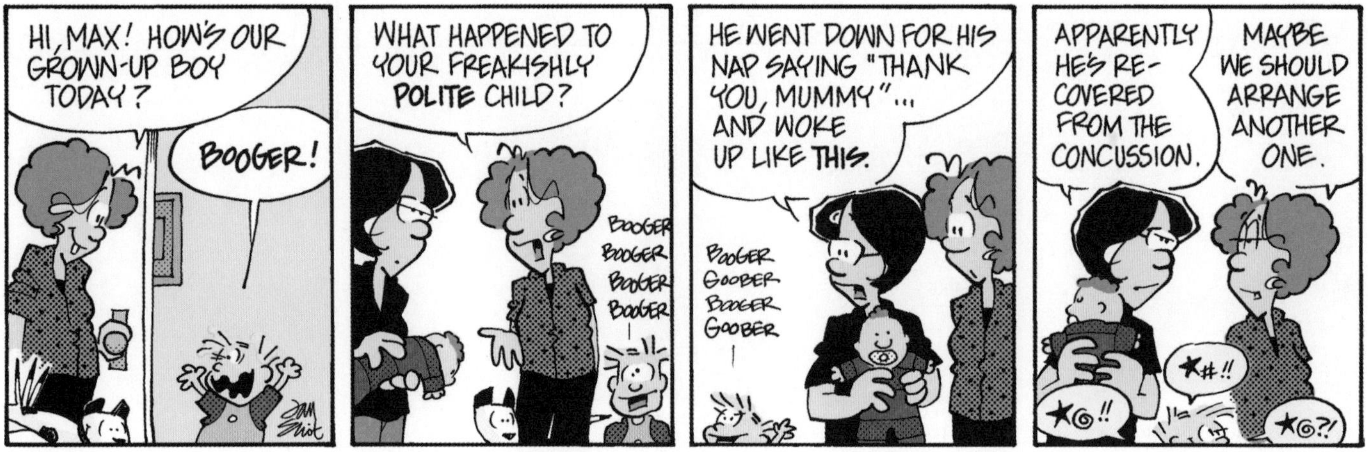
HI, MAX! HOW'S OUR GROWN-UP BOY TODAY?
BOOGER!
WHAT HAPPENED TO YOUR FREAKISHLY **POLITE** CHILD?
BOOGER BOOGER BOOGER BOOGER
HE WENT DOWN FOR HIS NAP SAYING "THANK YOU, MUMMY"... AND WOKE UP LIKE **THIS**.
BOOGER GOOBER BOOGER GOOBER
APPARENTLY HE'S RE-COVERED FROM THE CONCUSSION.
MAYBE WE SHOULD ARRANGE ANOTHER ONE.

Stone Soup

WAAAAWAAA AA
MAMA MAMA MAMA MAMA MAMA
WA WAAAWAA
MAMA MAMA MAM MA MA MA
NONONO MAMA MAMA MAMA MAMA MAMA MAMA !
WAAA WAAA AAA AAA
DING DONG
MAX! LET'S GO TO THE PARK!
BURP
NONO MAMA MAMA MA
BUT MAX! TODAY'S THE WORM AND PILL BUG "FESTIVAL"...
Jan Eliot
WE'LL HAVE TO DIG UP THAT "THING" WE BURIED.
HEE HEE HEE HEE HEE HEE
I'M HAPPY NOT TO ASK.

I WAS TALKING TO MY FRIEND CONNIE VICTOR THE OTHER DAY...

SHE WANTS ME TO LEARN HOW TO PLAY TENNIS.

SHE SAYS, "TENNIS IS SOMETHING WE CAN PLAY UNTIL WE'RE OLD LADIES!"

"UNTIL"?

IGNORE HER.

DOES SHE KNOW HOW OLD YOU ARE NOW?

UM...

I DO LOSE MY BALANCE SOMETIMES...

OOPS! YOUR FLAP-JACKS FELL ON THE GROUND!!

THOSE WERE MINE?!

WHO KNOWS IF I CAN REMEMBER HOW TO MAKE MORE!

28

Stone Soup

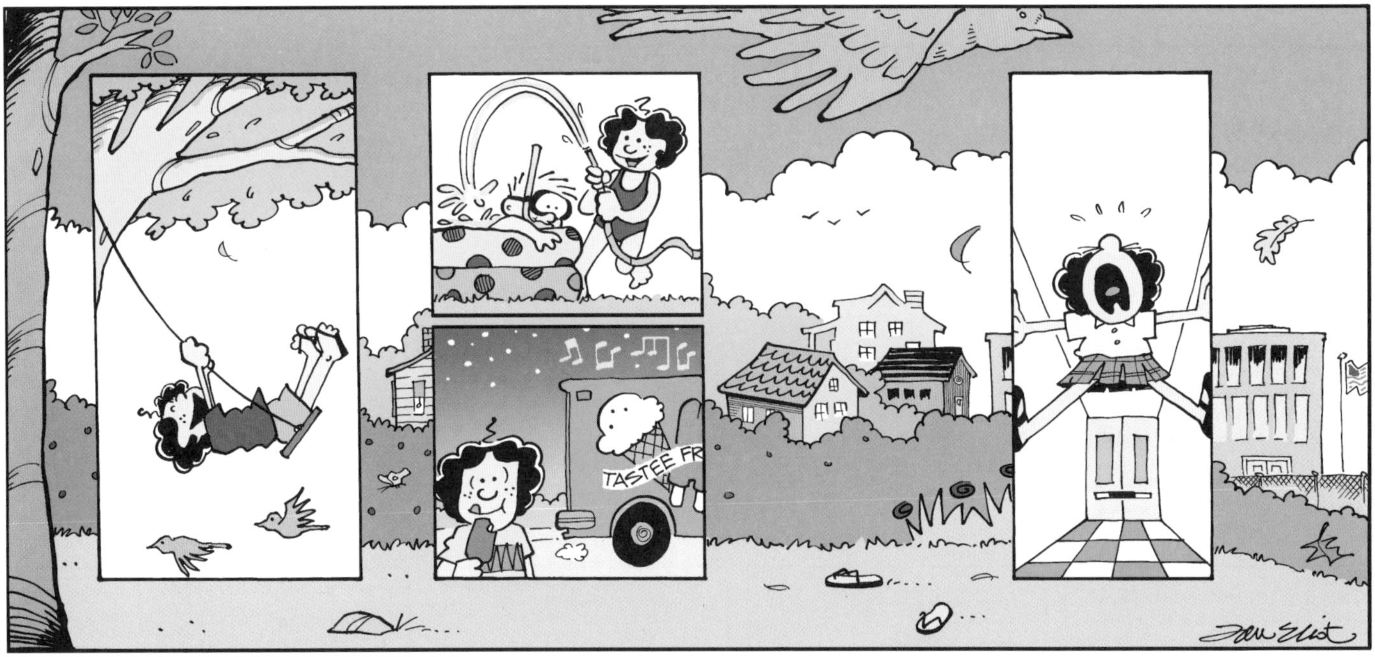
TASTEE FR

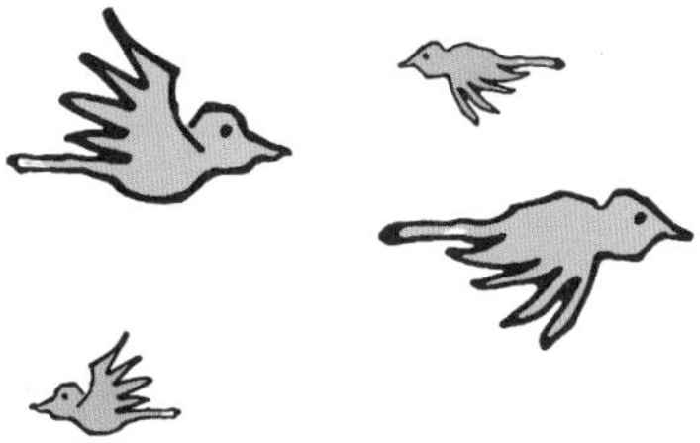

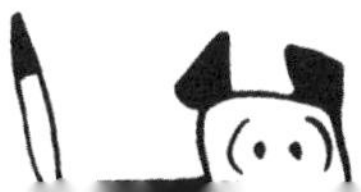

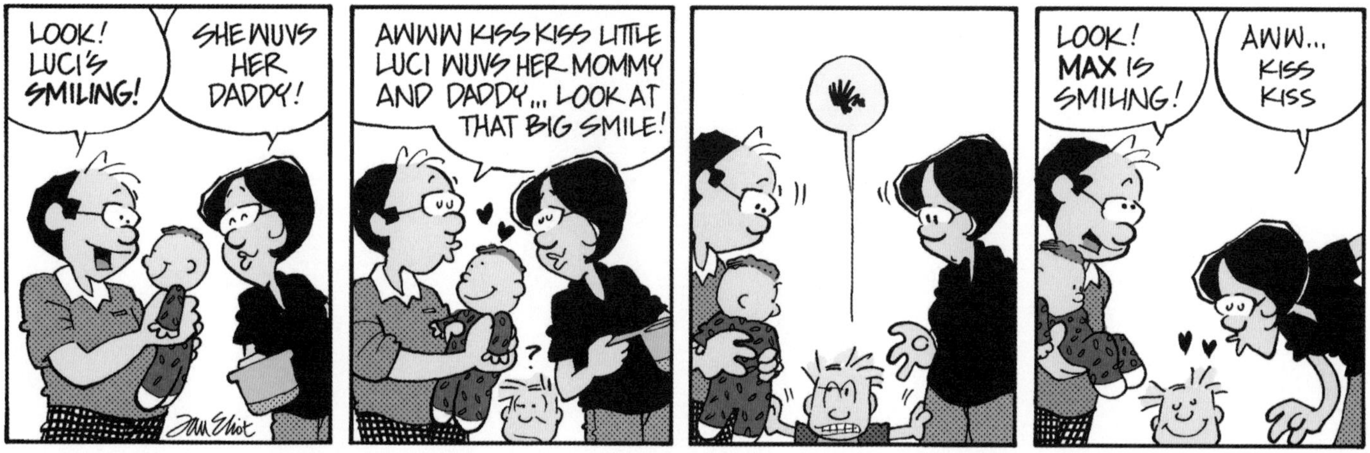
LOOK! LUCI'S SMILING!
SHE WUVS HER DADDY!
AWWW KISS KISS LITTLE LUCI WUVS HER MOMMY AND DADDY... LOOK AT THAT BIG SMILE!
?
LOOK! MAX IS SMILING!
AWW... KISS KISS

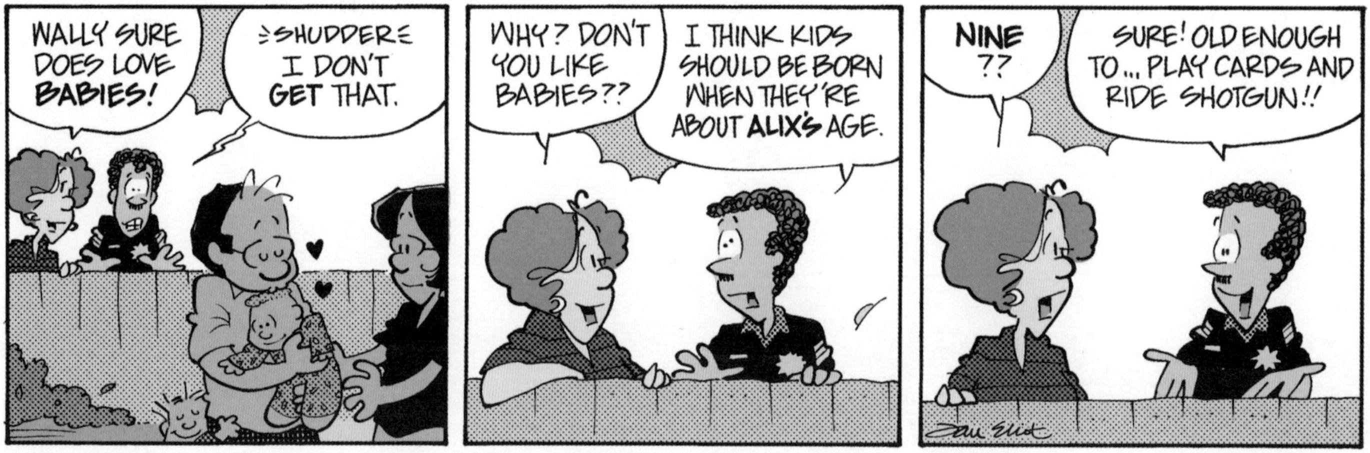
WALLY SURE DOES LOVE BABIES!
SHUDDER I DON'T GET THAT.
WHY? DON'T YOU LIKE BABIES??
I THINK KIDS SHOULD BE BORN WHEN THEY'RE ABOUT ALIX'S AGE.
NINE ??
SURE! OLD ENOUGH TO... PLAY CARDS AND RIDE SHOTGUN!!

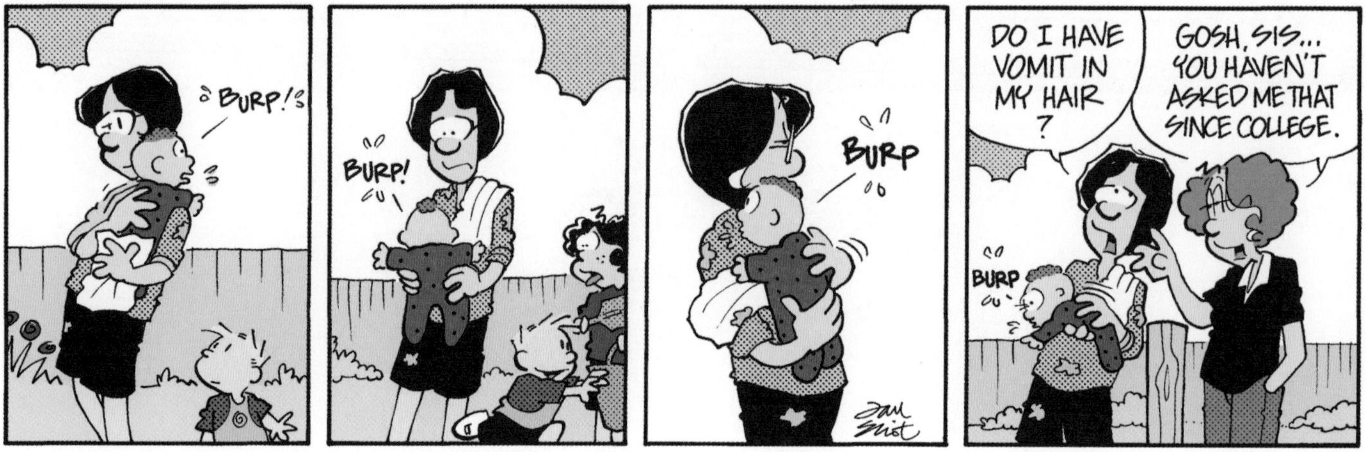
BURP!
BURP!
BURP
DO I HAVE VOMIT IN MY HAIR ?
GOSH, SIS... YOU HAVEN'T ASKED ME THAT SINCE COLLEGE.
BURP

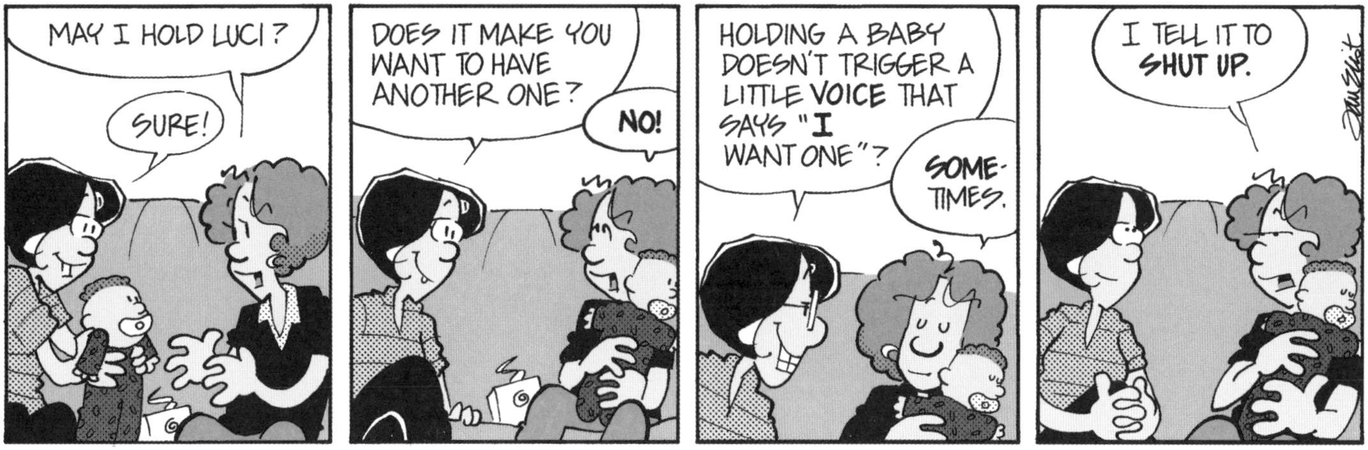
MAY I HOLD LUCI?
SURE!
DOES IT MAKE YOU WANT TO HAVE ANOTHER ONE?
NO!
HOLDING A BABY DOESN'T TRIGGER A LITTLE **VOICE** THAT SAYS "**I** WANT ONE"?
SOME-TIMES.
I TELL IT TO **SHUT UP.**

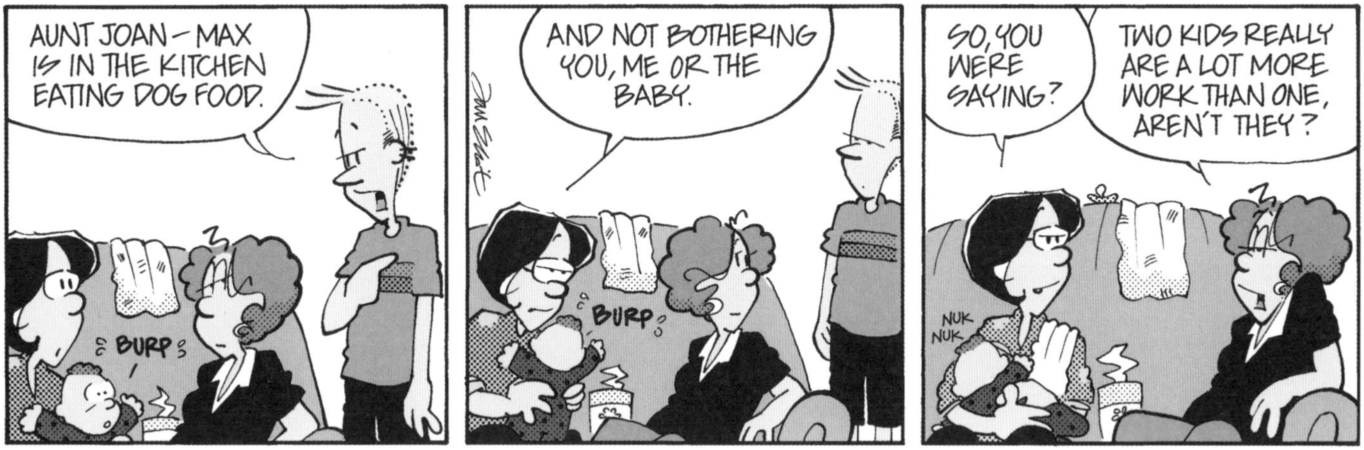
AUNT JOAN – MAX IS IN THE KITCHEN EATING DOG FOOD.
BURP
AND NOT BOTHERING YOU, ME OR THE BABY.
BURP
SO, YOU WERE SAYING?
TWO KIDS REALLY ARE A LOT MORE WORK THAN ONE, AREN'T THEY?
NUK NUK

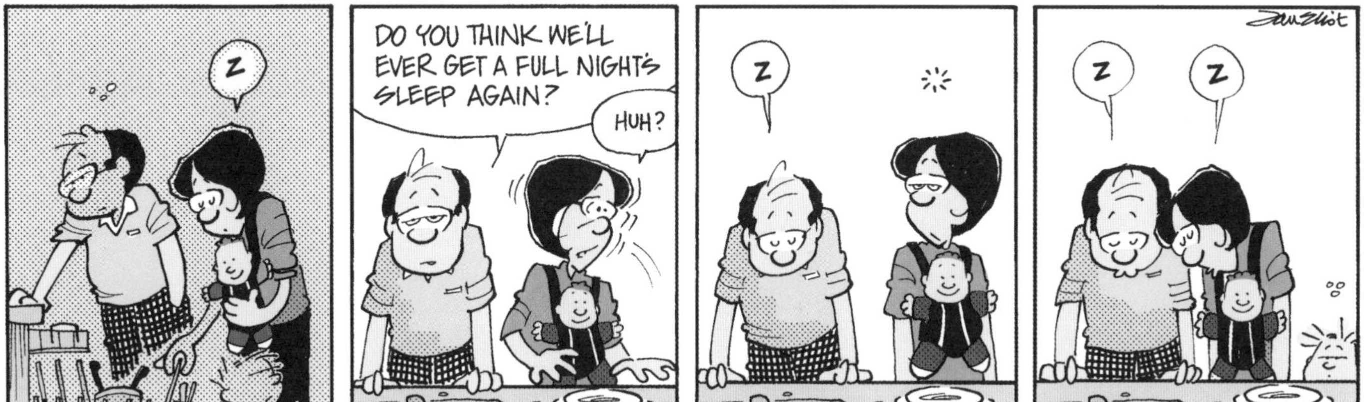
Z
DO YOU THINK WE'LL EVER GET A FULL NIGHT'S SLEEP AGAIN?
HUH?
Z
Z
Z

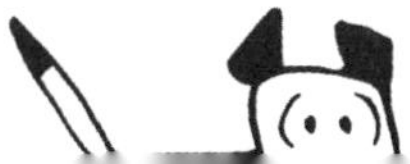

Stone Soup

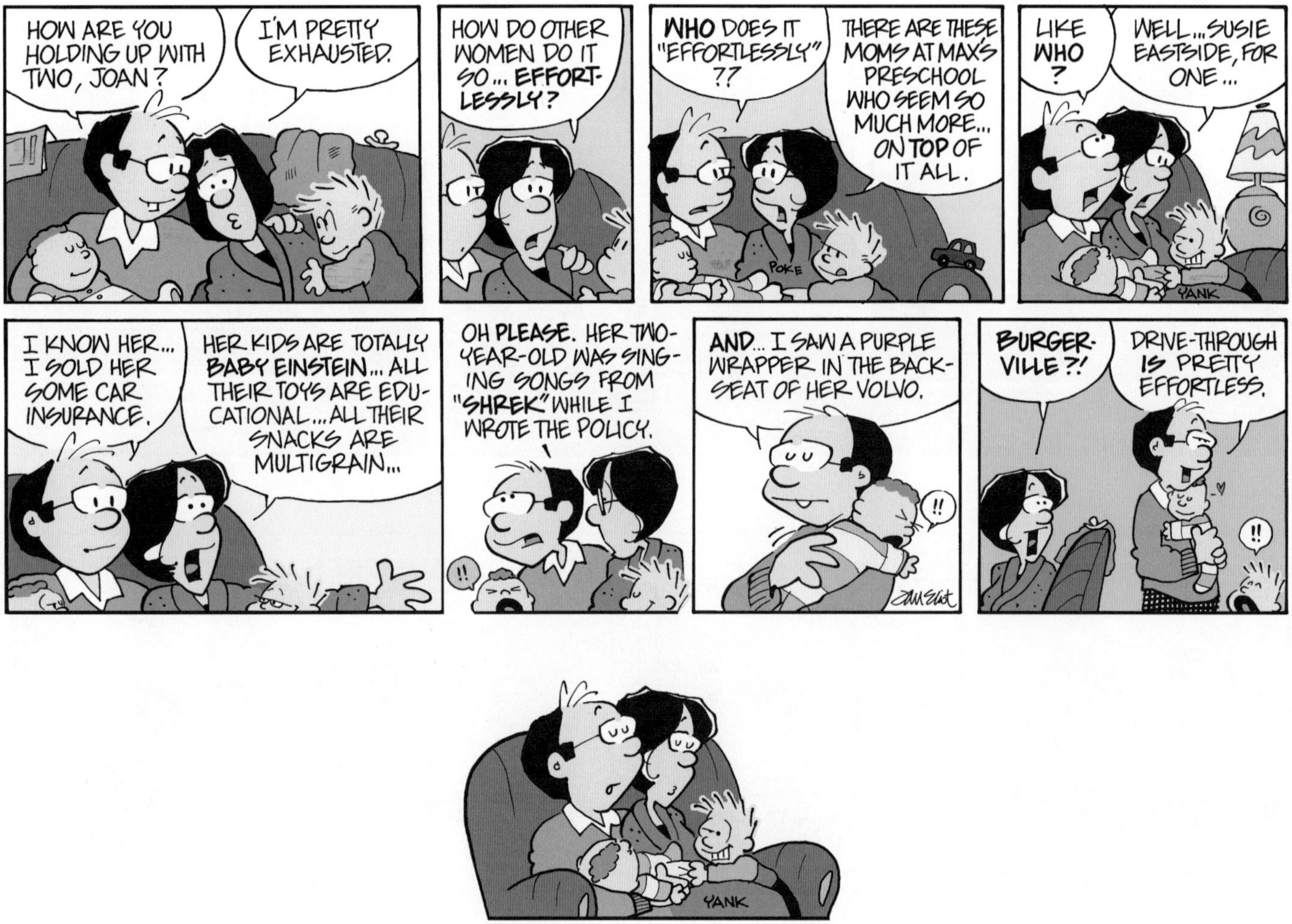

HOW ARE YOU HOLDING UP WITH TWO, JOAN?
I'M PRETTY EXHAUSTED.
HOW DO OTHER WOMEN DO IT SO... **EFFORTLESSLY?**
WHO DOES IT "EFFORTLESSLY"??
THERE ARE THESE MOMS AT MAX'S PRESCHOOL WHO SEEM SO MUCH MORE... ON **TOP** OF IT ALL.
POKE
LIKE **WHO**?
WELL... SUSIE EASTSIDE, FOR ONE...
YANK
I KNOW HER... I SOLD HER SOME CAR INSURANCE.
HER KIDS ARE TOTALLY **BABY EINSTEIN**... ALL THEIR TOYS ARE EDUCATIONAL... ALL THEIR SNACKS ARE MULTIGRAIN...
OH **PLEASE.** HER TWO-YEAR-OLD WAS SINGING SONGS FROM "**SHREK**" WHILE I WROTE THE POLICY.
!!
AND... I SAW A PURPLE WRAPPER IN THE BACKSEAT OF HER VOLVO.
!!
BURGERVILLE?!
DRIVE-THROUGH **IS** PRETTY EFFORTLESS.
!!
YANK

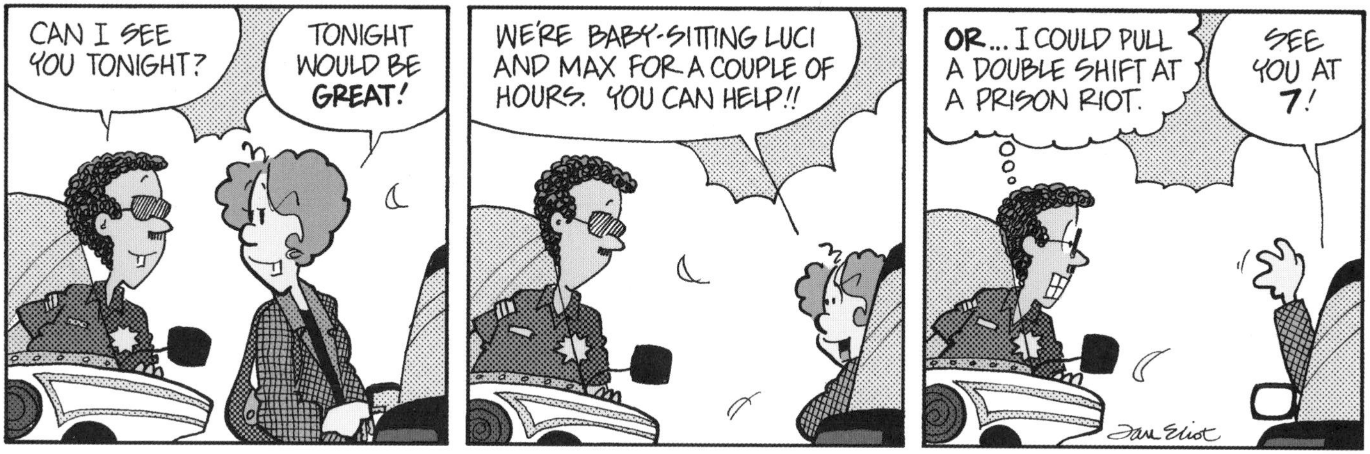
CAN I SEE YOU TONIGHT?
TONIGHT WOULD BE **GREAT**!
WE'RE BABY-SITTING LUCI AND MAX FOR A COUPLE OF HOURS. YOU CAN HELP!!
OR... I COULD PULL A DOUBLE SHIFT AT A PRISON RIOT.
SEE YOU AT **7**!
Jan Eliot

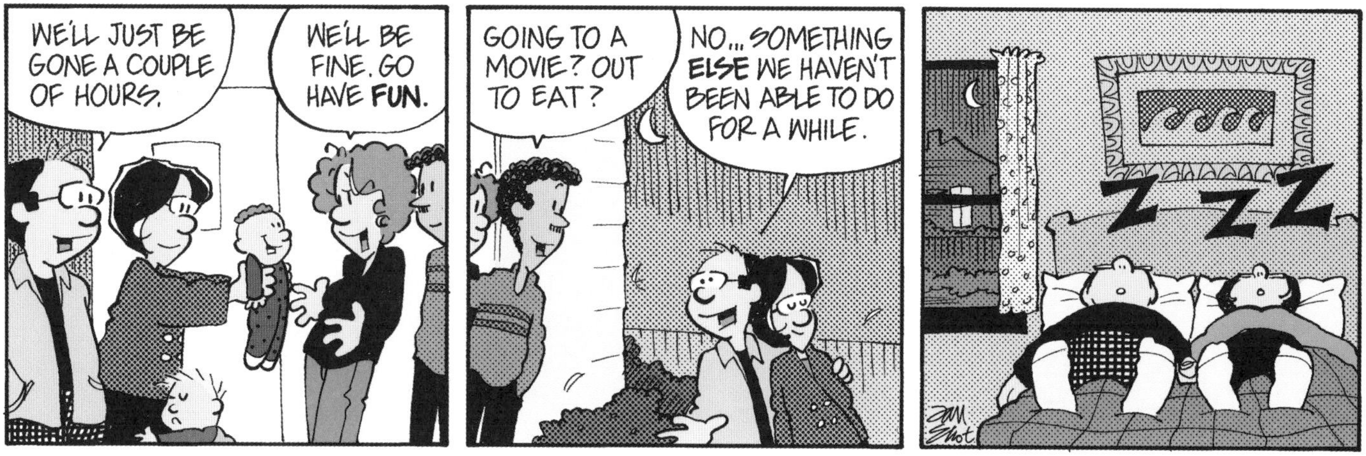
WE'LL JUST BE GONE A COUPLE OF HOURS.
WE'LL BE FINE. GO HAVE **FUN**.
GOING TO A MOVIE? OUT TO EAT?
NO... SOMETHING **ELSE** WE HAVEN'T BEEN ABLE TO DO FOR A WHILE.
Z Z Z

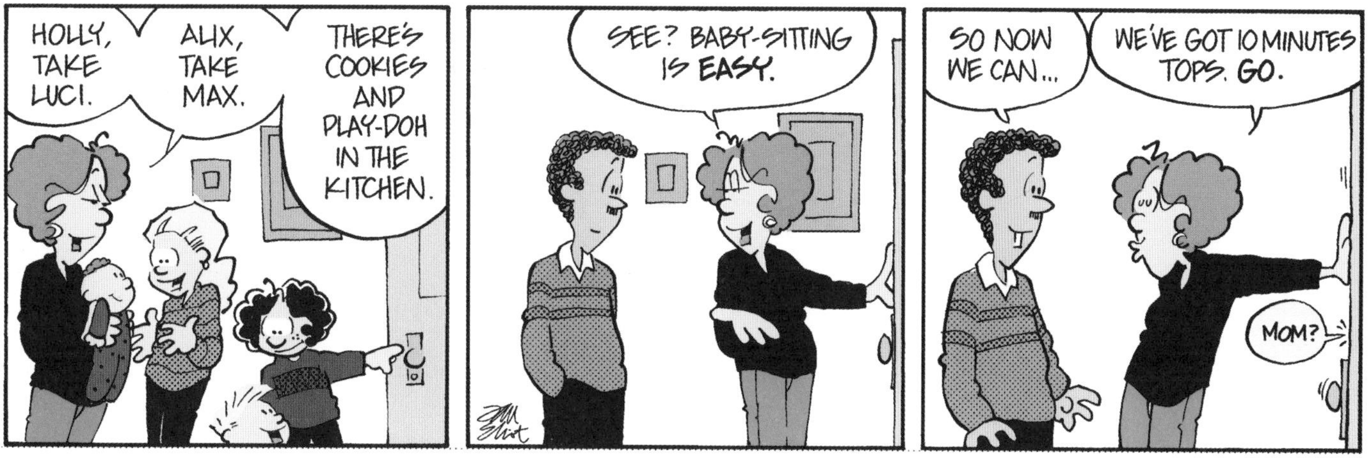
HOLLY, TAKE LUCI.
ALIX, TAKE MAX.
THERE'S COOKIES AND PLAY-DOH IN THE KITCHEN.
SEE? BABY-SITTING IS **EASY**.
SO NOW WE CAN...
WE'VE GOT 10 MINUTES TOPS. **GO**.
MOM?

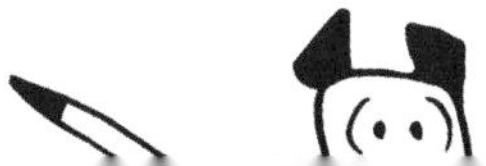

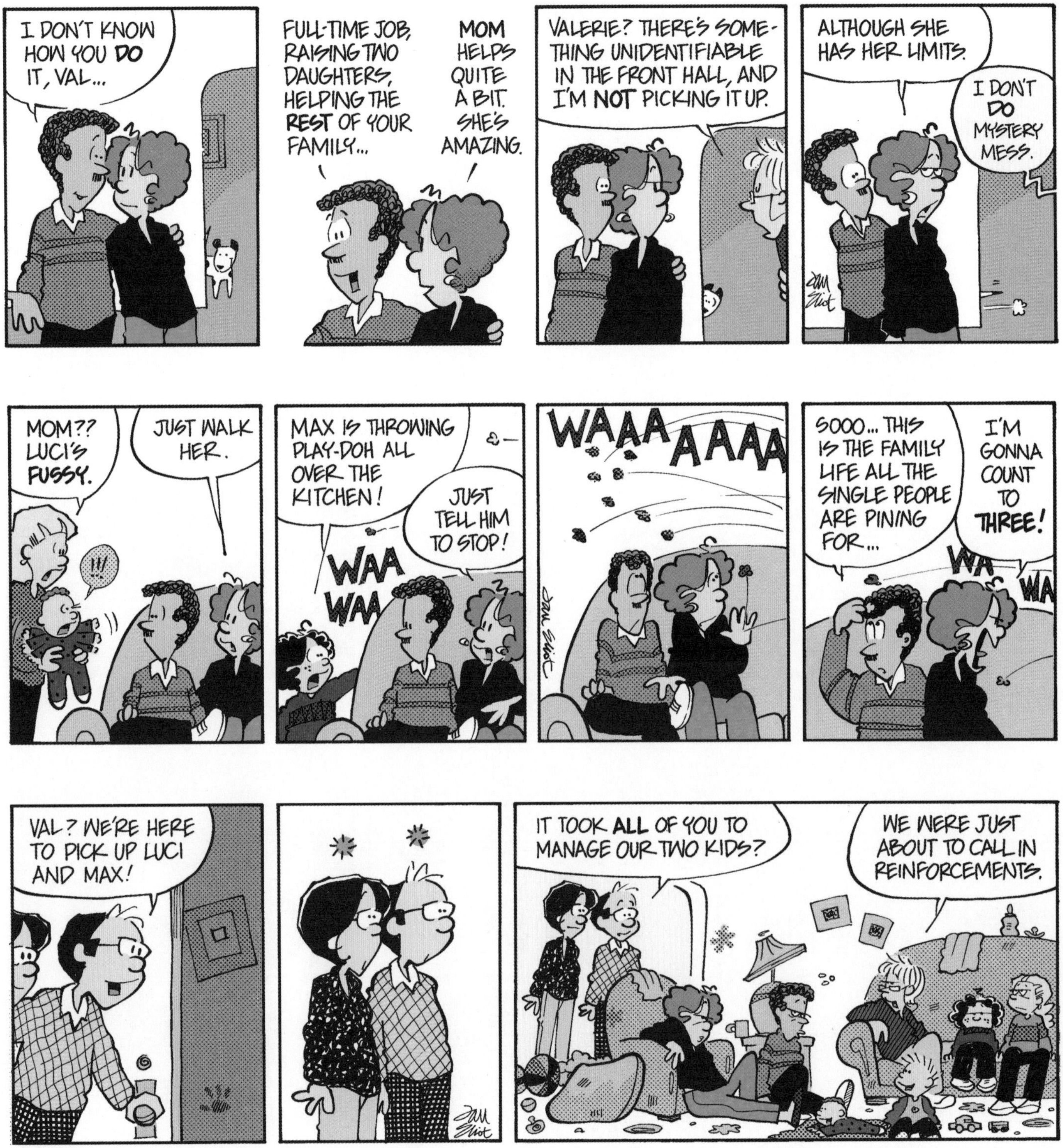
I DON'T KNOW HOW YOU DO IT, VAL...
FULL-TIME JOB, RAISING TWO DAUGHTERS, HELPING THE REST OF YOUR FAMILY...
MOM HELPS QUITE A BIT. SHE'S AMAZING.
VALERIE? THERE'S SOME-THING UNIDENTIFIABLE IN THE FRONT HALL, AND I'M NOT PICKING IT UP.
ALTHOUGH SHE HAS HER LIMITS.
I DON'T DO MYSTERY MESS.
MOM?? LUCI'S FUSSY.
!!/
JUST WALK HER.
MAX IS THROWING PLAY-DOH ALL OVER THE KITCHEN!
WAA WAA
JUST TELL HIM TO STOP!
WAAAAAAA
SOOO... THIS IS THE FAMILY LIFE ALL THE SINGLE PEOPLE ARE PINING FOR...
I'M GONNA COUNT TO THREE!
WA WA
VAL? WE'RE HERE TO PICK UP LUCI AND MAX!
IT TOOK ALL OF YOU TO MANAGE OUR TWO KIDS?
WE WERE JUST ABOUT TO CALL IN REINFORCEMENTS.

Stone Soup

WHAT ARE YOU DOING, ALIX?
WRITING A COMIC BOOK.
I KNEW IT WAS SOMETHING DORKY.
IT'S NOT DORKY.
IT'S SUPER TEDDY VS. DR. BUGGY...
A CLASSIC STRUGGLE BETWEEN GOOD AND EVIL.
WHAT'S DR. BUGGY HOLDING?
THINK OF IT AS A BEE BATTERING RAM.
OK, I'M HOOKED. TELL ME MORE.
SUPER TEDDY HAS A SIDEKICK NAMED AUNT EATER.
HOW'D YOU KNOW?!
LET ME GUESS ...SHE'S AN ANTEATER.
RAINY SUNDAYS AREN'T SO BAD...

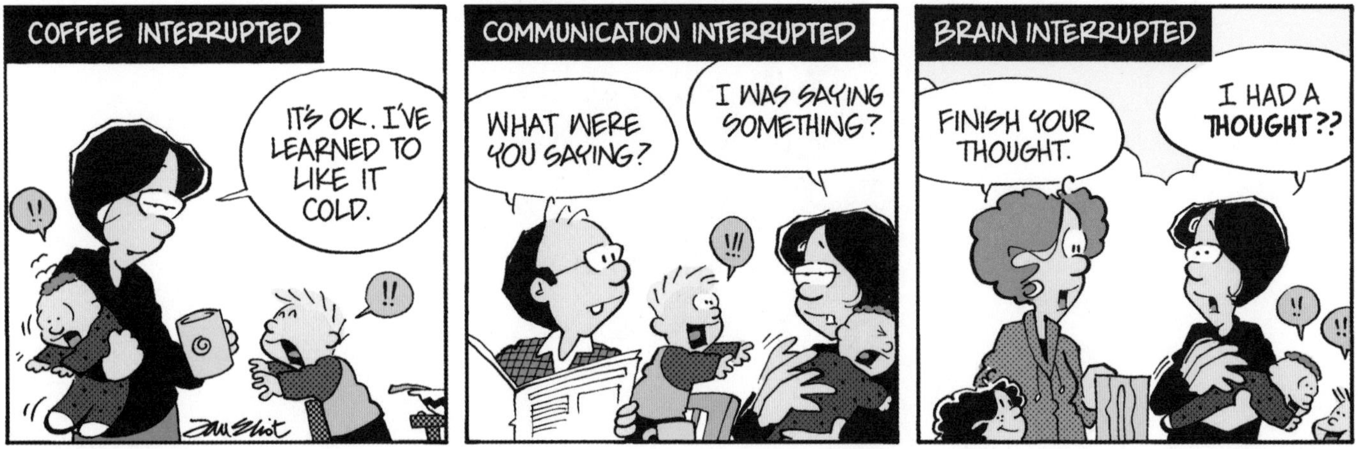
COFFEE INTERRUPTED
!!
IT'S OK. I'VE LEARNED TO LIKE IT COLD.
!!
COMMUNICATION INTERRUPTED
WHAT WERE YOU SAYING?
I WAS SAYING SOMETHING?
!!!
BRAIN INTERRUPTED
FINISH YOUR THOUGHT.
I HAD A **THOUGHT**??
!!
!!

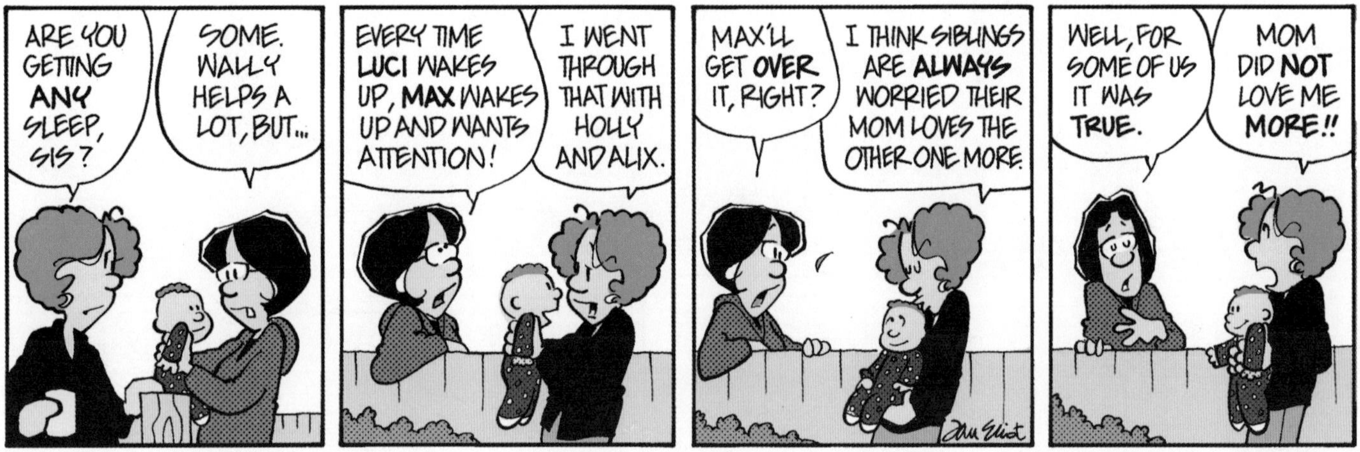
ARE YOU GETTING **ANY** SLEEP, SIS?
SOME. WALLY HELPS A LOT, BUT...
EVERY TIME **LUCI** WAKES UP, **MAX** WAKES UP AND WANTS ATTENTION!
I WENT THROUGH THAT WITH HOLLY AND ALIX.
MAX'LL GET **OVER** IT, RIGHT?
I THINK SIBLINGS ARE **ALWAYS** WORRIED THEIR MOM LOVES THE OTHER ONE MORE.
WELL, FOR SOME OF US IT WAS **TRUE**.
MOM DID **NOT** LOVE ME **MORE**!!

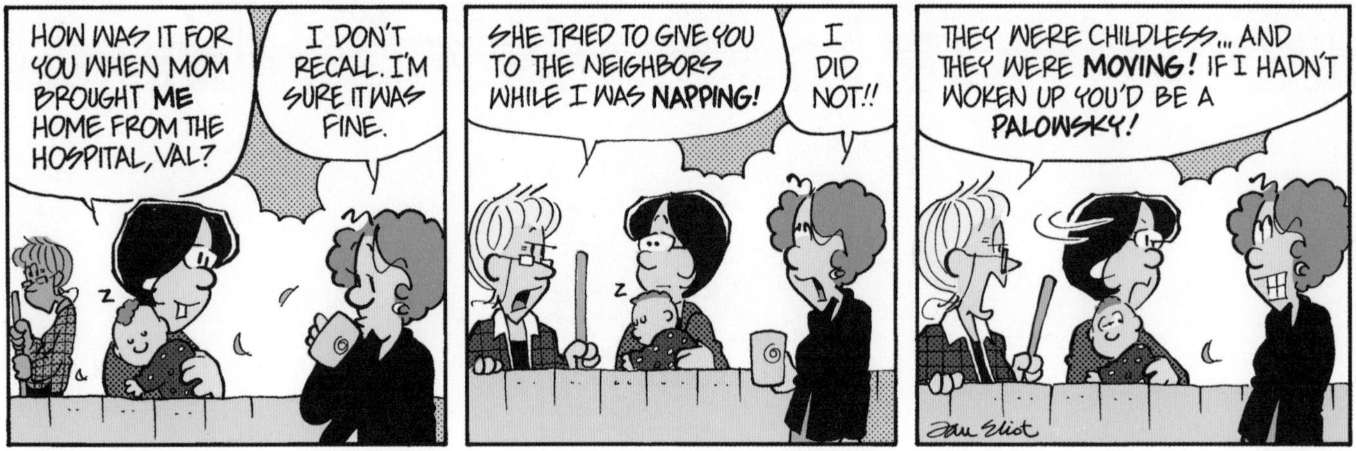
HOW WAS IT FOR YOU WHEN MOM BROUGHT **ME** HOME FROM THE HOSPITAL, VAL?
I DON'T RECALL. I'M SURE IT WAS FINE.
SHE TRIED TO GIVE YOU TO THE NEIGHBORS WHILE I WAS **NAPPING**!
I DID NOT!!
THEY WERE CHILDLESS... AND THEY WERE **MOVING**! IF I HADN'T WOKEN UP YOU'D BE A **PALOWSKY**!

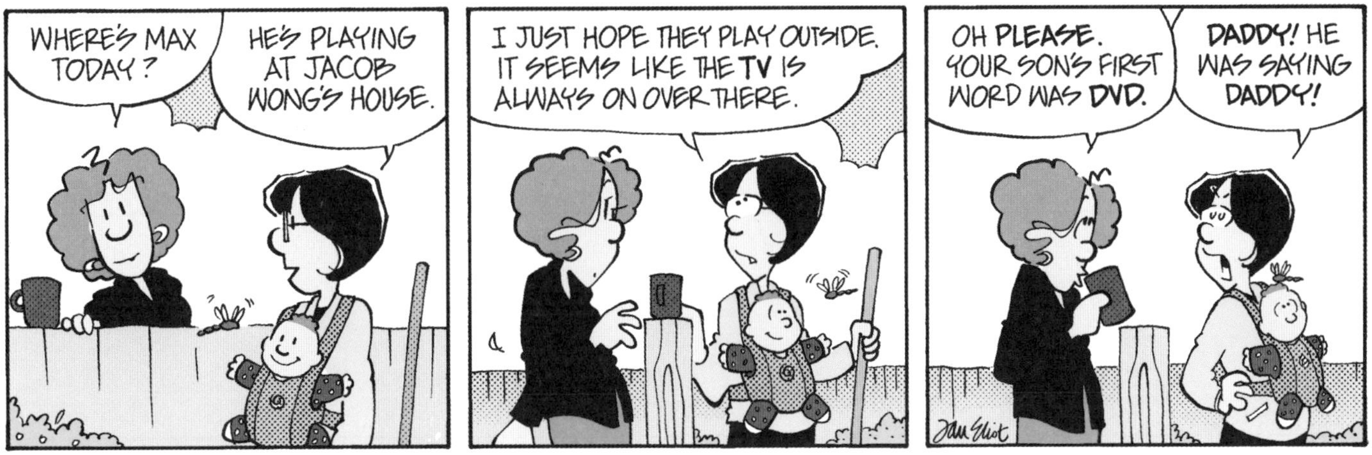
WHERE'S MAX TODAY?
HE'S PLAYING AT JACOB WONG'S HOUSE.
I JUST HOPE THEY PLAY OUTSIDE. IT SEEMS LIKE THE **TV** IS ALWAYS ON OVER THERE.
OH **PLEASE**. YOUR SON'S FIRST WORD WAS **DVD**.
DADDY! HE WAS SAYING **DADDY!**

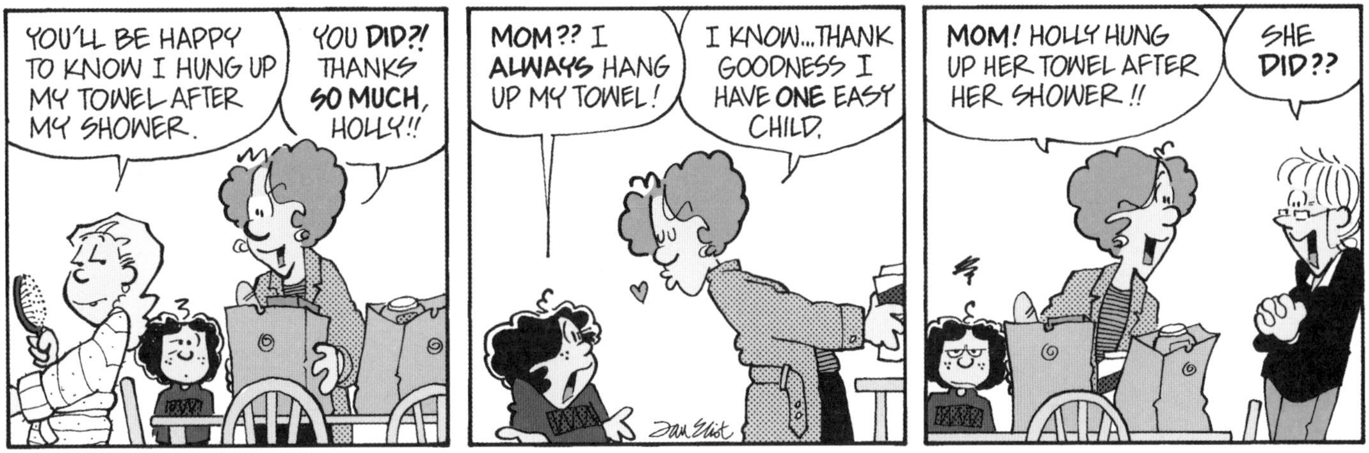
YOU'LL BE HAPPY TO KNOW I HUNG UP MY TOWEL AFTER MY SHOWER.
YOU **DID?!** THANKS **SO MUCH**, HOLLY!!
MOM?? I **ALWAYS** HANG UP MY TOWEL!
I KNOW...THANK GOODNESS I HAVE **ONE** EASY CHILD.
MOM! HOLLY HUNG UP HER TOWEL AFTER HER SHOWER!!
SHE **DID??**

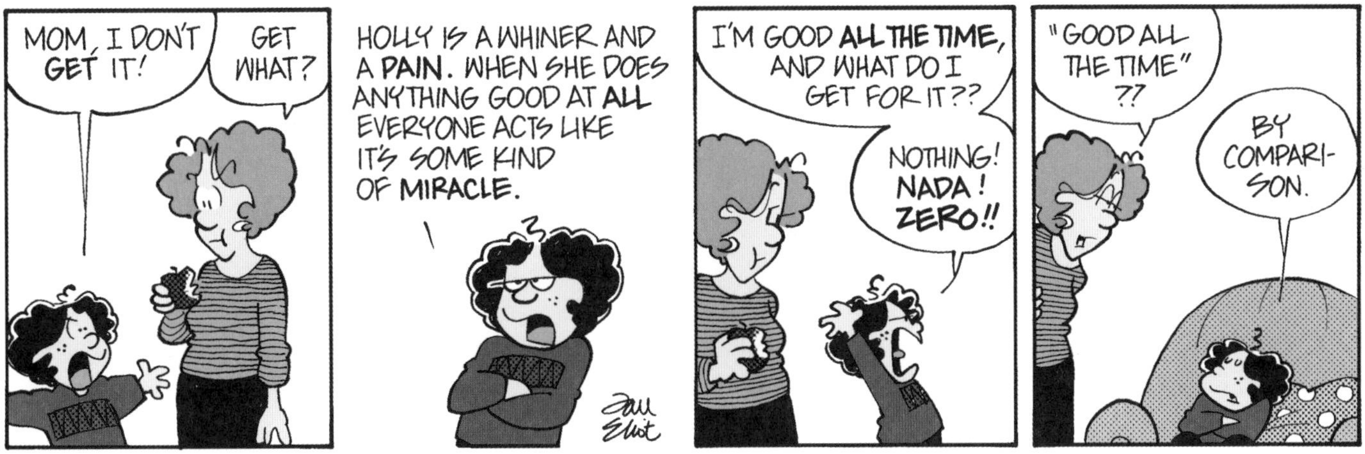
MOM, I DON'T **GET** IT!
GET WHAT?
HOLLY IS A WHINER AND A **PAIN**. WHEN SHE DOES ANYTHING GOOD AT **ALL** EVERYONE ACTS LIKE IT'S SOME KIND OF **MIRACLE**.
I'M GOOD **ALL THE TIME**, AND WHAT DO I GET FOR IT??
NOTHING! **NADA! ZERO!!**
"GOOD ALL THE TIME"??
BY COMPARISON.

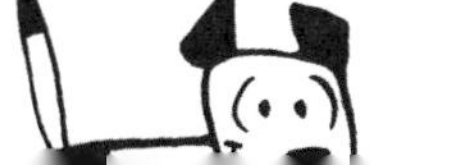

Stone Soup

CAN I TAKE YOU TO DINNER?
I'D LOVE THAT!
BUT... I'VE HAD TO WORK SO MUCH LATELY, I'D FEEL BAD LEAVING THE GIRLS HOME ALONE AGAIN...
BRING THEM!
BUT THEN I HATE TO THINK OF MOM EATING ALL BY HERSELF...
BRING HER TOO!
OH WAIT! I'M SUPPOSED TO TAKE DINNER TO MY SISTER'S ... THEY HAVEN'T HAD MUCH TIME TO COOK SINCE THE BABY CAME...
INVITE THEM. WE'LL ALL GO.
ARE YOU SURE?
WHEN YOU DATE THE MOM, YOU DATE THE VILLAGE.
IF YOU REALLY LOVE OUR MOM, YOU'LL LET US ORDER WHATEVER WE WANT.
I LIKE STEAK.

VROOOOOOOM!

Stone Soup

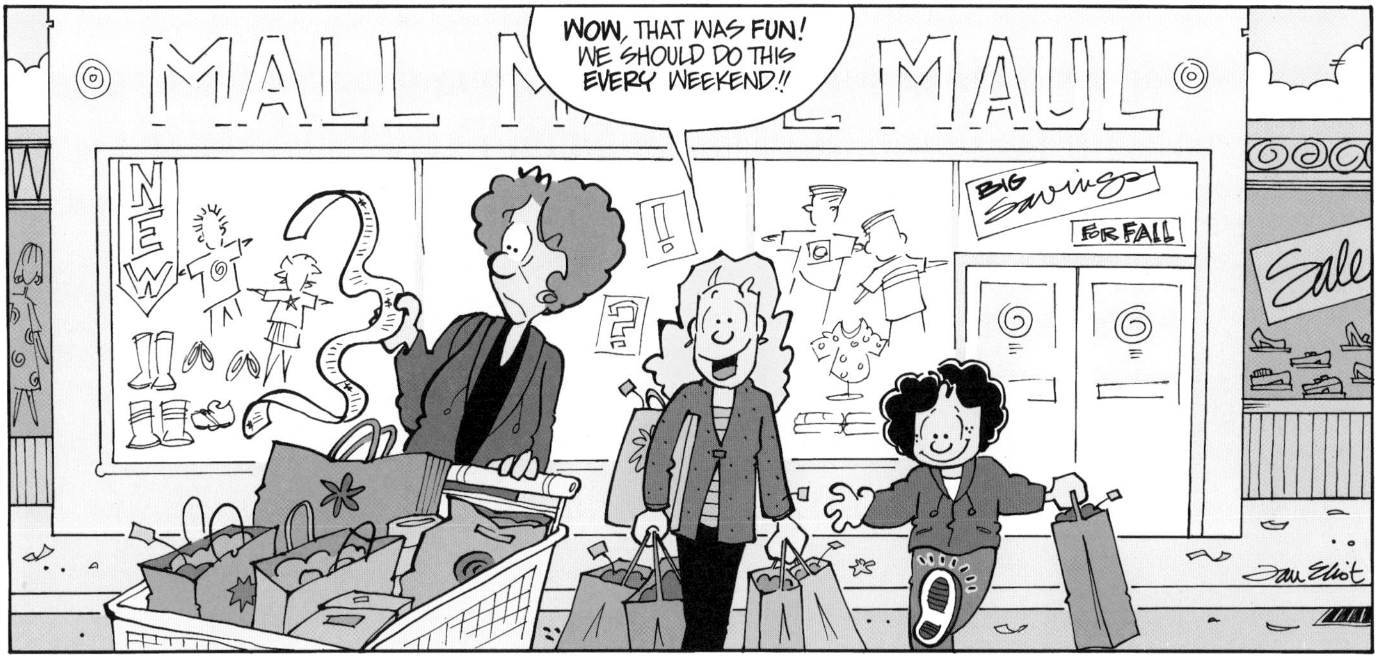
MALL
MAUL
WOW, THAT WAS FUN! WE SHOULD DO THIS EVERY WEEKEND!!
NEW
BIG Savings
FOR FALL
Sale
Jan Eliot

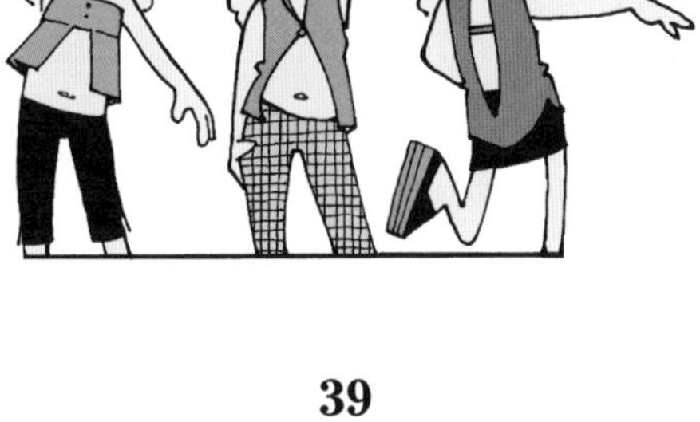

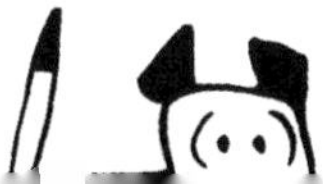

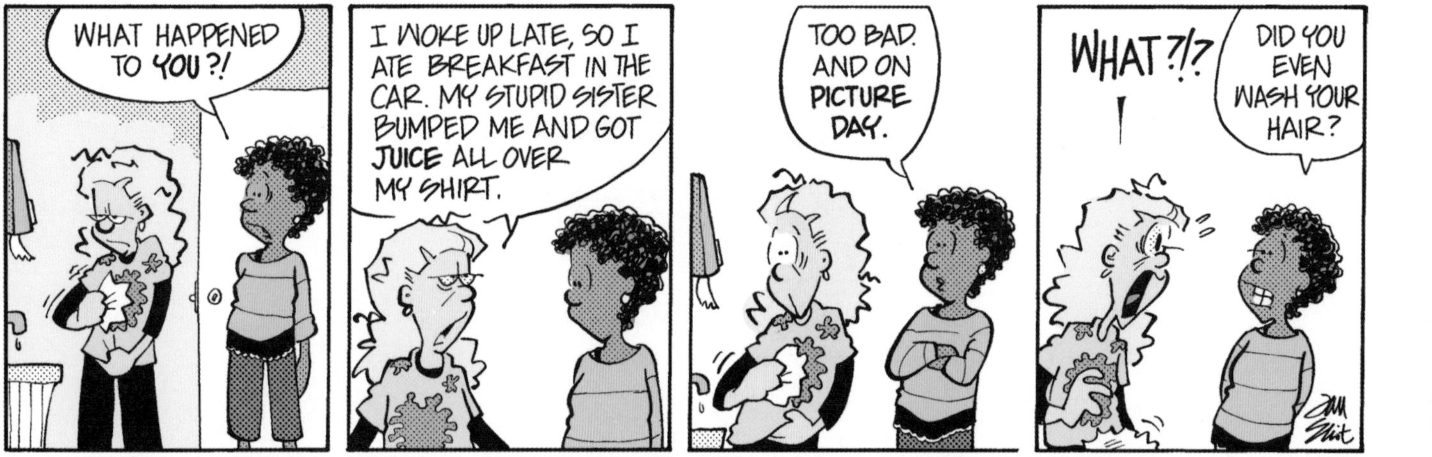
WHAT HAPPENED TO YOU?!
I WOKE UP LATE, SO I ATE BREAKFAST IN THE CAR. MY STUPID SISTER BUMPED ME AND GOT JUICE ALL OVER MY SHIRT.
TOO BAD. AND ON PICTURE DAY.
WHAT?!?
DID YOU EVEN WASH YOUR HAIR?

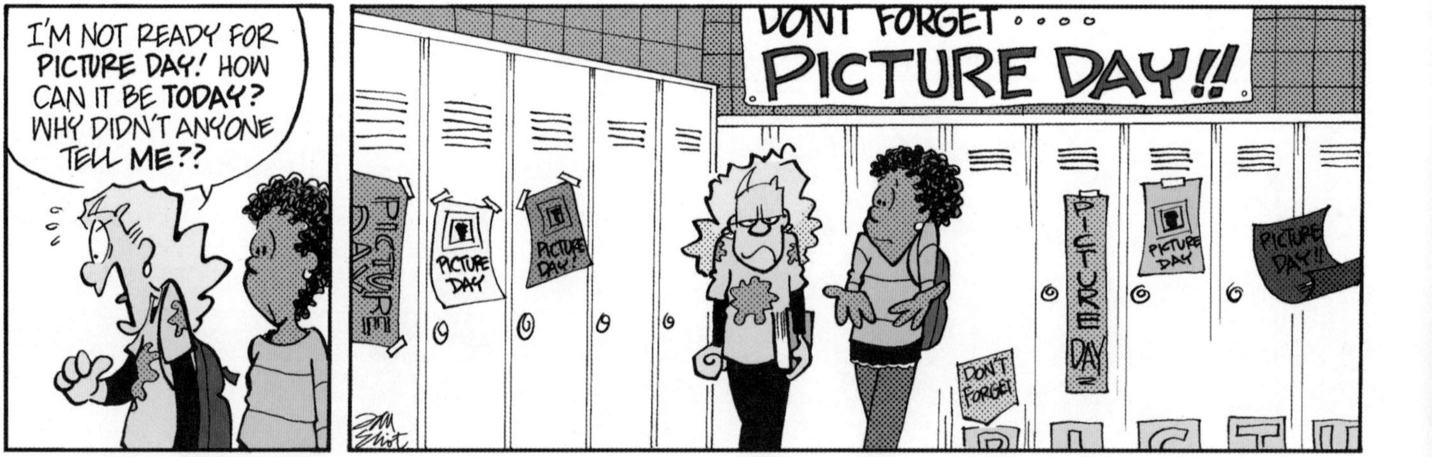
I'M NOT READY FOR PICTURE DAY! HOW CAN IT BE TODAY? WHY DIDN'T ANYONE TELL ME??
DON'T FORGET ....
PICTURE DAY!!
PICTURE DAY
PICTURE DAY
PICTURE DAY
PICTURE DAY
PICTURE DAY!!
PICTURE DAY
DON'T FORGET

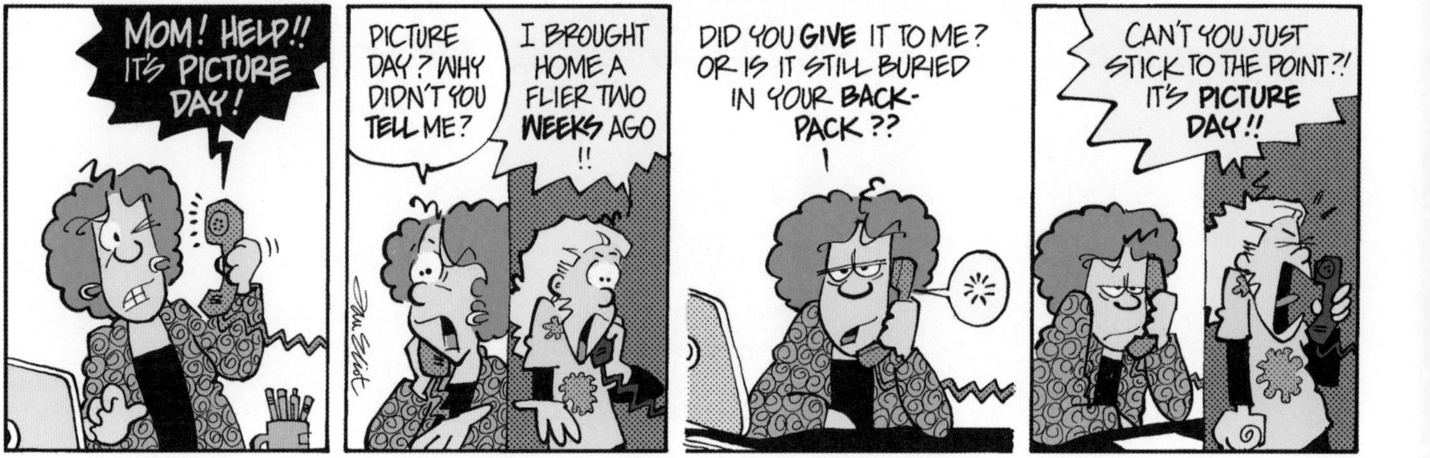
MOM! HELP!! IT'S PICTURE DAY!
PICTURE DAY? WHY DIDN'T YOU TELL ME?
I BROUGHT HOME A FLIER TWO WEEKS AGO!!
DID YOU GIVE IT TO ME? OR IS IT STILL BURIED IN YOUR BACK-PACK??
CAN'T YOU JUST STICK TO THE POINT?! IT'S PICTURE DAY!!

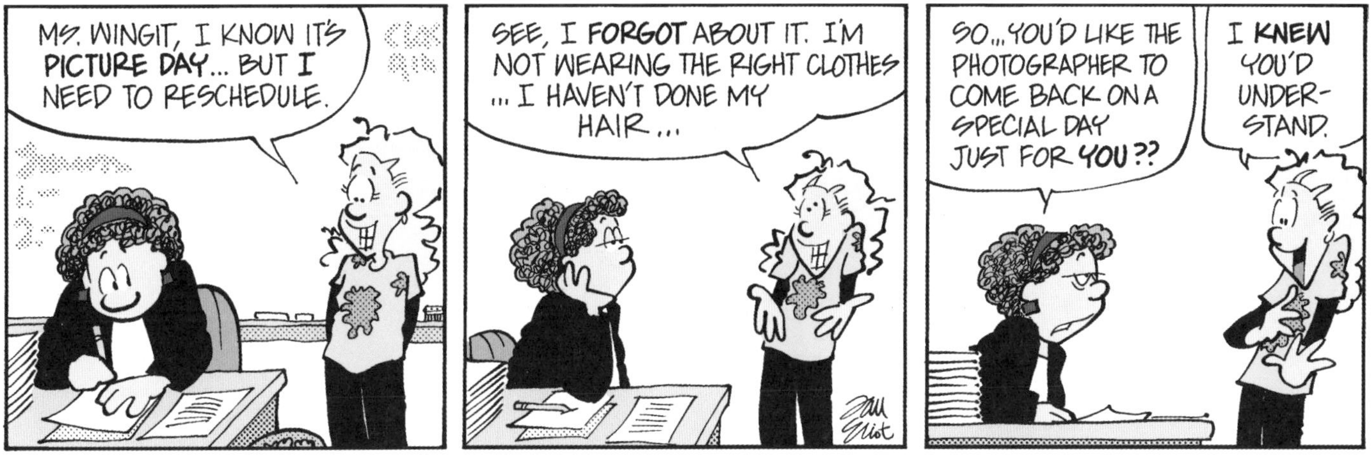
MS. WINGIT, I KNOW IT'S **PICTURE DAY**... BUT **I** NEED TO RESCHEDULE.
SEE, I **FORGOT** ABOUT IT. I'M NOT WEARING THE RIGHT CLOTHES ... I HAVEN'T DONE MY HAIR...
SO... YOU'D LIKE THE PHOTOGRAPHER TO COME BACK ON A SPECIAL DAY JUST FOR **YOU**??
I **KNEW** YOU'D UNDERSTAND.

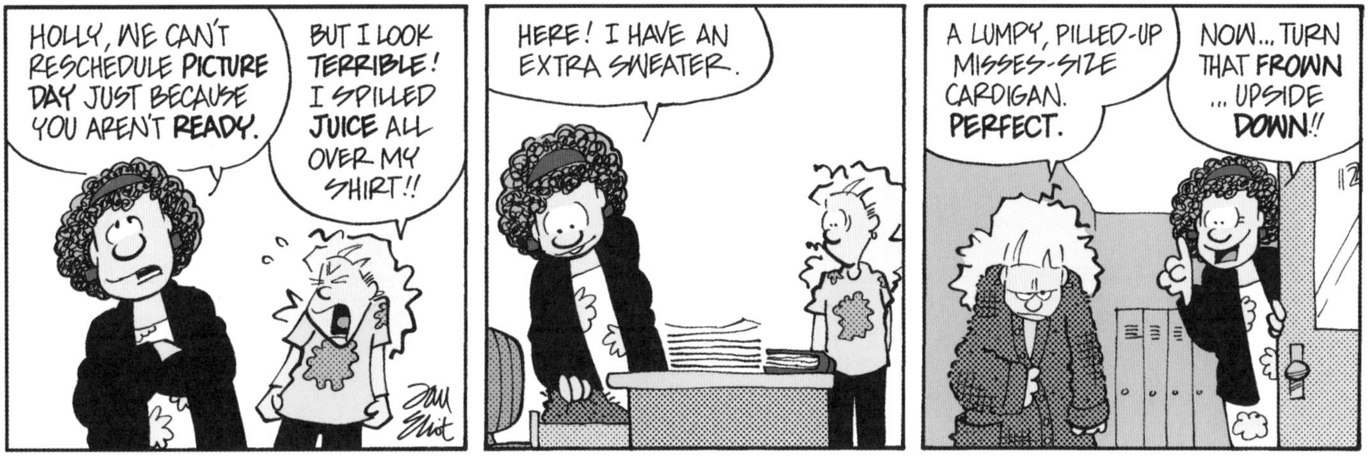
HOLLY, WE CAN'T RESCHEDULE **PICTURE DAY** JUST BECAUSE YOU AREN'T **READY**.
BUT I LOOK **TERRIBLE**! I SPILLED **JUICE** ALL OVER MY SHIRT!!
HERE! I HAVE AN EXTRA SWEATER.
A LUMPY, PILLED-UP MISSES-SIZE CARDIGAN. **PERFECT**.
NOW... TURN THAT **FROWN** ... UPSIDE **DOWN**!!

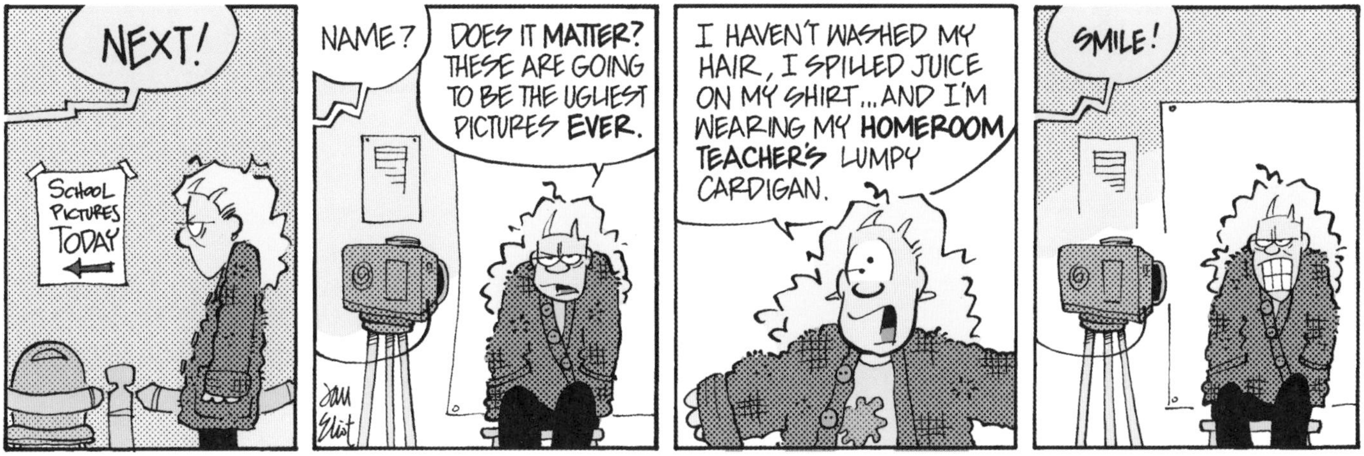
NEXT!
SCHOOL PICTURES TODAY
NAME?
DOES IT **MATTER**? THESE ARE GOING TO BE THE UGLIEST PICTURES **EVER**.
I HAVEN'T WASHED MY HAIR, I SPILLED JUICE ON MY SHIRT... AND I'M WEARING MY **HOMEROOM TEACHER'S** LUMPY CARDIGAN.
SMILE!

Stone Soup

HOW ARE THINGS WITH YOU AND VAL, PHIL?
OK...
BUT IT'S A LITTLE WEIRD FOR ME... SORT OF BEING THE "DAD."
DATE A SINGLE MOM AND YOU'RE IN THE DAD ROLE FOR SURE.
YOU'RE REALLY GOOD AT BEING MAX AND ANDY'S DAD...
THEY NEEDED ME. ANYONE WOULD DO IT.
I SUPPOSE GIRLS ARE EASIER THAN BOYS...
HA! BOYS BREAK THINGS... THEY'RE UNCOMMUNICATIVE ...BUT GIRLS...
OFFICER JACKSON? DO YOU REALIZE THAT YOUR ROLE AS CAMPUS COP AND SOMEONE WHO DATES MY MOTHER COULD HAVE COMPLICATED SOCIAL CONSEQUENCES FOR ME? WE SERIOUSLY NEED TO TALK... AND—
GIRLS HAVE ISSUES.
LEAVE OFFICER JACKSON ALONE, HONEY. HE'S NOT WEARING HIS BODY ARMOR.

WHAT?

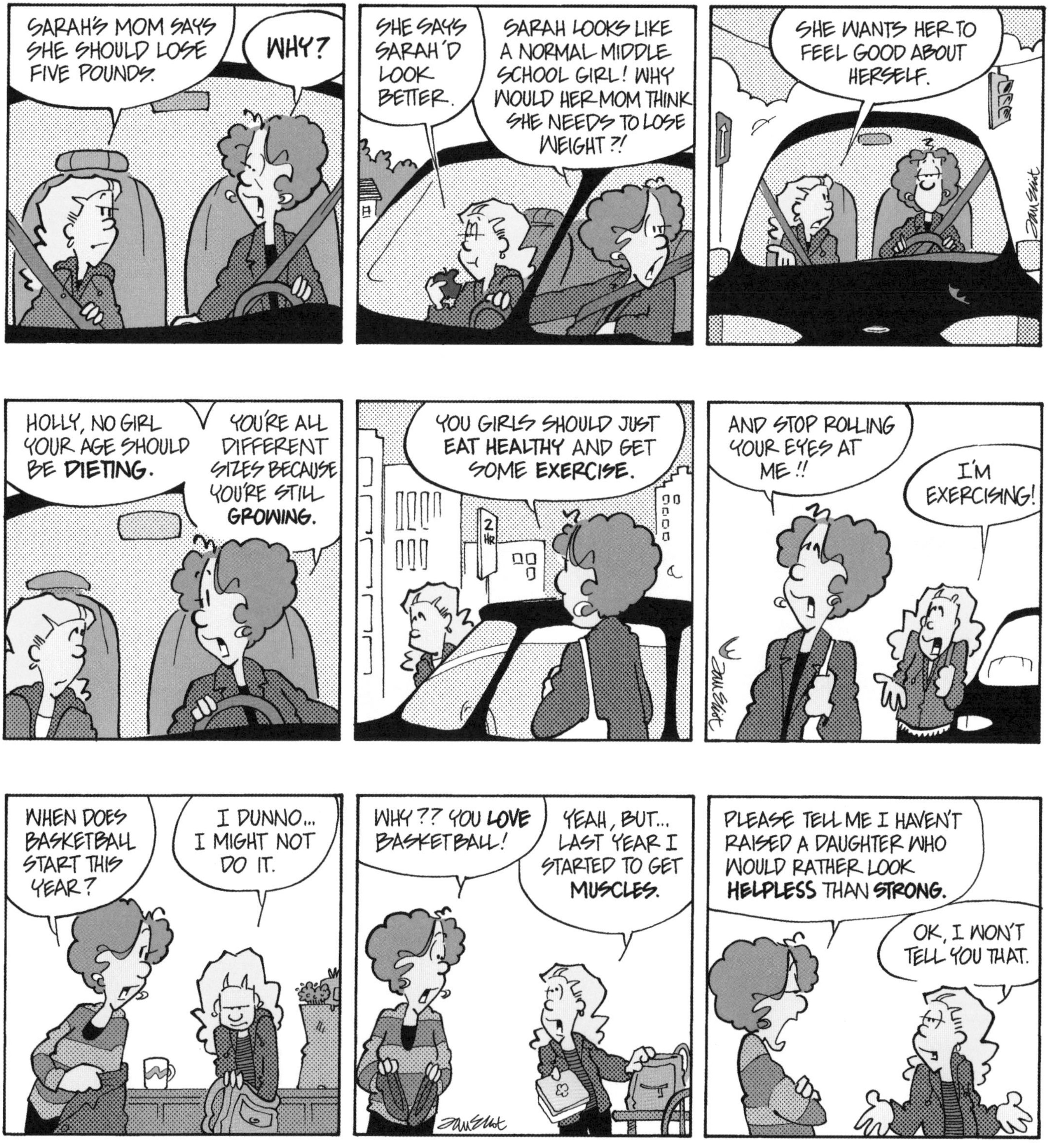
SARAH'S MOM SAYS SHE SHOULD LOSE FIVE POUNDS.
WHY?
SHE SAYS SARAH'D LOOK BETTER.
SARAH LOOKS LIKE A NORMAL MIDDLE SCHOOL GIRL! WHY WOULD HER MOM THINK SHE NEEDS TO LOSE WEIGHT?!
SHE WANTS HER TO FEEL GOOD ABOUT HERSELF.
HOLLY, NO GIRL YOUR AGE SHOULD BE DIETING.
YOU'RE ALL DIFFERENT SIZES BECAUSE YOU'RE STILL GROWING.
YOU GIRLS SHOULD JUST EAT HEALTHY AND GET SOME EXERCISE.
AND STOP ROLLING YOUR EYES AT ME!!
I'M EXERCISING!
WHEN DOES BASKETBALL START THIS YEAR?
I DUNNO... I MIGHT NOT DO IT.
WHY?? YOU LOVE BASKETBALL!
YEAH, BUT... LAST YEAR I STARTED TO GET MUSCLES.
PLEASE TELL ME I HAVEN'T RAISED A DAUGHTER WHO WOULD RATHER LOOK HELPLESS THAN STRONG.
OK, I WON'T TELL YOU THAT.

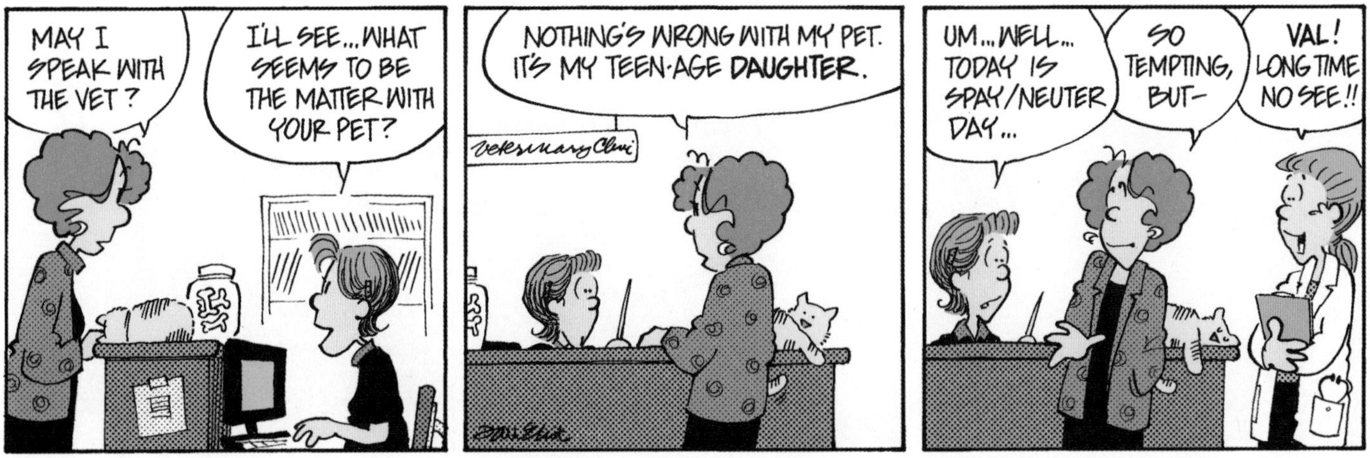
MAY I SPEAK WITH THE VET?
I'LL SEE... WHAT SEEMS TO BE THE MATTER WITH YOUR PET?
NOTHING'S WRONG WITH MY PET. IT'S MY TEEN-AGE DAUGHTER.
UM... WELL... TODAY IS SPAY/NEUTER DAY...
SO TEMPTING, BUT-
VAL! LONG TIME NO SEE!!

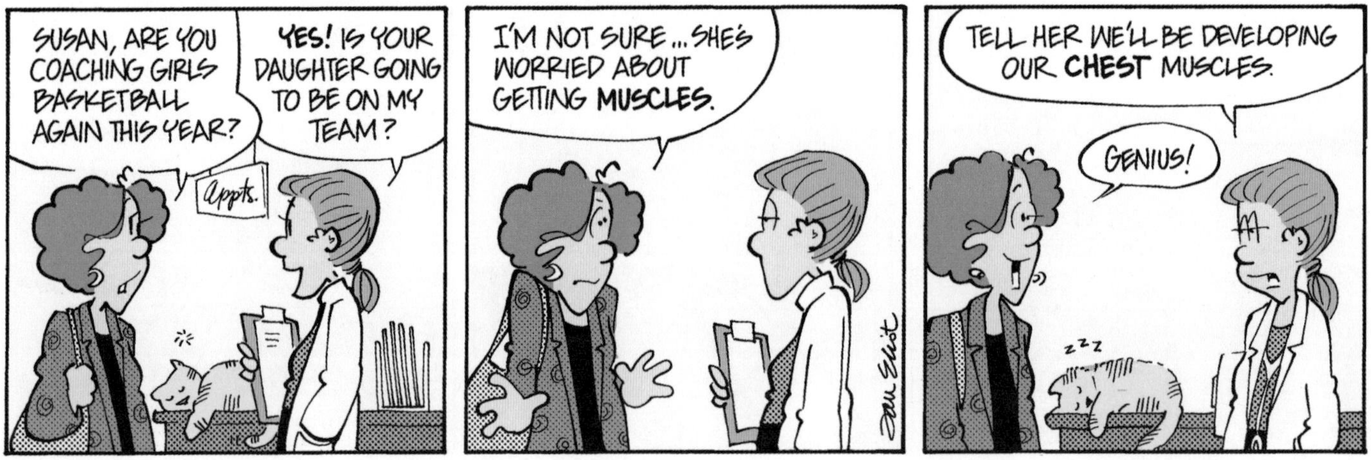
SUSAN, ARE YOU COACHING GIRLS BASKETBALL AGAIN THIS YEAR?
YES! IS YOUR DAUGHTER GOING TO BE ON MY TEAM?
Appts.
I'M NOT SURE... SHE'S WORRIED ABOUT GETTING MUSCLES.
TELL HER WE'LL BE DEVELOPING OUR CHEST MUSCLES.
GENIUS!

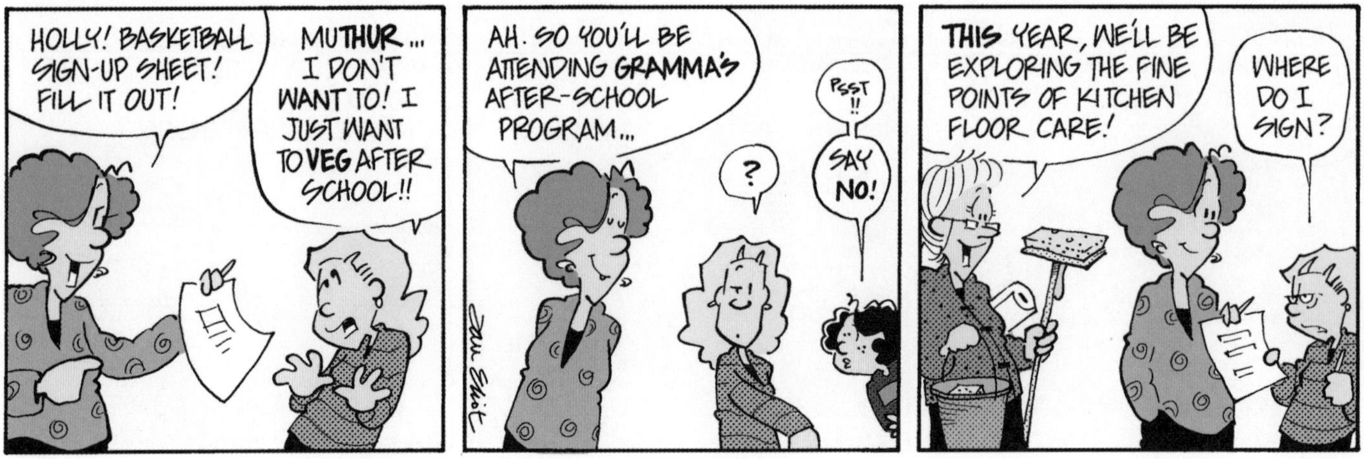
HOLLY! BASKETBALL SIGN-UP SHEET! FILL IT OUT!
MUTHUR... I DON'T WANT TO! I JUST WANT TO VEG AFTER SCHOOL!!
AH. SO YOU'LL BE ATTENDING GRAMMA'S AFTER-SCHOOL PROGRAM...
?
PSST!!
SAY NO!
THIS YEAR, WE'LL BE EXPLORING THE FINE POINTS OF KITCHEN FLOOR CARE!
WHERE DO I SIGN?

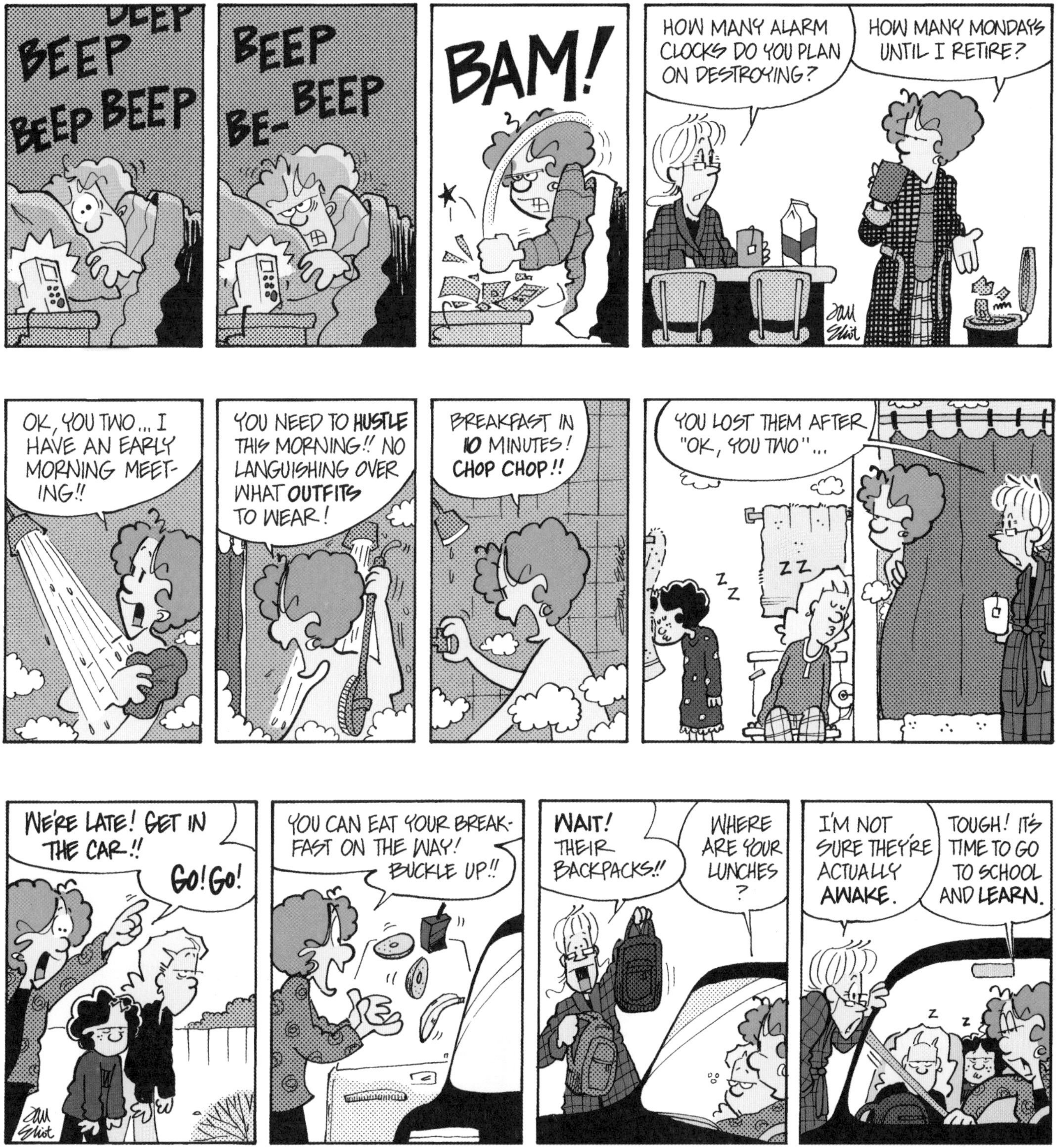
BEEP
BEEP BEEP
BEEP
BE- BEEP
BAM!
HOW MANY ALARM CLOCKS DO YOU PLAN ON DESTROYING?
HOW MANY MONDAYS UNTIL I RETIRE?
OK, YOU TWO... I HAVE AN EARLY MORNING MEET-ING!!
YOU NEED TO HUSTLE THIS MORNING!! NO LANGUISHING OVER WHAT OUTFITS TO WEAR!
BREAKFAST IN 10 MINUTES! CHOP CHOP!!
YOU LOST THEM AFTER "OK, YOU TWO"...
Z Z
Z Z
WE'RE LATE! GET IN THE CAR!!
GO! GO!
YOU CAN EAT YOUR BREAK-FAST ON THE WAY! BUCKLE UP!!
WAIT! THEIR BACKPACKS!!
WHERE ARE YOUR LUNCHES?
I'M NOT SURE THEY'RE ACTUALLY AWAKE.
TOUGH! IT'S TIME TO GO TO SCHOOL AND LEARN.
Z Z

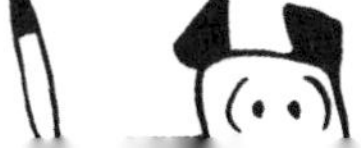

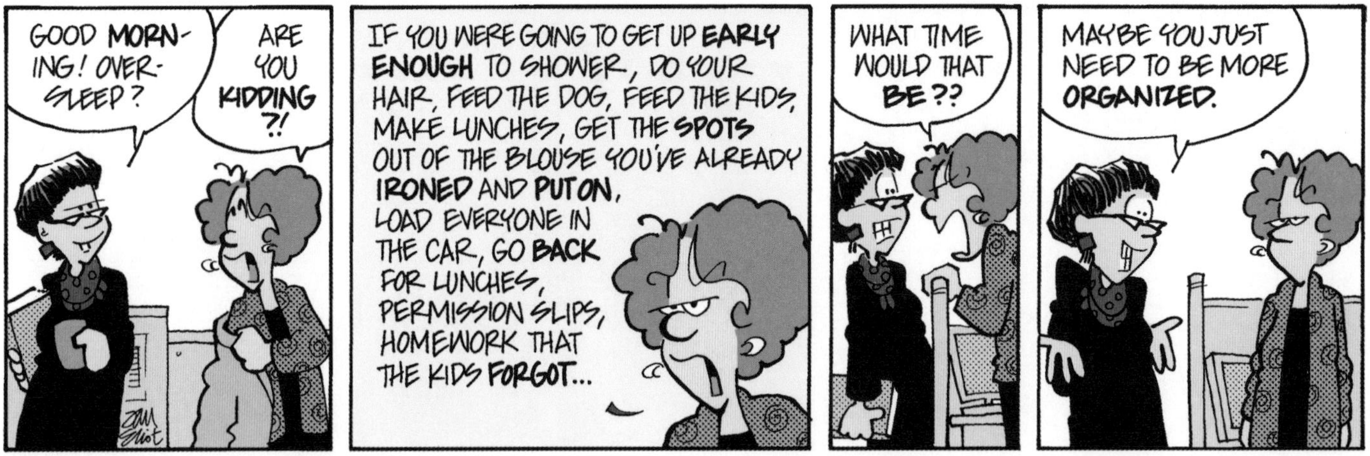
GOOD MORNING! OVERSLEEP?
ARE YOU KIDDING?!
IF YOU WERE GOING TO GET UP EARLY ENOUGH TO SHOWER, DO YOUR HAIR, FEED THE DOG, FEED THE KIDS, MAKE LUNCHES, GET THE SPOTS OUT OF THE BLOUSE YOU'VE ALREADY IRONED AND PUT ON, LOAD EVERYONE IN THE CAR, GO BACK FOR LUNCHES, PERMISSION SLIPS, HOMEWORK THAT THE KIDS FORGOT...
WHAT TIME WOULD THAT BE??
MAYBE YOU JUST NEED TO BE MORE ORGANIZED.

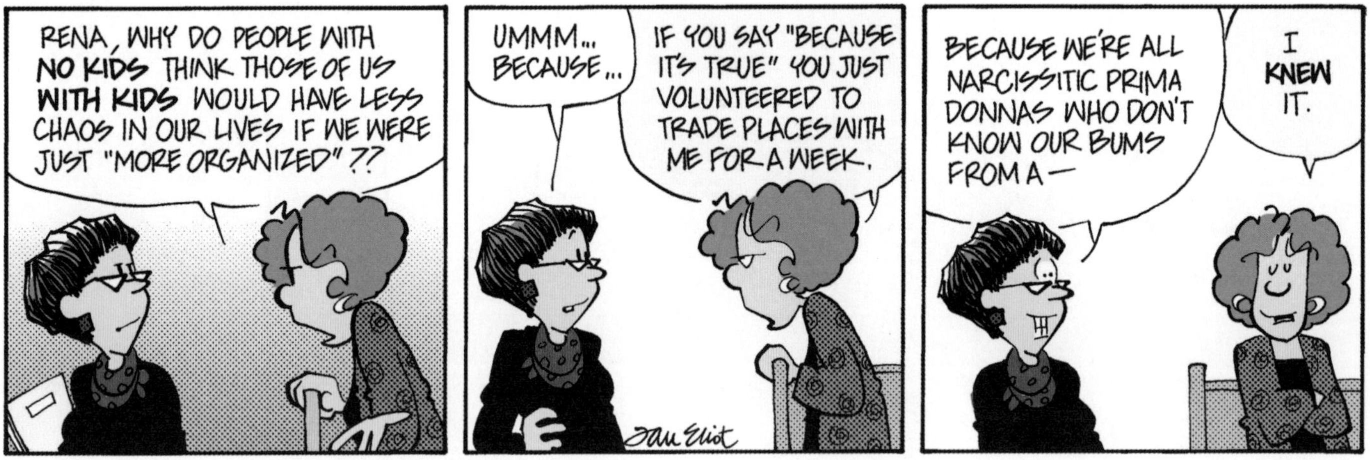
RENA, WHY DO PEOPLE WITH NO KIDS THINK THOSE OF US WITH KIDS WOULD HAVE LESS CHAOS IN OUR LIVES IF WE WERE JUST "MORE ORGANIZED"??
UMMM... BECAUSE...
IF YOU SAY "BECAUSE IT'S TRUE" YOU JUST VOLUNTEERED TO TRADE PLACES WITH ME FOR A WEEK.
BECAUSE WE'RE ALL NARCISSISTIC PRIMA DONNAS WHO DON'T KNOW OUR BUMS FROM A—
I KNEW IT.

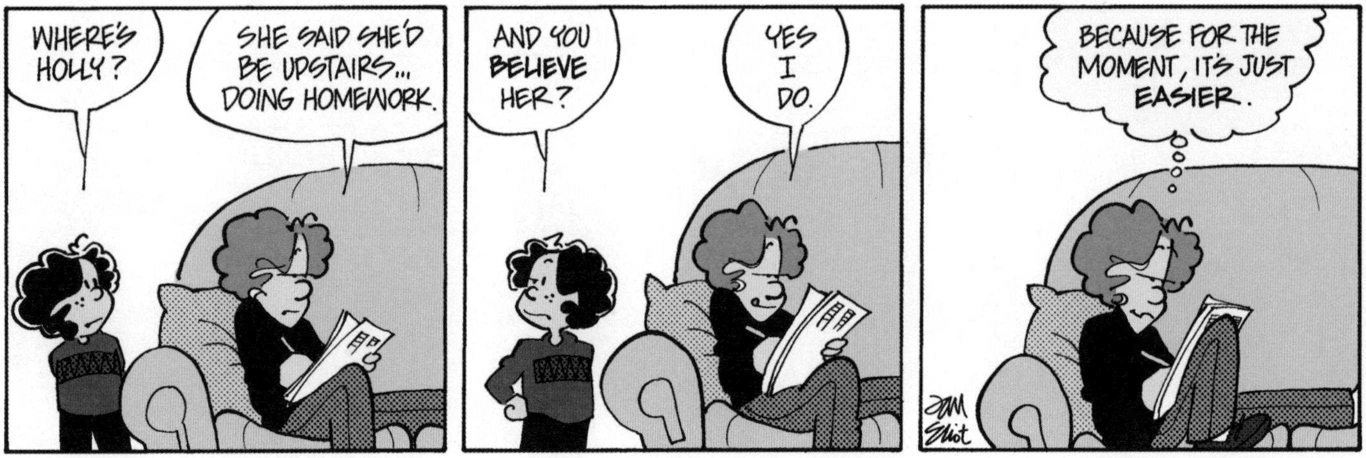
WHERE'S HOLLY?
SHE SAID SHE'D BE UPSTAIRS... DOING HOMEWORK.
AND YOU BELIEVE HER?
YES I DO.
BECAUSE FOR THE MOMENT, IT'S JUST EASIER.

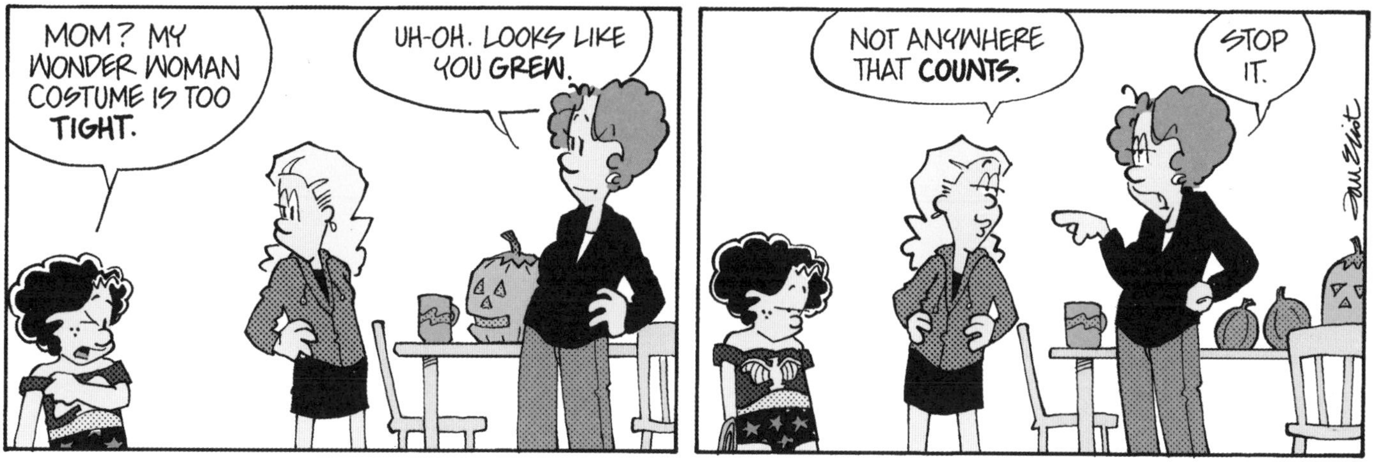
MOM? MY WONDER WOMAN COSTUME IS TOO TIGHT.
UH-OH. LOOKS LIKE YOU GREW.
NOT ANYWHERE THAT COUNTS.
STOP IT.

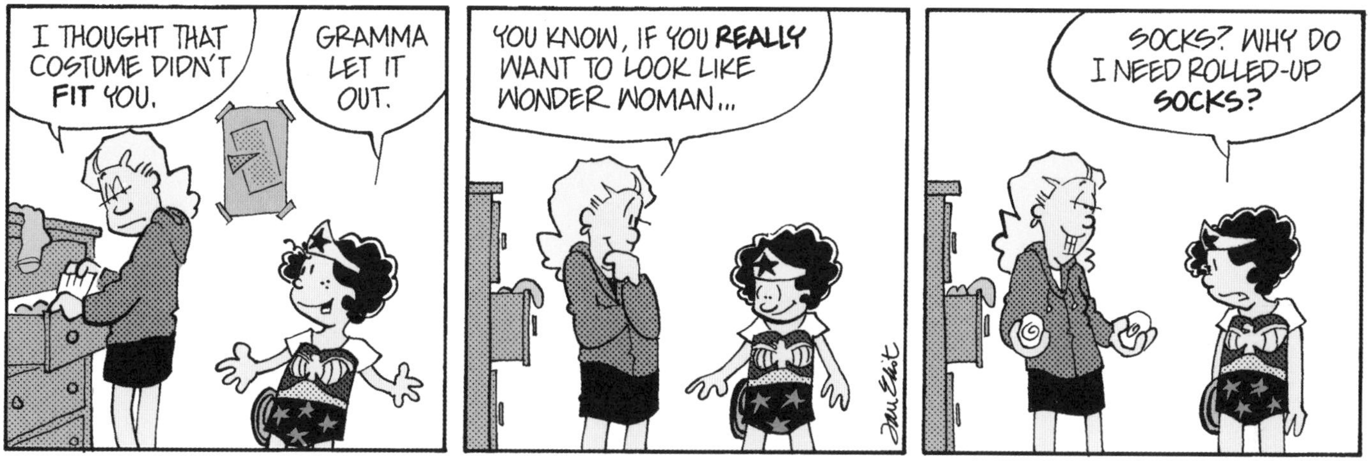
I THOUGHT THAT COSTUME DIDN'T FIT YOU.
GRAMMA LET IT OUT.
YOU KNOW, IF YOU REALLY WANT TO LOOK LIKE WONDER WOMAN...
SOCKS? WHY DO I NEED ROLLED-UP SOCKS?

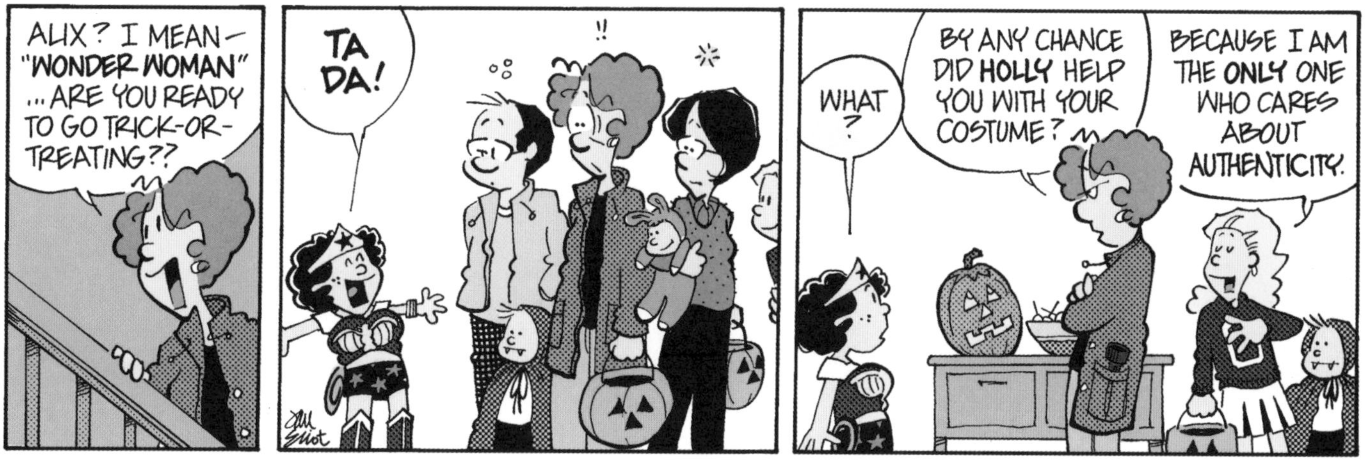
ALIX? I MEAN– "WONDER WOMAN" ...ARE YOU READY TO GO TRICK-OR-TREATING??
TA DA!
!!
WHAT?
BY ANY CHANCE DID HOLLY HELP YOU WITH YOUR COSTUME?
BECAUSE I AM THE ONLY ONE WHO CARES ABOUT AUTHENTICITY.

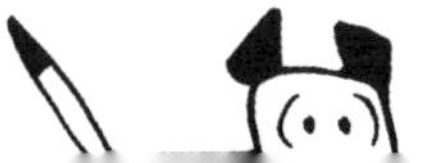

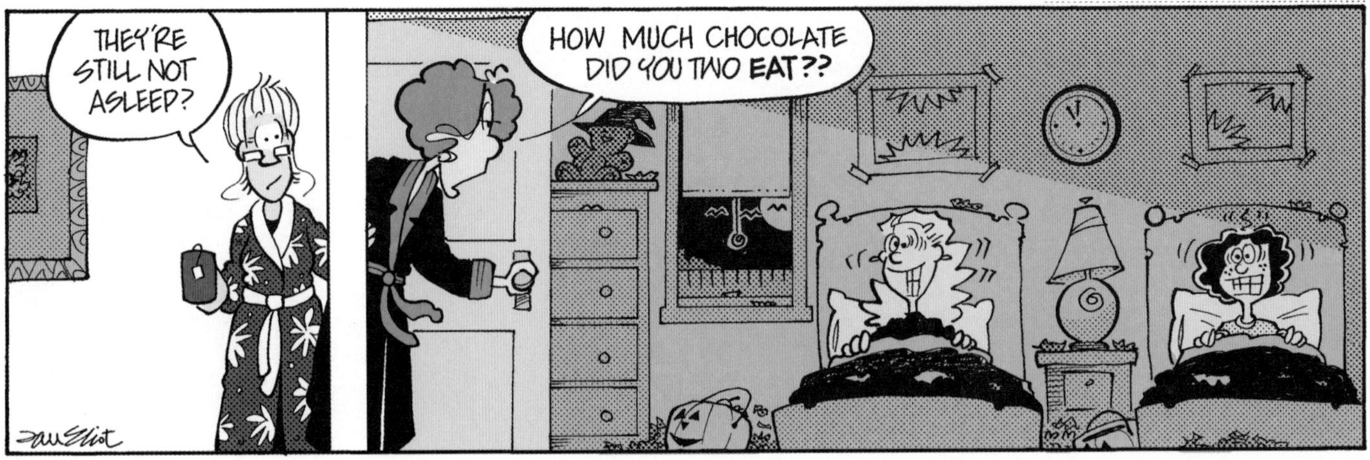
THEY'RE STILL NOT ASLEEP?
HOW MUCH CHOCOLATE DID YOU TWO **EAT**??

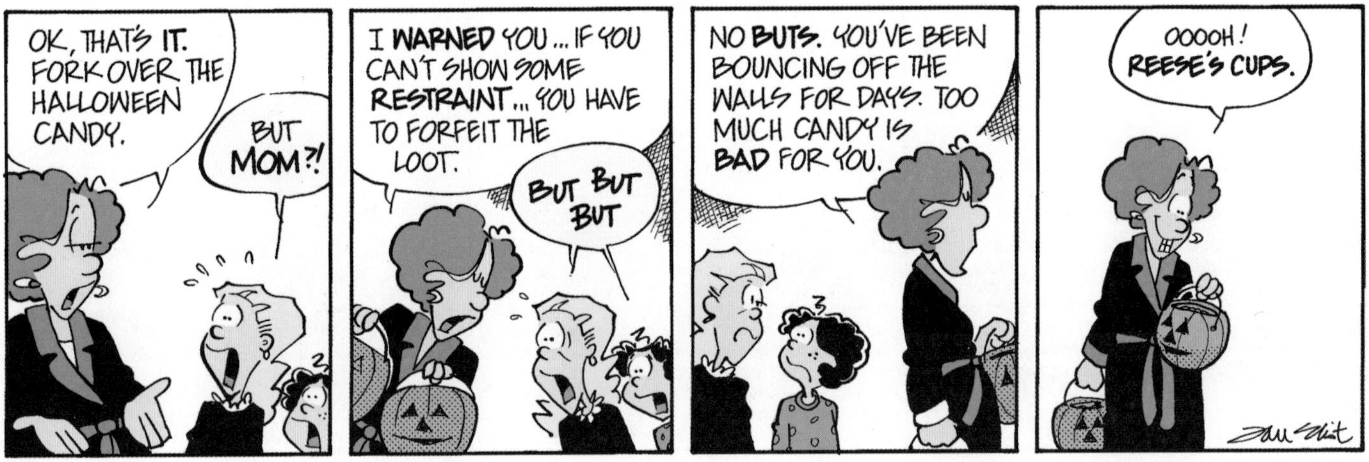
OK, THAT'S **IT.** FORK OVER THE HALLOWEEN CANDY.
BUT **MOM**?!
I **WARNED** YOU ... IF YOU CAN'T SHOW SOME **RESTRAINT**... YOU HAVE TO FORFEIT THE LOOT.
BUT BUT BUT
NO **BUTS.** YOU'VE BEEN BOUNCING OFF THE WALLS FOR DAYS. TOO MUCH CANDY IS **BAD** FOR YOU.
OOOOH! **REESE'S CUPS.**

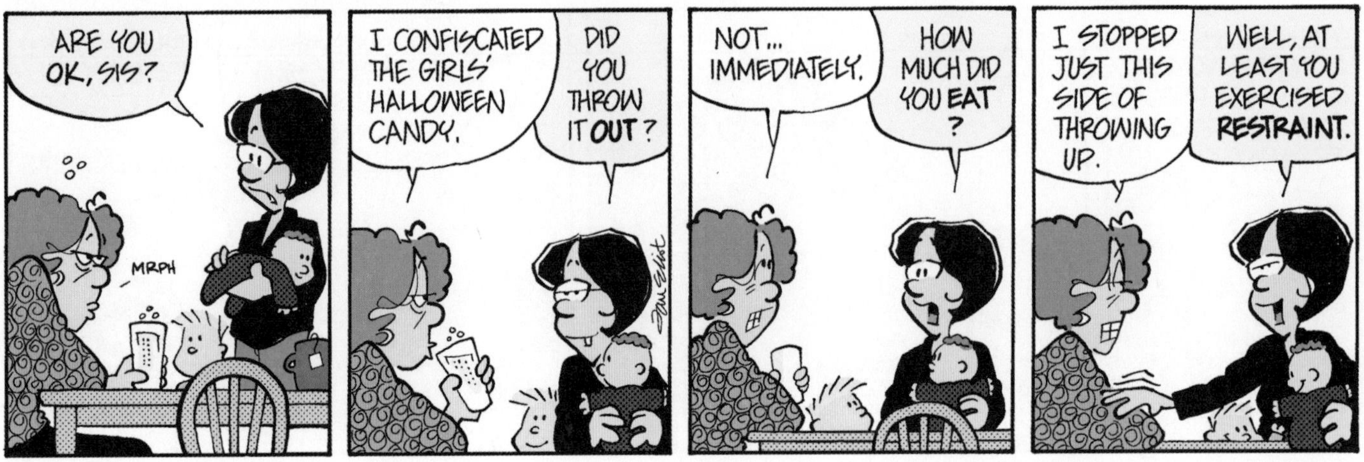
ARE YOU **OK**, SIS?
MRPH
I CONFISCATED THE GIRLS' HALLOWEEN CANDY.
DID YOU THROW IT **OUT**?
NOT... IMMEDIATELY.
HOW MUCH DID YOU **EAT**?
I STOPPED JUST THIS SIDE OF THROWING UP.
WELL, AT LEAST YOU EXERCISED **RESTRAINT.**

Stone Soup

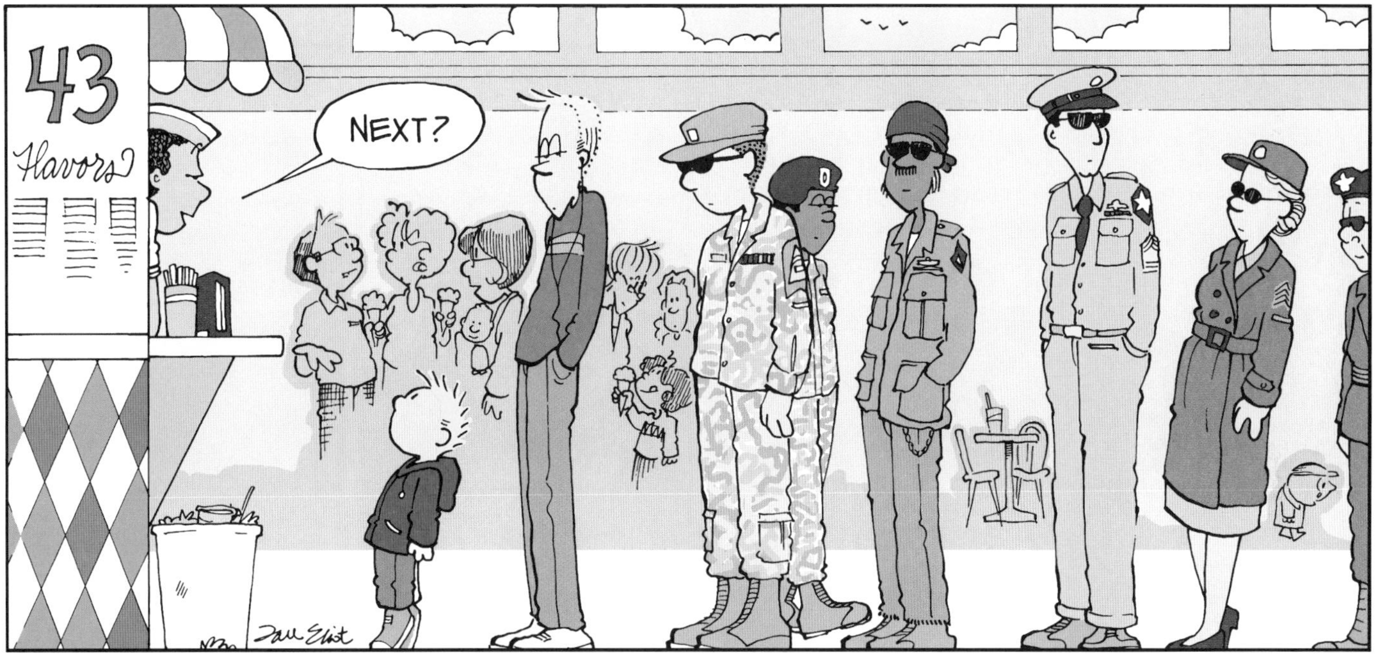
43
Flavors
NEXT?

This strip was created as a tribute for Veterans Day. Each soldier wears a uniform from a different war. 43 flavors refers to 43 presidential administrations. The setting is a mall—a protected, clean place—as we Americans are protected from the realities of war.

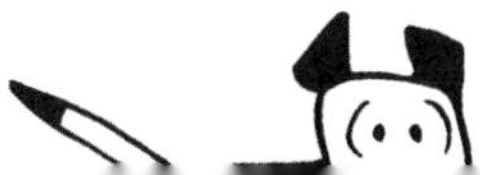

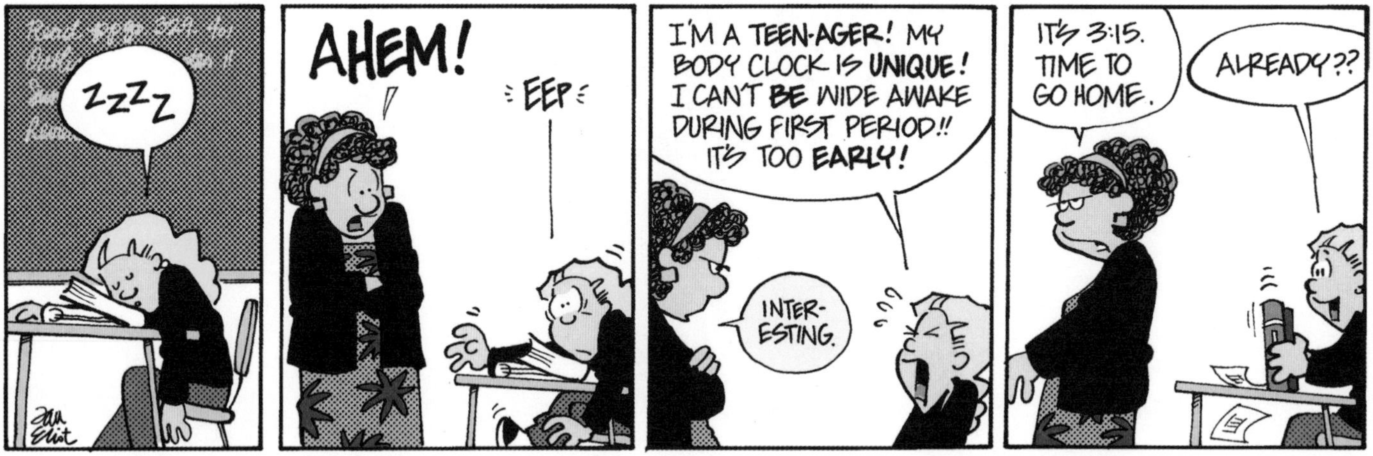
ZZZZ
AHEM!
EEP
I'M A TEEN-AGER! MY BODY CLOCK IS UNIQUE! I CAN'T BE WIDE AWAKE DURING FIRST PERIOD!! IT'S TOO EARLY!
INTER-ESTING.
IT'S 3:15. TIME TO GO HOME.
ALREADY??

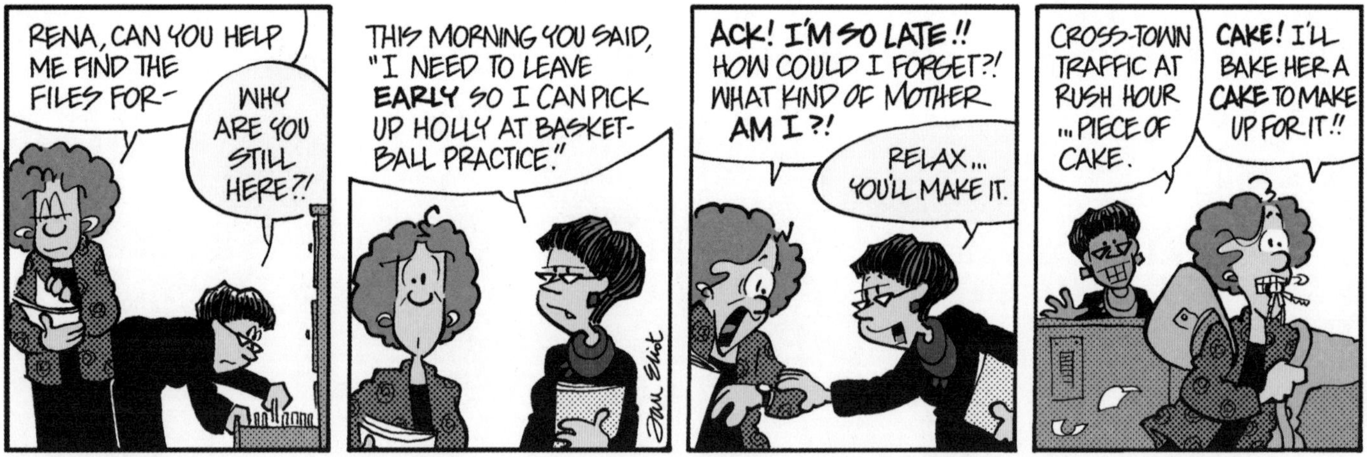
RENA, CAN YOU HELP ME FIND THE FILES FOR-
WHY ARE YOU STILL HERE?!
THIS MORNING YOU SAID, "I NEED TO LEAVE EARLY SO I CAN PICK UP HOLLY AT BASKET-BALL PRACTICE."
ACK! I'M SO LATE!! HOW COULD I FORGET?! WHAT KIND OF MOTHER AM I?!
RELAX... YOU'LL MAKE IT.
CROSS-TOWN TRAFFIC AT RUSH HOUR ... PIECE OF CAKE.
CAKE! I'LL BAKE HER A CAKE TO MAKE UP FOR IT!!

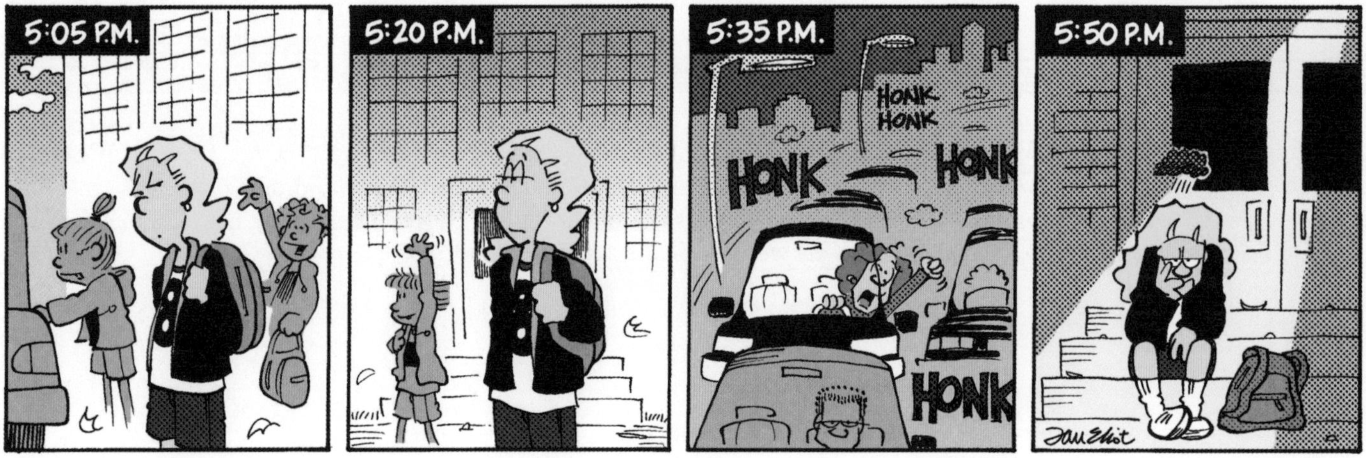
5:05 P.M.
5:20 P.M.
5:35 P.M.
HONK HONK
HONK
HONK
HONK
5:50 P.M.

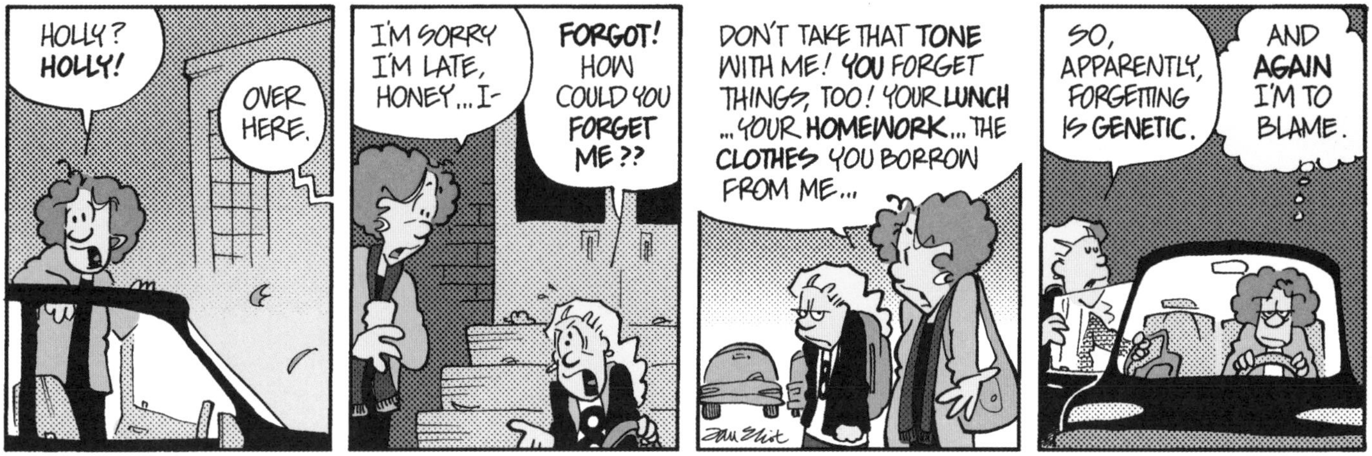
HOLLY? HOLLY!
OVER HERE.
I'M SORRY I'M LATE, HONEY... I-
FORGOT! HOW COULD YOU FORGET ME??
DON'T TAKE THAT TONE WITH ME! YOU FORGET THINGS, TOO! YOUR LUNCH ...YOUR HOMEWORK... THE CLOTHES YOU BORROW FROM ME...
SO, APPARENTLY, FORGETTING IS GENETIC.
AND AGAIN I'M TO BLAME.

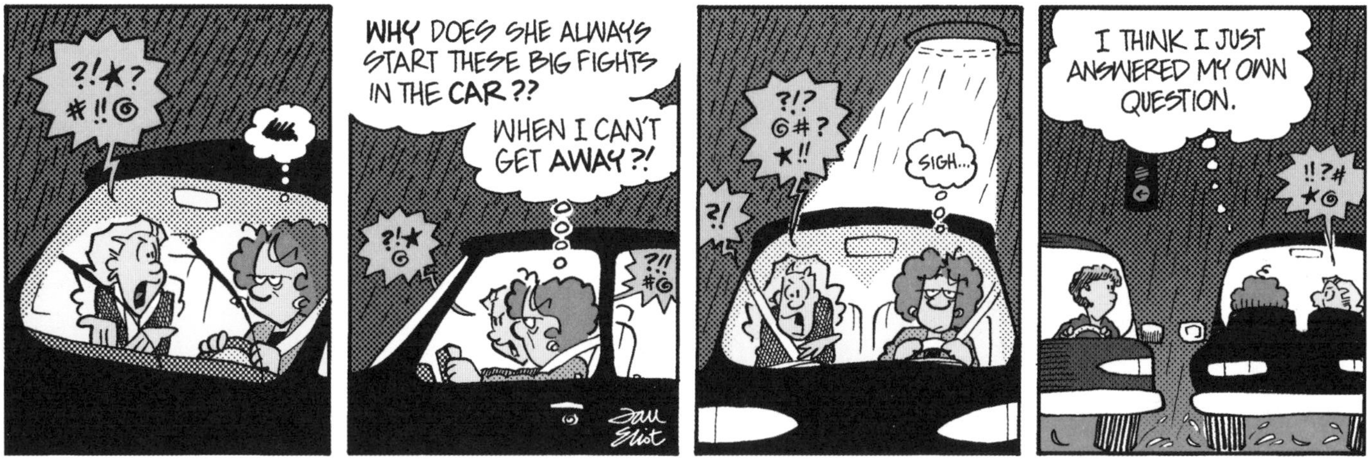
WHY DOES SHE ALWAYS START THESE BIG FIGHTS IN THE CAR??
WHEN I CAN'T GET AWAY?!
SIGH...
I THINK I JUST ANSWERED MY OWN QUESTION.

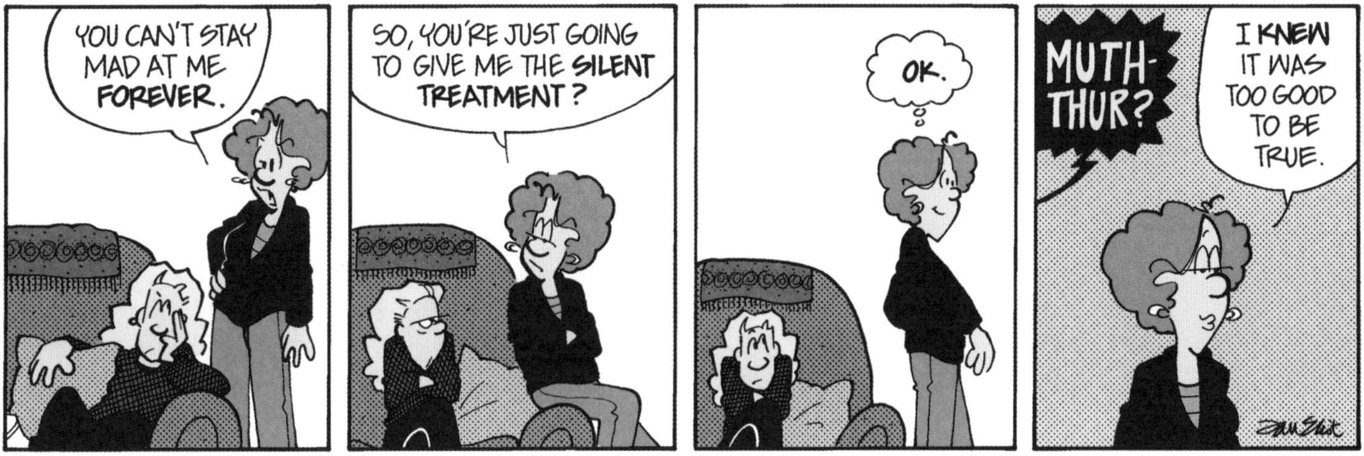
YOU CAN'T STAY MAD AT ME FOREVER.
SO, YOU'RE JUST GOING TO GIVE ME THE SILENT TREATMENT?
OK.
MUTH-THUR?
I KNEW IT WAS TOO GOOD TO BE TRUE.

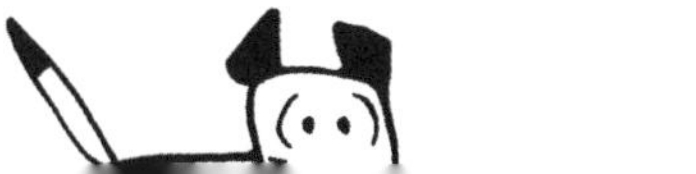

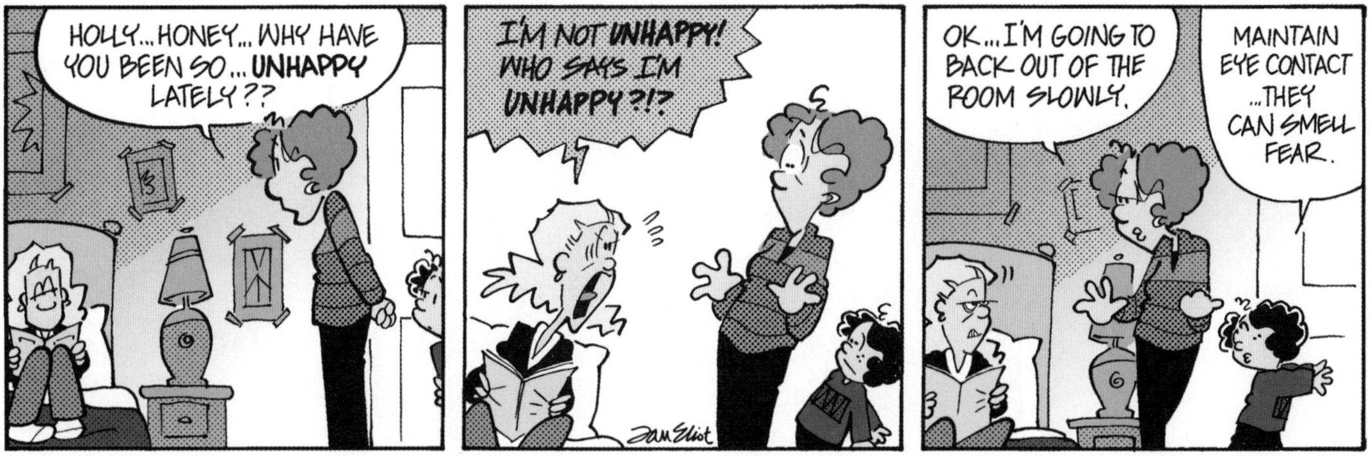
HOLLY... HONEY... WHY HAVE YOU BEEN SO... UNHAPPY LATELY??
I'M NOT UNHAPPY! WHO SAYS I'M UNHAPPY?!?
OK... I'M GOING TO BACK OUT OF THE ROOM SLOWLY.
MAINTAIN EYE CONTACT ...THEY CAN SMELL FEAR.
Jan Eliot

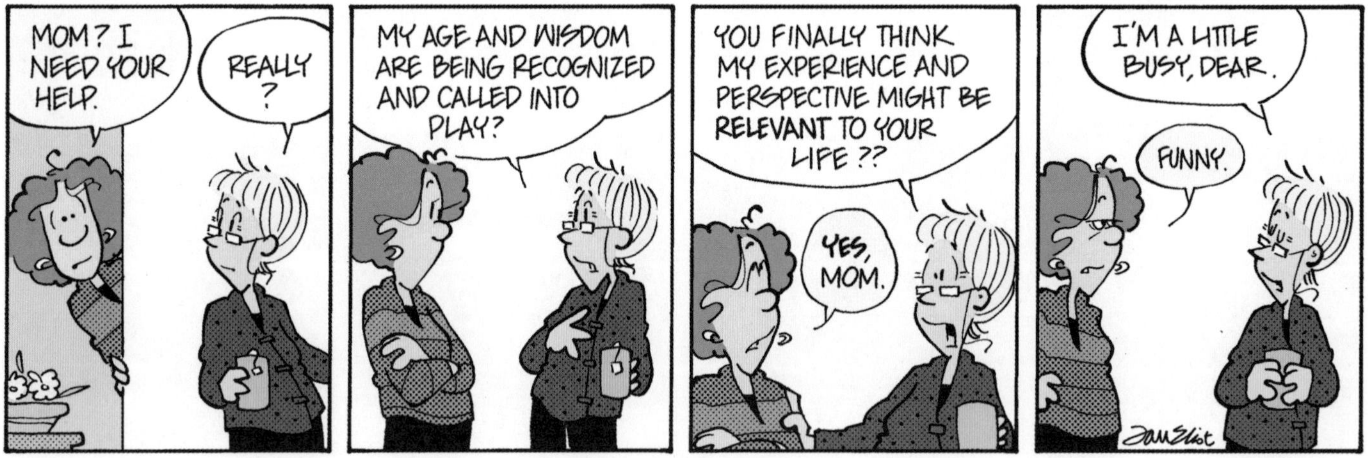
MOM? I NEED YOUR HELP.
REALLY?
MY AGE AND WISDOM ARE BEING RECOGNIZED AND CALLED INTO PLAY?
YOU FINALLY THINK MY EXPERIENCE AND PERSPECTIVE MIGHT BE RELEVANT TO YOUR LIFE??
YES, MOM.
I'M A LITTLE BUSY, DEAR.
FUNNY.
Jan Eliot

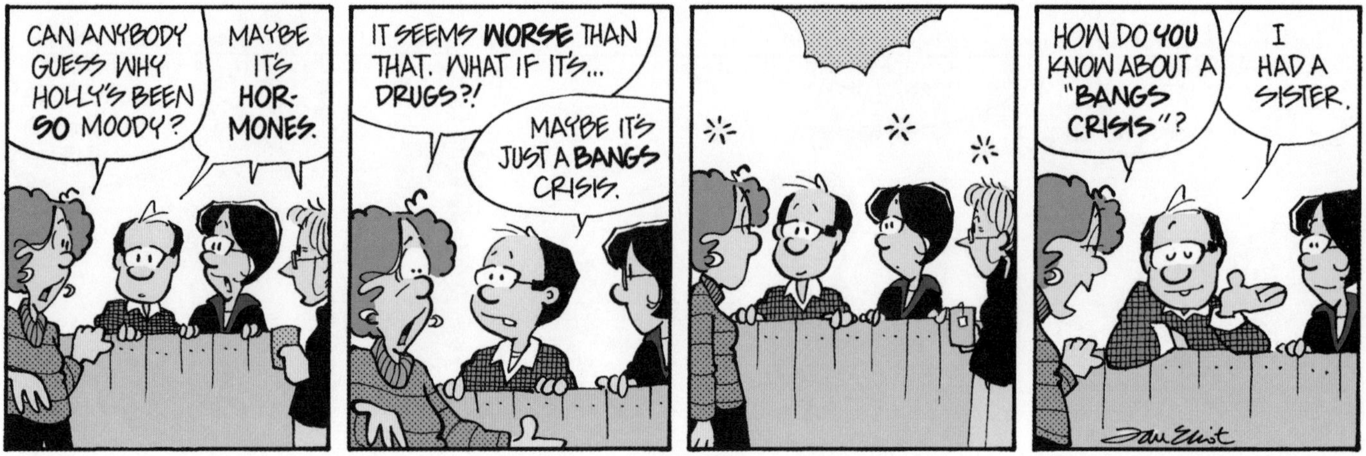
CAN ANYBODY GUESS WHY HOLLY'S BEEN SO MOODY?
MAYBE IT'S HOR-MONES.
IT SEEMS WORSE THAN THAT. WHAT IF IT'S... DRUGS?!
MAYBE IT'S JUST A BANGS CRISIS.
HOW DO YOU KNOW ABOUT A "BANGS CRISIS"?
I HAD A SISTER.
Jan Eliot

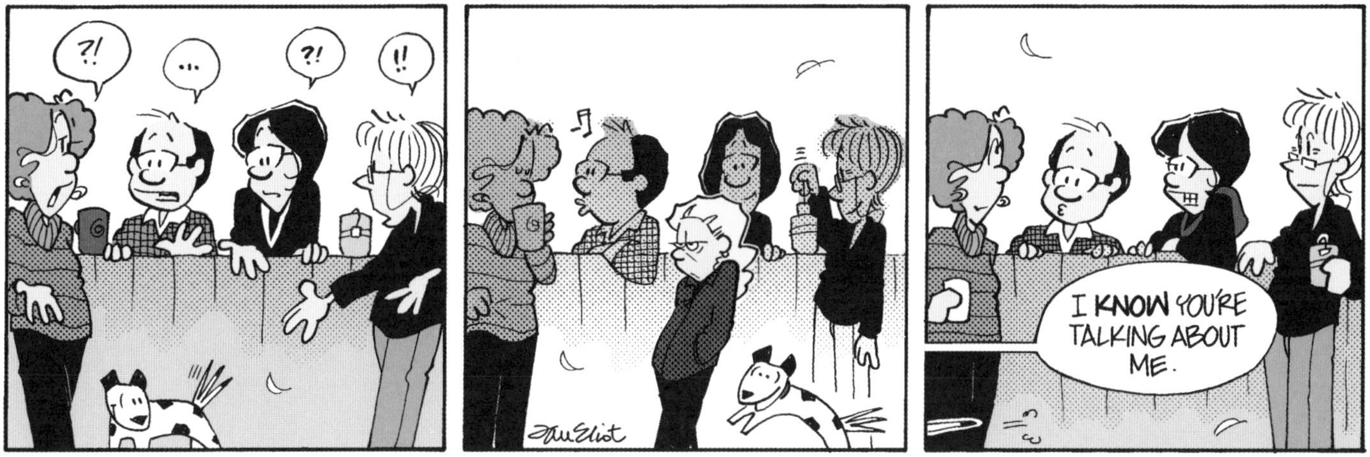
?!
...
?!
!!
I **KNOW** YOU'RE TALKING ABOUT ME.

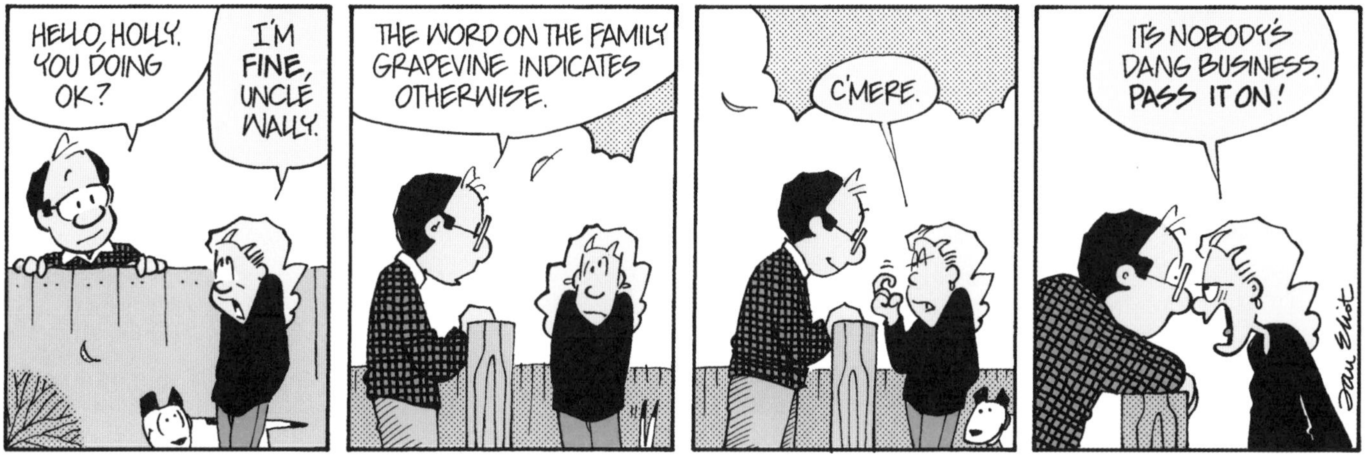
HELLO, HOLLY. YOU DOING OK?
I'M **FINE,** UNCLE WALLY.
THE WORD ON THE FAMILY GRAPEVINE INDICATES OTHERWISE.
C'MERE.
IT'S NOBODY'S DANG BUSINESS. **PASS IT ON!**

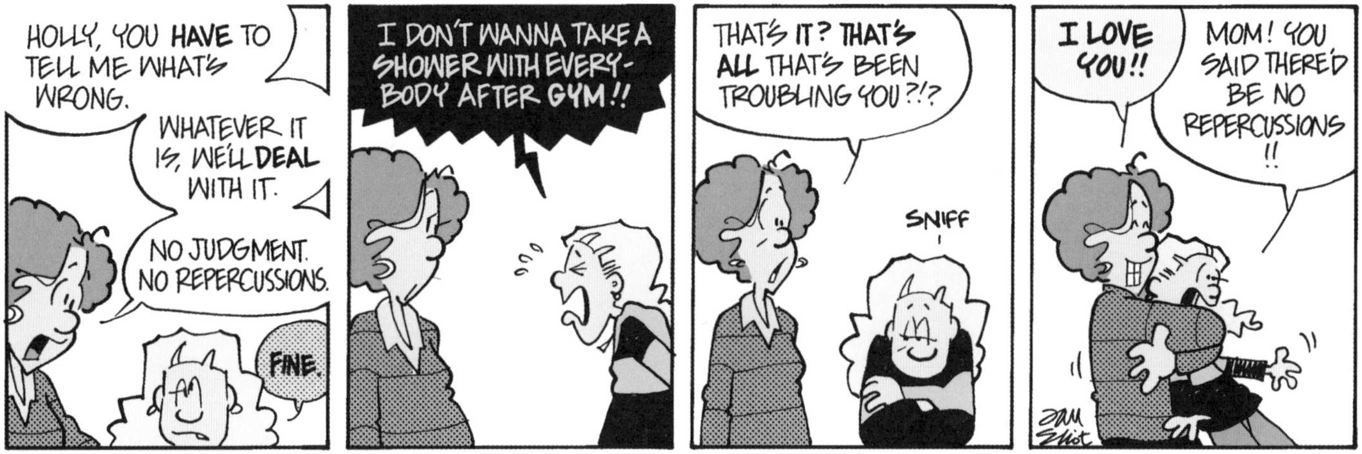
HOLLY, YOU **HAVE** TO TELL ME WHAT'S WRONG.
WHATEVER IT IS, WE'LL **DEAL** WITH IT.
NO JUDGMENT. NO REPERCUSSIONS.
FINE.
I DON'T WANNA TAKE A SHOWER WITH EVERY-BODY AFTER **GYM!!**
THAT'S **IT? THAT'S ALL** THAT'S BEEN TROUBLING YOU?!?
SNIFF
I LOVE YOU!!
MOM! YOU SAID THERE'D BE NO REPERCUSSIONS !!

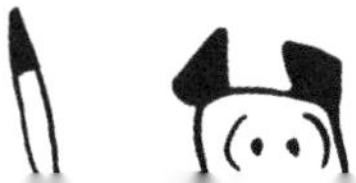

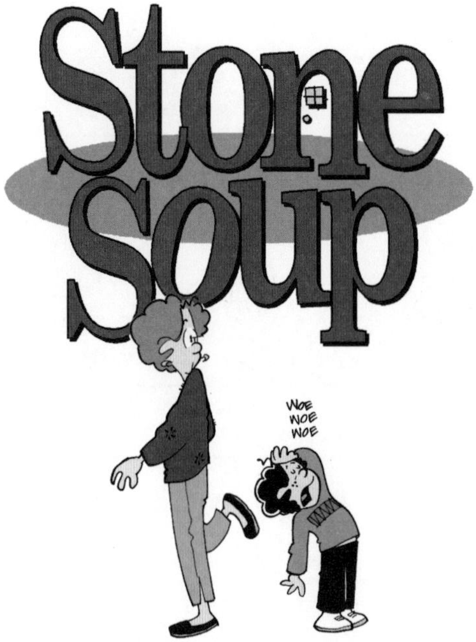
Stone Soup
WOE
WOE
WOE

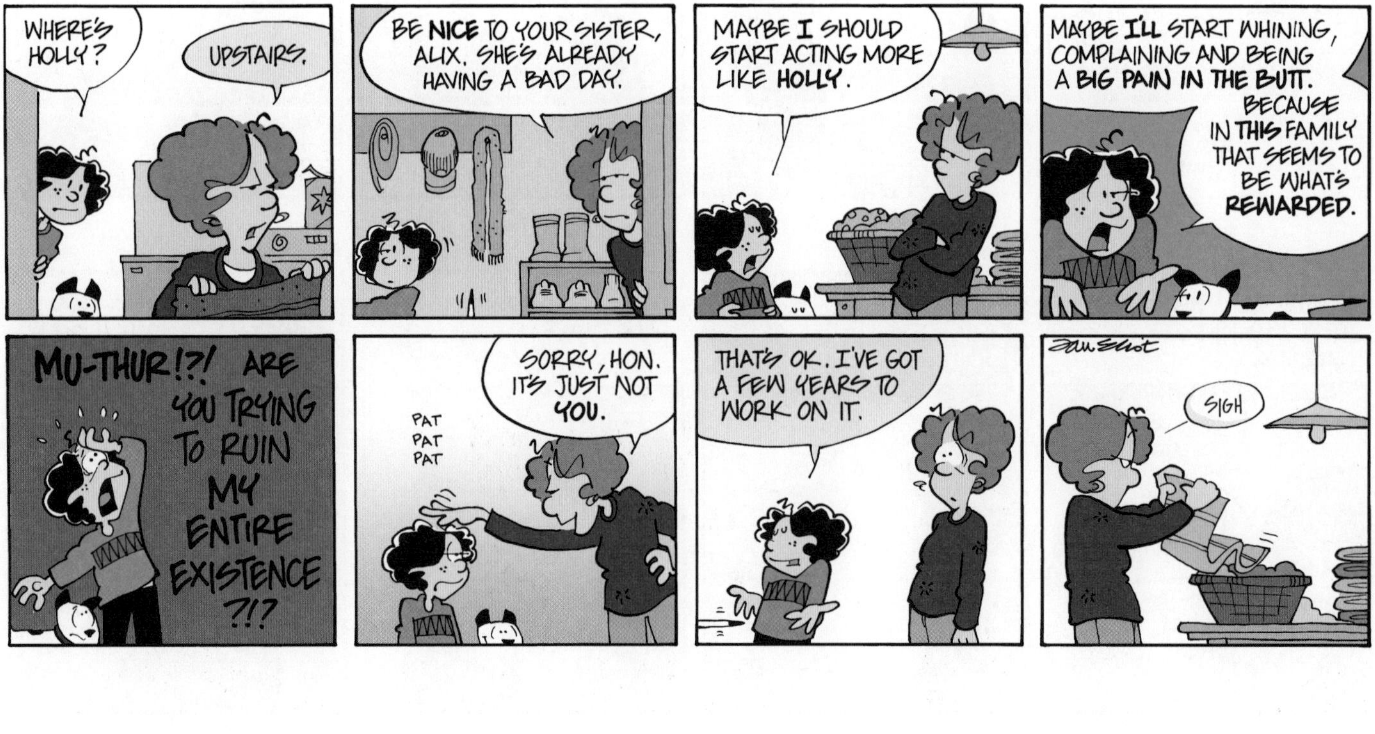
WHERE'S HOLLY?
UPSTAIRS.
BE NICE TO YOUR SISTER, ALIX. SHE'S ALREADY HAVING A BAD DAY.
MAYBE I SHOULD START ACTING MORE LIKE HOLLY.
MAYBE I'LL START WHINING, COMPLAINING AND BEING A BIG PAIN IN THE BUTT.
BECAUSE IN THIS FAMILY THAT SEEMS TO BE WHAT'S REWARDED.
MU-THUR!?! ARE YOU TRYING TO RUIN MY ENTIRE EXISTENCE ?!?
PAT
PAT
PAT
SORRY, HON. IT'S JUST NOT YOU.
THAT'S OK. I'VE GOT A FEW YEARS TO WORK ON IT.
SIGH

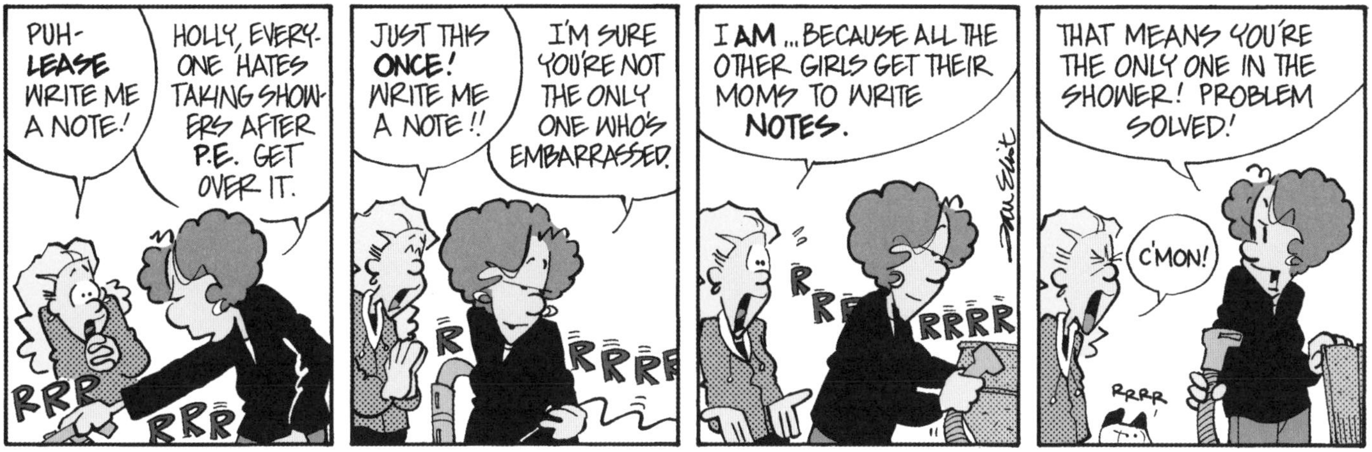
PUH-LEASE WRITE ME A NOTE!
HOLLY, EVERYONE HATES TAKING SHOWERS AFTER P.E. GET OVER IT.
RRR
RRR
JUST THIS ONCE! WRITE ME A NOTE!!
I'M SURE YOU'RE NOT THE ONLY ONE WHO'S EMBARRASSED.
R
RRRR
I AM ... BECAUSE ALL THE OTHER GIRLS GET THEIR MOMS TO WRITE NOTES.
RRRRR
THAT MEANS YOU'RE THE ONLY ONE IN THE SHOWER! PROBLEM SOLVED!
C'MON!
RRRR

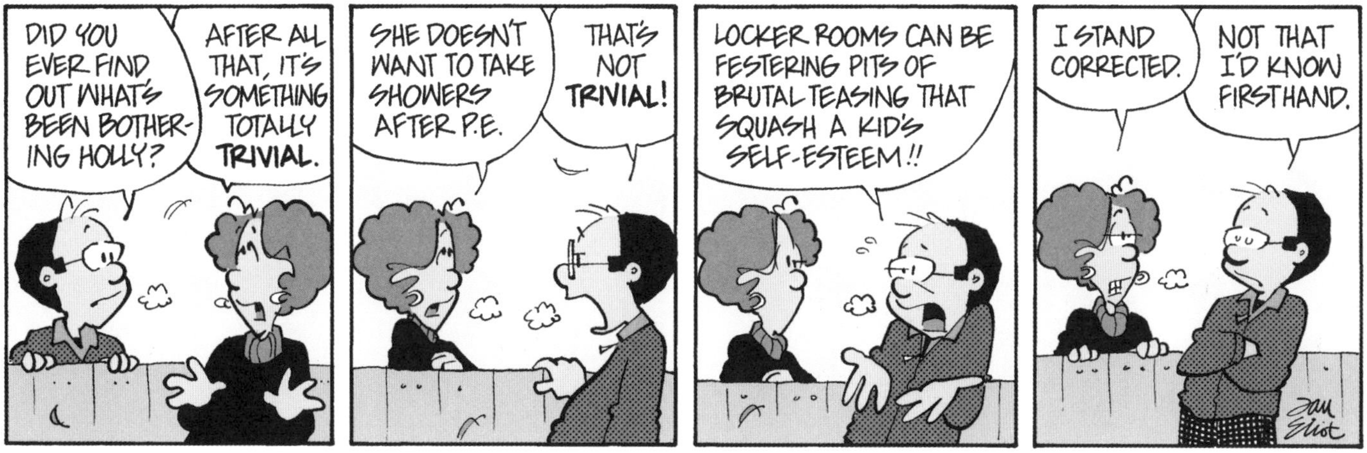
DID YOU EVER FIND OUT WHAT'S BEEN BOTHERING HOLLY?
AFTER ALL THAT, IT'S SOMETHING TOTALLY TRIVIAL.
SHE DOESN'T WANT TO TAKE SHOWERS AFTER P.E.
THAT'S NOT TRIVIAL!
LOCKER ROOMS CAN BE FESTERING PITS OF BRUTAL TEASING THAT SQUASH A KID'S SELF-ESTEEM!!
I STAND CORRECTED.
NOT THAT I'D KNOW FIRSTHAND.

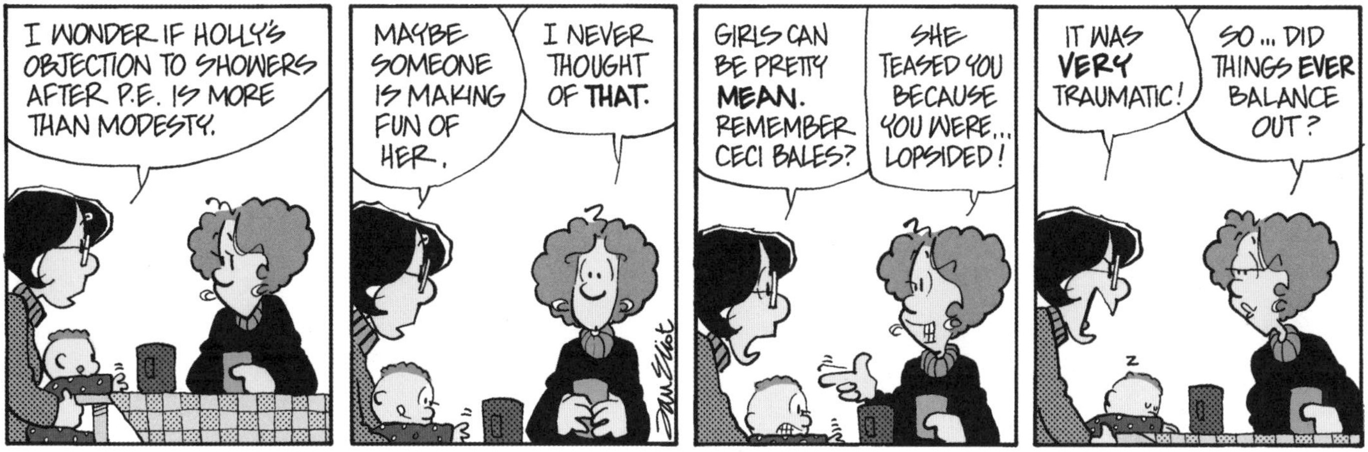
I WONDER IF HOLLY'S OBJECTION TO SHOWERS AFTER P.E. IS MORE THAN MODESTY.
MAYBE SOMEONE IS MAKING FUN OF HER.
I NEVER THOUGHT OF THAT.
GIRLS CAN BE PRETTY MEAN. REMEMBER CECI BALES?
SHE TEASED YOU BECAUSE YOU WERE... LOPSIDED!
IT WAS VERY TRAUMATIC!
SO ... DID THINGS EVER BALANCE OUT?

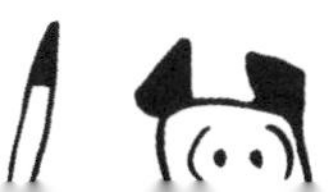

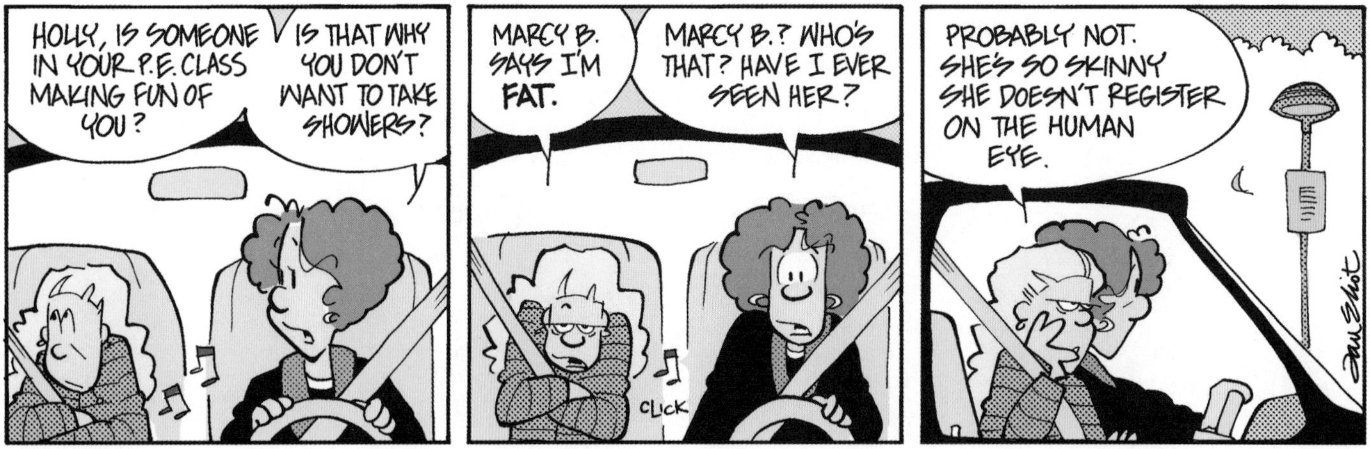
HOLLY, IS SOMEONE IN YOUR P.E. CLASS MAKING FUN OF YOU?
IS THAT WHY YOU DON'T WANT TO TAKE SHOWERS?
MARCY B. SAYS I'M **FAT.**
MARCY B.? WHO'S THAT? HAVE I EVER SEEN HER?
CLICK
PROBABLY NOT. SHE'S SO SKINNY SHE DOESN'T REGISTER ON THE HUMAN EYE.

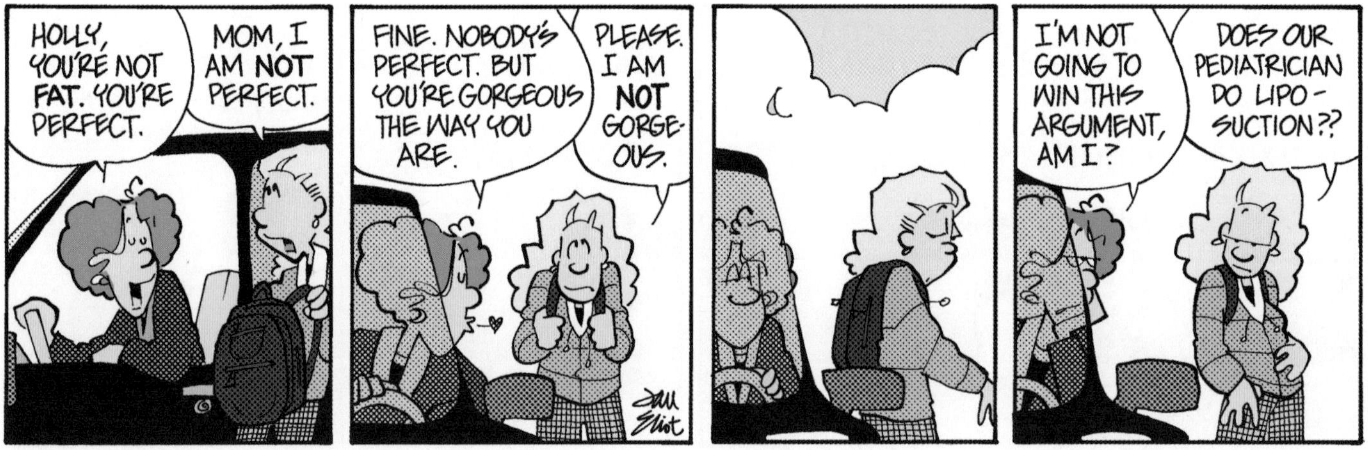
HOLLY, YOU'RE NOT **FAT.** YOU'RE PERFECT.
MOM, I AM **NOT** PERFECT.
FINE. NOBODY'S PERFECT. BUT YOU'RE GORGEOUS THE WAY YOU ARE.
PLEASE. I AM **NOT** GORGE-OUS.
I'M NOT GOING TO WIN THIS ARGUMENT, AM I?
DOES OUR PEDIATRICIAN DO LIPO-SUCTION??

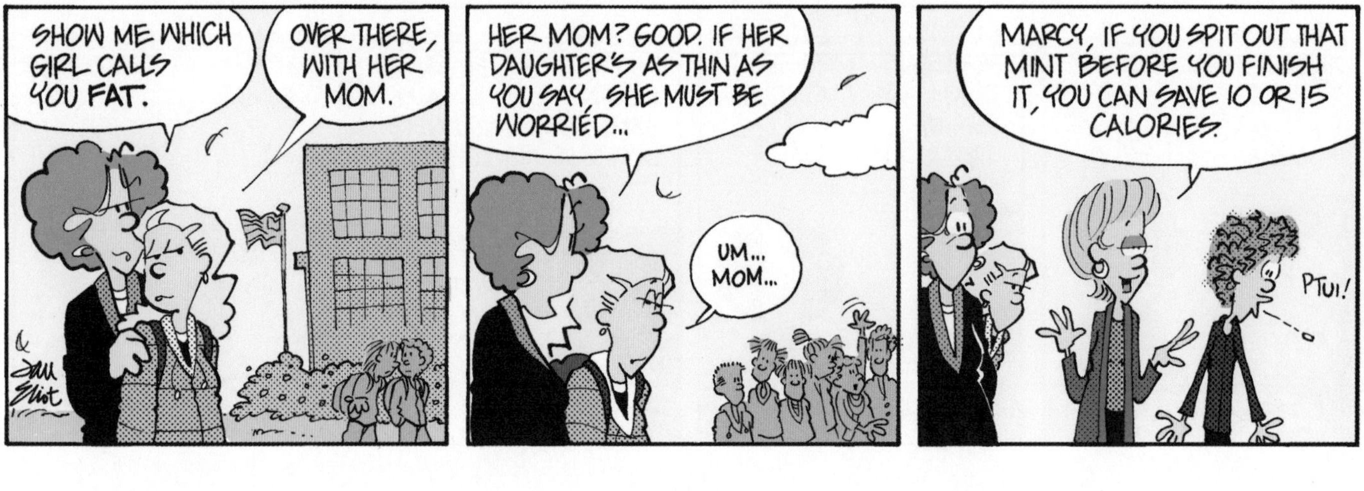
SHOW ME WHICH GIRL CALLS YOU **FAT.**
OVER THERE, WITH HER MOM.
HER MOM? GOOD. IF HER DAUGHTER'S AS THIN AS YOU SAY, SHE MUST BE WORRIED...
UM... MOM...
MARCY, IF YOU SPIT OUT THAT MINT BEFORE YOU FINISH IT, YOU CAN SAVE 10 OR 15 CALORIES.
PTUI!

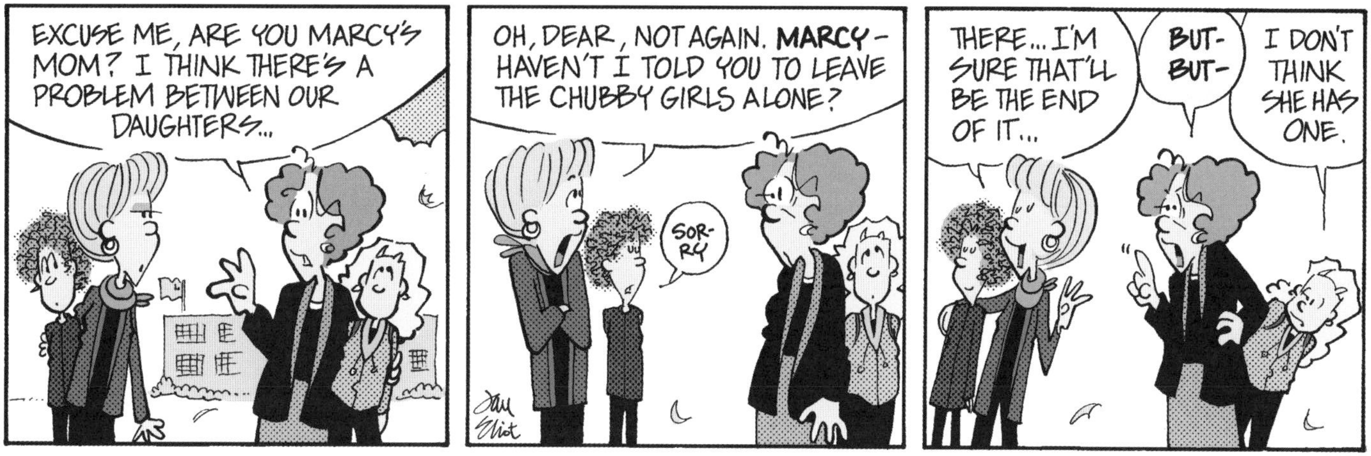
EXCUSE ME, ARE YOU MARCY'S MOM? I THINK THERE'S A PROBLEM BETWEEN OUR DAUGHTERS...
OH, DEAR, NOT AGAIN. **MARCY** - HAVEN'T I TOLD YOU TO LEAVE THE CHUBBY GIRLS ALONE?
SORRY
THERE... I'M SURE THAT'LL BE THE END OF IT...
BUT- BUT-
I DON'T THINK SHE HAS ONE.

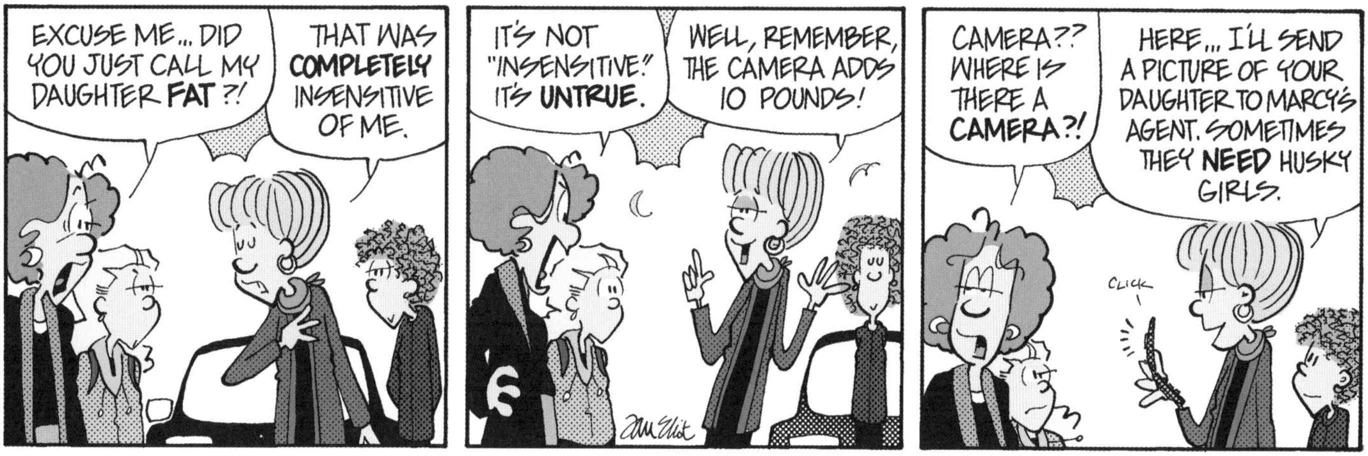
EXCUSE ME... DID YOU JUST CALL MY DAUGHTER **FAT** ?!
THAT WAS **COMPLETELY** INSENSITIVE OF ME.
IT'S NOT "INSENSITIVE." IT'S **UNTRUE**.
WELL, REMEMBER, THE CAMERA ADDS 10 POUNDS!
CAMERA?? WHERE IS THERE A **CAMERA**?!
HERE... I'LL SEND A PICTURE OF YOUR DAUGHTER TO MARCY'S AGENT. SOMETIMES THEY **NEED** HUSKY GIRLS.
CLICK

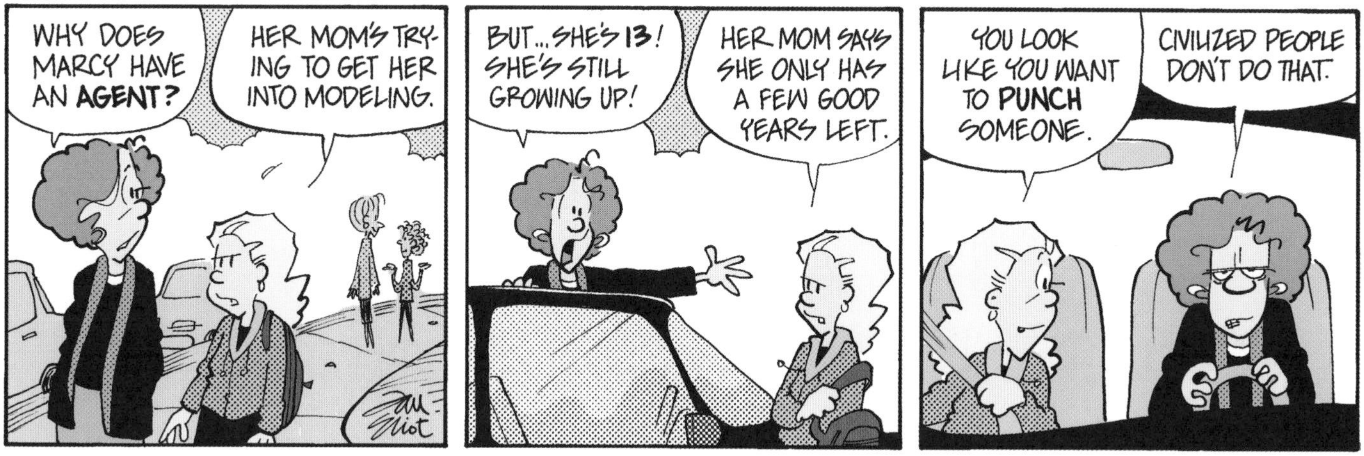
WHY DOES MARCY HAVE AN **AGENT**?
HER MOM'S TRYING TO GET HER INTO MODELING.
BUT... SHE'S **13**! SHE'S STILL GROWING UP!
HER MOM SAYS SHE ONLY HAS A FEW GOOD YEARS LEFT.
YOU LOOK LIKE YOU WANT TO **PUNCH** SOMEONE.
CIVILIZED PEOPLE DON'T DO THAT.

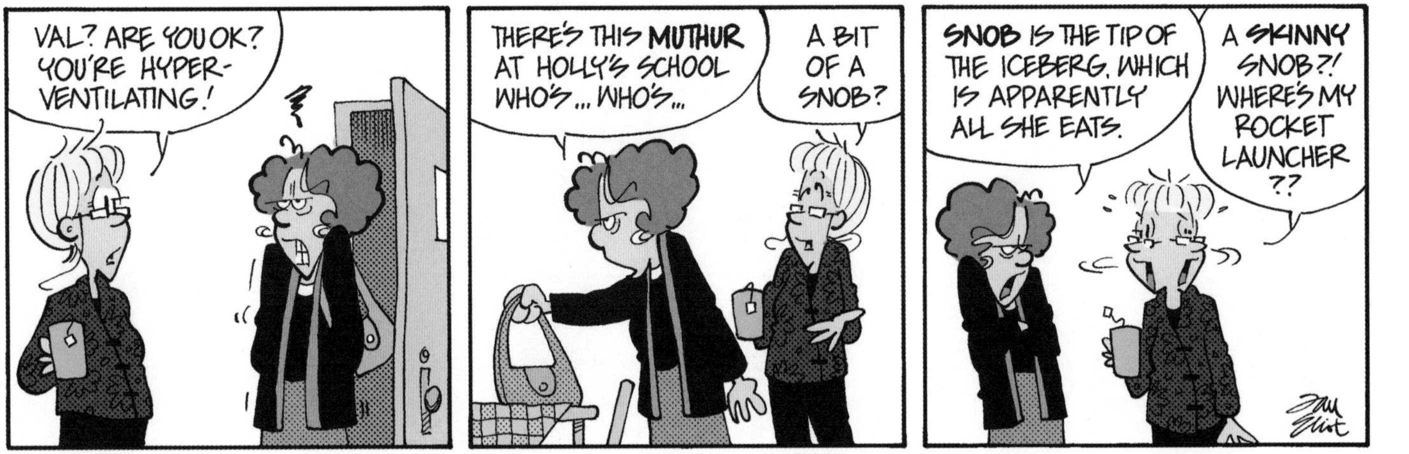
VAL? ARE YOU OK? YOU'RE HYPER-VENTILATING!
THERE'S THIS **MUTHUR** AT HOLLY'S SCHOOL WHO'S... WHO'S...
A BIT OF A SNOB?
SNOB IS THE TIP OF THE ICEBERG, WHICH IS APPARENTLY ALL SHE EATS.
A **SKINNY** SNOB?! WHERE'S MY ROCKET LAUNCHER ??

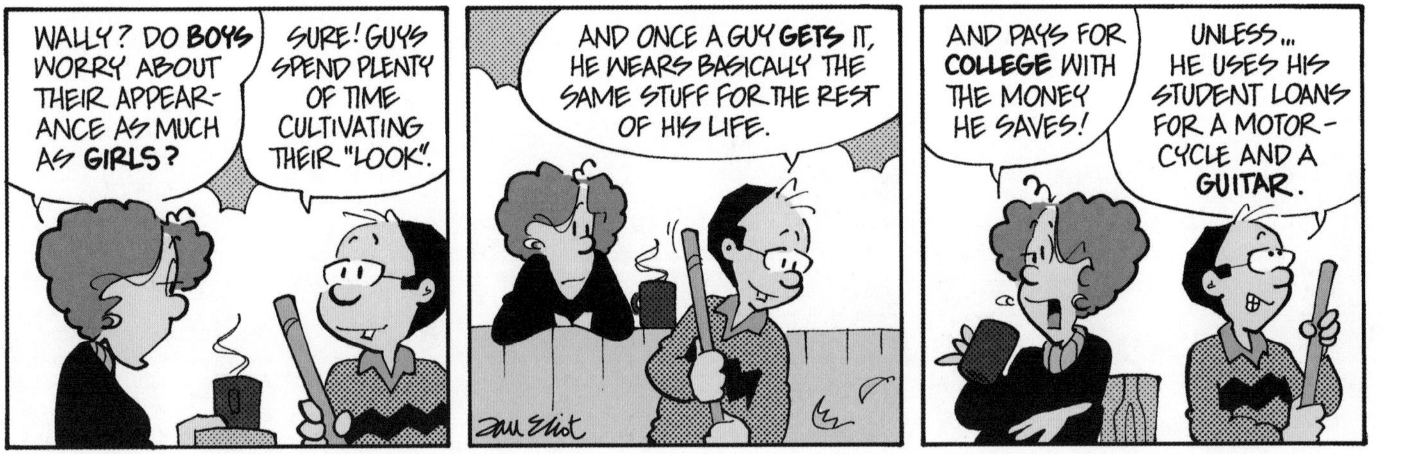
WALLY? DO **BOYS** WORRY ABOUT THEIR APPEARANCE AS MUCH AS **GIRLS**?
SURE! GUYS SPEND PLENTY OF TIME CULTIVATING THEIR "LOOK".
AND ONCE A GUY **GETS** IT, HE WEARS BASICALLY THE SAME STUFF FOR THE REST OF HIS LIFE.
AND PAYS FOR **COLLEGE** WITH THE MONEY HE SAVES!
UNLESS... HE USES HIS STUDENT LOANS FOR A MOTOR-CYCLE AND A **GUITAR**.

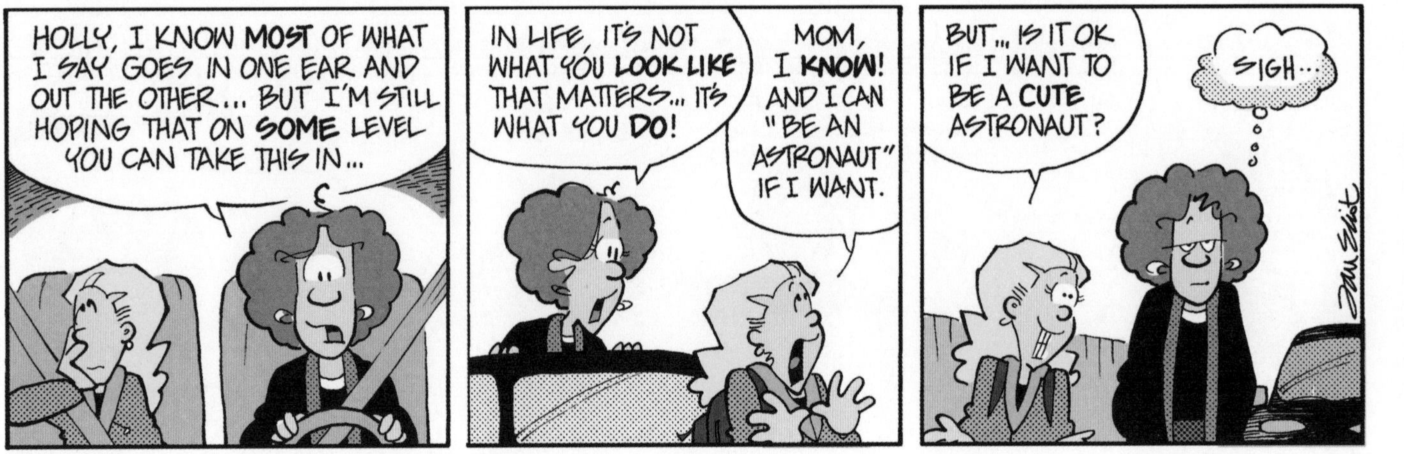
HOLLY, I KNOW **MOST** OF WHAT I SAY GOES IN ONE EAR AND OUT THE OTHER... BUT I'M STILL HOPING THAT ON **SOME** LEVEL YOU CAN TAKE THIS IN...
IN LIFE, IT'S NOT WHAT YOU **LOOK LIKE** THAT MATTERS... IT'S WHAT YOU **DO**!
MOM, I **KNOW**! AND I CAN "BE AN ASTRONAUT" IF I WANT.
BUT... IS IT OK IF I WANT TO BE A **CUTE** ASTRONAUT?
SIGH...

Stone Soup

LADIES... THIS DESSERT IS **ON ME**.

YOU'RE ALL SO CUTE!

I HOPE WHEN **I'M YOUR AGE** I'LL STILL BE GOING OUT FOR LUNCH AND HAVING COCKTAILS WITH MY **GIRL-FRIENDS**!

SHE THINKS WE'RE **OLD**?!

SO?

NO KIDDING! WE SHOULD HAVE ORDERED **THREE** DESSERTS!

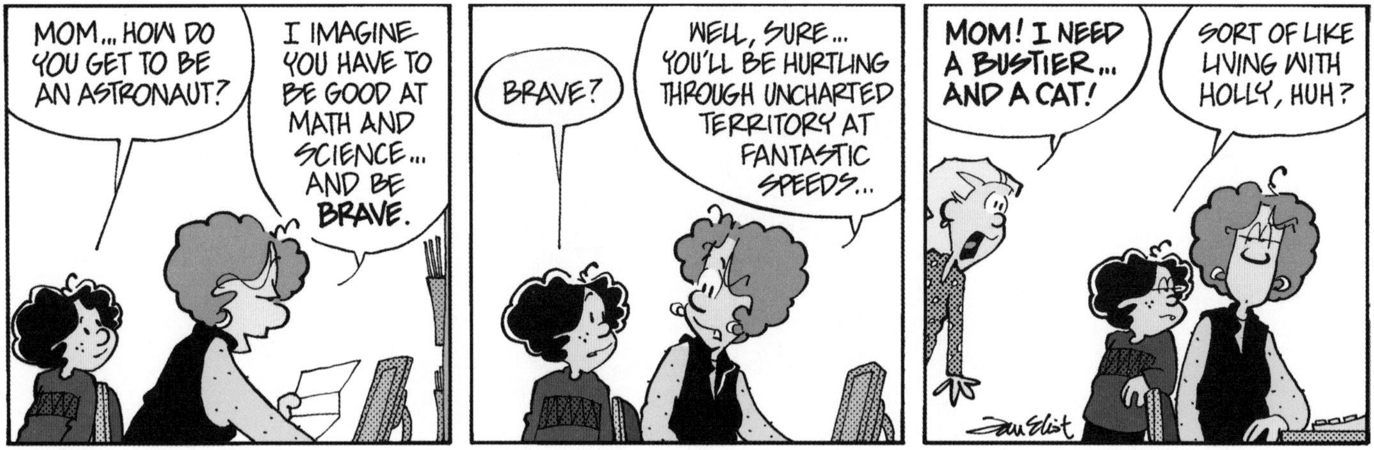
MOM... HOW DO YOU GET TO BE AN ASTRONAUT?
I IMAGINE YOU HAVE TO BE GOOD AT MATH AND SCIENCE... AND BE BRAVE.
BRAVE?
WELL, SURE... YOU'LL BE HURTLING THROUGH UNCHARTED TERRITORY AT FANTASTIC SPEEDS...
MOM! I NEED A BUSTIER... AND A CAT!
SORT OF LIKE LIVING WITH HOLLY, HUH?

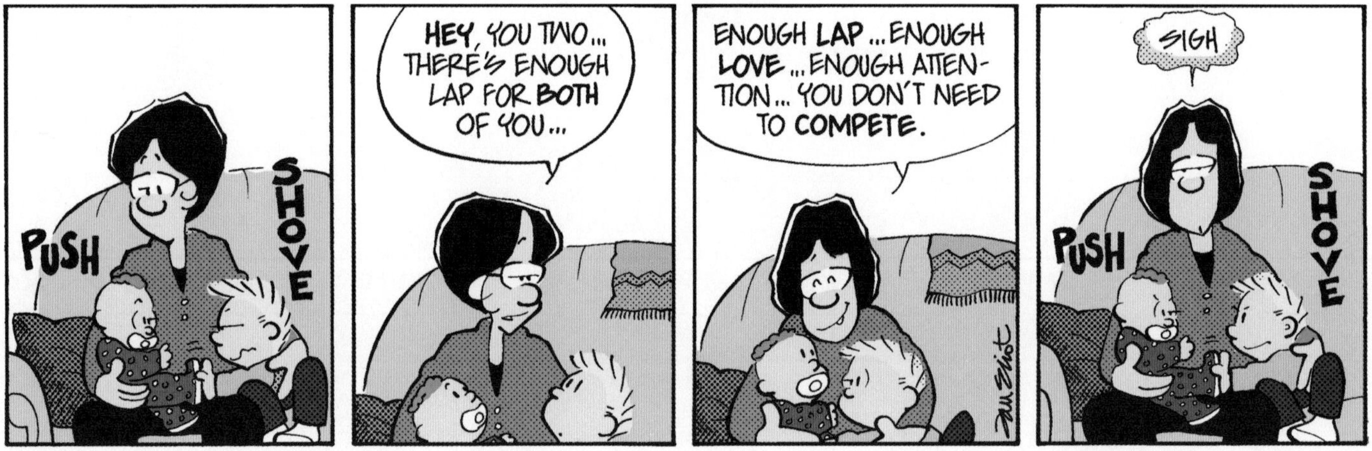
PUSH
SHOVE
HEY, YOU TWO... THERE'S ENOUGH LAP FOR BOTH OF YOU...
ENOUGH LAP... ENOUGH LOVE... ENOUGH ATTENTION... YOU DON'T NEED TO COMPETE.
SIGH
PUSH
SHOVE

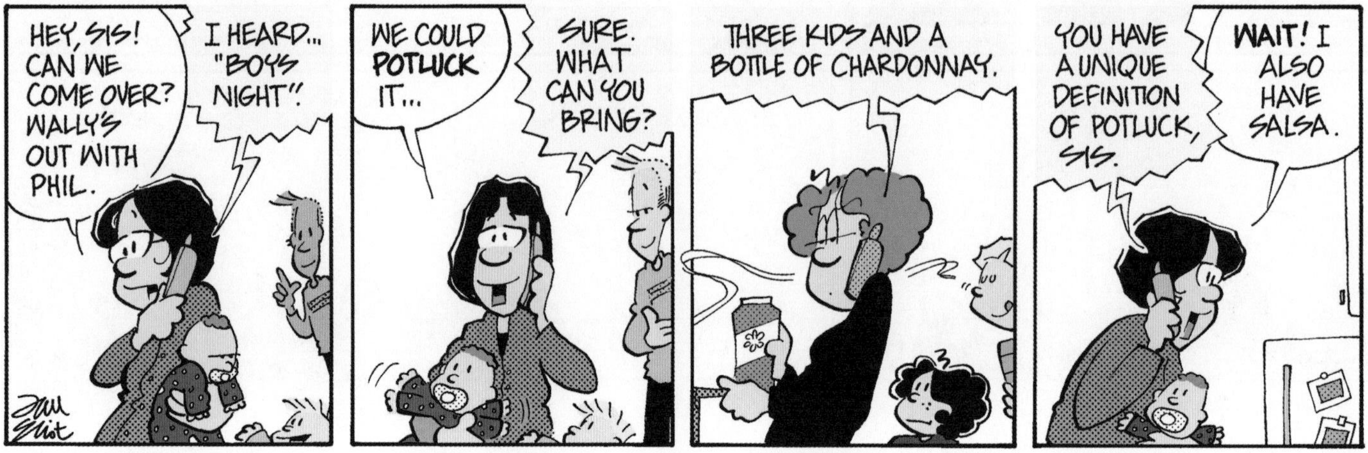
HEY, SIS! CAN WE COME OVER? WALLY'S OUT WITH PHIL.
I HEARD... "BOYS NIGHT".
WE COULD POTLUCK IT...
SURE. WHAT CAN YOU BRING?
THREE KIDS AND A BOTTLE OF CHARDONNAY.
YOU HAVE A UNIQUE DEFINITION OF POTLUCK, SIS.
WAIT! I ALSO HAVE SALSA.

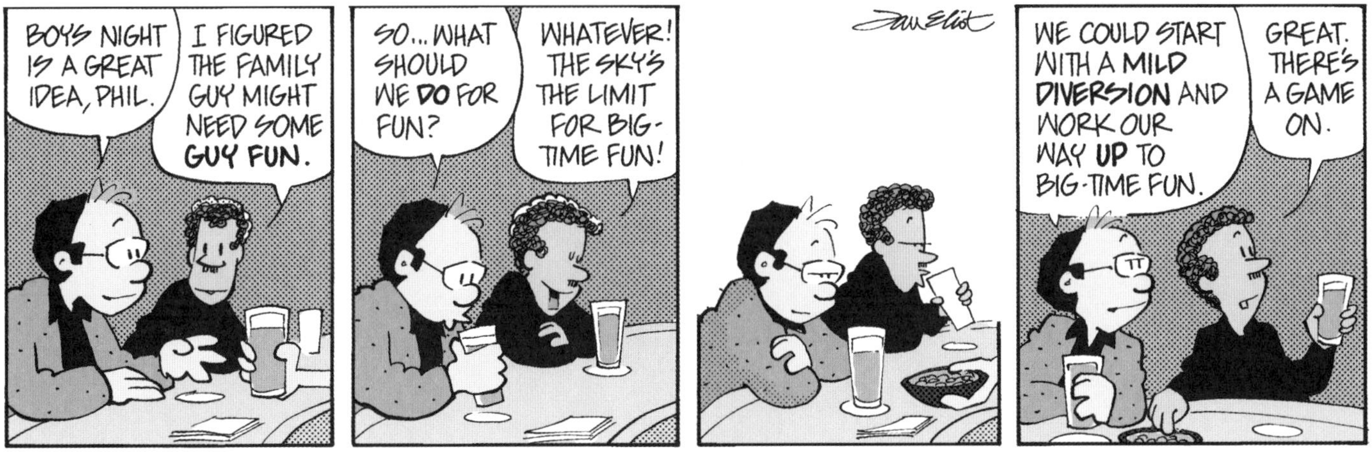
BOYS NIGHT IS A GREAT IDEA, PHIL.
I FIGURED THE FAMILY GUY MIGHT NEED SOME GUY FUN.
SO... WHAT SHOULD WE DO FOR FUN?
WHATEVER! THE SKY'S THE LIMIT FOR BIG-TIME FUN!
WE COULD START WITH A MILD DIVERSION AND WORK OUR WAY UP TO BIG-TIME FUN.
GREAT. THERE'S A GAME ON.

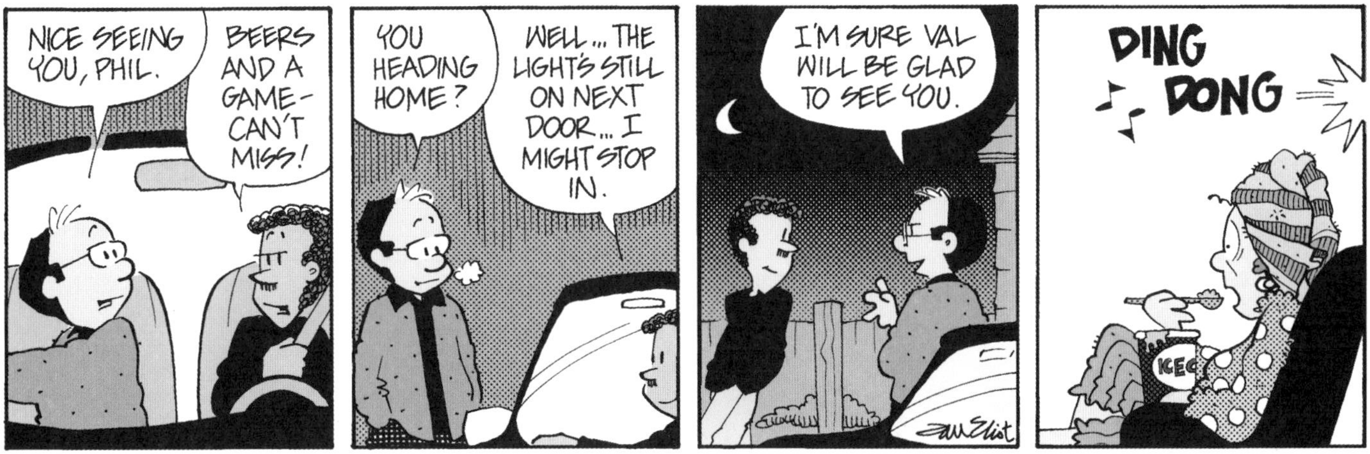
NICE SEEING YOU, PHIL.
BEERS AND A GAME- CAN'T MISS!
YOU HEADING HOME?
WELL... THE LIGHT'S STILL ON NEXT DOOR... I MIGHT STOP IN.
I'M SURE VAL WILL BE GLAD TO SEE YOU.
DING DONG
ICE

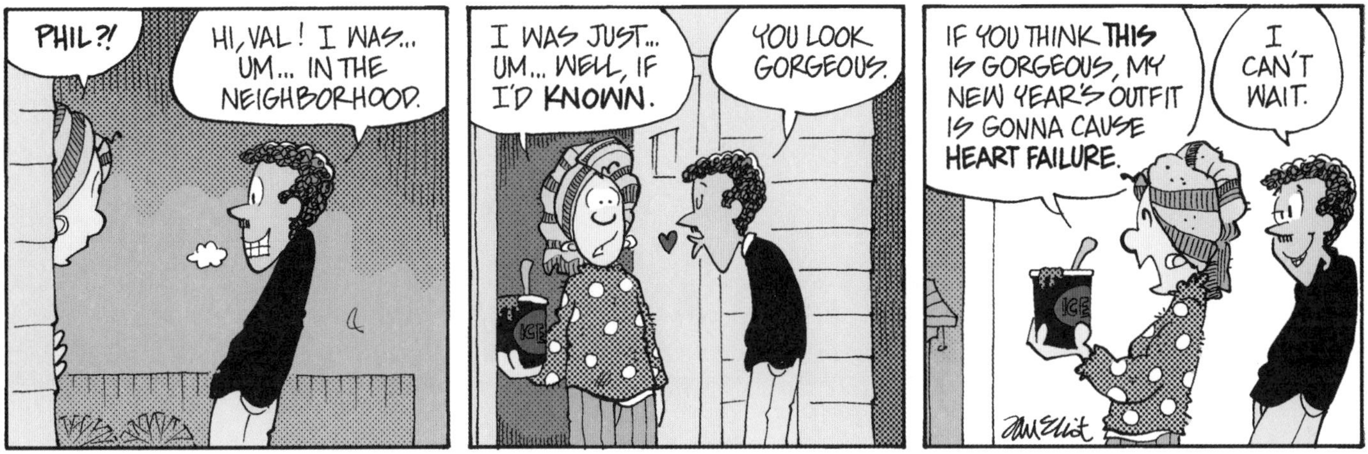
PHIL?!
HI, VAL! I WAS... UM... IN THE NEIGHBORHOOD.
I WAS JUST... UM... WELL, IF I'D KNOWN.
YOU LOOK GORGEOUS.
IF YOU THINK THIS IS GORGEOUS, MY NEW YEAR'S OUTFIT IS GONNA CAUSE HEART FAILURE.
I CAN'T WAIT.
ICE
ICE

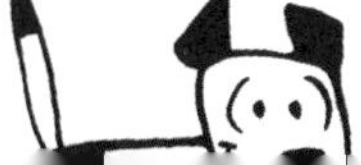

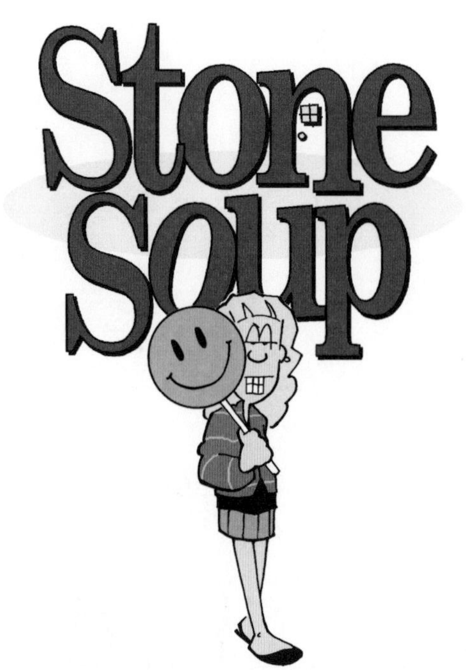
Stone Soup

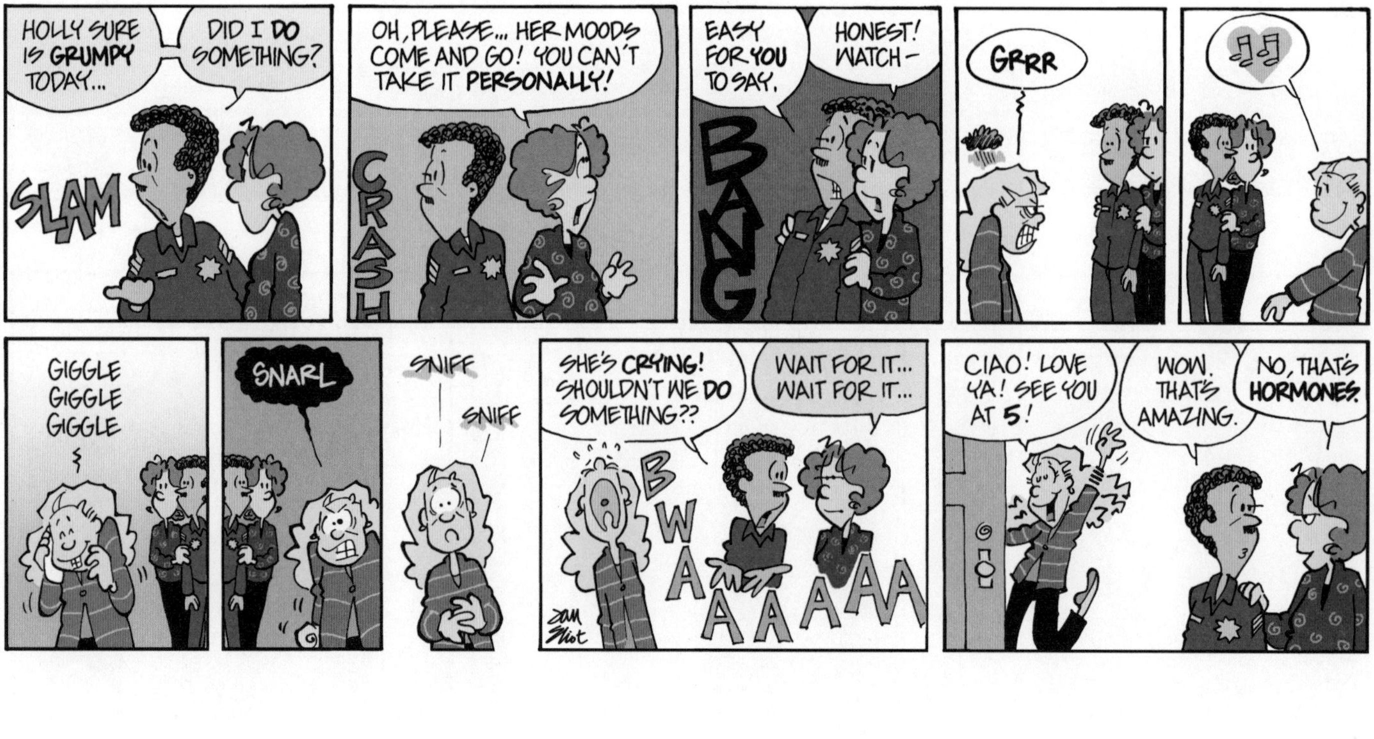
HOLLY SURE IS GRUMPY TODAY...
DID I DO SOMETHING?
SLAM
OH, PLEASE... HER MOODS COME AND GO! YOU CAN'T TAKE IT PERSONALLY!
CRASH
EASY FOR YOU TO SAY.
HONEST! WATCH—
BANG
GRRR
GIGGLE GIGGLE GIGGLE
SNARL
SNIFF
SNIFF
SHE'S CRYING! SHOULDN'T WE DO SOMETHING??
WAIT FOR IT... WAIT FOR IT...
BWAAAAAA
CIAO! LOVE YA! SEE YOU AT 5!
WOW. THAT'S AMAZING.
NO, THAT'S HORMONES.

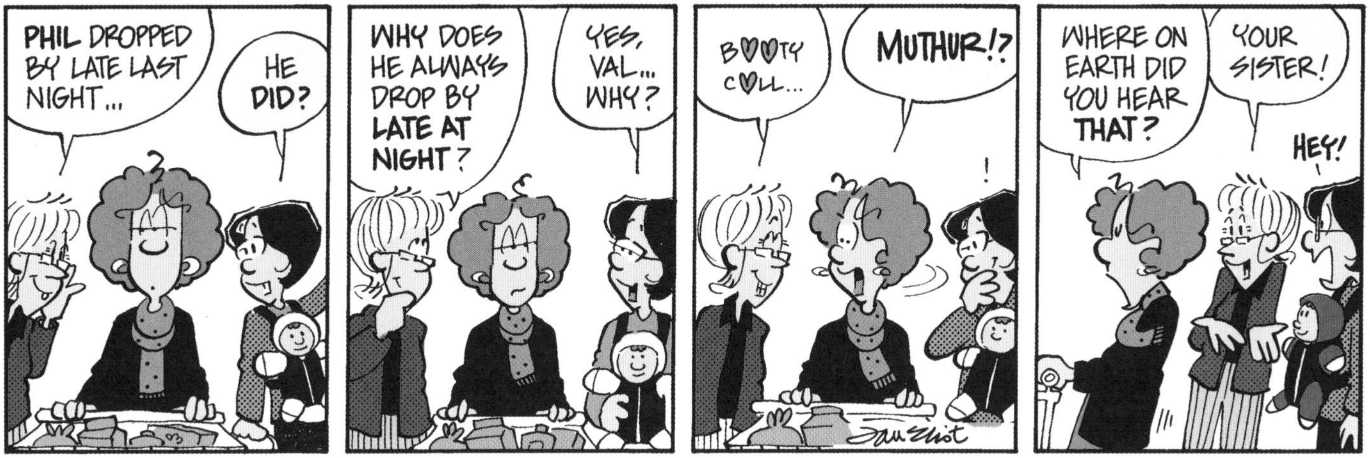
PHIL DROPPED BY LATE LAST NIGHT...
HE DID?
WHY DOES HE ALWAYS DROP BY LATE AT NIGHT?
YES, VAL... WHY?
B♥♥TY C♥LL...
MUTHUR!?
!
WHERE ON EARTH DID YOU HEAR THAT?
YOUR SISTER!
HEY!

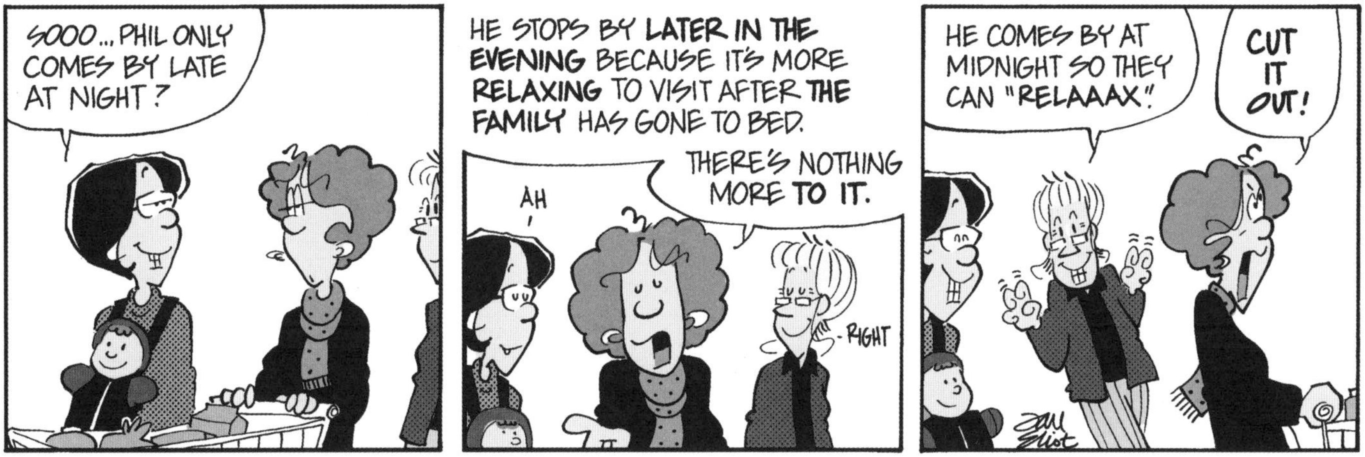
SOOO... PHIL ONLY COMES BY LATE AT NIGHT?
HE STOPS BY LATER IN THE EVENING BECAUSE IT'S MORE RELAXING TO VISIT AFTER THE FAMILY HAS GONE TO BED.
AH
THERE'S NOTHING MORE TO IT.
-RIGHT
HE COMES BY AT MIDNIGHT SO THEY CAN "RELAAAX."
CUT IT OUT!

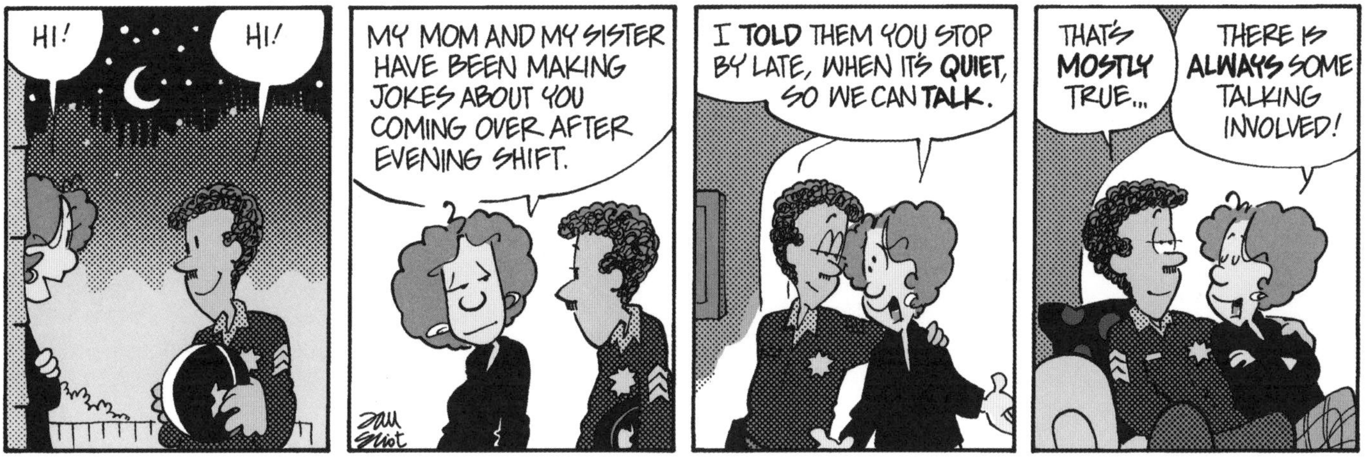
HI!
HI!
MY MOM AND MY SISTER HAVE BEEN MAKING JOKES ABOUT YOU COMING OVER AFTER EVENING SHIFT.
I TOLD THEM YOU STOP BY LATE, WHEN IT'S QUIET, SO WE CAN TALK.
THAT'S MOSTLY TRUE...
THERE IS ALWAYS SOME TALKING INVOLVED!

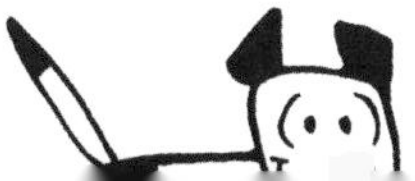

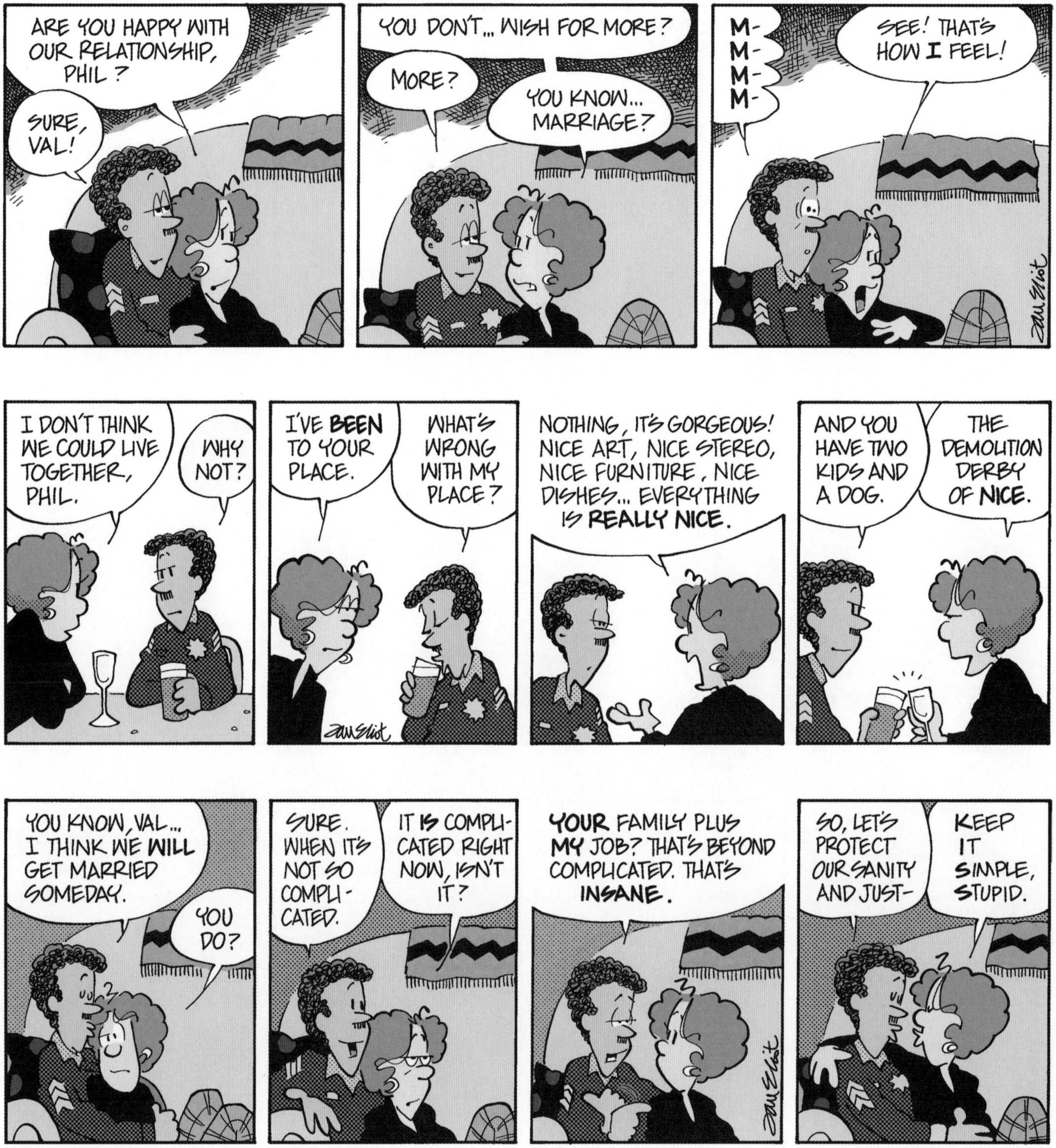
ARE YOU HAPPY WITH OUR RELATIONSHIP, PHIL ?
SURE, VAL!
YOU DON'T... WISH FOR MORE?
MORE?
YOU KNOW... MARRIAGE?
M-M-M-M-
SEE! THAT'S HOW I FEEL!
I DON'T THINK WE COULD LIVE TOGETHER, PHIL.
WHY NOT?
I'VE BEEN TO YOUR PLACE.
WHAT'S WRONG WITH MY PLACE?
NOTHING, IT'S GORGEOUS! NICE ART, NICE STEREO, NICE FURNITURE, NICE DISHES... EVERYTHING IS REALLY NICE.
AND YOU HAVE TWO KIDS AND A DOG.
THE DEMOLITION DERBY OF NICE.
YOU KNOW, VAL... I THINK WE WILL GET MARRIED SOMEDAY.
YOU DO?
SURE. WHEN IT'S NOT SO COMPLICATED.
IT IS COMPLICATED RIGHT NOW, ISN'T IT?
YOUR FAMILY PLUS MY JOB? THAT'S BEYOND COMPLICATED. THAT'S INSANE.
SO, LET'S PROTECT OUR SANITY AND JUST-
KEEP IT SIMPLE, STUPID.

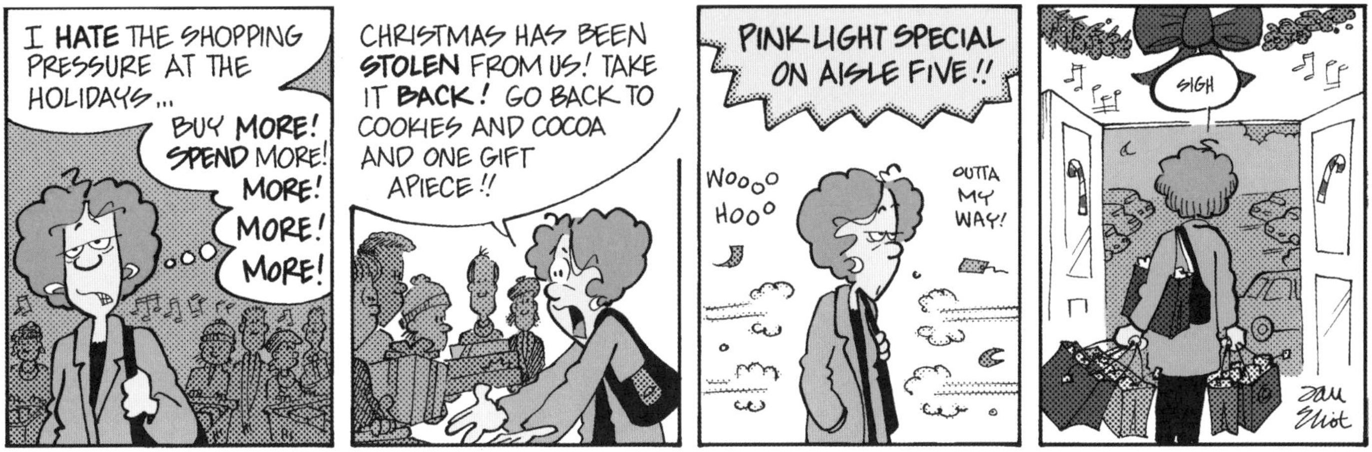
I HATE THE SHOPPING PRESSURE AT THE HOLIDAYS...
BUY MORE! SPEND MORE! MORE! MORE! MORE!
CHRISTMAS HAS BEEN STOLEN FROM US! TAKE IT BACK! GO BACK TO COOKIES AND COCOA AND ONE GIFT APIECE!!
PINK LIGHT SPECIAL ON AISLE FIVE!!
WOOOO HOOO
OUTTA MY WAY!
SIGH
JAN ELIOT

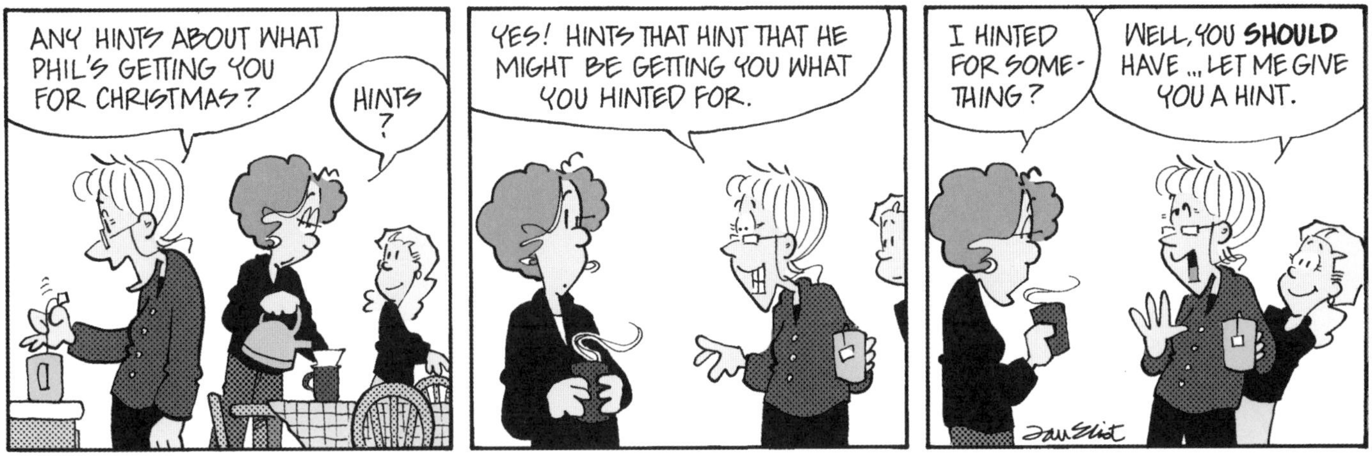
ANY HINTS ABOUT WHAT PHIL'S GETTING YOU FOR CHRISTMAS?
HINTS?
YES! HINTS THAT HINT THAT HE MIGHT BE GETTING YOU WHAT YOU HINTED FOR.
I HINTED FOR SOME-THING?
WELL, YOU SHOULD HAVE ... LET ME GIVE YOU A HINT.
JAN ELIOT

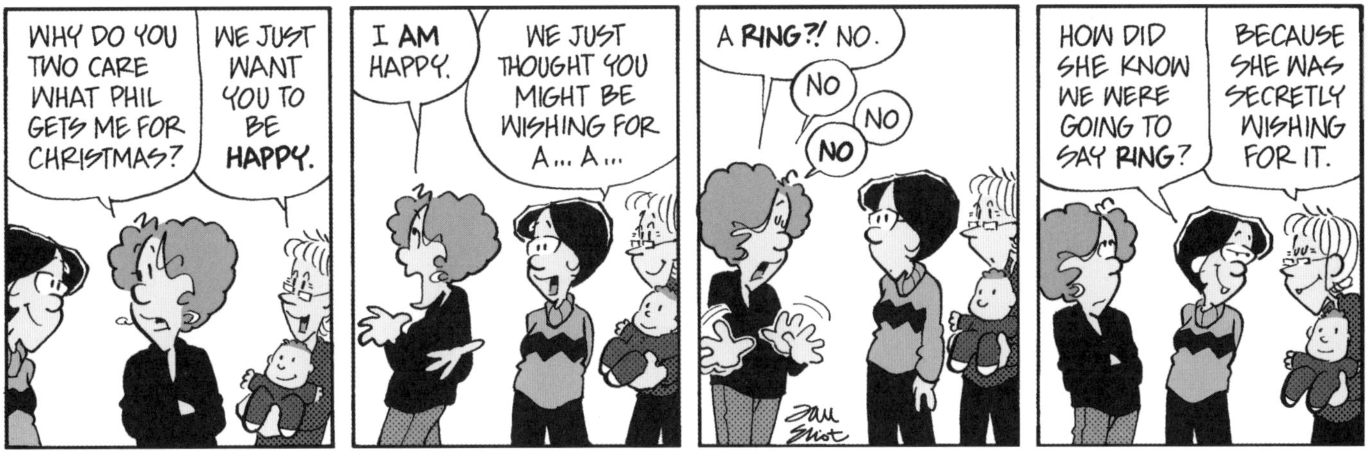
WHY DO YOU TWO CARE WHAT PHIL GETS ME FOR CHRISTMAS?
WE JUST WANT YOU TO BE HAPPY.
I AM HAPPY.
WE JUST THOUGHT YOU MIGHT BE WISHING FOR A... A...
A RING?! NO.
NO
NO
NO
JAN ELIOT
HOW DID SHE KNOW WE WERE GOING TO SAY RING?
BECAUSE SHE WAS SECRETLY WISHING FOR IT.

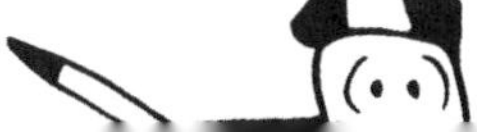

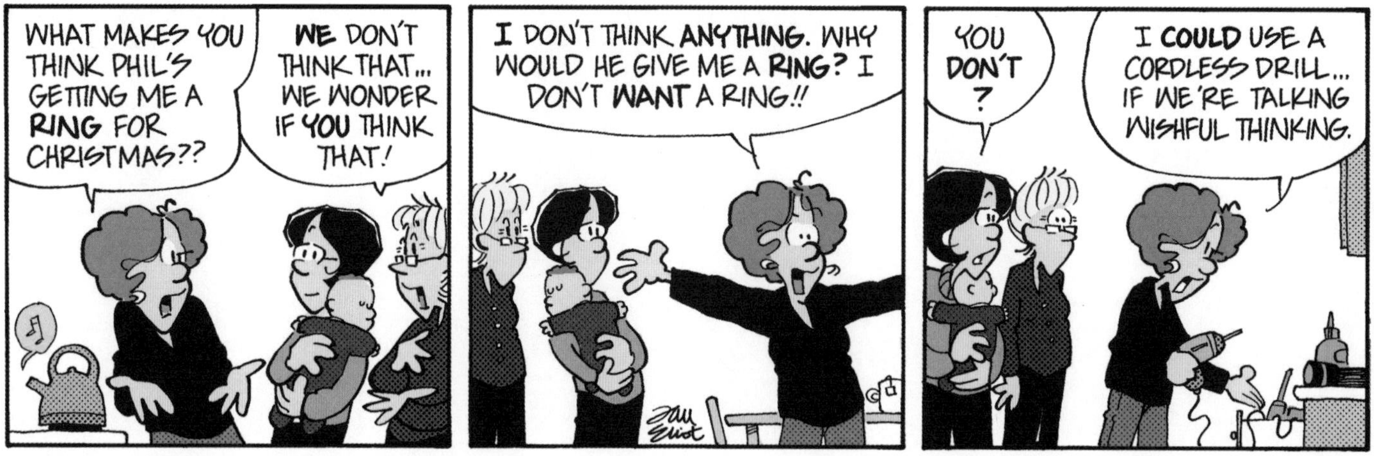
WHAT MAKES YOU THINK PHIL'S GETTING ME A **RING** FOR CHRISTMAS??
WE DON'T THINK THAT... WE WONDER IF **YOU** THINK THAT!
I DON'T THINK **ANYTHING**. WHY WOULD HE GIVE ME A **RING?** I DON'T **WANT** A RING!!
YOU **DON'T** ?
I **COULD** USE A CORDLESS DRILL... IF WE'RE TALKING WISHFUL THINKING.

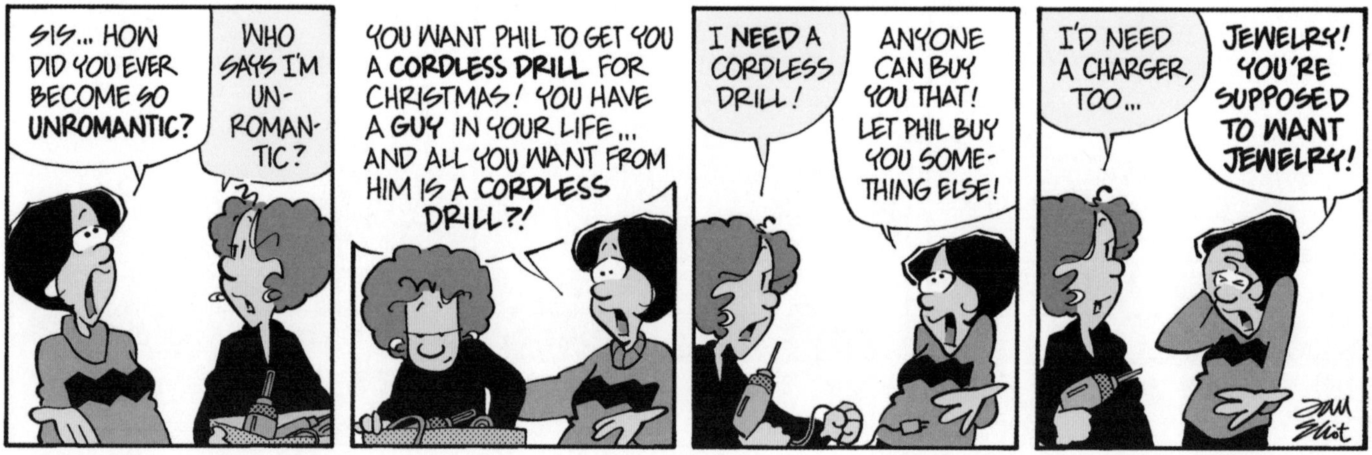
SIS... HOW DID YOU EVER BECOME SO **UNROMANTIC?**
WHO SAYS I'M UN-ROMAN-TIC?
YOU WANT PHIL TO GET YOU A **CORDLESS DRILL** FOR CHRISTMAS! YOU HAVE A **GUY** IN YOUR LIFE... AND ALL YOU WANT FROM HIM IS A **CORDLESS DRILL?!**
I **NEED** A CORDLESS DRILL!
ANYONE CAN BUY YOU THAT! LET PHIL BUY YOU SOME-THING ELSE!
I'D NEED A CHARGER, TOO...
JEWELRY! YOU'RE SUPPOSED TO WANT JEWELRY!

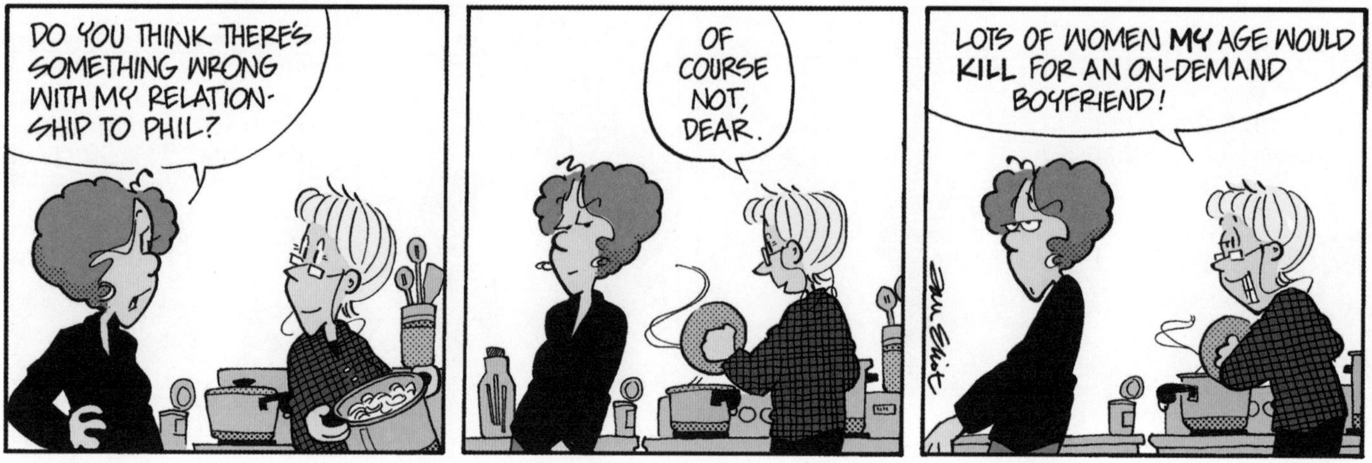
DO YOU THINK THERE'S SOMETHING WRONG WITH MY RELATION-SHIP TO PHIL?
OF COURSE NOT, DEAR.
LOTS OF WOMEN **MY** AGE WOULD **KILL** FOR AN ON-DEMAND BOYFRIEND!

Stone Soup

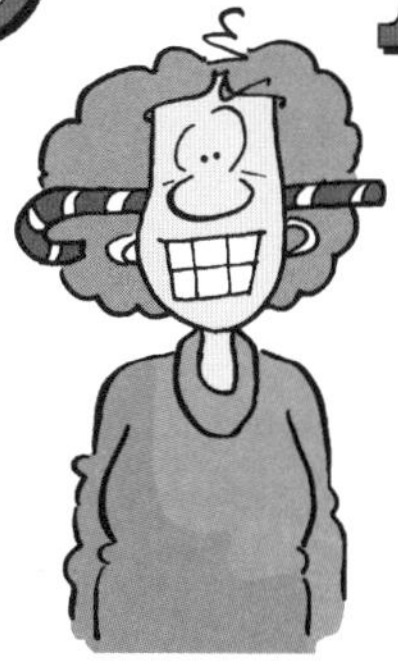

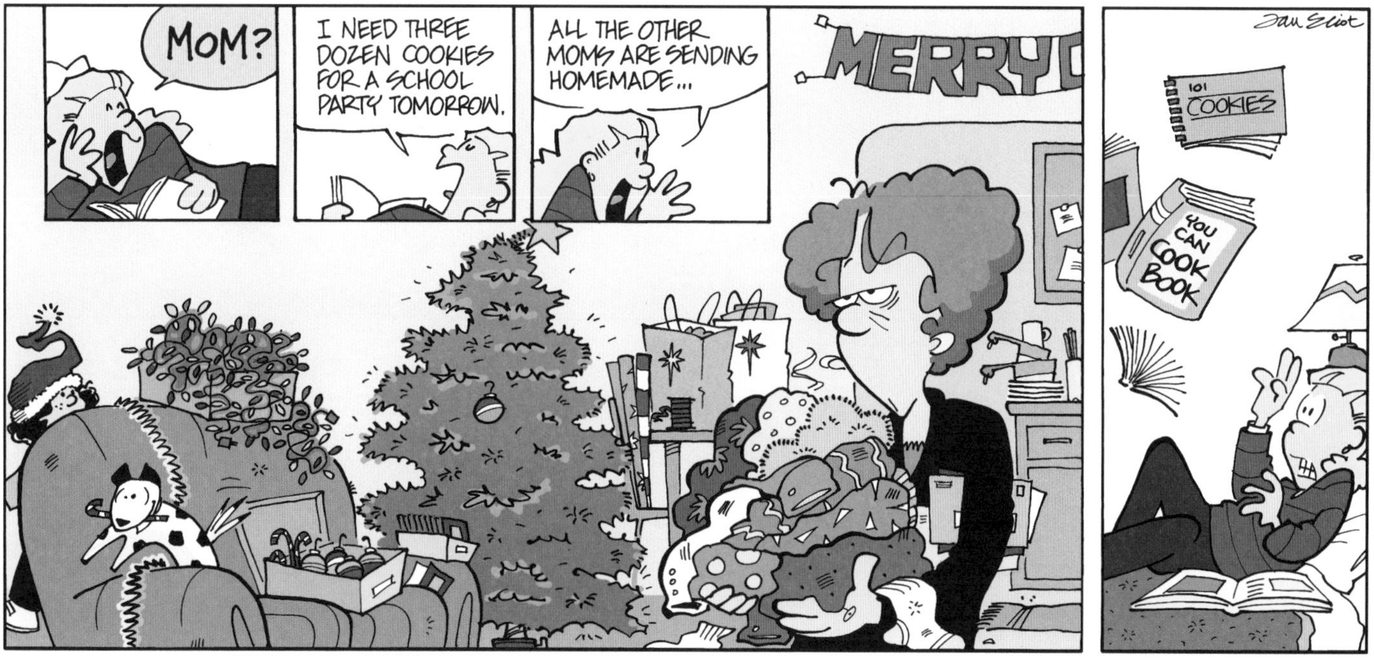
MOM?
I NEED THREE DOZEN COOKIES FOR A SCHOOL PARTY TOMORROW.
ALL THE OTHER MOMS ARE SENDING HOMEMADE...
MERRY
Jan Eliot
101 COOKIES
YOU CAN COOK BOOK

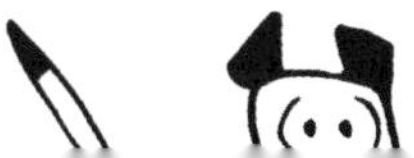

Stone Soup

MOM? AREN'T YOU AND PHIL DONE WRAPPING PACKAGES YET?

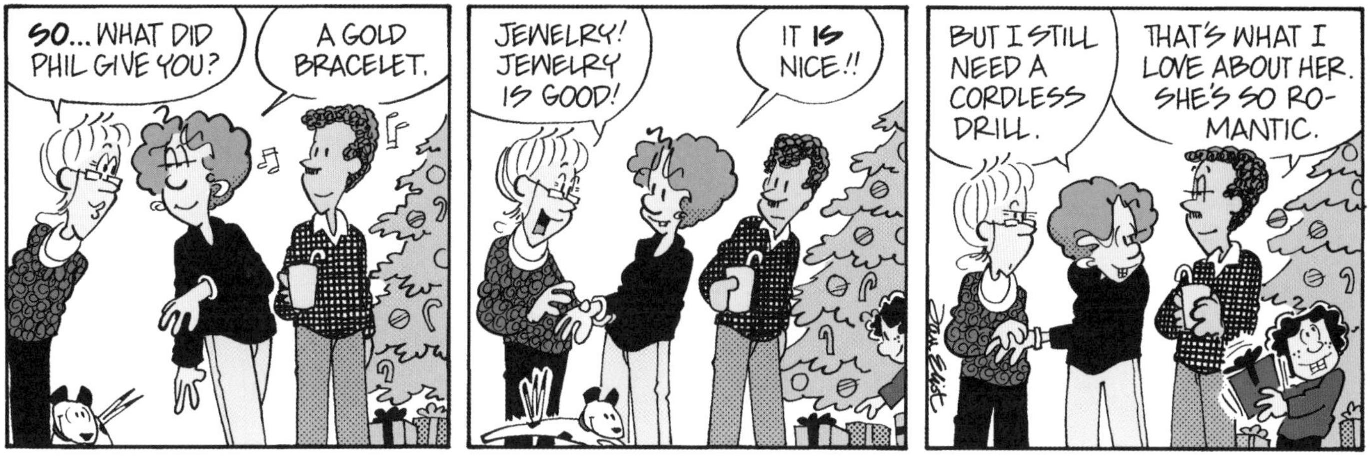
SO... WHAT DID PHIL GIVE YOU?
A GOLD BRACELET.
JEWELRY! JEWELRY IS GOOD!
IT IS NICE!!
BUT I STILL NEED A CORDLESS DRILL.
THAT'S WHAT I LOVE ABOUT HER. SHE'S SO RO-MANTIC.

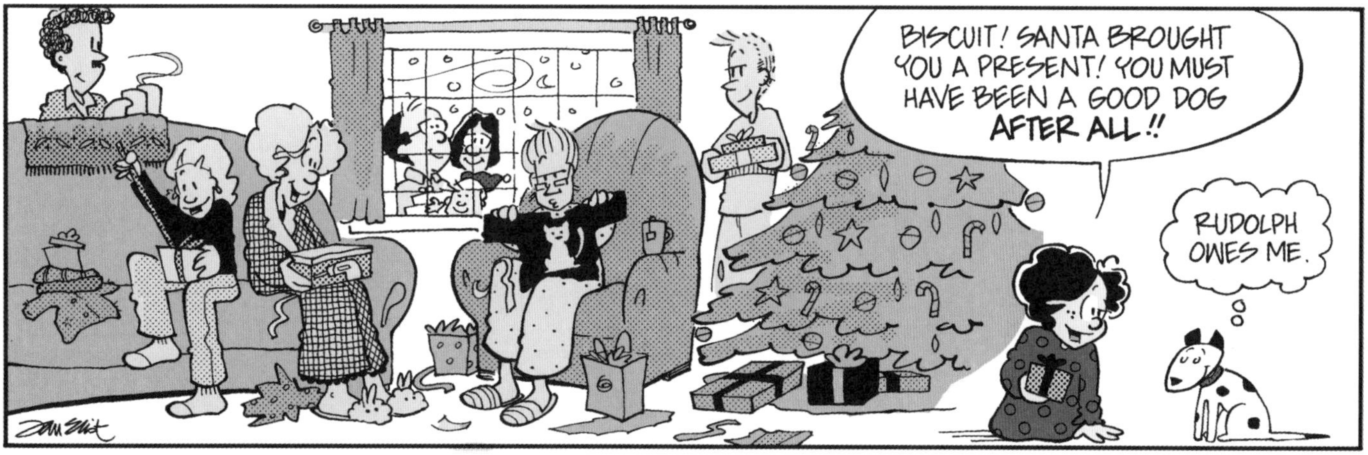
BISCUIT! SANTA BROUGHT YOU A PRESENT! YOU MUST HAVE BEEN A GOOD DOG AFTER ALL!!
RUDOLPH OWES ME.

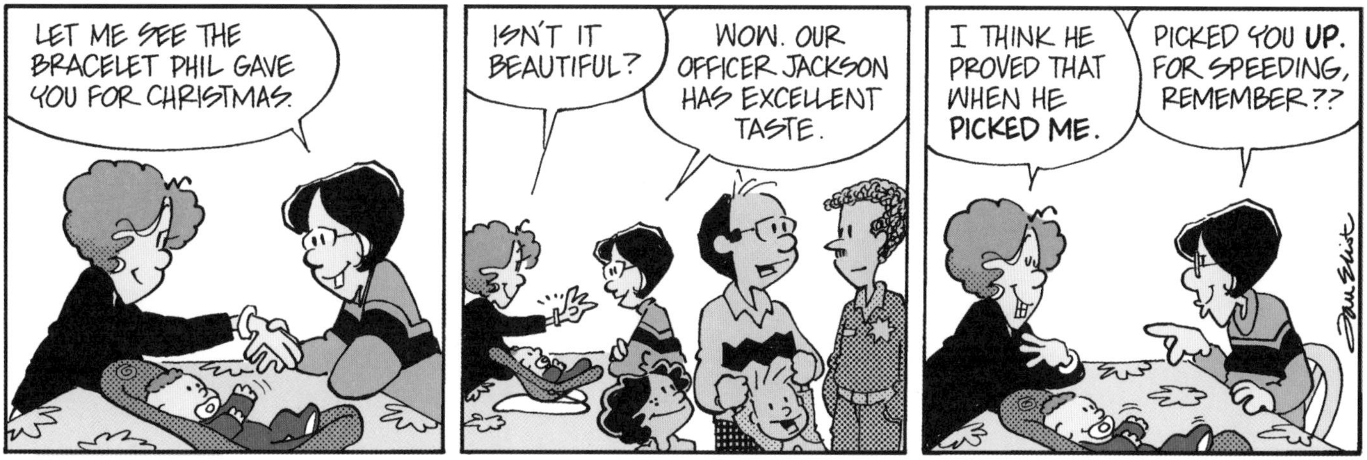
LET ME SEE THE BRACELET PHIL GAVE YOU FOR CHRISTMAS.
ISN'T IT BEAUTIFUL?
WOW. OUR OFFICER JACKSON HAS EXCELLENT TASTE.
I THINK HE PROVED THAT WHEN HE PICKED ME.
PICKED YOU UP. FOR SPEEDING, REMEMBER??

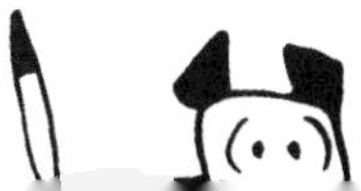

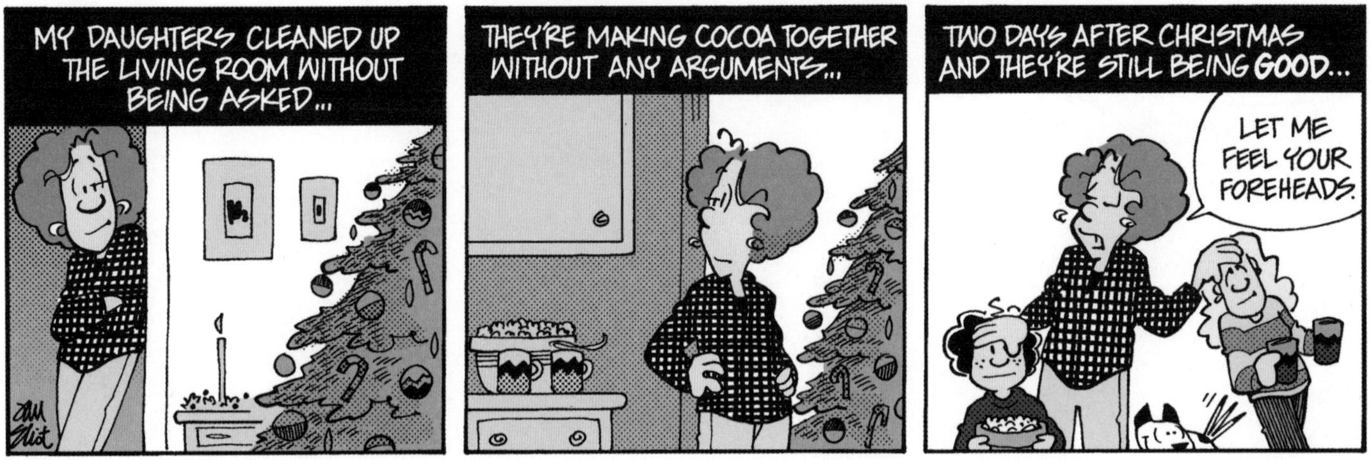
MY DAUGHTERS CLEANED UP THE LIVING ROOM WITHOUT BEING ASKED...
THEY'RE MAKING COCOA TOGETHER WITHOUT ANY ARGUMENTS...
TWO DAYS AFTER CHRISTMAS AND THEY'RE STILL BEING **GOOD**...
LET ME FEEL YOUR FOREHEADS.

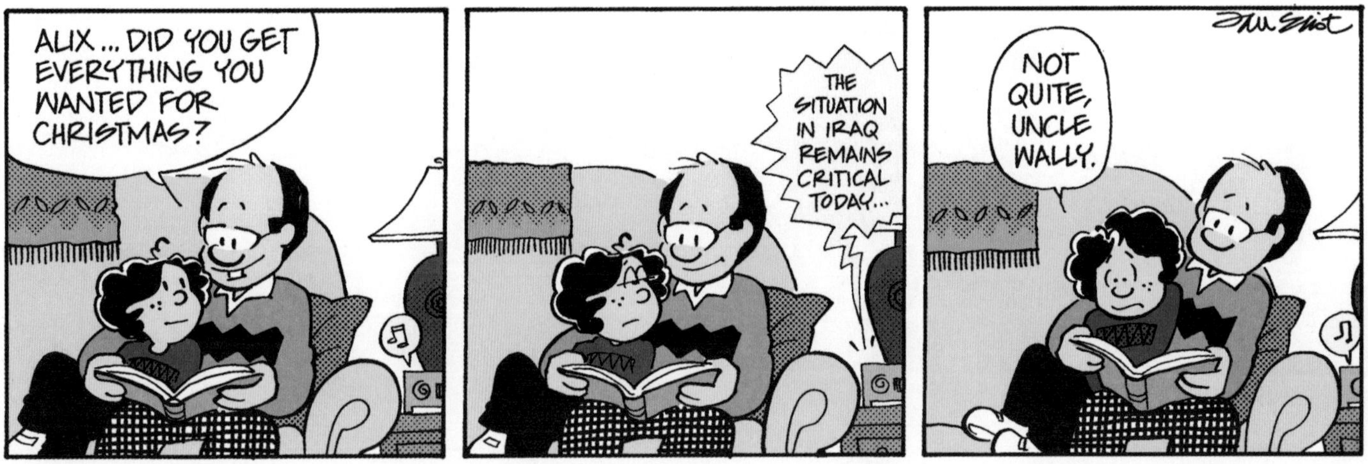
ALIX... DID YOU GET EVERYTHING YOU WANTED FOR CHRISTMAS?
THE SITUATION IN IRAQ REMAINS CRITICAL TODAY...
NOT QUITE, UNCLE WALLY.

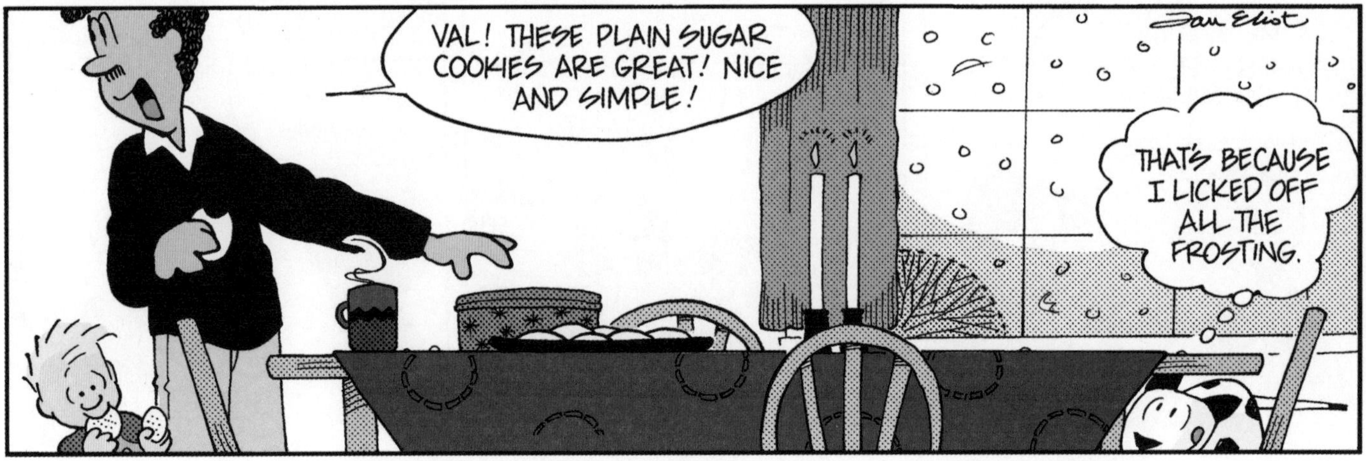
VAL! THESE PLAIN SUGAR COOKIES ARE GREAT! NICE AND SIMPLE!
THAT'S BECAUSE I LICKED OFF ALL THE FROSTING.

Stone Soup

I JUST LOVE THE BRACELET PHIL GAVE ME FOR CHRISTMAS.

YES... NICE... BUT... WHAT EXACTLY DOES A BRACELET **MEAN**?

IS IT MORE... OR **LESS**... SERIOUS THAN A NECKLACE?

WHAT DOES A BRACELET SAY? "YOU'RE **SWELL**"?

A **RING**... NOW, THAT'S A CLEAR MESSAGE! DOES HE KNOW YOUR RING SIZE?

PITY HE—

MOM.

WHAT I **WANTED** WAS A BRACELET.

VANESSA ANDERSON AND DAVID PADGALSKAS JUST GOT ENGAGED.

APPARENTLY, YOU AND I ARE THE ONLY ONES WHO DON'T THINK WE'RE READY FOR MARRIAGE.

YOU KNOW, IN FLOWER GIRL YEARS, I'M GETTIN' PRETTY **OLD**.

VROOOOOOOM!

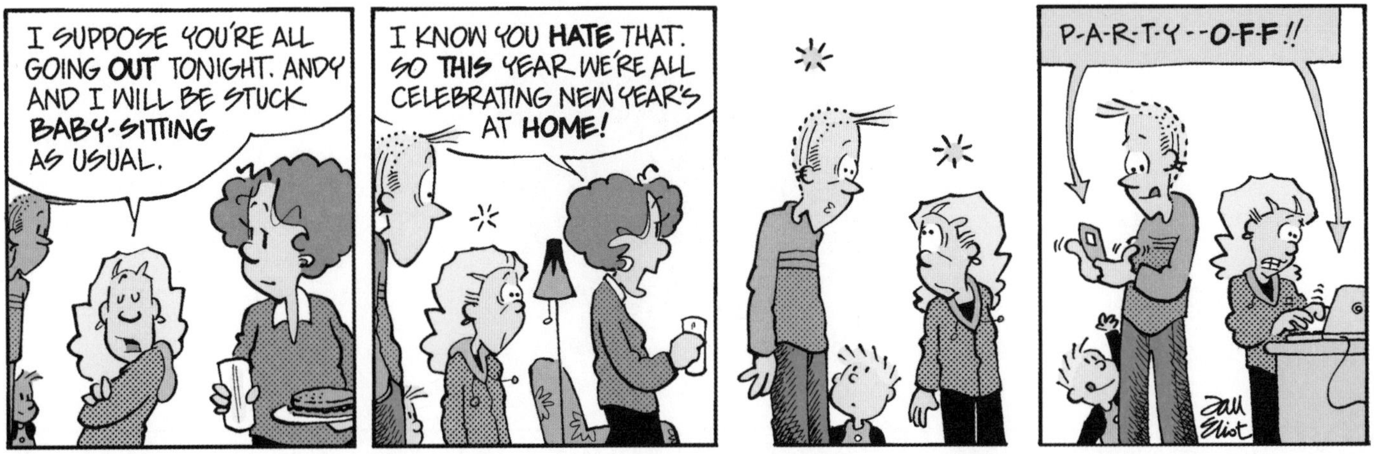
I SUPPOSE YOU'RE ALL GOING **OUT** TONIGHT. ANDY AND I WILL BE STUCK **BABY-SITTING** AS USUAL.
I KNOW YOU **HATE** THAT. SO **THIS** YEAR WE'RE ALL CELEBRATING NEW YEAR'S AT **HOME**!
P-A-R-T-Y--**O-F-F**!!

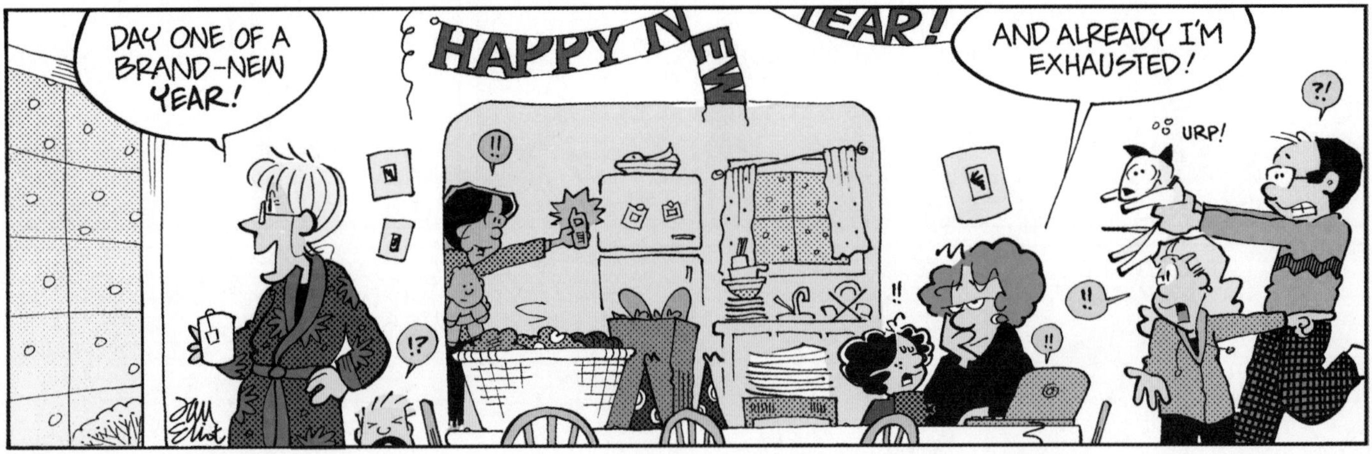
DAY ONE OF A BRAND-NEW **YEAR**!
HAPPY NEW YEAR!
AND ALREADY I'M EXHAUSTED!
!!
URP!
?!
!?
!!
!!
!!

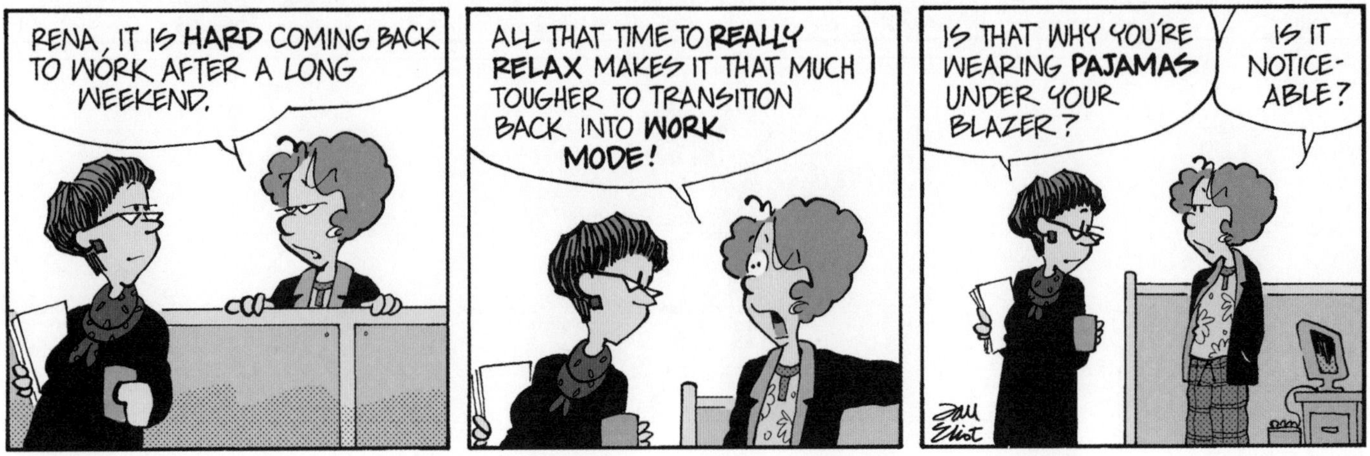
RENA, IT IS **HARD** COMING BACK TO WORK AFTER A LONG WEEKEND.
ALL THAT TIME TO **REALLY RELAX** MAKES IT THAT MUCH TOUGHER TO TRANSITION BACK INTO **WORK MODE**!
IS THAT WHY YOU'RE WEARING **PAJAMAS** UNDER YOUR BLAZER?
IS IT NOTICE-ABLE?

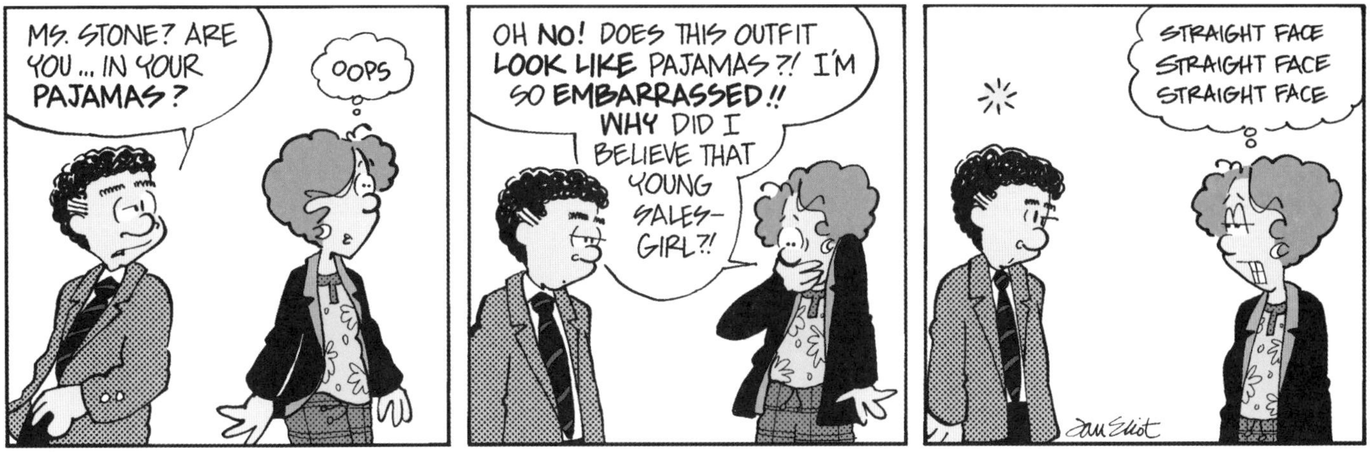
MS. STONE? ARE YOU ... IN YOUR PAJAMAS?
OOPS
OH NO! DOES THIS OUTFIT LOOK LIKE PAJAMAS?! I'M SO EMBARRASSED!! WHY DID I BELIEVE THAT YOUNG SALES-GIRL?!
STRAIGHT FACE STRAIGHT FACE STRAIGHT FACE

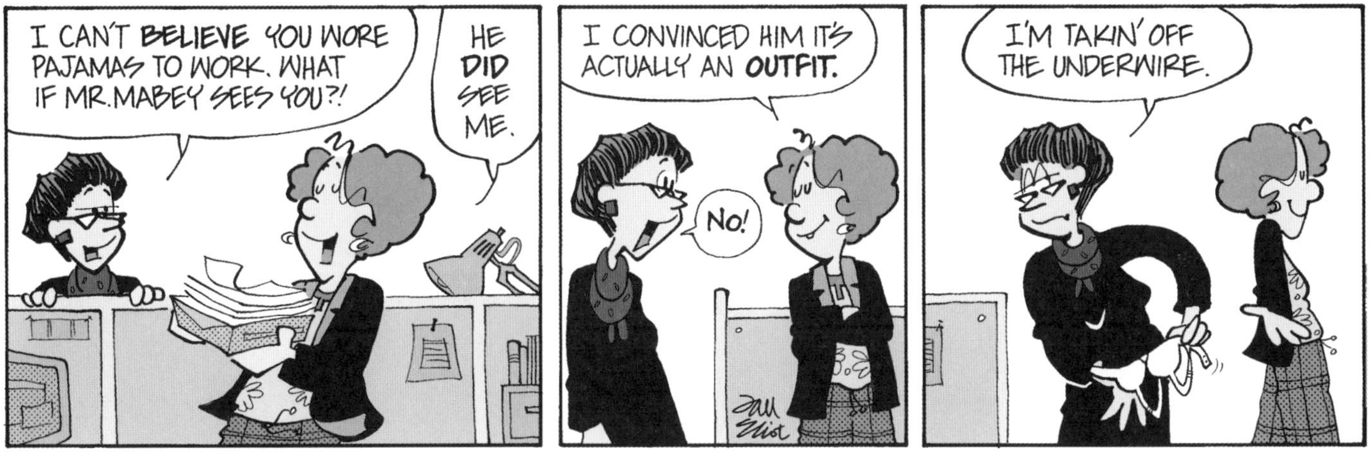
I CAN'T BELIEVE YOU WORE PAJAMAS TO WORK. WHAT IF MR. MABEY SEES YOU?!
HE DID SEE ME.
I CONVINCED HIM IT'S ACTUALLY AN OUTFIT.
NO!
I'M TAKIN' OFF THE UNDERWIRE.

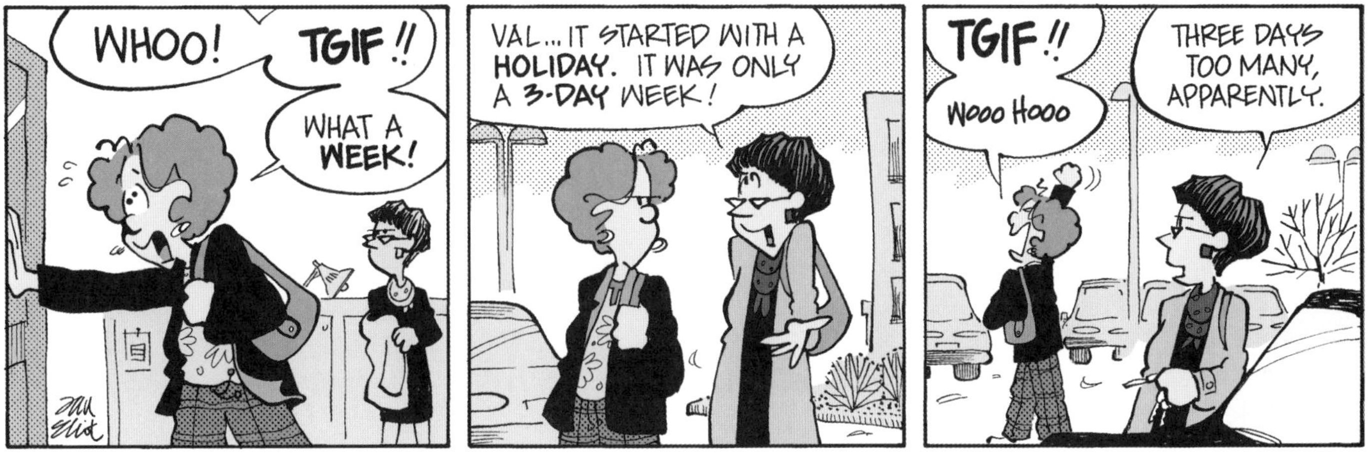
WHOO! TGIF!!
WHAT A WEEK!
VAL... IT STARTED WITH A HOLIDAY. IT WAS ONLY A 3-DAY WEEK!
TGIF!!
WOOO HOOO
THREE DAYS TOO MANY, APPARENTLY.

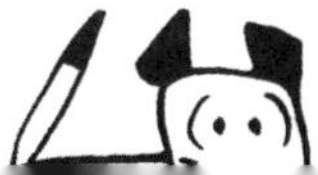

Stone Soup

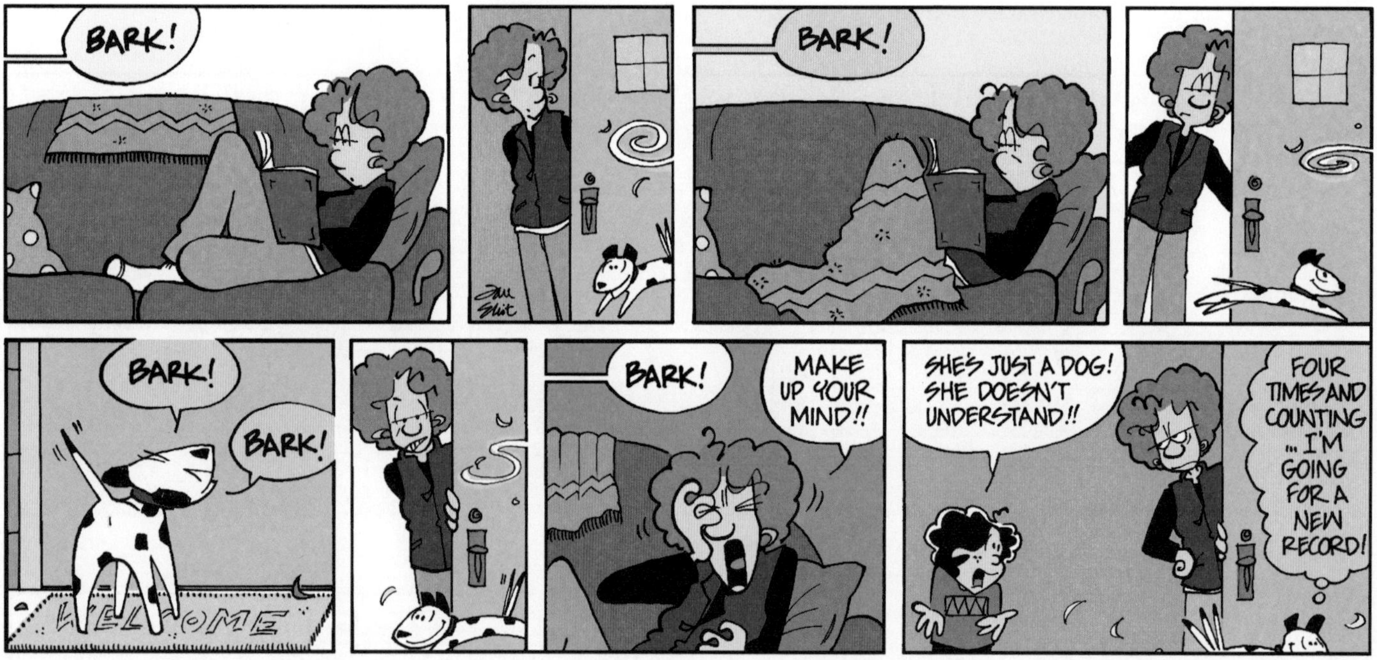

BARK!
BARK!
BARK!
BARK!
BARK!
MAKE UP YOUR MIND!!
SHE'S JUST A DOG! SHE DOESN'T UNDERSTAND!!
FOUR TIMES AND COUNTING ... I'M GOING FOR A NEW RECORD!

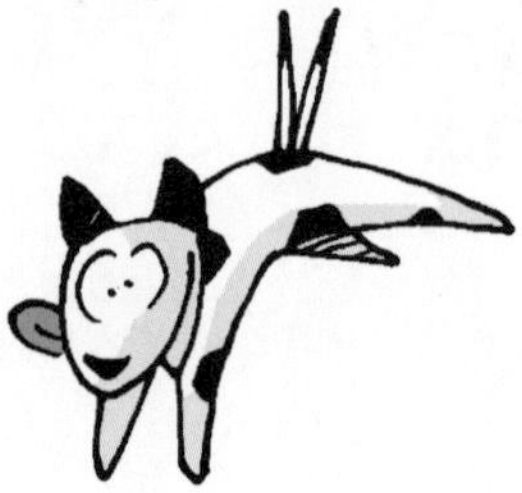

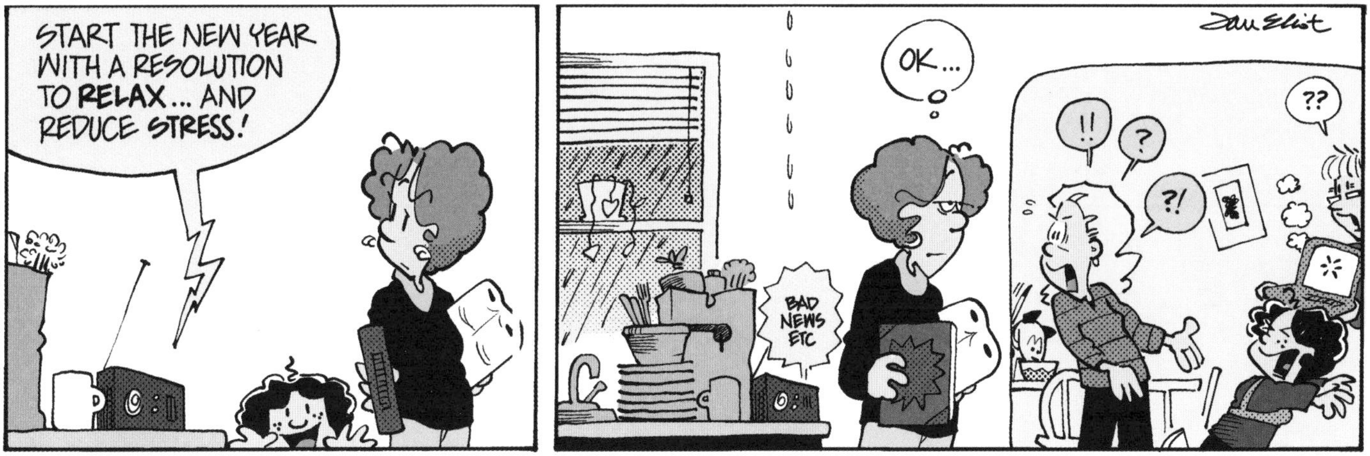
START THE NEW YEAR WITH A RESOLUTION TO **RELAX**... AND REDUCE **STRESS**!
BAD NEWS ETC
OK...
!!
?
?!
??

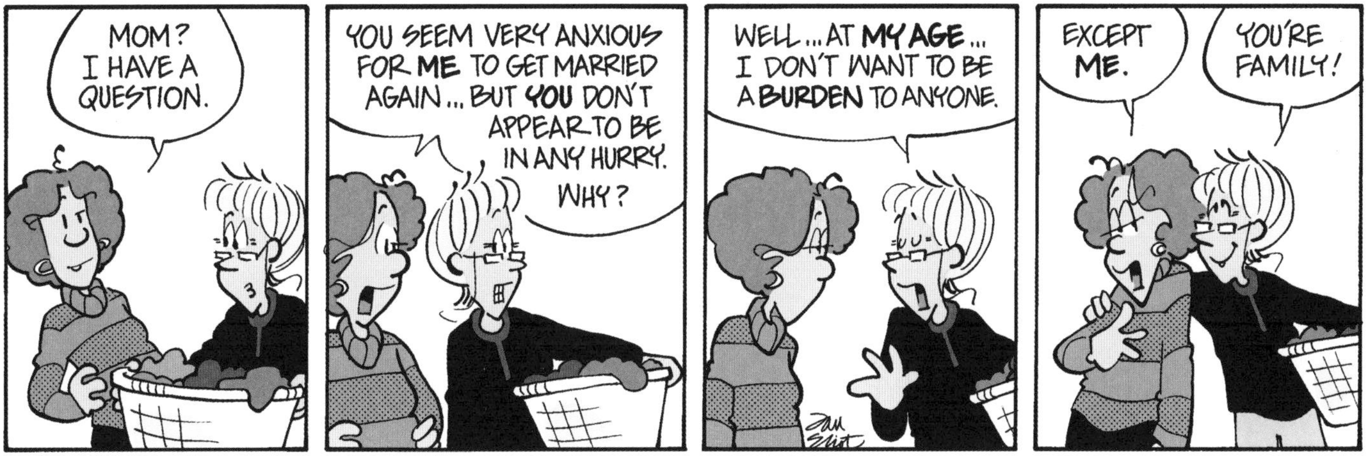
MOM? I HAVE A QUESTION.
YOU SEEM VERY ANXIOUS FOR **ME** TO GET MARRIED AGAIN... BUT **YOU** DON'T APPEAR TO BE IN ANY HURRY. WHY?
WELL... AT **MY AGE**... I DON'T WANT TO BE A **BURDEN** TO ANYONE.
EXCEPT **ME**.
YOU'RE FAMILY!

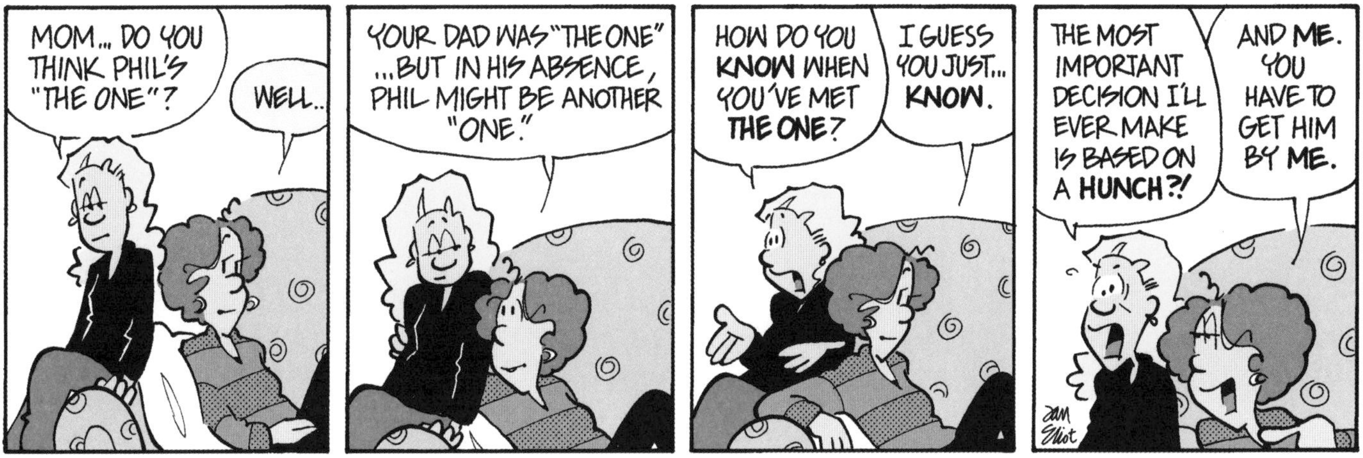
MOM... DO YOU THINK PHIL'S "THE ONE"?
WELL...
YOUR DAD WAS "THE ONE" ...BUT IN HIS ABSENCE, PHIL MIGHT BE ANOTHER "ONE."
HOW DO YOU **KNOW** WHEN YOU'VE MET **THE ONE**?
I GUESS YOU JUST... **KNOW**.
THE MOST IMPORTANT DECISION I'LL EVER MAKE IS BASED ON A **HUNCH**?!
AND **ME**. YOU HAVE TO GET HIM BY **ME**.

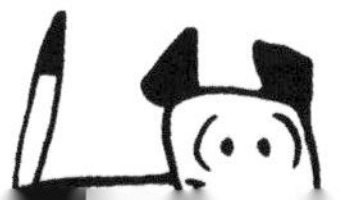

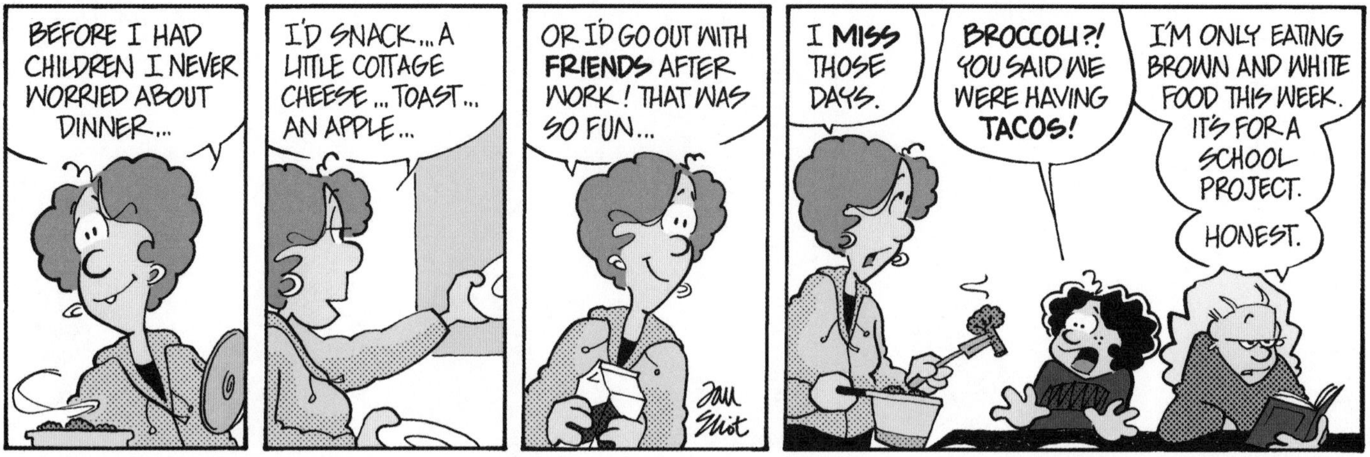
BEFORE I HAD CHILDREN I NEVER WORRIED ABOUT DINNER...
I'D SNACK... A LITTLE COTTAGE CHEESE... TOAST... AN APPLE...
OR I'D GO OUT WITH **FRIENDS** AFTER WORK! THAT WAS SO FUN...
I **MISS** THOSE DAYS.
BROCCOLI?! YOU SAID WE WERE HAVING **TACOS!**
I'M ONLY EATING BROWN AND WHITE FOOD THIS WEEK. IT'S FOR A SCHOOL PROJECT.
HONEST.

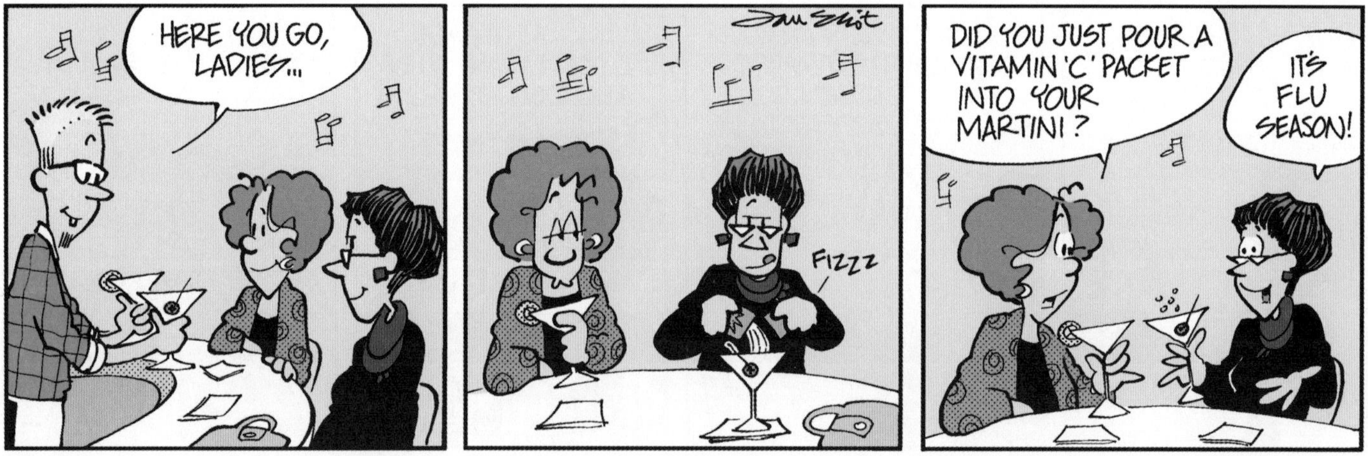
HERE YOU GO, LADIES...
FIZZZ
DID YOU JUST POUR A VITAMIN 'C' PACKET INTO YOUR MARTINI?
IT'S FLU SEASON!

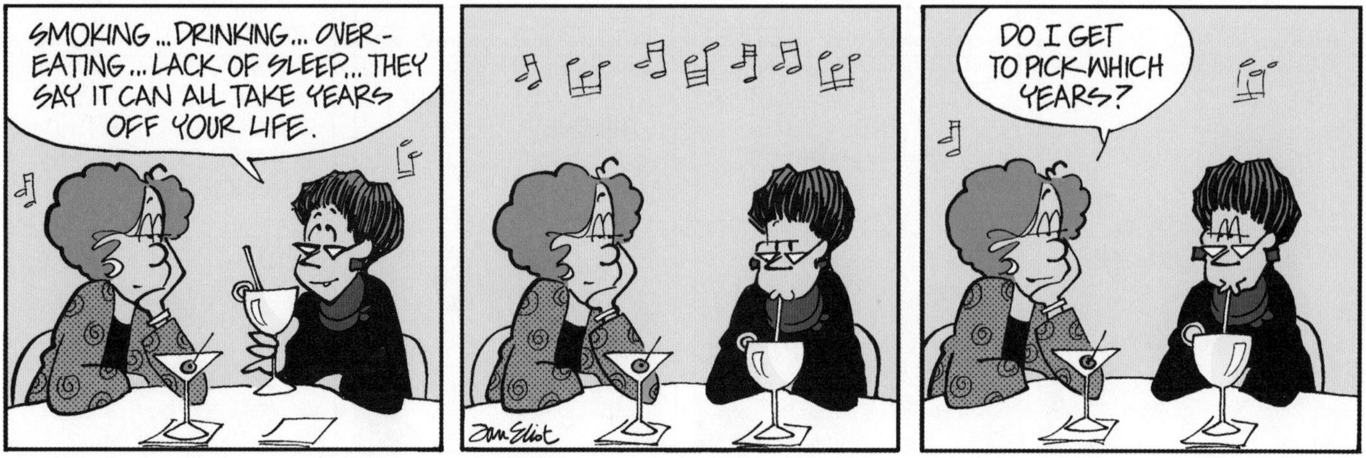
SMOKING... DRINKING... OVER-EATING... LACK OF SLEEP... THEY SAY IT CAN ALL TAKE YEARS OFF YOUR LIFE.
DO I GET TO PICK WHICH YEARS?

Stone Soup

FROM: VAL
RE: MEET?
TO: <BOOK CLUB>

DID WE DECIDE ON A DATE FOR NEXT MONTH'S MTG?
–Val

FROM: CATHY
RE: MEET?
TO: <BOOK CLUB>

I DON'T THINK SO. HOW'S THE 13TH FOR EVERYONE?
–Cathy

FROM: LYNN
FWD: RE: MEET?
TO: <BOOK CLUB>

CAN'T DO THE 13TH, BUT WHAT ABOUT THE 18TH, EVEN THO IT'S A SCHOOL HOLIDAY?
–Lynn

FWD: RE: MEET?
TO: <BOOK CLUB>

MONDAY THE 18TH IS NOT GOOD FOR JOAN OR CONNIE AND ALICE IS OUT OF TOWN THEN. CATHY'S ALONE THAT WEEK AND NEEDS COMPANY, BUT WED/THUR ARE NOT GOOD FOR ME. –Val

FWD: RE: MEET?
TO: <BOOK CLUB>

I'M OK TUES THE 12TH, OR TUES THE 19TH, OR THE 25TH, 26TH, 27TH. CATHY, WHEN DOES IRVING GET BACK? OR DOES IT MATTER?
–Connie

FROM: VAL
FWD: RE: RE: MEET?
TO: <BOOK CLUB>

TUES, HMM. 12TH BAD, 19TH GOOD. NEVER WEDNESDAY. I HAVE A WORKSHOP 25-27. THAT LEAVES ME WITH 19, 22, 23, 28 ...
–Val

TO: <BOOK CL
YIKES! TOO MANY #S FOR ME! TUES ARE BAD, THAT'S ALL. –Rose

AFTER YOU NAIL DOWN BOOK CLUB, LET'S PLAN POKER NIGHT!

DING!

DING!

DING!

DING!

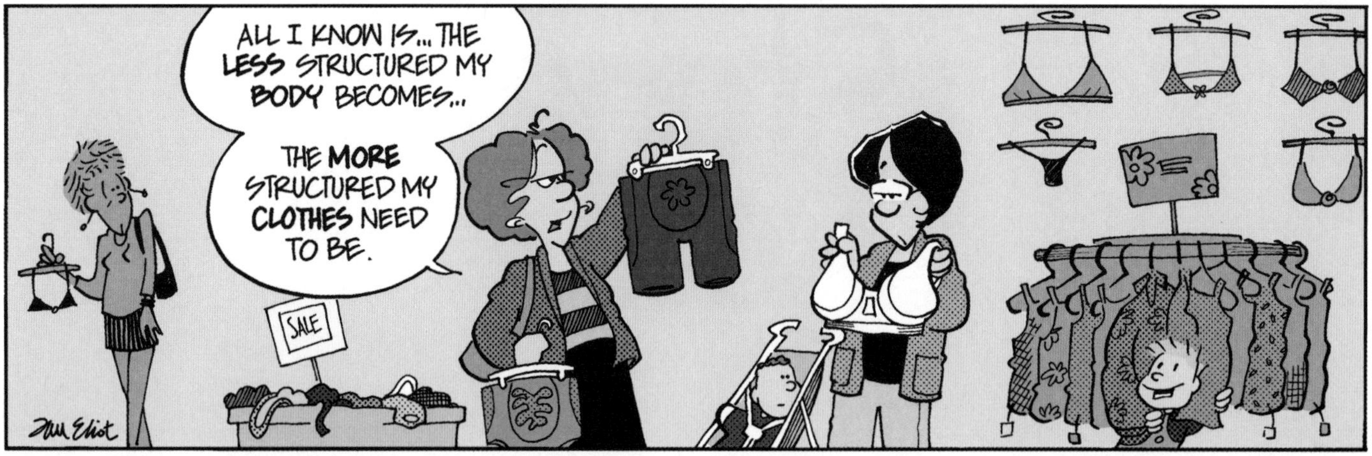
ALL I KNOW IS... THE LESS STRUCTURED MY BODY BECOMES...
THE MORE STRUCTURED MY CLOTHES NEED TO BE.
SALE

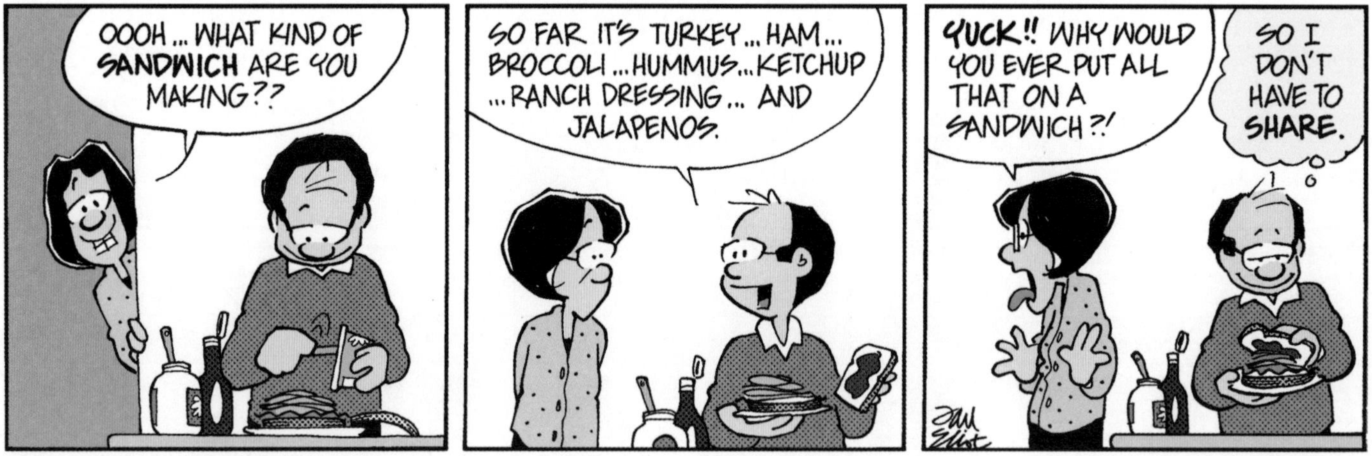
OOOH... WHAT KIND OF SANDWICH ARE YOU MAKING??
SO FAR IT'S TURKEY... HAM... BROCCOLI... HUMMUS... KETCHUP ...RANCH DRESSING... AND JALAPENOS.
YUCK!! WHY WOULD YOU EVER PUT ALL THAT ON A SANDWICH?!
SO I DON'T HAVE TO SHARE.

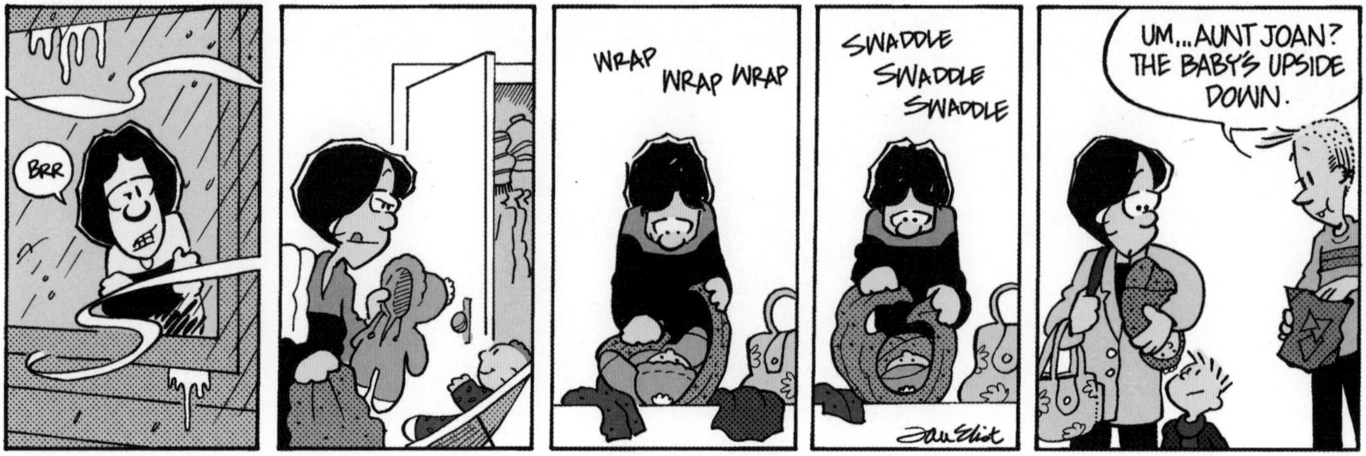
BRR
WRAP WRAP WRAP
SWADDLE SWADDLE SWADDLE
UM... AUNT JOAN? THE BABY'S UPSIDE DOWN.

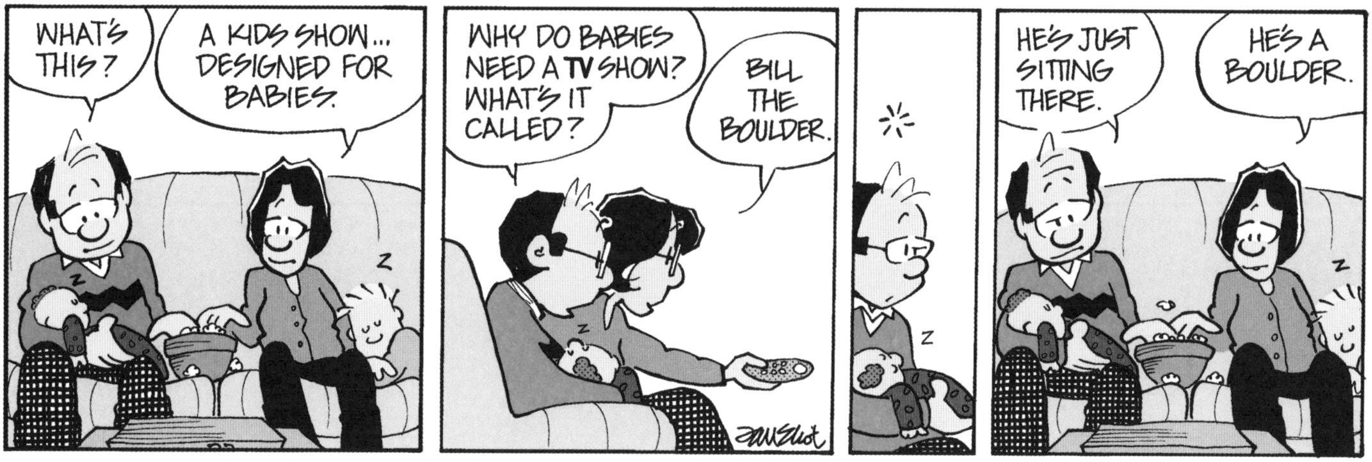
WHAT'S THIS?
A KIDS SHOW... DESIGNED FOR BABIES.
WHY DO BABIES NEED A **TV** SHOW? WHAT'S IT CALLED?
BILL THE BOULDER.
Z
HE'S JUST SITTING THERE.
HE'S A BOULDER.

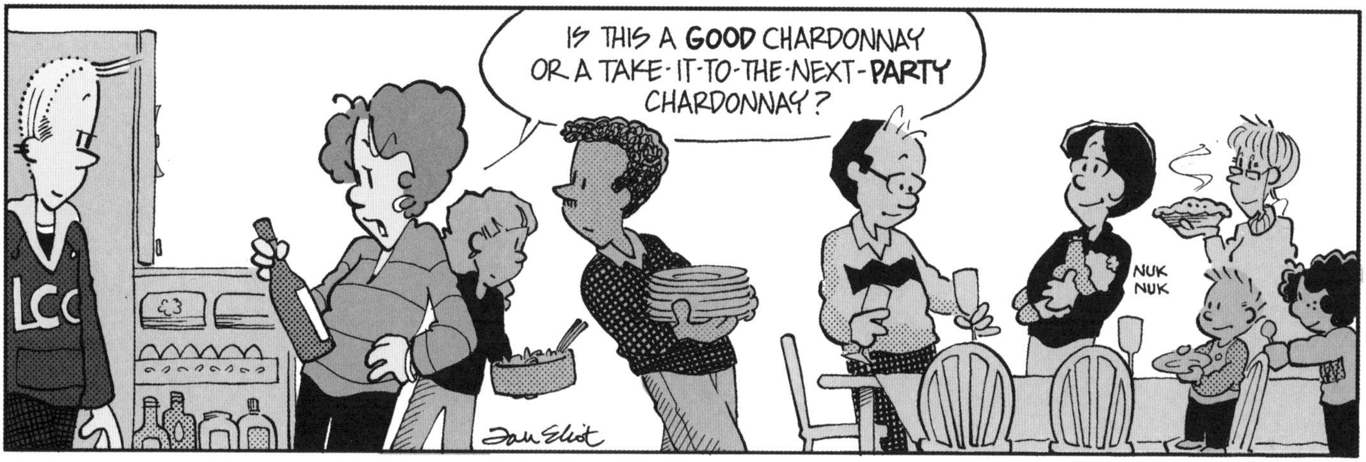
IS THIS A **GOOD** CHARDONNAY OR A TAKE-IT-TO-THE-NEXT-**PARTY** CHARDONNAY?
NUK NUK
LCC

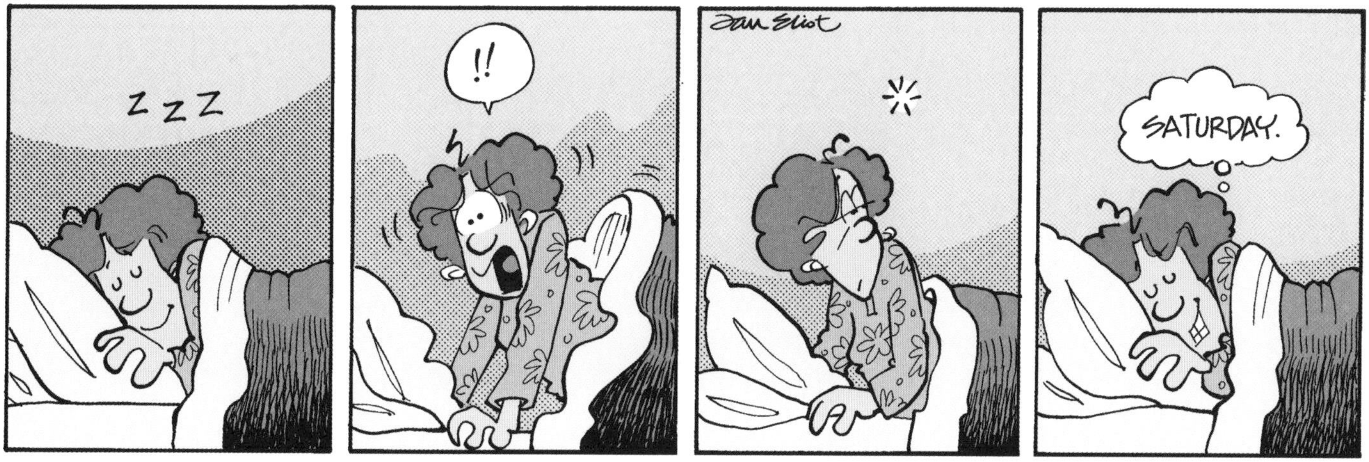
Z Z Z
!!
SATURDAY.

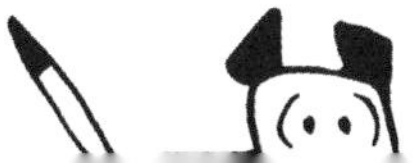

Stone Soup

MAY I HAVE THESE IN A 12, PLEASE?
YOU LOOK LIKE A 10 TO ME.
I WANT TO BREATHE. BRING ME A 12, OK?
SIGH
I'D PREFER A DARKER DENIM...
THIS LOOK IS TOTALLY IN.
BUT... THIS JUST LOOKS SORT OF ...DIRTY.
SIGH
HEY! DON'T ROLL YOUR EYES AT ME!! I GET ENOUGH OF THAT AT HOME. I DON'T NEED IT WHEN I GO SHOPPING!!
GASP
GASP
GASP
EYEROLL
EYEROLL
EYEROLL
EYE ROLL
SIGH

Something SQUARE
SIGH

Stone Soup

WALLY!
HOO HOO HOO
10K
WALLY!
WALLY ?!
WALLY!?
YOU FELL ASLEEP!!
I DID?
I DREAMT I WAS IN FANTASTIC SHAPE.
VISUALIZATION IS A GOOD FIRST STEP.

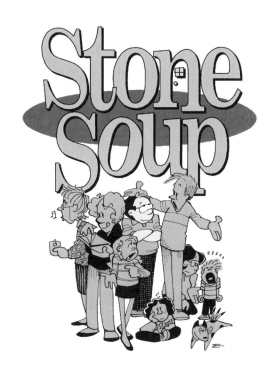

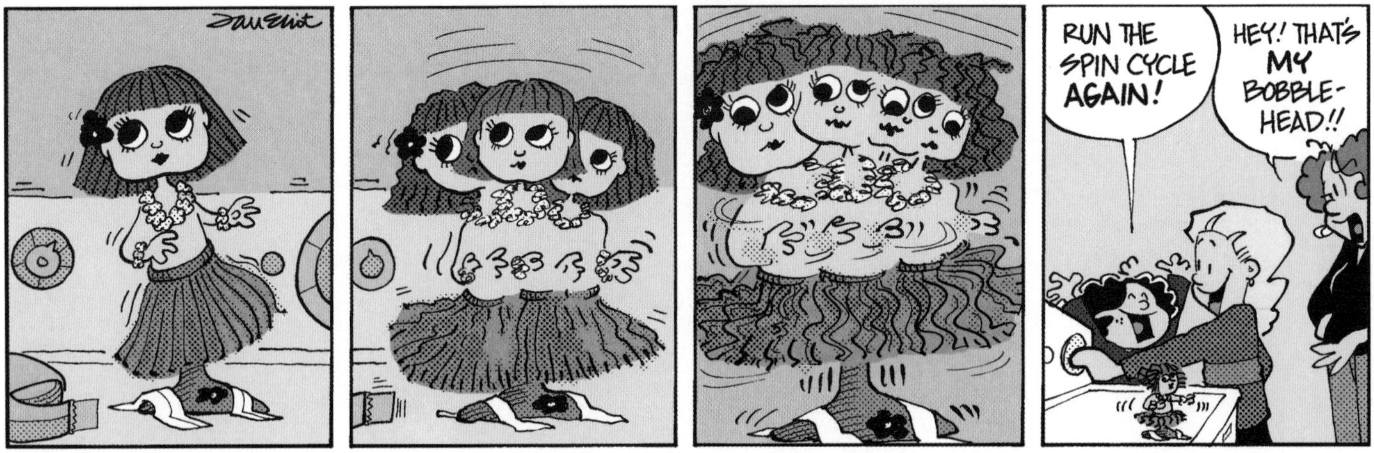
RUN THE SPIN CYCLE AGAIN!
HEY! THAT'S MY BOBBLE-HEAD!!

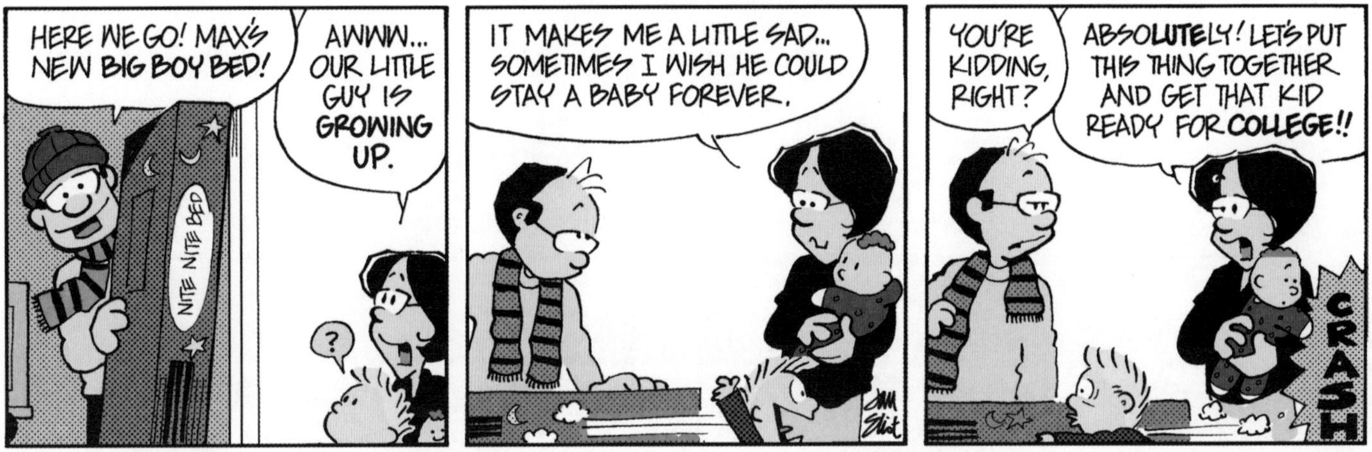
HERE WE GO! MAX'S NEW BIG BOY BED!
NITE NITE BED
AWWW... OUR LITTLE GUY IS GROWING UP.
?
IT MAKES ME A LITTLE SAD... SOMETIMES I WISH HE COULD STAY A BABY FOREVER.
YOU'RE KIDDING, RIGHT?
ABSOLUTELY! LET'S PUT THIS THING TOGETHER AND GET THAT KID READY FOR COLLEGE!!
CRASH

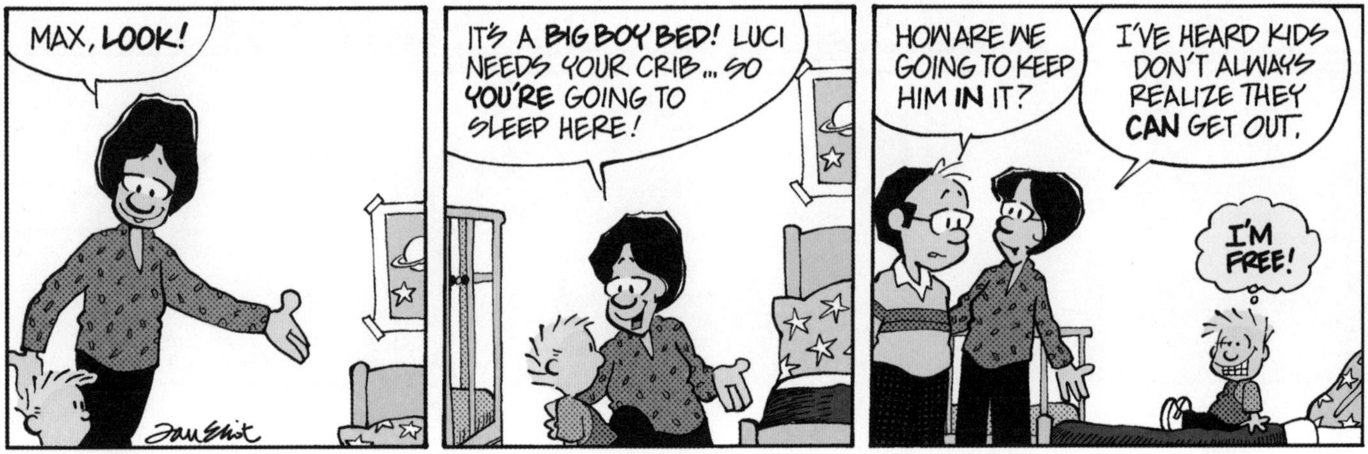
MAX, LOOK!
IT'S A BIG BOY BED! LUCI NEEDS YOUR CRIB... SO YOU'RE GOING TO SLEEP HERE!
HOW ARE WE GOING TO KEEP HIM IN IT?
I'VE HEARD KIDS DON'T ALWAYS REALIZE THEY CAN GET OUT.
I'M FREE!

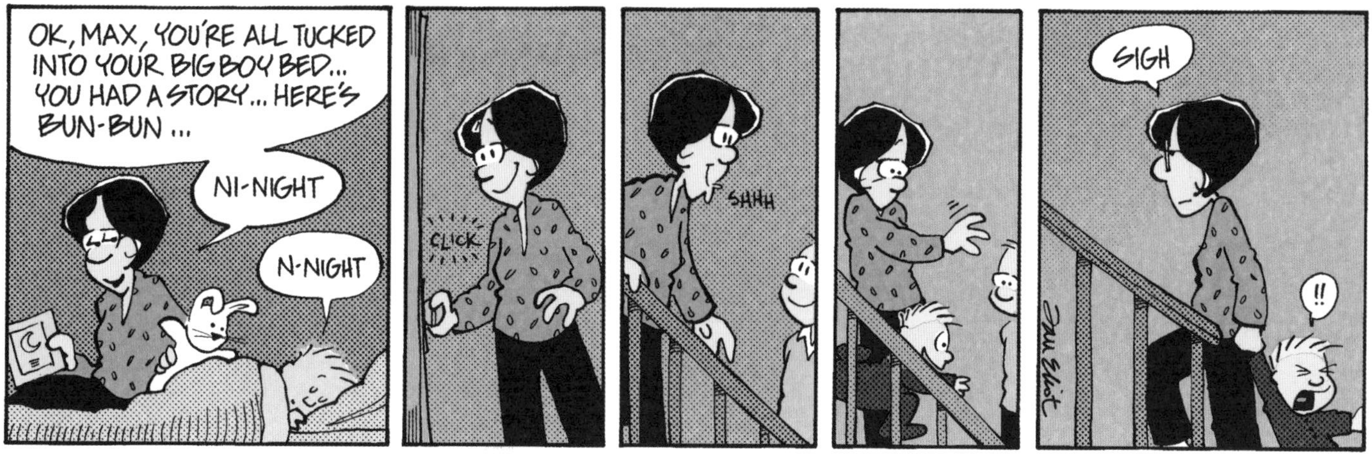
OK, MAX, YOU'RE ALL TUCKED INTO YOUR BIG BOY BED... YOU HAD A STORY... HERE'S BUN-BUN...
NI-NIGHT
N-NIGHT
CLICK
SHHH
SIGH
!!

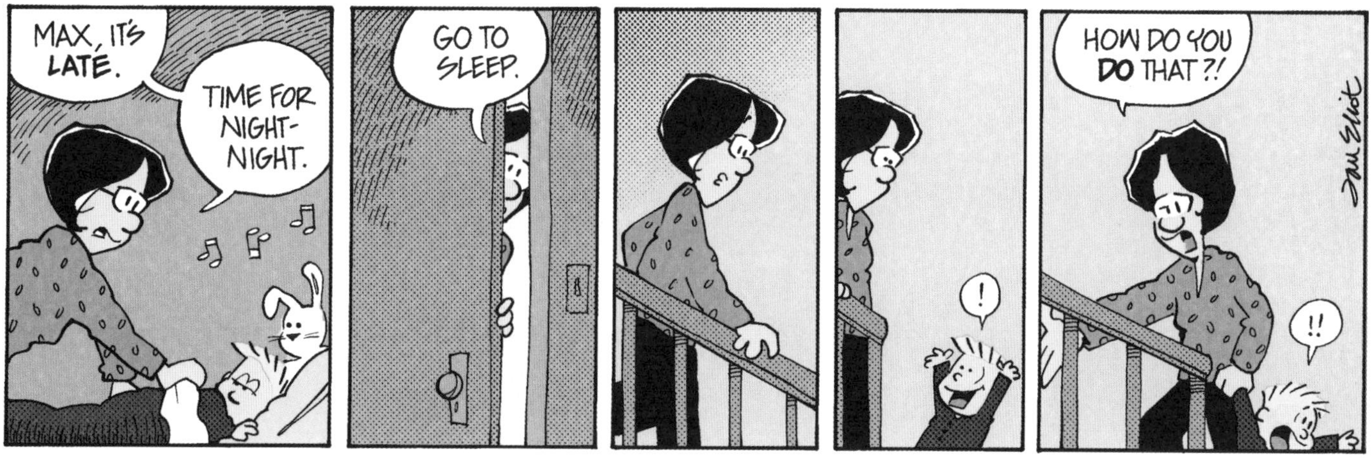
MAX, IT'S **LATE**.
TIME FOR NIGHT-NIGHT.
GO TO SLEEP.
!
HOW DO YOU **DO** THAT?!
!!

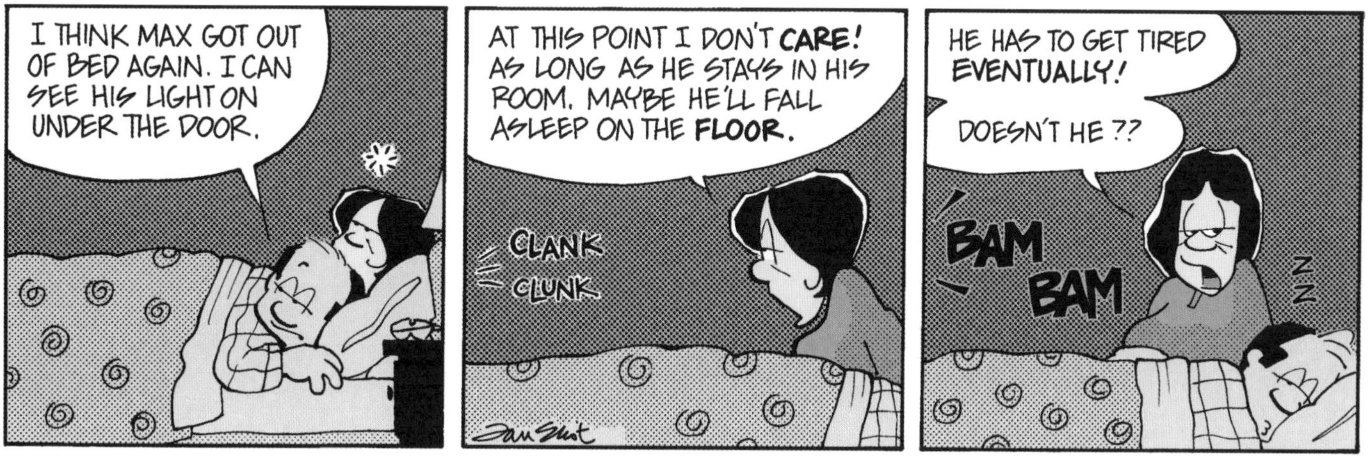
I THINK MAX GOT OUT OF BED AGAIN. I CAN SEE HIS LIGHT ON UNDER THE DOOR.
AT THIS POINT I DON'T **CARE!** AS LONG AS HE STAYS IN HIS ROOM. MAYBE HE'LL FALL ASLEEP ON THE **FLOOR**.
CLANK
CLUNK
HE HAS TO GET TIRED **EVENTUALLY!**
DOESN'T HE??
BAM
BAM
Z Z

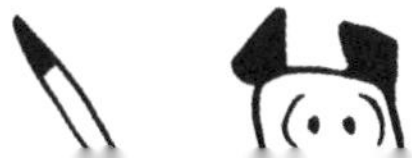

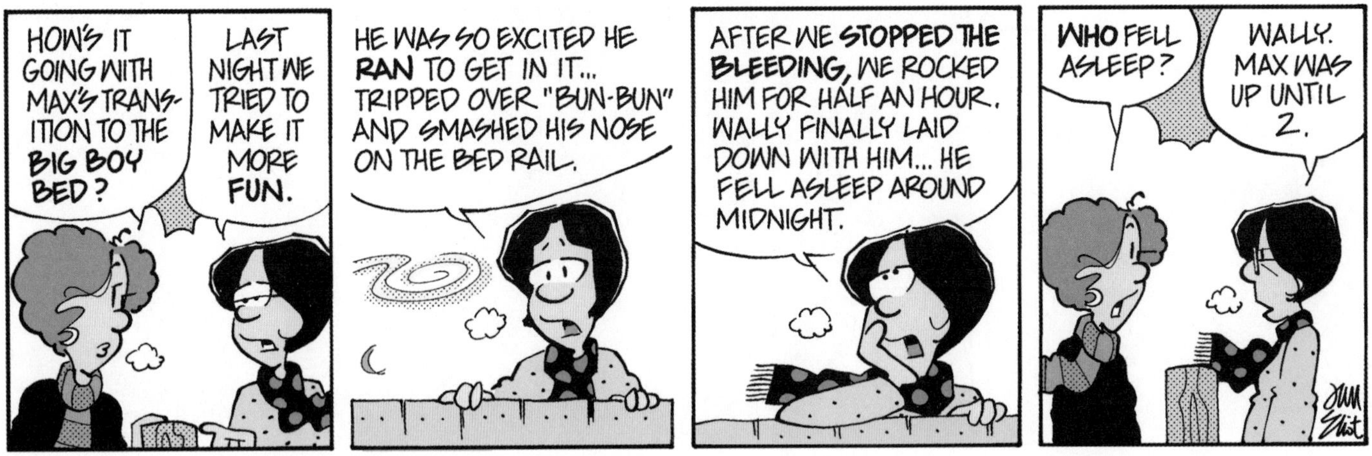
HOW'S IT GOING WITH MAX'S TRANSITION TO THE **BIG BOY BED**?
LAST NIGHT WE TRIED TO MAKE IT MORE **FUN**.
HE WAS SO EXCITED HE **RAN** TO GET IN IT... TRIPPED OVER "BUN-BUN" AND SMASHED HIS NOSE ON THE BED RAIL.
AFTER WE **STOPPED THE BLEEDING,** WE ROCKED HIM FOR HALF AN HOUR. WALLY FINALLY LAID DOWN WITH HIM... HE FELL ASLEEP AROUND MIDNIGHT.
WHO FELL ASLEEP?
WALLY. MAX WAS UP UNTIL 2.
JAN ELIOT

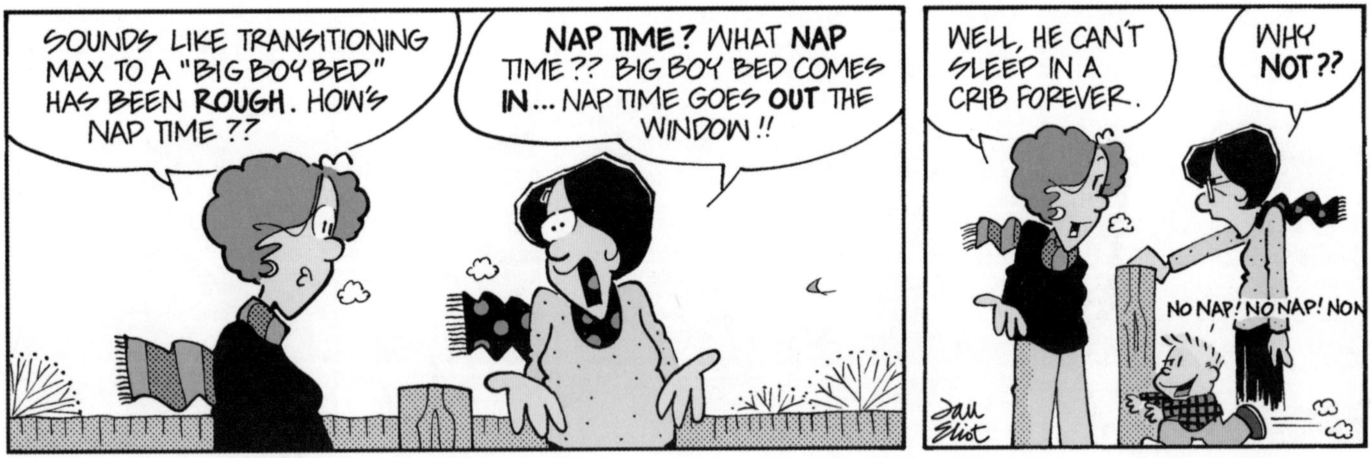
SOUNDS LIKE TRANSITIONING MAX TO A "BIG BOY BED" HAS BEEN **ROUGH**. HOW'S NAP TIME??
NAP TIME? WHAT **NAP** TIME?? BIG BOY BED COMES **IN**... NAP TIME GOES **OUT** THE WINDOW!!
WELL, HE CAN'T SLEEP IN A CRIB FOREVER.
WHY **NOT**??
NO NAP! NO NAP! NON
JAN ELIOT

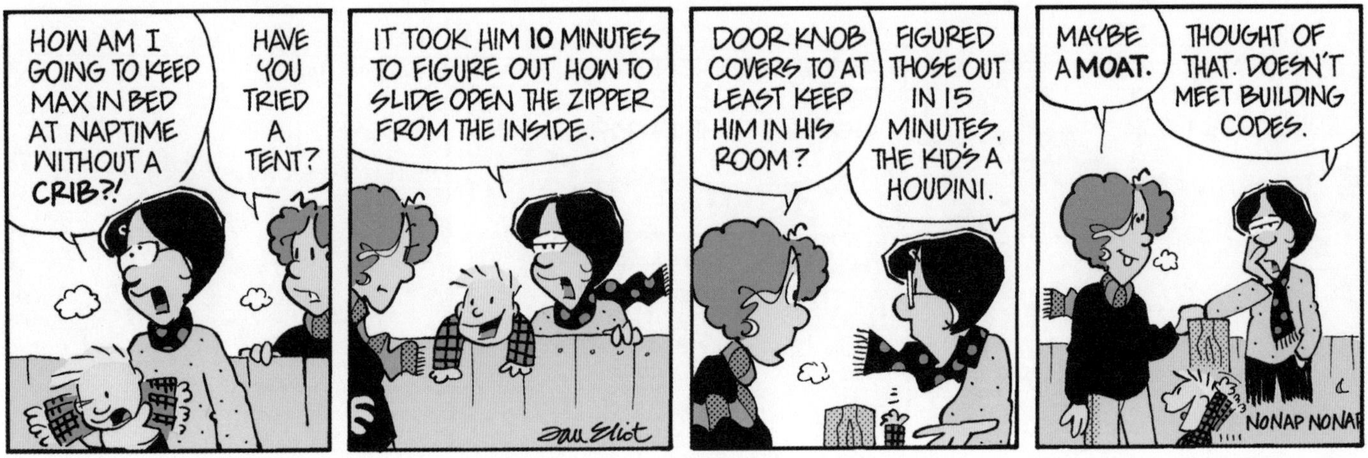
HOW AM I GOING TO KEEP MAX IN BED AT NAPTIME WITHOUT A **CRIB**?!
HAVE YOU TRIED A TENT?
IT TOOK HIM **10** MINUTES TO FIGURE OUT HOW TO SLIDE OPEN THE ZIPPER FROM THE INSIDE.
JAN ELIOT
DOOR KNOB COVERS TO AT LEAST KEEP HIM IN HIS ROOM?
FIGURED THOSE OUT IN 15 MINUTES. THE KID'S A HOUDINI.
MAYBE A **MOAT**.
THOUGHT OF THAT. DOESN'T MEET BUILDING CODES.
NONAP NONAP

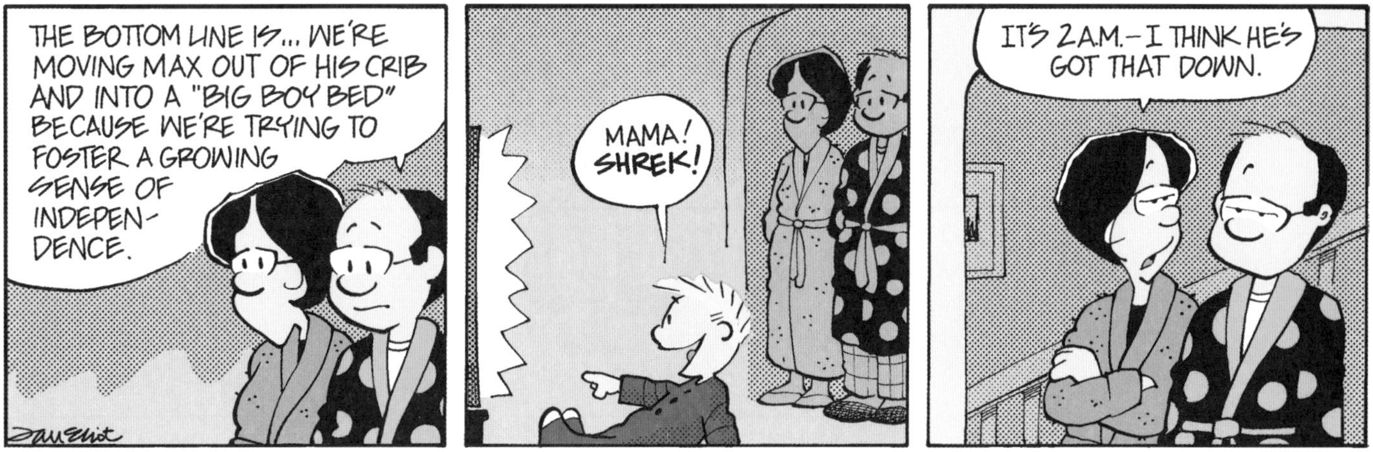
THE BOTTOM LINE IS... WE'RE MOVING MAX OUT OF HIS CRIB AND INTO A "BIG BOY BED" BECAUSE WE'RE TRYING TO FOSTER A GROWING SENSE OF INDEPEN- DENCE.
MAMA! SHREK!
IT'S 2 A.M.– I THINK HE'S GOT THAT DOWN.

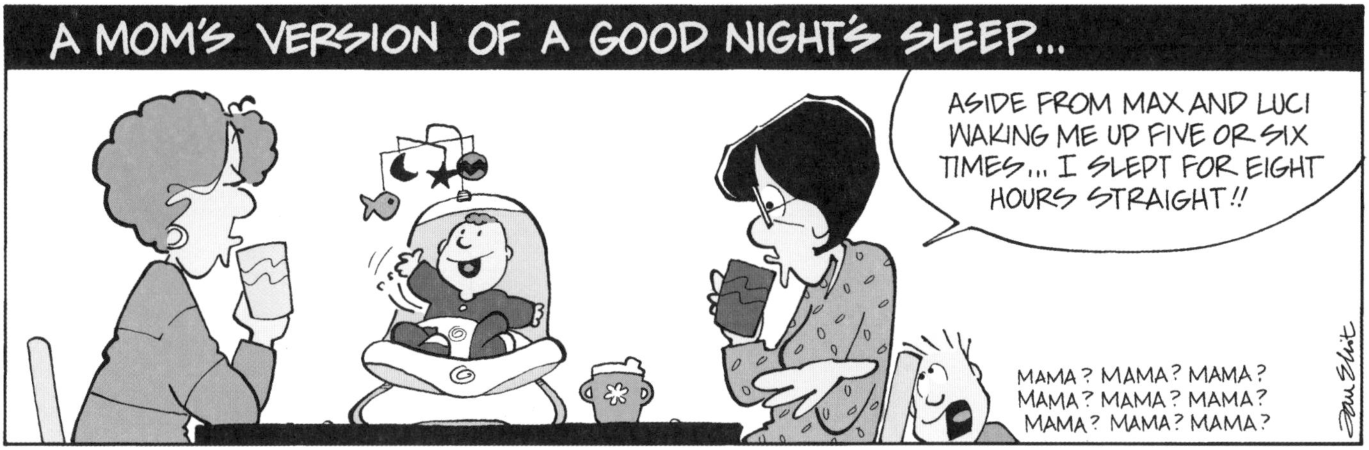
A MOM'S VERSION OF A GOOD NIGHT'S SLEEP...
ASIDE FROM MAX AND LUCI WAKING ME UP FIVE OR SIX TIMES... I SLEPT FOR EIGHT HOURS STRAIGHT!!
MAMA? MAMA? MAMA? MAMA? MAMA? MAMA? MAMA? MAMA? MAMA?

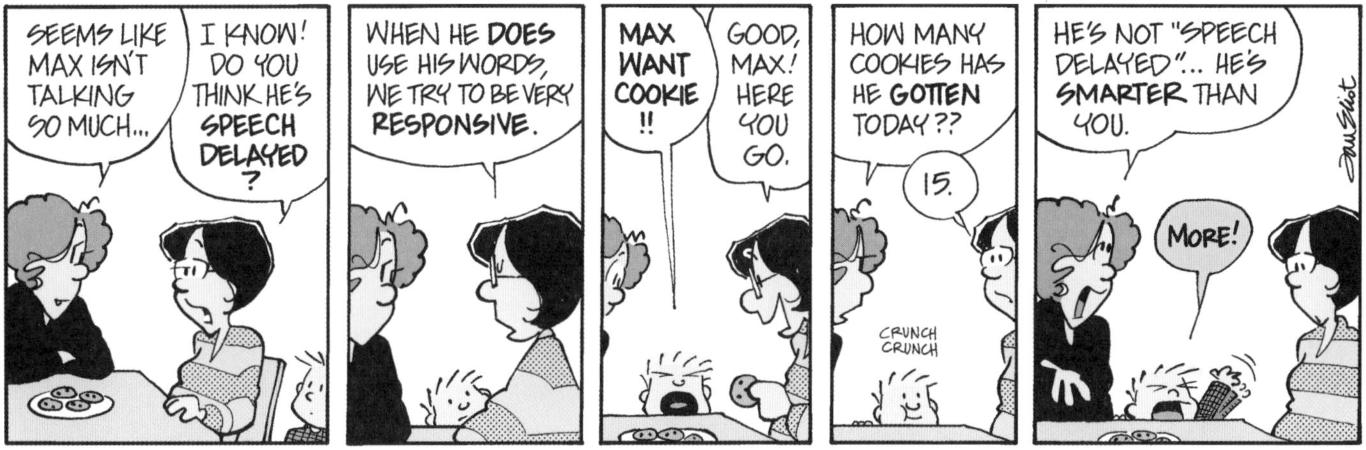
SEEMS LIKE MAX ISN'T TALKING SO MUCH...
I KNOW! DO YOU THINK HE'S SPEECH DELAYED?
WHEN HE DOES USE HIS WORDS, WE TRY TO BE VERY RESPONSIVE.
MAX WANT COOKIE!!
GOOD, MAX! HERE YOU GO.
HOW MANY COOKIES HAS HE GOTTEN TODAY??
15.
CRUNCH CRUNCH
HE'S NOT "SPEECH DELAYED"... HE'S SMARTER THAN YOU.
MORE!

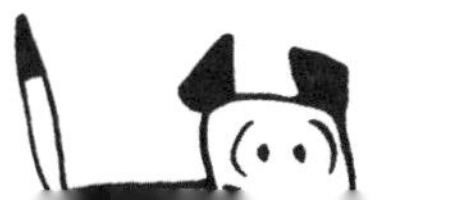

Stone Soup

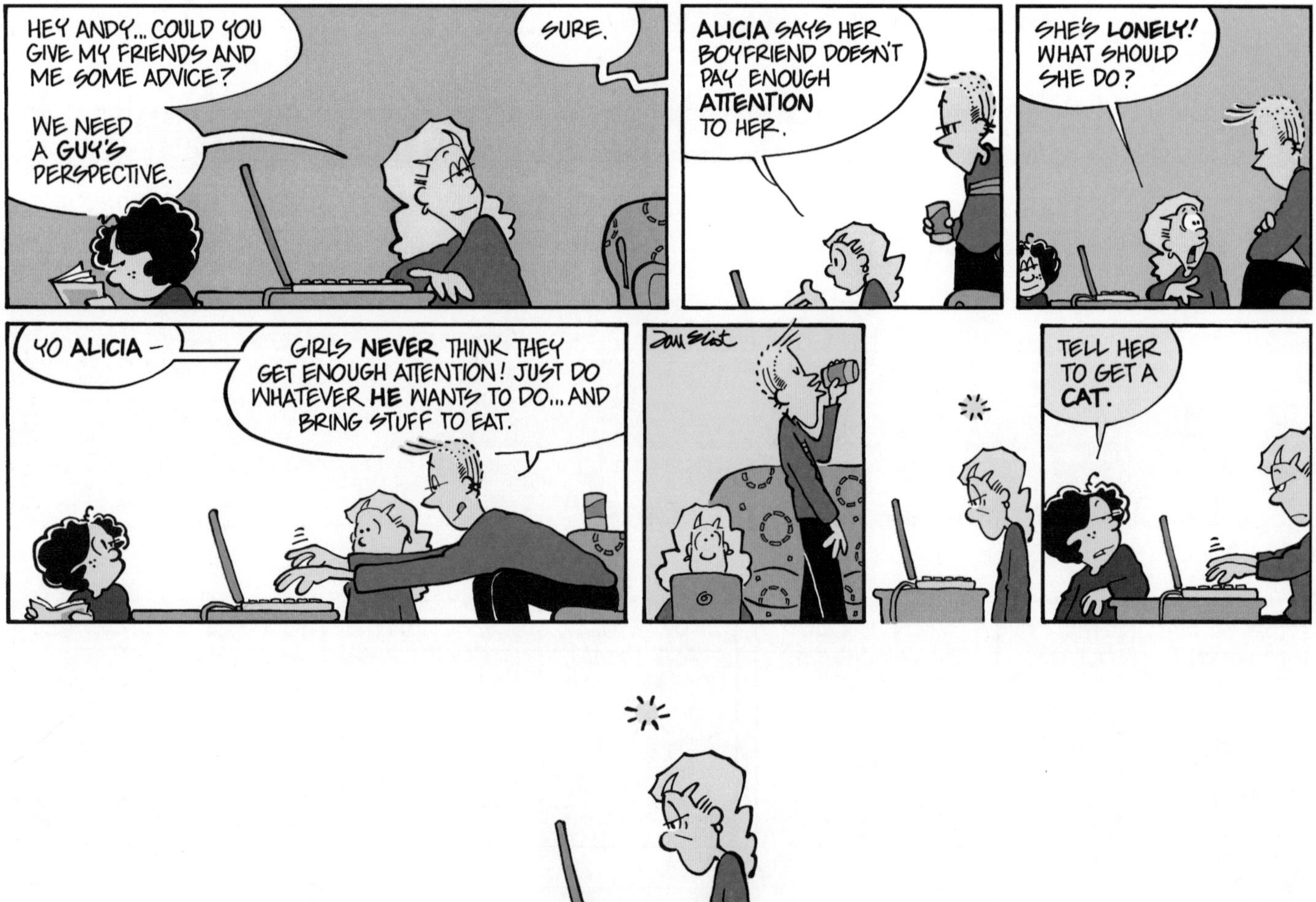
HEY ANDY... COULD YOU GIVE MY FRIENDS AND ME SOME ADVICE?
WE NEED A GUY'S PERSPECTIVE.
SURE.
ALICIA SAYS HER BOYFRIEND DOESN'T PAY ENOUGH ATTENTION TO HER.
SHE'S LONELY! WHAT SHOULD SHE DO?
YO ALICIA –
GIRLS NEVER THINK THEY GET ENOUGH ATTENTION! JUST DO WHATEVER HE WANTS TO DO... AND BRING STUFF TO EAT.
TELL HER TO GET A CAT.

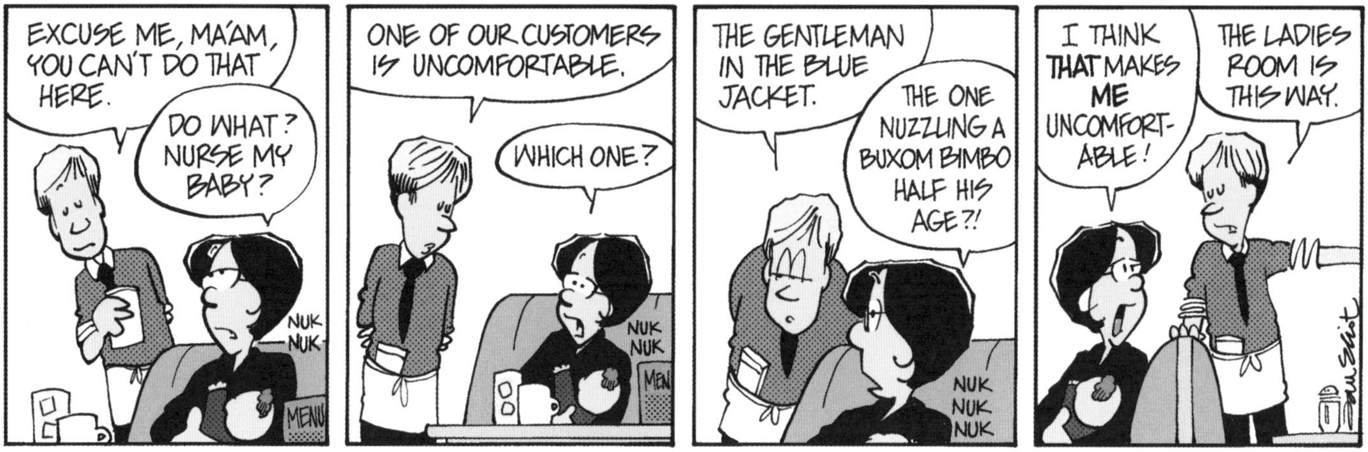
EXCUSE ME, MA'AM, YOU CAN'T DO THAT HERE.
DO WHAT? NURSE MY BABY?
NUK NUK
ONE OF OUR CUSTOMERS IS UNCOMFORTABLE.
WHICH ONE?
NUK NUK
THE GENTLEMAN IN THE BLUE JACKET.
THE ONE NUZZLING A BUXOM BIMBO HALF HIS AGE?!
NUK NUK NUK
I THINK **THAT** MAKES **ME** UNCOMFORTABLE!
THE LADIES ROOM IS THIS WAY.

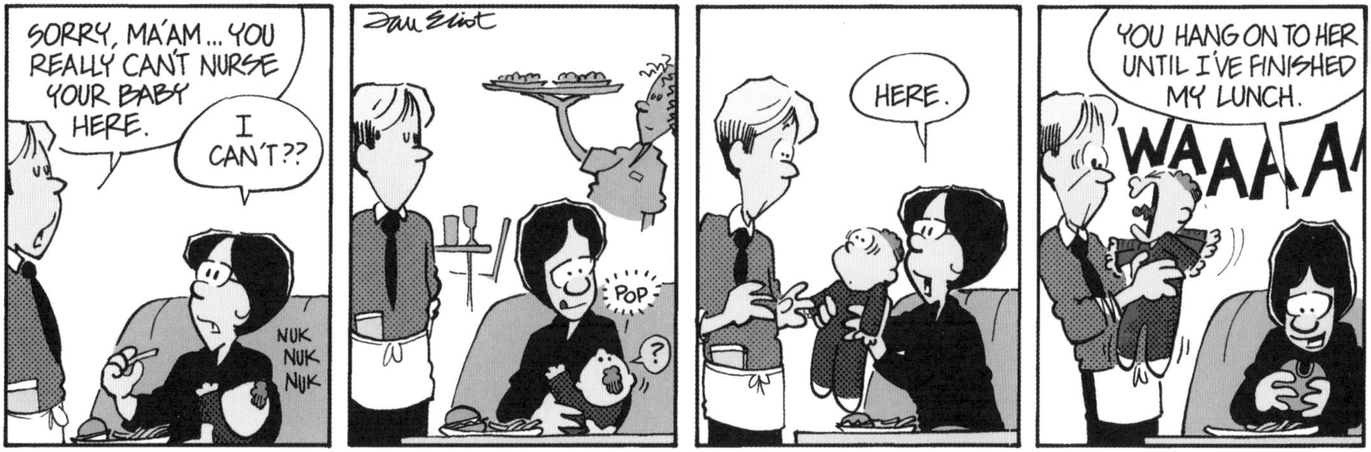
SORRY, MA'AM... YOU REALLY CAN'T NURSE YOUR BABY HERE.
I CAN'T??
NUK NUK NUK
POP
?
HERE.
YOU HANG ON TO HER UNTIL I'VE FINISHED MY LUNCH.
WAAAA

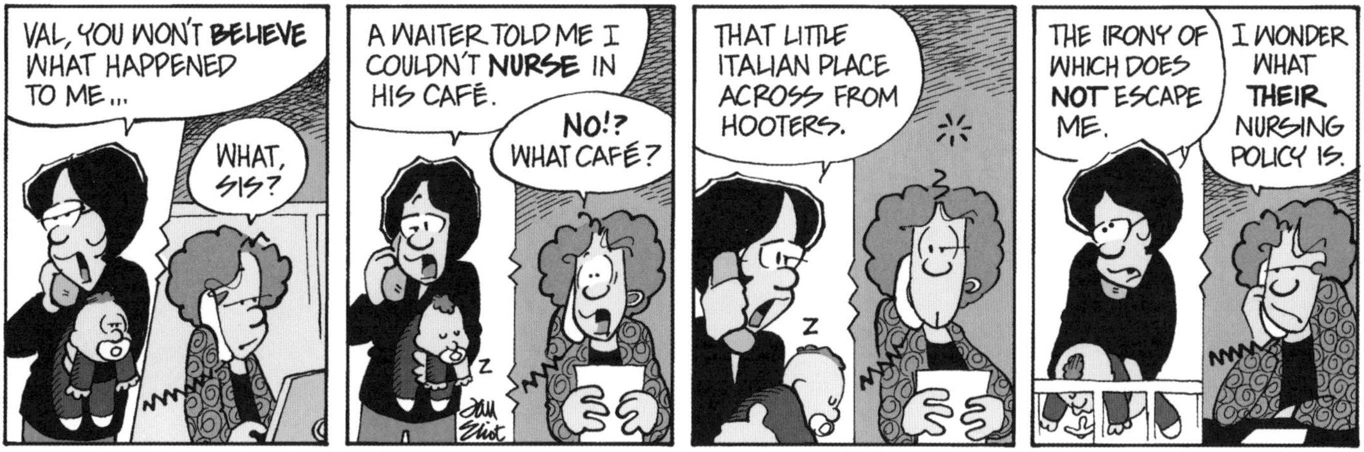
VAL, YOU WON'T **BELIEVE** WHAT HAPPENED TO ME...
WHAT, SIS?
A WAITER TOLD ME I COULDN'T **NURSE** IN HIS CAFÉ.
NO!? WHAT CAFÉ?
THAT LITTLE ITALIAN PLACE ACROSS FROM HOOTERS.
Z
THE IRONY OF WHICH DOES **NOT** ESCAPE ME.
I WONDER WHAT **THEIR** NURSING POLICY IS.

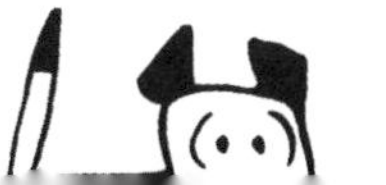

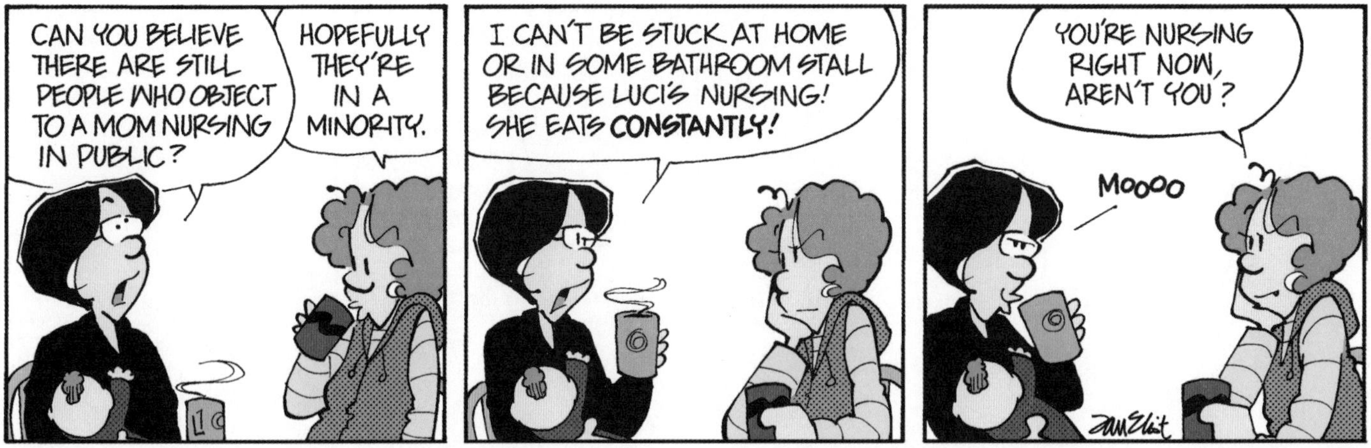
CAN YOU BELIEVE THERE ARE STILL PEOPLE WHO OBJECT TO A MOM NURSING IN PUBLIC?
HOPEFULLY THEY'RE IN A MINORITY.
I CAN'T BE STUCK AT HOME OR IN SOME BATHROOM STALL BECAUSE LUCI'S NURSING! SHE EATS CONSTANTLY!
MOOOO
YOU'RE NURSING RIGHT NOW, AREN'T YOU?

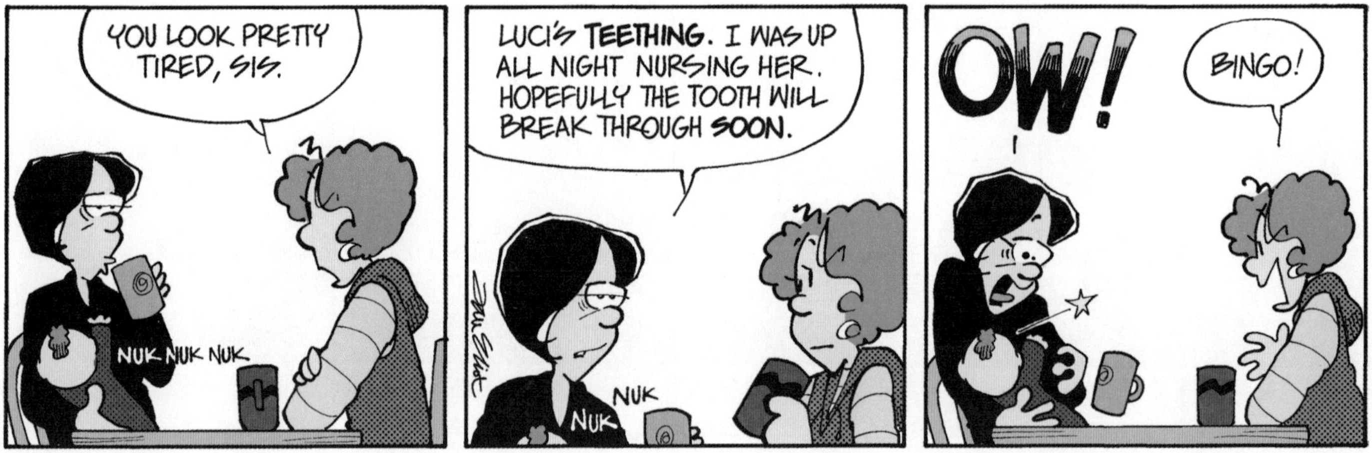
YOU LOOK PRETTY TIRED, SIS.
NUK NUK NUK
LUCI'S TEETHING. I WAS UP ALL NIGHT NURSING HER. HOPEFULLY THE TOOTH WILL BREAK THROUGH SOON.
NUK
NUK
OW!
BINGO!

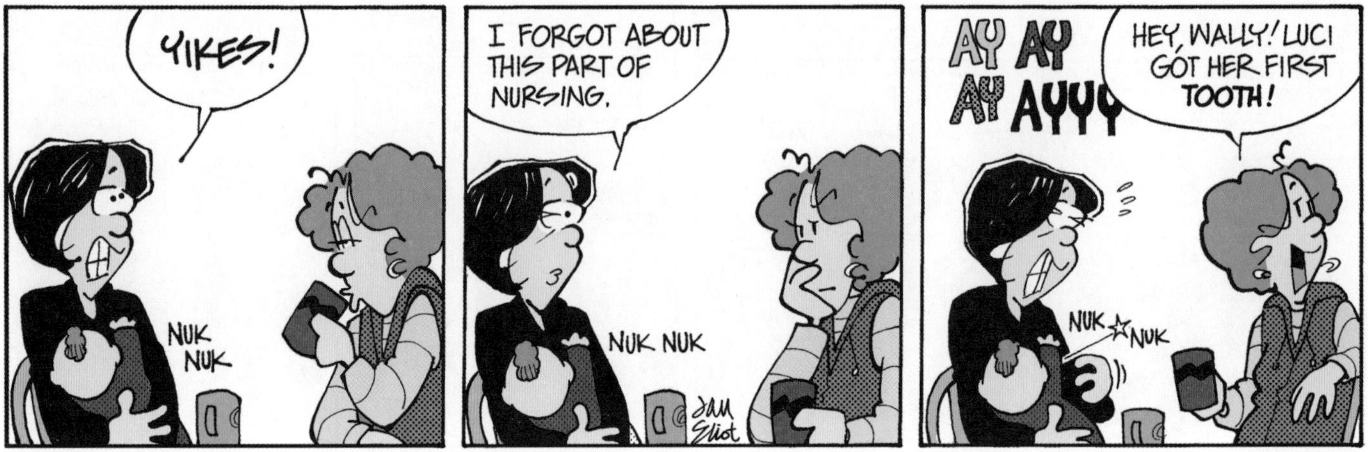
YIKES!
NUK NUK
I FORGOT ABOUT THIS PART OF NURSING.
NUK NUK
AY AY AY AYYY
HEY, WALLY! LUCI GOT HER FIRST TOOTH!
NUK NUK

Stone Soup

MOM? WHAT'S IT FEEL LIKE TO BE IN LOVE?
UM...
OOH! OOH! LET **ME** ANSWER THIS ONE!!
OK!
THE FIRST TIME **I** FELL HEAD OVER HEELS I FELT ALL **WARM** AND **FUZZY**...
AND REALLY **GIDDY**...
AND LIKE I COULD DO **ANYTHING!**
OR, WAIT... THAT MIGHT HAVE BEEN THE **TEQUILA**...
NEVER MIND.
I THOUGHT AUNT JOAN WAS SUPPOSED TO BE A **ROLE MODEL**.
WARNING! SHE'S A **WARNING!**

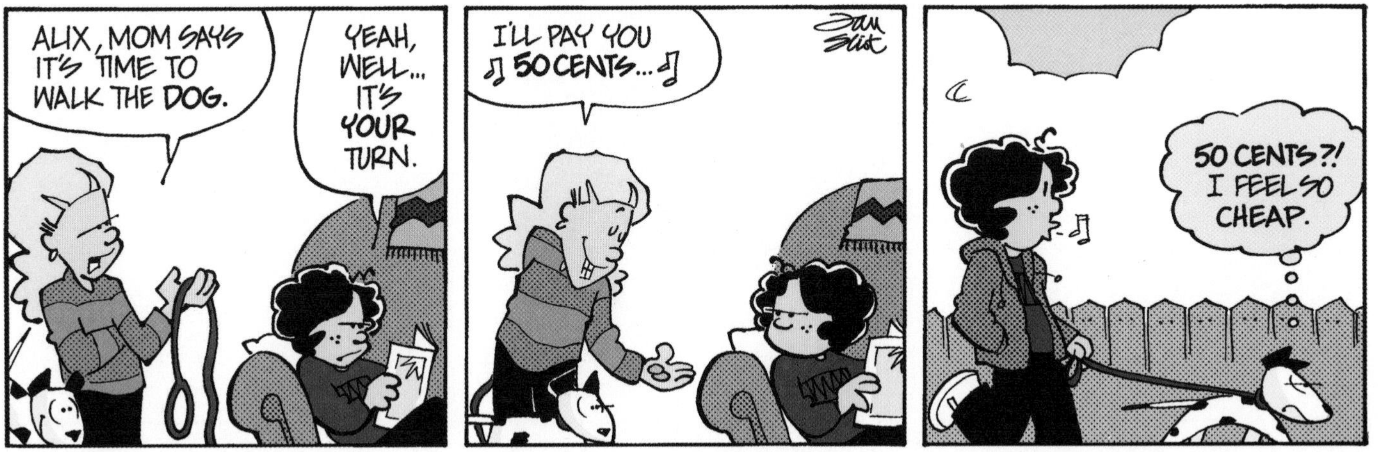
ALIX, MOM SAYS IT'S TIME TO WALK THE **DOG**.
YEAH, WELL... IT'S **YOUR** TURN.
I'LL PAY YOU ♫ **50 CENTS**... ♫
50 CENTS?! I FEEL SO **CHEAP**.

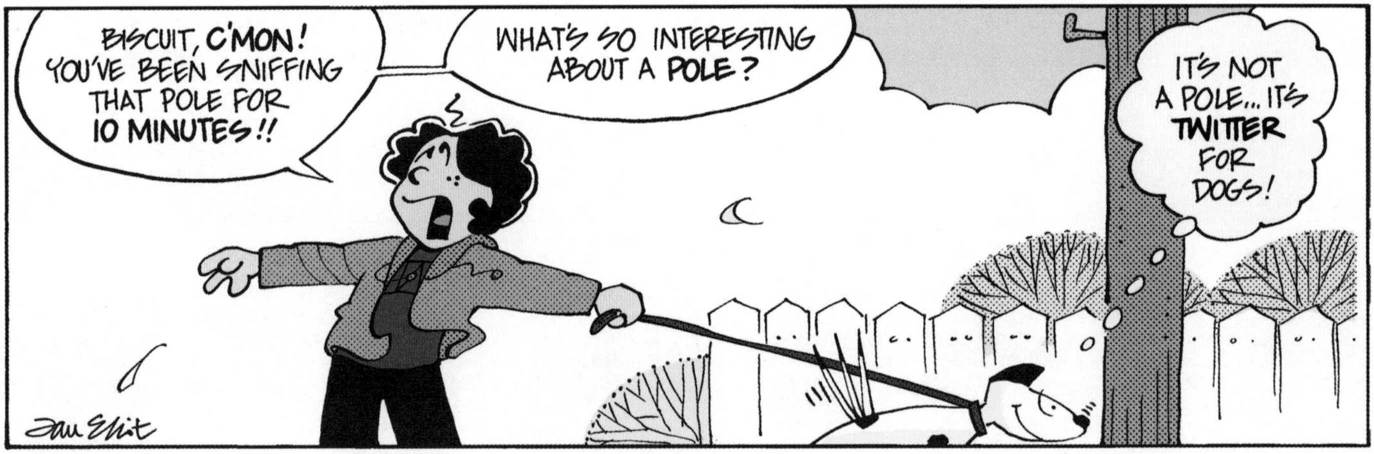
BISCUIT, **C'MON**! YOU'VE BEEN SNIFFING THAT POLE FOR **10 MINUTES**!!
WHAT'S SO INTERESTING ABOUT A **POLE**?
IT'S NOT A POLE... IT'S **TWITTER** FOR DOGS!

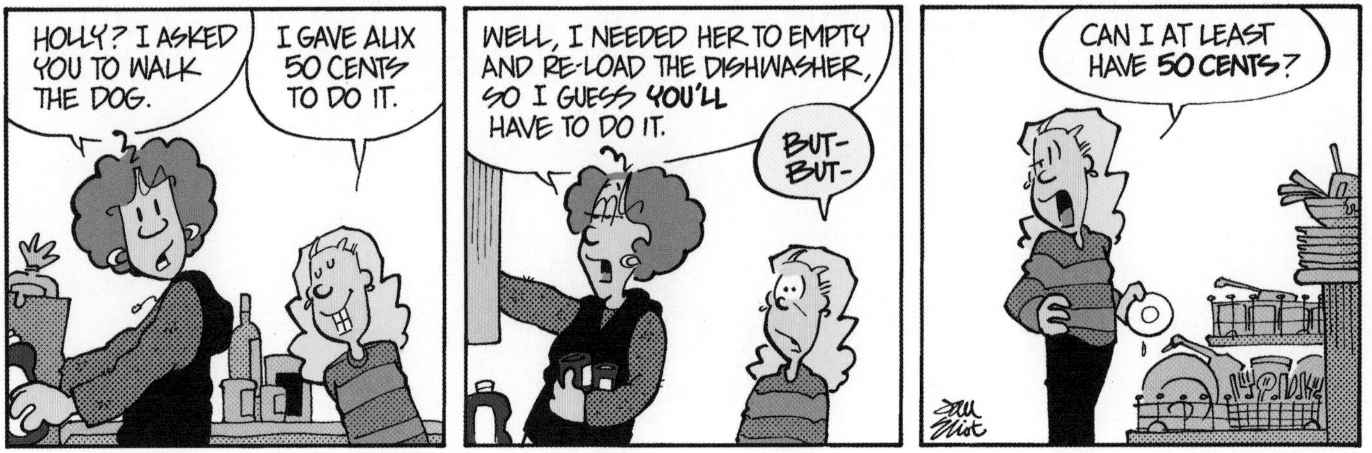
HOLLY? I ASKED YOU TO WALK THE DOG.
I GAVE ALIX 50 CENTS TO DO IT.
WELL, I NEEDED HER TO EMPTY AND RE-LOAD THE DISHWASHER, SO I GUESS **YOU'LL** HAVE TO DO IT.
BUT- BUT-
CAN I AT LEAST HAVE **50 CENTS**?

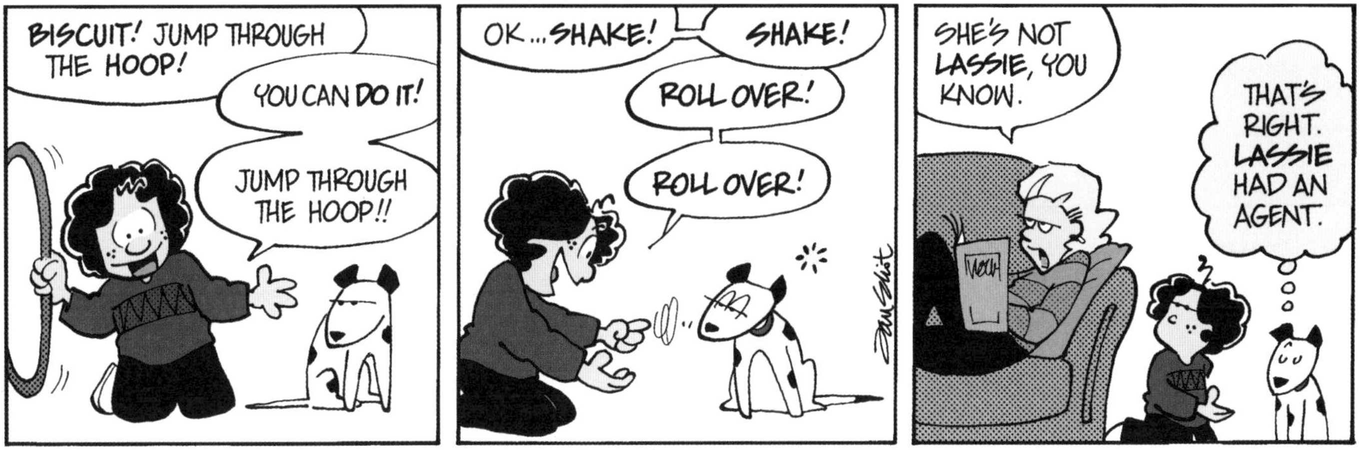
BISCUIT! JUMP THROUGH THE HOOP!
YOU CAN DO IT!
JUMP THROUGH THE HOOP!!
OK... SHAKE!
SHAKE!
ROLL OVER!
ROLL OVER!
SHE'S NOT LASSIE, YOU KNOW.
THAT'S RIGHT. LASSIE HAD AN AGENT.

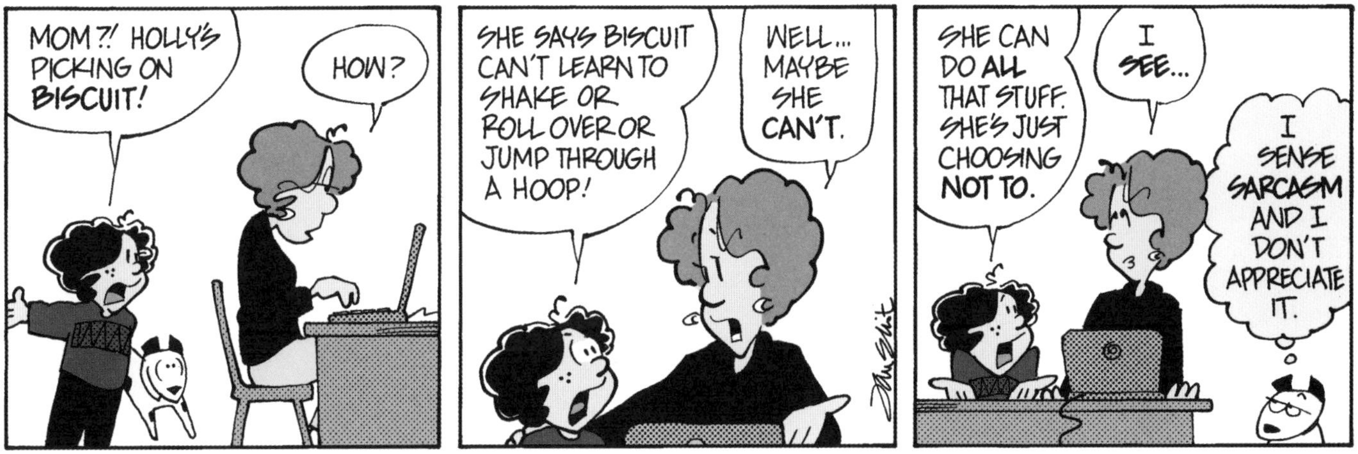
MOM?! HOLLY'S PICKING ON BISCUIT!
HOW?
SHE SAYS BISCUIT CAN'T LEARN TO SHAKE OR ROLL OVER OR JUMP THROUGH A HOOP!
WELL... MAYBE SHE CAN'T.
SHE CAN DO ALL THAT STUFF. SHE'S JUST CHOOSING NOT TO.
I SEE...
I SENSE SARCASM AND I DON'T APPRECIATE IT.

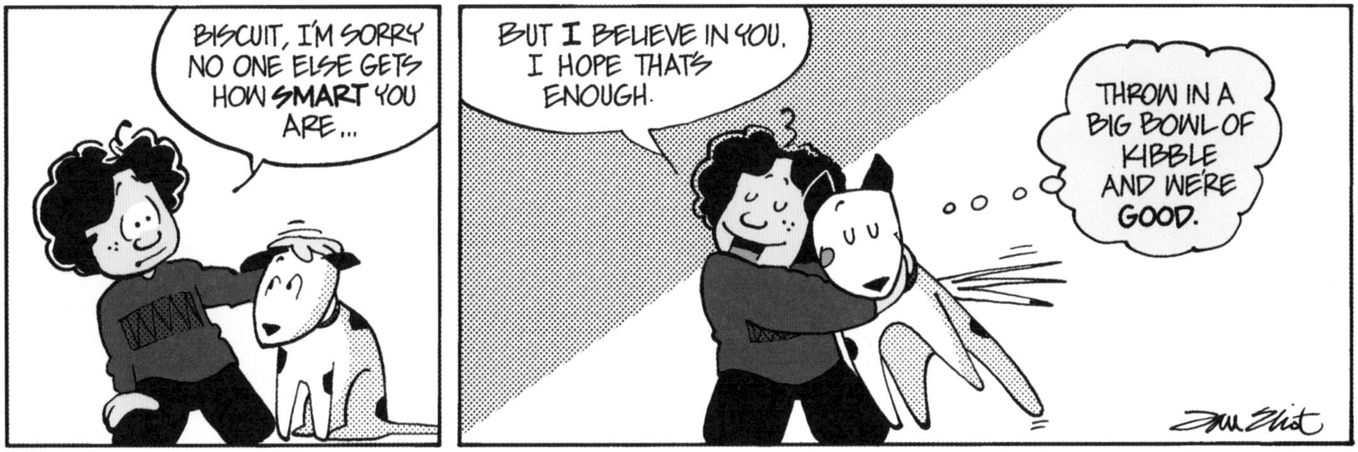
BISCUIT, I'M SORRY NO ONE ELSE GETS HOW SMART YOU ARE...
BUT I BELIEVE IN YOU. I HOPE THAT'S ENOUGH.
THROW IN A BIG BOWL OF KIBBLE AND WE'RE GOOD.

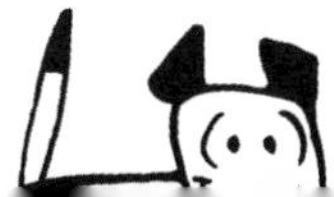

Stone Soup

MOM? WHEN YOU AND AUNT JOAN WERE MY AGE, WHAT KIND OF TROUBLE DID YOU GET INTO?
TROUBLE?
WE DIDN'T GET INTO ANY TROUBLE.
I'LL GO ASK GRAMMA.
WHEN HOLLY FINDS YOU, YOU DON'T REMEMBER A THING, GOT IT??
WHEN ARE YOU GOING TO TELL YOUR DAUGHTER ABOUT YOUR WILD YEARS?
THE DAY YOU TELL ME ABOUT YOURS.
HEY, GRAMMA? WHEN MOM WAS—
NOTHING! I REMEMBER NOTHING!

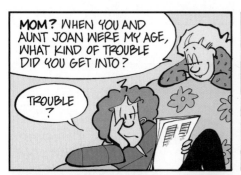

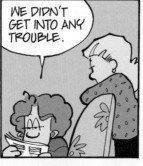

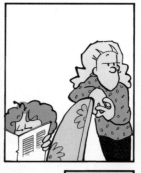

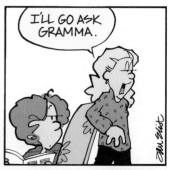

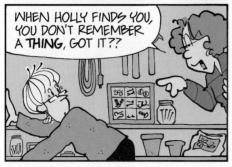

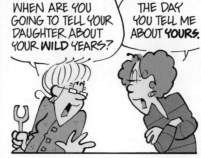

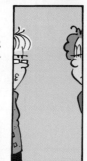

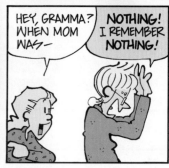

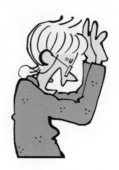

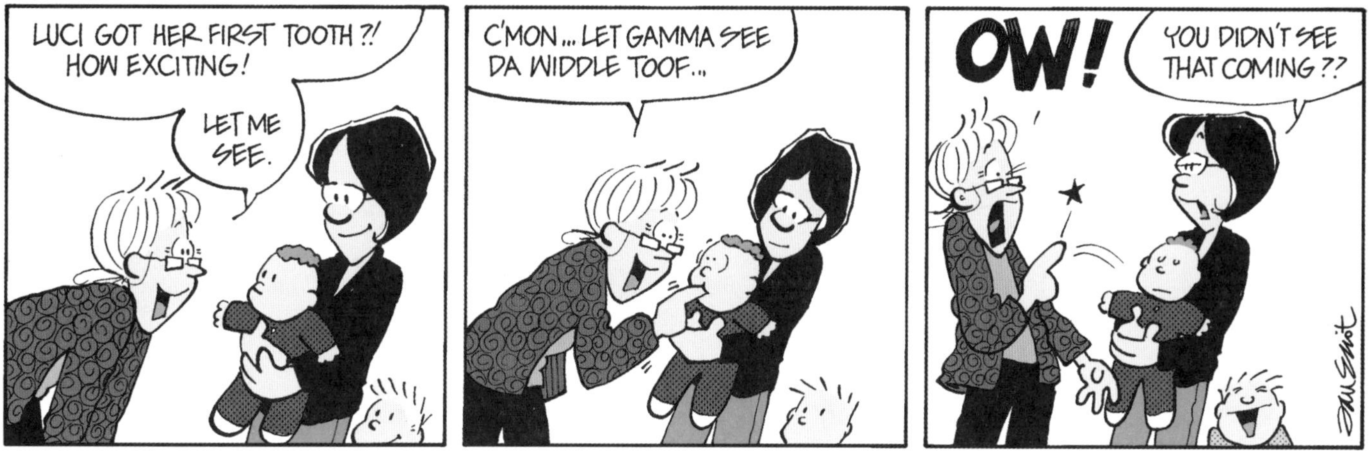
LUCI GOT HER FIRST TOOTH ?! HOW EXCITING!
LET ME SEE.
C'MON ... LET GAMMA SEE DA WIDDLE TOOF...
OW!
YOU DIDN'T SEE THAT COMING ??
Jan Eliot

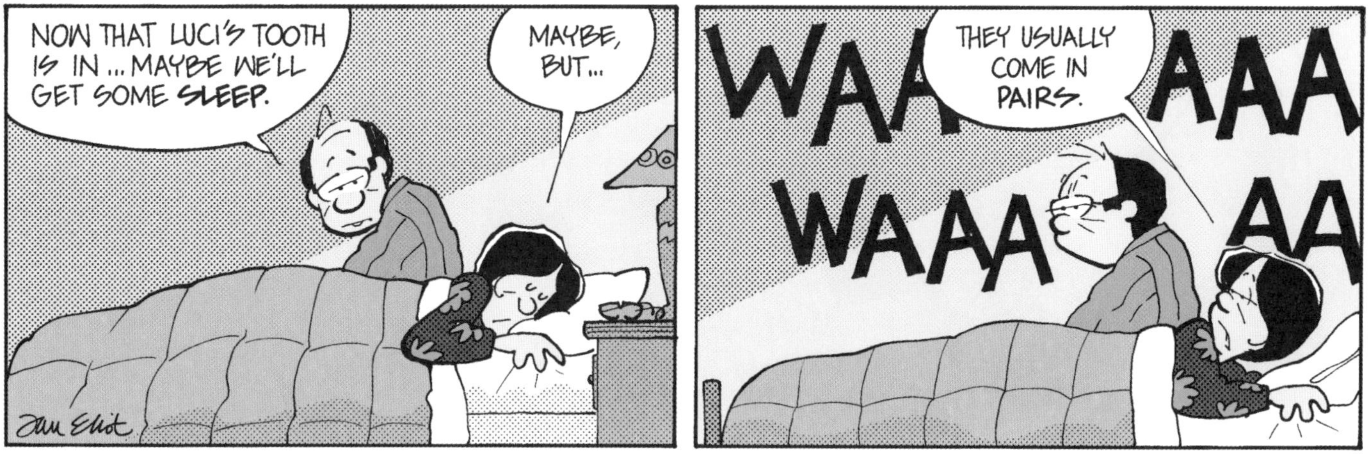
NOW THAT LUCI'S TOOTH IS IN ... MAYBE WE'LL GET SOME **SLEEP**.
MAYBE, BUT...
Jan Eliot
WAA
THEY USUALLY COME IN **PAIRS**.
AAA
WAAA
AA

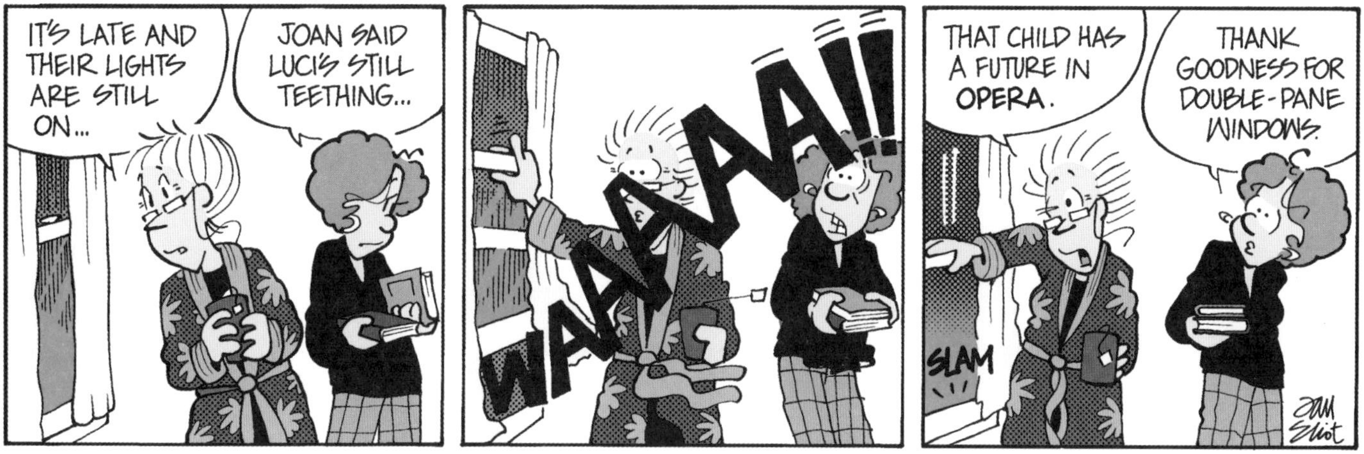
IT'S LATE AND THEIR LIGHTS ARE STILL ON...
JOAN SAID LUCI'S STILL TEETHING...
WAAAAAA!!
THAT CHILD HAS A FUTURE IN **OPERA**.
THANK GOODNESS FOR DOUBLE-PANE WINDOWS.
SLAM
Jan Eliot

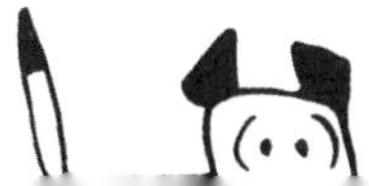

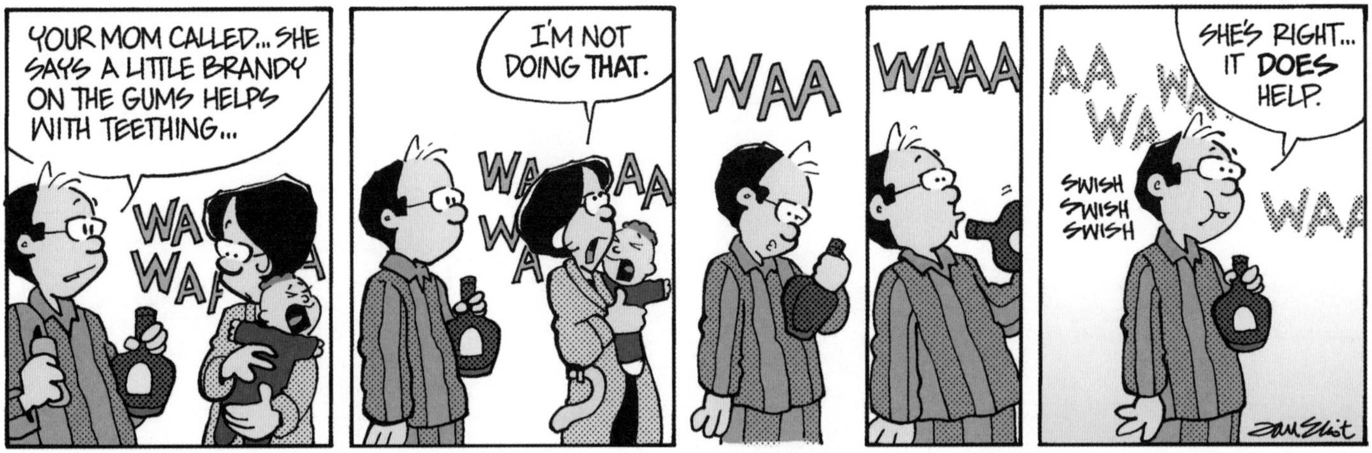
YOUR MOM CALLED... SHE SAYS A LITTLE BRANDY ON THE GUMS HELPS WITH TEETHING...
I'M NOT DOING **THAT**.
WAA
WAAA
SWISH SWISH SWISH
SHE'S RIGHT... IT **DOES** HELP.
WAA

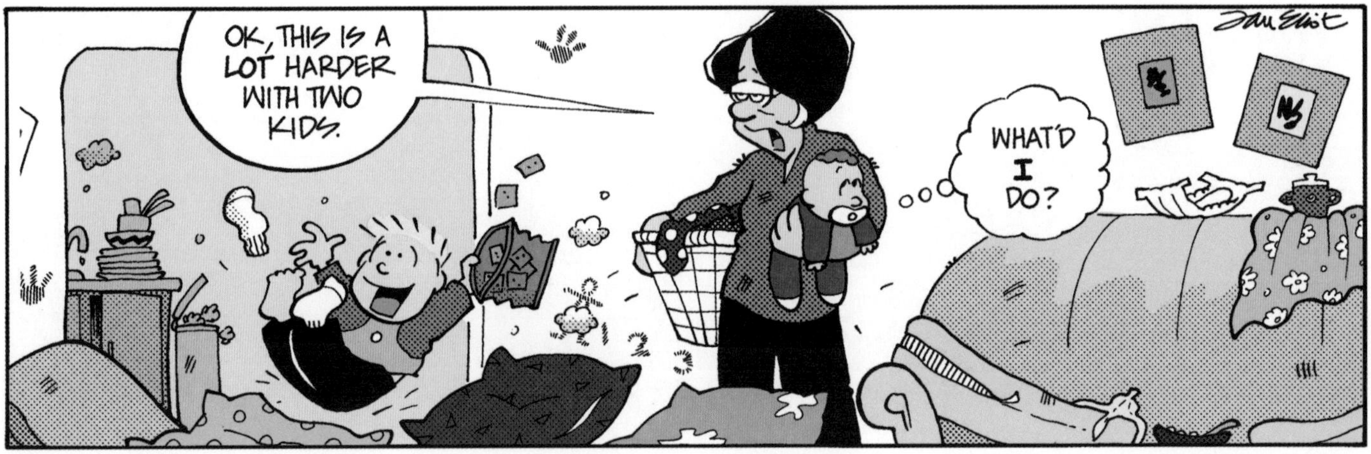
OK, THIS IS A **LOT** HARDER WITH TWO KIDS.
WHAT'D **I** DO?

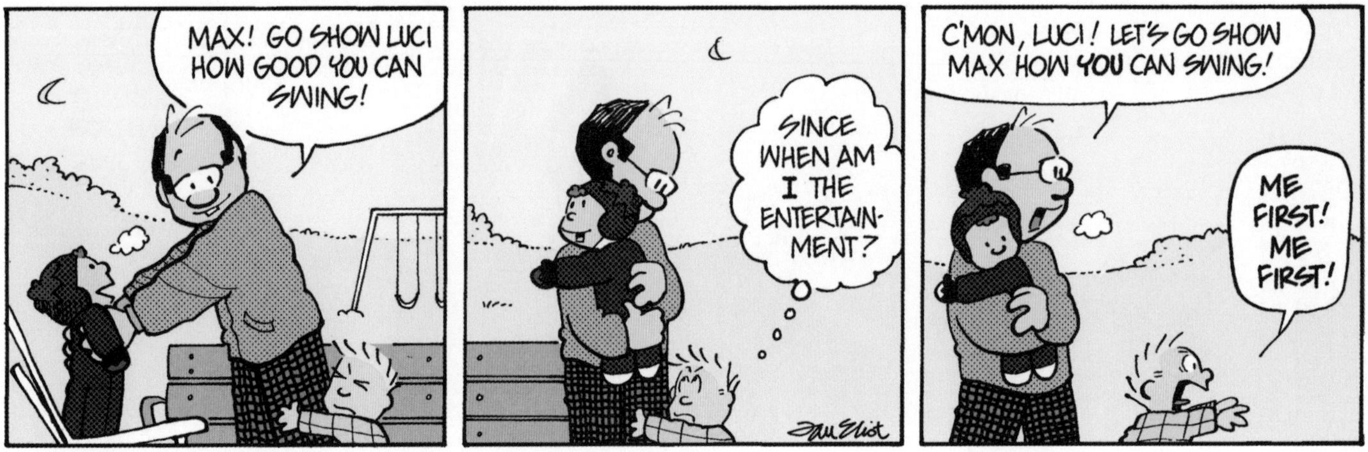
MAX! GO SHOW LUCI HOW GOOD YOU CAN SWING!
SINCE WHEN AM **I** THE ENTERTAIN-MENT?
C'MON, LUCI! LET'S GO SHOW MAX HOW **YOU** CAN SWING!
ME FIRST! ME FIRST!

Stone Soup

?!
!!!
THWEET!
RRRR
BRUM! BRUM BRUM
!!!
HEY, LOOK! IT'S SNOWING!
IT IS!
SLEDDING! SNOWMEN! SNOW FORTS!!
COATS! HATS! MITTENS!!
OH BOY!
LUCI'S FIRST SNOW! I'LL GET THE CAMERA!
CLICK
JOAN? ARE YOU COMING OUTSIDE? JOAN??

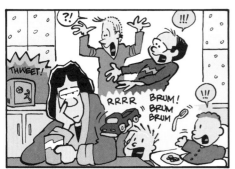

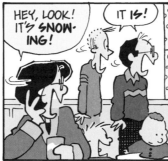

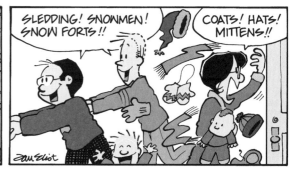

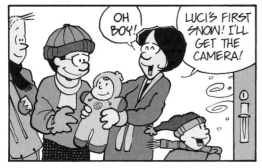

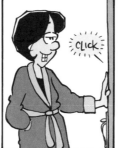

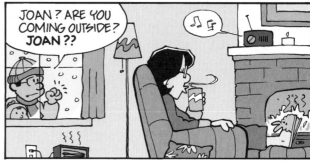

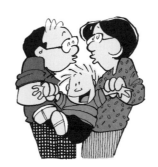

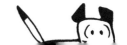

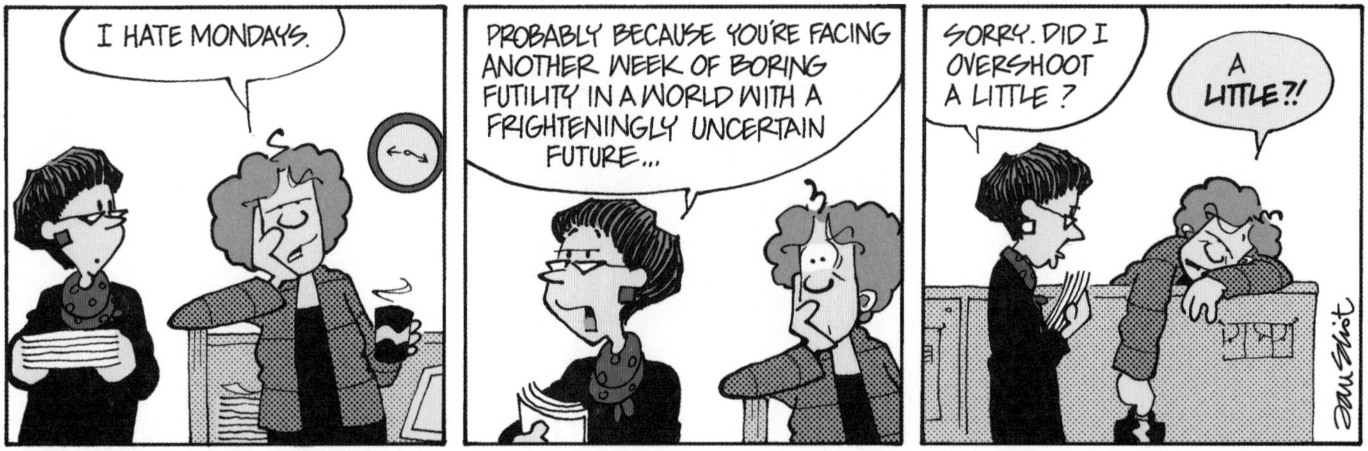
I HATE MONDAYS.
PROBABLY BECAUSE YOU'RE FACING ANOTHER WEEK OF BORING FUTILITY IN A WORLD WITH A FRIGHTENINGLY UNCERTAIN FUTURE...
SORRY. DID I OVERSHOOT A LITTLE ?
A **LITTLE?!**

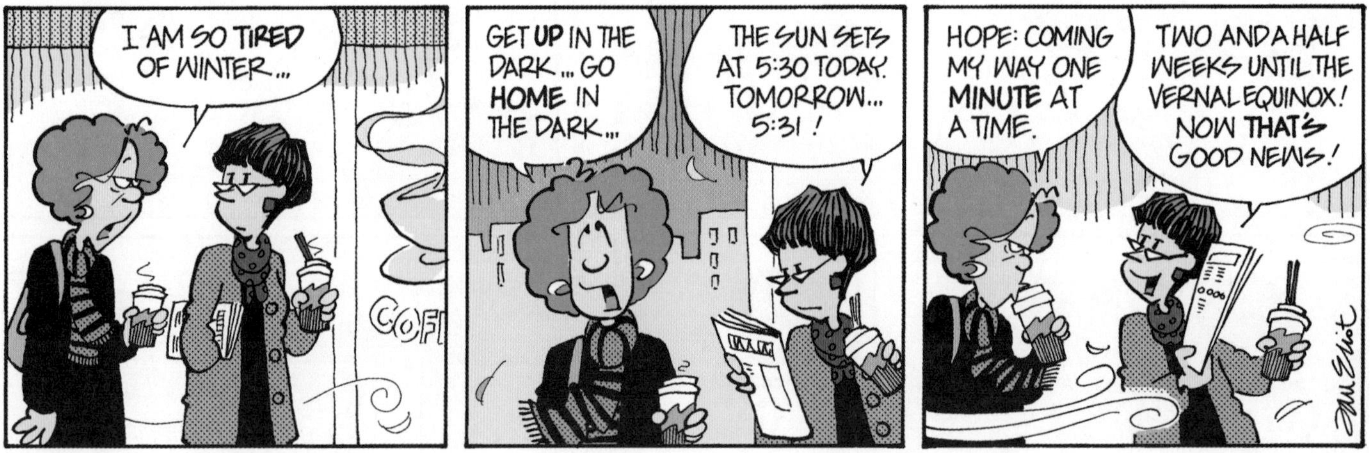
I AM SO **TIRED** OF WINTER...
GET **UP** IN THE DARK... GO **HOME** IN THE DARK...
THE SUN SETS AT 5:30 TODAY. TOMORROW... 5:31 !
HOPE: COMING MY WAY ONE **MINUTE** AT A TIME.
TWO AND A HALF WEEKS UNTIL THE VERNAL EQUINOX! NOW **THAT'S** GOOD NEWS!

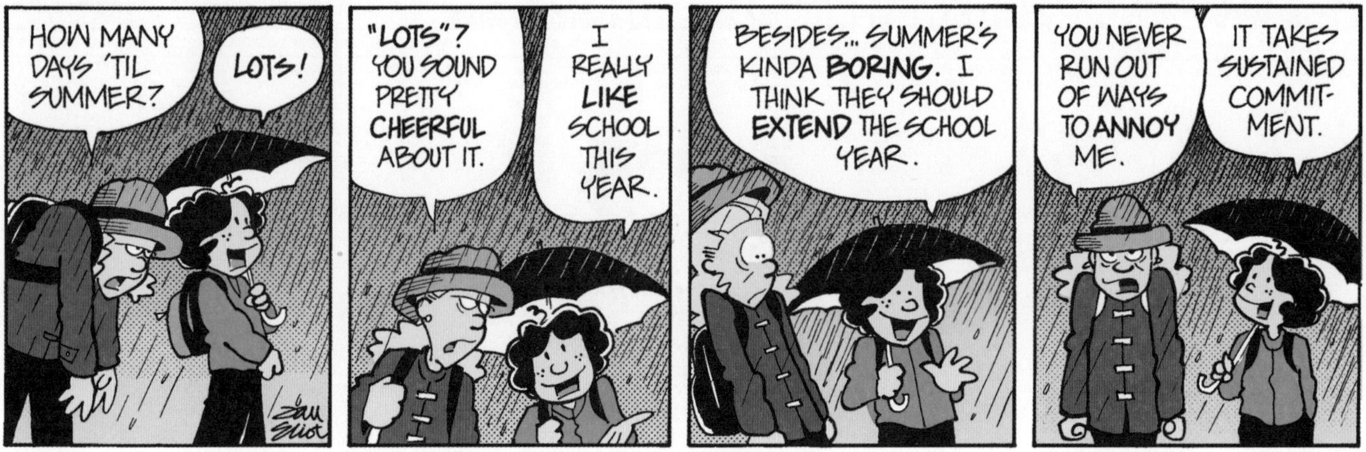
HOW MANY DAYS 'TIL SUMMER?
LOTS!
"**LOTS**"? YOU SOUND PRETTY **CHEERFUL** ABOUT IT.
I REALLY **LIKE** SCHOOL THIS YEAR.
BESIDES... SUMMER'S KINDA **BORING**. I THINK THEY SHOULD **EXTEND** THE SCHOOL YEAR.
YOU NEVER RUN OUT OF WAYS TO **ANNOY** ME.
IT TAKES SUSTAINED COMMIT-MENT.

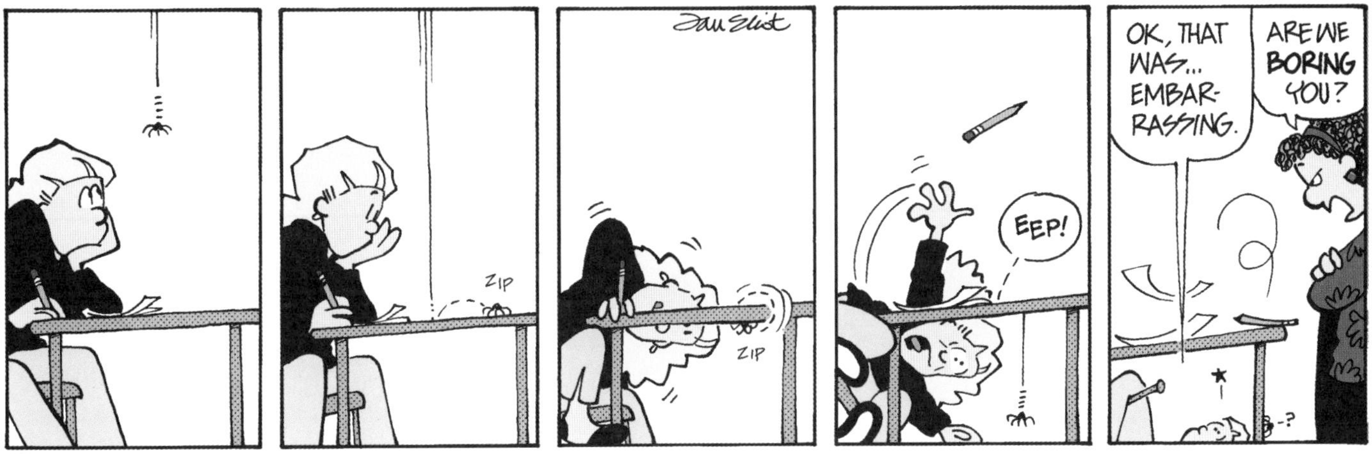
ZIP
ZIP
EEP!
OK, THAT WAS... EMBARRASSING.
ARE WE **BORING** YOU?

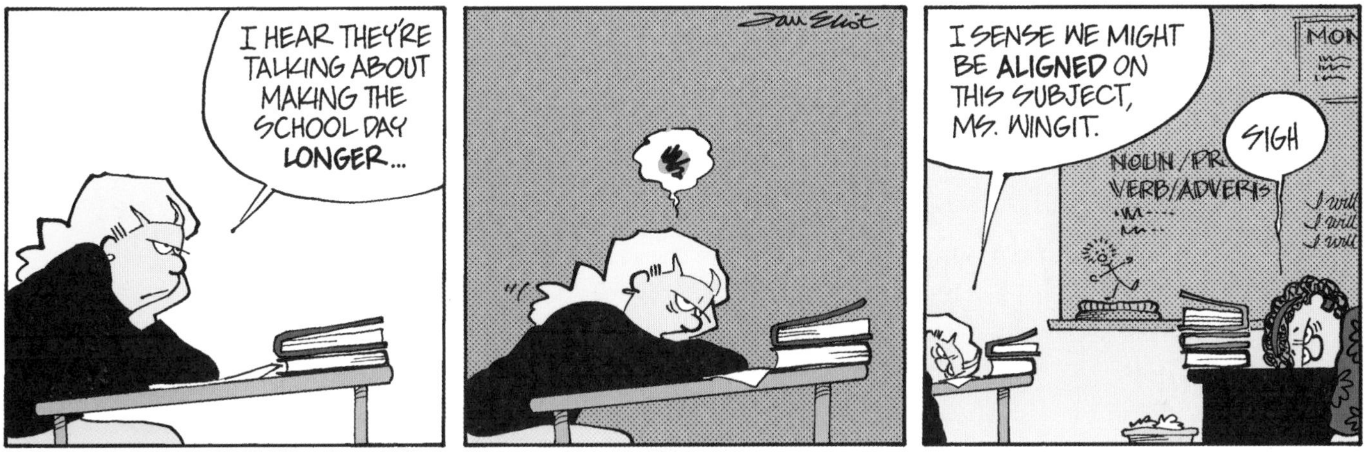
I HEAR THEY'RE TALKING ABOUT MAKING THE SCHOOL DAY **LONGER**...
I SENSE WE MIGHT BE **ALIGNED** ON THIS SUBJECT, MS. WINGIT.
SIGH

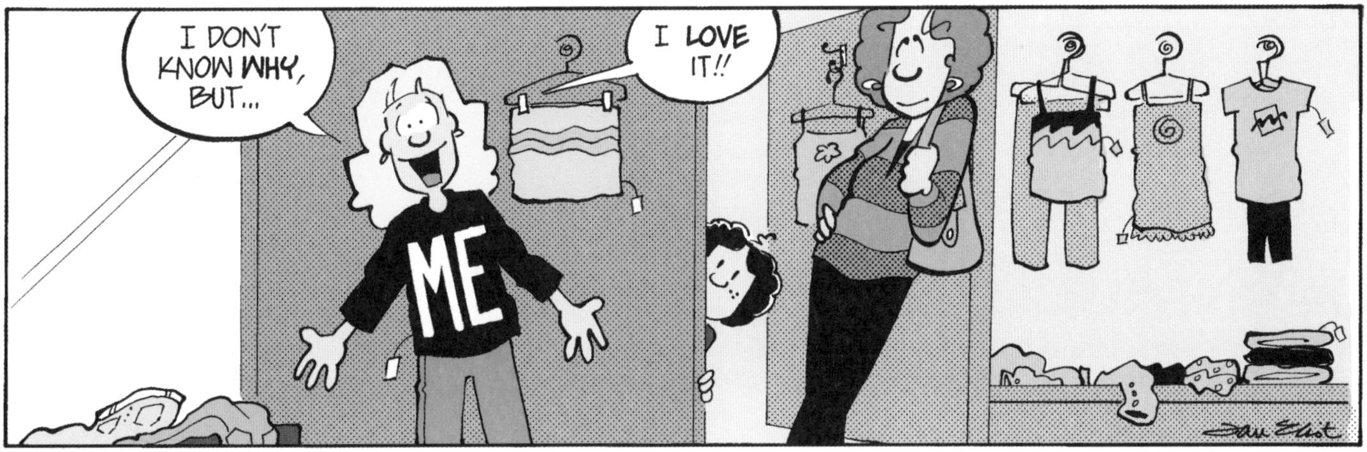
I DON'T KNOW **WHY**, BUT...
I **LOVE** IT!!
ME

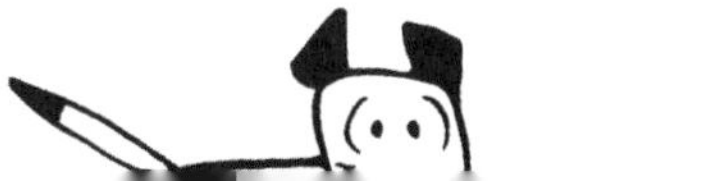

Stone Soup

"EXPIRATION DATES DON'T REALLY MATTER"
HOW BAD COULD IT BE?
"IT TASTES OK TO ME!"
"THAT'S NEVER HAPPENED BEFORE"
"I'VE ALWAYS DONE IT THIS WAY"
"THEY WOULDN'T SELL IT IF IT WEREN'T GOOD FOR YOU"
"OH C'MON IT'LL BE FUN!"
GRAVEYARD OF THE NOT-SO-ETERNAL OPTIMISTS...

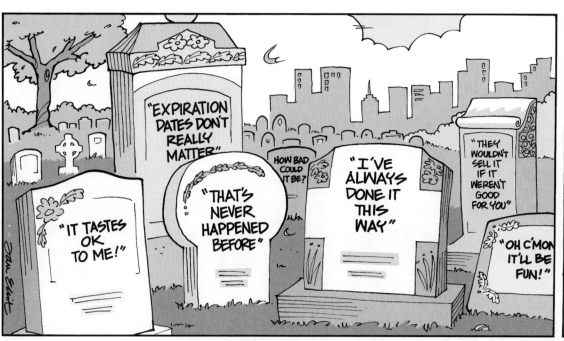

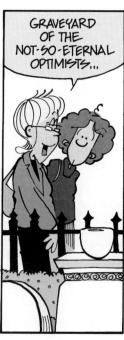

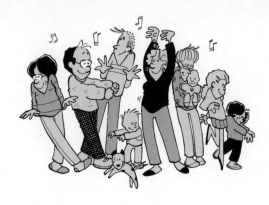

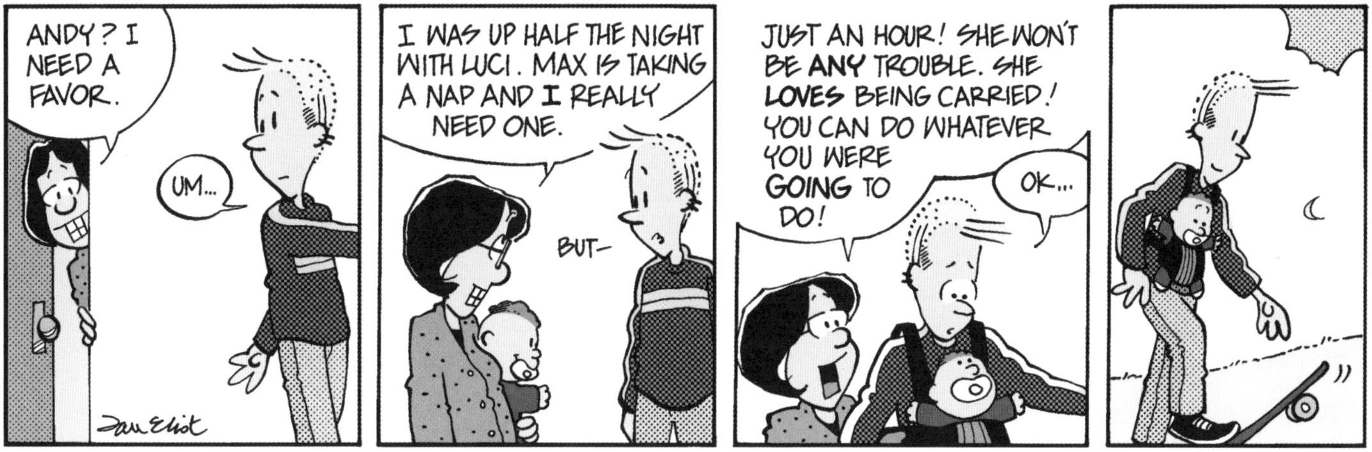
ANDY? I NEED A FAVOR.
UM...
I WAS UP HALF THE NIGHT WITH LUCI. MAX IS TAKING A NAP AND **I** REALLY NEED ONE.
BUT–
JUST AN HOUR! SHE WON'T BE **ANY** TROUBLE. SHE **LOVES** BEING CARRIED! YOU CAN DO WHATEVER YOU WERE **GOING** TO DO!
OK...

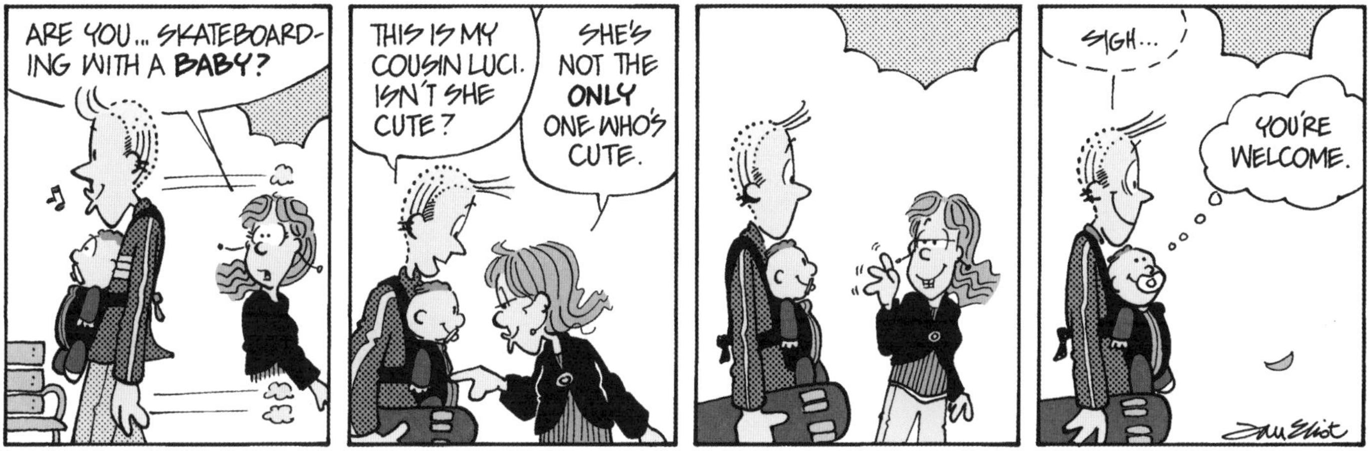
ARE YOU... SKATEBOARDING WITH A **BABY?**
THIS IS MY COUSIN LUCI. ISN'T SHE CUTE?
SHE'S NOT THE **ONLY** ONE WHO'S CUTE.
SIGH...
YOU'RE WELCOME.

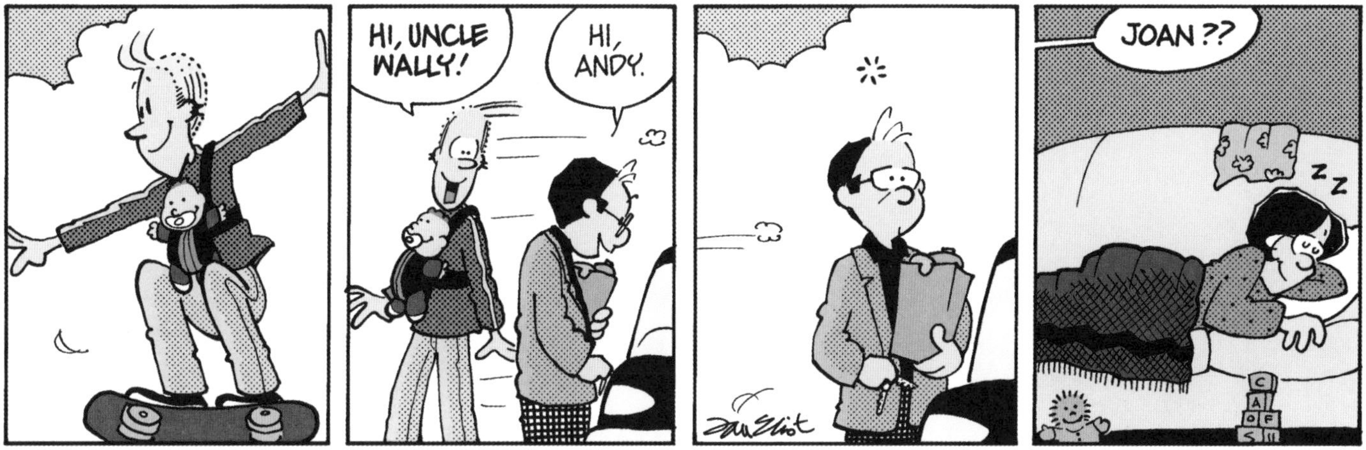
HI, UNCLE WALLY!
HI, ANDY.
JOAN??

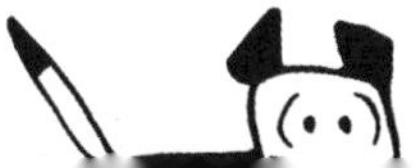

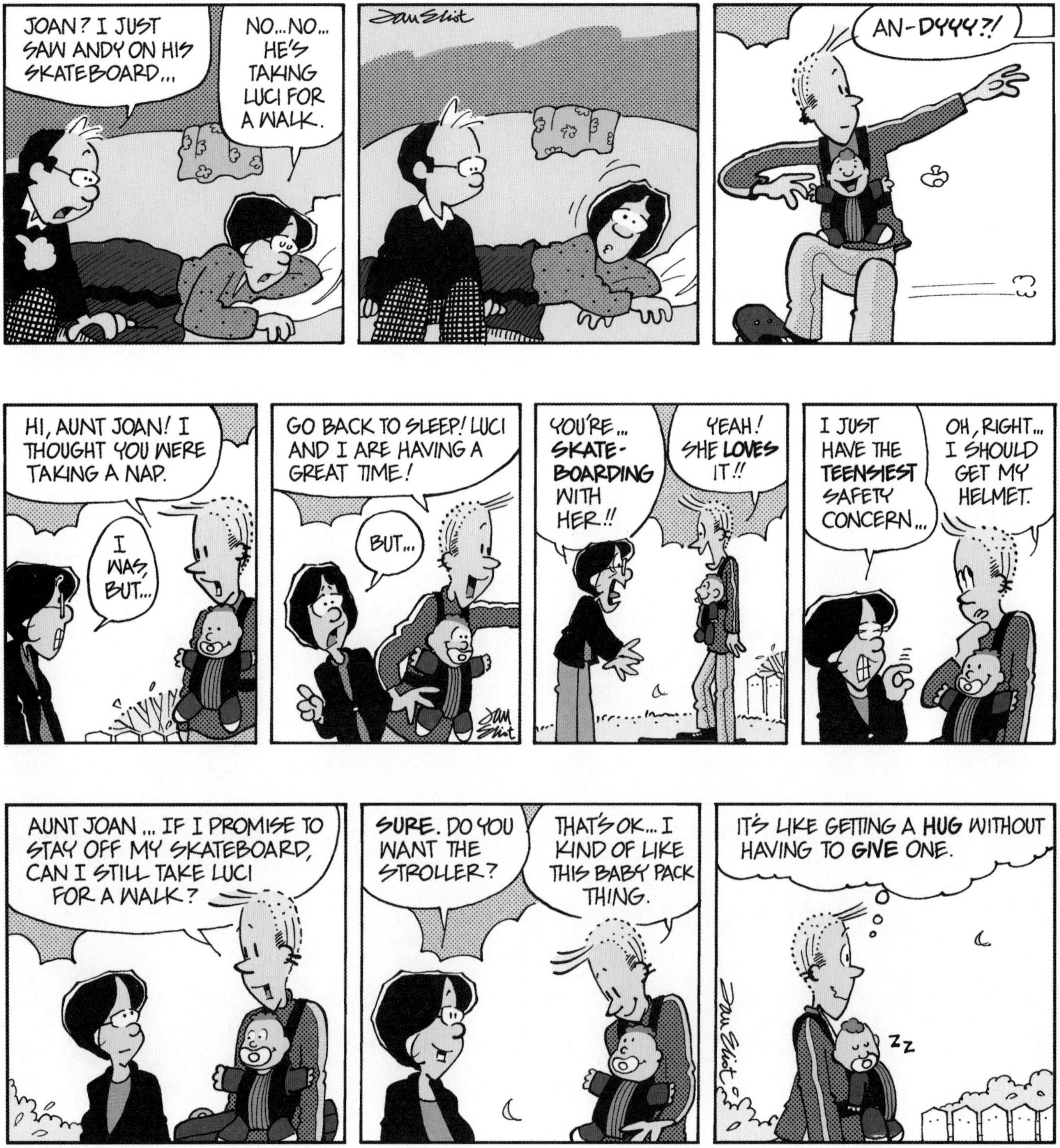
JOAN? I JUST SAW ANDY ON HIS SKATEBOARD...
NO...NO... HE'S TAKING LUCI FOR A WALK.
AN-DYYY?!
HI, AUNT JOAN! I THOUGHT YOU WERE TAKING A NAP.
I WAS, BUT...
GO BACK TO SLEEP! LUCI AND I ARE HAVING A GREAT TIME!
BUT...
YOU'RE... SKATE-BOARDING WITH HER!!
YEAH! SHE LOVES IT!!
I JUST HAVE THE TEENSIEST SAFETY CONCERN...
OH, RIGHT... I SHOULD GET MY HELMET.
AUNT JOAN ... IF I PROMISE TO STAY OFF MY SKATEBOARD, CAN I STILL TAKE LUCI FOR A WALK?
SURE. DO YOU WANT THE STROLLER?
THAT'S OK... I KIND OF LIKE THIS BABY PACK THING.
IT'S LIKE GETTING A HUG WITHOUT HAVING TO GIVE ONE.
Z Z

Stone Soup

WAA
MAM
WAAA

HOW'S IT GOING?

LUCI'S BEEN **CRUDDING** ALL OVER ME... MAX IS **TANTRUMING BIG-TIME** AND I'M **HORMONING** LIKE CRAZY.

NICE **VERBING**, AUNT JOAN.

COMPLETE AND TOTAL **VERBICIDE**.

PAT PAT PAT

KIND OF SURPRISES ME THAT A PROFESSIONAL **WRITER** LIKE YOU COULD SUCCUMB TO MAKING UP NONSENSE WORDS THAT—

WE'LL JUST TAKE THESE KIDDOS OFF YOUR HANDS.

GOOD, BECAUSE I WAS ABOUT TO START **MELTDOWNING** ALL OVER YOU.

SNIFF

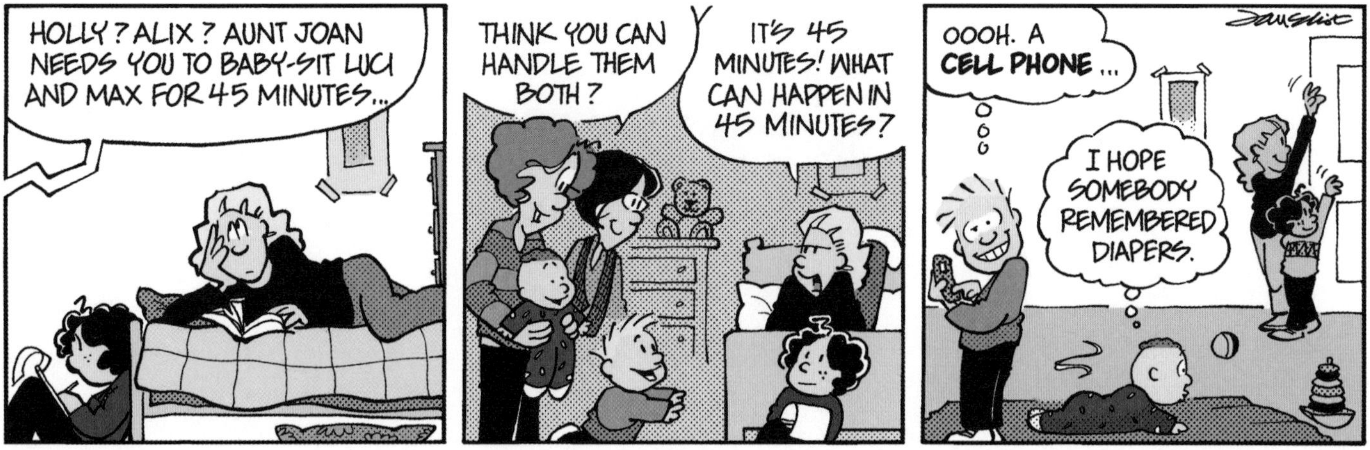
HOLLY? ALIX? AUNT JOAN NEEDS YOU TO BABY-SIT LUCI AND MAX FOR 45 MINUTES...
THINK YOU CAN HANDLE THEM BOTH?
IT'S 45 MINUTES! WHAT CAN HAPPEN IN 45 MINUTES?
OOOH. A **CELL PHONE**...
I HOPE SOMEBODY REMEMBERED DIAPERS.

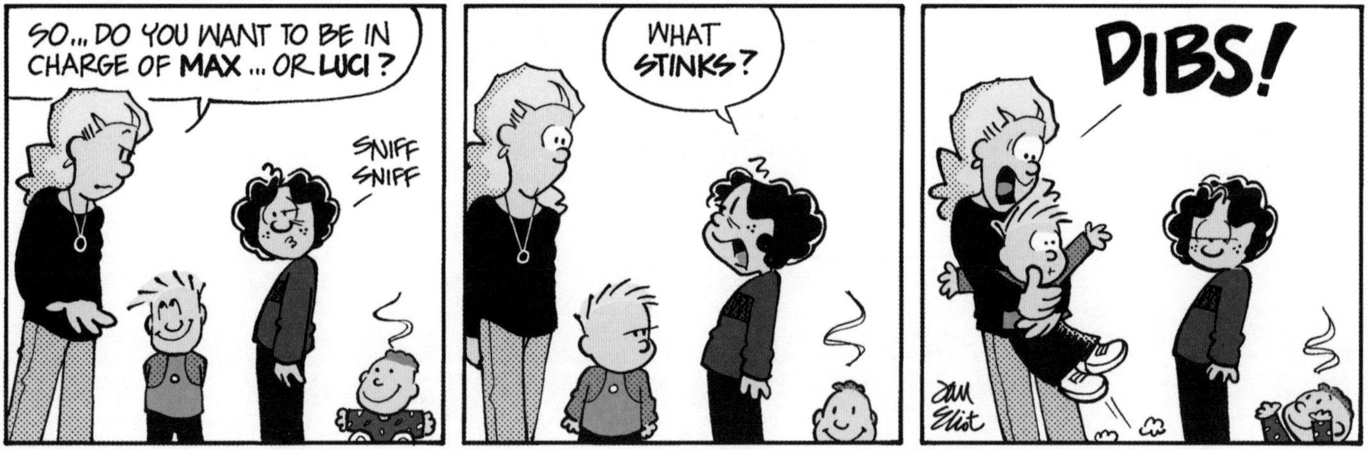
SO... DO YOU WANT TO BE IN CHARGE OF **MAX** ... OR **LUCI**?
SNIFF SNIFF
WHAT **STINKS**?
DIBS!

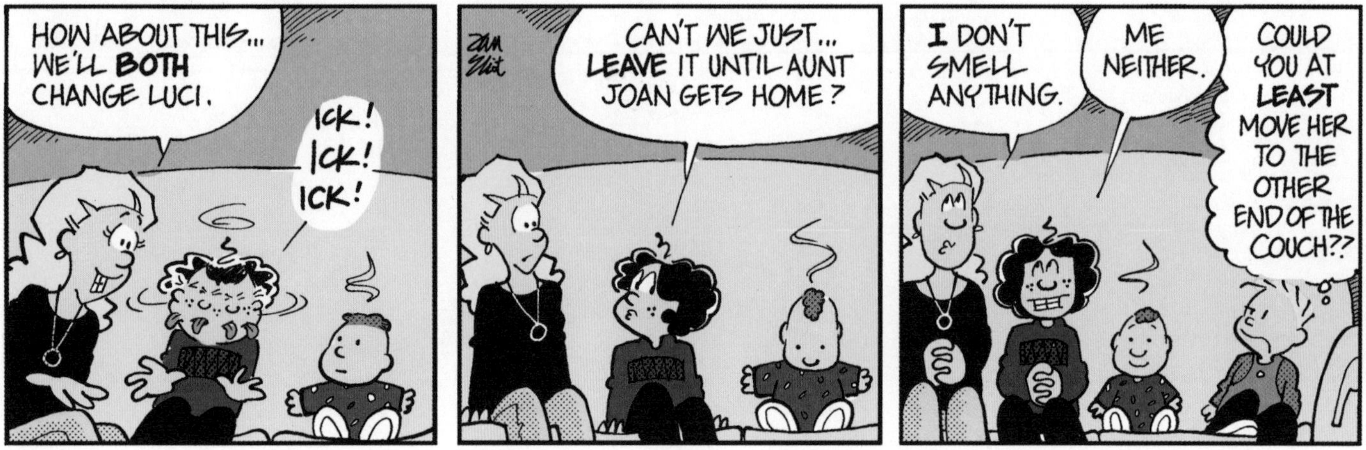
HOW ABOUT THIS... WE'LL **BOTH** CHANGE LUCI.
ICK! ICK! ICK!
CAN'T WE JUST... **LEAVE** IT UNTIL AUNT JOAN GETS HOME?
I DON'T SMELL ANYTHING.
ME NEITHER.
COULD YOU AT **LEAST** MOVE HER TO THE OTHER END OF THE COUCH??

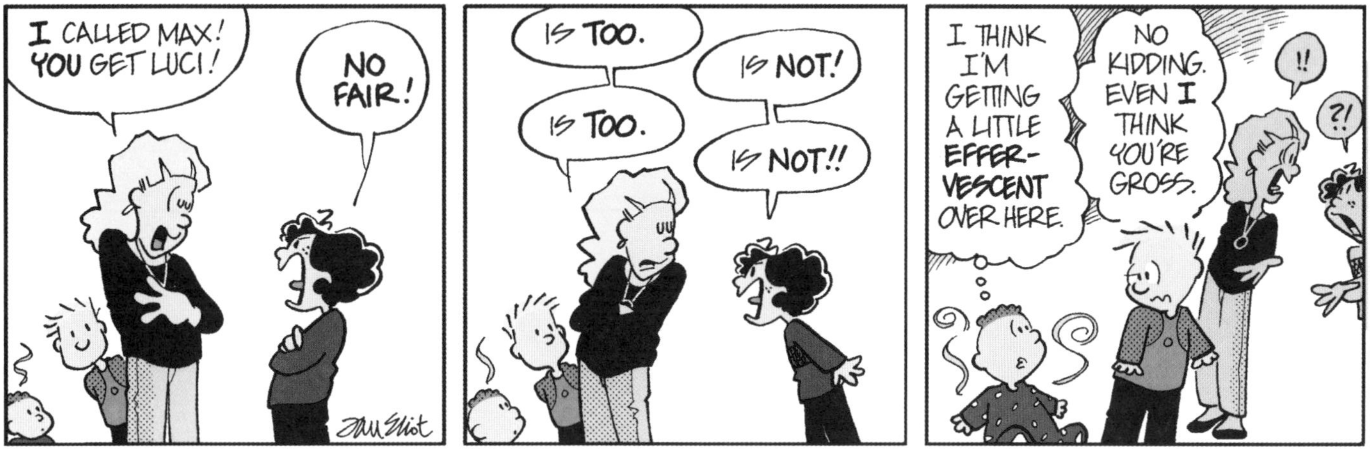
I CALLED MAX! YOU GET LUCI!
NO FAIR!
IS TOO.
IS NOT!
IS TOO.
IS NOT!!
I THINK I'M GETTING A LITTLE EFFER-VESCENT OVER HERE.
NO KIDDING. EVEN I THINK YOU'RE GROSS.
!!
?!

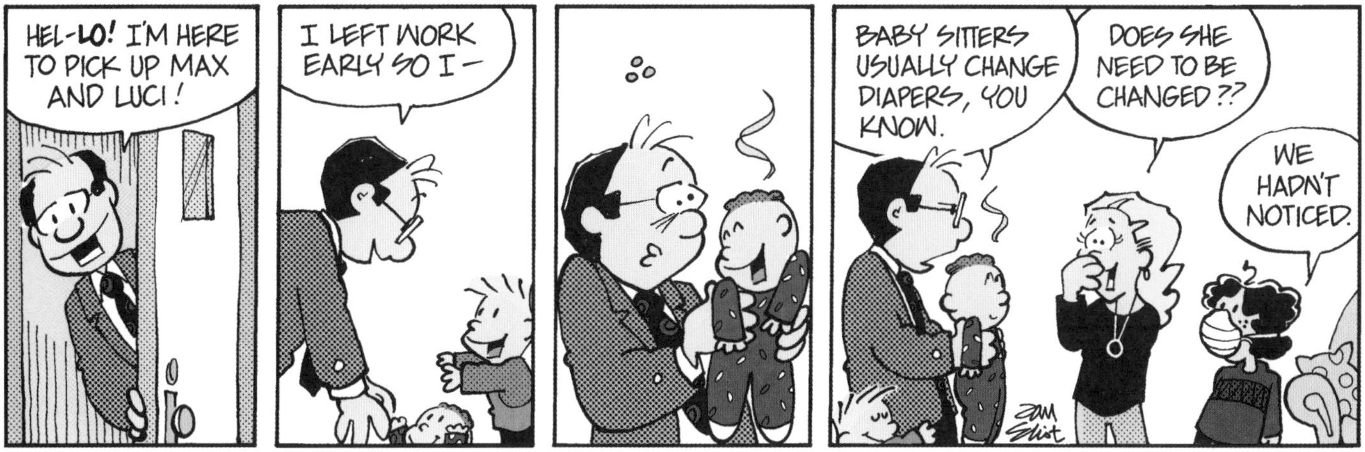
HEL-LO! I'M HERE TO PICK UP MAX AND LUCI!
I LEFT WORK EARLY SO I—
BABY SITTERS USUALLY CHANGE DIAPERS, YOU KNOW.
DOES SHE NEED TO BE CHANGED??
WE HADN'T NOTICED.

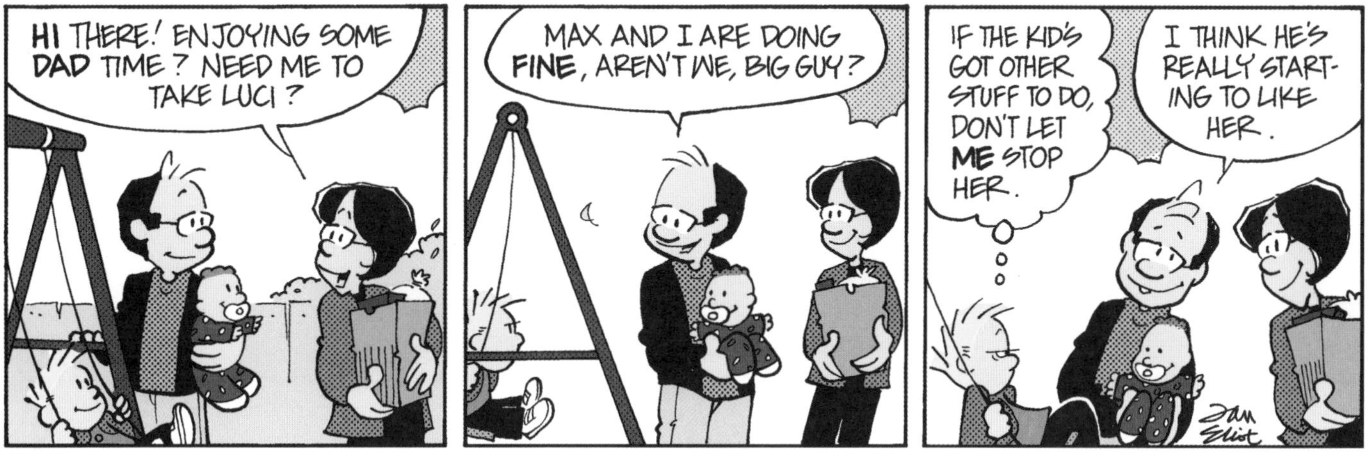
HI THERE! ENJOYING SOME DAD TIME? NEED ME TO TAKE LUCI?
MAX AND I ARE DOING FINE, AREN'T WE, BIG GUY?
IF THE KID'S GOT OTHER STUFF TO DO, DON'T LET ME STOP HER.
I THINK HE'S REALLY STARTING TO LIKE HER.

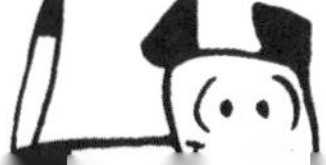

Stone
Soup

OOPS...
NOW?
NOW?
NOW??
JUST A SEC!
JUST A SEC!
JUST A SEC!!

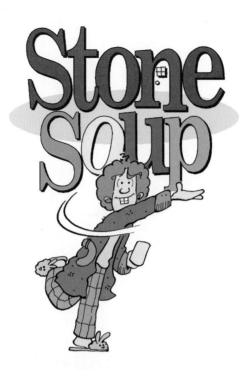

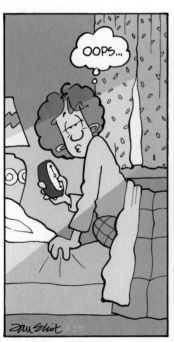

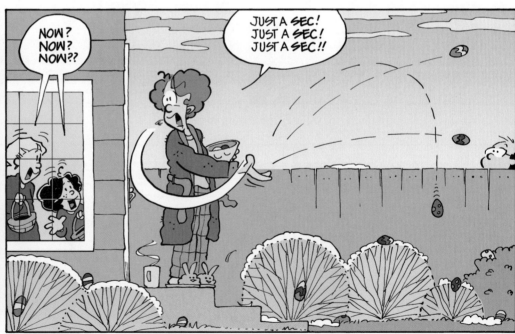

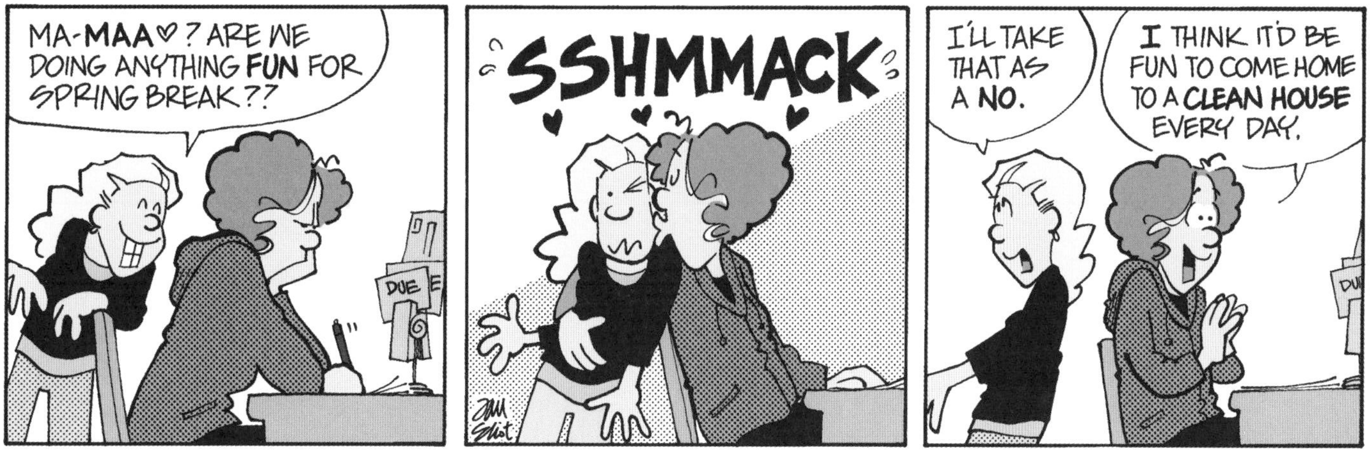
MA-**MAA**♡? ARE WE DOING ANYTHING **FUN** FOR SPRING BREAK??
SSHMMACK
I'LL TAKE THAT AS A **NO**.
I THINK IT'D BE FUN TO COME HOME TO A **CLEAN HOUSE** EVERY DAY.

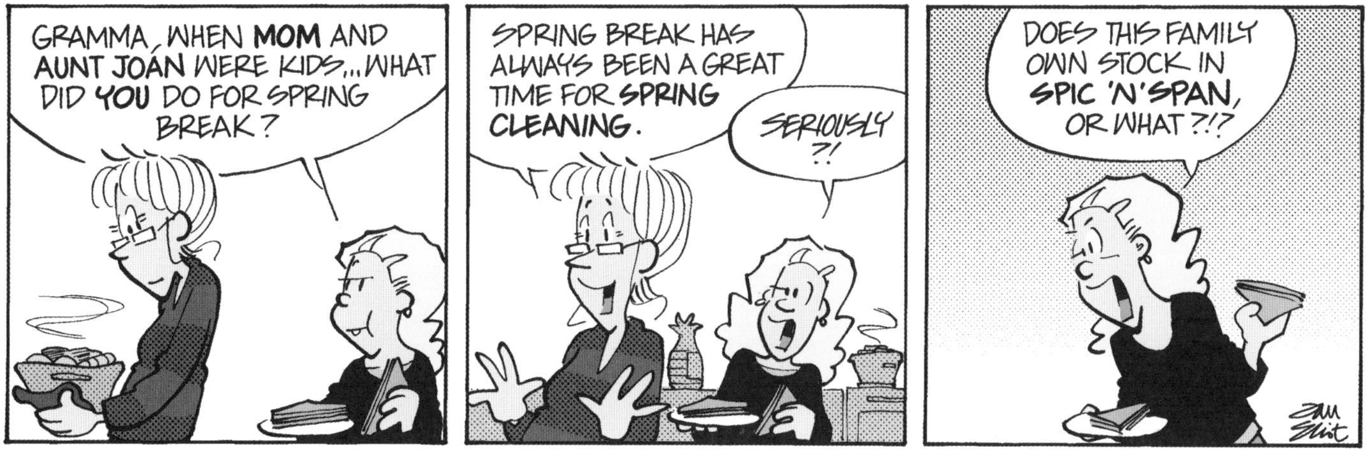
GRAMMA, WHEN **MOM** AND **AUNT JOAN** WERE KIDS... WHAT DID **YOU** DO FOR SPRING BREAK?
SPRING BREAK HAS ALWAYS BEEN A GREAT TIME FOR **SPRING CLEANING**.
SERIOUSLY?!
DOES THIS FAMILY OWN STOCK IN **SPIC 'N' SPAN**, OR WHAT?!?

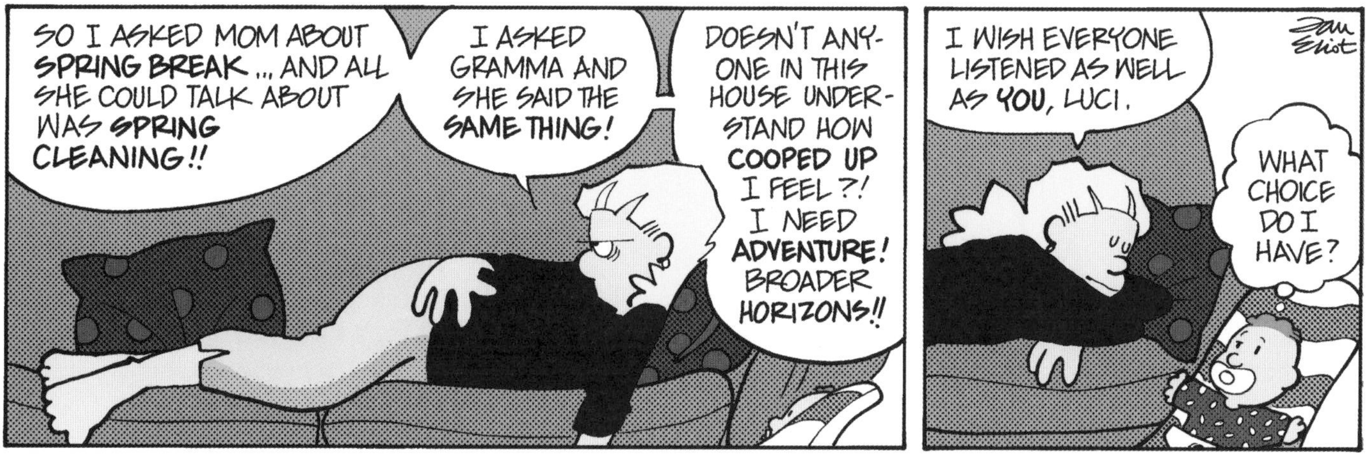
SO I ASKED MOM ABOUT **SPRING BREAK**... AND ALL SHE COULD TALK ABOUT WAS **SPRING CLEANING**!!
I ASKED GRAMMA AND SHE SAID THE **SAME THING**!
DOESN'T ANYONE IN THIS HOUSE UNDERSTAND HOW **COOPED UP** I FEEL?! I NEED **ADVENTURE**! BROADER **HORIZONS**!!
I WISH EVERYONE LISTENED AS WELL AS **YOU**, LUCI.
WHAT CHOICE DO I HAVE?

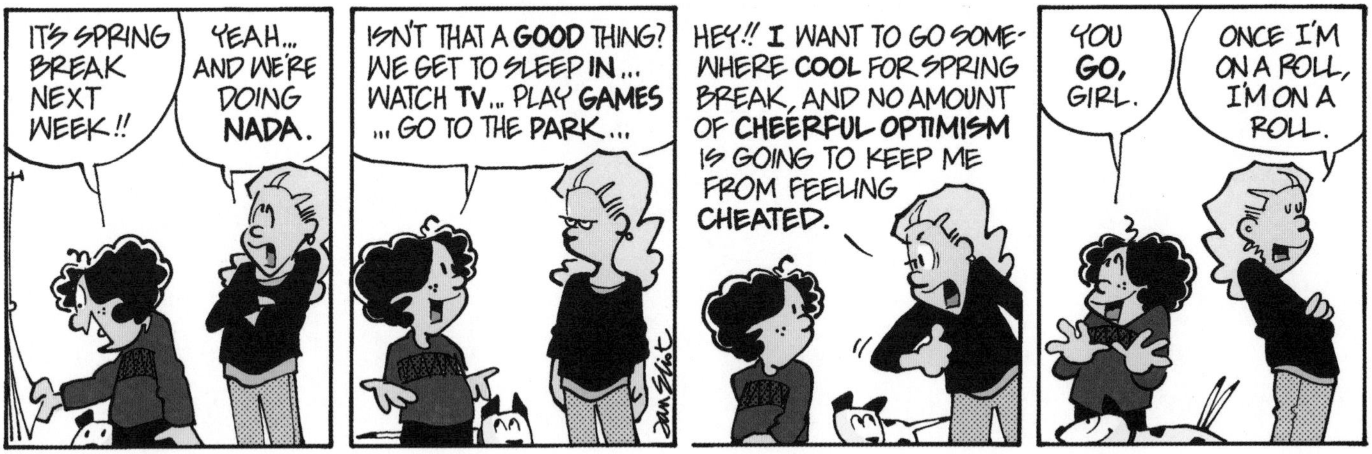
IT'S SPRING BREAK NEXT WEEK!!
YEAH... AND WE'RE DOING **NADA**.
ISN'T THAT A **GOOD** THING? WE GET TO SLEEP **IN**... WATCH **TV**... PLAY **GAMES** ... GO TO THE **PARK**...
HEY!! **I** WANT TO GO SOMEWHERE **COOL** FOR SPRING BREAK, AND NO AMOUNT OF **CHEERFUL OPTIMISM** IS GOING TO KEEP ME FROM FEELING **CHEATED**.
YOU **GO,** GIRL.
ONCE I'M ON A ROLL, I'M ON A ROLL.

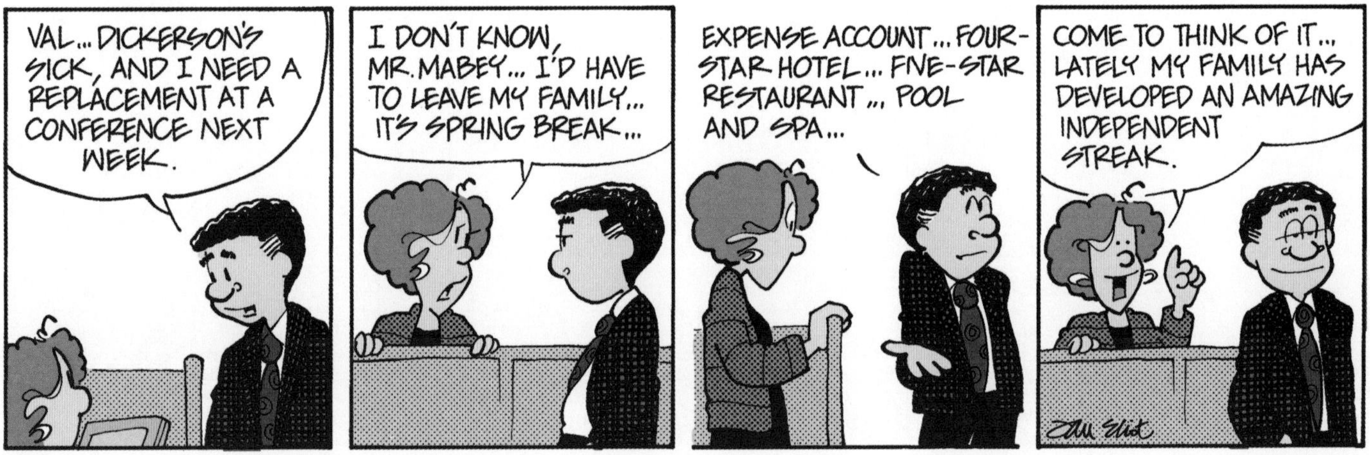
VAL... DICKERSON'S SICK, AND I NEED A REPLACEMENT AT A CONFERENCE NEXT WEEK.
I DON'T KNOW, MR. MABEY... I'D HAVE TO LEAVE MY FAMILY... IT'S SPRING BREAK...
EXPENSE ACCOUNT... FOUR-STAR HOTEL... FIVE-STAR RESTAURANT... POOL AND SPA...
COME TO THINK OF IT... LATELY MY FAMILY HAS DEVELOPED AN AMAZING INDEPENDENT STREAK.

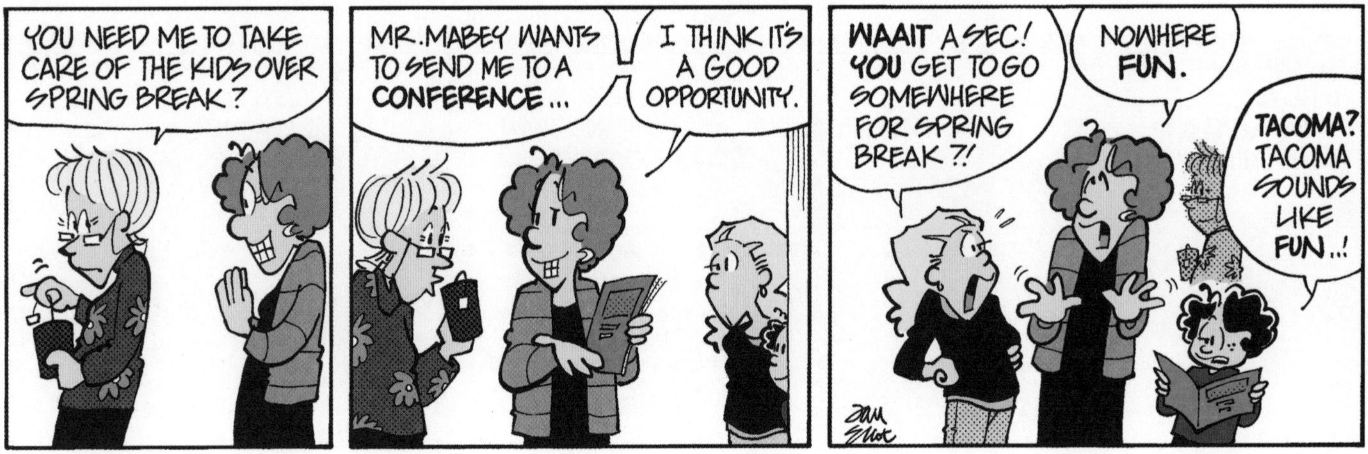
YOU NEED ME TO TAKE CARE OF THE KIDS OVER SPRING BREAK?
MR. MABEY WANTS TO SEND ME TO A **CONFERENCE**...
I THINK IT'S A GOOD OPPORTUNITY.
WAAIT A SEC! **YOU** GET TO GO SOMEWHERE FOR SPRING BREAK?!
NOWHERE **FUN**.
TACOMA? TACOMA SOUNDS LIKE **FUN**..!

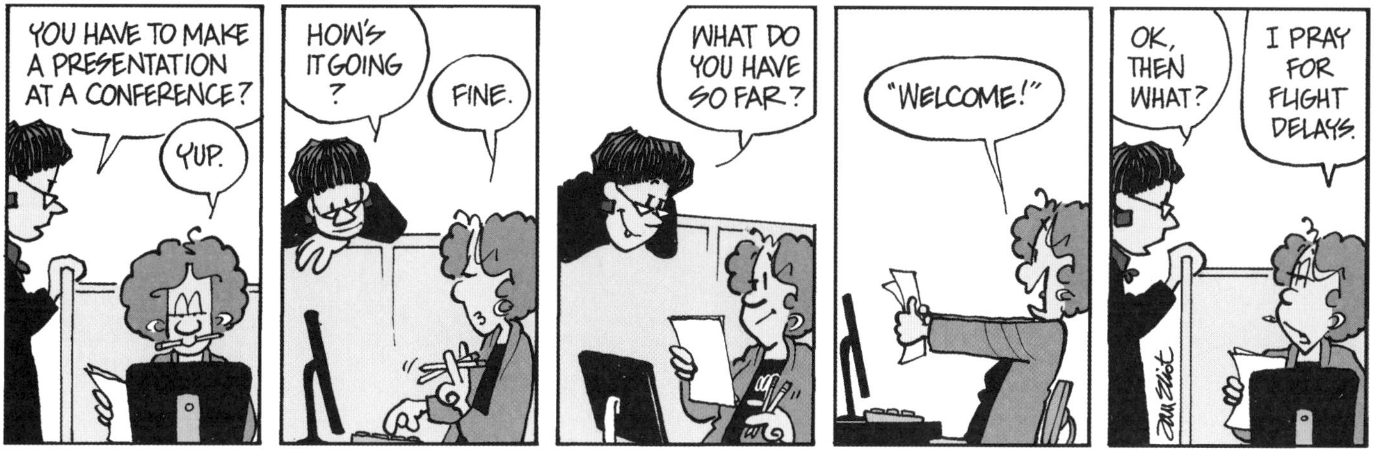
YOU HAVE TO MAKE A PRESENTATION AT A CONFERENCE?
YUP.
HOW'S IT GOING?
FINE.
WHAT DO YOU HAVE SO FAR?
"WELCOME!"
OK, THEN WHAT?
I PRAY FOR FLIGHT DELAYS.

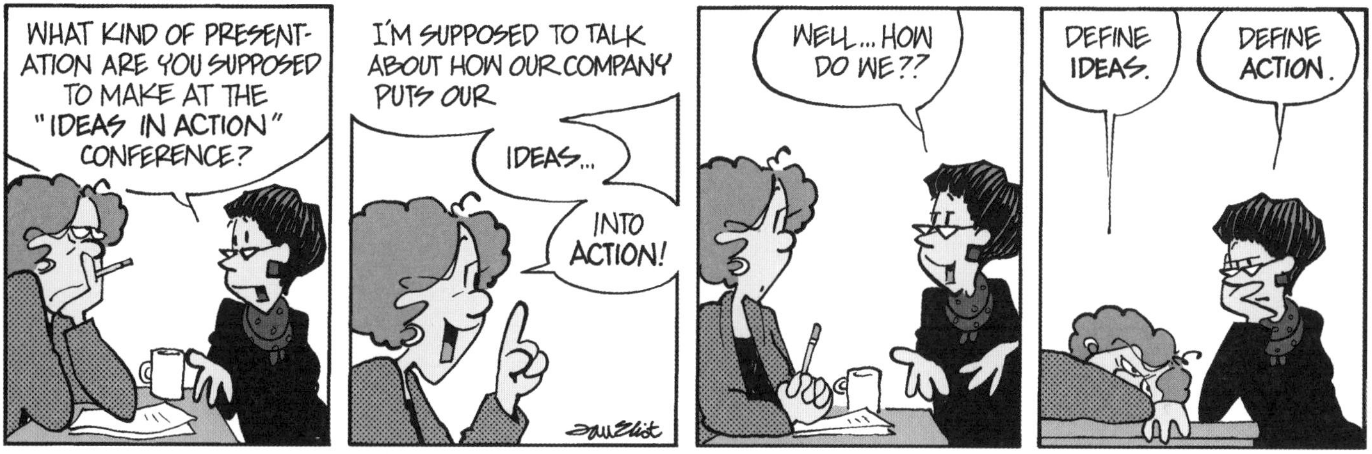
WHAT KIND OF PRESENTATION ARE YOU SUPPOSED TO MAKE AT THE "IDEAS IN ACTION" CONFERENCE?
I'M SUPPOSED TO TALK ABOUT HOW OUR COMPANY PUTS OUR
IDEAS...
INTO ACTION!
WELL... HOW DO WE??
DEFINE IDEAS.
DEFINE ACTION.

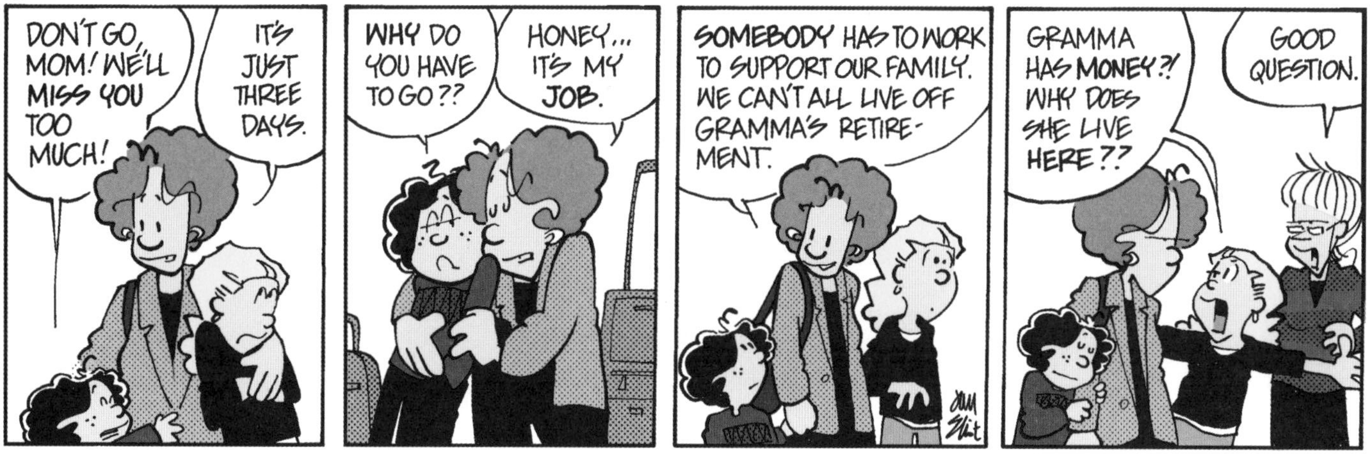
DON'T GO, MOM! WE'LL MISS YOU TOO MUCH!
IT'S JUST THREE DAYS.
WHY DO YOU HAVE TO GO??
HONEY... IT'S MY JOB.
SOMEBODY HAS TO WORK TO SUPPORT OUR FAMILY. WE CAN'T ALL LIVE OFF GRAMMA'S RETIREMENT.
GRAMMA HAS MONEY?! WHY DOES SHE LIVE HERE??
GOOD QUESTION.

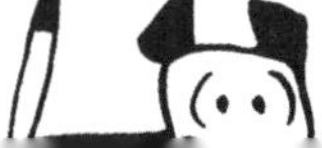

Stone Soup

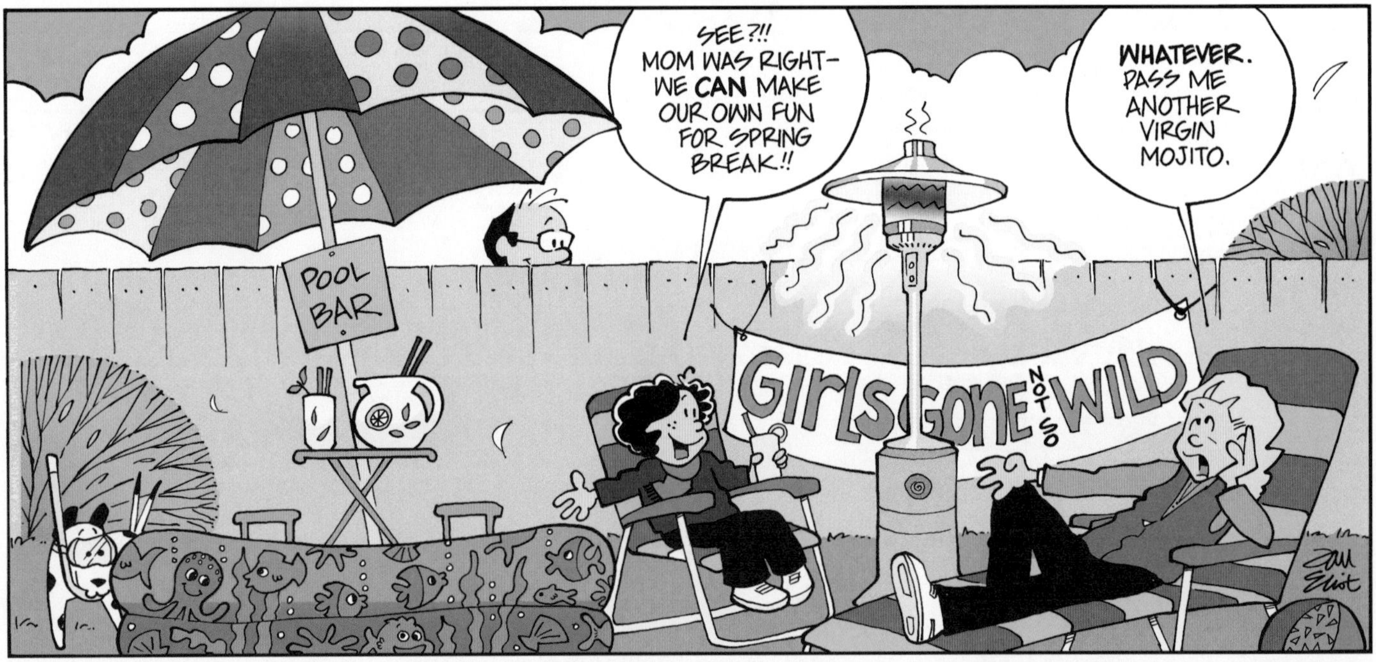
SEE?!! MOM WAS RIGHT— WE **CAN** MAKE OUR OWN FUN FOR SPRING BREAK!!
WHATEVER. PASS ME ANOTHER VIRGIN MOJITO.
POOL BAR
GIRLS GONE NOT SO WILD

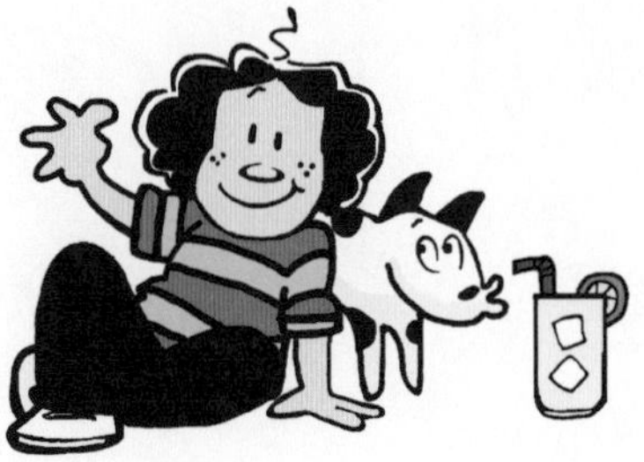

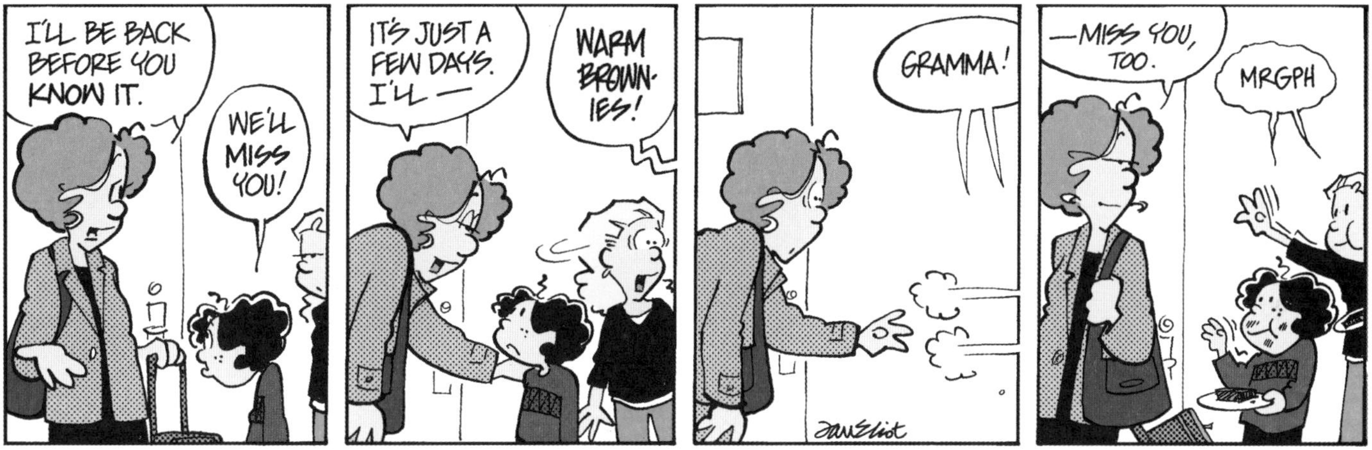
I'LL BE BACK BEFORE YOU KNOW IT.
WE'LL MISS YOU!
IT'S JUST A FEW DAYS. I'LL —
WARM BROWNIES!
GRAMMA!
— MISS YOU, TOO.
MRGPH
Jan Eliot

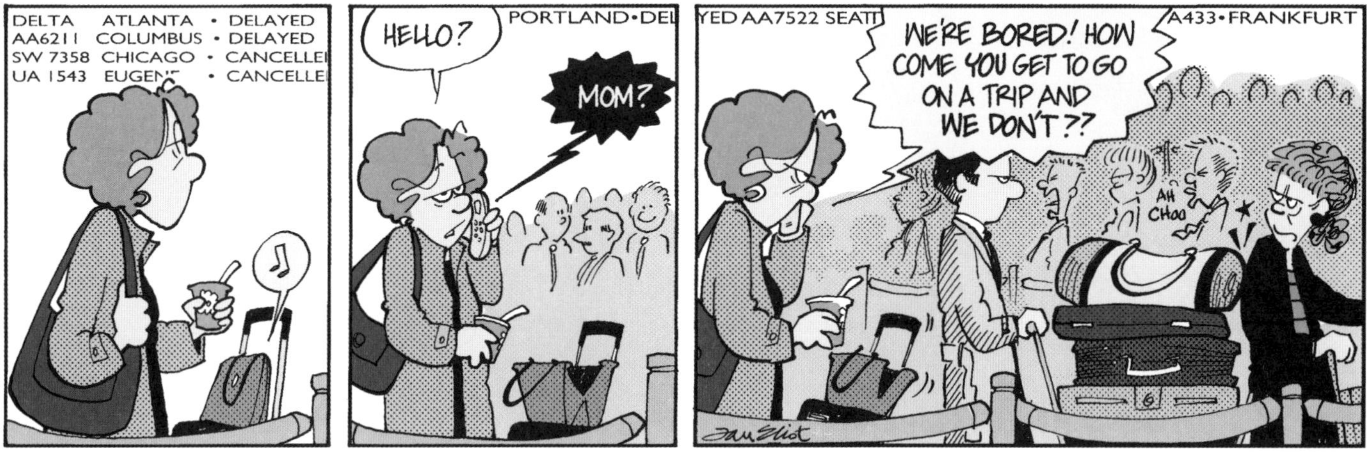
DELTA ATLANTA • DELAYED
AA6211 COLUMBUS • DELAYED
SW 7358 CHICAGO • CANCELLE
UA 1543 EUGEN • CANCELLE
HELLO?
PORTLAND•DEL
MOM?
YED AA7522 SEATT
A433•FRANKFURT
WE'RE BORED! HOW COME YOU GET TO GO ON A TRIP AND WE DON'T??
AH CHOO
Jan Eliot

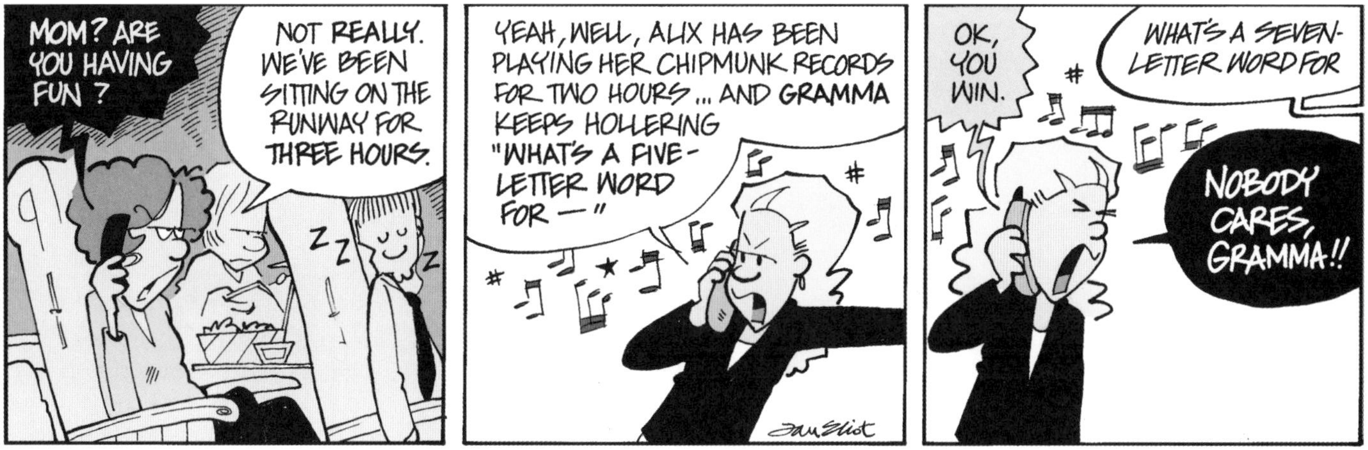
MOM? ARE YOU HAVING FUN ?
NOT REALLY. WE'VE BEEN SITTING ON THE RUNWAY FOR THREE HOURS.
Z Z Z
YEAH, WELL, ALIX HAS BEEN PLAYING HER CHIPMUNK RECORDS FOR TWO HOURS ... AND GRAMMA KEEPS HOLLERING "WHAT'S A FIVE-LETTER WORD FOR —"
Jan Eliot
OK, YOU WIN.
WHAT'S A SEVEN-LETTER WORD FOR
NOBODY CARES, GRAMMA!!

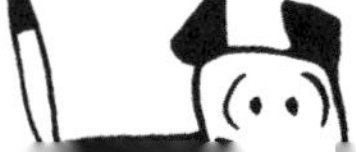

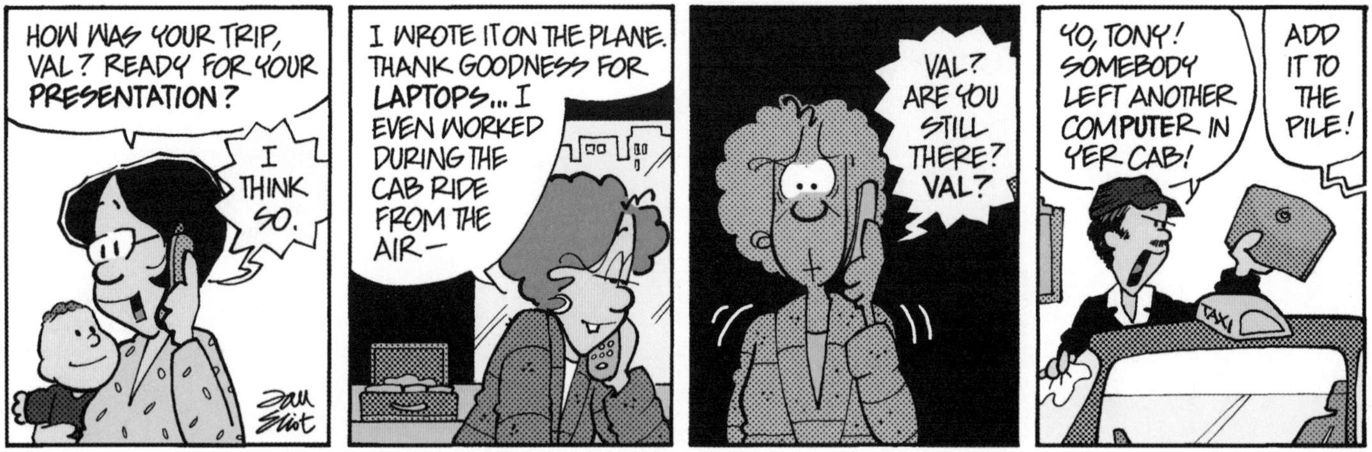
HOW WAS YOUR TRIP, VAL? READY FOR YOUR **PRESENTATION**?
I THINK SO.
I WROTE IT ON THE PLANE. THANK GOODNESS FOR **LAPTOPS**... I EVEN WORKED DURING THE CAB RIDE FROM THE AIR—
VAL? ARE YOU STILL THERE? **VAL?**
YO, TONY! SOMEBODY LEFT ANOTHER **COMPUTER** IN YER CAB!
ADD IT TO THE PILE!
TAXI

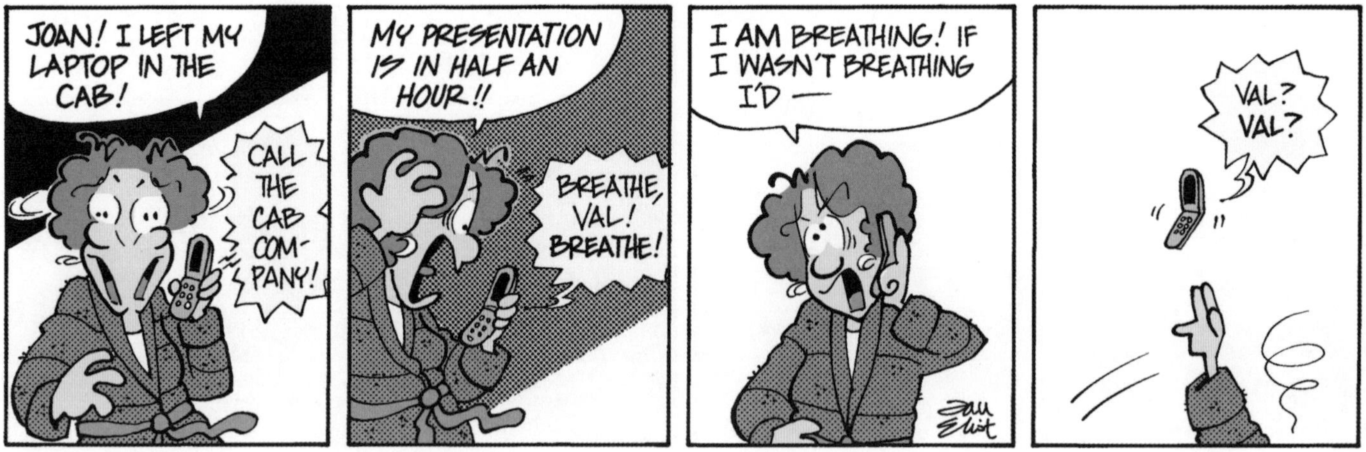
JOAN! I LEFT MY LAPTOP IN THE CAB!
CALL THE CAB COM-PANY!
MY PRESENTATION IS IN HALF AN HOUR!!
BREATHE, VAL! **BREATHE!**
I **AM** BREATHING! IF I WASN'T BREATHING I'D —
VAL? **VAL?**

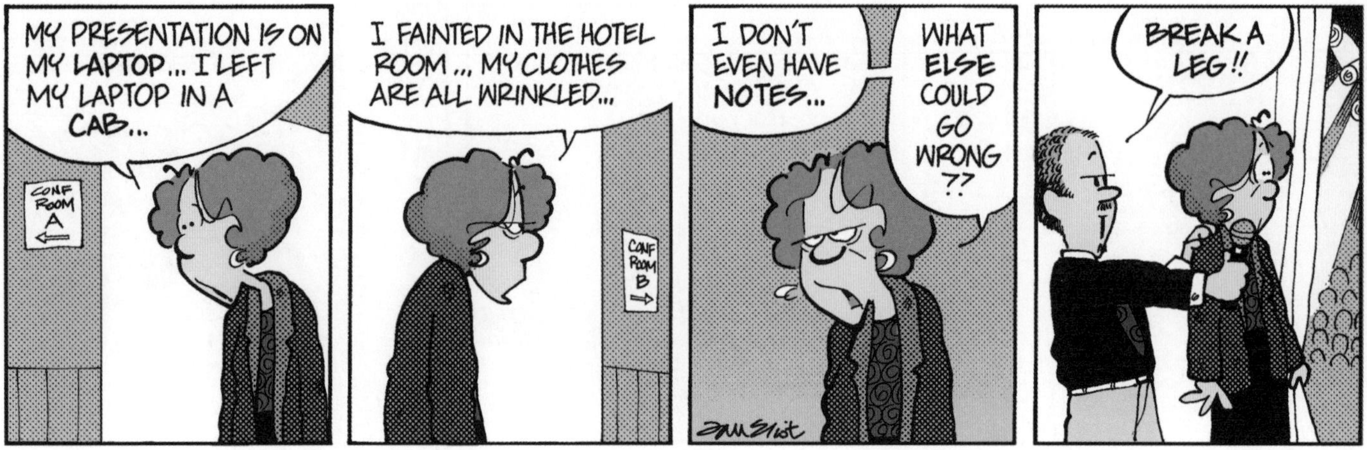
MY PRESENTATION IS ON MY **LAPTOP**... I LEFT MY LAPTOP IN A **CAB**...
CONF ROOM A
I FAINTED IN THE HOTEL ROOM ... MY CLOTHES ARE ALL WRINKLED...
CONF ROOM B
I DON'T EVEN HAVE **NOTES**...
WHAT **ELSE** COULD GO WRONG??
BREAK A LEG!!

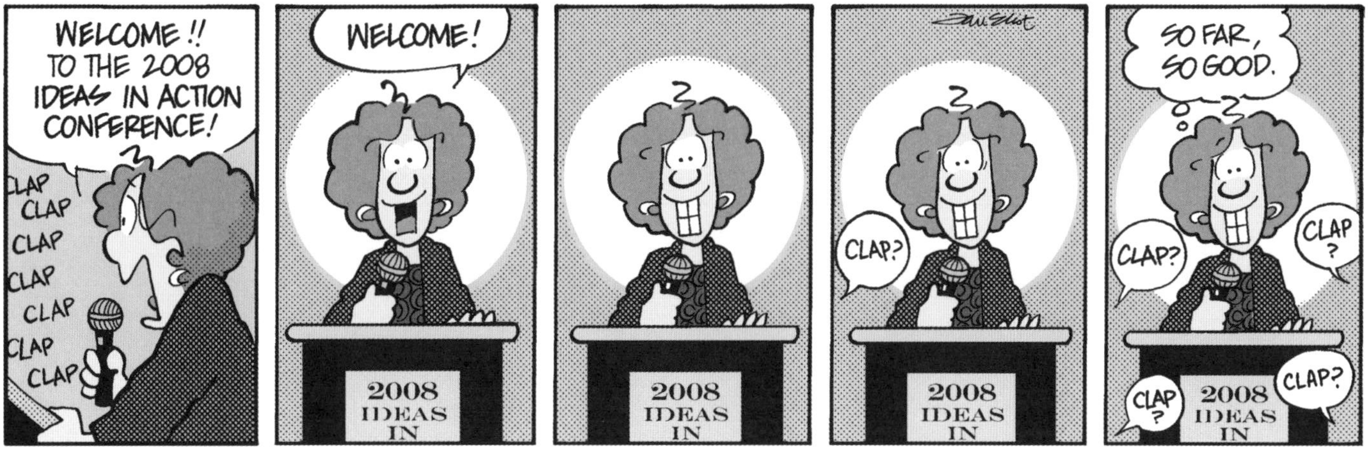
WELCOME !! TO THE 2008 IDEAS IN ACTION CONFERENCE!
CLAP CLAP CLAP CLAP CLAP CLAP CLAP
WELCOME!
2008 IDEAS IN
CLAP?
SO FAR, SO GOOD.
CLAP?
CLAP ?
CLAP ?
CLAP?

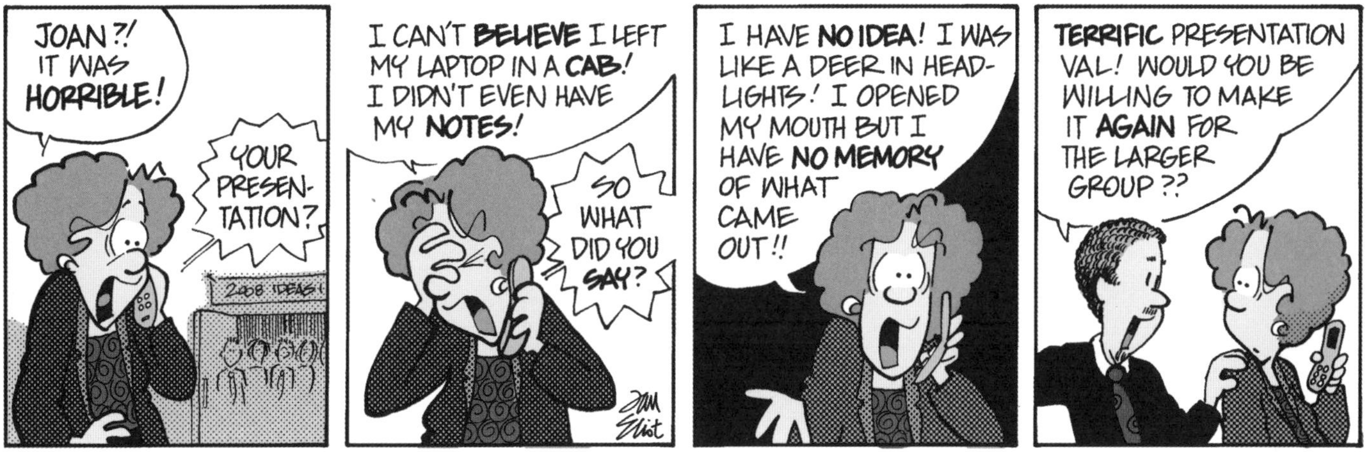
JOAN ?! IT WAS HORRIBLE!
YOUR PRESEN-TATION?
2008 IDEAS
I CAN'T BELIEVE I LEFT MY LAPTOP IN A CAB! I DIDN'T EVEN HAVE MY NOTES!
SO WHAT DID YOU SAY?
I HAVE NO IDEA! I WAS LIKE A DEER IN HEAD-LIGHTS! I OPENED MY MOUTH BUT I HAVE NO MEMORY OF WHAT CAME OUT!!
TERRIFIC PRESENTATION VAL! WOULD YOU BE WILLING TO MAKE IT AGAIN FOR THE LARGER GROUP ??

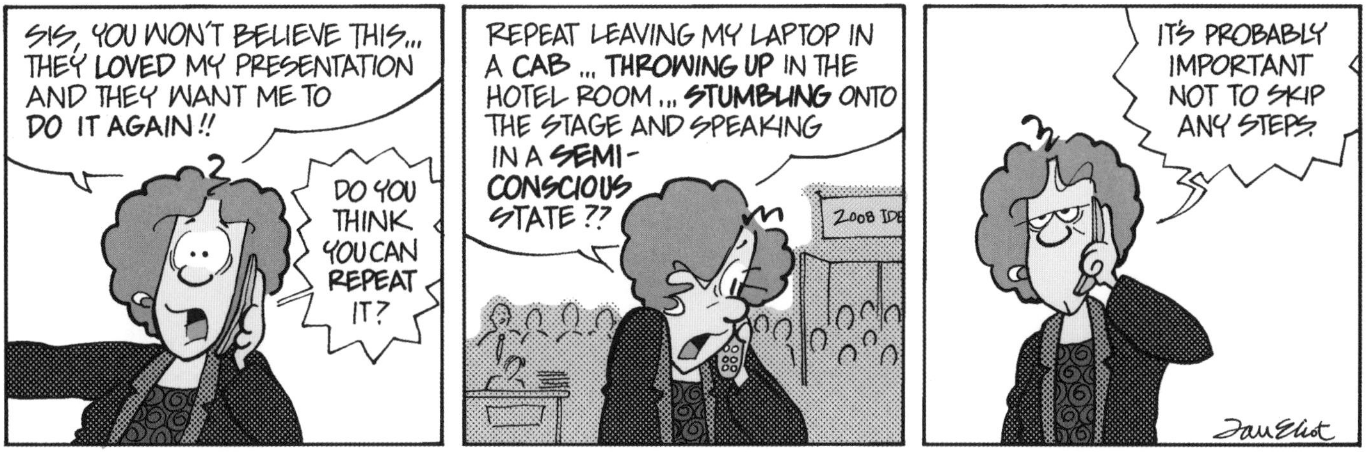
SIS, YOU WON'T BELIEVE THIS... THEY LOVED MY PRESENTATION AND THEY WANT ME TO DO IT AGAIN!!
DO YOU THINK YOU CAN REPEAT IT?
REPEAT LEAVING MY LAPTOP IN A CAB ... THROWING UP IN THE HOTEL ROOM ... STUMBLING ONTO THE STAGE AND SPEAKING IN A SEMI-CONSCIOUS STATE ??
2008 IDE
IT'S PROBABLY IMPORTANT NOT TO SKIP ANY STEPS.

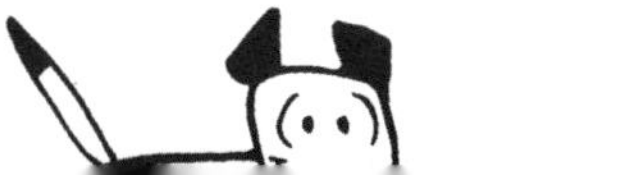

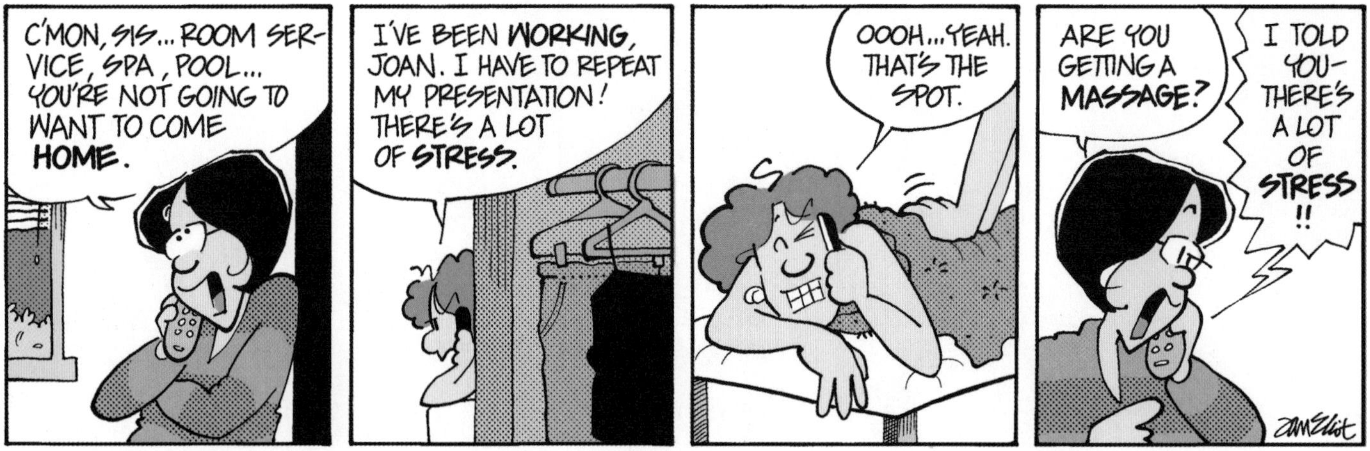
C'MON, SIS... ROOM SERVICE, SPA, POOL... YOU'RE NOT GOING TO WANT TO COME **HOME**.
I'VE BEEN **WORKING**, JOAN. I HAVE TO REPEAT MY PRESENTATION! THERE'S A LOT OF **STRESS**.
OOOH... YEAH. THAT'S THE SPOT.
ARE YOU GETTING A **MASSAGE**?
I TOLD YOU- THERE'S A LOT OF **STRESS** !!

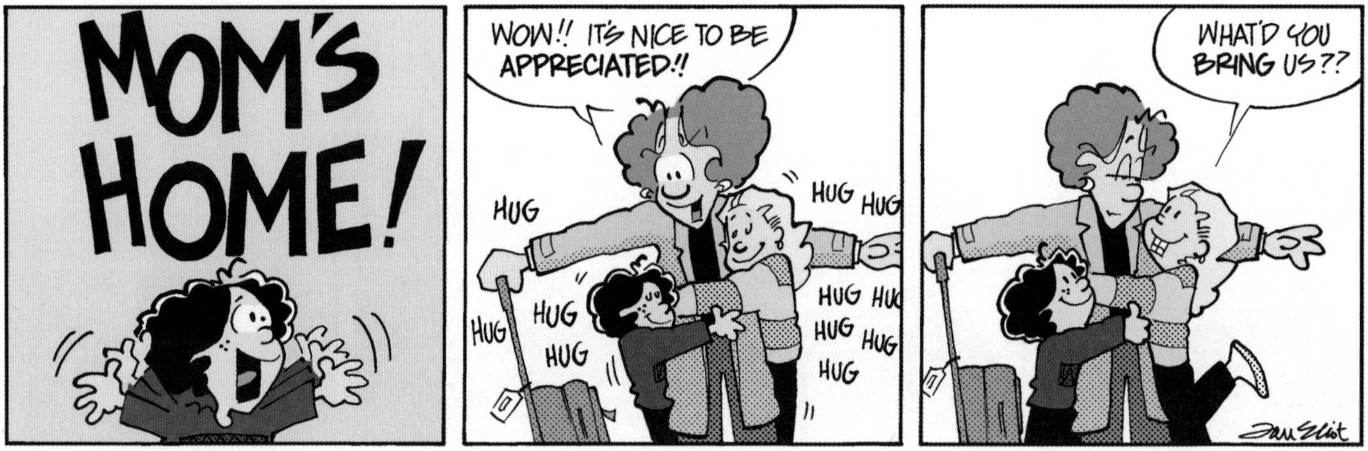
MOM'S HOME!
WOW!! IT'S NICE TO BE **APPRECIATED**!!
HUG
HUG HUG
HUG
HUG
HUG
HUG HUG
HUG HUG
HUG
WHAT'D YOU **BRING** US??

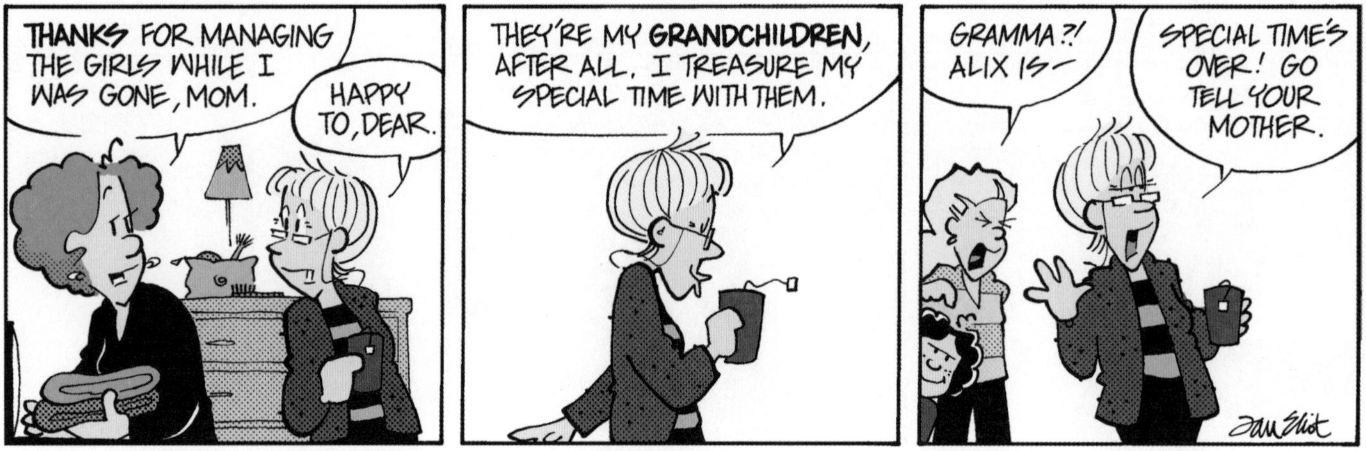
THANKS FOR MANAGING THE GIRLS WHILE I WAS GONE, MOM.
HAPPY TO, DEAR.
THEY'RE MY **GRANDCHILDREN**, AFTER ALL. I TREASURE MY SPECIAL TIME WITH THEM.
GRAMMA?! ALIX IS—
SPECIAL TIME'S OVER! GO TELL YOUR MOTHER.

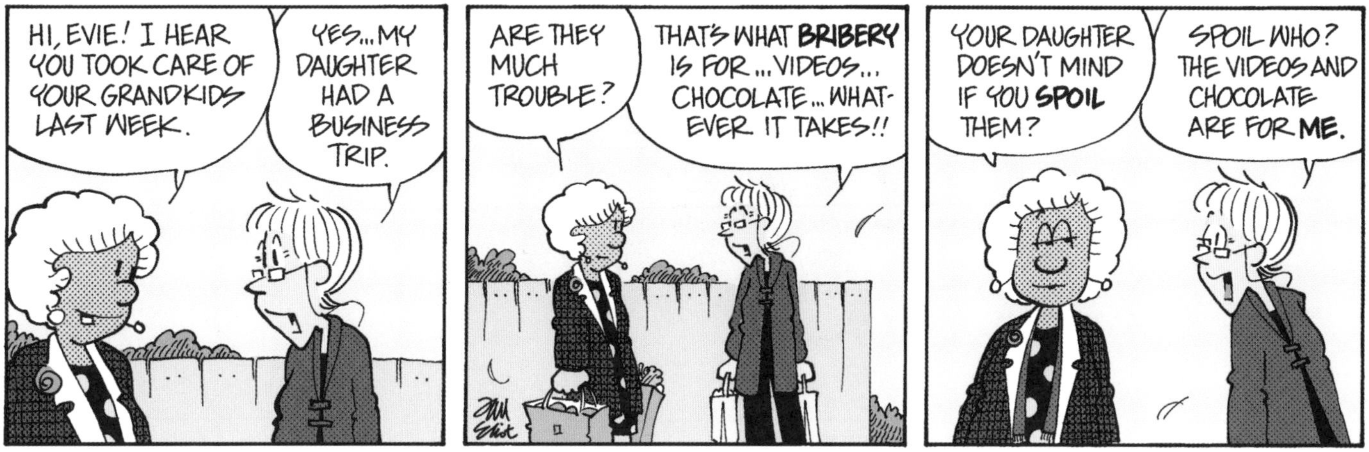
HI, EVIE! I HEAR YOU TOOK CARE OF YOUR GRANDKIDS LAST WEEK.
YES... MY DAUGHTER HAD A BUSINESS TRIP.
ARE THEY MUCH TROUBLE?
THAT'S WHAT **BRIBERY** IS FOR ... VIDEOS... CHOCOLATE... WHATEVER IT TAKES!!
YOUR DAUGHTER DOESN'T MIND IF YOU **SPOIL** THEM?
SPOIL WHO? THE VIDEOS AND CHOCOLATE ARE FOR **ME.**

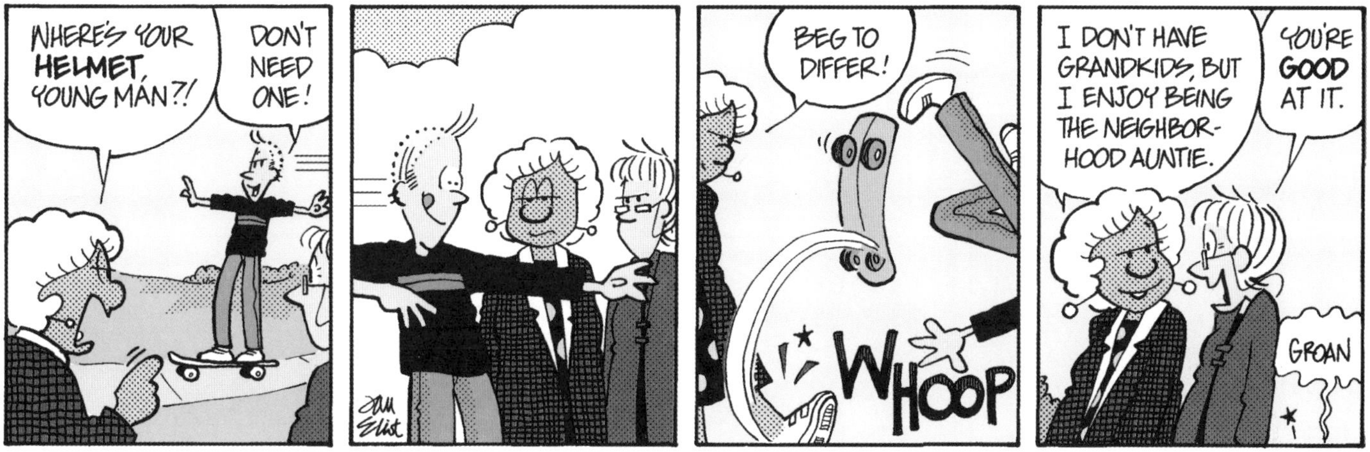
WHERE'S YOUR **HELMET**, YOUNG MAN?!
DON'T NEED ONE!
BEG TO DIFFER!
WHOOP
I DON'T HAVE GRANDKIDS, BUT I ENJOY BEING THE NEIGHBORHOOD AUNTIE.
YOU'RE **GOOD** AT IT.
GROAN

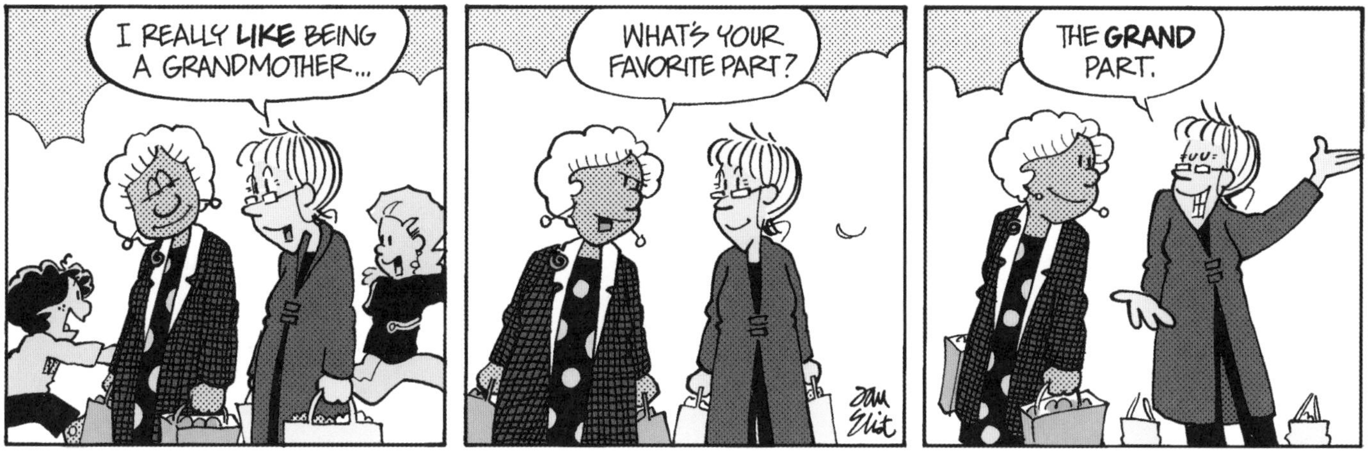
I REALLY **LIKE** BEING A GRANDMOTHER...
WHAT'S YOUR FAVORITE PART?
THE **GRAND** PART.

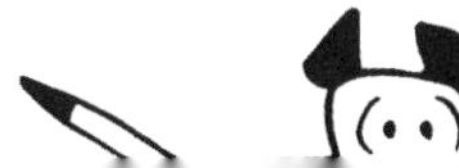

Stone Soup

SO VAL... HOW'S PHIL??
FINE.
I MEAN... HOW'S THE RE-LAA-TION-SHIP?
WELL, WE'RE STILL AFLOAT.
ALTHOUGH WE RARELY LEAVE THE HARBOR...
MAYBE I DON'T REALLY WANT TO RISK IT ON THE HIGH SEAS.
BUT IF I DON'T... HOW WILL I KNOW HOW IT HANDLES IN STORMY WEATHER??
PUH-LEASE TELL ME YOU'VE RUN OUT OF METAPHORS!!
AND IF WE EVER ACTUALLY DO SET SAIL... WHO'LL BE CAPTAIN?!?

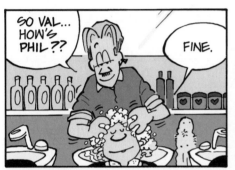

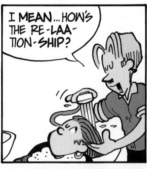

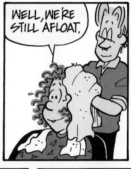

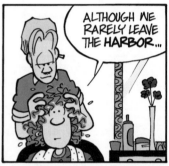

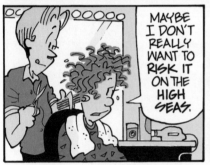

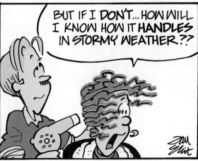

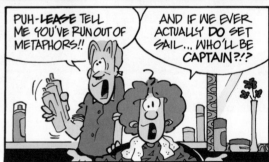

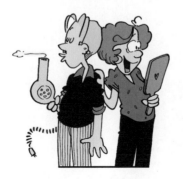

WHERE'S THAT LITTLE BRUSH WE USE TO CLEAN UPHOLSTERY?

10:20 am

IT WAS UNDER HERE ... IN A CUP WITH —

TOOTHBRUSHES, STEEL WOOL ... HEY— THERE'S WATER IN HERE!

WHERE'D THAT COME FROM? IS ANYTHING ELSE WET??

MAYBE THIS PIPE IS CLOGGED...

I'VE BEEN MEANING TO CLEAN IT OUT...

GROSS! AND THE WASHER ROTTED...

I'M GOING TO THE HARDWARE STORE!

FIXED IT!

WHERE'S THAT LITTLE BRUSH WE USE TO CLEAN UPHOLSTERY?

3:30 pm

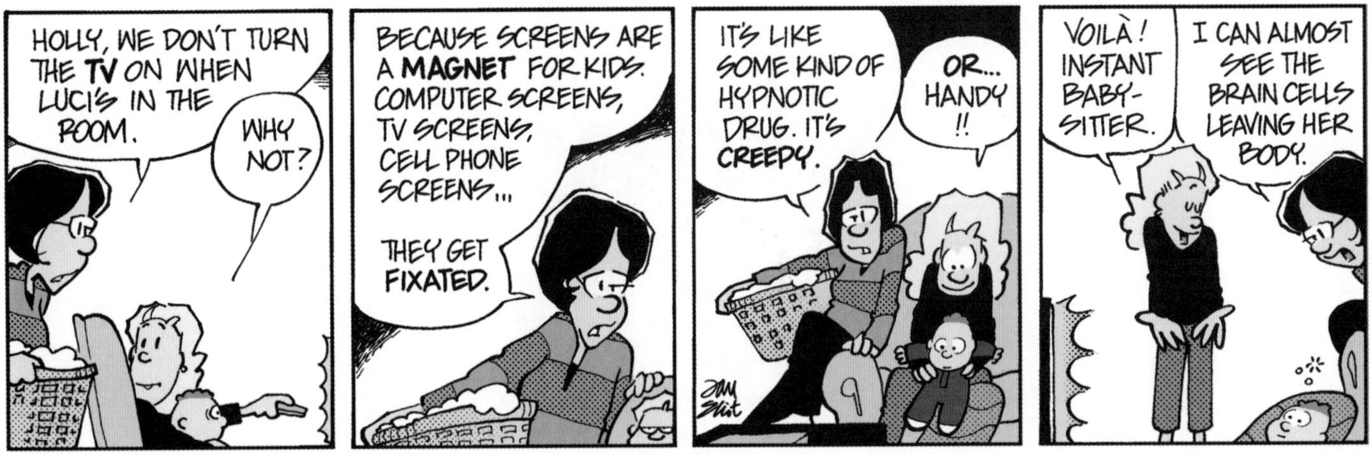
HOLLY, WE DON'T TURN THE **TV** ON WHEN LUCI'S IN THE ROOM.
WHY NOT?
BECAUSE SCREENS ARE A **MAGNET** FOR KIDS. COMPUTER SCREENS, TV SCREENS, CELL PHONE SCREENS...
THEY GET **FIXATED**.
IT'S LIKE SOME KIND OF HYPNOTIC DRUG. IT'S **CREEPY**.
OR... HANDY !!
VOILÀ! INSTANT BABY-SITTER.
I CAN ALMOST SEE THE BRAIN CELLS LEAVING HER BODY.

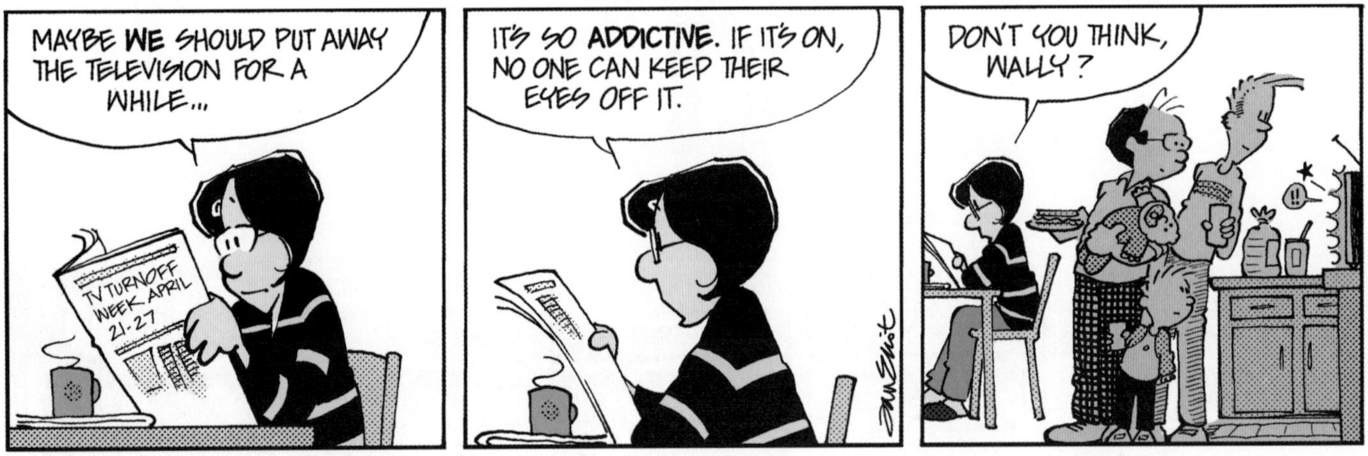
MAYBE **WE** SHOULD PUT AWAY THE TELEVISION FOR A WHILE...
TV TURNOFF WEEK APRIL 21-27
IT'S SO **ADDICTIVE**. IF IT'S ON, NO ONE CAN KEEP THEIR EYES OFF IT.
DON'T YOU THINK, WALLY?

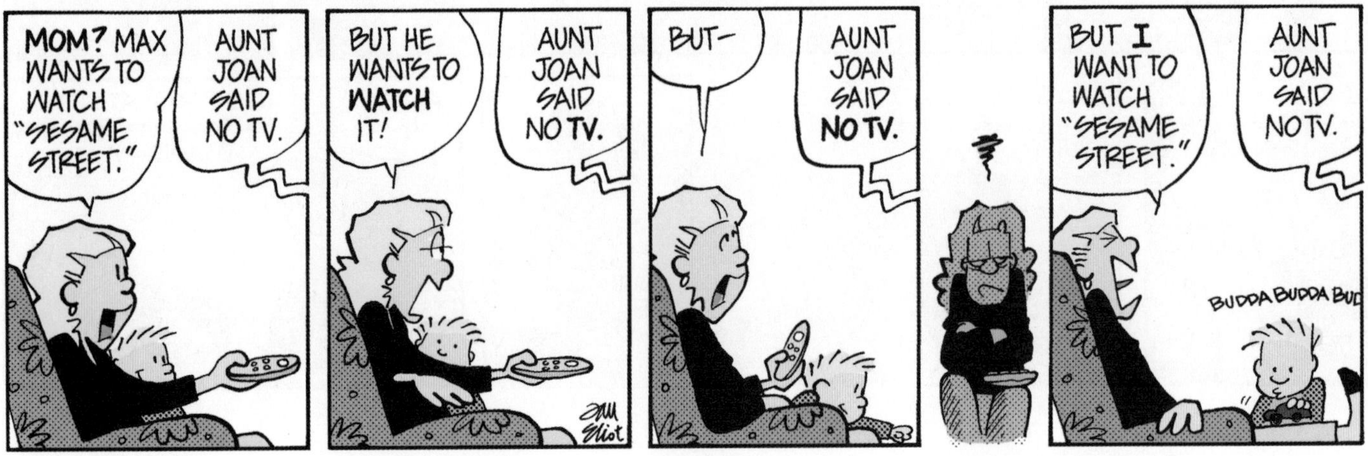
MOM? MAX WANTS TO WATCH "SESAME STREET."
AUNT JOAN SAID NO TV.
BUT HE WANTS TO **WATCH** IT!
AUNT JOAN SAID NO **TV.**
BUT-
AUNT JOAN SAID **NO TV.**
BUT **I** WANT TO WATCH "SESAME STREET."
AUNT JOAN SAID NO TV.
BUDDA BUDDA BUD

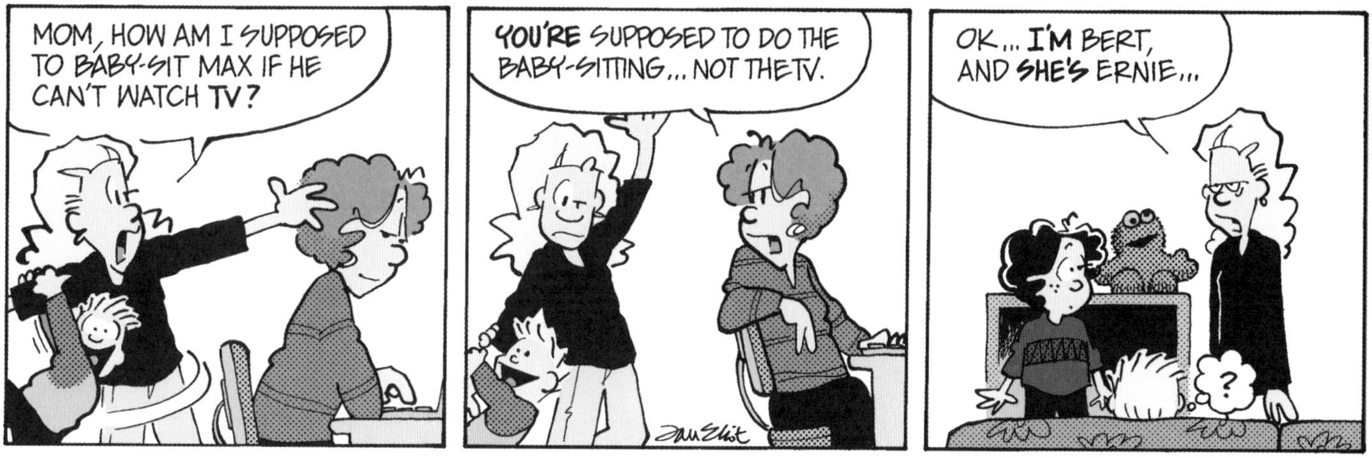
MOM, HOW AM I SUPPOSED TO BABY-SIT MAX IF HE CAN'T WATCH TV?
YOU'RE SUPPOSED TO DO THE BABY-SITTING... NOT THE TV.
OK... I'M BERT, AND SHE'S ERNIE...
?

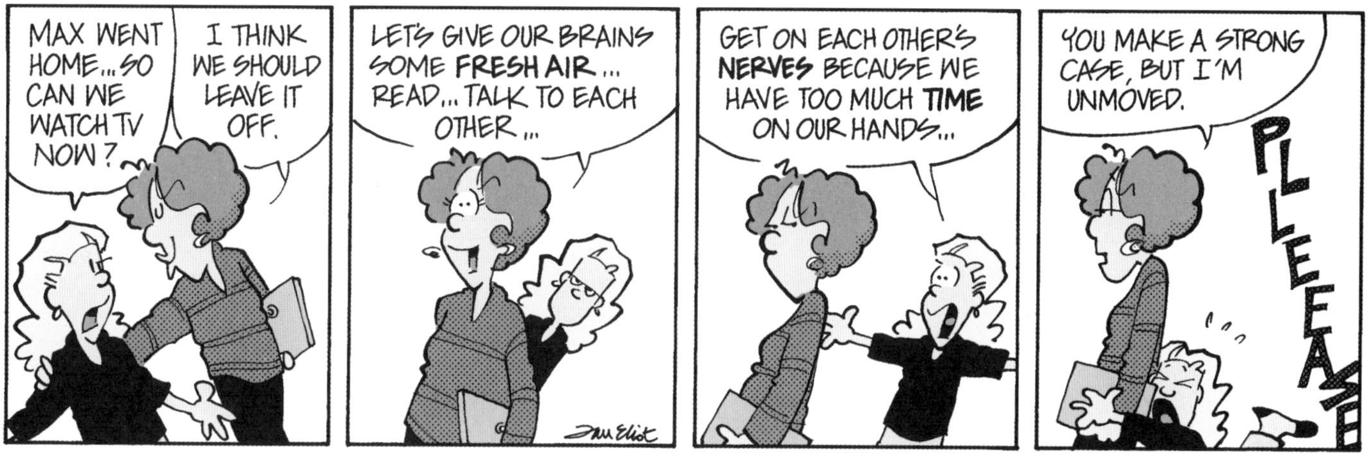
MAX WENT HOME... SO CAN WE WATCH TV NOW?
I THINK WE SHOULD LEAVE IT OFF.
LET'S GIVE OUR BRAINS SOME FRESH AIR... READ... TALK TO EACH OTHER...
GET ON EACH OTHER'S NERVES BECAUSE WE HAVE TOO MUCH TIME ON OUR HANDS...
YOU MAKE A STRONG CASE, BUT I'M UNMOVED.
PLLEEEASE

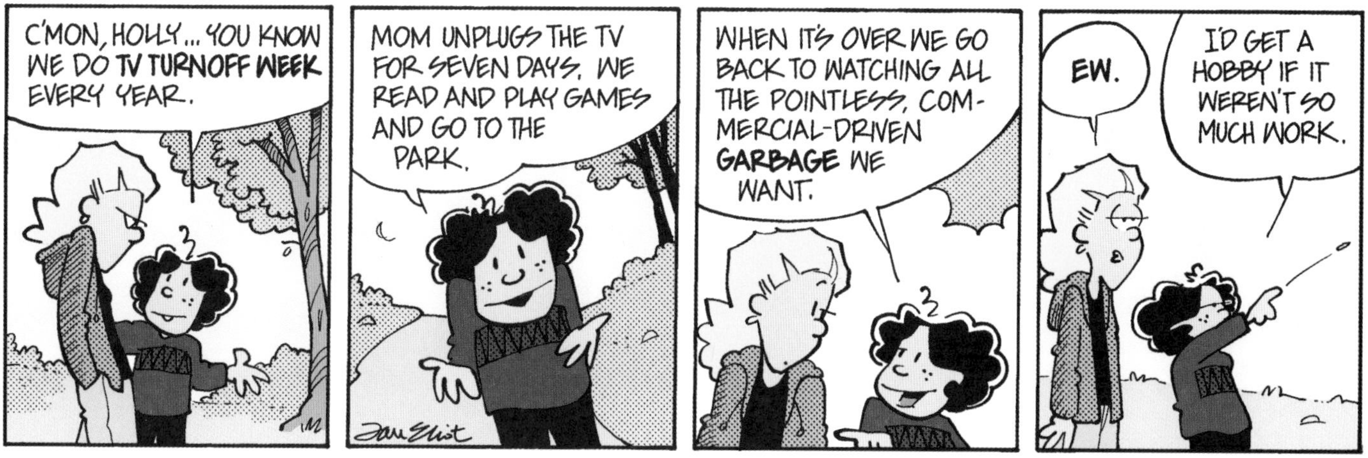
C'MON, HOLLY... YOU KNOW WE DO TV TURNOFF WEEK EVERY YEAR.
MOM UNPLUGS THE TV FOR SEVEN DAYS. WE READ AND PLAY GAMES AND GO TO THE PARK.
WHEN IT'S OVER WE GO BACK TO WATCHING ALL THE POINTLESS, COM-MERCIAL-DRIVEN GARBAGE WE WANT.
EW.
I'D GET A HOBBY IF IT WEREN'T SO MUCH WORK.

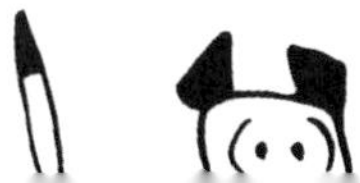

Stone Soup

OH, FOR THE LOVE OF SIMONE de B.!!
WHAT ??
LOOK AT THIS KIDS' FURNITURE CATALOG.
NUK NUK
CUTE BEDROOM SETS! NAUTICAL THEME... SURFER THEME... SUPER HEROES...
THOSE ARE THE BOYS BEDROOMS.
OK... AND FOR THE GIRLS...
WHOA. A TOTALLY ...PINK...PRETEND KITCHEN...
AND ON THIS PAGE...
A PINK, PRETEND—
VACUUM CLEANER ?!
SEND YOUR DAUGHTER BACK TO THE '50s!! OVERNIGHT SHIPPING AVAILABLE!!
NUK NUK
WHAT'S IN THE LITTLE BOTTLES?
PRETEND VALIUM. ORDER ME SOME.

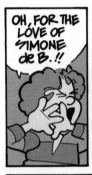

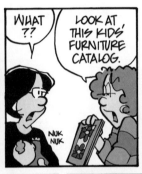

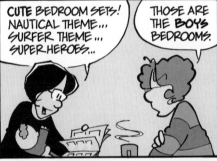

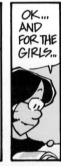

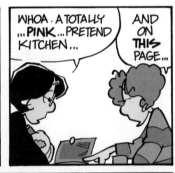

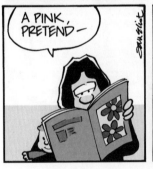

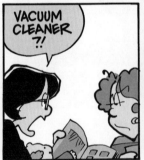

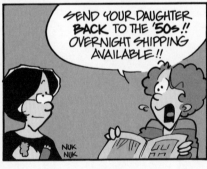

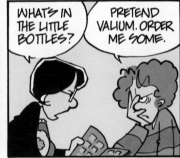

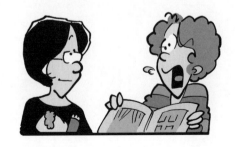

Stone Soup
KABOOM

SIGH
!!
!!?
!!
HAVE YOU TRIED THE PLUNGER?!
I'M HAVIN' A GREAT DAY...

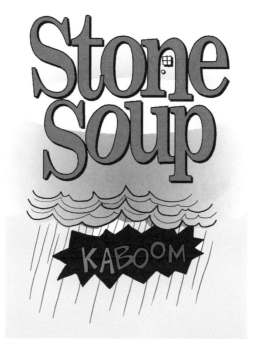

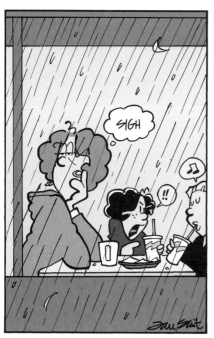

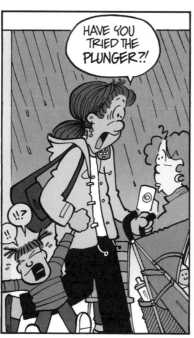

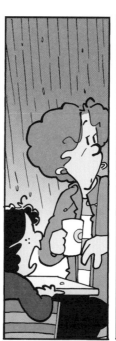

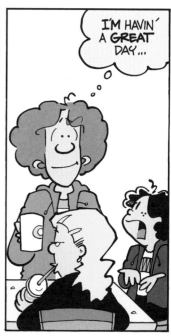

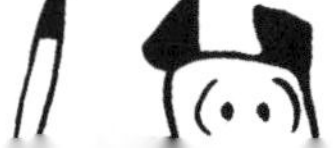

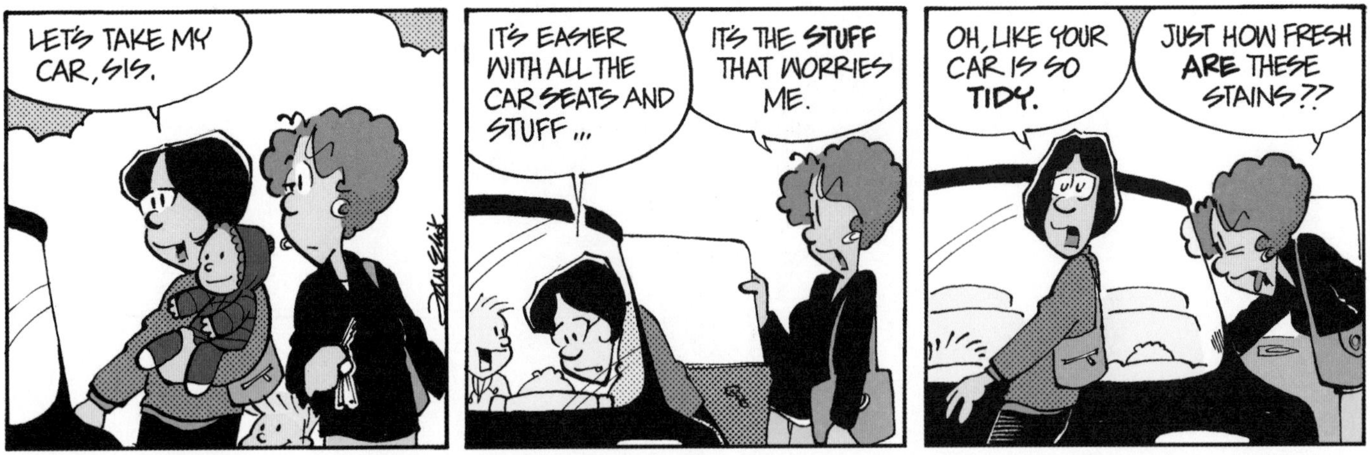
LET'S TAKE MY CAR, SIS.
IT'S EASIER WITH ALL THE CAR SEATS AND STUFF...
IT'S THE **STUFF** THAT WORRIES ME.
OH, LIKE YOUR CAR IS SO **TIDY.**
JUST HOW FRESH **ARE** THESE STAINS??

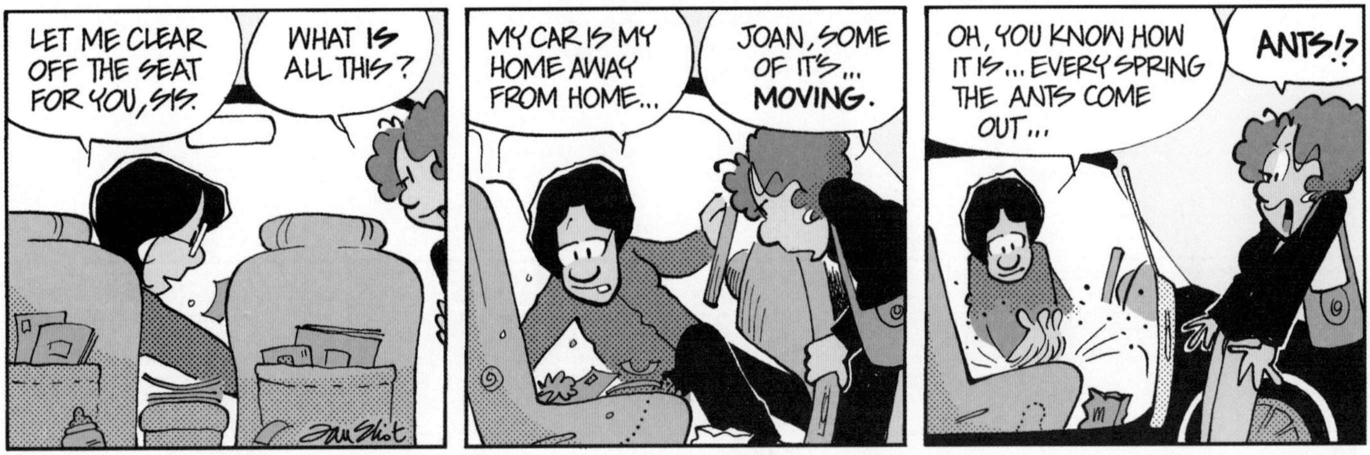
LET ME CLEAR OFF THE SEAT FOR YOU, SIS.
WHAT **IS** ALL THIS?
MY CAR IS MY HOME AWAY FROM HOME...
JOAN, SOME OF IT'S... **MOVING.**
OH, YOU KNOW HOW IT IS... EVERY SPRING THE ANTS COME OUT...
ANTS!?

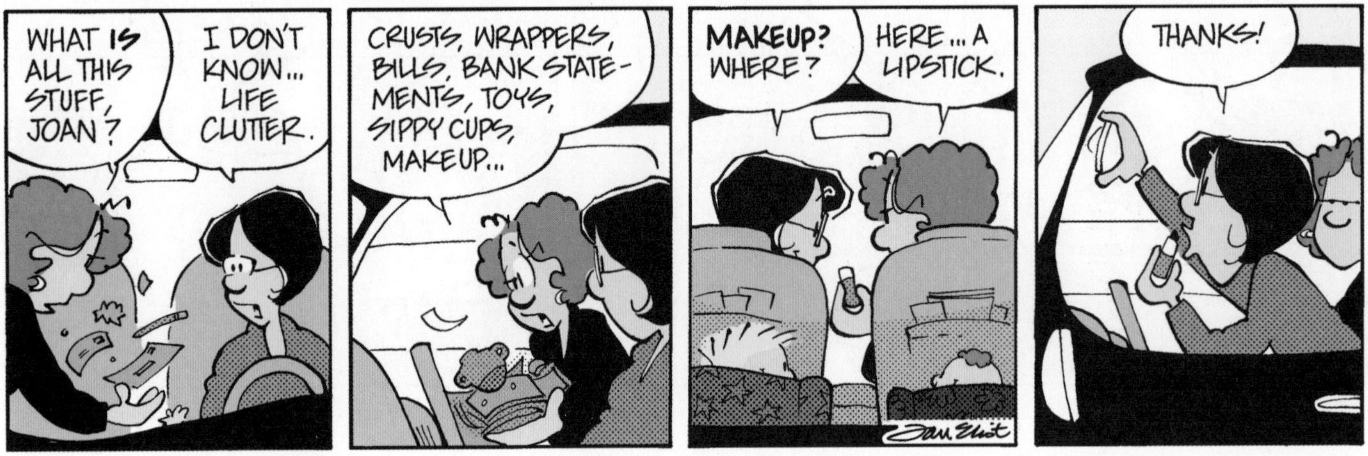
WHAT **IS** ALL THIS STUFF, JOAN?
I DON'T KNOW... LIFE CLUTTER.
CRUSTS, WRAPPERS, BILLS, BANK STATE-MENTS, TOYS, SIPPY CUPS, MAKEUP...
MAKEUP? WHERE?
HERE... A LIPSTICK.
THANKS!

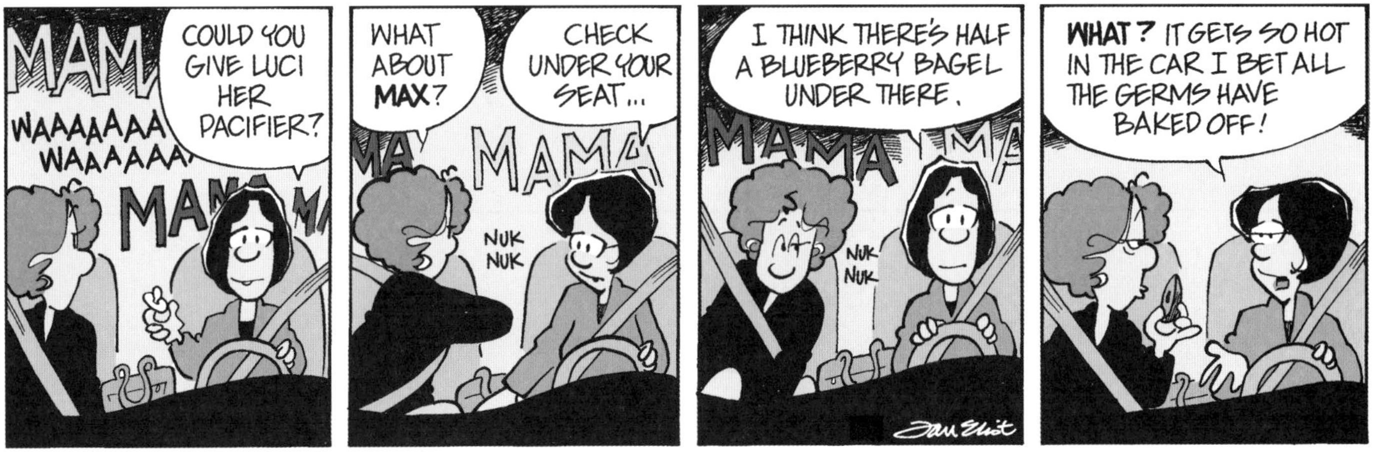
MAM
WAAAAAAA WAAAAAA
MAMA MA
COULD YOU GIVE LUCI HER PACIFIER?
WHAT ABOUT MAX?
CHECK UNDER YOUR SEAT...
MAMA
NUK NUK
I THINK THERE'S HALF A BLUEBERRY BAGEL UNDER THERE.
MAMA MA
NUK NUK
WHAT? IT GETS SO HOT IN THE CAR I BET ALL THE GERMS HAVE BAKED OFF!

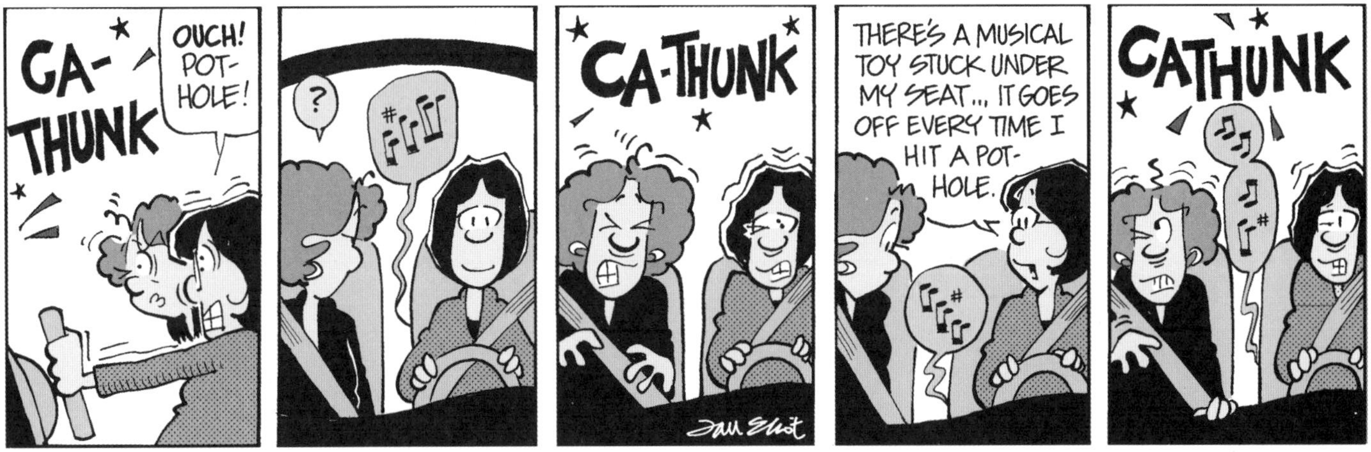
CA-THUNK
OUCH! POT-HOLE!
?
CA-THUNK
THERE'S A MUSICAL TOY STUCK UNDER MY SEAT... IT GOES OFF EVERY TIME I HIT A POT-HOLE.
CATHUNK

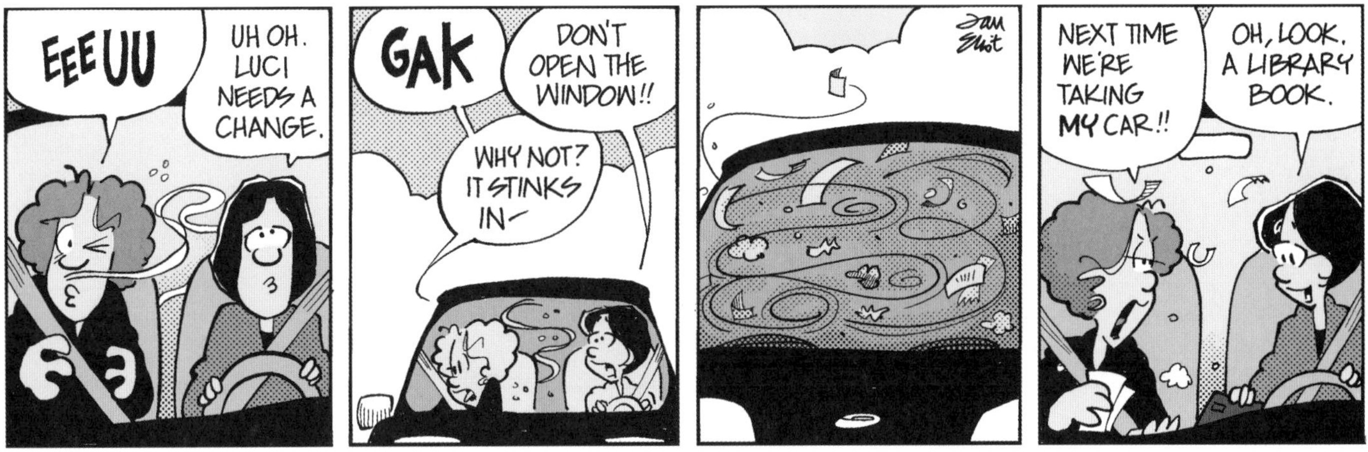
EEEUU
UH OH. LUCI NEEDS A CHANGE.
GAK
DON'T OPEN THE WINDOW!!
WHY NOT? IT STINKS IN—
NEXT TIME WE'RE TAKING MY CAR!!
OH, LOOK. A LIBRARY BOOK.

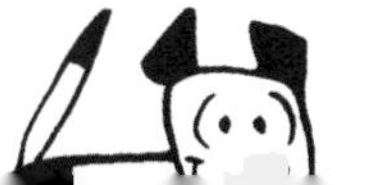

Stone Soup

Z Z
BIP
BIP BIP
BIP BIP
BIP
BIP–
–PLINK
WELCOME TO THE NIGHTLY NEWS–
ONE OF THOSE TIMES YOU'RE SO **GRATEFUL** YOU'RE ALONE.

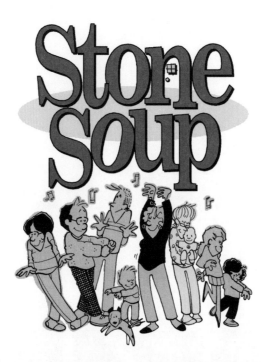

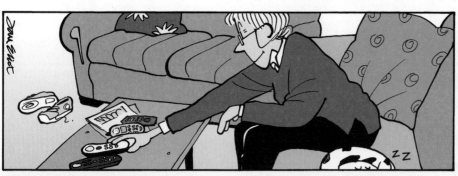

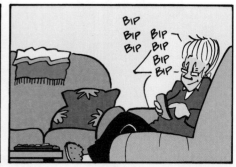

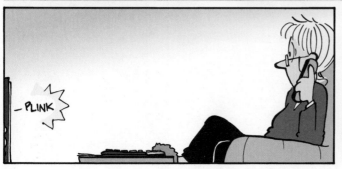

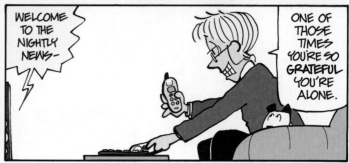

Stone Soup

ANDY? YOU SAID YOU'D HELP ME IN THE YARD!
I WANT TO HELP, UNCLE WALLY... BUT I WAS JUST ABOUT TO UPDATE MY ONLINE PROFILE!
YEAH, UNCLE WALLY. IF YOU DON'T UPDATE ... THINGS REALLY GET OUT OF HAND!!
OH...
AND HOW COULD YOU EXIST IF YOU COULDN'T POST YOUR MOST PRIVATE THOUGHTS FOR YOUR 50,000 CLOSEST "FRIENDS"??
BY THE WAY..., WHAT'S THIS?
OUR ROUTER! WE NEED THAT TO GET ONLINE!
FOR AN OLD GUY, HE'S PRETTY SAVVY.
!★@

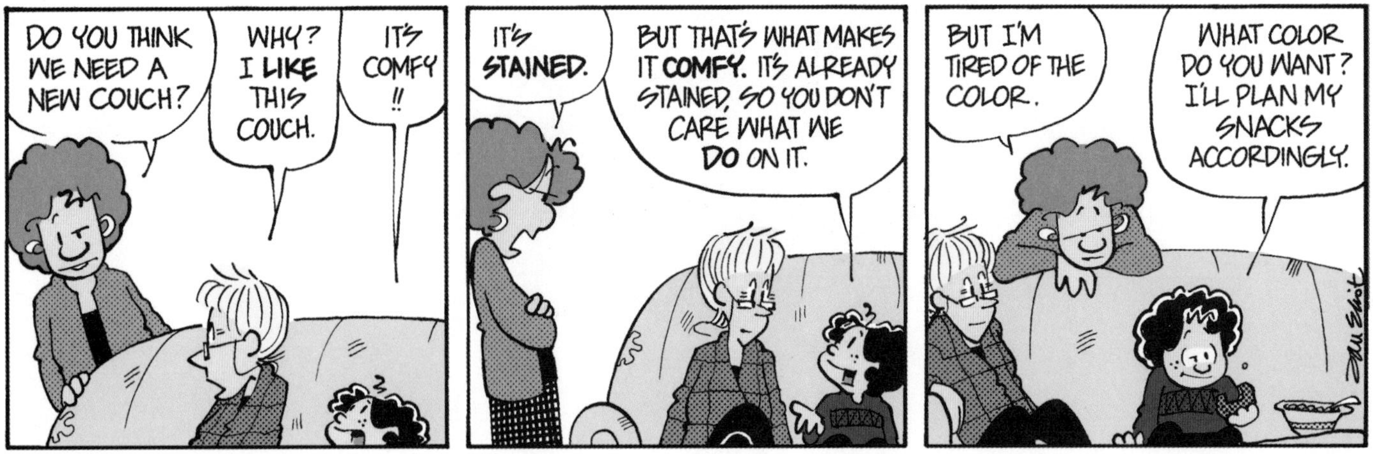
DO YOU THINK WE NEED A NEW COUCH?
WHY? I **LIKE** THIS COUCH.
IT'S COMFY !!
IT'S **STAINED.**
BUT THAT'S WHAT MAKES IT **COMFY.** IT'S ALREADY STAINED, SO YOU DON'T CARE WHAT WE **DO** ON IT.
BUT I'M TIRED OF THE COLOR.
WHAT COLOR DO YOU WANT? I'LL PLAN MY SNACKS ACCORDINGLY.

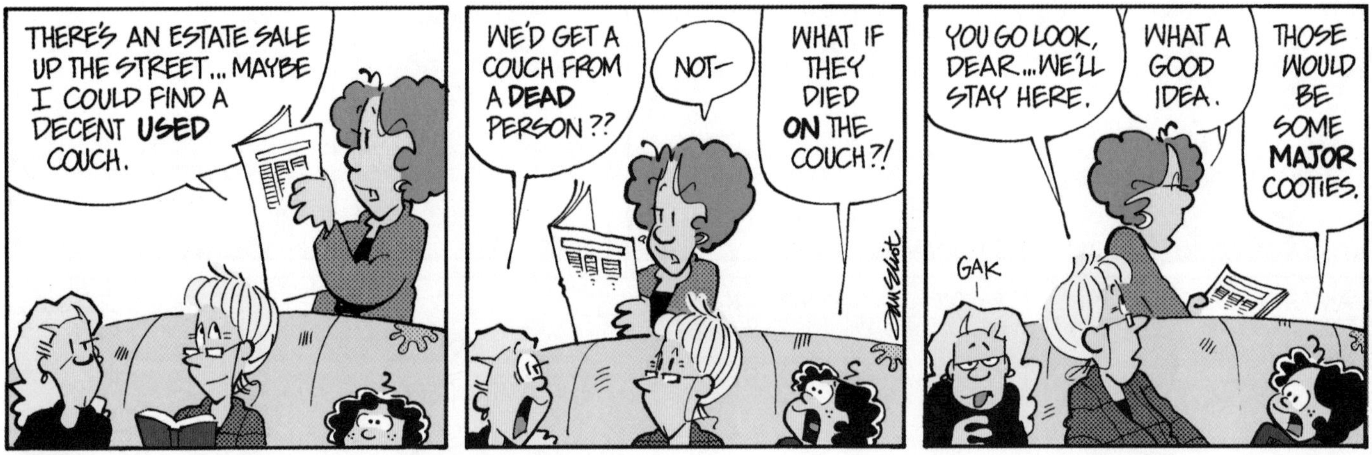
THERE'S AN ESTATE SALE UP THE STREET... MAYBE I COULD FIND A DECENT **USED** COUCH.
WE'D GET A COUCH FROM A **DEAD** PERSON??
NOT-
WHAT IF THEY DIED **ON** THE COUCH?!
GAK
YOU GO LOOK, DEAR... WE'LL STAY HERE.
WHAT A GOOD IDEA.
THOSE WOULD BE SOME **MAJOR** COOTIES.

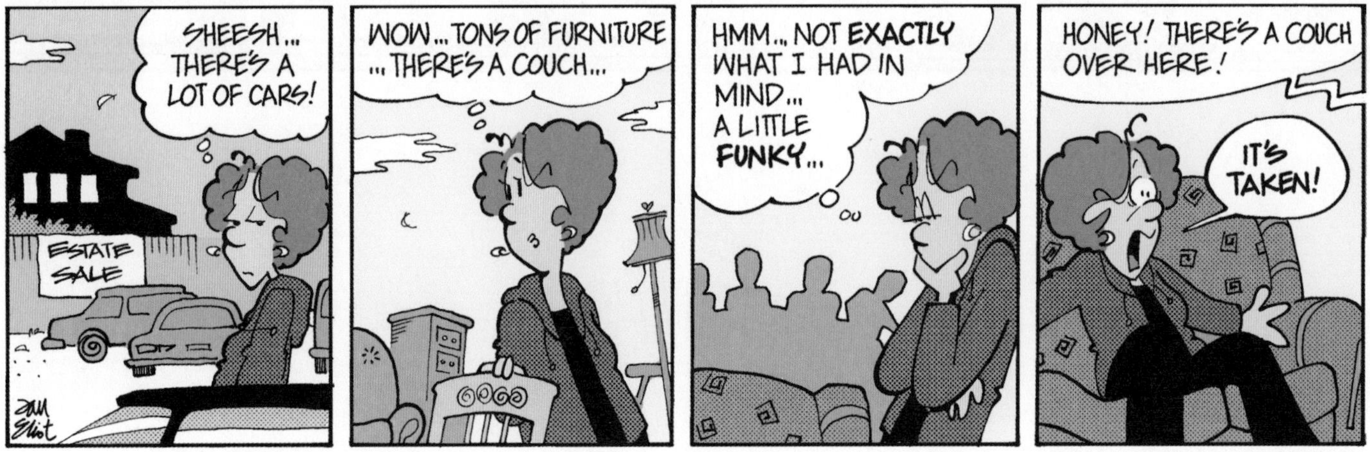
SHEESH... THERE'S A LOT OF CARS!
ESTATE SALE
WOW... TONS OF FURNITURE ... THERE'S A COUCH...
HMM... NOT **EXACTLY** WHAT I HAD IN MIND... A LITTLE **FUNKY**...
HONEY! THERE'S A COUCH OVER HERE!
IT'S TAKEN!

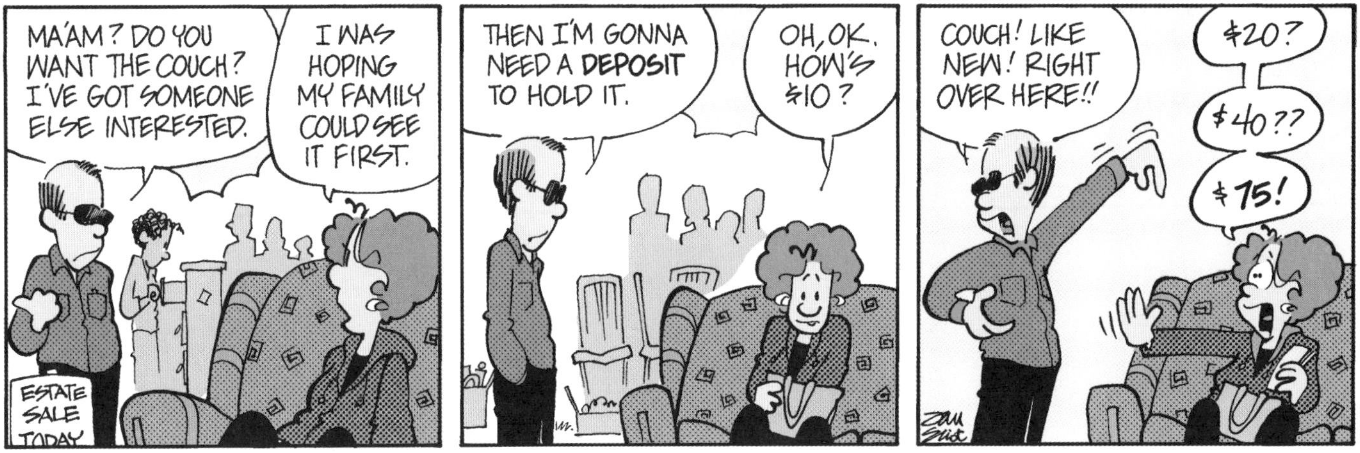
MA'AM? DO YOU WANT THE COUCH? I'VE GOT SOMEONE ELSE INTERESTED.
I WAS HOPING MY FAMILY COULD SEE IT FIRST.
ESTATE SALE TODAY
THEN I'M GONNA NEED A **DEPOSIT** TO HOLD IT.
OH, OK. HOW'S $10?
COUCH! LIKE NEW! RIGHT OVER HERE!!
$20?
$40??
$75!

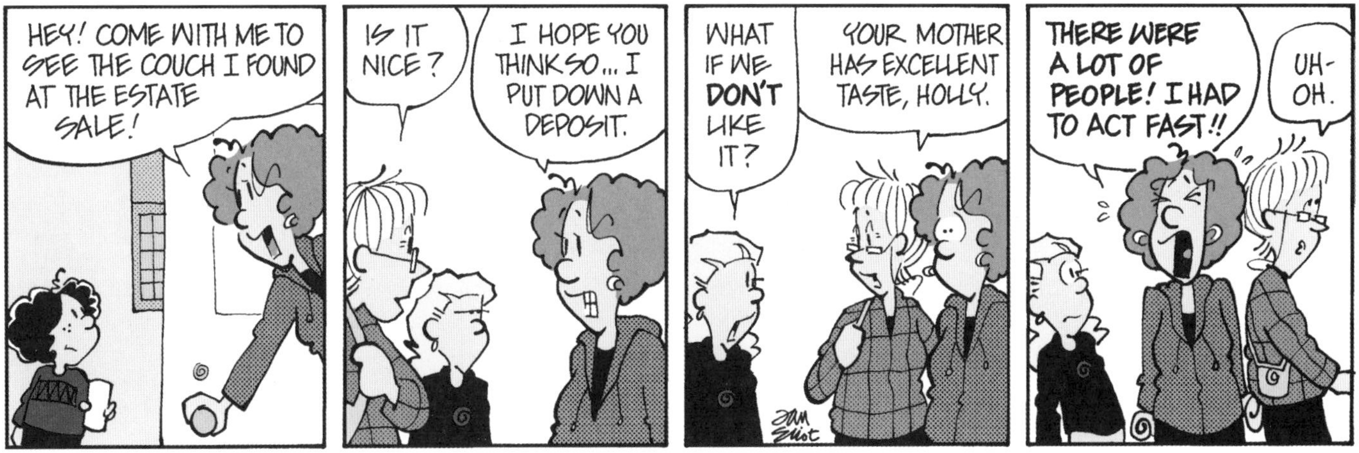
HEY! COME WITH ME TO SEE THE COUCH I FOUND AT THE ESTATE SALE!
IS IT NICE?
I HOPE YOU THINK SO... I PUT DOWN A DEPOSIT.
WHAT IF WE **DON'T** LIKE IT?
YOUR MOTHER HAS EXCELLENT TASTE, HOLLY.
THERE WERE A LOT OF PEOPLE! I HAD TO ACT FAST!!
UH-OH.

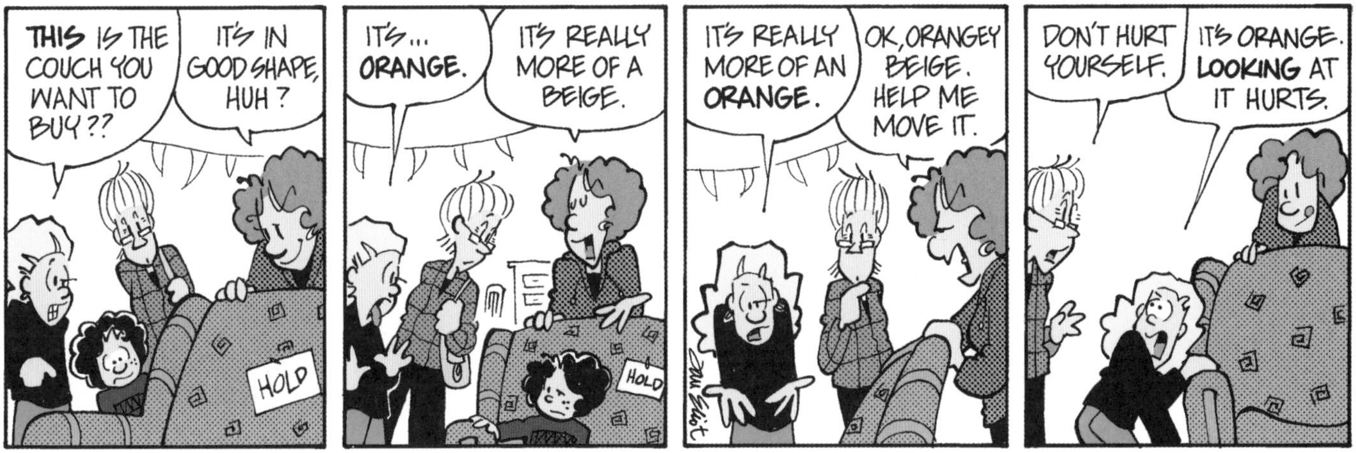
THIS IS THE COUCH YOU WANT TO BUY??
IT'S IN GOOD SHAPE, HUH?
HOLD
IT'S... **ORANGE.**
IT'S REALLY MORE OF A BEIGE.
HOLD
IT'S REALLY MORE OF AN **ORANGE.**
OK, ORANGEY BEIGE. HELP ME MOVE IT.
DON'T HURT YOURSELF.
IT'S ORANGE. **LOOKING** AT IT HURTS.

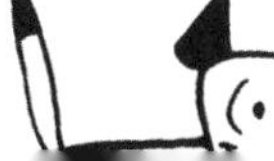

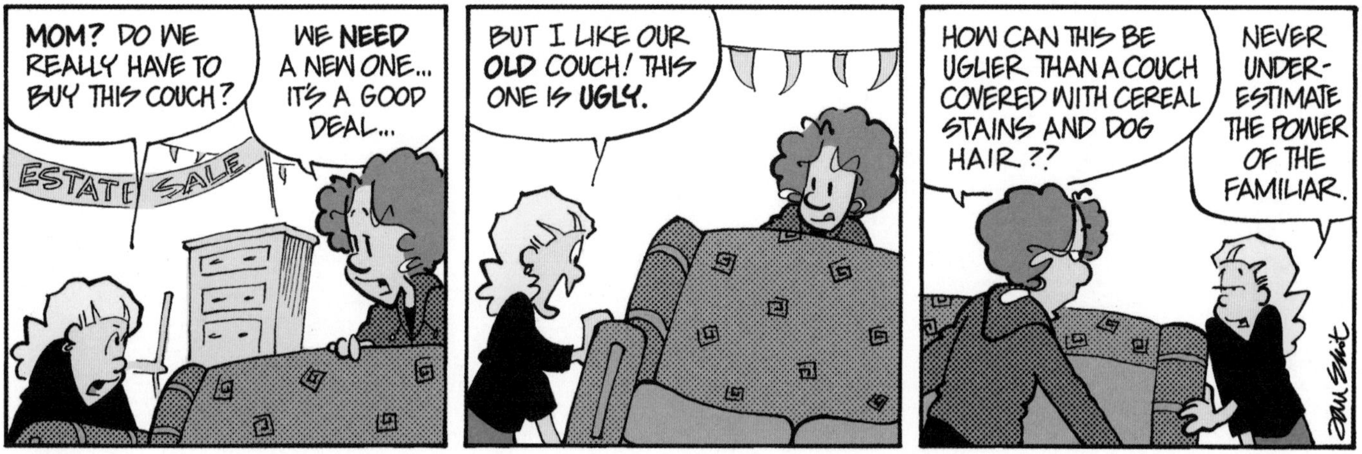
MOM? DO WE REALLY HAVE TO BUY THIS COUCH?
WE NEED A NEW ONE... IT'S A GOOD DEAL...
ESTATE SALE
BUT I LIKE OUR OLD COUCH! THIS ONE IS UGLY.
HOW CAN THIS BE UGLIER THAN A COUCH COVERED WITH CEREAL STAINS AND DOG HAIR??
NEVER UNDER-ESTIMATE THE POWER OF THE FAMILIAR.

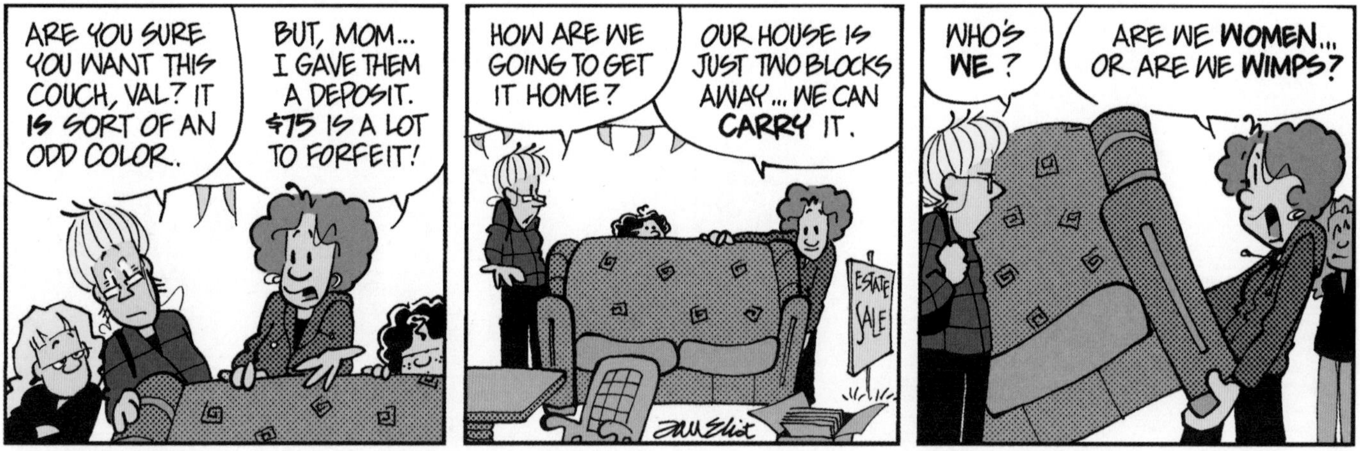
ARE YOU SURE YOU WANT THIS COUCH, VAL? IT IS SORT OF AN ODD COLOR.
BUT, MOM... I GAVE THEM A DEPOSIT. $75 IS A LOT TO FORFEIT!
HOW ARE WE GOING TO GET IT HOME?
OUR HOUSE IS JUST TWO BLOCKS AWAY... WE CAN CARRY IT.
ESTATE SALE
WHO'S WE?
ARE WE WOMEN... OR ARE WE WIMPS?

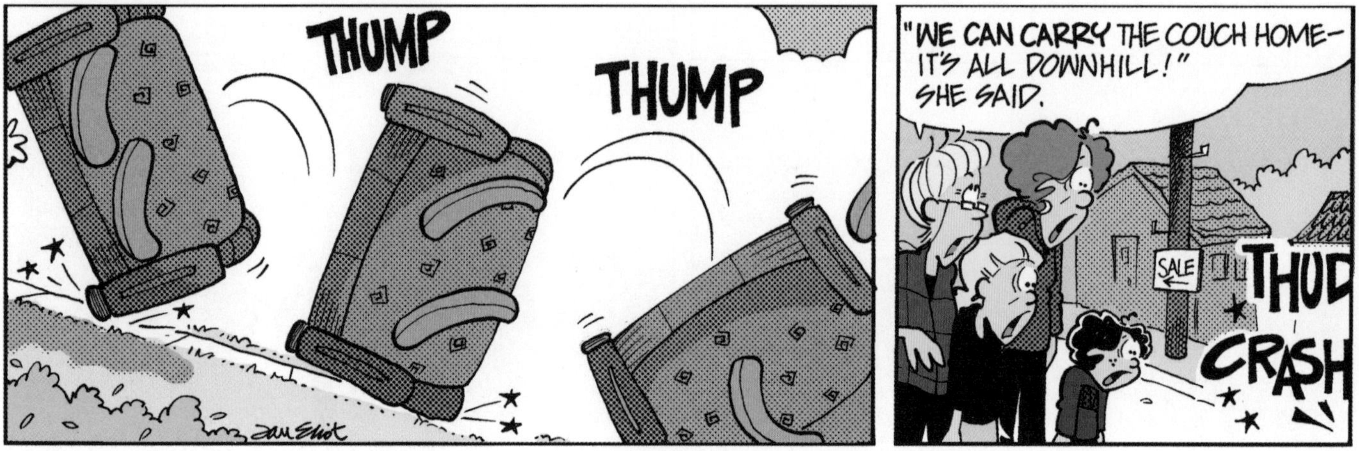
THUMP
THUMP
"WE CAN CARRY THE COUCH HOME- IT'S ALL DOWNHILL!" SHE SAID.
SALE
THUD
CRASH

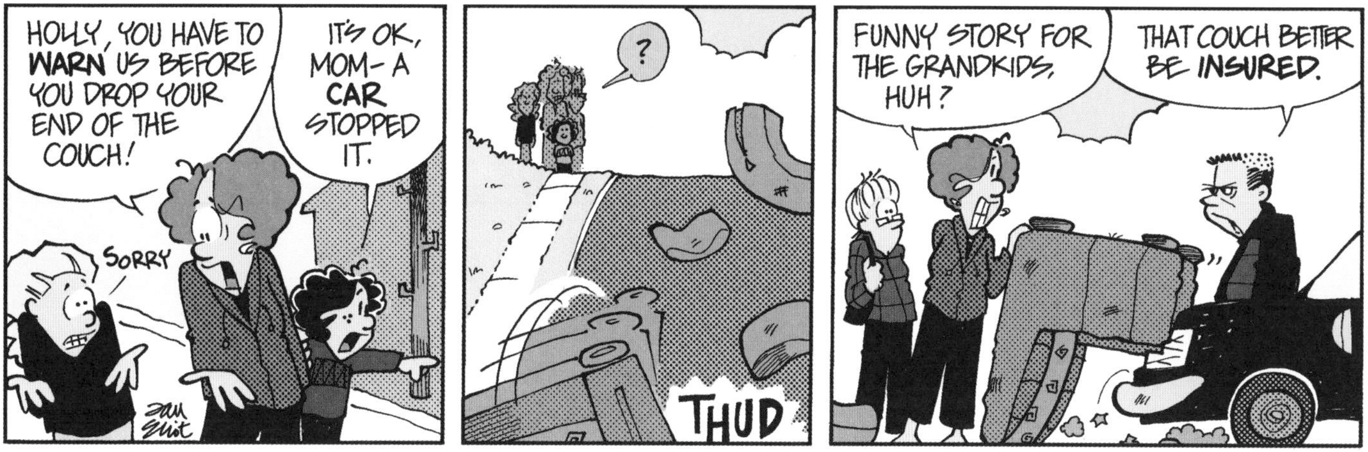
HOLLY, YOU HAVE TO WARN US BEFORE YOU DROP YOUR END OF THE COUCH!
SORRY
IT'S OK, MOM– A CAR STOPPED IT.
?
THUD
FUNNY STORY FOR THE GRANDKIDS, HUH?
THAT COUCH BETTER BE INSURED.

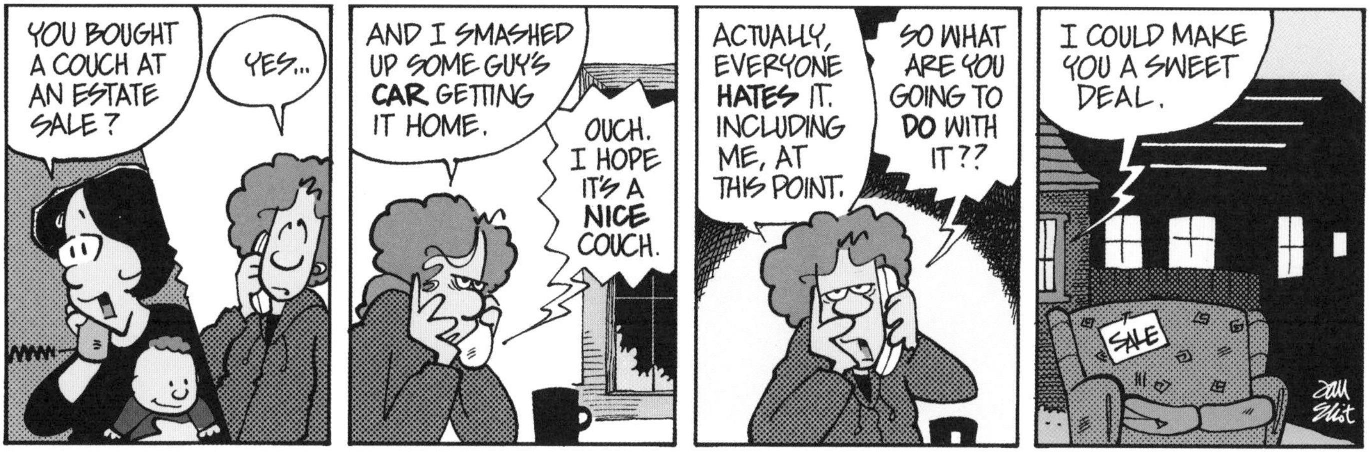
YOU BOUGHT A COUCH AT AN ESTATE SALE?
YES...
AND I SMASHED UP SOME GUY'S CAR GETTING IT HOME.
OUCH. I HOPE IT'S A NICE COUCH.
ACTUALLY, EVERYONE HATES IT. INCLUDING ME, AT THIS POINT.
SO WHAT ARE YOU GOING TO DO WITH IT??
I COULD MAKE YOU A SWEET DEAL.
SALE

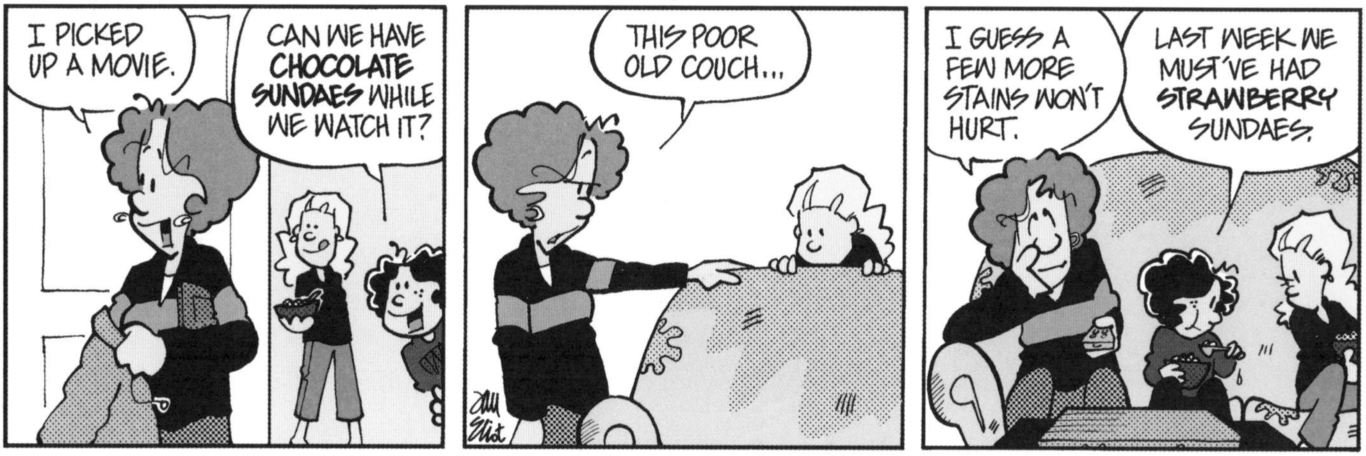
I PICKED UP A MOVIE.
CAN WE HAVE CHOCOLATE SUNDAES WHILE WE WATCH IT?
THIS POOR OLD COUCH...
I GUESS A FEW MORE STAINS WON'T HURT.
LAST WEEK WE MUST'VE HAD STRAWBERRY SUNDAES.

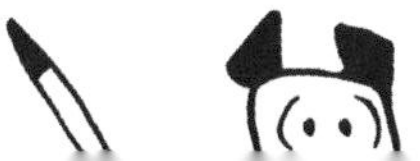

Stone Soup

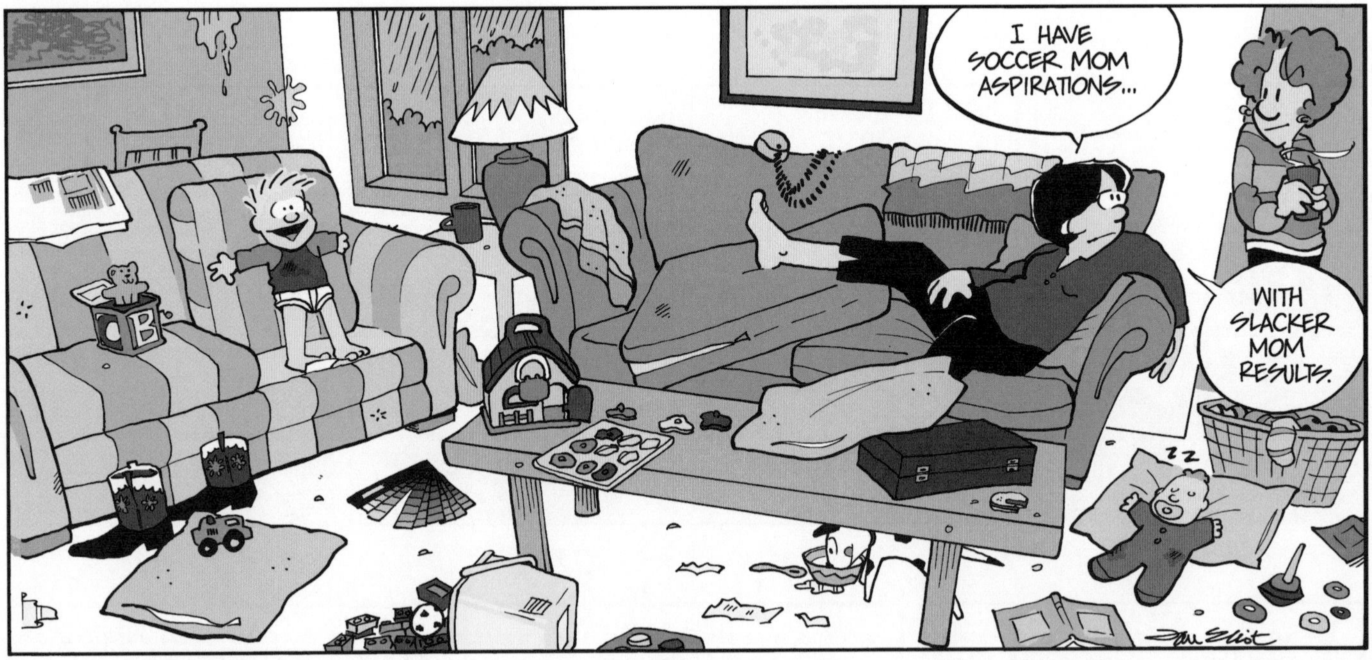
I HAVE SOCCER MOM ASPIRATIONS...
WITH SLACKER MOM RESULTS.

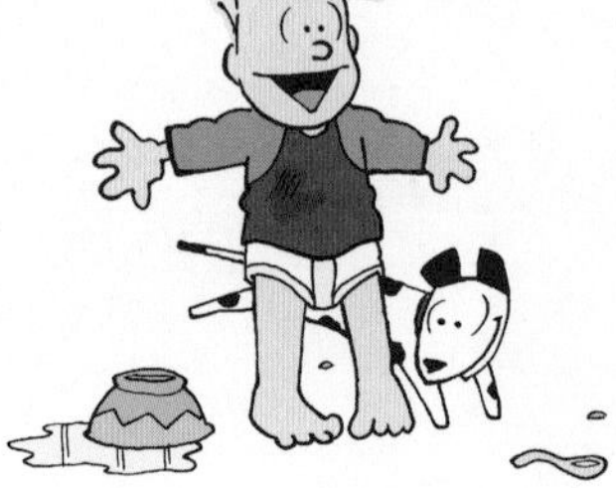

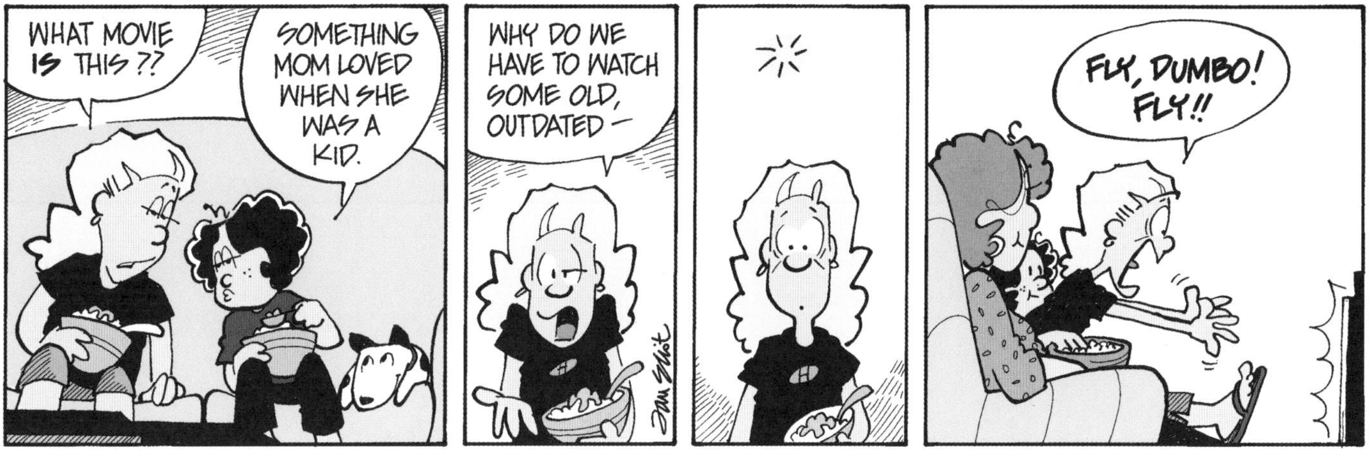
WHAT MOVIE IS THIS??
SOMETHING MOM LOVED WHEN SHE WAS A KID.
WHY DO WE HAVE TO WATCH SOME OLD, OUTDATED –
FLY, DUMBO! FLY!!

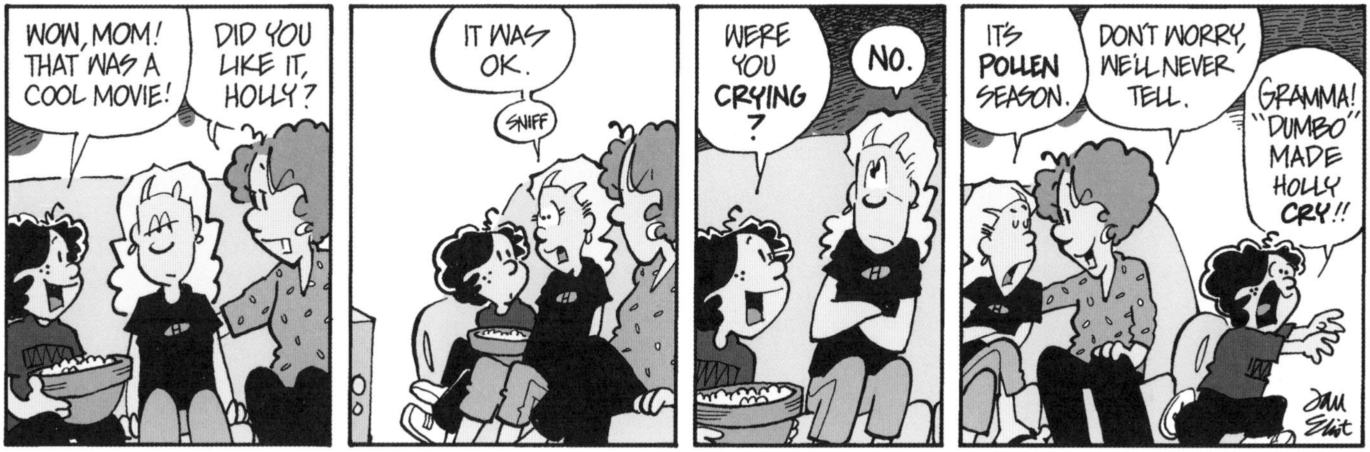
WOW, MOM! THAT WAS A COOL MOVIE!
DID YOU LIKE IT, HOLLY?
IT WAS OK.
SNIFF
WERE YOU CRYING?
NO.
IT'S POLLEN SEASON.
DON'T WORRY, WE'LL NEVER TELL.
GRAMMA! "DUMBO" MADE HOLLY CRY!!

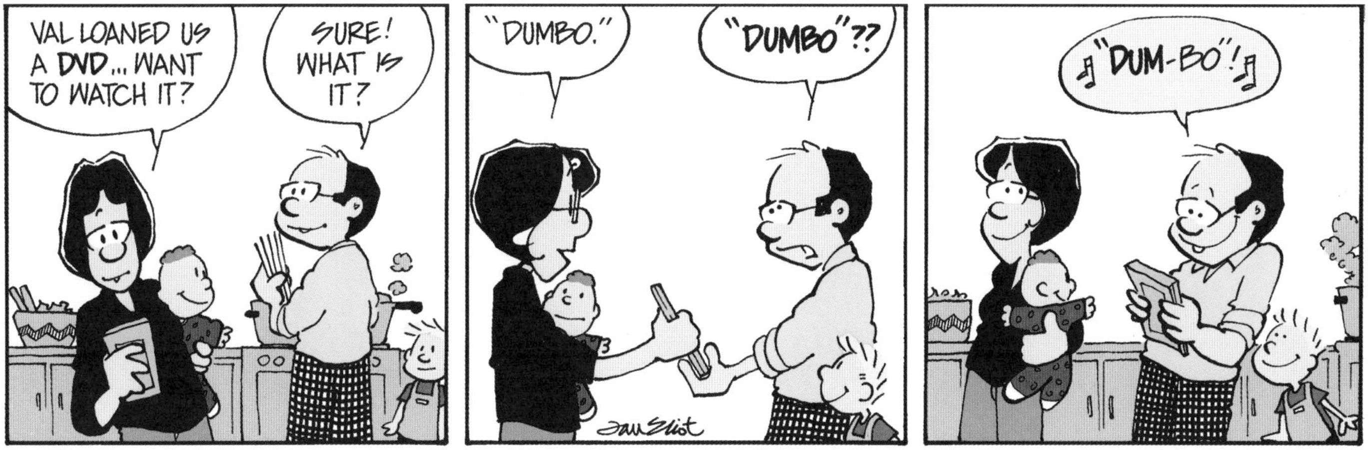
VAL LOANED US A DVD... WANT TO WATCH IT?
SURE! WHAT IS IT?
"DUMBO."
"DUMBO"??
"DUM-BO"!

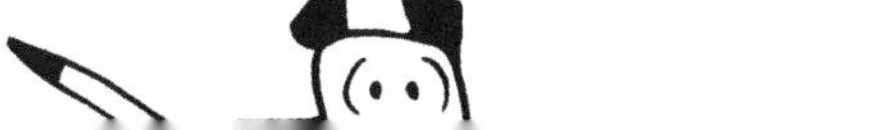

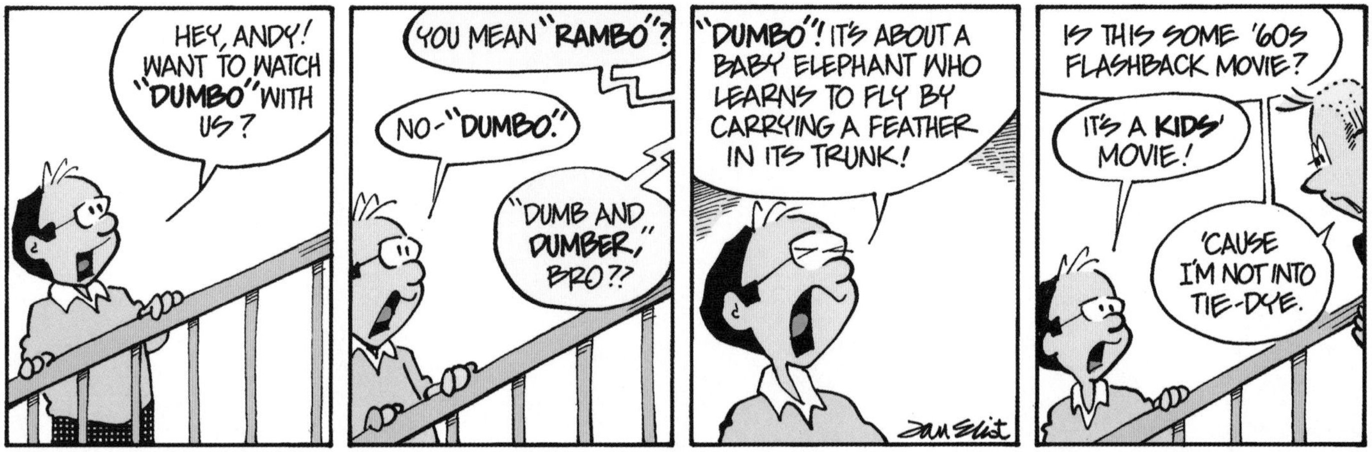
HEY, ANDY! WANT TO WATCH "DUMBO" WITH US?
YOU MEAN "RAMBO"?
NO- "DUMBO."
"DUMB AND DUMBER," BRO??
"DUMBO"! IT'S ABOUT A BABY ELEPHANT WHO LEARNS TO FLY BY CARRYING A FEATHER IN ITS TRUNK!
IS THIS SOME '60S FLASHBACK MOVIE?
IT'S A KIDS' MOVIE!
'CAUSE I'M NOT INTO TIE-DYE.

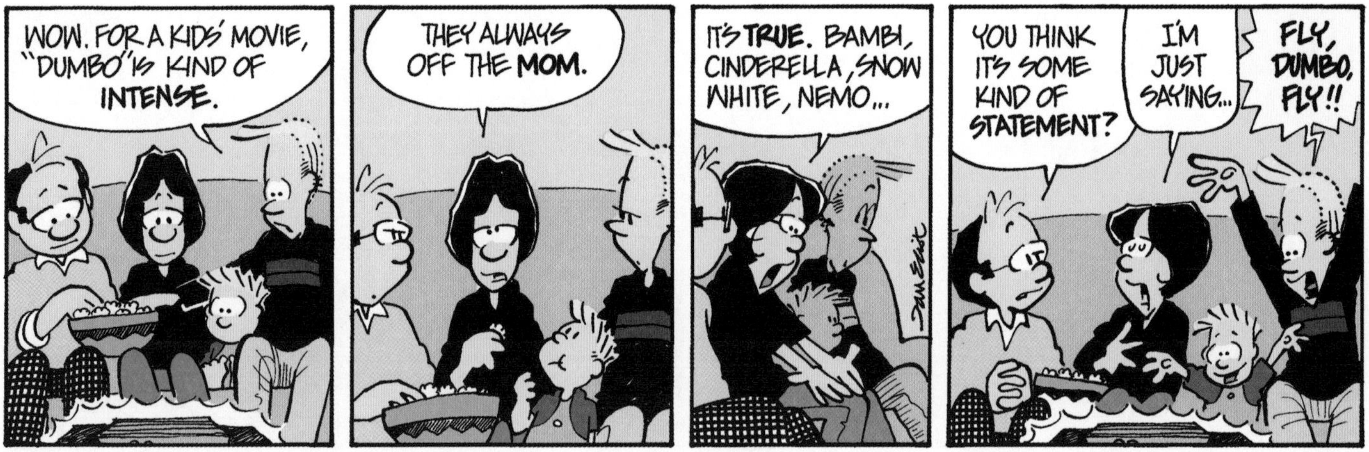
WOW. FOR A KIDS' MOVIE, "DUMBO" IS KIND OF INTENSE.
THEY ALWAYS OFF THE MOM.
IT'S TRUE. BAMBI, CINDERELLA, SNOW WHITE, NEMO...
YOU THINK IT'S SOME KIND OF STATEMENT?
I'M JUST SAYING...
FLY, DUMBO, FLY!!

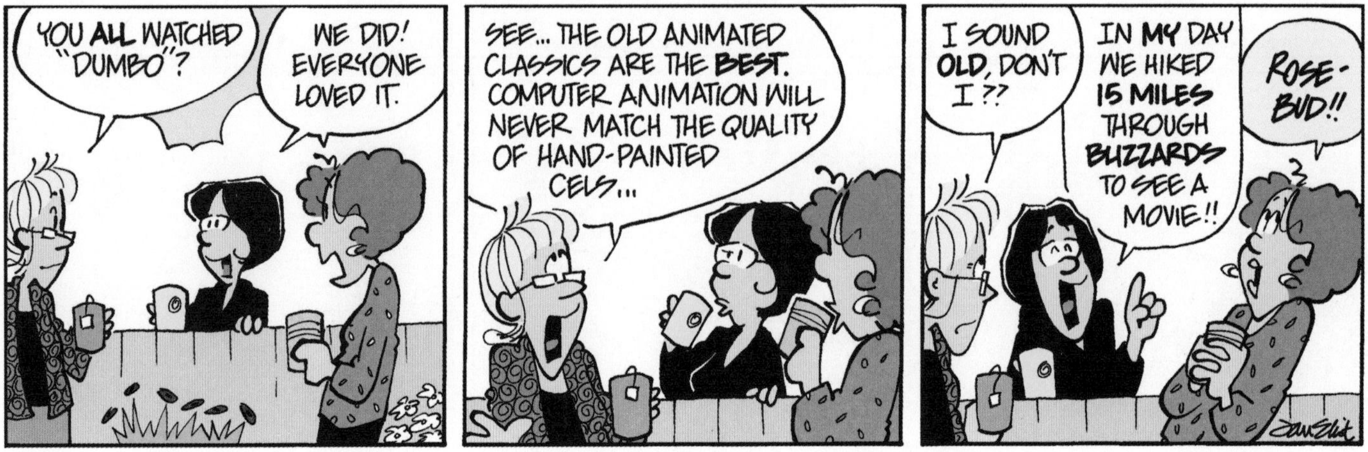
YOU ALL WATCHED "DUMBO"?
WE DID! EVERYONE LOVED IT.
SEE... THE OLD ANIMATED CLASSICS ARE THE BEST. COMPUTER ANIMATION WILL NEVER MATCH THE QUALITY OF HAND-PAINTED CELS...
I SOUND OLD, DON'T I??
IN MY DAY WE HIKED 15 MILES THROUGH BLIZZARDS TO SEE A MOVIE!!
ROSE-BUD!!

Stone Soup

I KNOW YOU HAVE A DOUGHNUT.

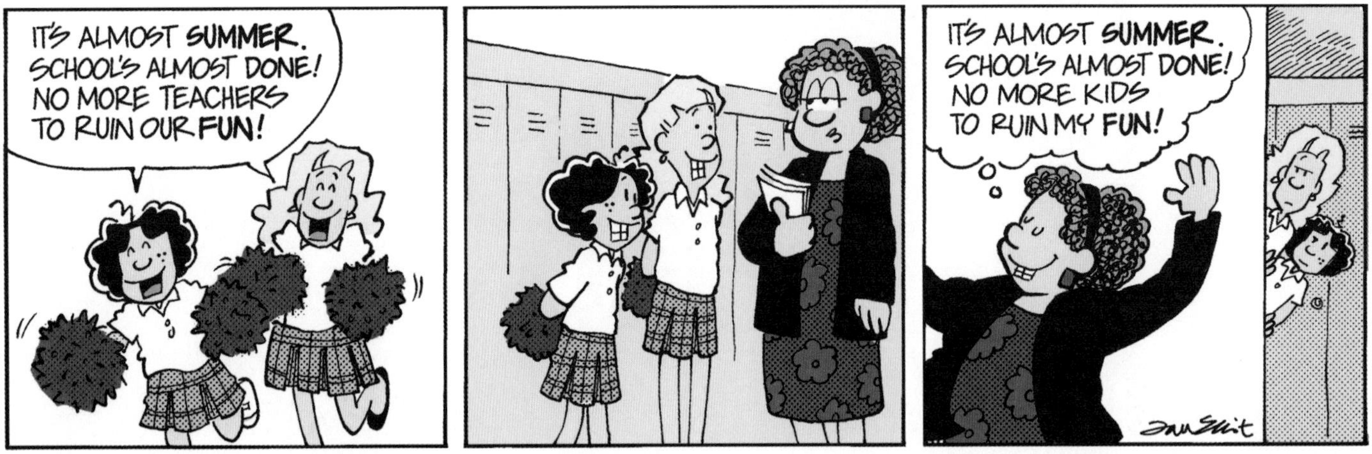
IT'S ALMOST SUMMER. SCHOOL'S ALMOST DONE! NO MORE TEACHERS TO RUIN OUR FUN!
IT'S ALMOST SUMMER. SCHOOL'S ALMOST DONE! NO MORE KIDS TO RUIN MY FUN!

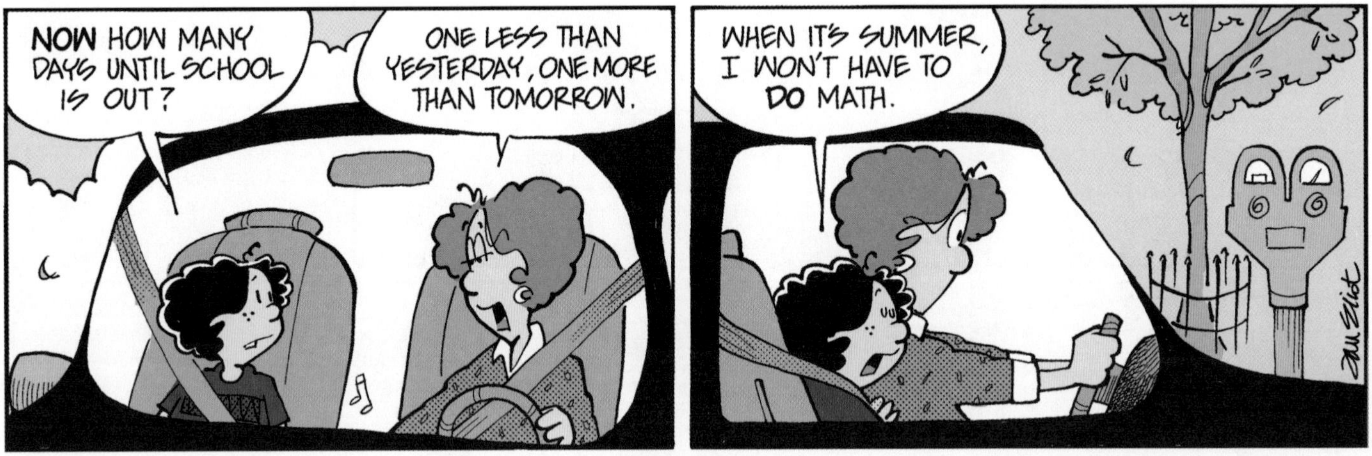
NOW HOW MANY DAYS UNTIL SCHOOL IS OUT?
ONE LESS THAN YESTERDAY, ONE MORE THAN TOMORROW.
WHEN IT'S SUMMER, I WON'T HAVE TO DO MATH.

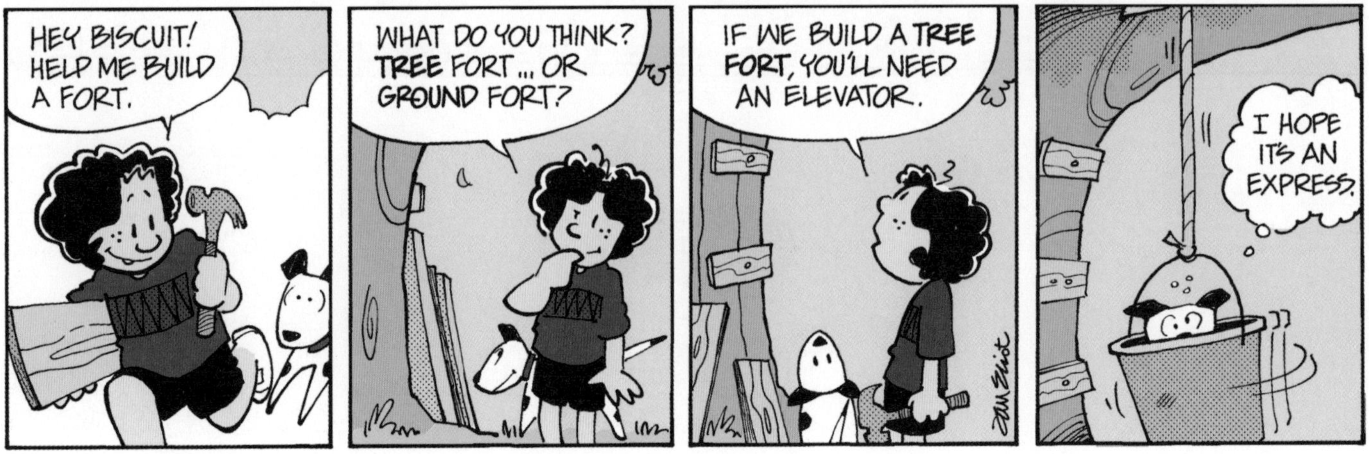
HEY BISCUIT! HELP ME BUILD A FORT.
WHAT DO YOU THINK? TREE FORT... OR GROUND FORT?
IF WE BUILD A TREE FORT, YOU'LL NEED AN ELEVATOR.
I HOPE IT'S AN EXPRESS.

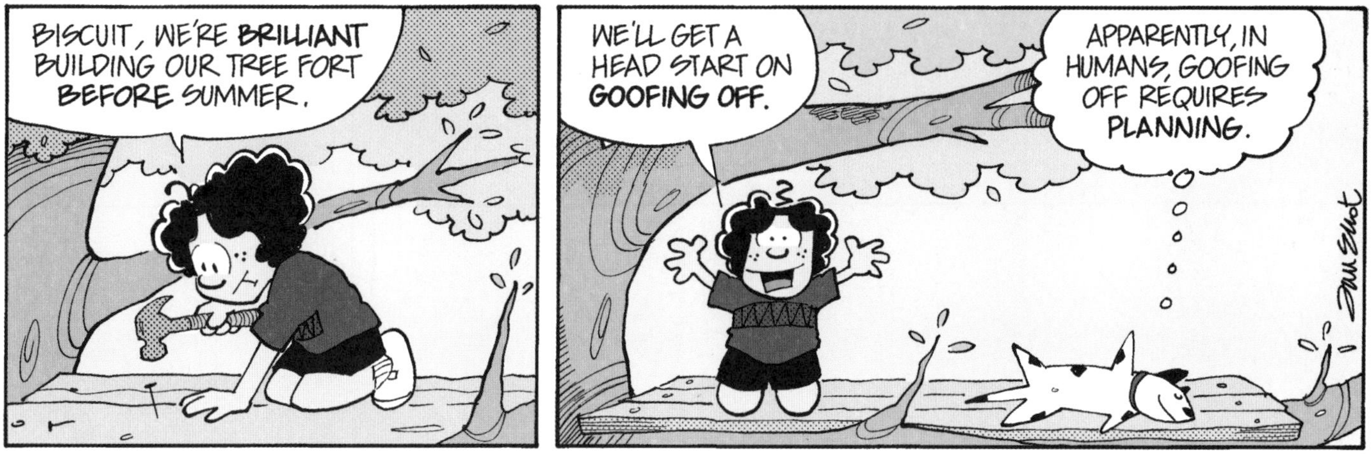
BISCUIT, WE'RE **BRILLIANT** BUILDING OUR TREE FORT **BEFORE** SUMMER.
WE'LL GET A HEAD START ON **GOOFING OFF.**
APPARENTLY, IN HUMANS, GOOFING OFF REQUIRES **PLANNING.**

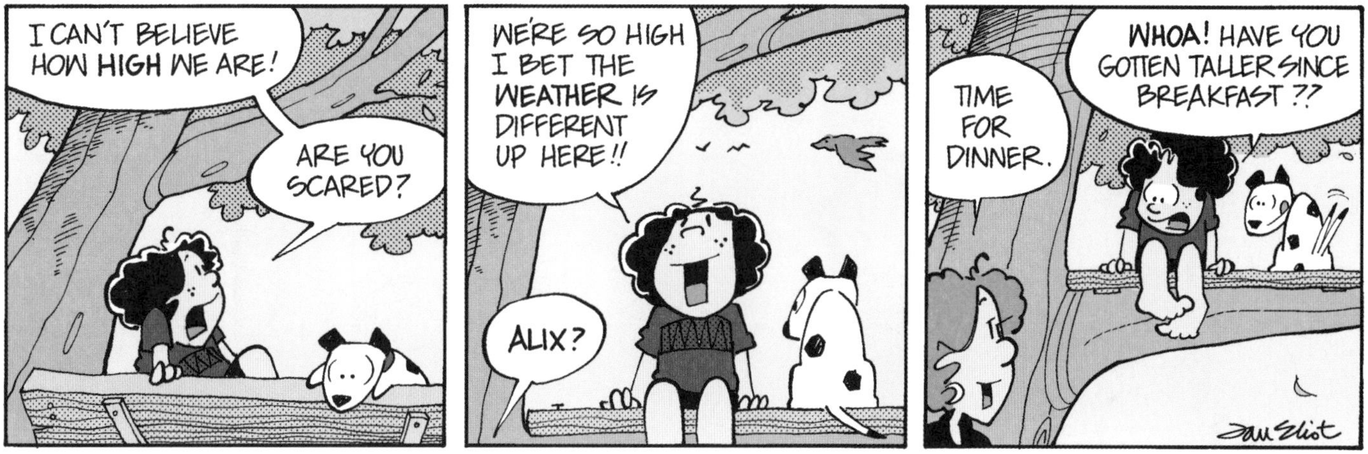
I CAN'T BELIEVE HOW **HIGH** WE ARE!
ARE YOU SCARED?
WE'RE SO HIGH I BET THE **WEATHER** IS DIFFERENT UP HERE!!
ALIX?
TIME FOR DINNER.
WHOA! HAVE YOU GOTTEN TALLER SINCE BREAKFAST??

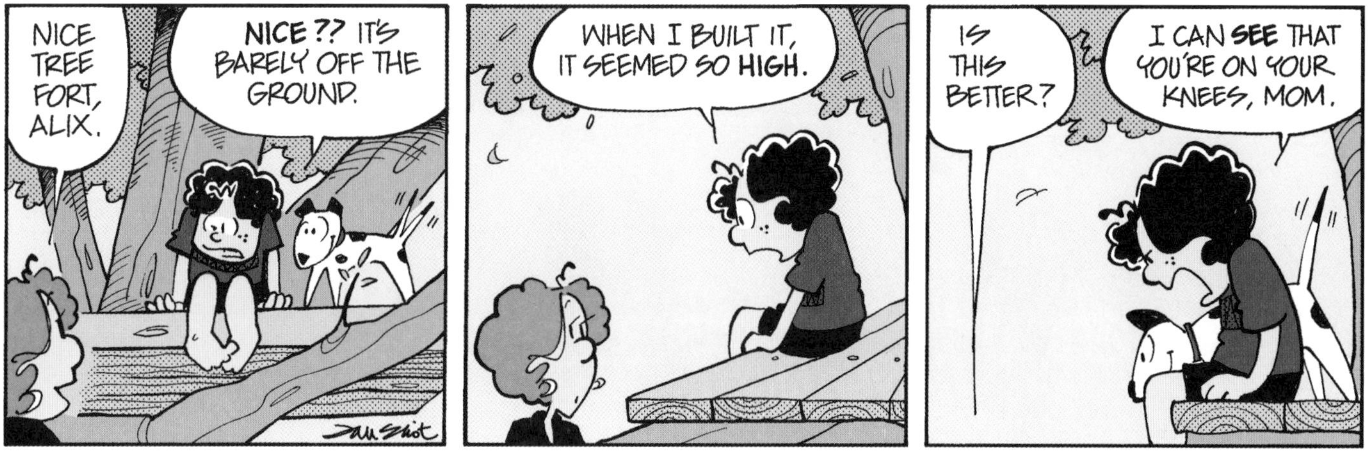
NICE TREE FORT, ALIX.
NICE?? IT'S BARELY OFF THE GROUND.
WHEN I BUILT IT, IT SEEMED SO **HIGH.**
IS THIS BETTER?
I CAN **SEE** THAT YOU'RE ON YOUR KNEES, MOM.

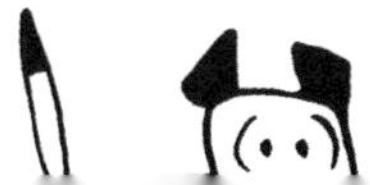

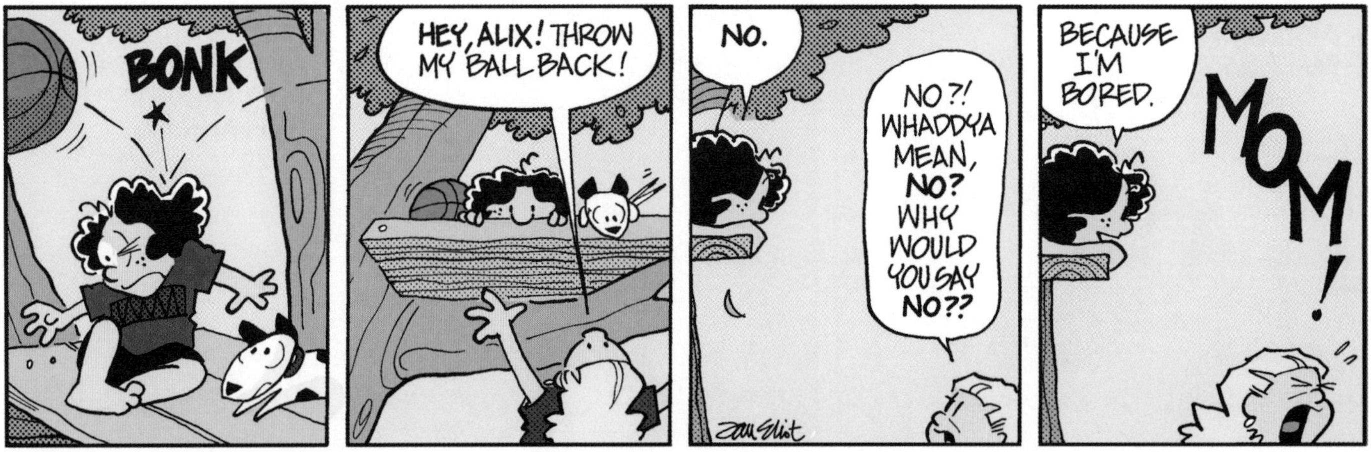
BONK
HEY, ALIX! THROW MY BALL BACK!
NO.
NO?! WHADDYA MEAN, NO? WHY WOULD YOU SAY NO??
BECAUSE I'M BORED.
MOM!

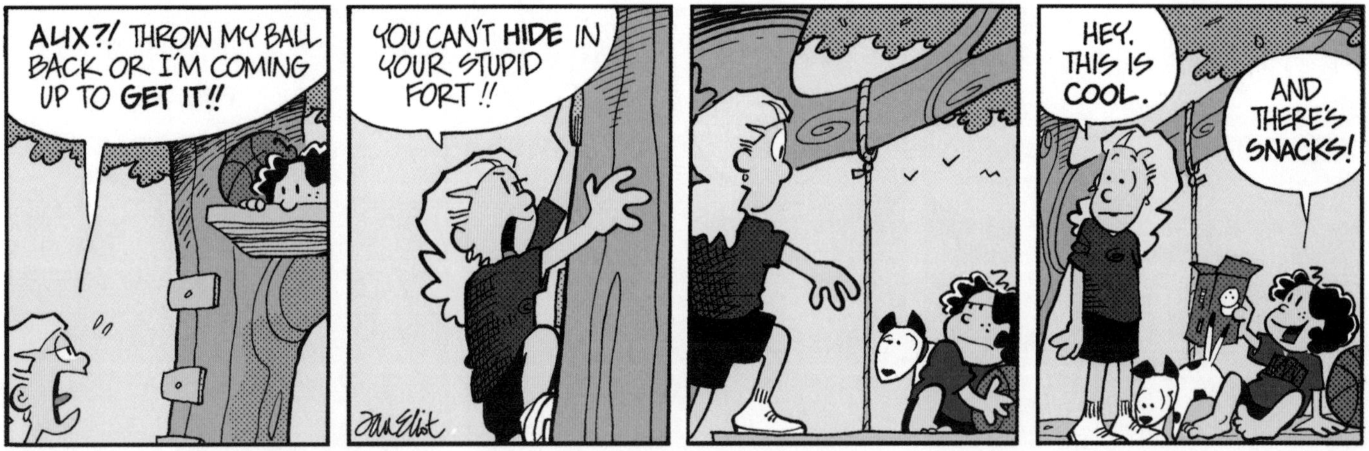
ALIX?! THROW MY BALL BACK OR I'M COMING UP TO GET IT!!
YOU CAN'T HIDE IN YOUR STUPID FORT!!
HEY. THIS IS COOL.
AND THERE'S SNACKS!

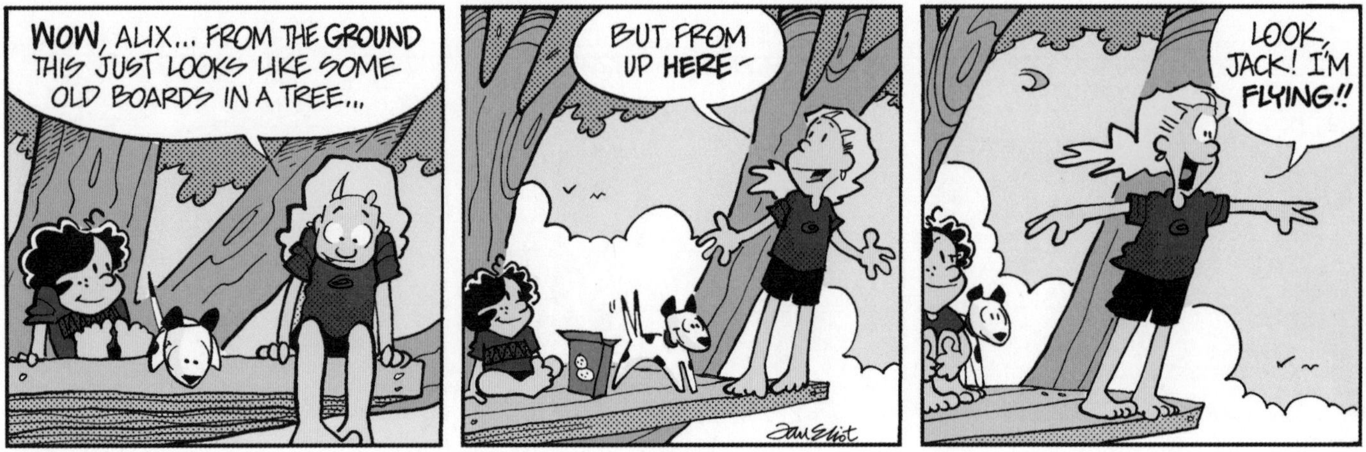
WOW, ALIX... FROM THE GROUND THIS JUST LOOKS LIKE SOME OLD BOARDS IN A TREE...
BUT FROM UP HERE -
LOOK, JACK! I'M FLYING!!

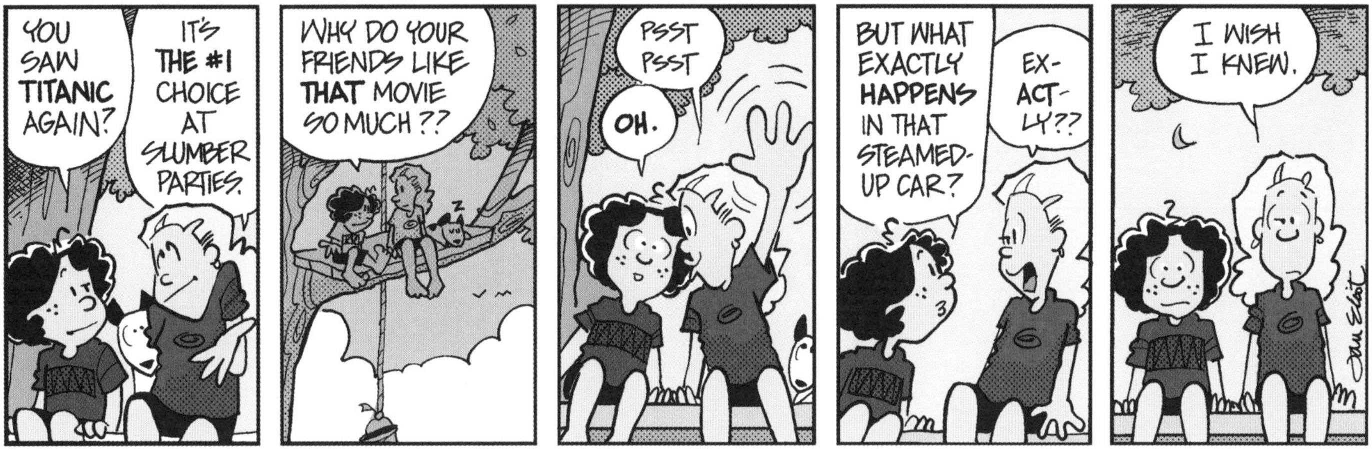
YOU SAW TITANIC AGAIN?
IT'S THE #1 CHOICE AT SLUMBER PARTIES.
WHY DO YOUR FRIENDS LIKE THAT MOVIE SO MUCH??
PSST PSST
OH.
BUT WHAT EXACTLY HAPPENS IN THAT STEAMED-UP CAR?
EX-ACT-LY??
I WISH I KNEW.
Jan Eliot

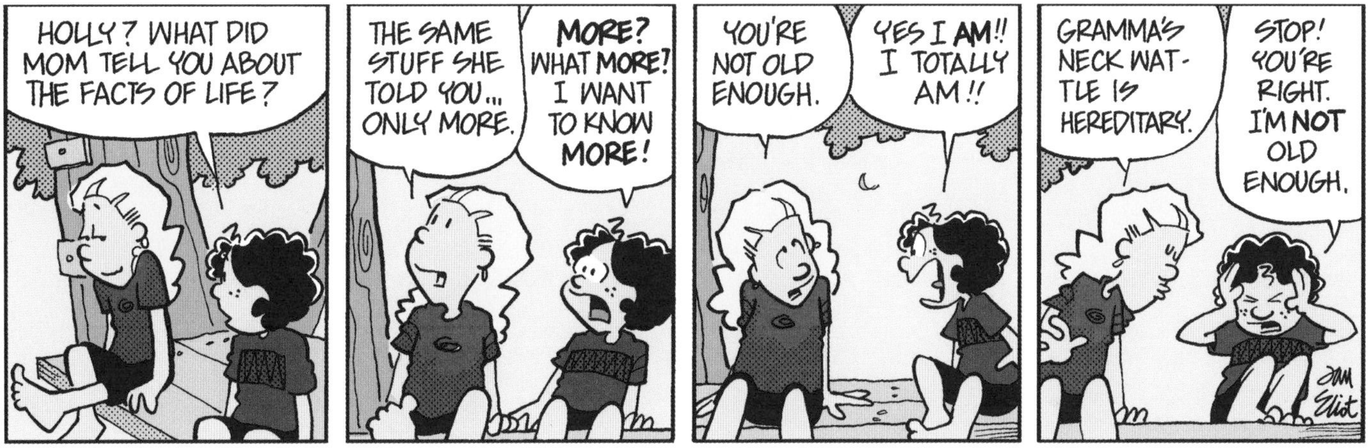
HOLLY? WHAT DID MOM TELL YOU ABOUT THE FACTS OF LIFE?
THE SAME STUFF SHE TOLD YOU... ONLY MORE.
MORE? WHAT MORE? I WANT TO KNOW MORE!
YOU'RE NOT OLD ENOUGH.
YES I AM!! I TOTALLY AM!!
GRAMMA'S NECK WAT-TLE IS HEREDITARY.
STOP! YOU'RE RIGHT. I'M NOT OLD ENOUGH.
Jan Eliot

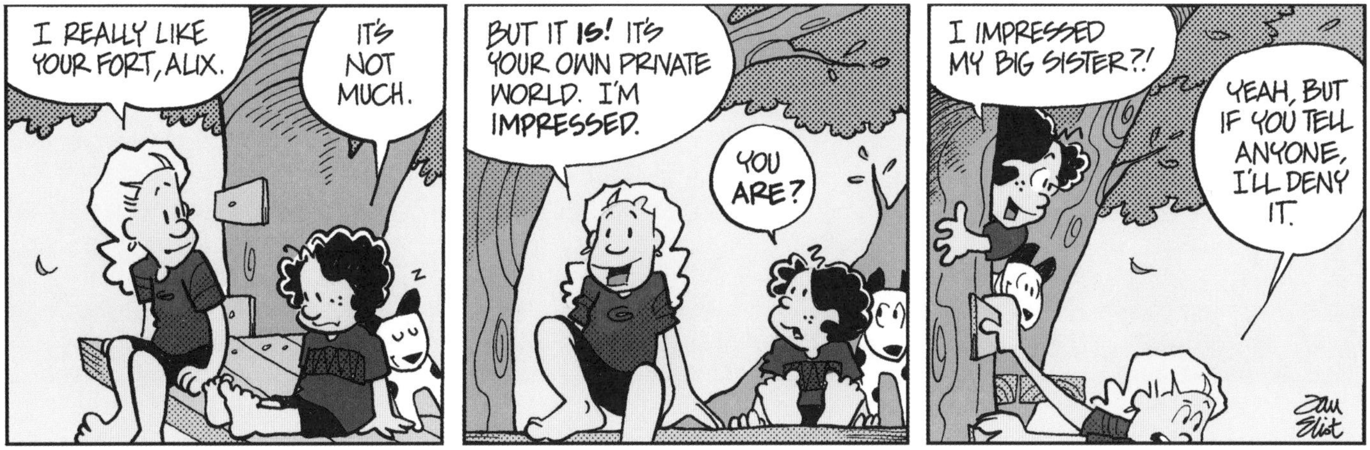
I REALLY LIKE YOUR FORT, ALIX.
IT'S NOT MUCH.
BUT IT IS! IT'S YOUR OWN PRIVATE WORLD. I'M IMPRESSED.
YOU ARE?
I IMPRESSED MY BIG SISTER?!
YEAH, BUT IF YOU TELL ANYONE, I'LL DENY IT.
Jan Eliot

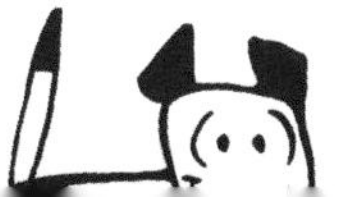

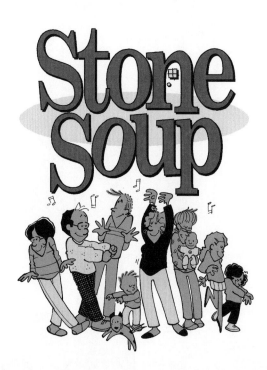

Stone Soup

AVERAGE AMERICANS EVERYWHERE ARE FEELING THE **PINCH** OF THE UNCERTAIN ECONOMY...

TONIGHT WE VISIT WITH THE HARRISONS.

WITH RISING OIL PRICES AND THE DECLINING VALUE OF THE DOLLAR...THE HARRISONS ARE ABANDONING THEIR PLANS FOR A **EUROPEAN TOUR** THIS SUMMER.

" WE HAVE TO SETTLE FOR EIGHT DAYS IN MARTHA'S VINEYARD INSTEAD!"

OMIGOSH, THOSE POOR, **POOR** PEOPLE.

SNIFF

I **LOVE** HER SARCASM WHEN IT'S NOT DIRECTED AT **US.**

NEXT THING YOU KNOW THEY'LL HAVE TO GIVE UP THE **HUMMER.**

Stone Soup

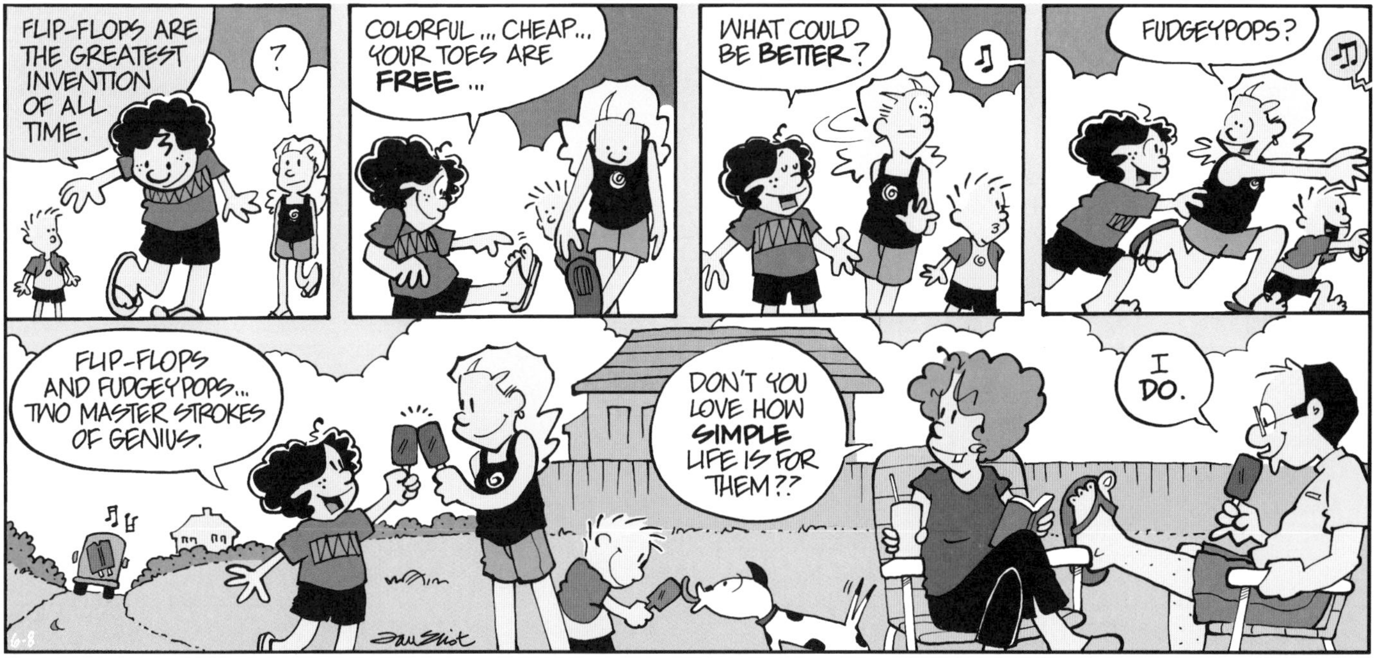
FLIP-FLOPS ARE THE GREATEST INVENTION OF ALL TIME.
?
COLORFUL ... CHEAP... YOUR TOES ARE **FREE** ...
WHAT COULD BE **BETTER**?
FUDGEYPOPS?
FLIP-FLOPS AND FUDGEYPOPS... TWO MASTER STROKES OF GENIUS.
DON'T YOU LOVE HOW **SIMPLE** LIFE IS FOR THEM??
I **DO**.
6-8

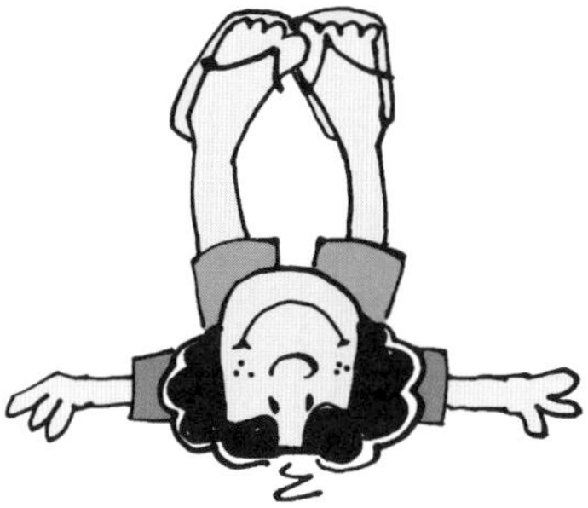

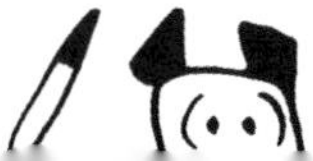

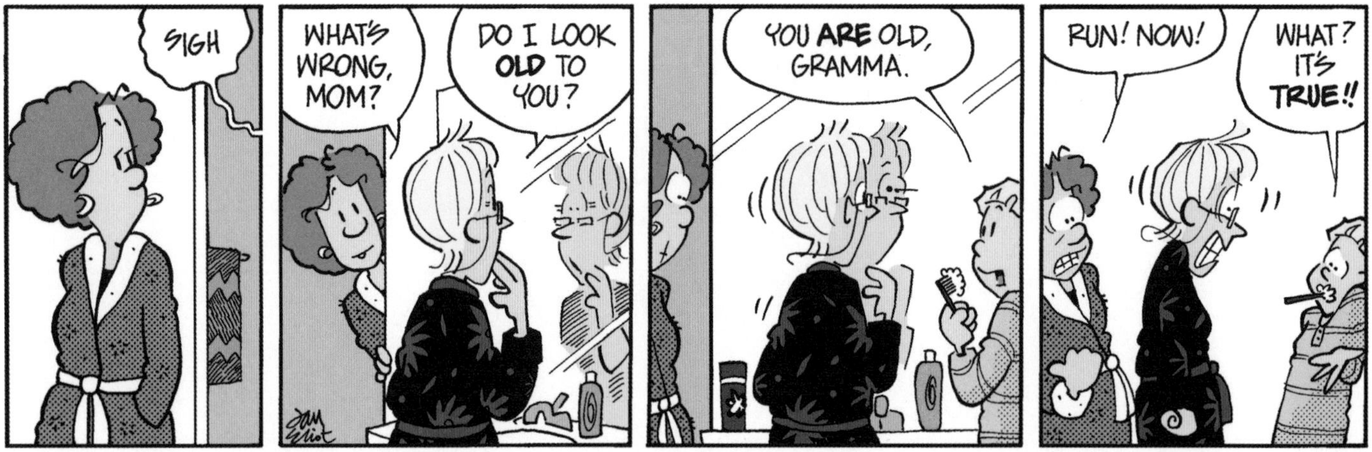
SIGH
WHAT'S WRONG, MOM?
DO I LOOK **OLD** TO YOU?
YOU **ARE** OLD, GRAMMA.
RUN! NOW!
WHAT? IT'S **TRUE!!**
Jan Eliot

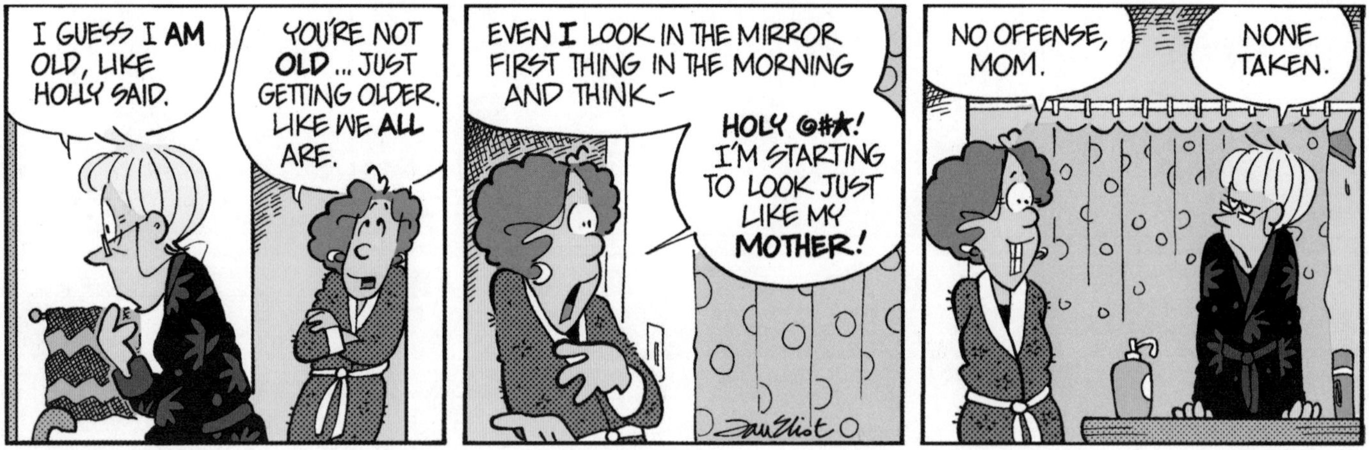
I GUESS I **AM** OLD, LIKE HOLLY SAID.
YOU'RE NOT **OLD**... JUST GETTING OLDER. LIKE WE **ALL** ARE.
EVEN **I** LOOK IN THE MIRROR FIRST THING IN THE MORNING AND THINK –
HOLY @#★! I'M STARTING TO LOOK JUST LIKE MY **MOTHER!**
NO OFFENSE, MOM.
NONE TAKEN.
Jan Eliot

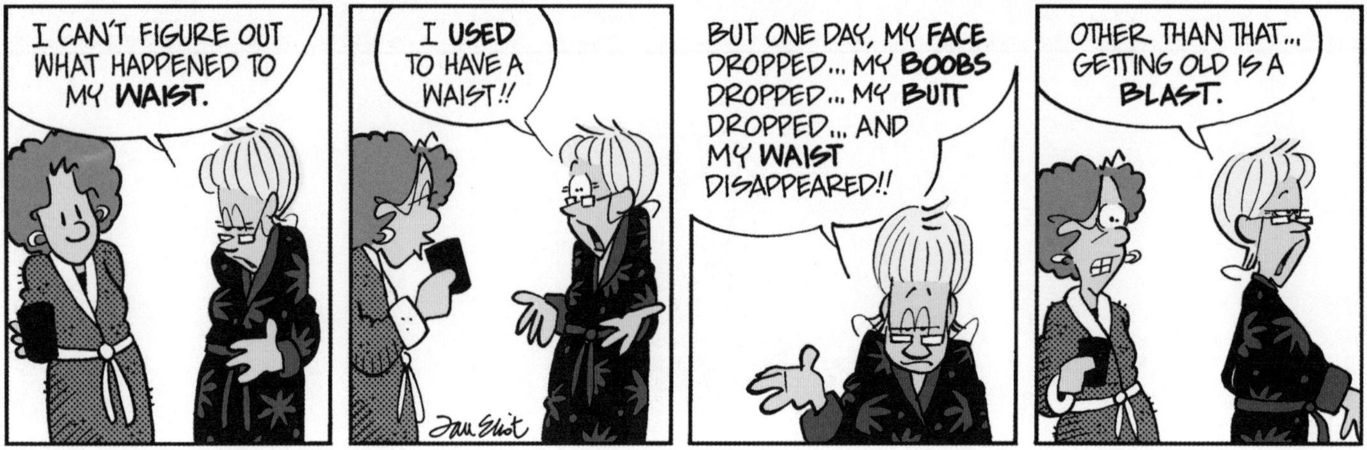
I CAN'T FIGURE OUT WHAT HAPPENED TO MY **WAIST.**
I **USED** TO HAVE A WAIST!!
BUT ONE DAY, MY **FACE** DROPPED... MY **BOOBS** DROPPED... MY **BUTT** DROPPED... AND MY **WAIST** DISAPPEARED!!
OTHER THAN THAT... GETTING OLD IS A **BLAST.**
Jan Eliot

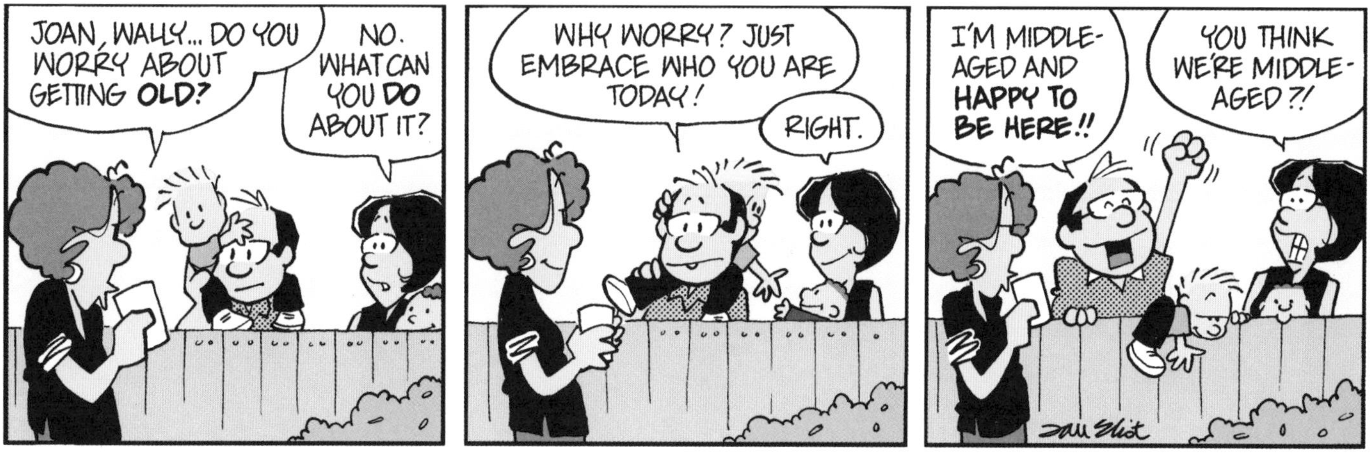
JOAN, WALLY... DO YOU WORRY ABOUT GETTING **OLD?**
NO. WHAT CAN YOU **DO** ABOUT IT?
WHY WORRY? JUST EMBRACE WHO YOU ARE TODAY!
RIGHT.
I'M MIDDLE-AGED AND **HAPPY TO BE HERE!!**
YOU THINK WE'RE MIDDLE-AGED?!

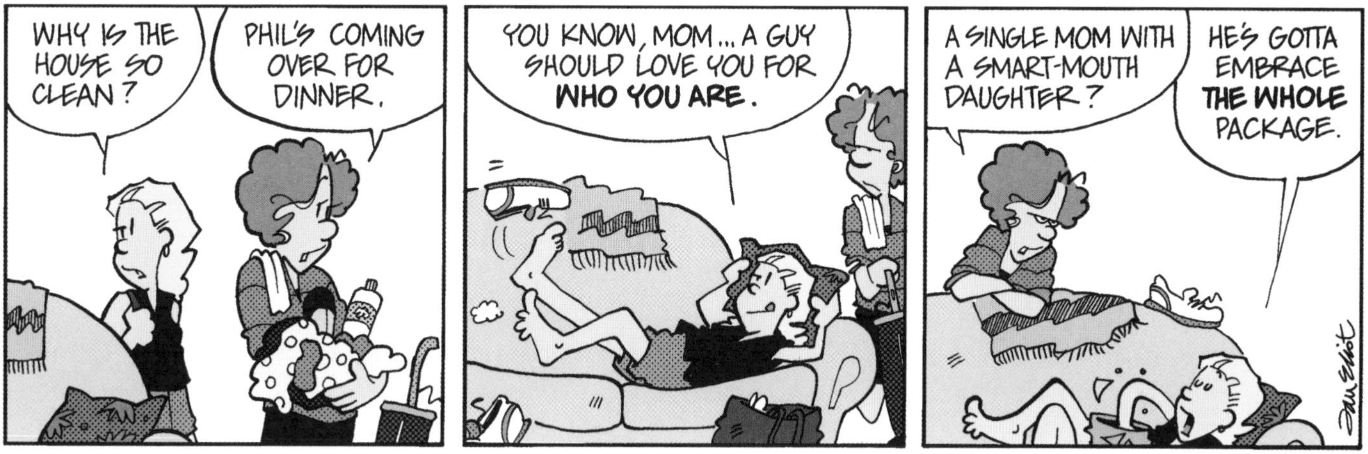
WHY IS THE HOUSE SO CLEAN?
PHIL'S COMING OVER FOR DINNER.
YOU KNOW, MOM... A GUY SHOULD LOVE YOU FOR **WHO YOU ARE.**
A SINGLE MOM WITH A SMART-MOUTH DAUGHTER?
HE'S GOTTA EMBRACE **THE WHOLE** PACKAGE.

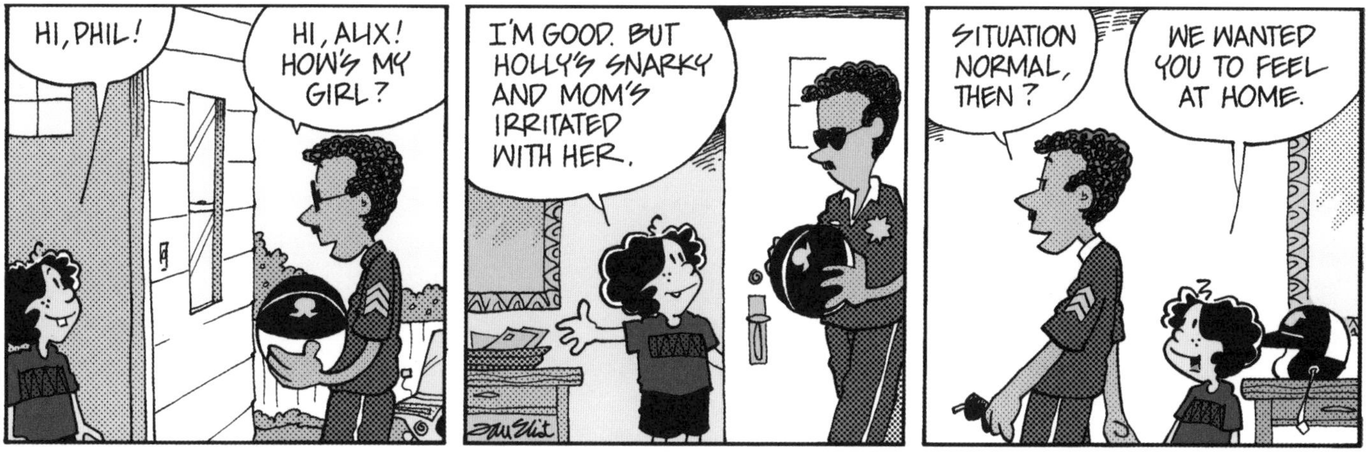
HI, PHIL!
HI, ALIX! HOW'S MY GIRL?
I'M GOOD. BUT HOLLY'S SNARKY AND MOM'S IRRITATED WITH HER.
SITUATION NORMAL, THEN?
WE WANTED YOU TO FEEL AT HOME.

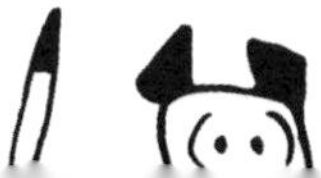

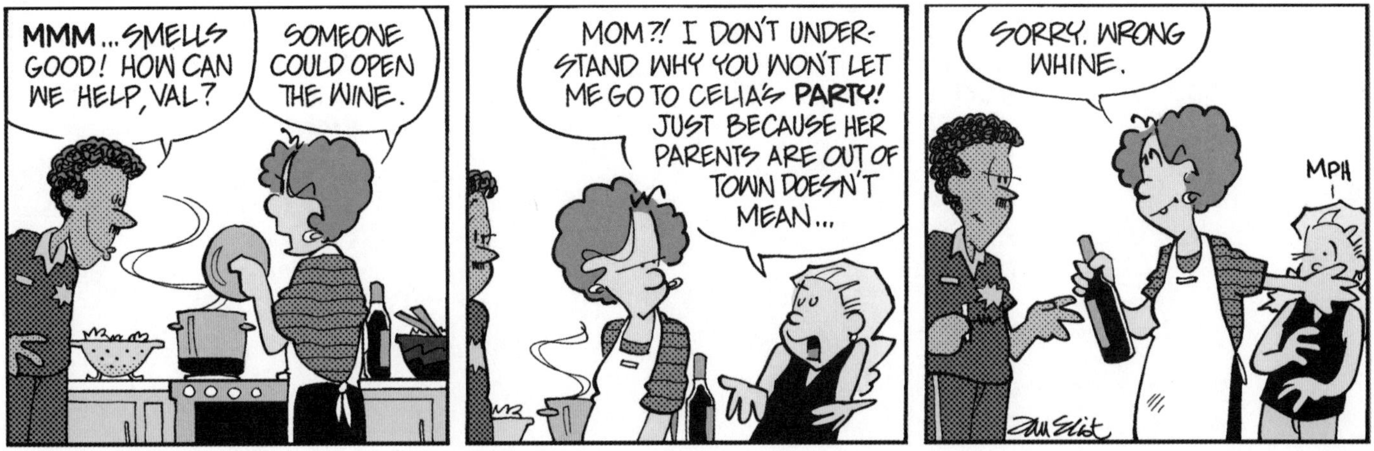
MMM...SMELLS GOOD! HOW CAN WE HELP, VAL?
SOMEONE COULD OPEN THE WINE.
MOM?! I DON'T UNDERSTAND WHY YOU WON'T LET ME GO TO CELIA'S PARTY! JUST BECAUSE HER PARENTS ARE OUT OF TOWN DOESN'T MEAN...
SORRY. WRONG WHINE.
MPH

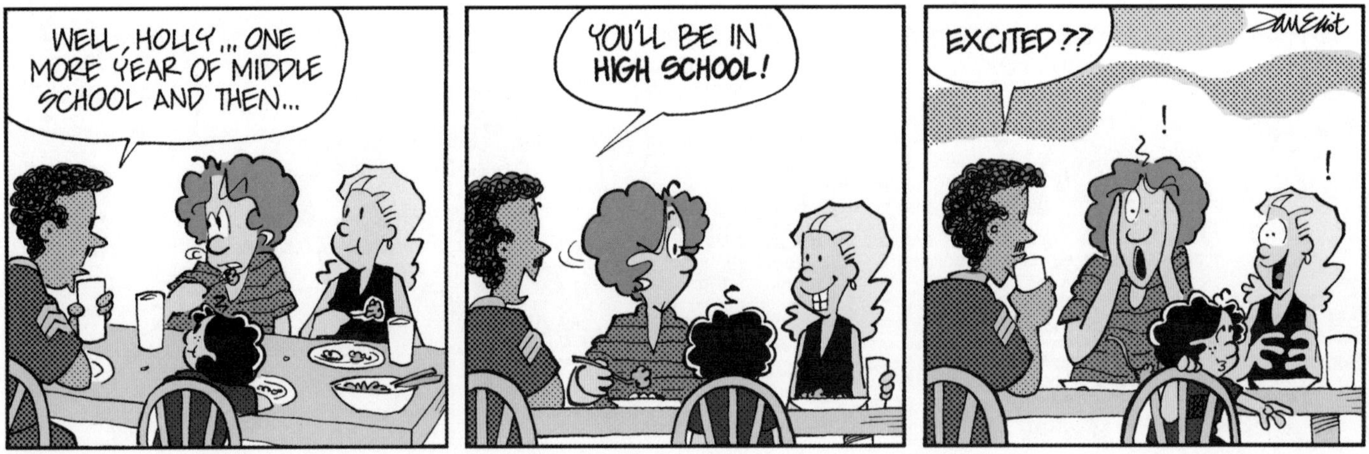
WELL, HOLLY... ONE MORE YEAR OF MIDDLE SCHOOL AND THEN...
YOU'LL BE IN HIGH SCHOOL!
EXCITED??
!
!

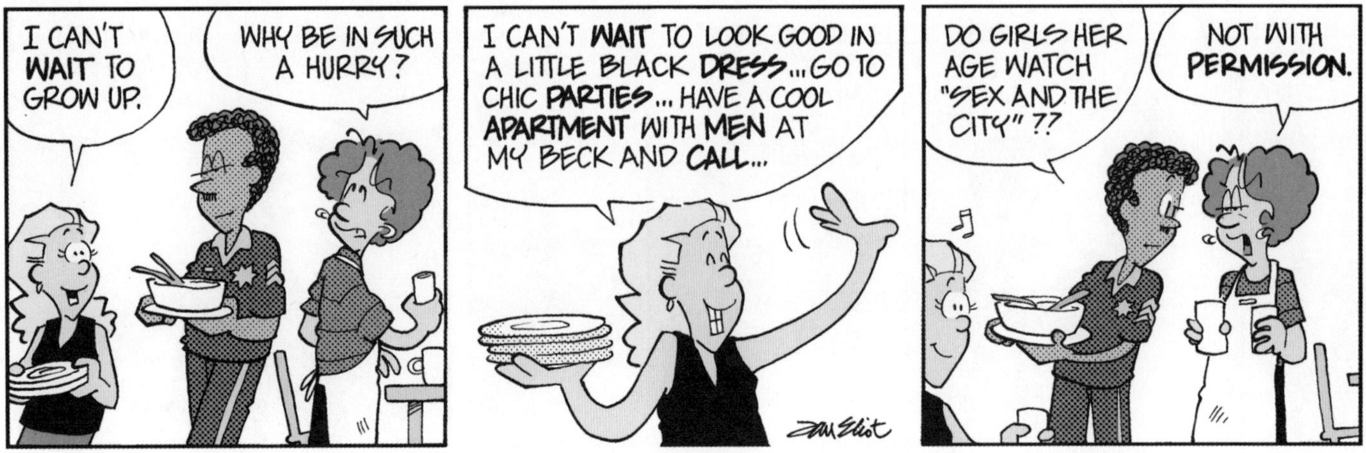
I CAN'T WAIT TO GROW UP.
WHY BE IN SUCH A HURRY?
I CAN'T WAIT TO LOOK GOOD IN A LITTLE BLACK DRESS... GO TO CHIC PARTIES... HAVE A COOL APARTMENT WITH MEN AT MY BECK AND CALL...
DO GIRLS HER AGE WATCH "SEX AND THE CITY"??
NOT WITH PERMISSION.

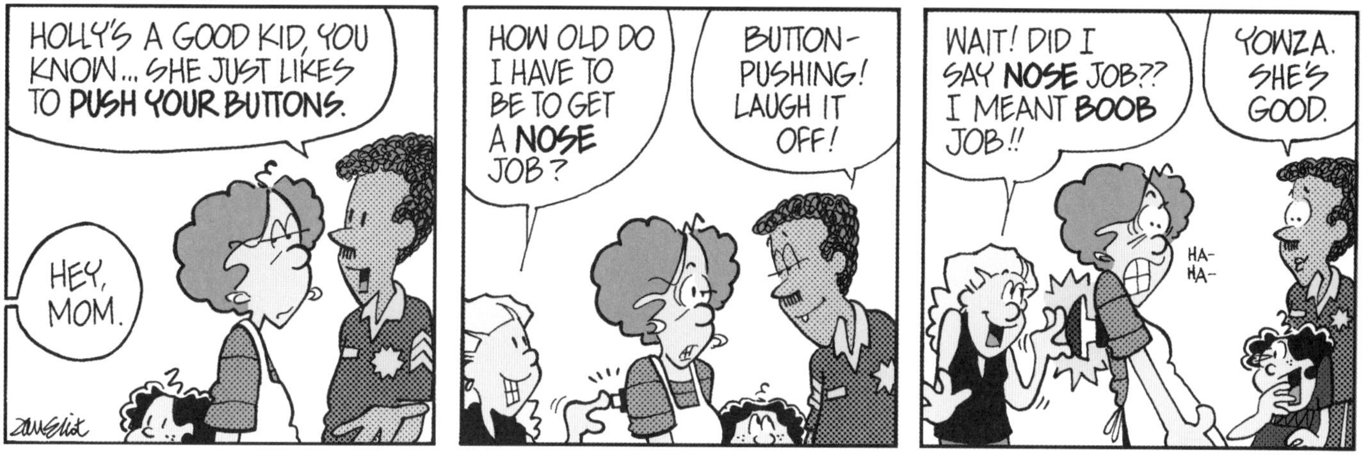
HOLLY'S A GOOD KID, YOU KNOW... SHE JUST LIKES TO PUSH YOUR BUTTONS.
HEY, MOM.
HOW OLD DO I HAVE TO BE TO GET A NOSE JOB?
BUTTON-PUSHING! LAUGH IT OFF!
WAIT! DID I SAY NOSE JOB?? I MEANT BOOB JOB!!
HA-HA--
YOWZA. SHE'S GOOD.

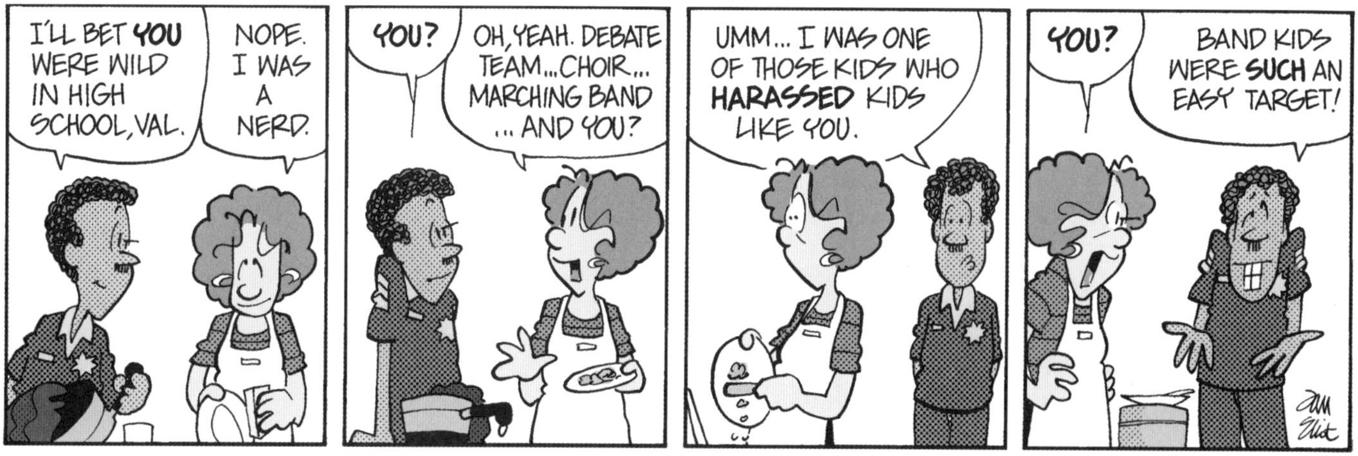
I'LL BET YOU WERE WILD IN HIGH SCHOOL, VAL.
NOPE. I WAS A NERD.
YOU?
OH, YEAH. DEBATE TEAM... CHOIR... MARCHING BAND ... AND YOU?
UMM... I WAS ONE OF THOSE KIDS WHO HARASSED KIDS LIKE YOU.
YOU?
BAND KIDS WERE SUCH AN EASY TARGET!

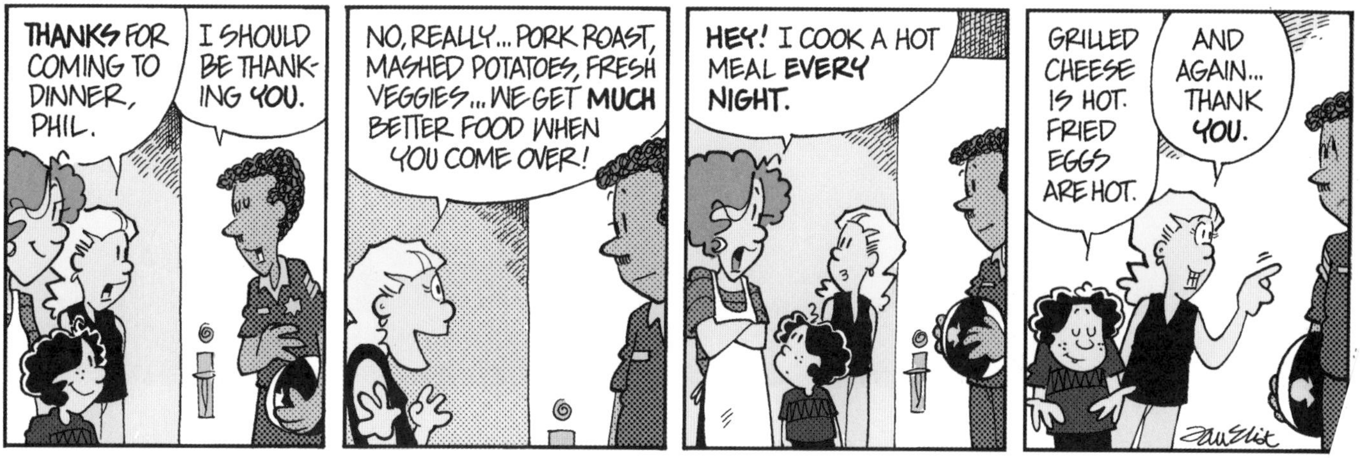
THANKS FOR COMING TO DINNER, PHIL.
I SHOULD BE THANKING YOU.
NO, REALLY... PORK ROAST, MASHED POTATOES, FRESH VEGGIES... WE GET MUCH BETTER FOOD WHEN YOU COME OVER!
HEY! I COOK A HOT MEAL EVERY NIGHT.
GRILLED CHEESE IS HOT. FRIED EGGS ARE HOT.
AND AGAIN... THANK YOU.

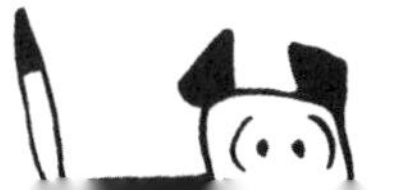

Stone Soup

WOW... SO MANY GORGEOUS **FLOWERS** IN BLOOM.
LOOK! **QUAIL!**
SMELL THE PINE NEEDLES.
LISTEN TO THE **WIND.**
DO WE REALLY GET TO HAVE LUNCH BY A **LAKE?**
OMIGAWD, MY LIFE IS **SOOO BORING.**

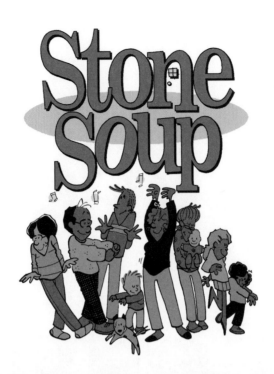

Stone Soup

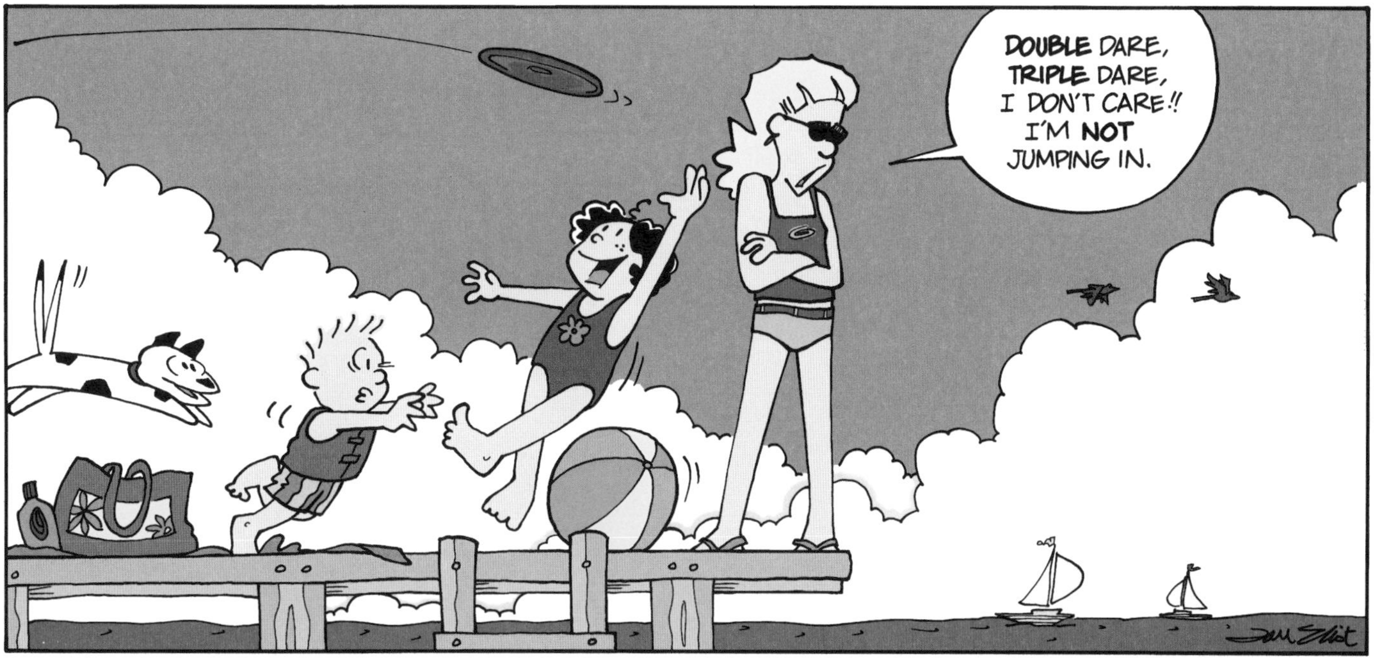
DOUBLE DARE, **TRIPLE** DARE, I DON'T CARE!! I'M **NOT** JUMPING IN.

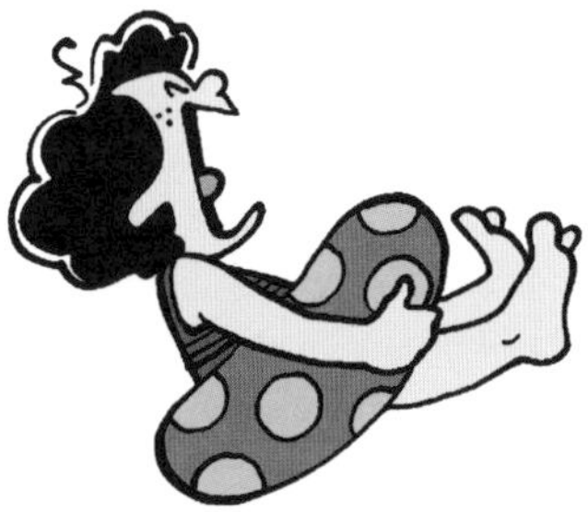

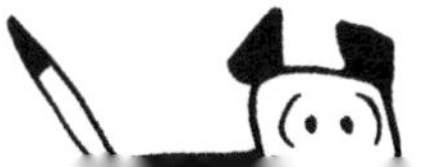

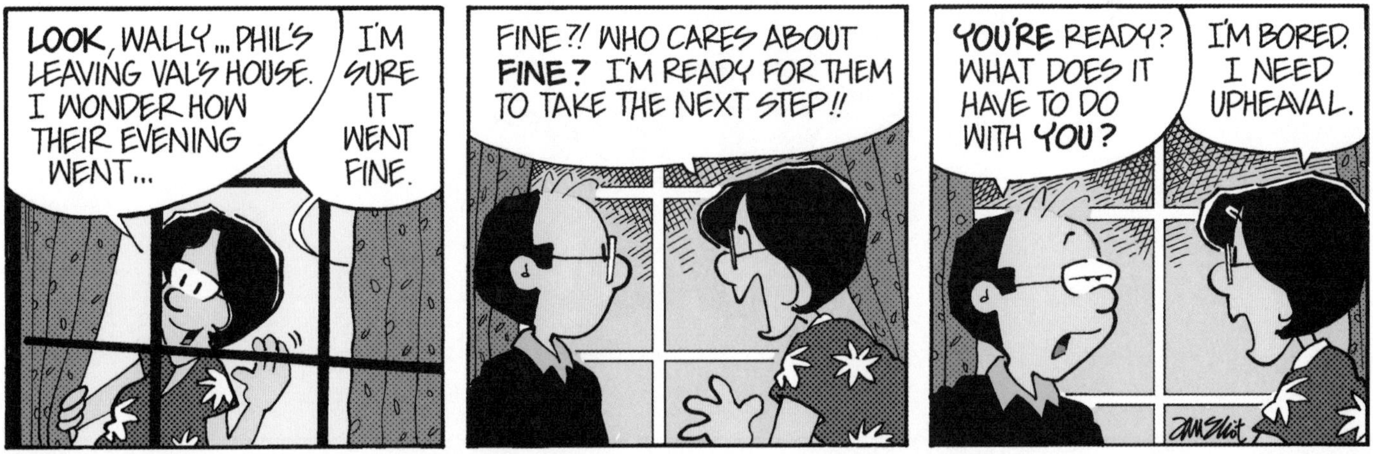
LOOK, WALLY... PHIL'S LEAVING VAL'S HOUSE. I WONDER HOW THEIR EVENING WENT...
I'M SURE IT WENT FINE.
FINE?! WHO CARES ABOUT FINE? I'M READY FOR THEM TO TAKE THE NEXT STEP!!
YOU'RE READY? WHAT DOES IT HAVE TO DO WITH YOU?
I'M BORED. I NEED UPHEAVAL.

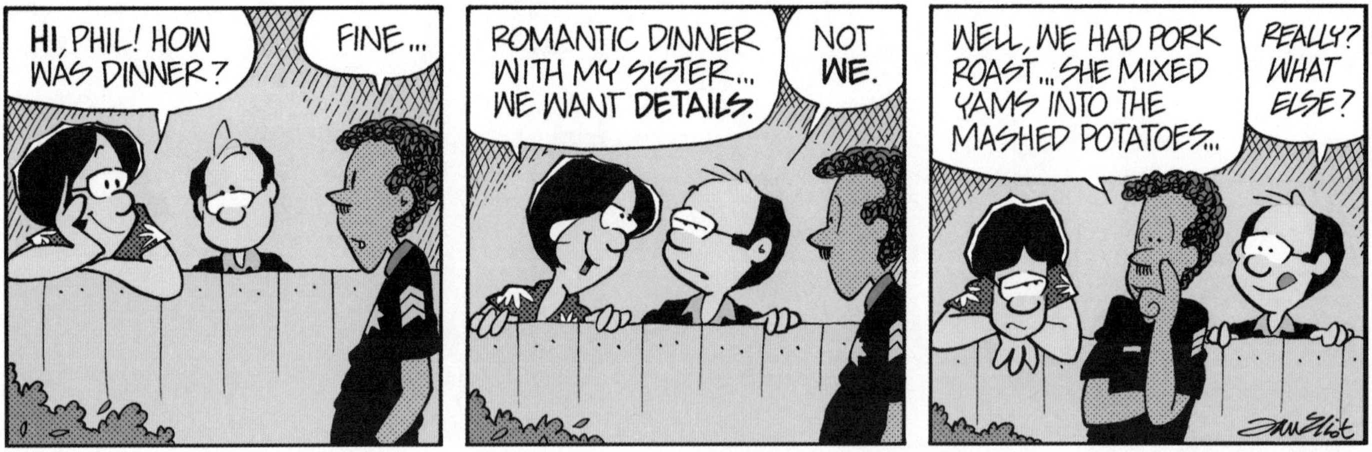
HI, PHIL! HOW WAS DINNER?
FINE...
ROMANTIC DINNER WITH MY SISTER... WE WANT DETAILS.
NOT WE.
WELL, WE HAD PORK ROAST... SHE MIXED YAMS INTO THE MASHED POTATOES...
REALLY? WHAT ELSE?

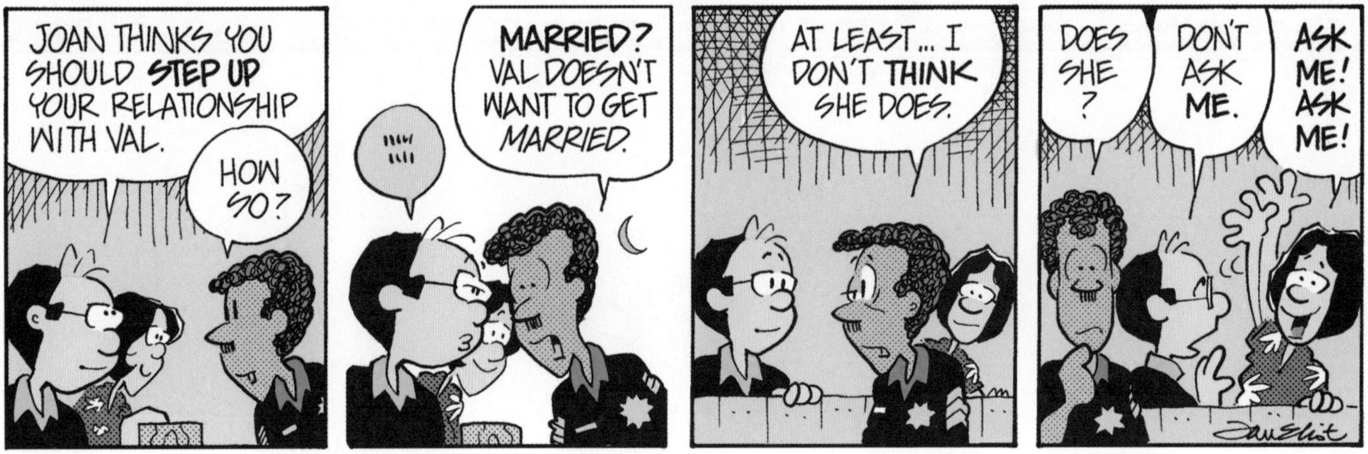
JOAN THINKS YOU SHOULD STEP UP YOUR RELATIONSHIP WITH VAL.
HOW SO?
MARRIED? VAL DOESN'T WANT TO GET MARRIED.
AT LEAST... I DON'T THINK SHE DOES.
DOES SHE?
DON'T ASK ME.
ASK ME! ASK ME!

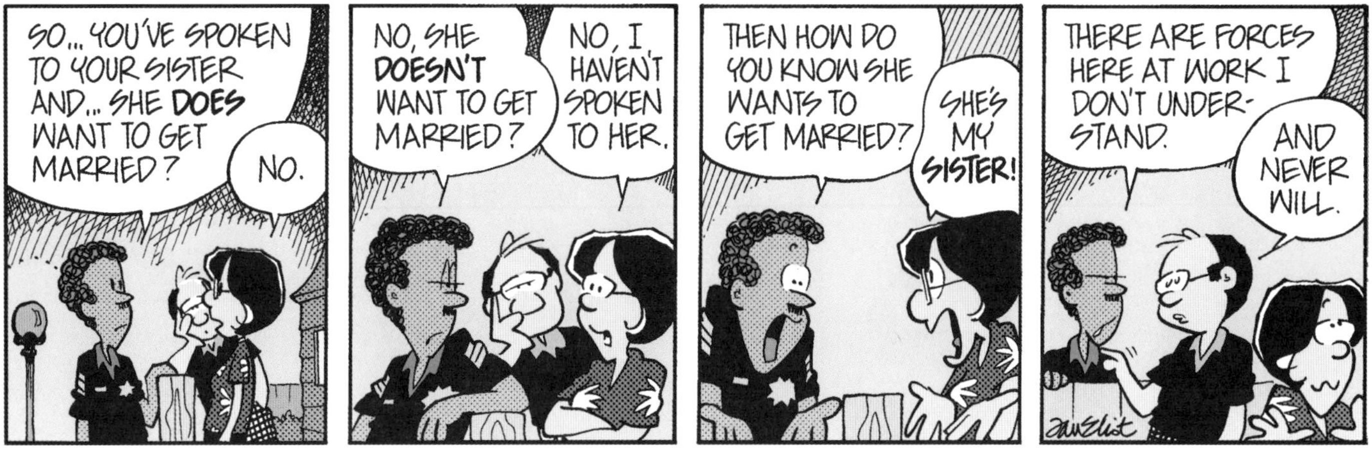
SO... YOU'VE SPOKEN TO YOUR SISTER AND... SHE **DOES** WANT TO GET MARRIED?
NO.
NO, SHE **DOESN'T** WANT TO GET MARRIED?
NO, I HAVEN'T SPOKEN TO HER.
THEN HOW DO YOU KNOW SHE WANTS TO GET MARRIED?
SHE'S MY **SISTER**!
THERE ARE FORCES HERE AT WORK I DON'T UNDERSTAND.
AND NEVER WILL.

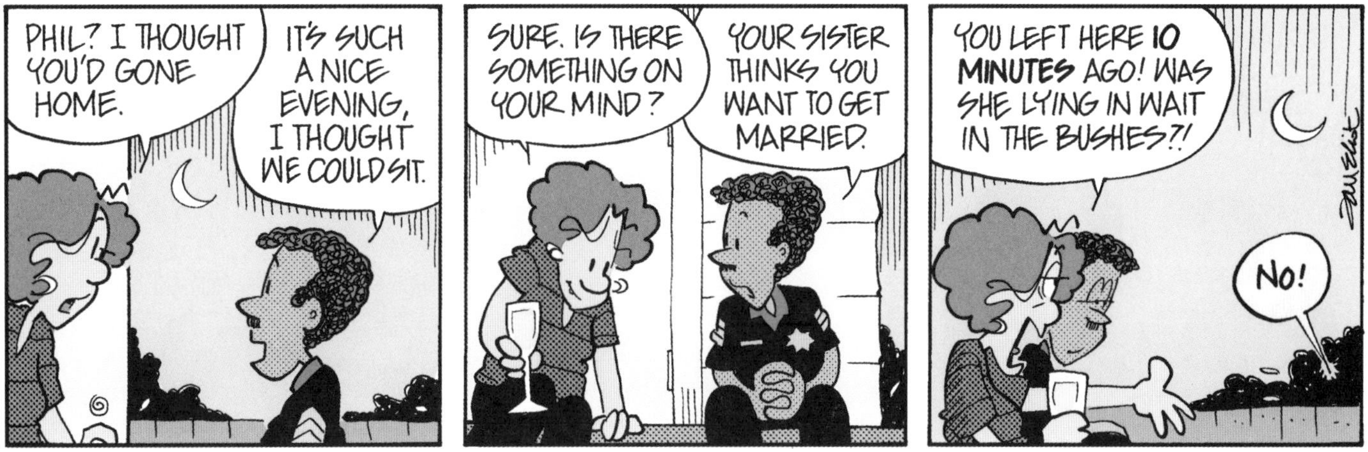
PHIL? I THOUGHT YOU'D GONE HOME.
IT'S SUCH A NICE EVENING, I THOUGHT WE COULD SIT.
SURE. IS THERE SOMETHING ON YOUR MIND?
YOUR SISTER THINKS YOU WANT TO GET MARRIED.
YOU LEFT HERE **10 MINUTES** AGO! WAS SHE LYING IN WAIT IN THE BUSHES?!
NO!

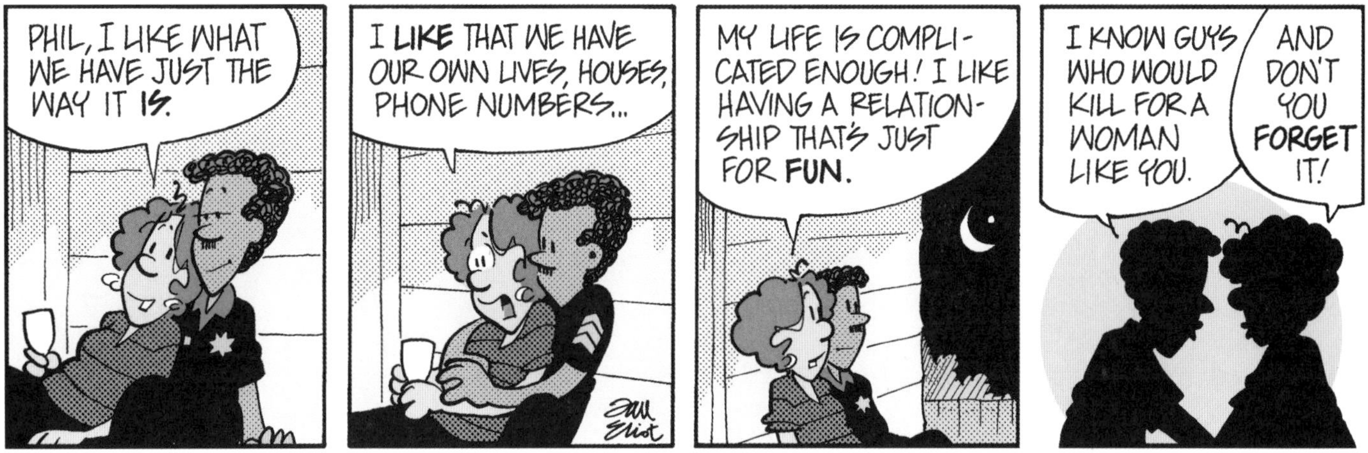
PHIL, I LIKE WHAT WE HAVE JUST THE WAY IT **IS**.
I **LIKE** THAT WE HAVE OUR OWN LIVES, HOUSES, PHONE NUMBERS...
MY LIFE IS COMPLICATED ENOUGH! I LIKE HAVING A RELATIONSHIP THAT'S JUST FOR **FUN**.
I KNOW GUYS WHO WOULD KILL FOR A WOMAN LIKE YOU.
AND DON'T YOU **FORGET** IT!

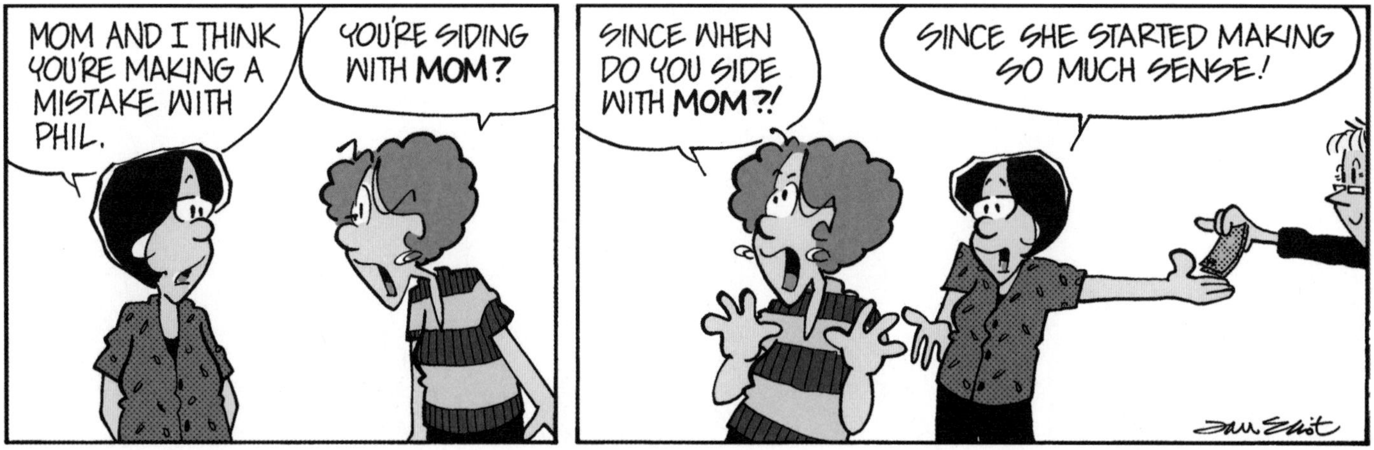
MOM AND I THINK YOU'RE MAKING A MISTAKE WITH PHIL.
YOU'RE SIDING WITH **MOM?**
SINCE WHEN DO YOU SIDE WITH **MOM?!**
SINCE SHE STARTED MAKING SO MUCH SENSE!

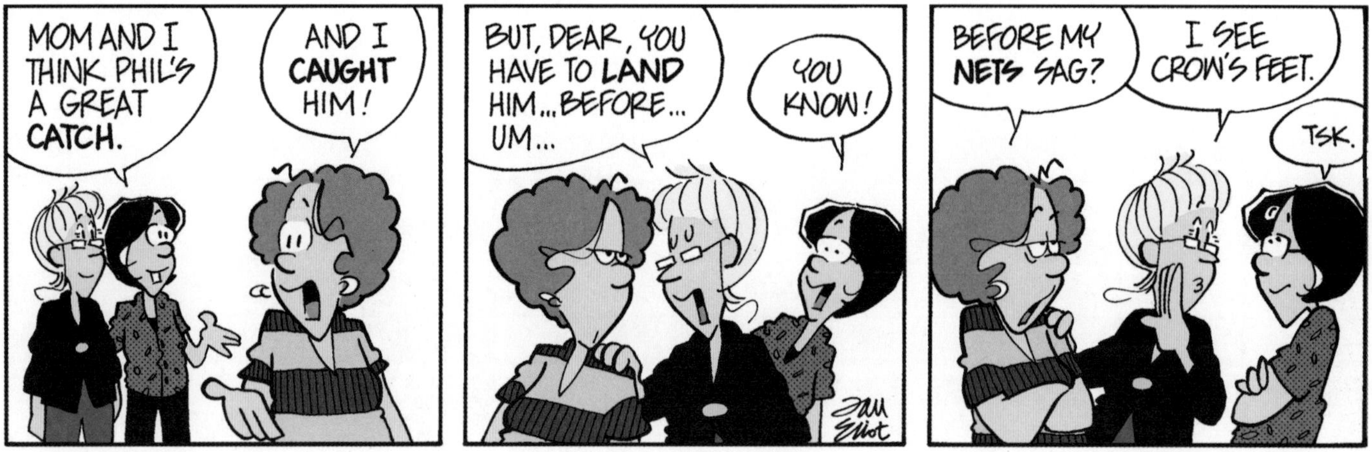
MOM AND I THINK PHIL'S A GREAT **CATCH.**
AND I **CAUGHT** HIM!
BUT, DEAR, YOU HAVE TO **LAND** HIM...BEFORE... UM...
YOU KNOW!
BEFORE MY **NETS** SAG?
I SEE CROW'S FEET.
TSK.

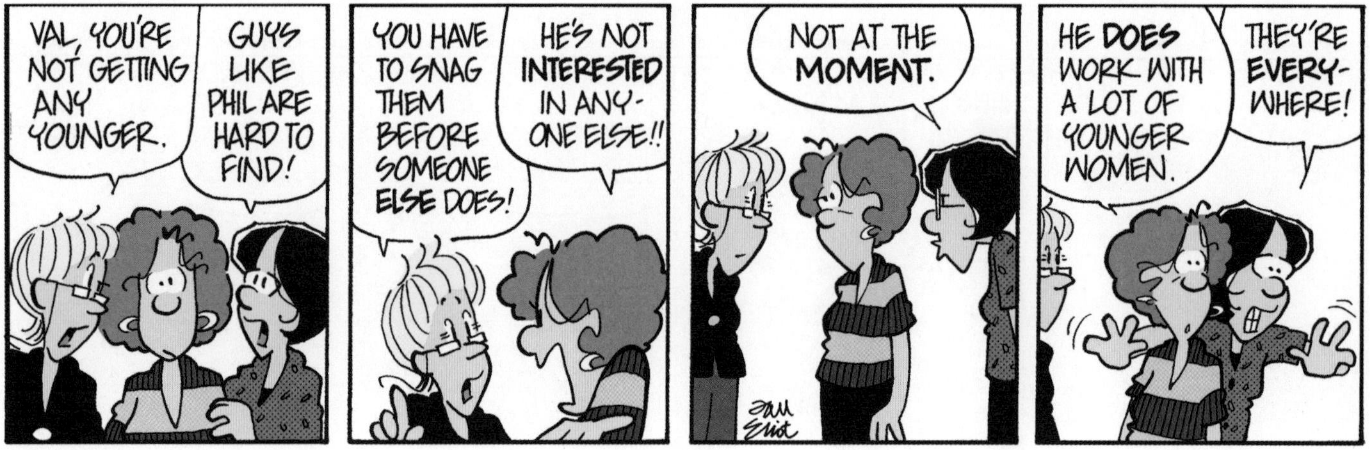
VAL, YOU'RE NOT GETTING ANY YOUNGER.
GUYS LIKE PHIL ARE HARD TO FIND!
YOU HAVE TO SNAG THEM BEFORE SOMEONE **ELSE** DOES!
HE'S NOT **INTERESTED** IN ANYONE ELSE!!
NOT AT THE **MOMENT.**
HE **DOES** WORK WITH A LOT OF YOUNGER WOMEN.
THEY'RE **EVERYWHERE!**

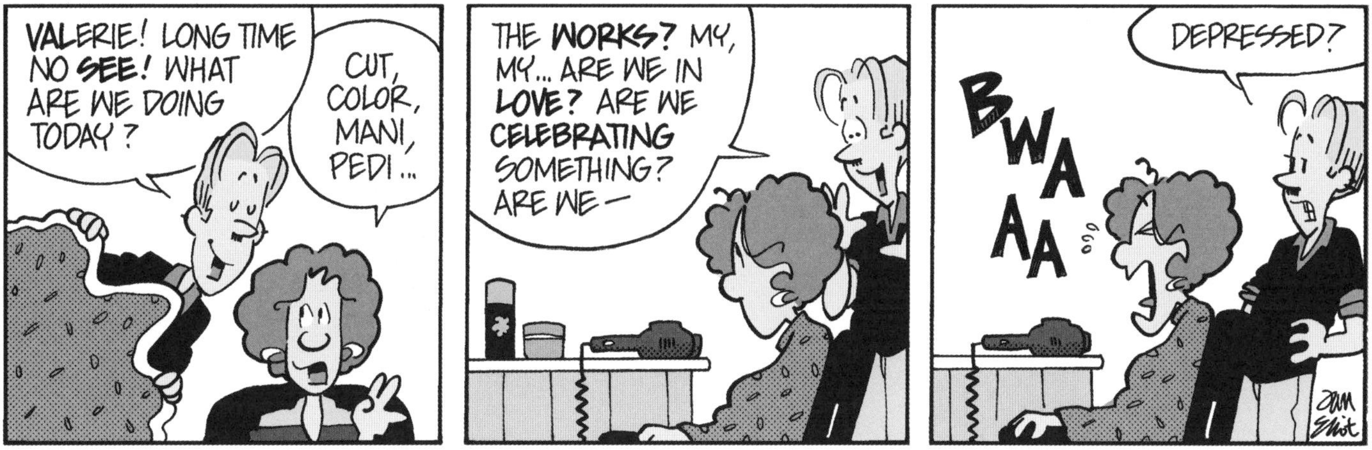
VALERIE! LONG TIME NO SEE! WHAT ARE WE DOING TODAY?
CUT, COLOR, MANI, PEDI...
THE WORKS? MY, MY... ARE WE IN LOVE? ARE WE CELEBRATING SOMETHING? ARE WE—
BWAAAA
DEPRESSED?

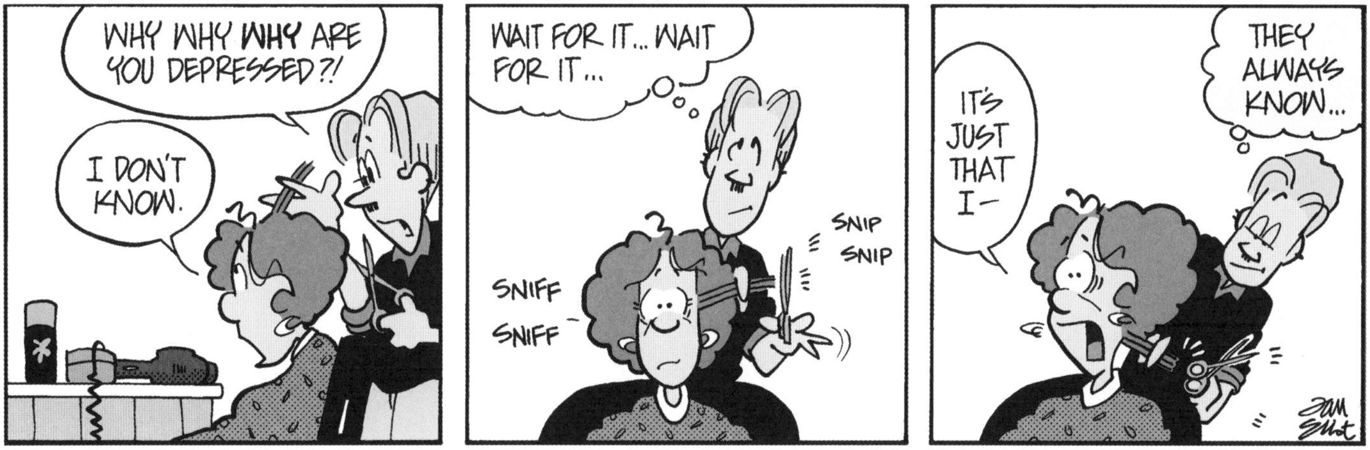
WHY WHY WHY ARE YOU DEPRESSED?!
I DON'T KNOW.
WAIT FOR IT... WAIT FOR IT...
SNIFF
SNIFF
SNIP
SNIP
IT'S JUST THAT I—
THEY ALWAYS KNOW...

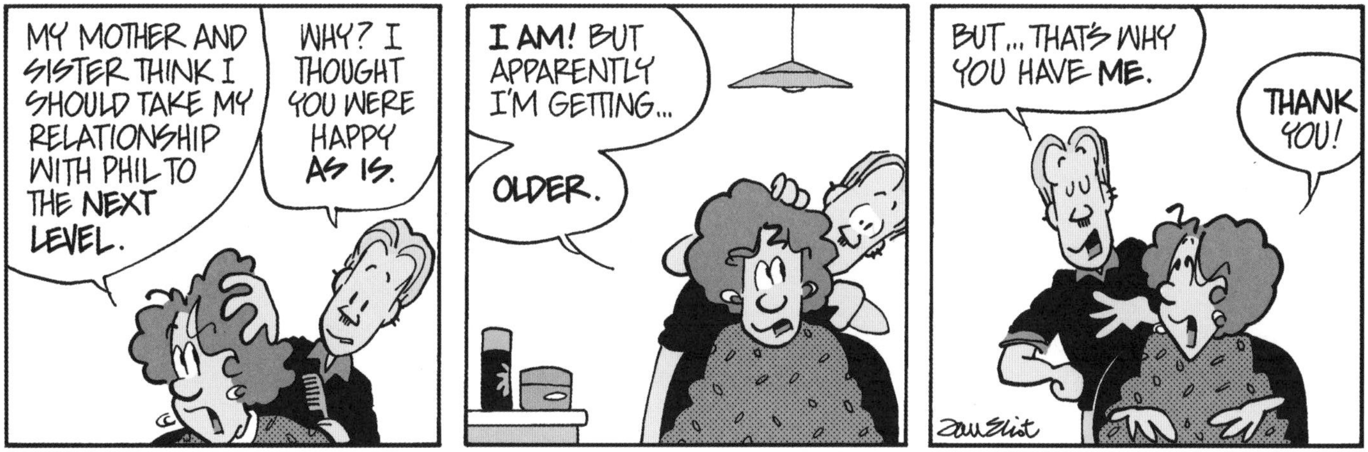
MY MOTHER AND SISTER THINK I SHOULD TAKE MY RELATIONSHIP WITH PHIL TO THE NEXT LEVEL.
WHY? I THOUGHT YOU WERE HAPPY AS IS.
I AM! BUT APPARENTLY I'M GETTING...
OLDER.
BUT... THAT'S WHY YOU HAVE ME.
THANK YOU!

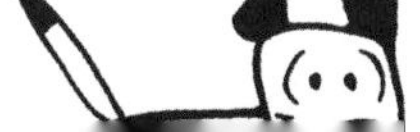

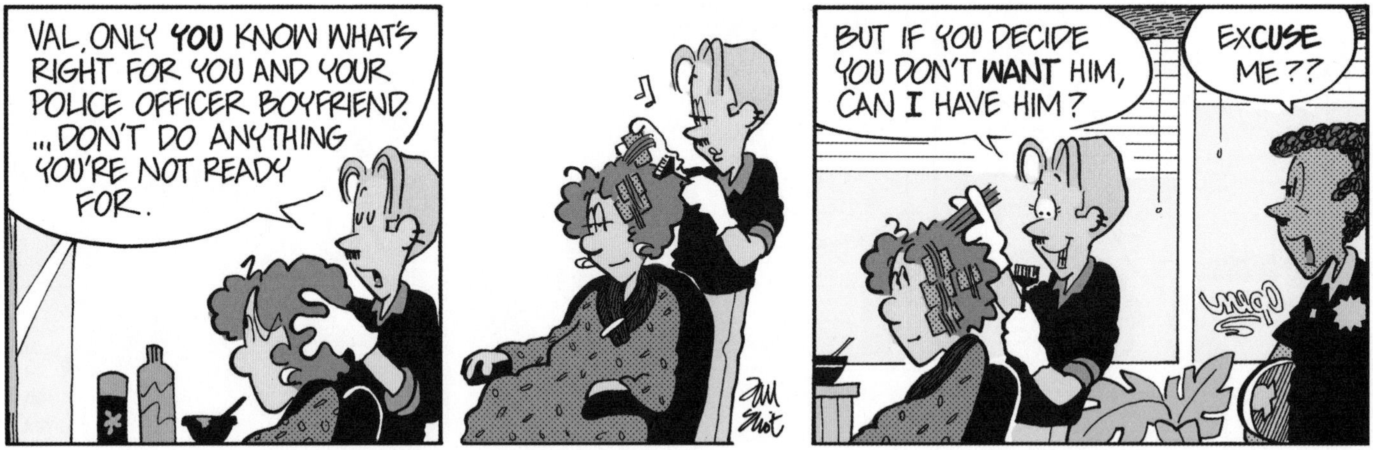
VAL, ONLY **YOU** KNOW WHAT'S RIGHT FOR YOU AND YOUR POLICE OFFICER BOYFRIEND. ...DON'T DO ANYTHING YOU'RE NOT READY FOR.
BUT IF YOU DECIDE YOU DON'T **WANT** HIM, CAN **I** HAVE HIM?
EX**CUSE** ME??

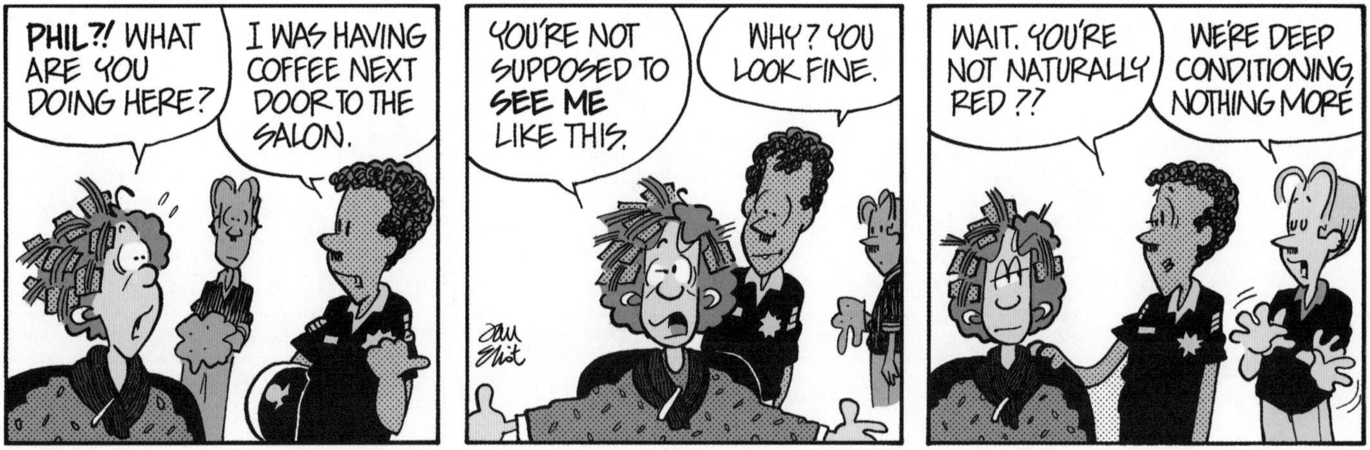
PHIL?! WHAT ARE YOU DOING HERE?
I WAS HAVING COFFEE NEXT DOOR TO THE SALON.
YOU'RE NOT SUPPOSED TO **SEE ME** LIKE THIS.
WHY? YOU LOOK FINE.
WAIT. YOU'RE NOT NATURALLY RED??
WE'RE DEEP CONDITIONING, NOTHING MORE

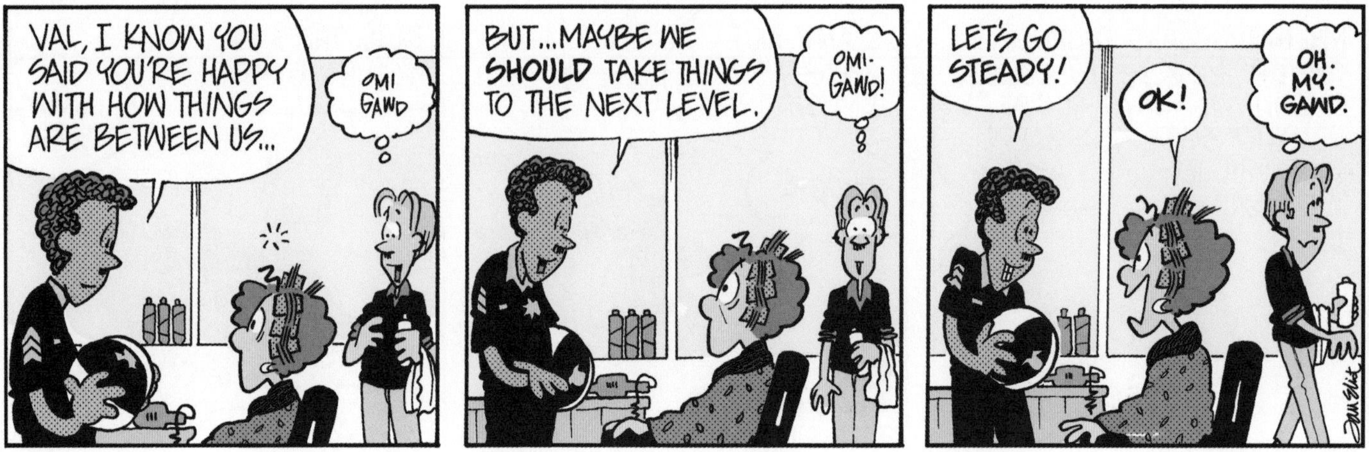
VAL, I KNOW YOU SAID YOU'RE HAPPY WITH HOW THINGS ARE BETWEEN US...
OMI GAWD
BUT...MAYBE WE **SHOULD** TAKE THINGS TO THE NEXT LEVEL.
OMI-GAWD!
LET'S GO STEADY!
OK!
OH. MY. GAWD.

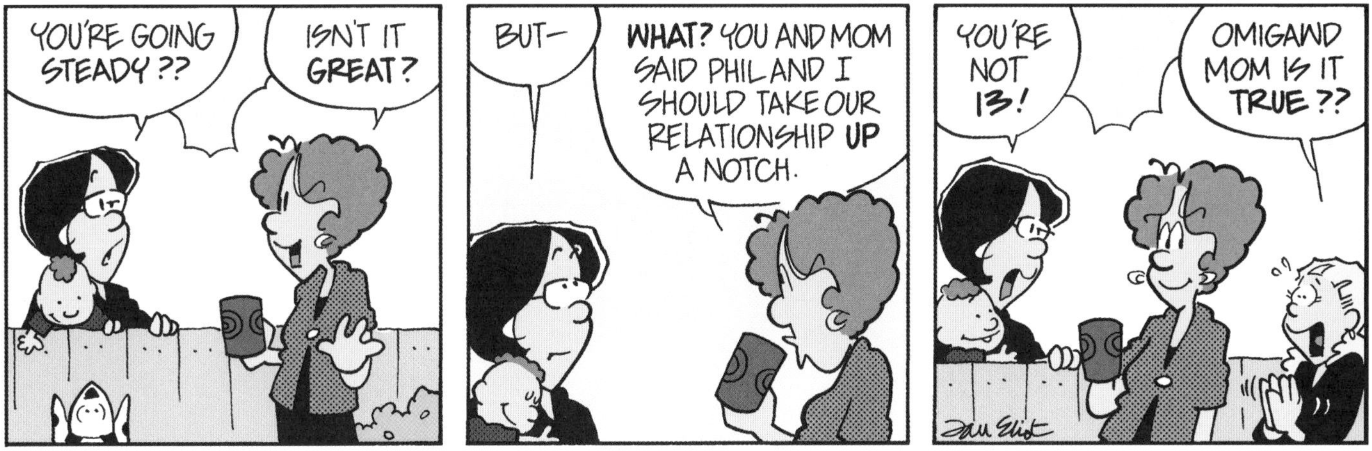
YOU'RE GOING STEADY ??
ISN'T IT GREAT?
BUT—
WHAT? YOU AND MOM SAID PHIL AND I SHOULD TAKE OUR RELATIONSHIP UP A NOTCH.
YOU'RE NOT 13!
OMIGAWD MOM IS IT TRUE??

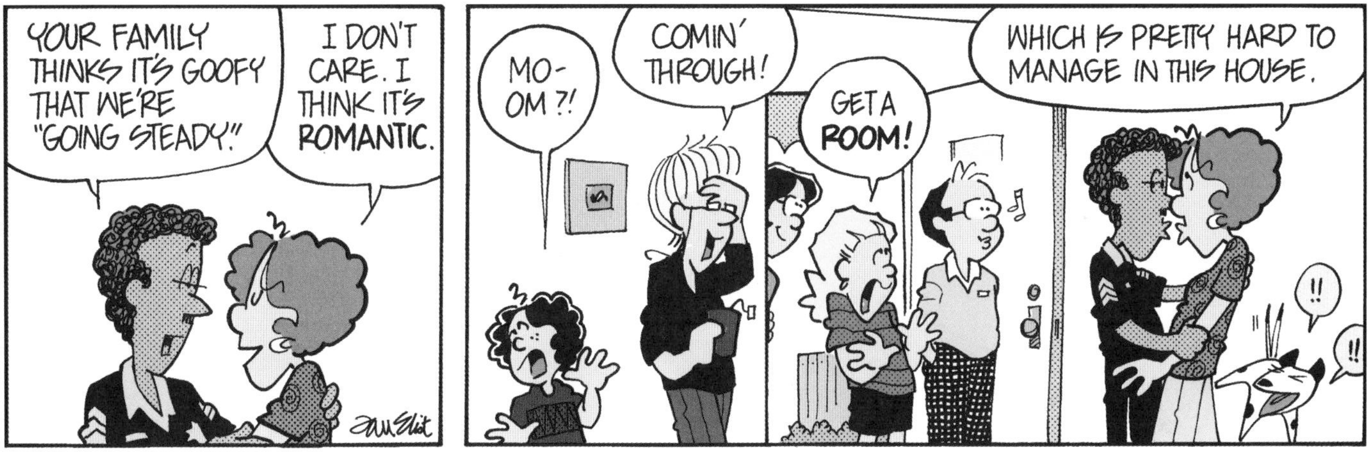
YOUR FAMILY THINKS IT'S GOOFY THAT WE'RE "GOING STEADY."
I DON'T CARE. I THINK IT'S ROMANTIC.
MO-OM ?!
COMIN' THROUGH!
GET A ROOM!
WHICH IS PRETTY HARD TO MANAGE IN THIS HOUSE.

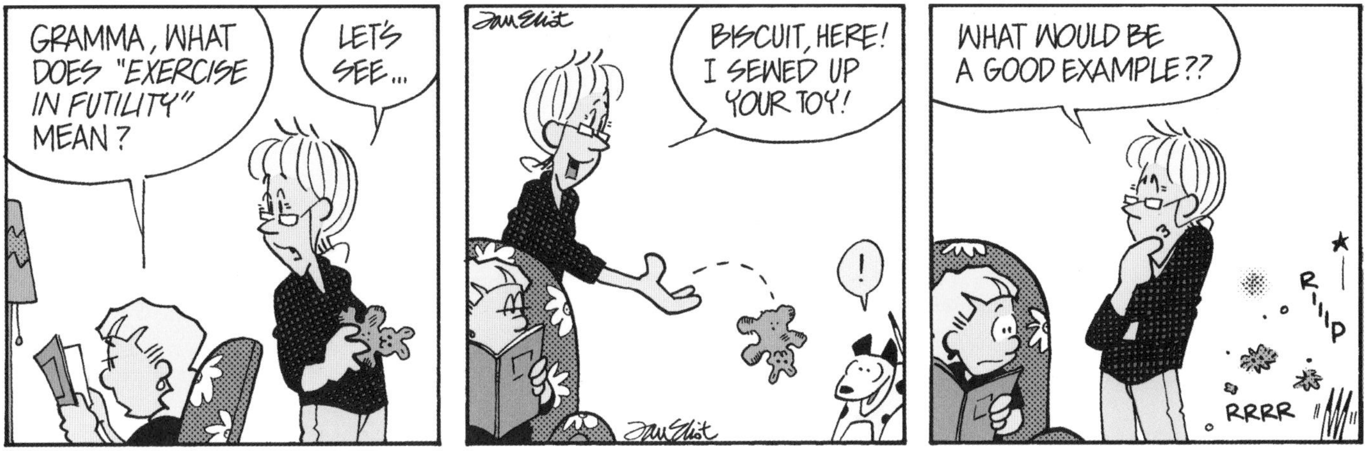
GRAMMA, WHAT DOES "EXERCISE IN FUTILITY" MEAN?
LET'S SEE...
BISCUIT, HERE! I SEWED UP YOUR TOY!
WHAT WOULD BE A GOOD EXAMPLE??
RIIIP
RRRR

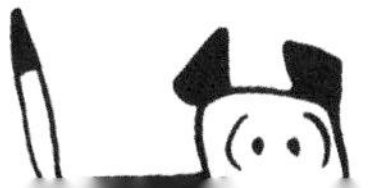

Stone Soup

OW
WHAT'S WRONG ??
I **PULLED** SOMETHING.
DID YOU LIFT WITH YOUR KNEES?
AH AH AH
WHAT'S WRONG?
I BET HE DIDN'T LIFT WITH HIS KNEES.
WALLY PULLED SOME-THING...
YOU'RE SUPPOSED TO LIFT WITH YOUR KNEES.
MAYBE I SHOULDN'T BE GARDENING.
BUT, GARDENING'S **GOOD** FOR YOU.
DUDE, LIFT WITH YOUR KNEES.

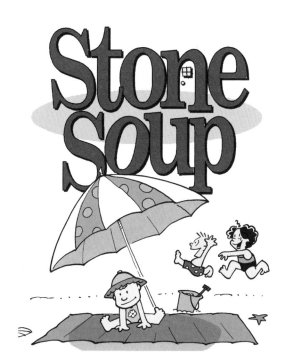

Stone Soup

UH-OH, VAL ... YOUR LEGS ARE GETTING PINK.

THE MINUTE I GET ANY SUN I TURN INTO A MASS OF **FRECKLES**.

TAKE MY HAT.

YOUR ARMS ARE RED, TOO! DID YOU USE SUNSCREEN?

YES, BUT IT'S OLD.

PUT ON MY SHIRT.

I JUST **LOVE** THE BEACH, DON'T YOU?!

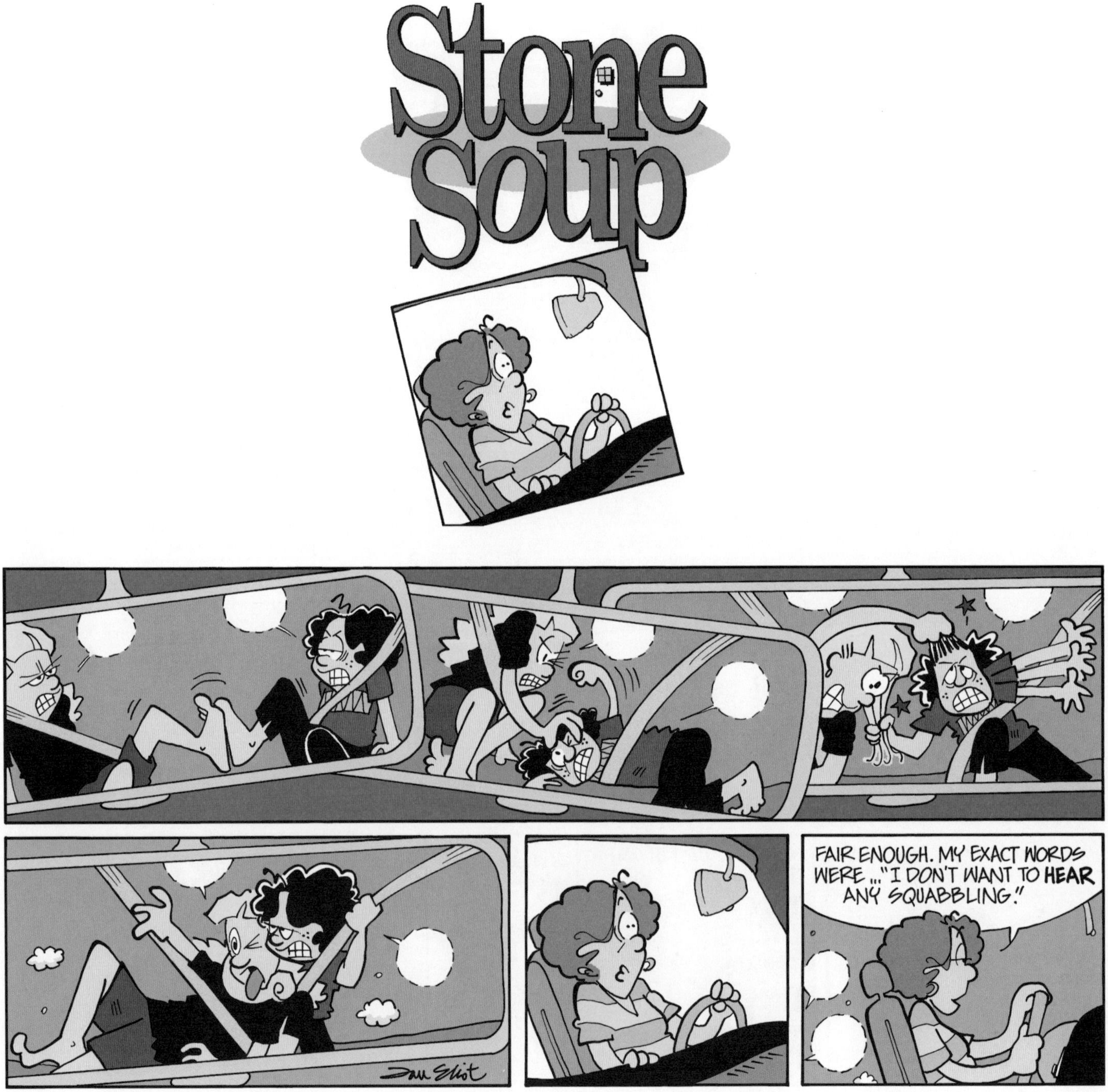
Stone Soup
FAIR ENOUGH. MY EXACT WORDS WERE ... "I DON'T WANT TO **HEAR** ANY SQUABBLING."

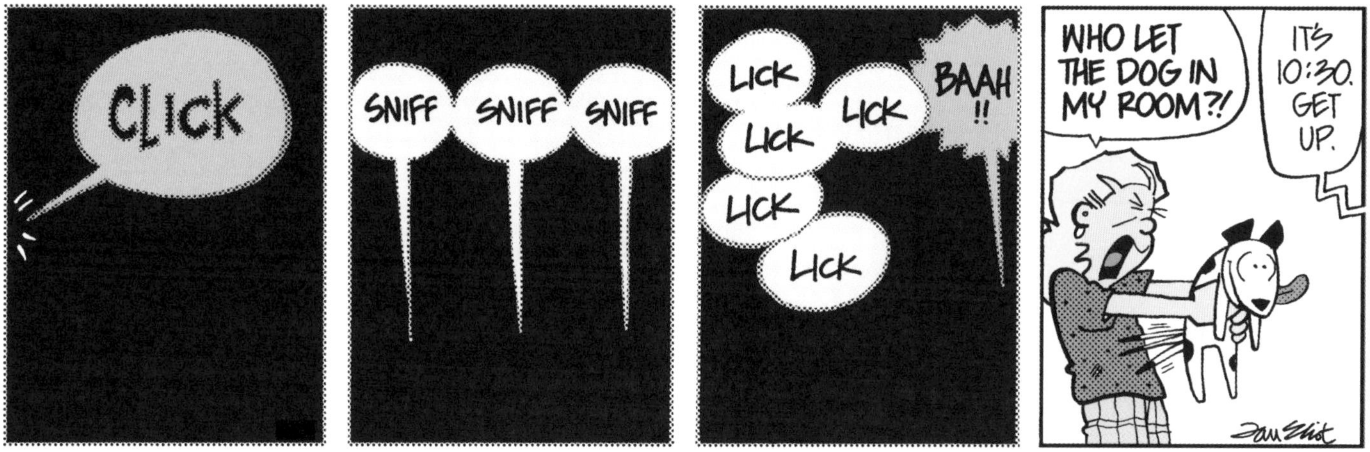
CLICK
SNIFF
SNIFF
SNIFF
LICK
LICK
LICK
LICK
LICK
BAAH !!
WHO LET THE DOG IN MY ROOM?!
IT'S 10:30. GET UP.

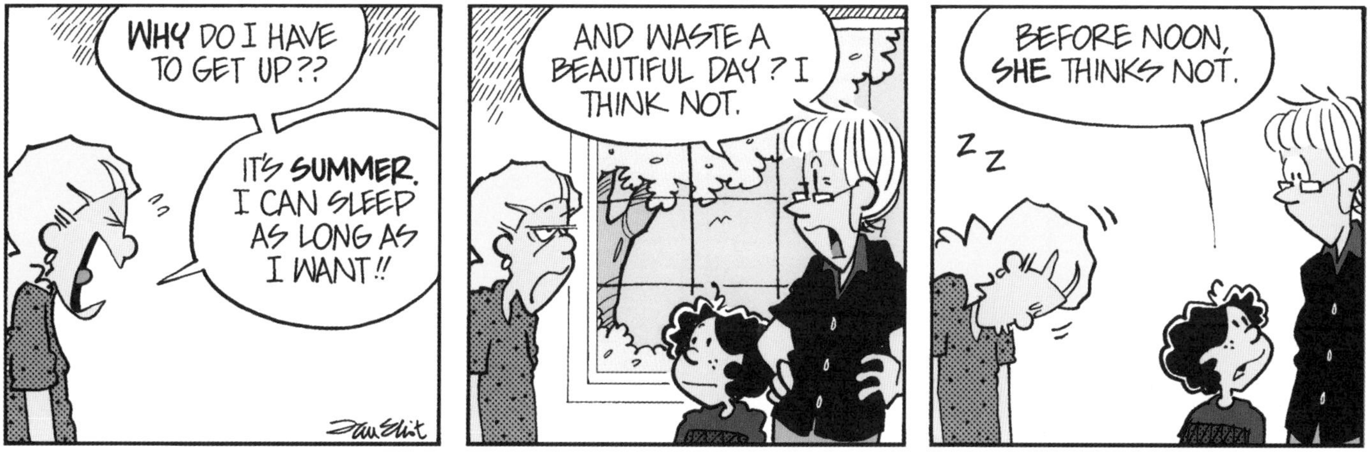
WHY DO I HAVE TO GET UP??
IT'S SUMMER. I CAN SLEEP AS LONG AS I WANT!!
AND WASTE A BEAUTIFUL DAY? I THINK NOT.
Z Z
BEFORE NOON, SHE THINKS NOT.

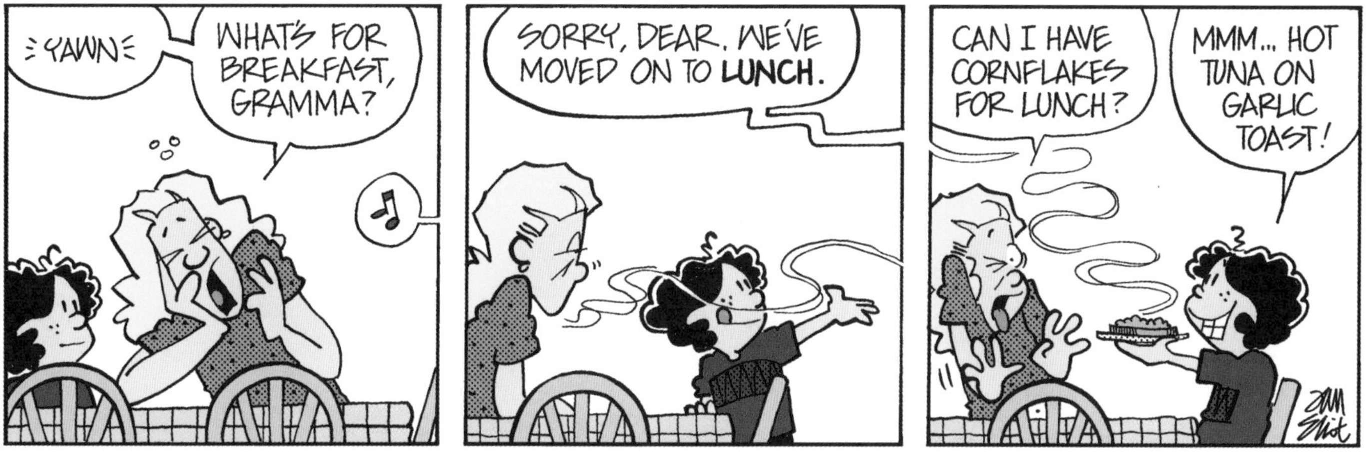
YAWN
WHAT'S FOR BREAKFAST, GRAMMA?
SORRY, DEAR. WE'VE MOVED ON TO LUNCH.
CAN I HAVE CORNFLAKES FOR LUNCH?
MMM... HOT TUNA ON GARLIC TOAST!

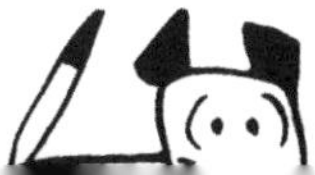

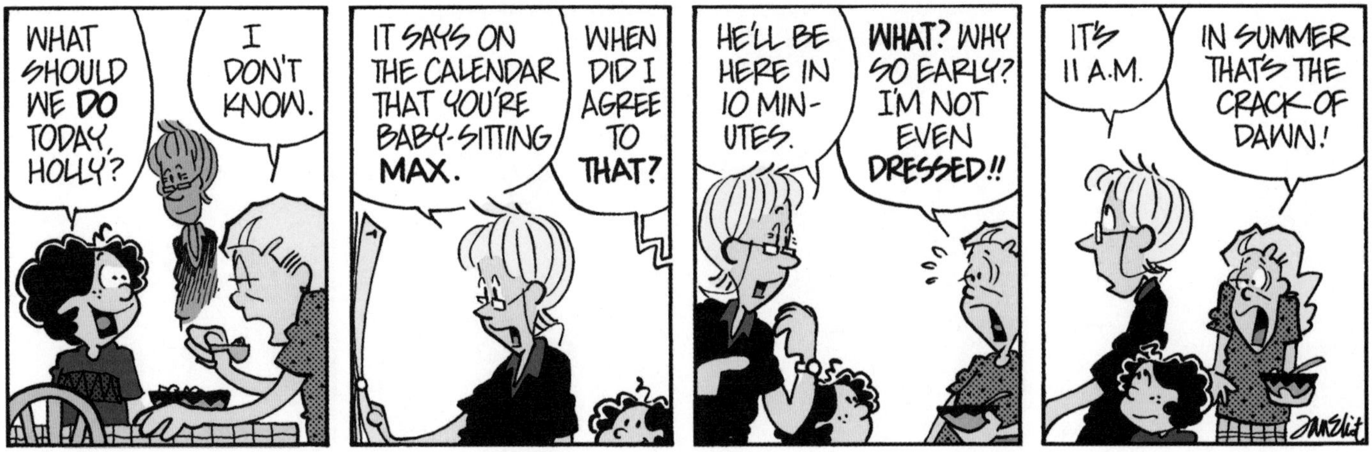
WHAT SHOULD WE **DO** TODAY, HOLLY?
I DON'T KNOW.
IT SAYS ON THE CALENDAR THAT YOU'RE BABY-SITTING **MAX**.
WHEN DID I AGREE TO **THAT?**
HE'LL BE HERE IN 10 MINUTES.
WHAT? WHY SO EARLY? I'M NOT EVEN **DRESSED!!**
IT'S 11 A.M.
IN SUMMER THAT'S THE CRACK OF DAWN!

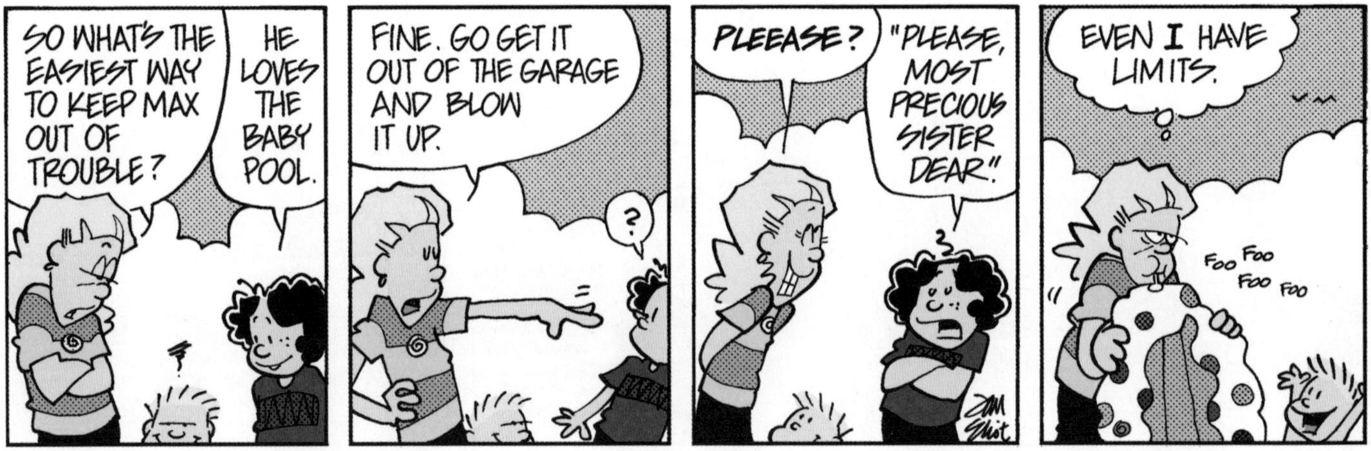
SO WHAT'S THE EASIEST WAY TO KEEP MAX OUT OF TROUBLE?
HE LOVES THE BABY POOL.
FINE. GO GET IT OUT OF THE GARAGE AND BLOW IT UP.
?
PLEEASE?
"PLEASE, MOST PRECIOUS SISTER DEAR."
EVEN **I** HAVE LIMITS.
FOO FOO FOO FOO FOO

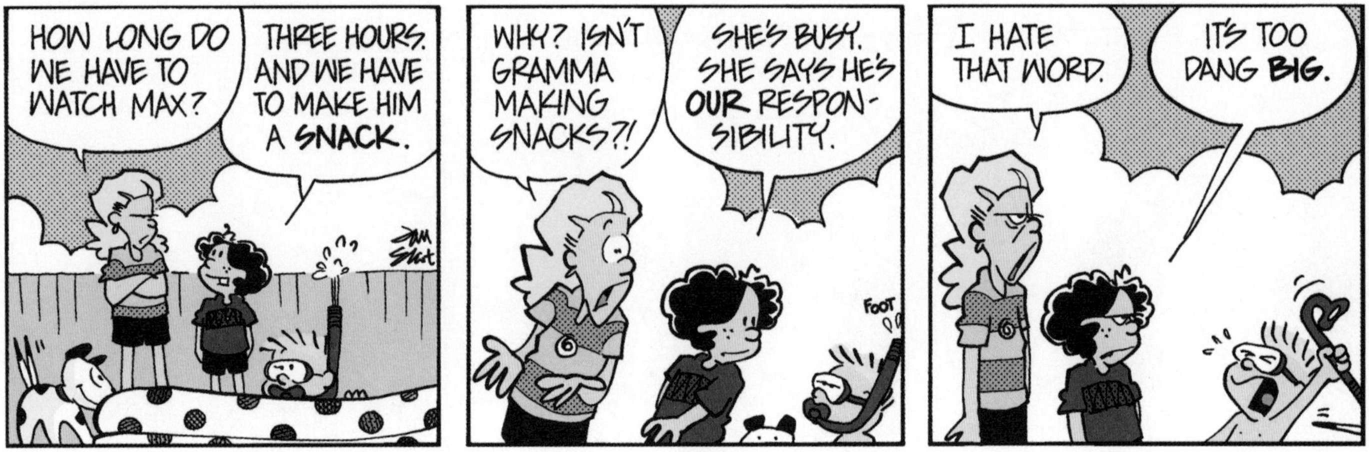
HOW LONG DO WE HAVE TO WATCH MAX?
THREE HOURS. AND WE HAVE TO MAKE HIM A **SNACK**.
WHY? ISN'T GRAMMA MAKING SNACKS?!
SHE'S BUSY. SHE SAYS HE'S **OUR** RESPONSIBILITY.
FOOT
I HATE THAT WORD.
IT'S TOO DANG **BIG**.

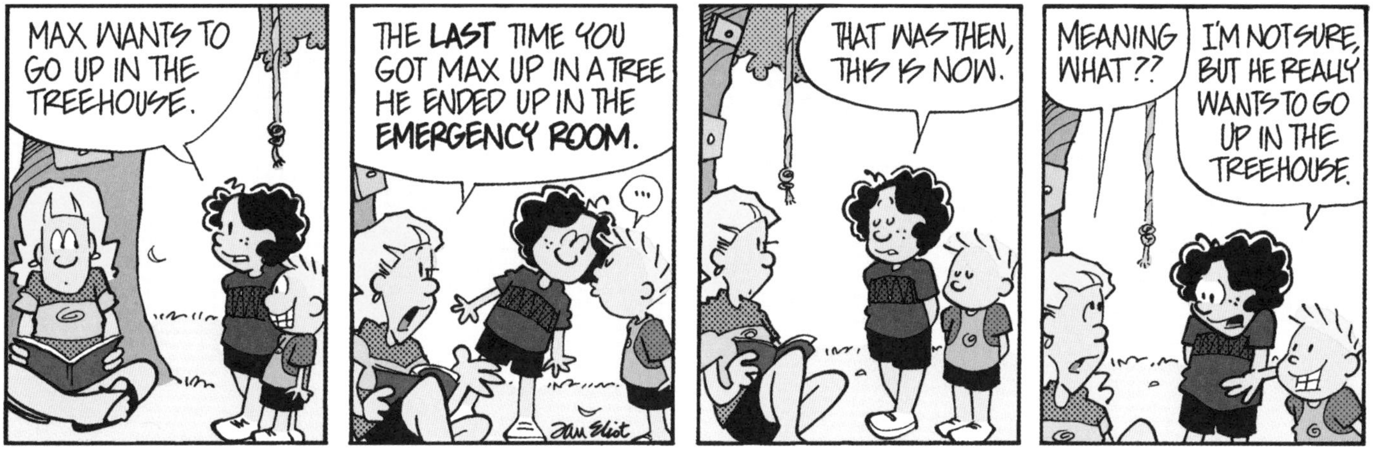
MAX WANTS TO GO UP IN THE TREEHOUSE.
THE **LAST** TIME YOU GOT MAX UP IN A TREE HE ENDED UP IN THE **EMERGENCY ROOM.**
...
THAT WAS THEN, THIS IS NOW.
MEANING WHAT??
I'M NOT SURE, BUT HE REALLY WANTS TO GO UP IN THE TREEHOUSE.

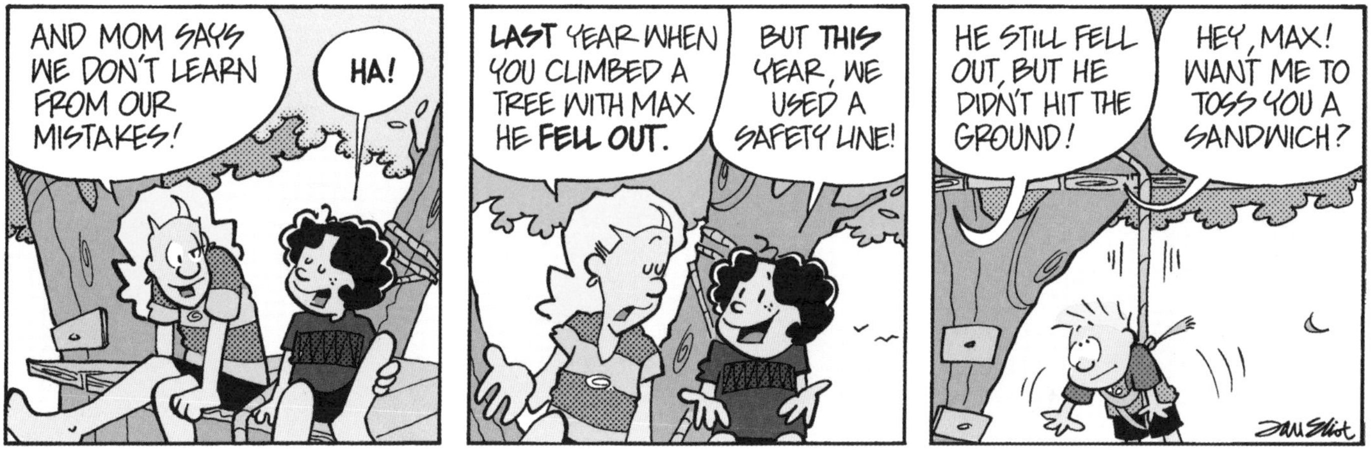
AND MOM SAYS WE DON'T LEARN FROM OUR MISTAKES!
HA!
LAST YEAR WHEN YOU CLIMBED A TREE WITH MAX HE **FELL OUT.**
BUT **THIS** YEAR, WE USED A SAFETY LINE!
HE STILL FELL OUT, BUT HE DIDN'T HIT THE GROUND!
HEY, MAX! WANT ME TO TOSS YOU A SANDWICH?

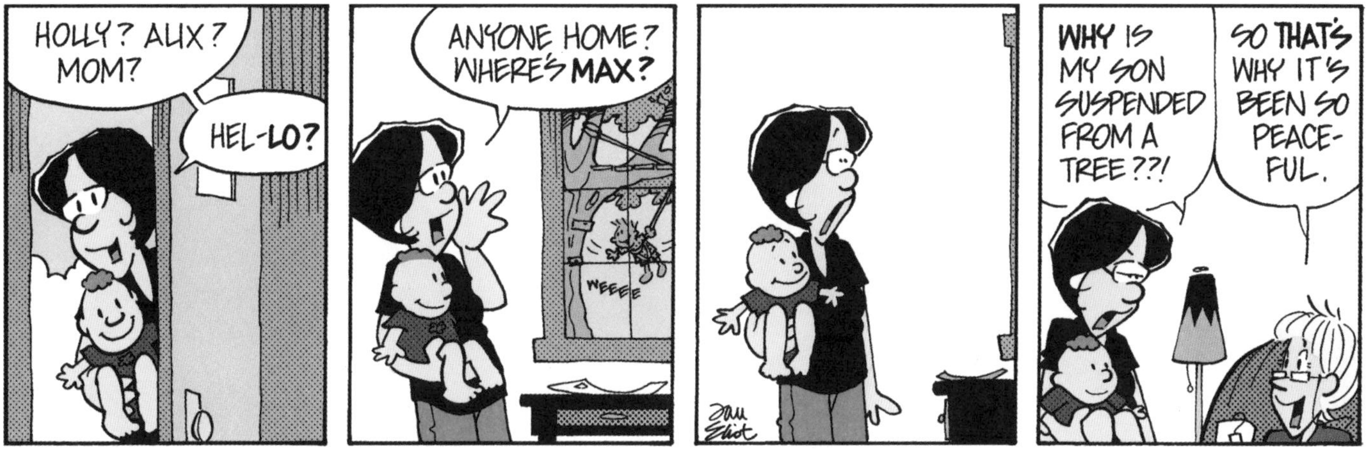
HOLLY? ALIX? MOM?
HEL-**LO?**
ANYONE HOME? WHERE'S **MAX?**
WEEEE
WHY IS MY SON SUSPENDED FROM A TREE??!
SO **THAT'S** WHY IT'S BEEN SO PEACE-FUL.

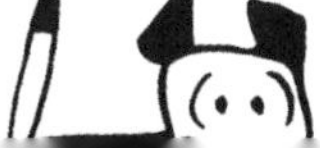

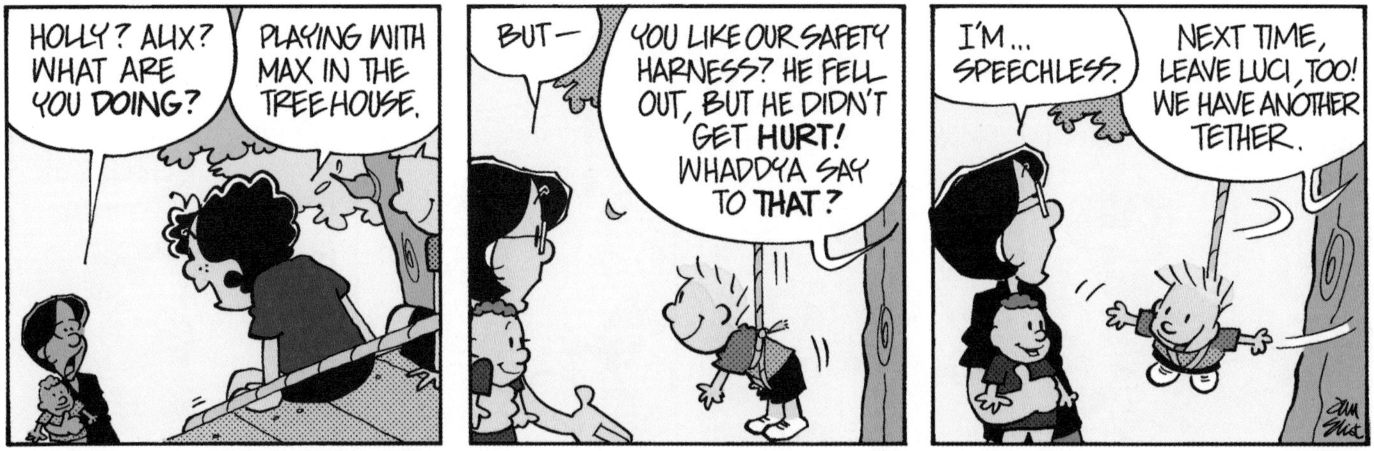
HOLLY? ALIX? WHAT ARE YOU DOING?
PLAYING WITH MAX IN THE TREEHOUSE.
BUT—
YOU LIKE OUR SAFETY HARNESS? HE FELL OUT, BUT HE DIDN'T GET HURT! WHADDYA SAY TO THAT?
I'M... SPEECHLESS.
NEXT TIME, LEAVE LUCI, TOO! WE HAVE ANOTHER TETHER.

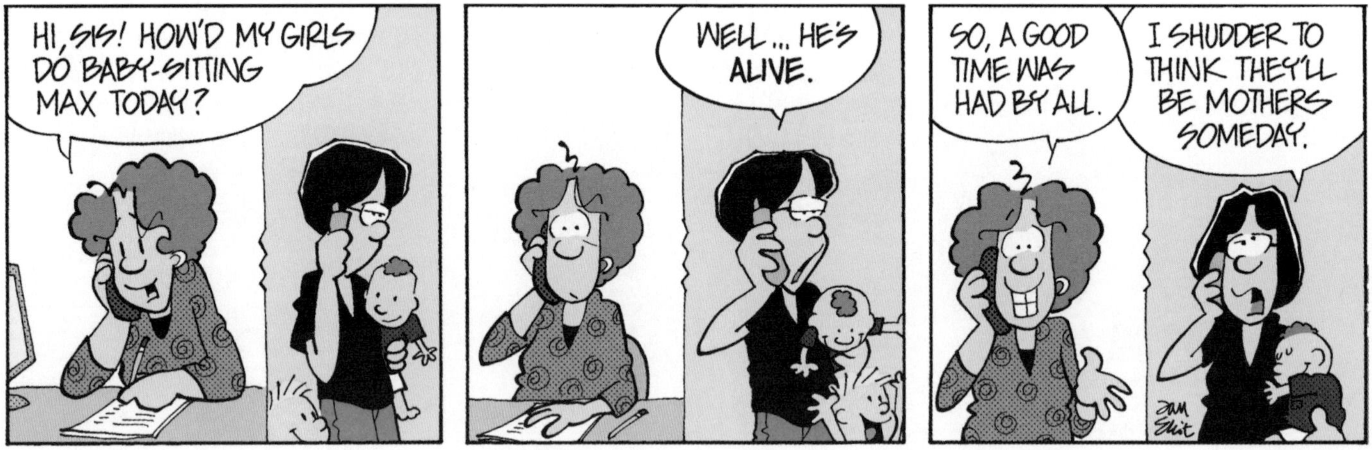
HI, SIS! HOW'D MY GIRLS DO BABY-SITTING MAX TODAY?
WELL... HE'S ALIVE.
SO, A GOOD TIME WAS HAD BY ALL.
I SHUDDER TO THINK THEY'LL BE MOTHERS SOMEDAY.

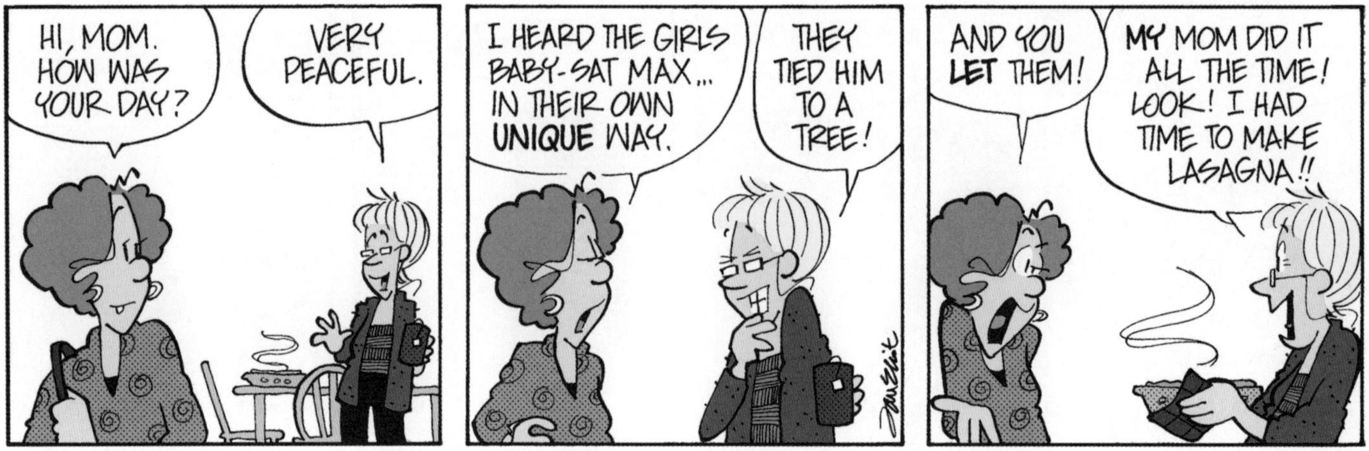
HI, MOM. HOW WAS YOUR DAY?
VERY PEACEFUL.
I HEARD THE GIRLS BABY-SAT MAX... IN THEIR OWN UNIQUE WAY.
THEY TIED HIM TO A TREE!
AND YOU LET THEM!
MY MOM DID IT ALL THE TIME! LOOK! I HAD TIME TO MAKE LASAGNA!!

Stone Soup

Jan Eliot
I HATE PEAK SEASON.

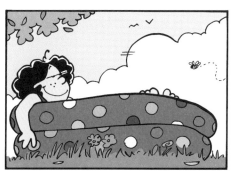

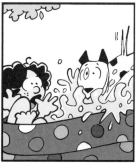

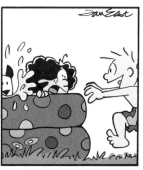

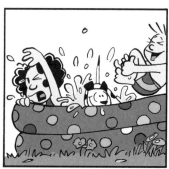

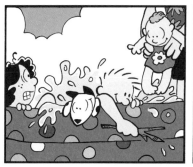

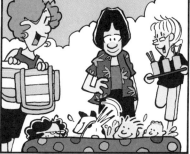

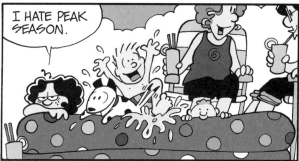

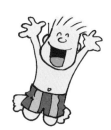

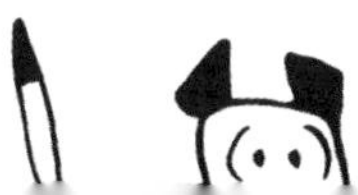

Stone Soup

WHAT ARE YOU DOING?

SETTING UP A NATURE PRESERVE.

IN OUR **BACKYARD**??

THIS COULD BE THE LAST WILD, UNDEVELOPED AREA IN THE NEIGHBORHOOD!

IT'S A **WEED** PATCH.

NATIVE SPECIES, WORTHY OF OUR PROTECTION.

LOOK! WE HAVE A RARE BUTTERFLY.

IT'S A CABBAGE MOTH.

WHAT **LUCK**! WE GET TO WITNESS THE MIRACLE OF SPIDER EGGS HATCHING!!

SPIDERS ARE GROSS.

I SPEAK FOR THE GROUP WHEN I SAY THE **FEELING** IS MUTUAL.

I LIKE SPIDERS. CAN I BE OFF-LEASH?

Stone Soup

THERE YOU GO... COMFY? GOT EVERYTHING YOU NEED?
'CAUSE YOU'RE SICK AND WE WANT YOU TO GET WELL.
WHAT A SHAME YOU CAUGHT A COLD.
HMPHLG
SUMMER COLDS ARE SUCH A DRAG.
ALIX HAS MAGAZINES. IF YOU NEED ANYTHING ELSE, LET US KNOW. PROMISE??
WOW, THANKS.
OH, WAIT. HOLLY'S ONLY 13.
MY TEA'S COLD.
HOT, COLD, IT'S STILL TEA. DRINK UP.

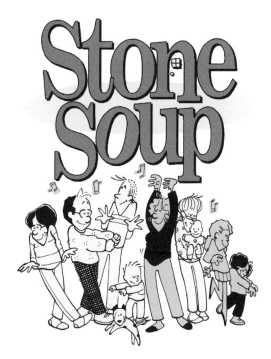

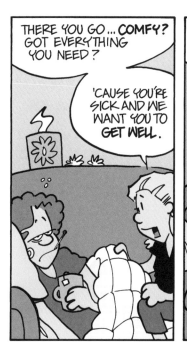

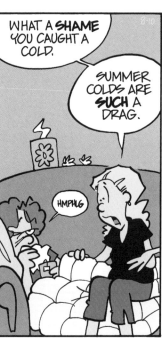

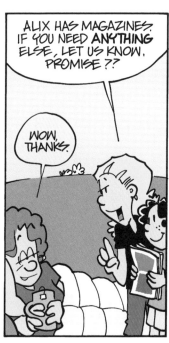

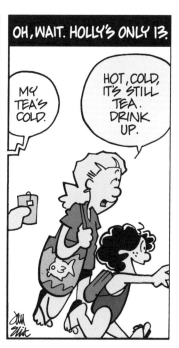

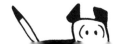

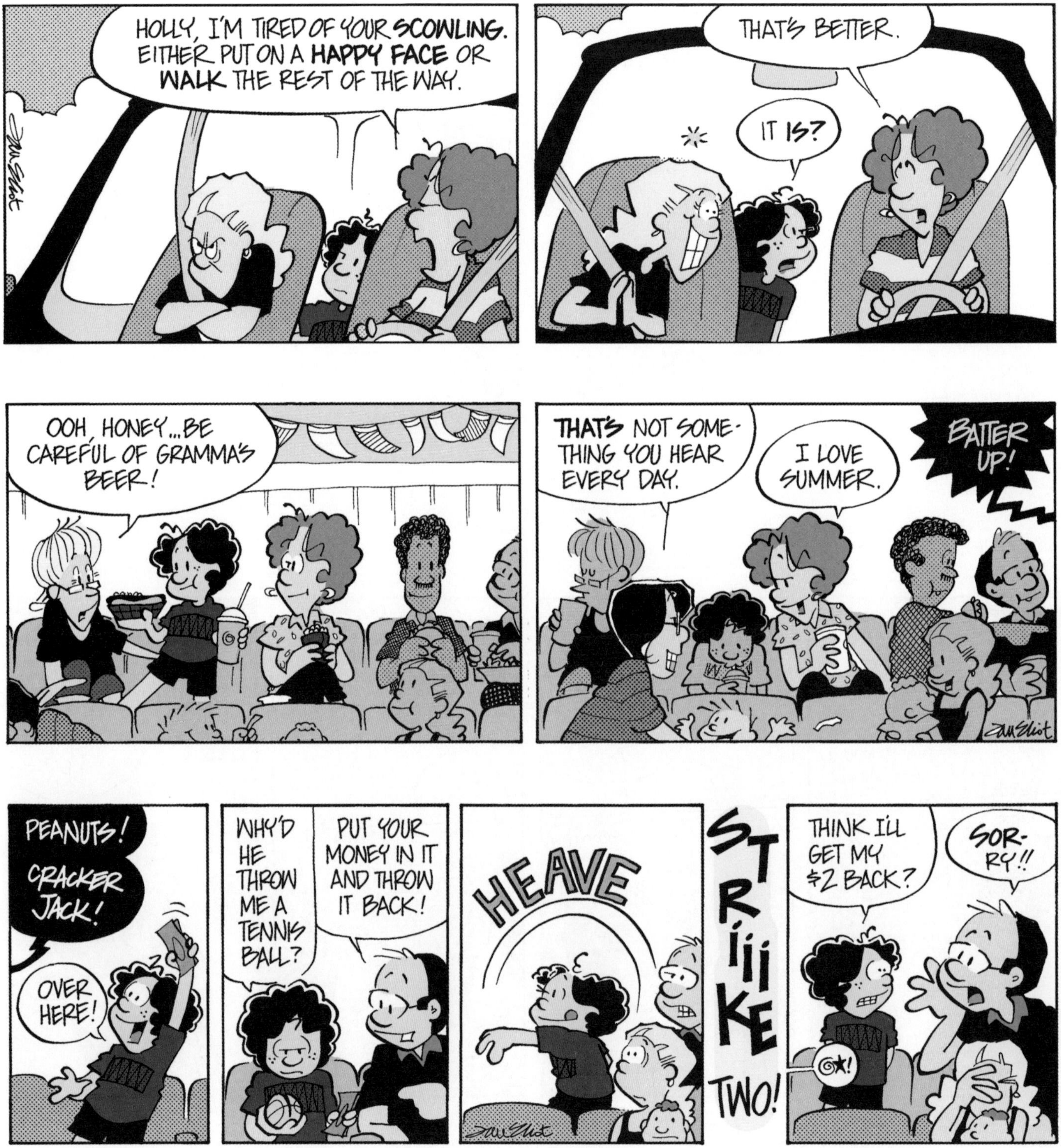
HOLLY, I'M TIRED OF YOUR SCOWLING. EITHER PUT ON A HAPPY FACE OR WALK THE REST OF THE WAY.
THAT'S BETTER.
IT IS?
OOH, HONEY...BE CAREFUL OF GRAMMA'S BEER!
THAT'S NOT SOMETHING YOU HEAR EVERY DAY.
I LOVE SUMMER.
BATTER UP!
PEANUTS! CRACKER JACK!
OVER HERE!
WHY'D HE THROW ME A TENNIS BALL?
PUT YOUR MONEY IN IT AND THROW IT BACK!
HEAVE
STRiiiKE TWO!
THINK I'LL GET MY $2 BACK?
SORRY!!

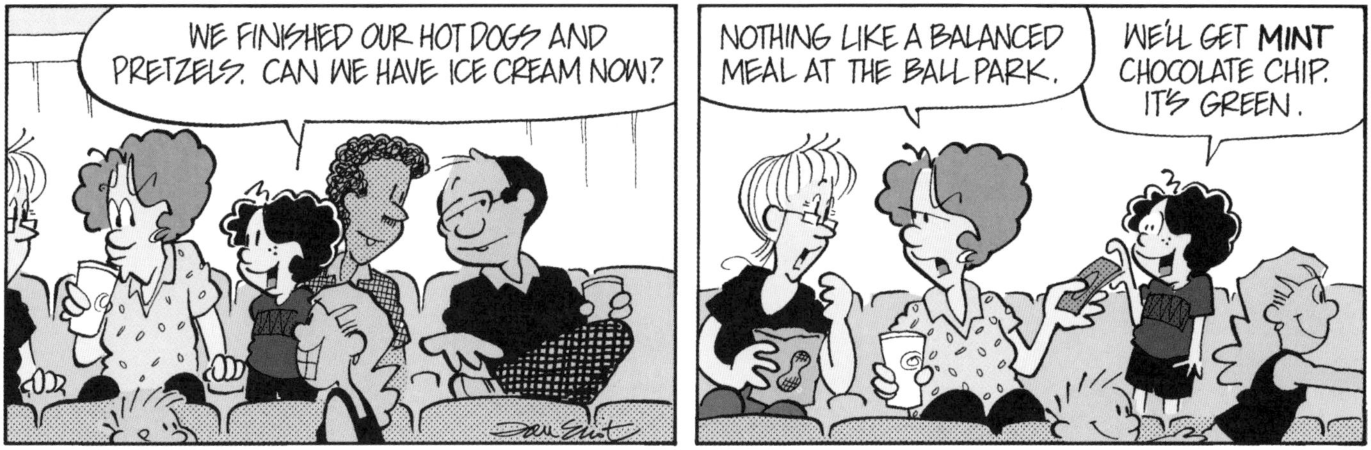
WE FINISHED OUR HOT DOGS AND PRETZELS. CAN WE HAVE ICE CREAM NOW?
NOTHING LIKE A BALANCED MEAL AT THE BALL PARK.
WE'LL GET **MINT** CHOCOLATE CHIP. IT'S GREEN.

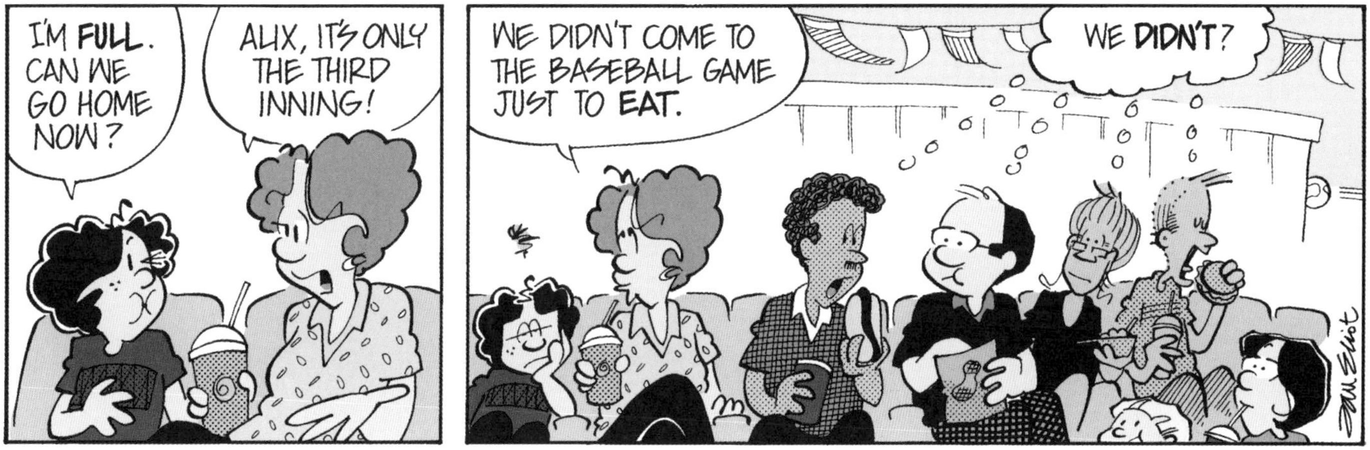
I'M **FULL**. CAN WE GO HOME NOW?
ALIX, IT'S ONLY THE THIRD INNING!
WE DIDN'T COME TO THE BASEBALL GAME JUST TO **EAT**.
WE **DIDN'T**?

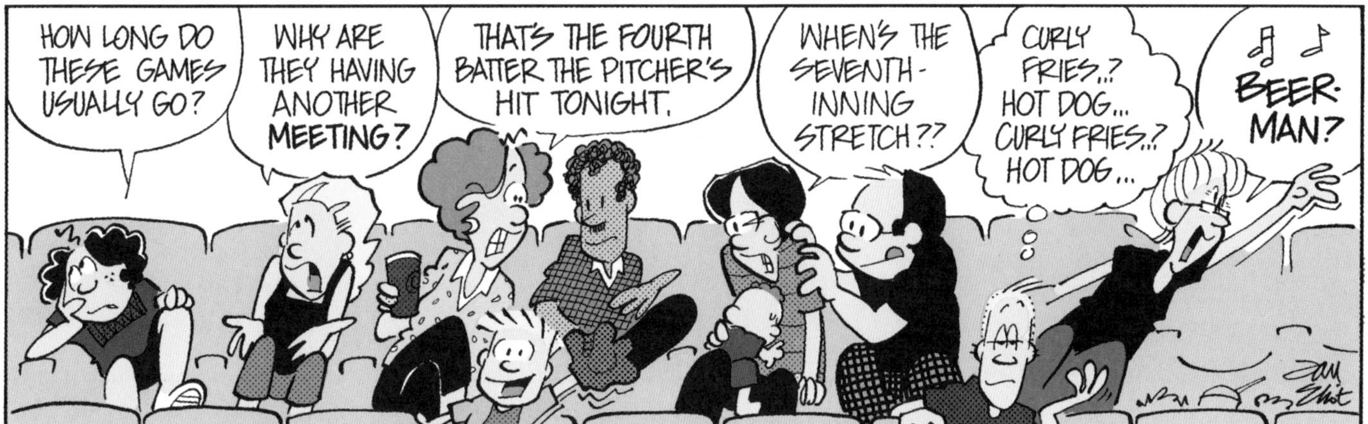
HOW LONG DO THESE GAMES USUALLY GO?
WHY ARE THEY HAVING ANOTHER **MEETING?**
THAT'S THE FOURTH BATTER THE PITCHER'S HIT TONIGHT.
WHEN'S THE SEVENTH-INNING STRETCH??
CURLY FRIES..? HOT DOG... CURLY FRIES..? HOT DOG...
BEER-MAN?

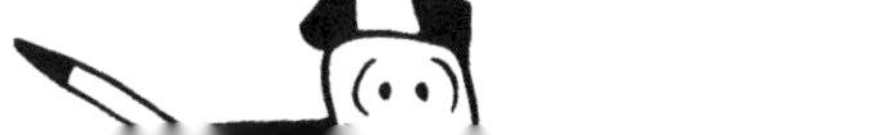

Stone Soup

Cafe Aloof
I LOVE THIS.
ME, TOO.
SUMMER WEATHER, OUTDOOR CAFE...
SITTING IN AN OUTDOOR CAFE HAS ALWAYS **SCREAMED** SUMMER TO ME.
SIP
SIP
BUT, WHEN WE WERE YOUNGER IT DIDN'T INVOLVE ACTUAL **SCREAMING**, DID IT?
HEY!?
!!!
!!!
!!!

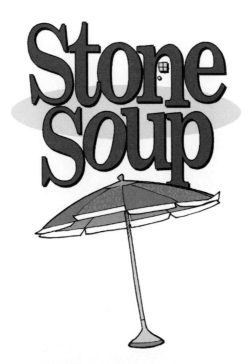

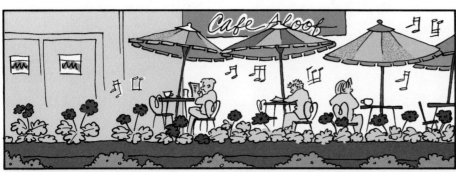

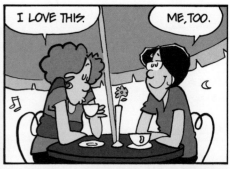

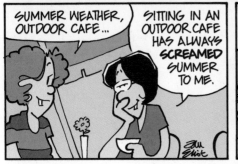

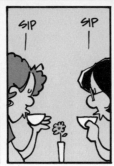

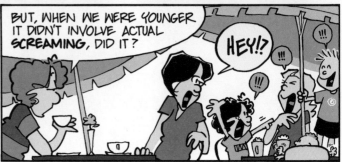

Stone Soup

REALLY... I SHOULD **DO** SOMETHING.

ME, TOO.

I JUST DON'T **FEEL** LIKE IT.

ME, NEITHER.

IT JUST SEEMS LIKE I SHOULD BE **ACCOMPLISH-ING** SOMETHING...

I SUPPOSE.

THEY SAY AMERICANS HAVE AN EXAGGERATED NEED FOR PRODUCTIVITY.

SO, BY DOING **NOTHING**... I'D PROVE A POINT?

SEEMS SO.

WELL, MY DAY'S SET.

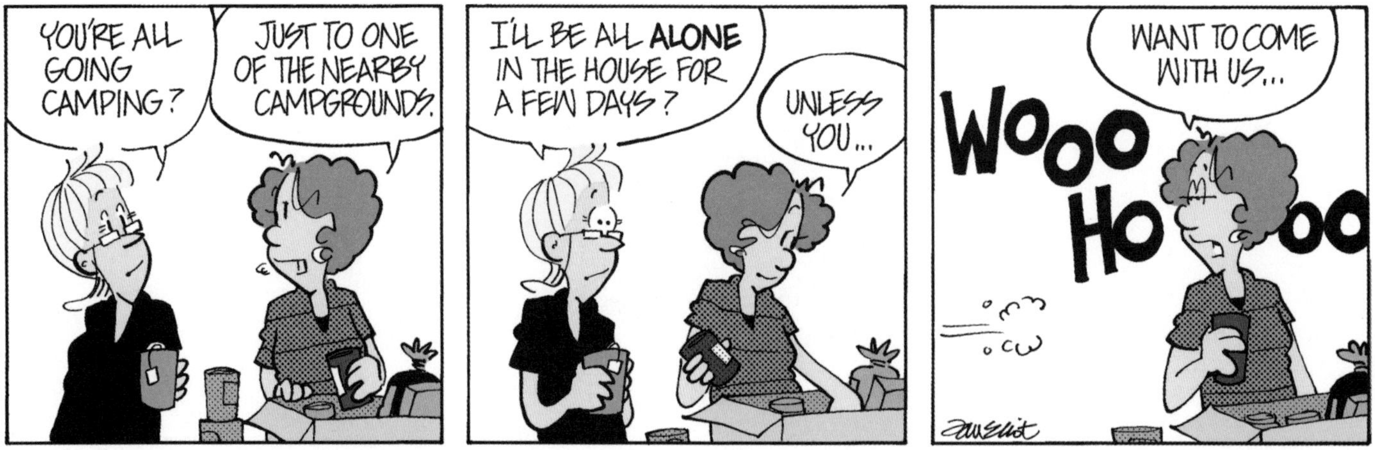
YOU'RE ALL GOING CAMPING?
JUST TO ONE OF THE NEARBY CAMPGROUNDS.
I'LL BE ALL **ALONE** IN THE HOUSE FOR A FEW DAYS?
UNLESS YOU...
WANT TO COME WITH US...
WOOO HOOOO

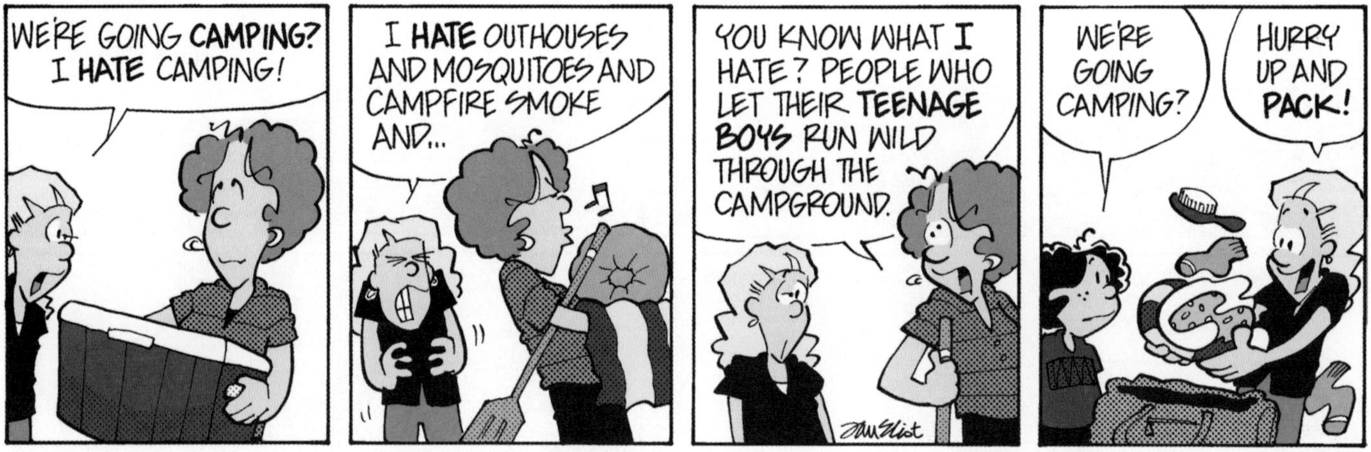
WE'RE GOING **CAMPING?** I **HATE** CAMPING!
I **HATE** OUTHOUSES AND MOSQUITOES AND CAMPFIRE SMOKE AND...
YOU KNOW WHAT **I** HATE? PEOPLE WHO LET THEIR **TEENAGE BOYS** RUN WILD THROUGH THE CAMPGROUND.
WE'RE GOING CAMPING?
HURRY UP AND **PACK**!

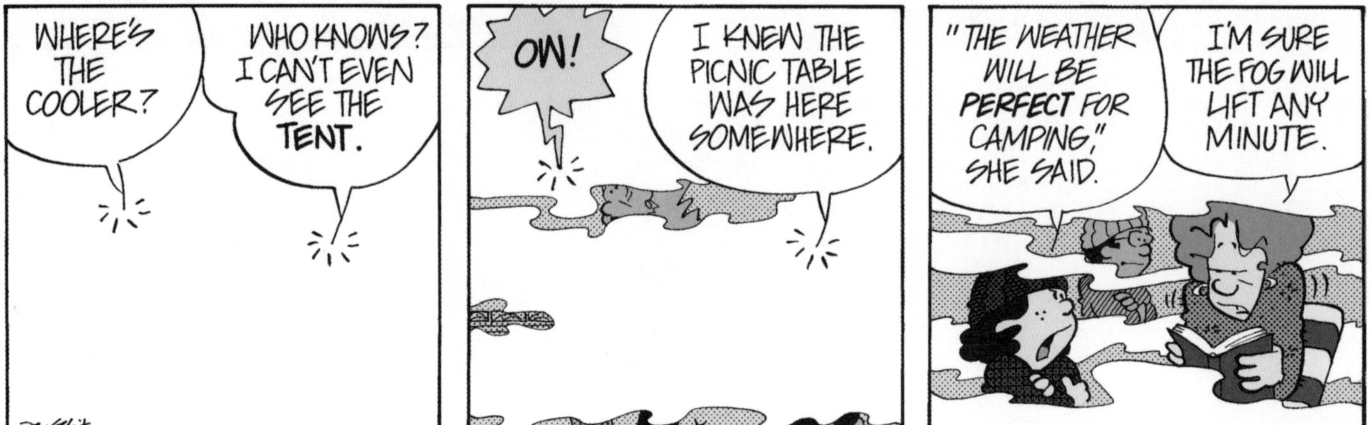
WHERE'S THE COOLER?
WHO KNOWS? I CAN'T EVEN SEE THE **TENT**.
OW!
I KNEW THE PICNIC TABLE WAS HERE SOMEWHERE.
"THE WEATHER WILL BE **PERFECT** FOR CAMPING," SHE SAID.
I'M SURE THE FOG WILL LIFT ANY MINUTE.

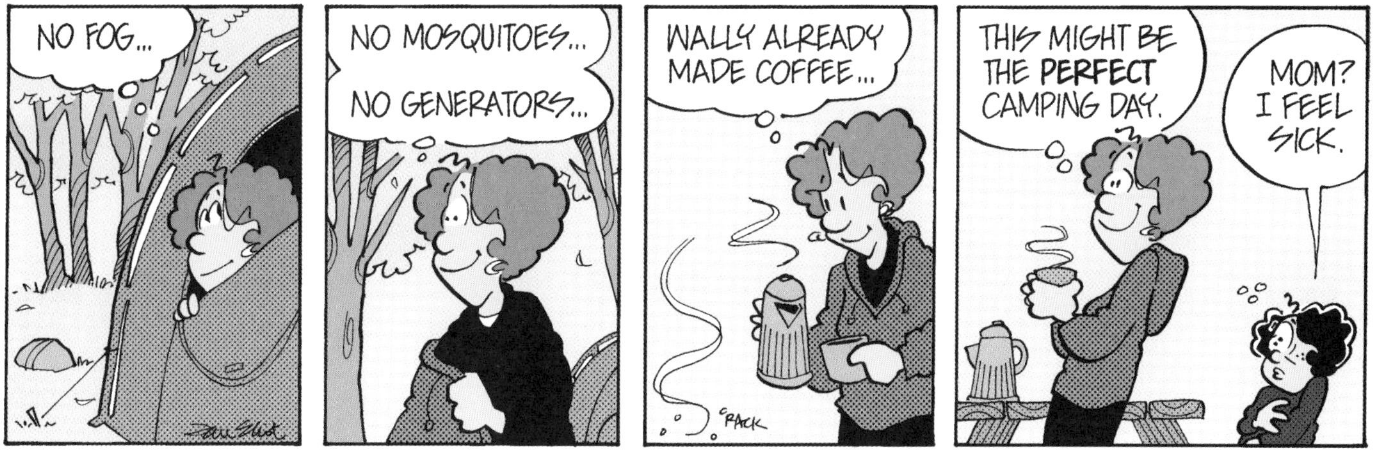
NO FOG...
NO MOSQUITOES...
NO GENERATORS...
WALLY ALREADY MADE COFFEE...
CRACK
THIS MIGHT BE THE **PERFECT** CAMPING DAY.
MOM? I FEEL SICK.

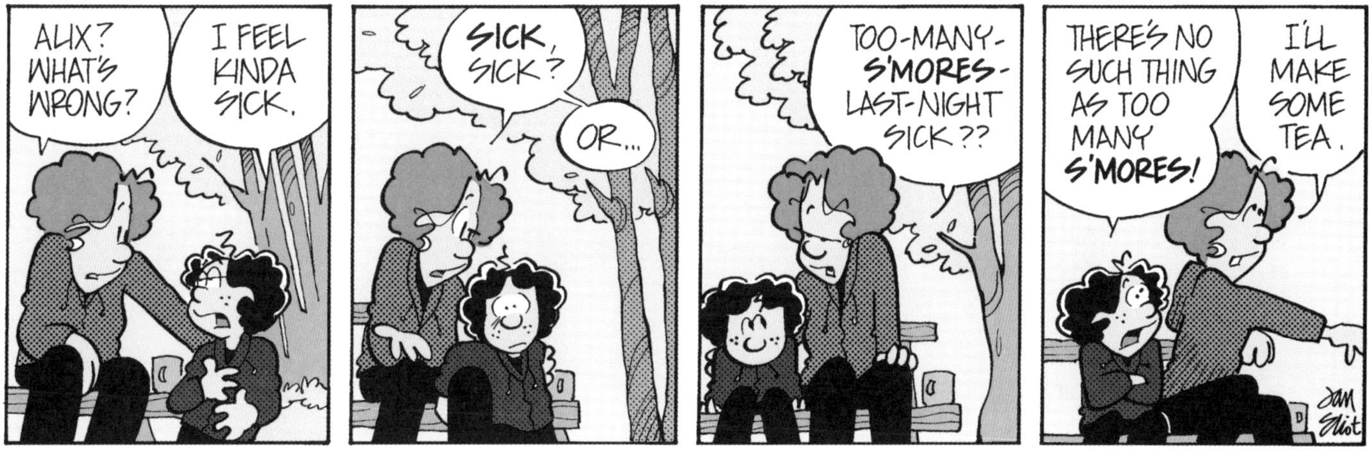
ALIX? WHAT'S WRONG?
I FEEL KINDA SICK.
SICK, SICK?
OR...
TOO-MANY-**S'MORES**-LAST-NIGHT SICK??
THERE'S NO SUCH THING AS TOO MANY **S'MORES!**
I'LL MAKE SOME TEA.

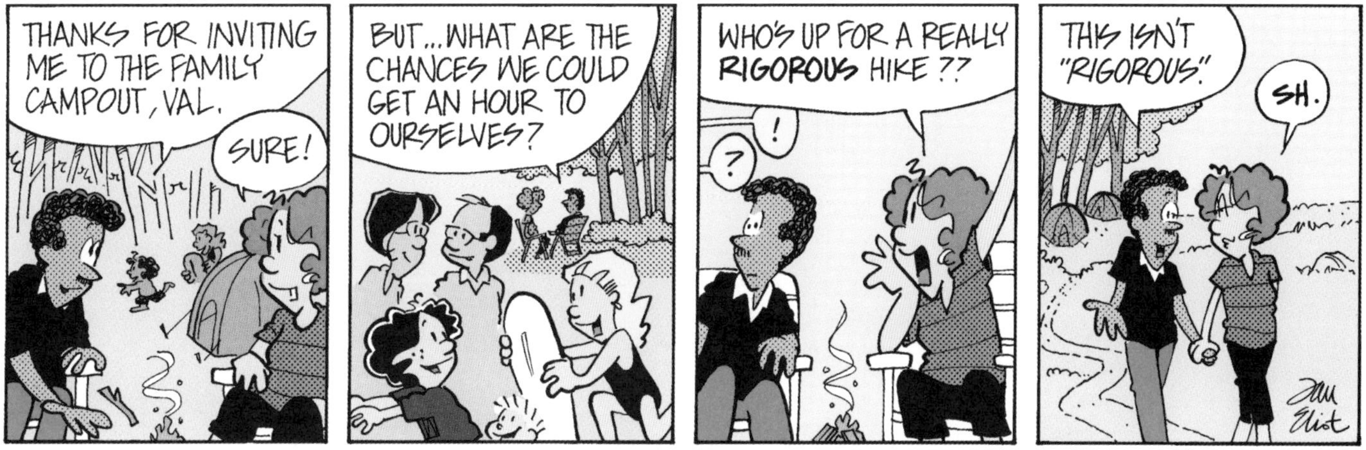
THANKS FOR INVITING ME TO THE FAMILY CAMPOUT, VAL.
SURE!
BUT...WHAT ARE THE CHANCES WE COULD GET AN HOUR TO OURSELVES?
WHO'S UP FOR A REALLY **RIGOROUS** HIKE??
?
!
THIS ISN'T "RIGOROUS."
SH.

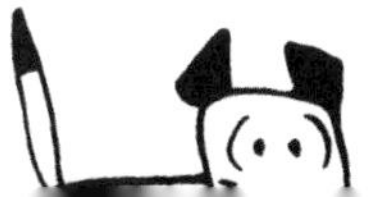

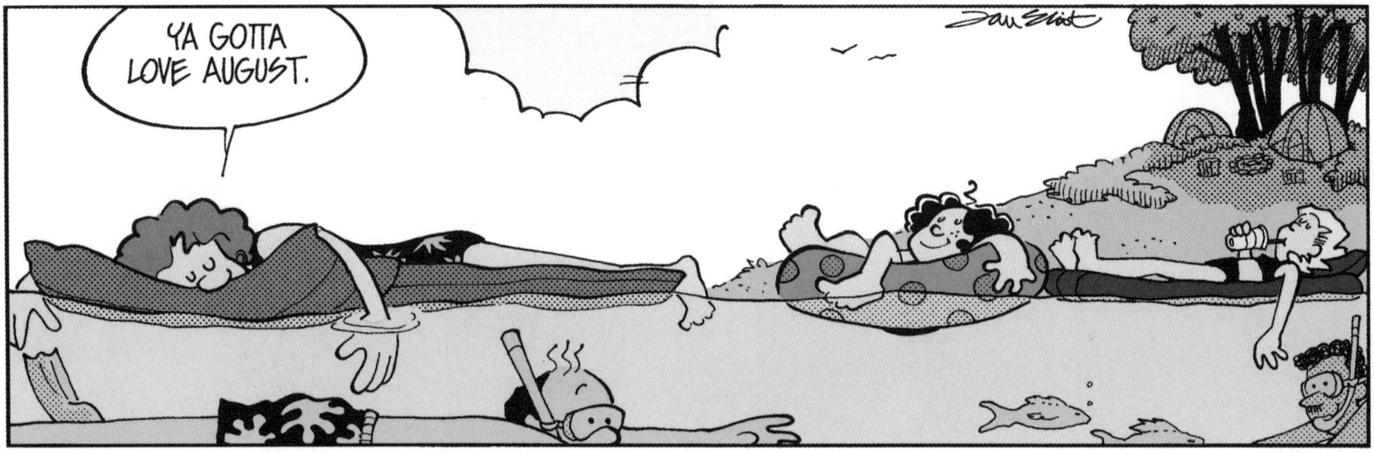
YA GOTTA LOVE AUGUST.

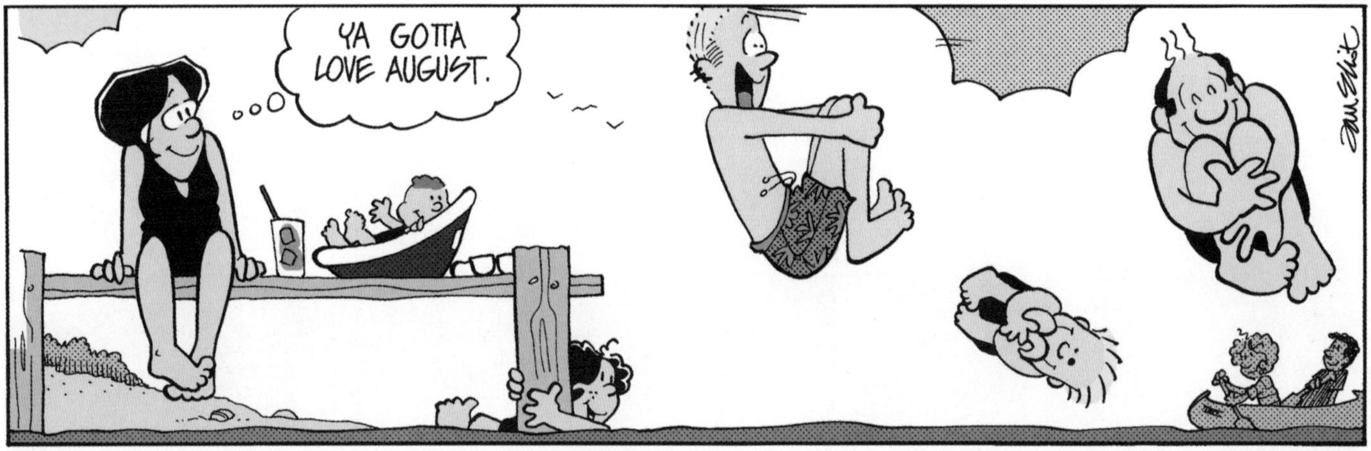
YA GOTTA LOVE AUGUST.

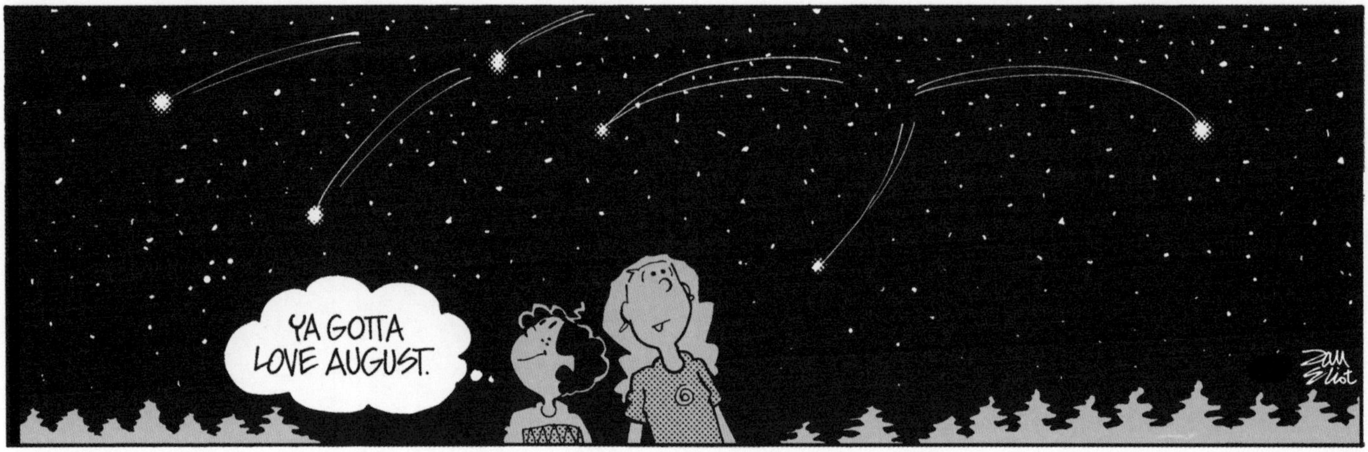
YA GOTTA LOVE AUGUST.

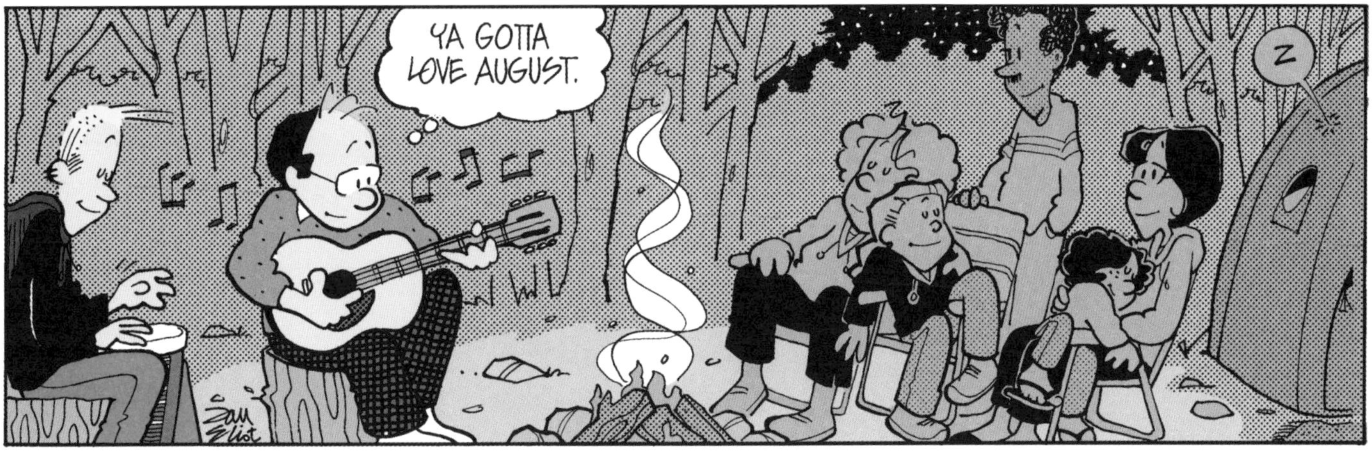
YA GOTTA LOVE AUGUST.
Z

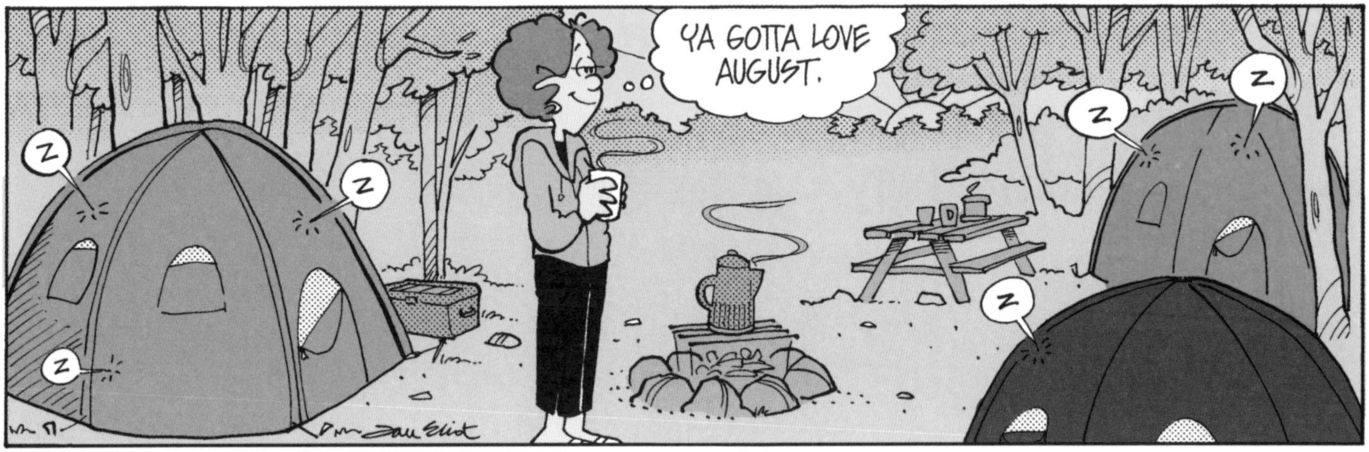
YA GOTTA LOVE AUGUST.
Z
Z
Z
Z
Z
Z

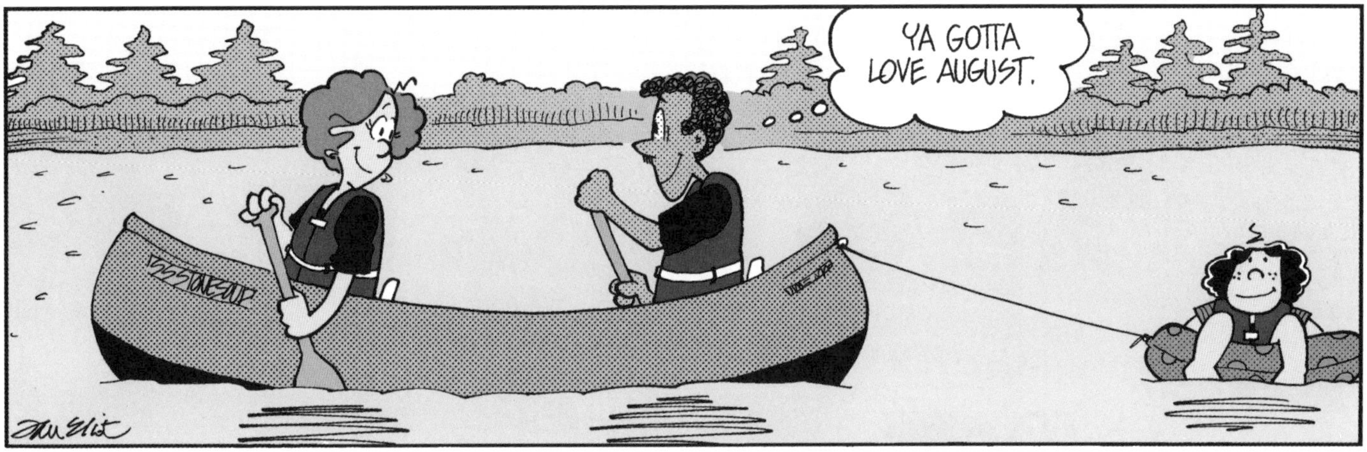
YA GOTTA LOVE AUGUST.

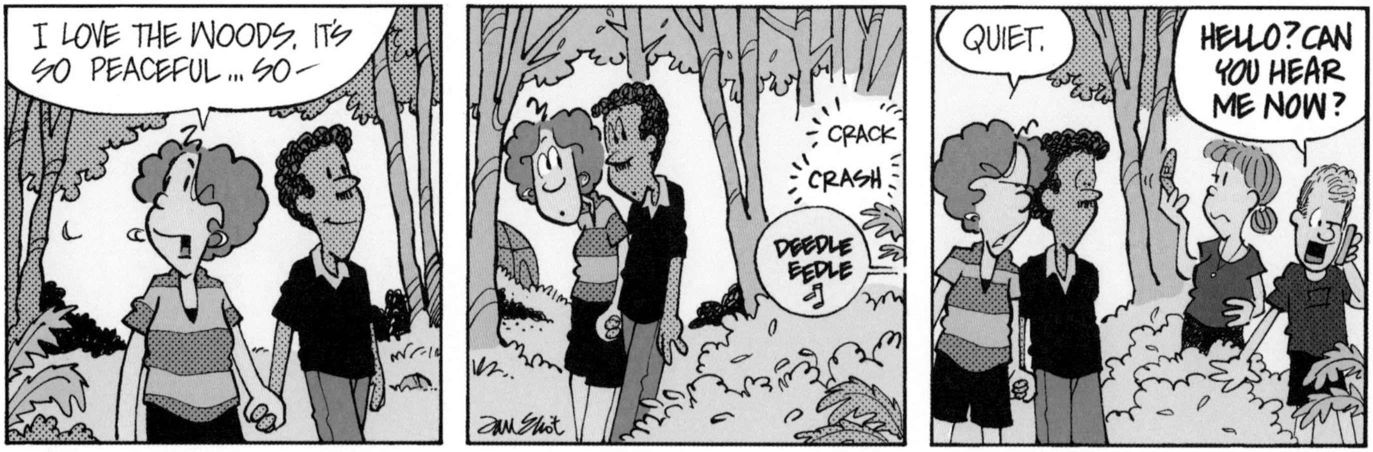
I LOVE THE WOODS. IT'S SO PEACEFUL... SO—
CRACK
CRASH
DEEDLE EEDLE
QUIET.
HELLO? CAN YOU HEAR ME NOW?

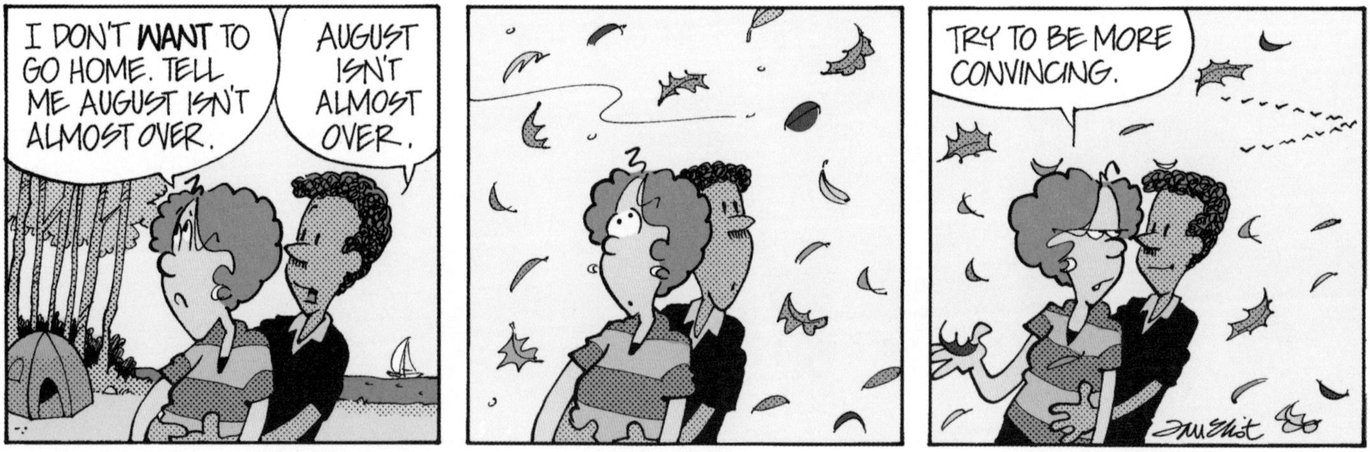
I DON'T **WANT** TO GO HOME. TELL ME AUGUST ISN'T ALMOST OVER.
AUGUST ISN'T ALMOST OVER.
TRY TO BE MORE CONVINCING.

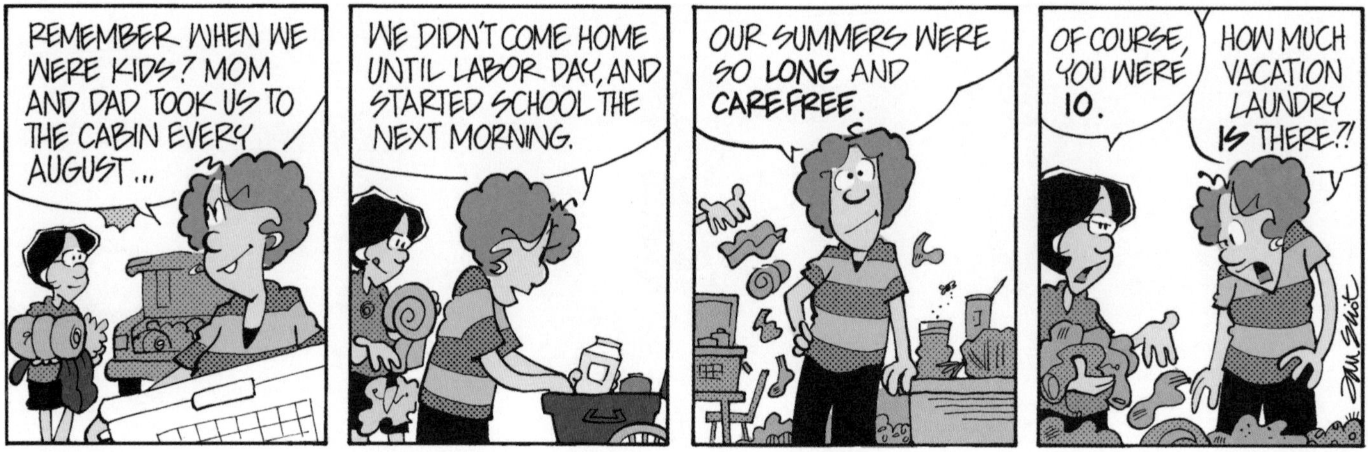
REMEMBER WHEN WE WERE KIDS? MOM AND DAD TOOK US TO THE CABIN EVERY AUGUST...
WE DIDN'T COME HOME UNTIL LABOR DAY, AND STARTED SCHOOL THE NEXT MORNING.
OUR SUMMERS WERE SO **LONG** AND **CAREFREE**.
OF COURSE, YOU WERE **10**.
HOW MUCH VACATION LAUNDRY **IS** THERE?!

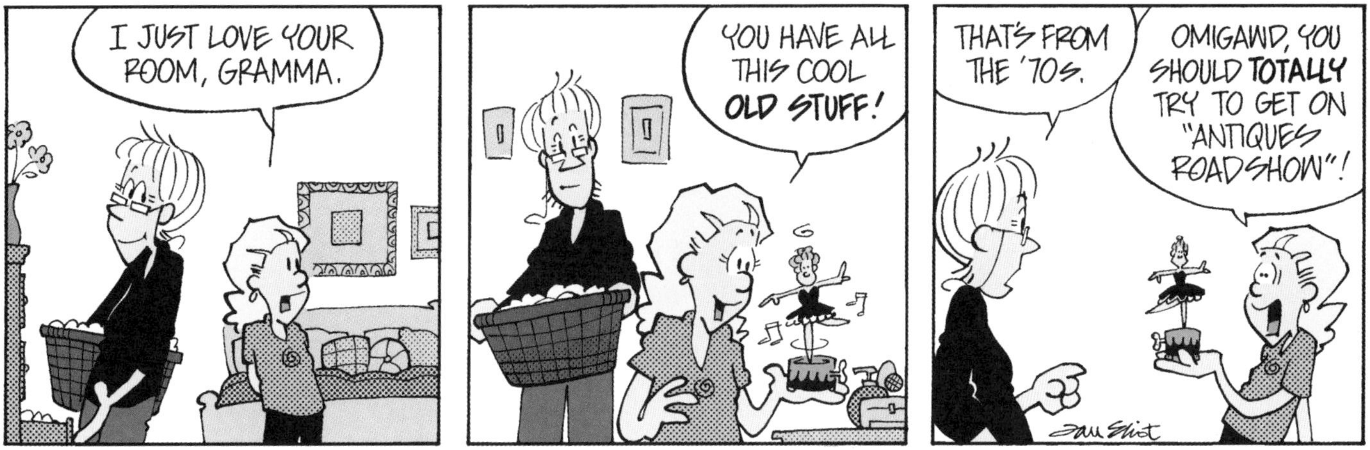
I JUST LOVE YOUR ROOM, GRAMMA.
YOU HAVE ALL THIS COOL **OLD STUFF**!
THAT'S FROM THE '70s.
OMIGAWD, YOU SHOULD **TOTALLY** TRY TO GET ON "ANTIQUES ROADSHOW"!

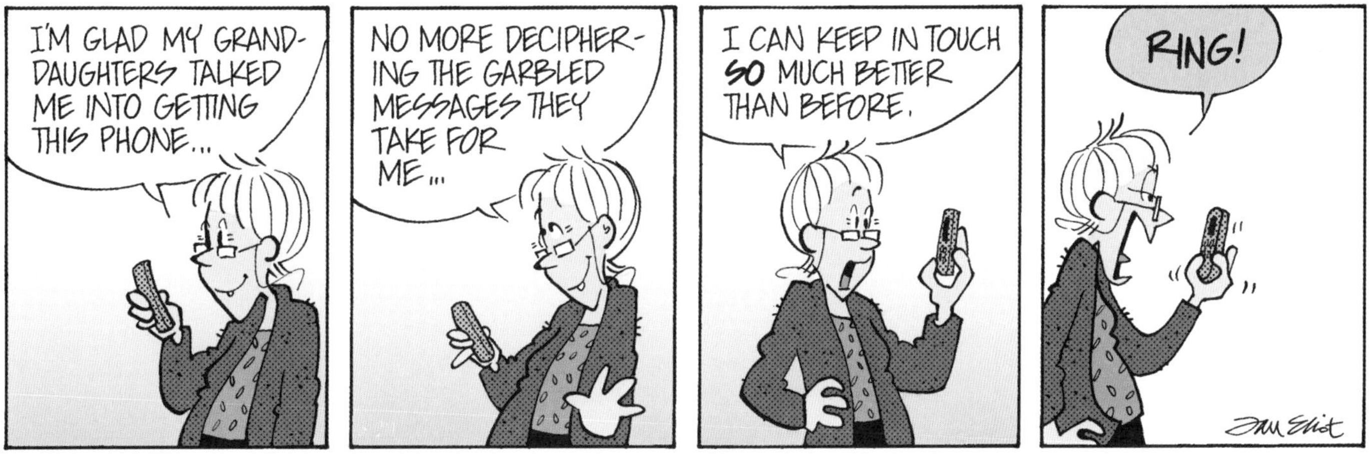
I'M GLAD MY GRAND-DAUGHTERS TALKED ME INTO GETTING THIS PHONE...
NO MORE DECIPHER-ING THE GARBLED MESSAGES THEY TAKE FOR ME...
I CAN KEEP IN TOUCH **SO** MUCH BETTER THAN BEFORE.
RING!

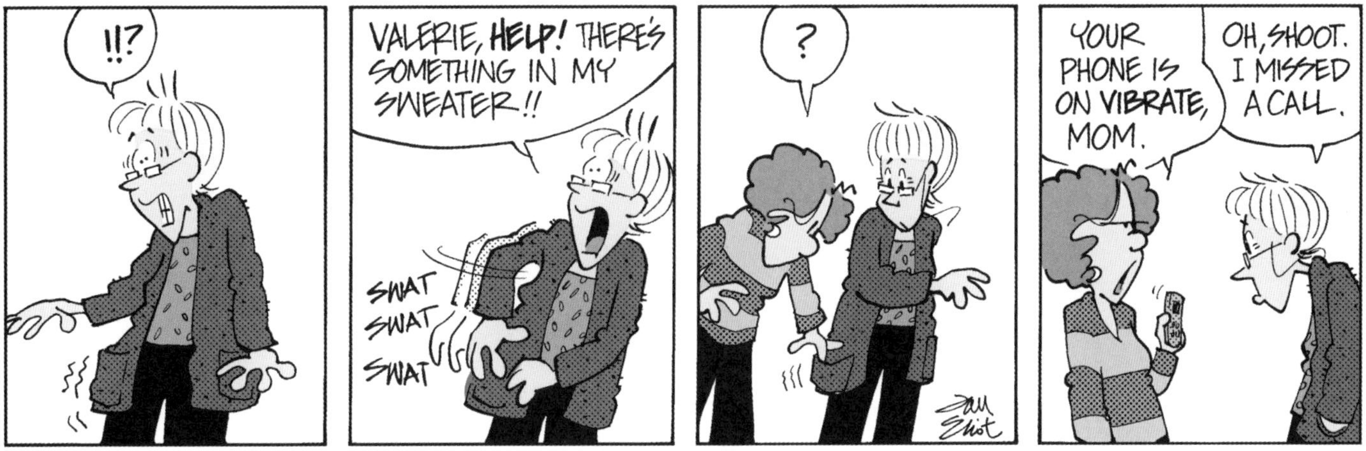
!!?
VALERIE, **HELP!** THERE'S SOMETHING IN MY SWEATER!!
SWAT
SWAT
SWAT
?
YOUR PHONE IS ON **VIBRATE**, MOM.
OH, SHOOT. I MISSED A CALL.

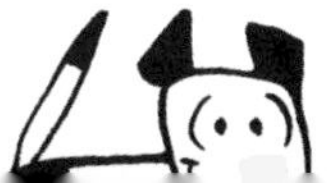

Stone Soup

SHOE
SUMMER IS NOT OFFICIALLY OVER UNTIL SEPTEMBER 22!
JUST STAND UP AND TELL ME HOW THEY FEEL.

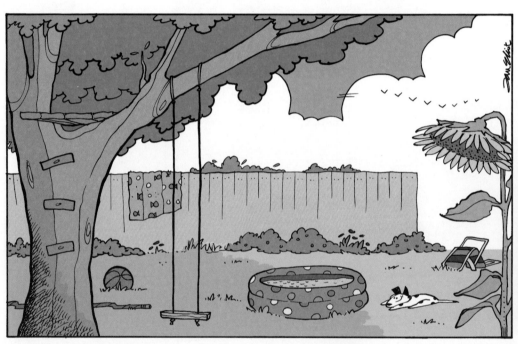

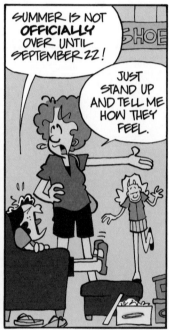

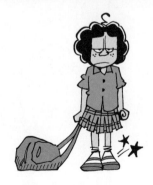

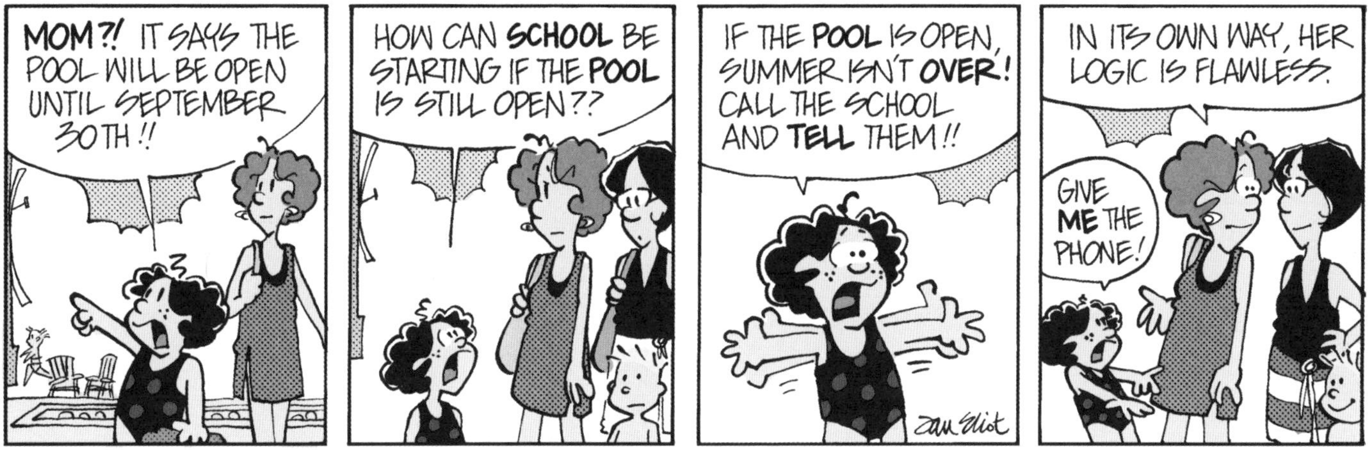
MOM?! IT SAYS THE POOL WILL BE OPEN UNTIL SEPTEMBER 30TH!!
HOW CAN SCHOOL BE STARTING IF THE POOL IS STILL OPEN??
IF THE POOL IS OPEN, SUMMER ISN'T OVER! CALL THE SCHOOL AND TELL THEM!!
IN ITS OWN WAY, HER LOGIC IS FLAWLESS.
GIVE ME THE PHONE!

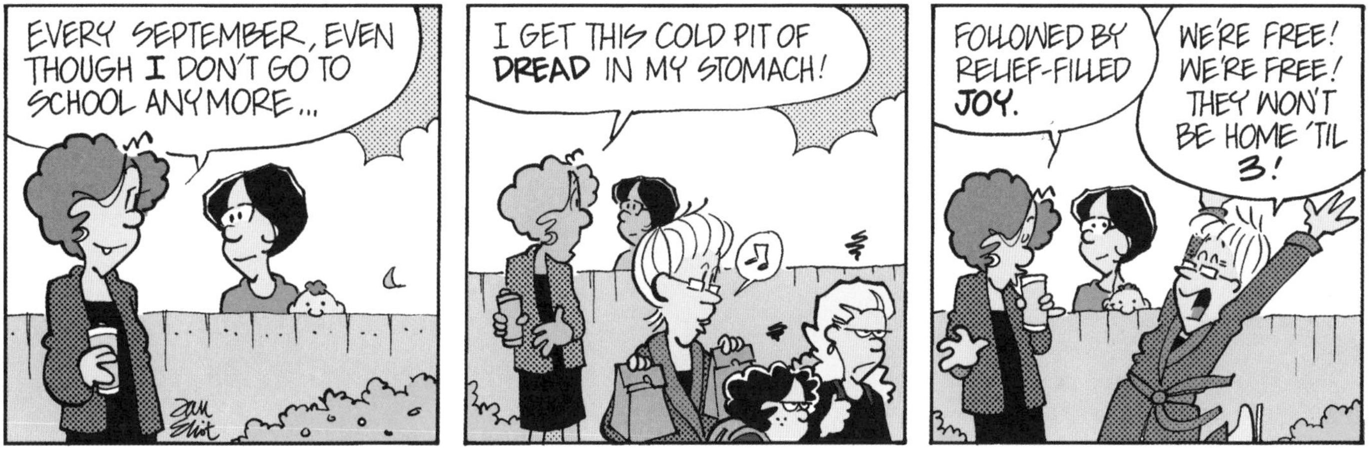
EVERY SEPTEMBER, EVEN THOUGH I DON'T GO TO SCHOOL ANYMORE...
I GET THIS COLD PIT OF DREAD IN MY STOMACH!
FOLLOWED BY RELIEF-FILLED JOY.
WE'RE FREE! WE'RE FREE! THEY WON'T BE HOME 'TIL 3!

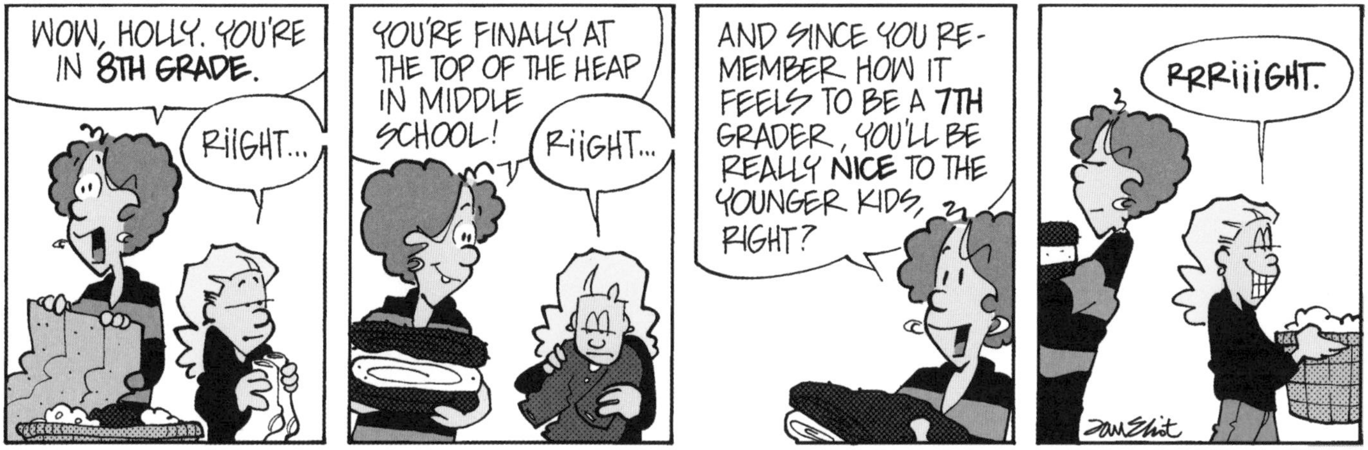
WOW, HOLLY. YOU'RE IN 8TH GRADE.
RiiGHT...
YOU'RE FINALLY AT THE TOP OF THE HEAP IN MIDDLE SCHOOL!
RiiGHT...
AND SINCE YOU RE-MEMBER HOW IT FEELS TO BE A 7TH GRADER, YOU'LL BE REALLY NICE TO THE YOUNGER KIDS, RIGHT?
RRRiiiGHT.

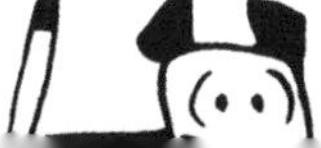

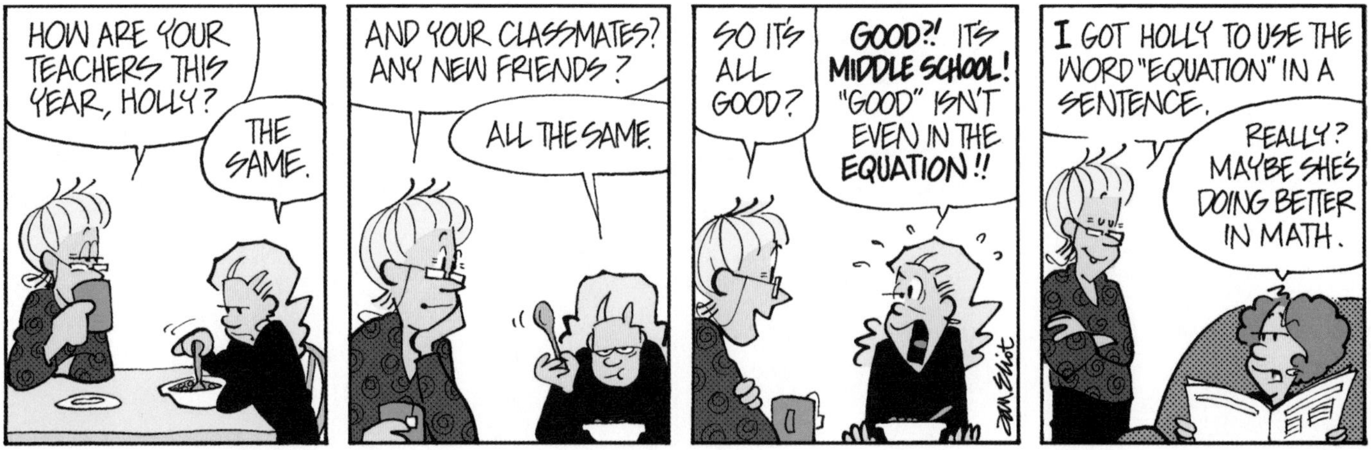
HOW ARE YOUR TEACHERS THIS YEAR, HOLLY?
THE SAME.
AND YOUR CLASSMATES? ANY NEW FRIENDS?
ALL THE SAME.
SO IT'S ALL GOOD?
GOOD?! IT'S MIDDLE SCHOOL! "GOOD" ISN'T EVEN IN THE EQUATION!!
I GOT HOLLY TO USE THE WORD "EQUATION" IN A SENTENCE.
REALLY? MAYBE SHE'S DOING BETTER IN MATH.

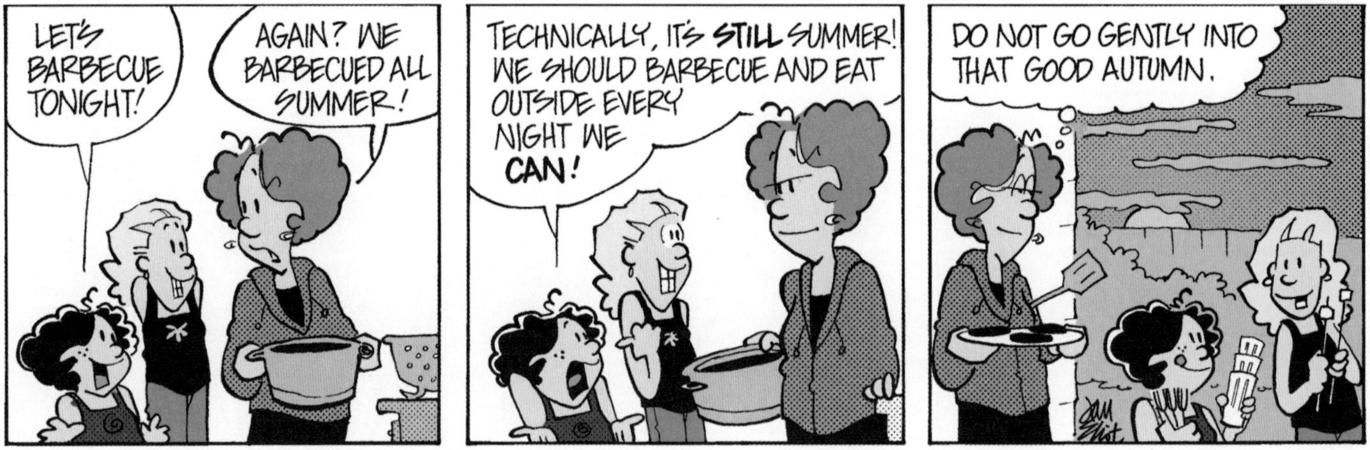
LET'S BARBECUE TONIGHT!
AGAIN? WE BARBECUED ALL SUMMER!
TECHNICALLY, IT'S STILL SUMMER! WE SHOULD BARBECUE AND EAT OUTSIDE EVERY NIGHT WE CAN!
DO NOT GO GENTLY INTO THAT GOOD AUTUMN.

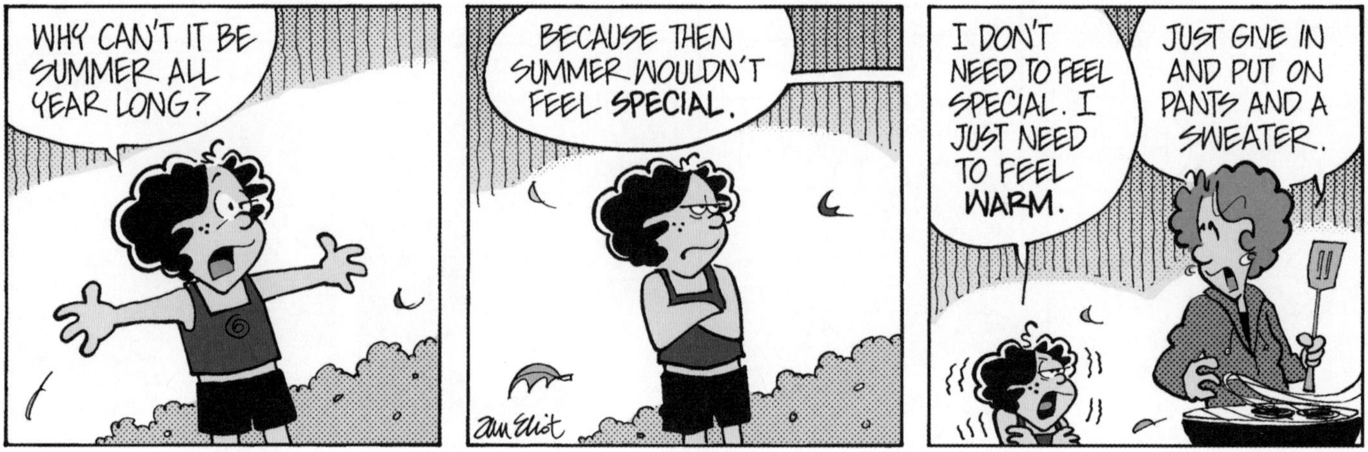
WHY CAN'T IT BE SUMMER ALL YEAR LONG?
BECAUSE THEN SUMMER WOULDN'T FEEL SPECIAL.
I DON'T NEED TO FEEL SPECIAL. I JUST NEED TO FEEL WARM.
JUST GIVE IN AND PUT ON PANTS AND A SWEATER.

WHAT ARE YOU DOING?

PRACTICING MY SCHOOL PICTURE FACE...

FAMOUS PEOPLE DON'T **SMILE** FOR THE CAMERA... THEY **SNEER**.

WHY?

'CAUSE SNEERING IS **COOL**.

IT IS?

SURE. BECAUSE SNEERING SAYS "**WHO CARES?**" TO EVERYONE AND EVERYTHING.

AND WE **LIKE** THEM FOR THAT?

SURE. BECAUSE THEY'RE **COOL**. HOW'S THIS?

THAT DEFINITELY SAYS "WHO CARES?"

MOM'S GONNA BE THRILLED.

WHO CARES??

OOH. CHECK OUT THE SHADES.

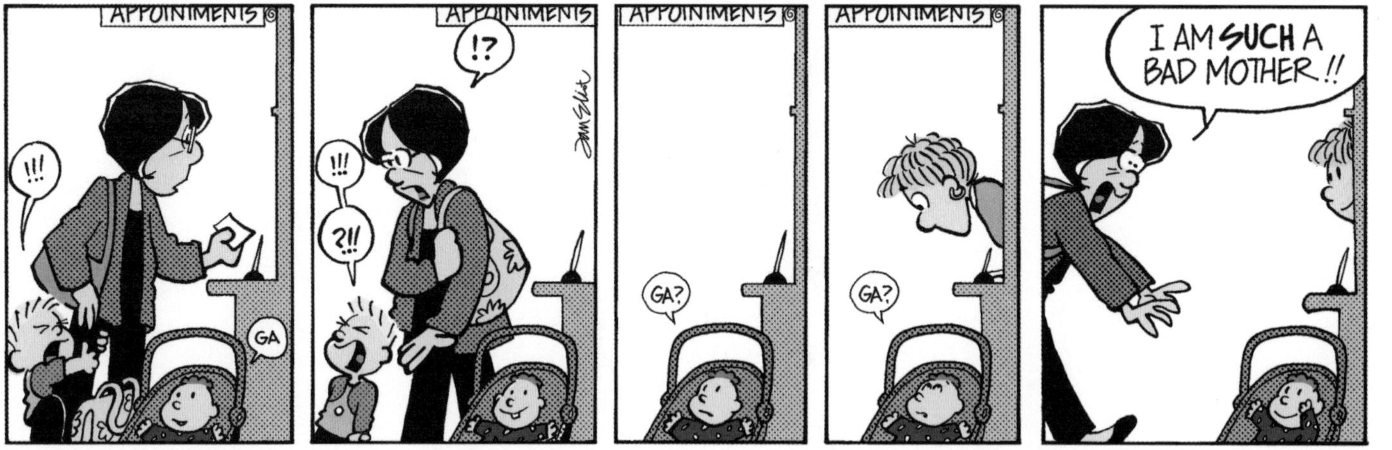
APPOINTMENTS
!!!
GA
APPOINTMENTS
!?
!!!
?!!
APPOINTMENTS
GA?
APPOINTMENTS
GA?
I AM **SUCH** A BAD MOTHER !!

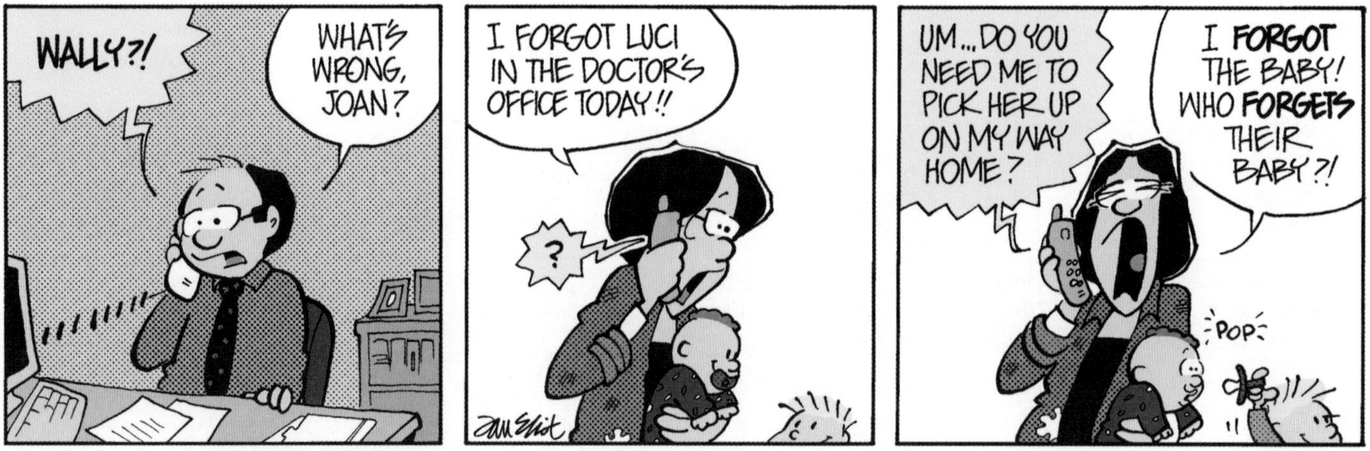
WALLY?!
WHAT'S WRONG, JOAN?
I FORGOT LUCI IN THE DOCTOR'S OFFICE TODAY!!
?
UM... DO YOU NEED ME TO PICK HER UP ON MY WAY HOME?
I **FORGOT** THE BABY! WHO **FORGETS** THEIR BABY?!
POP
!!

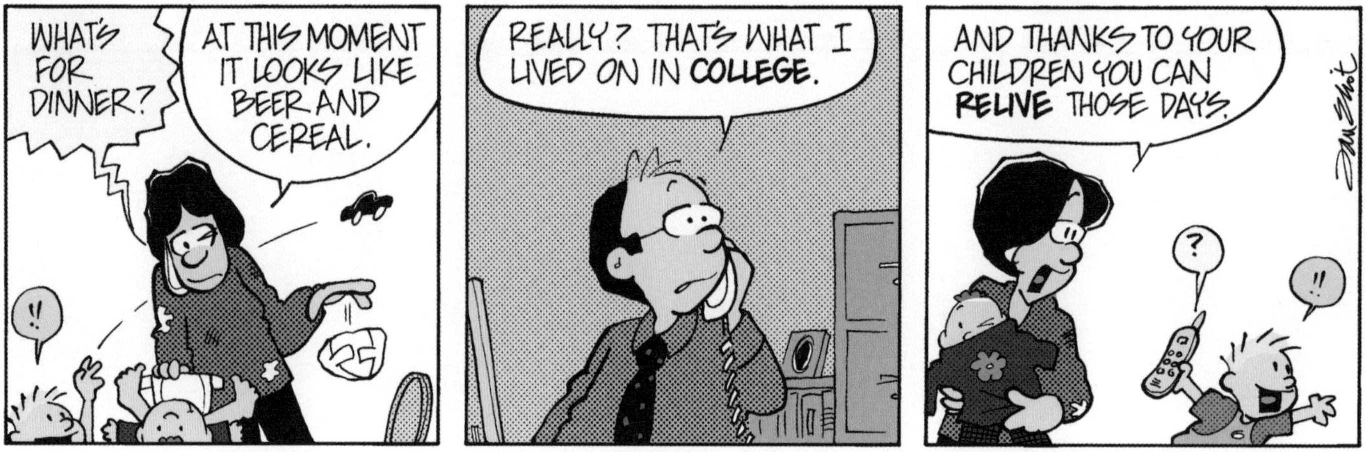
WHAT'S FOR DINNER?
AT THIS MOMENT IT LOOKS LIKE BEER AND CEREAL.
!!
REALLY? THAT'S WHAT I LIVED ON IN **COLLEGE**.
AND THANKS TO YOUR CHILDREN YOU CAN **RELIVE** THOSE DAYS.
?
!!

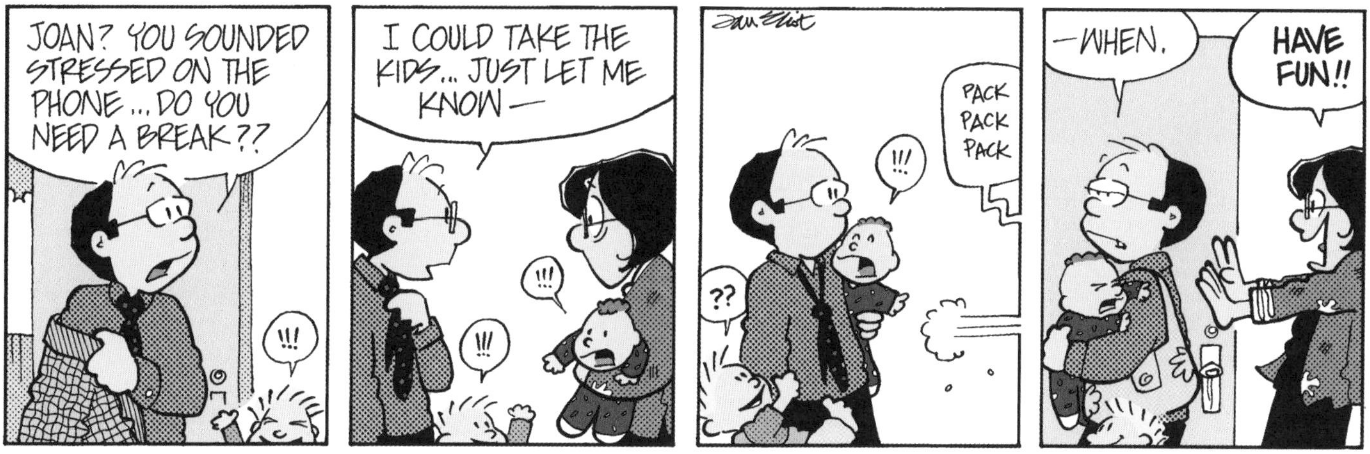
JOAN? YOU SOUNDED STRESSED ON THE PHONE ... DO YOU NEED A BREAK??
!!!
I COULD TAKE THE KIDS... JUST LET ME KNOW—
!!!
!!!
!!!
??
PACK PACK PACK
—WHEN.
HAVE FUN!!

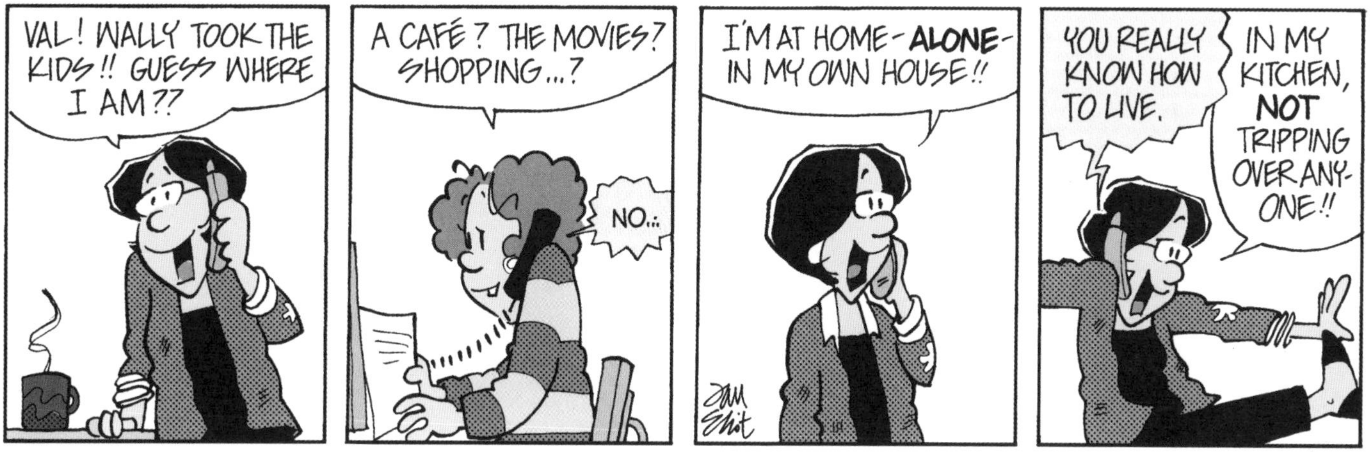
VAL! WALLY TOOK THE KIDS!! GUESS WHERE I AM??
A CAFÉ? THE MOVIES? SHOPPING...?
NO...
I'M AT HOME - ALONE - IN MY OWN HOUSE!!
YOU REALLY KNOW HOW TO LIVE.
IN MY KITCHEN, NOT TRIPPING OVER ANYONE!!

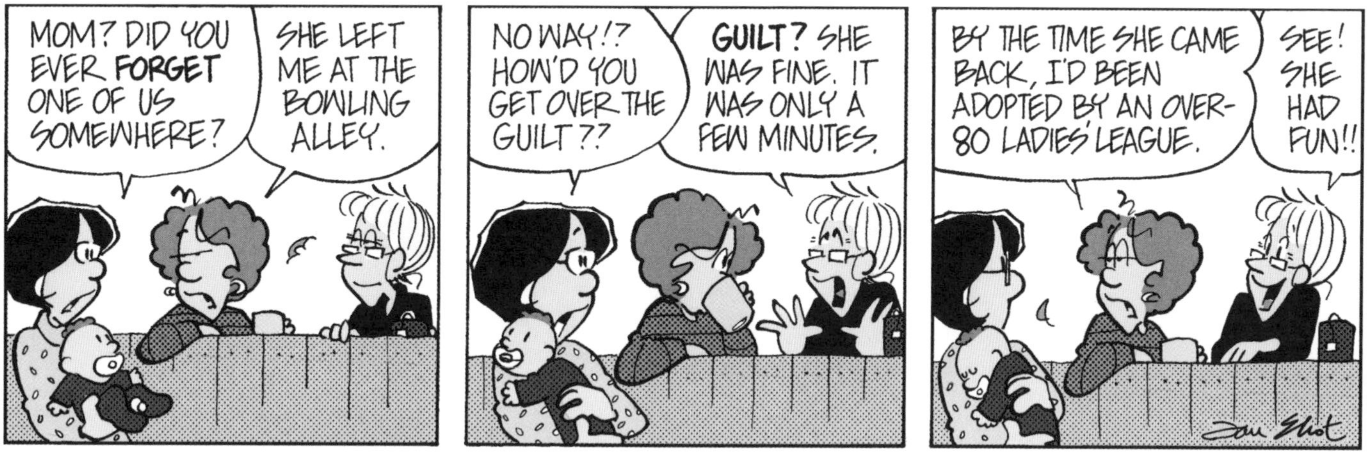
MOM? DID YOU EVER FORGET ONE OF US SOMEWHERE?
SHE LEFT ME AT THE BOWLING ALLEY.
NO WAY!? HOW'D YOU GET OVER THE GUILT??
GUILT? SHE WAS FINE. IT WAS ONLY A FEW MINUTES.
BY THE TIME SHE CAME BACK, I'D BEEN ADOPTED BY AN OVER-80 LADIES' LEAGUE.
SEE! SHE HAD FUN!!

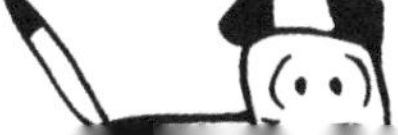

Stone Soup

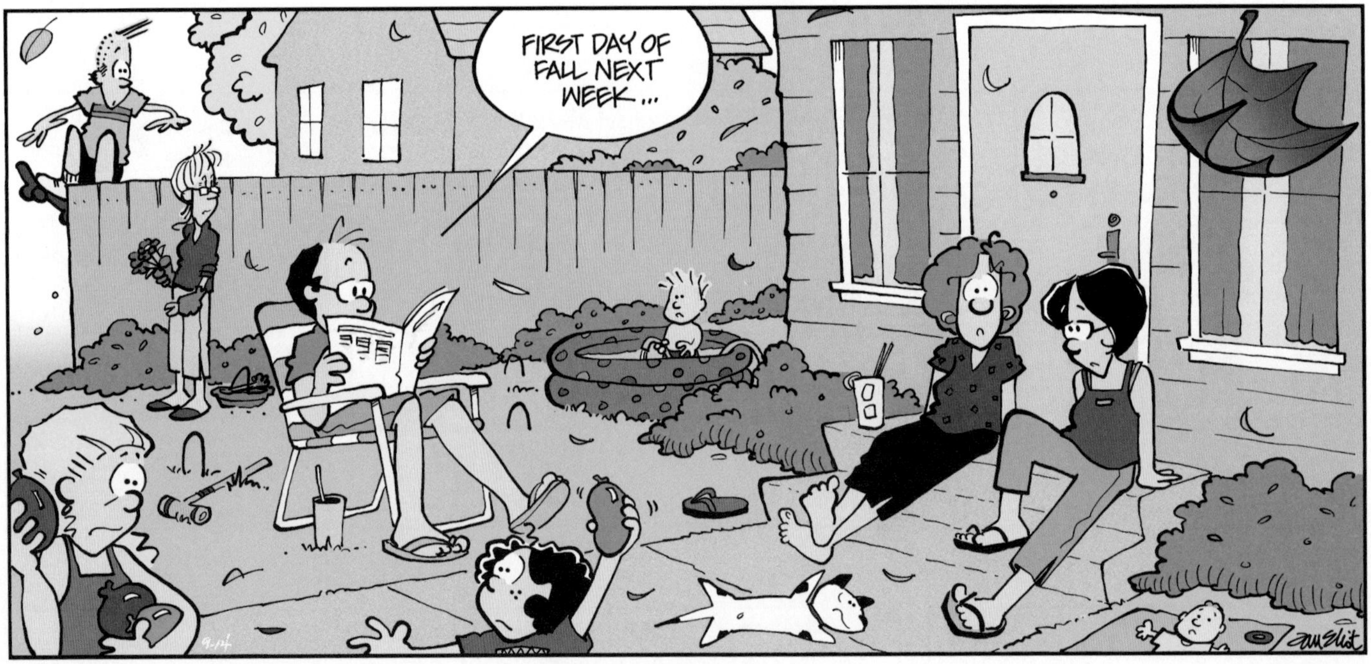
FIRST DAY OF FALL NEXT WEEK...

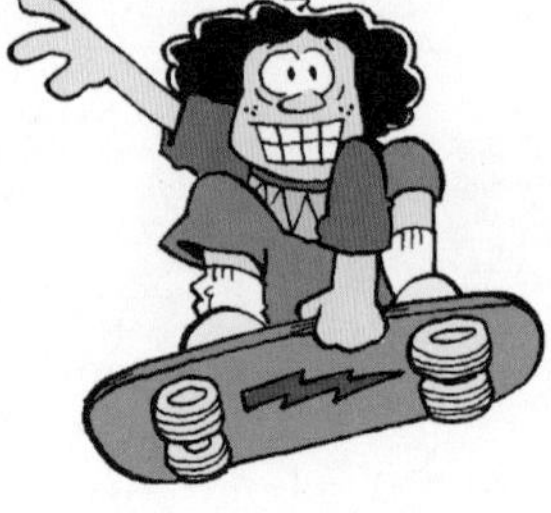

Stone Soup

MUMMY? WOULD YOU LIKE SOME **CHAI**?
WHY... SURE! THANKS!
SSIIIPP
TOAST?
MULTIGRAIN WITH HONEY? MY FAVORITE!!
AND HERE... YOU NEED MORE LIGHT...
MUNCH...?
SIP...?
HOLD IT.
WHY ARE YOU BEING SO NICE TO ME??
I **HIGHLY** RESENT THE IMPLICATION THAT I–
GLARE
FINE! I CONFESS! I'M GUILTY! I'LL PAY YOU ALL BACK!!
"ALL"?
HOLLY MADE US CHAI!

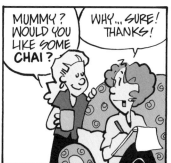

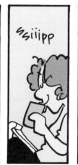

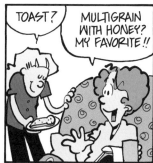

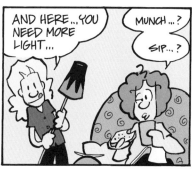

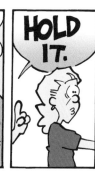

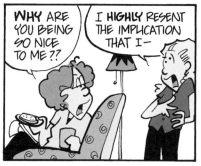

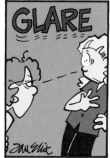

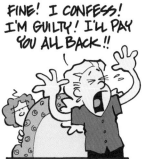

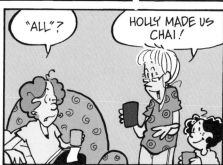

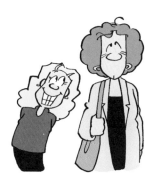

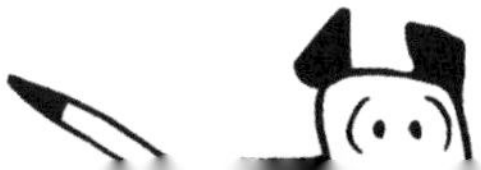

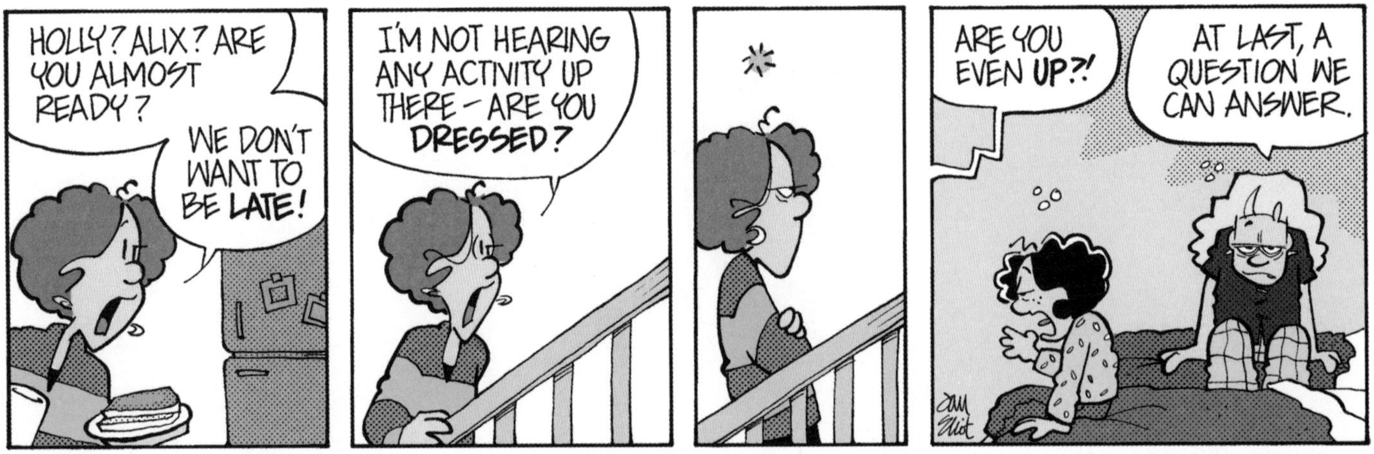
HOLLY? ALIX? ARE YOU ALMOST READY?
WE DON'T WANT TO BE **LATE**!
I'M NOT HEARING ANY ACTIVITY UP THERE – ARE YOU **DRESSED**?
ARE YOU EVEN **UP**?!
AT LAST, A QUESTION WE CAN ANSWER.

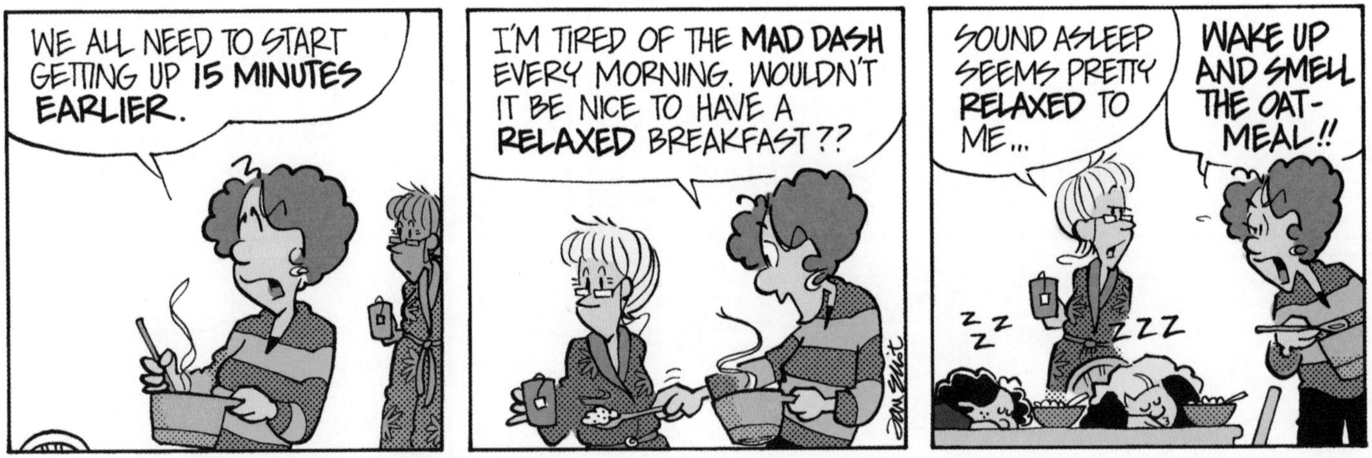
WE ALL NEED TO START GETTING UP **15 MINUTES EARLIER**.
I'M TIRED OF THE **MAD DASH** EVERY MORNING. WOULDN'T IT BE NICE TO HAVE A **RELAXED** BREAKFAST??
ZZZ
ZZZ
SOUND ASLEEP SEEMS PRETTY **RELAXED** TO ME...
WAKE UP AND SMELL THE OAT-MEAL!!

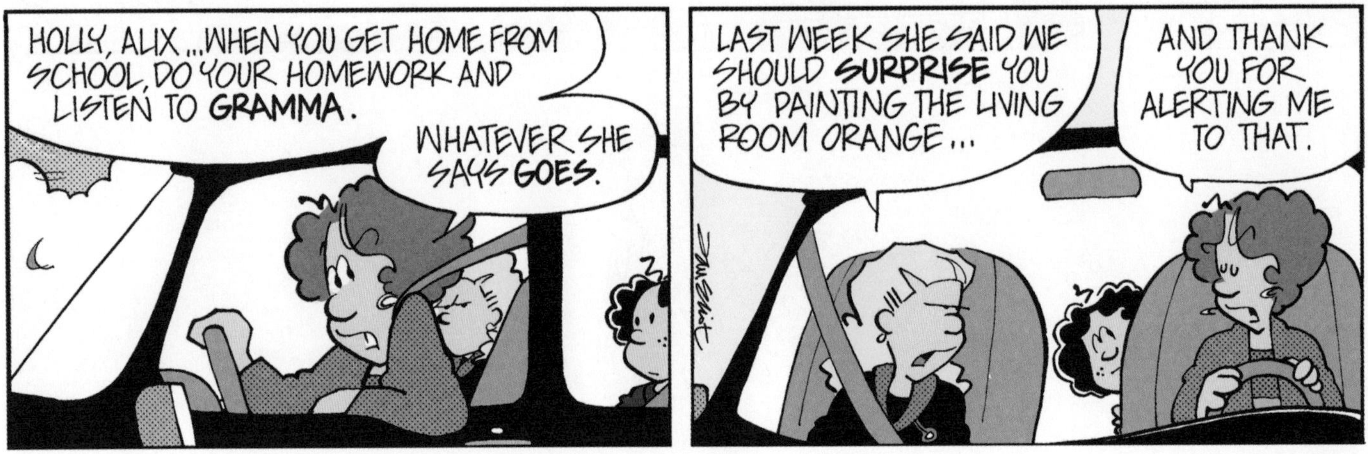
HOLLY, ALIX... WHEN YOU GET HOME FROM SCHOOL, DO YOUR HOMEWORK AND LISTEN TO **GRAMMA**.
WHATEVER SHE SAYS **GOES**.
LAST WEEK SHE SAID WE SHOULD **SURPRISE** YOU BY PAINTING THE LIVING ROOM ORANGE...
AND THANK YOU FOR ALERTING ME TO THAT.

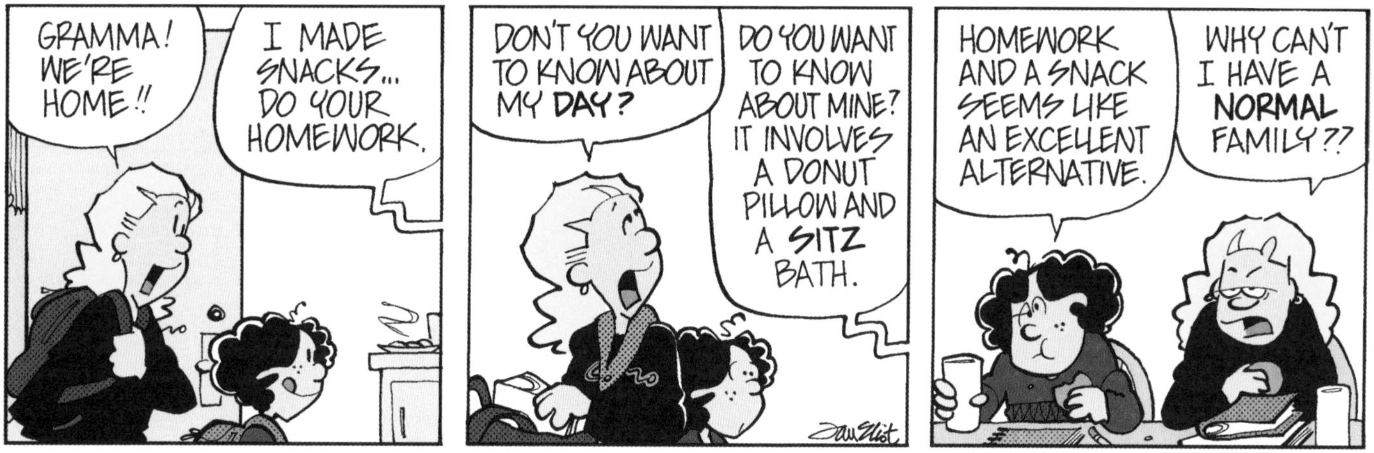
GRAMMA! WE'RE HOME!!
I MADE SNACKS... DO YOUR HOMEWORK.
DON'T YOU WANT TO KNOW ABOUT MY **DAY**?
DO YOU WANT TO KNOW ABOUT MINE? IT INVOLVES A DONUT PILLOW AND A **SITZ** BATH.
HOMEWORK AND A SNACK SEEMS LIKE AN EXCELLENT ALTERNATIVE.
WHY CAN'T I HAVE A **NORMAL** FAMILY??

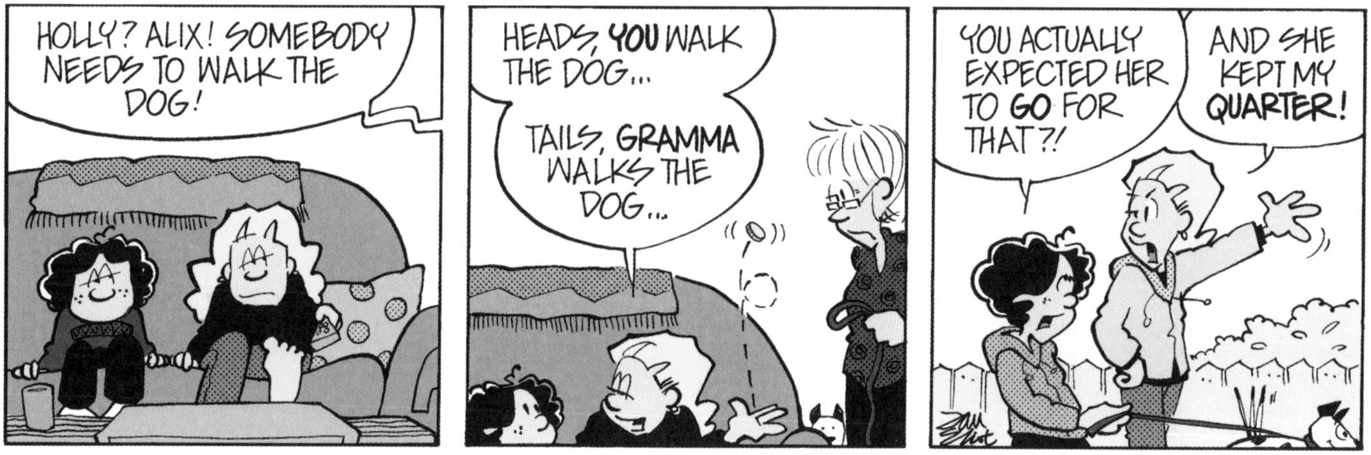
HOLLY? ALIX! SOMEBODY NEEDS TO WALK THE DOG!
HEADS, **YOU** WALK THE DOG...
TAILS, **GRAMMA** WALKS THE DOG...
YOU ACTUALLY EXPECTED HER TO **GO** FOR THAT?!
AND SHE KEPT MY **QUARTER**!

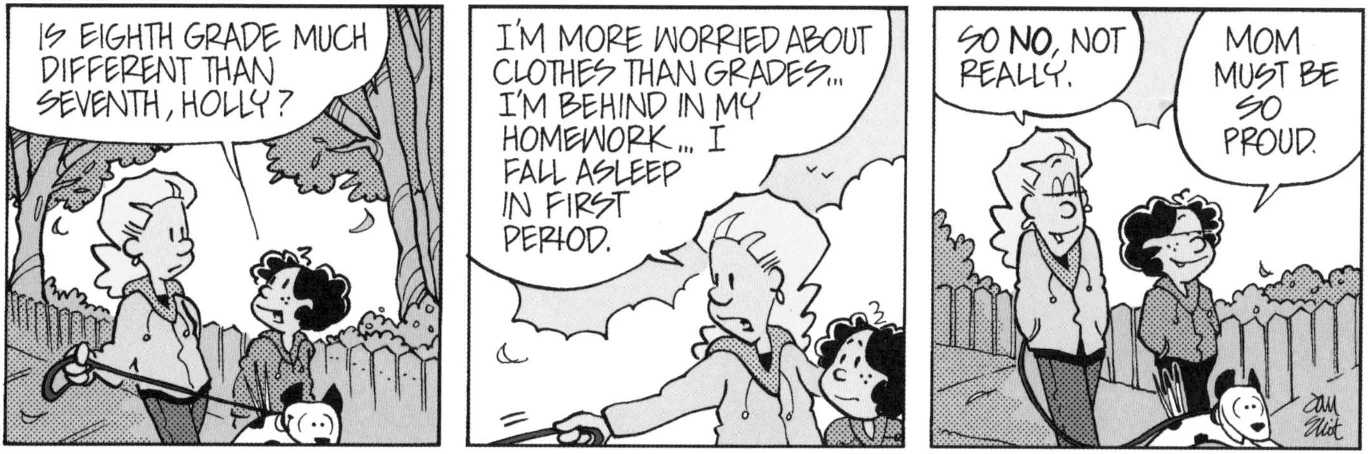
IS EIGHTH GRADE MUCH DIFFERENT THAN SEVENTH, HOLLY?
I'M MORE WORRIED ABOUT CLOTHES THAN GRADES... I'M BEHIND IN MY HOMEWORK... I FALL ASLEEP IN FIRST PERIOD.
SO **NO**, NOT REALLY.
MOM MUST BE SO PROUD.

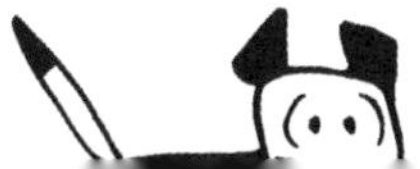

Stone Soup

HOLLY!? WHY ARE YOU WEARING ALL THAT MAKEUP AND PERFUME?

I DIDN'T PUT IT ON!!

THIS LADY IN THE DEPARTMENT STORE PRACTICALLY FORCED ME TO HAVE A MAKE-OVER!!

SHE TRIED TO GET ME TO BUY ALL THIS STUFF — I TOLD HER YOU WOULDN'T APPROVE, BUT SHE SAID SHE HAD A QUOTA TO FILL OR SHE'D BE FIRED!!

I BOUGHT THE EARRINGS TO HELP HER OUT.

I THINK SHE SAID SHE HAD A COUPLE OF KIDS.

YOU CAN KEEP THE EARRINGS, BUT WASH OFF ALL THAT MAKEUP AND (SNIFF) GAWD-AWFUL PERFUME.

OK

MOM'S LETTING YOU KEEP THOSE HUGE EARRINGS??

IT'S ALL IN HOW YOU ASK.

180

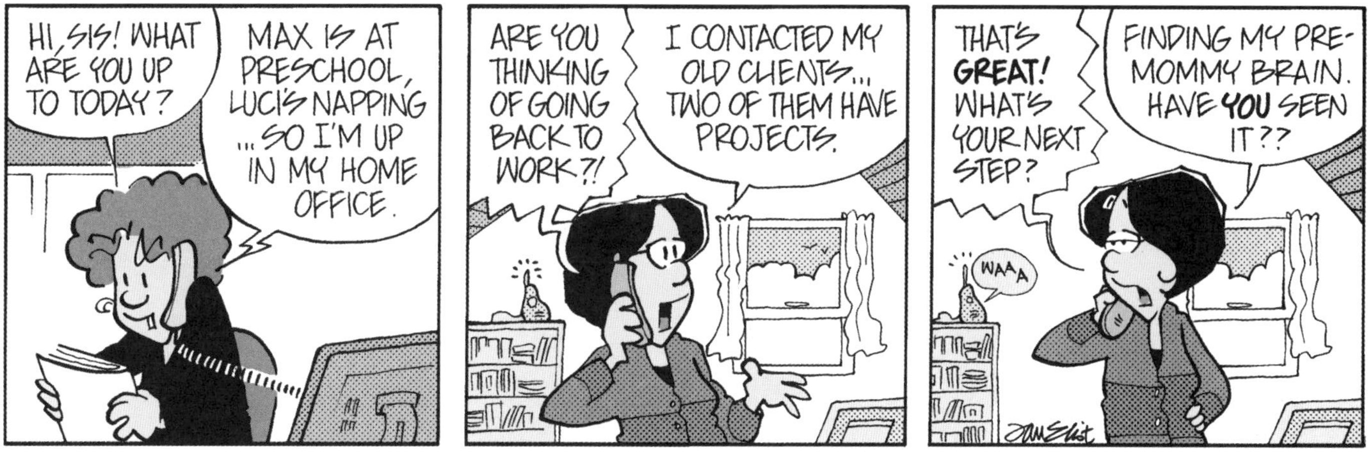
HI, SIS! WHAT ARE YOU UP TO TODAY?
MAX IS AT PRESCHOOL, LUCI'S NAPPING ... SO I'M UP IN MY HOME OFFICE.
ARE YOU THINKING OF GOING BACK TO WORK?!
I CONTACTED MY OLD CLIENTS... TWO OF THEM HAVE PROJECTS.
THAT'S **GREAT!** WHAT'S YOUR NEXT STEP?
FINDING MY PRE-MOMMY BRAIN. HAVE **YOU** SEEN IT??
WAAA

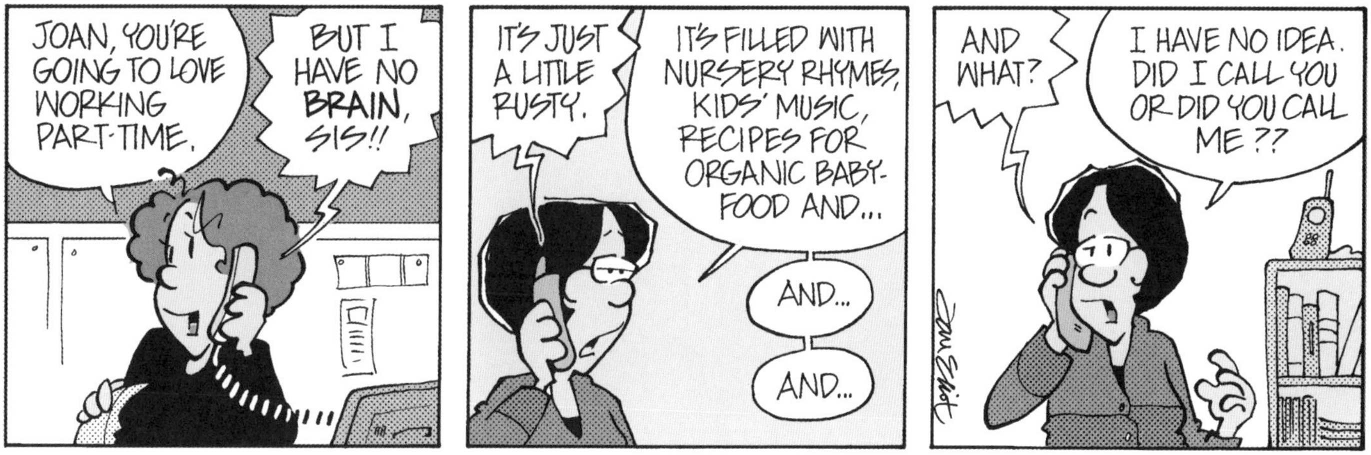
JOAN, YOU'RE GOING TO LOVE WORKING PART-TIME.
BUT I HAVE NO **BRAIN**, SIS!!
IT'S JUST A LITTLE RUSTY.
IT'S FILLED WITH NURSERY RHYMES, KIDS' MUSIC, RECIPES FOR ORGANIC BABY-FOOD AND...
AND...
AND...
AND WHAT?
I HAVE NO IDEA. DID I CALL YOU OR DID YOU CALL ME??

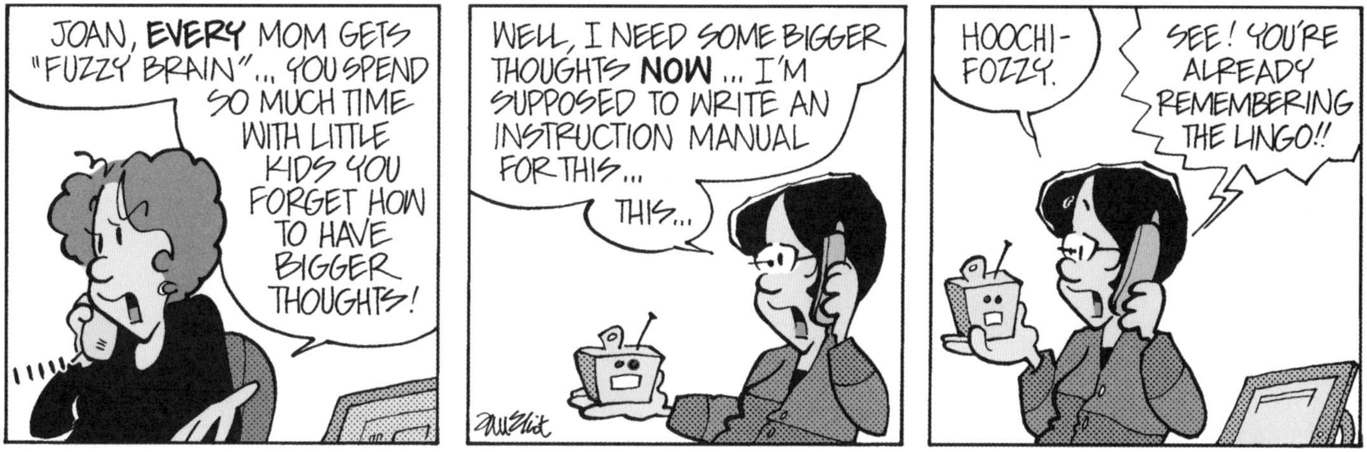
JOAN, **EVERY** MOM GETS "FUZZY BRAIN"... YOU SPEND SO MUCH TIME WITH LITTLE KIDS YOU FORGET HOW TO HAVE BIGGER THOUGHTS!
WELL, I NEED SOME BIGGER THOUGHTS **NOW** ... I'M SUPPOSED TO WRITE AN INSTRUCTION MANUAL FOR THIS...
THIS...
HOOCHI-FOZZY.
SEE! YOU'RE ALREADY REMEMBERING THE LINGO!!

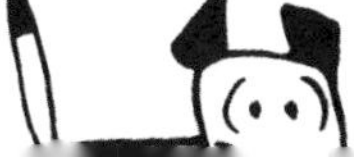

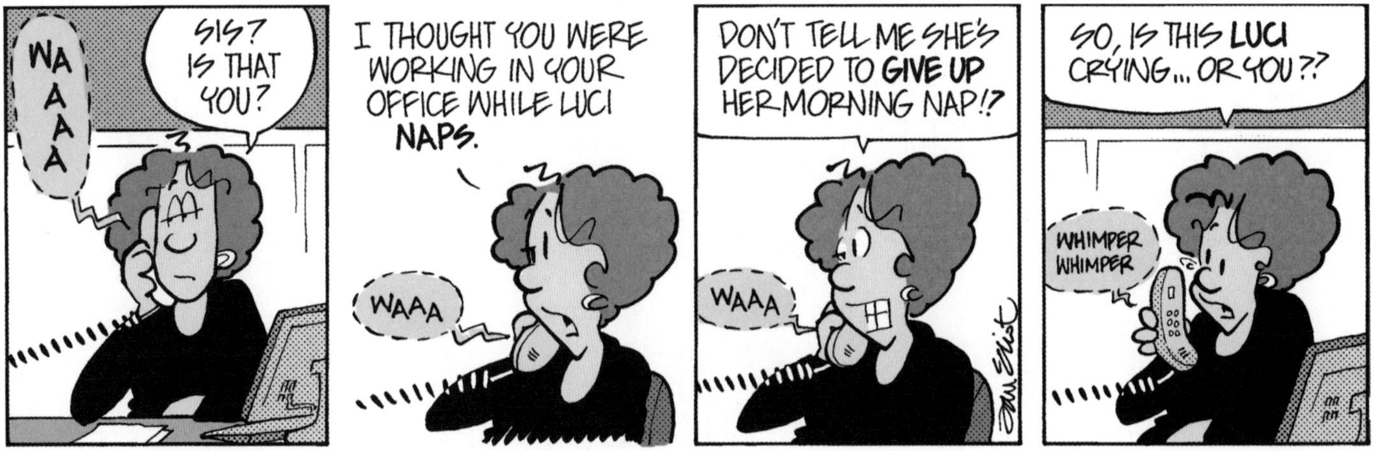
WAAAA
SIS? IS THAT YOU?
I THOUGHT YOU WERE WORKING IN YOUR OFFICE WHILE LUCI **NAPS**.
WAAA
DON'T TELL ME SHE'S DECIDED TO **GIVE UP** HER MORNING NAP!?
WAAA
SO, IS THIS **LUCI** CRYING... OR YOU??
WHIMPER WHIMPER

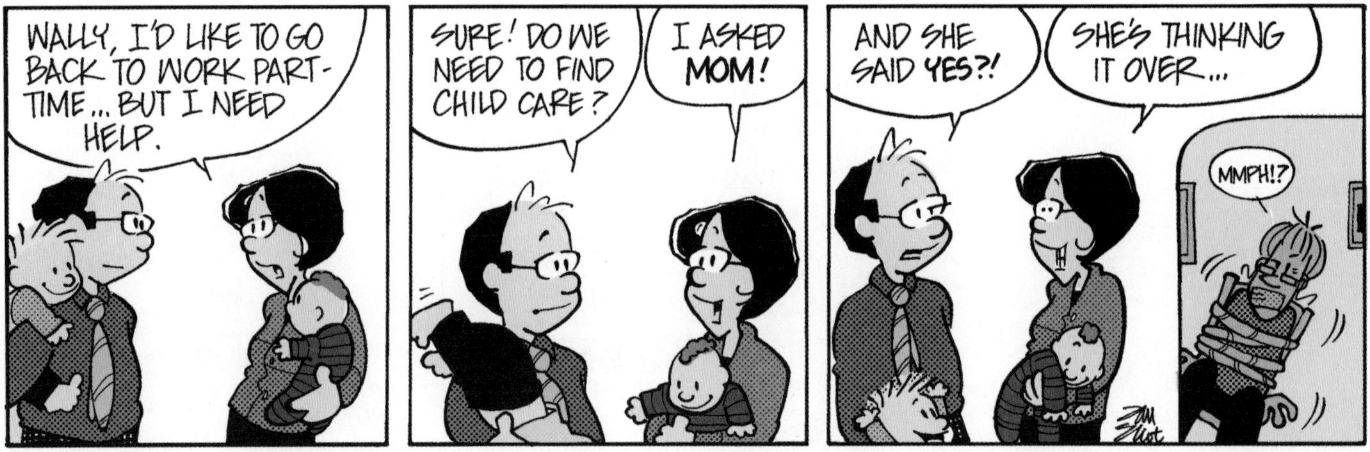
WALLY, I'D LIKE TO GO BACK TO WORK PART-TIME... BUT I NEED HELP.
SURE! DO WE NEED TO FIND CHILD CARE?
I ASKED **MOM**!
AND SHE SAID **YES**?!
SHE'S THINKING IT OVER...
MMPH!?

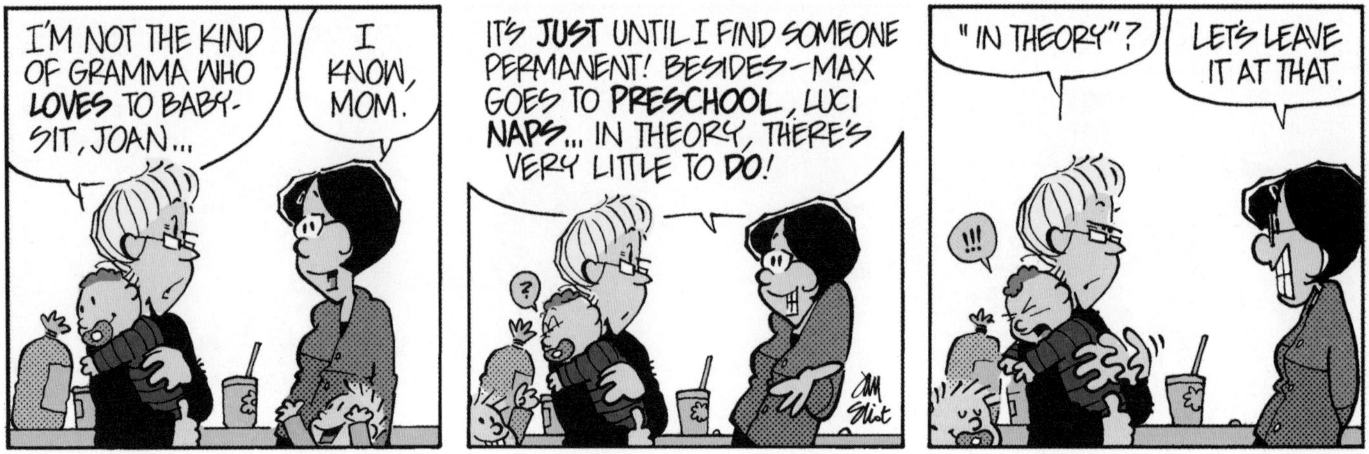
I'M NOT THE KIND OF GRAMMA WHO **LOVES** TO BABY-SIT, JOAN...
I KNOW, MOM.
IT'S **JUST** UNTIL I FIND SOMEONE PERMANENT! BESIDES—MAX GOES TO **PRESCHOOL**, LUCI **NAPS**... IN THEORY, THERE'S VERY LITTLE TO **DO**!
?
"IN THEORY"?
LET'S LEAVE IT AT THAT.
!!!

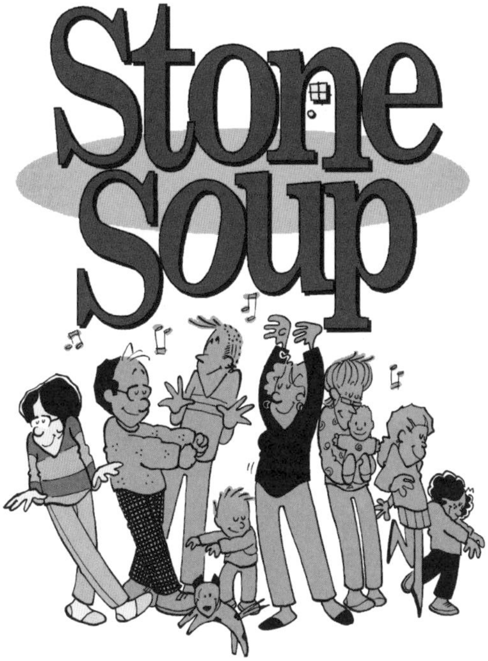
Stone Soup

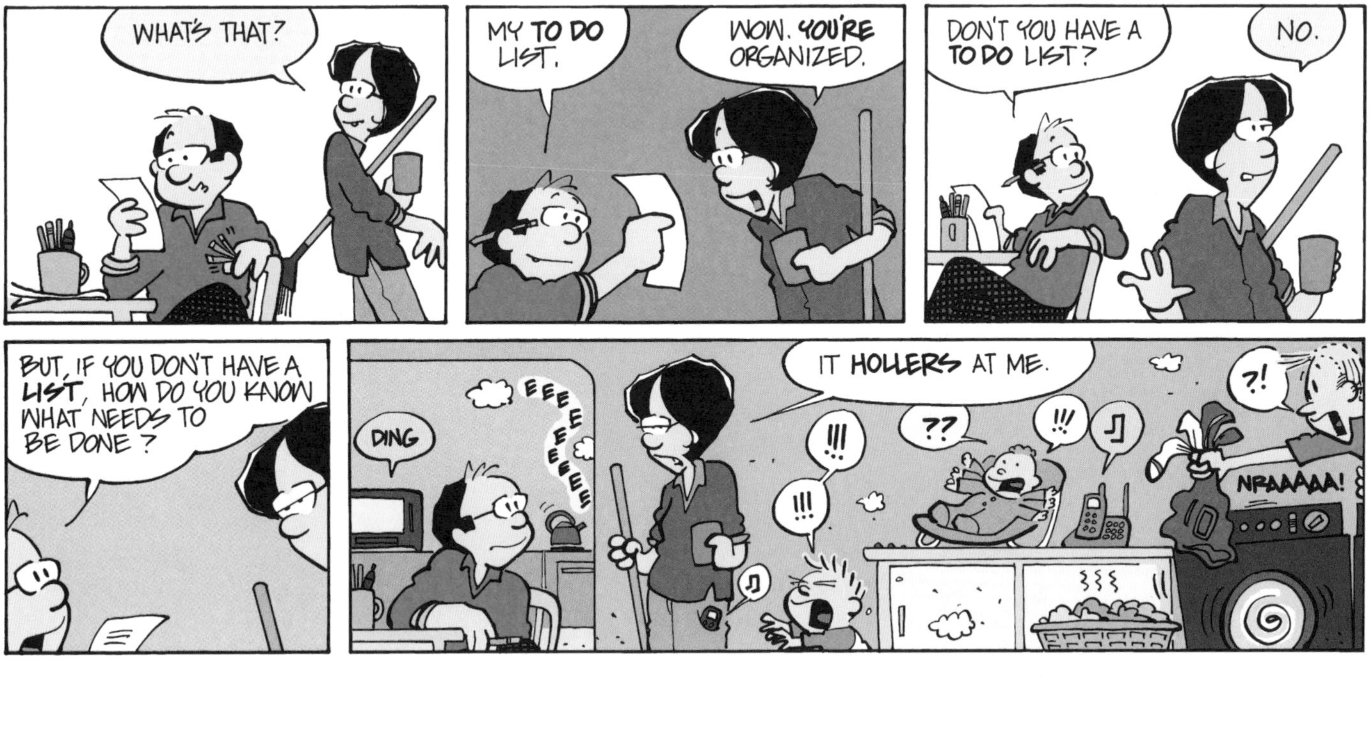
WHAT'S THAT?
MY **TO DO** LIST.
WOW. **YOU'RE** ORGANIZED.
DON'T YOU HAVE A **TO DO** LIST?
NO.
BUT, IF YOU DON'T HAVE A **LIST**, HOW DO YOU KNOW WHAT NEEDS TO BE DONE?
IT **HOLLERS** AT ME.
DING
EEEEEEEEEEE
!!!
!!!
??
!!!
?!
NRAAAAA!

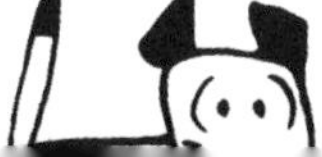

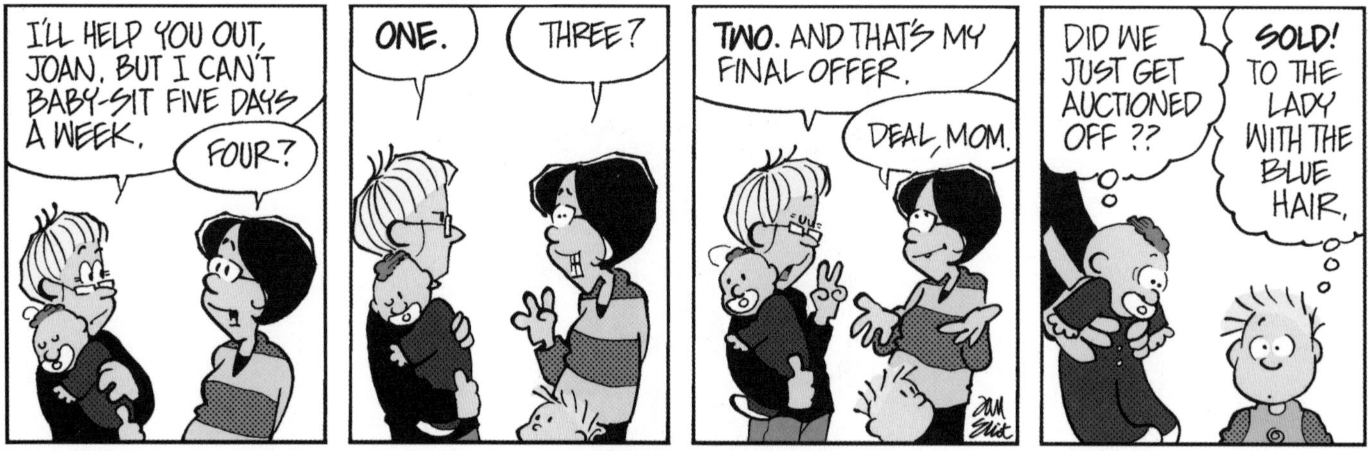
I'LL HELP YOU OUT, JOAN. BUT I CAN'T BABY-SIT FIVE DAYS A WEEK.
FOUR?
ONE.
THREE?
TWO. AND THAT'S MY FINAL OFFER.
DEAL, MOM.
DID WE JUST GET AUCTIONED OFF ??
SOLD! TO THE LADY WITH THE BLUE HAIR.

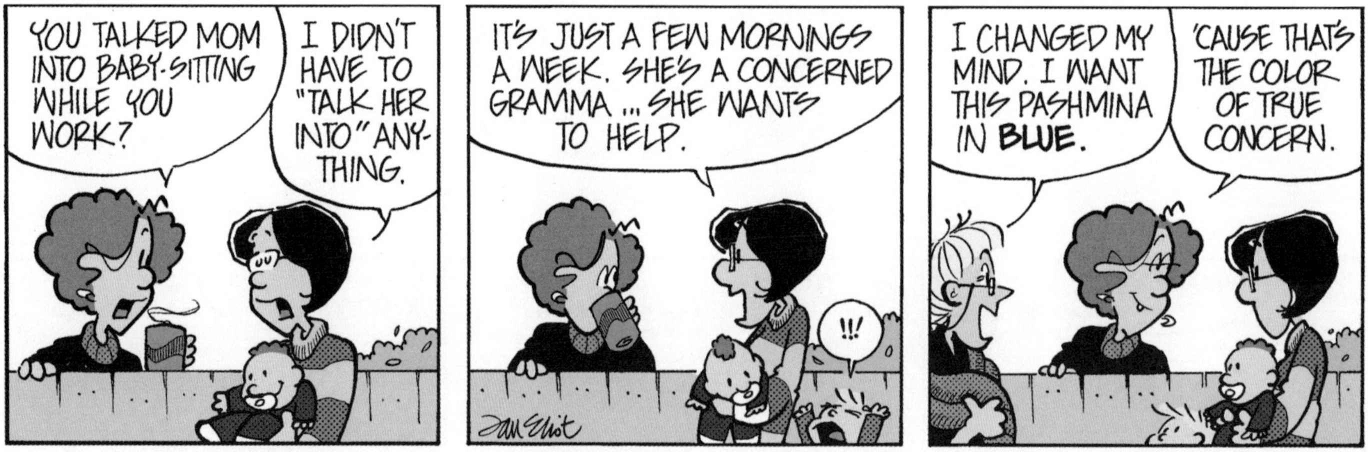
YOU TALKED MOM INTO BABY-SITTING WHILE YOU WORK?
I DIDN'T HAVE TO "TALK HER INTO" ANY-THING.
IT'S JUST A FEW MORNINGS A WEEK. SHE'S A CONCERNED GRAMMA ... SHE WANTS TO HELP.
!!!
I CHANGED MY MIND. I WANT THIS PASHMINA IN BLUE.
'CAUSE THAT'S THE COLOR OF TRUE CONCERN.

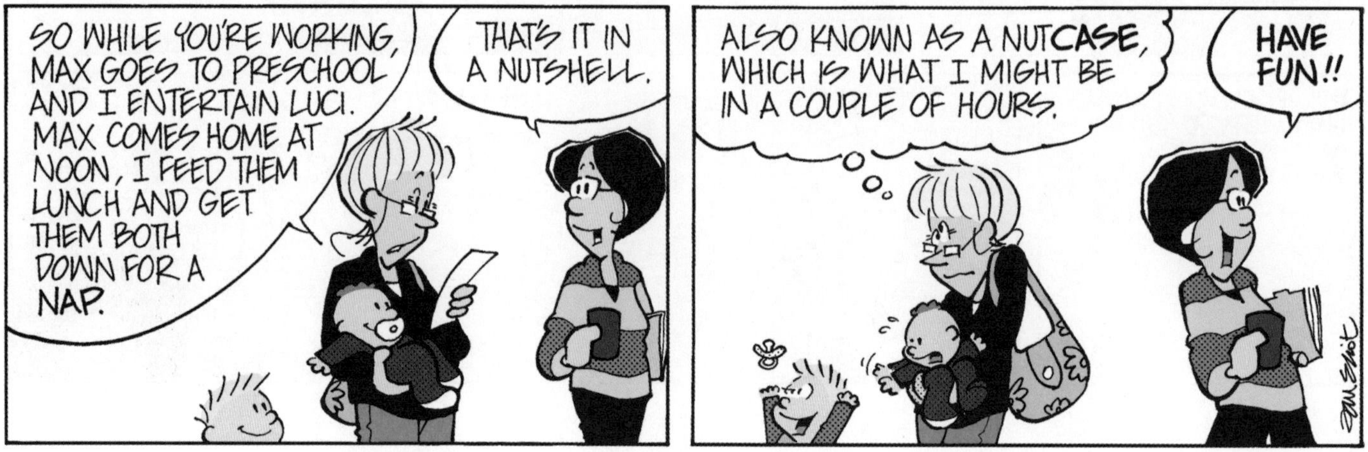
SO WHILE YOU'RE WORKING, MAX GOES TO PRESCHOOL AND I ENTERTAIN LUCI. MAX COMES HOME AT NOON, I FEED THEM LUNCH AND GET THEM BOTH DOWN FOR A NAP.
THAT'S IT IN A NUTSHELL.
ALSO KNOWN AS A NUTCASE, WHICH IS WHAT I MIGHT BE IN A COUPLE OF HOURS.
HAVE FUN!!

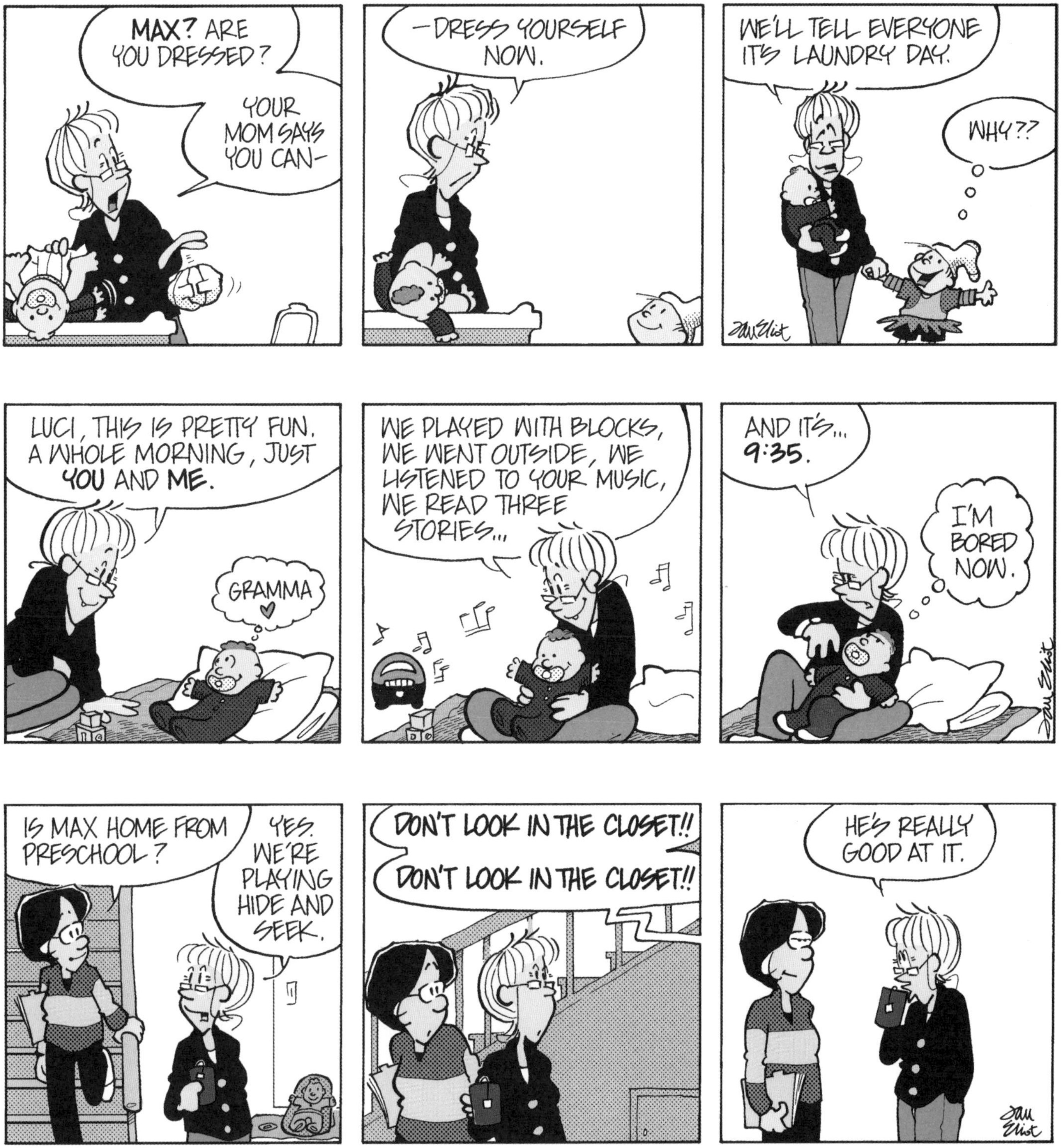
MAX? ARE YOU DRESSED?
YOUR MOM SAYS YOU CAN-
-DRESS YOURSELF NOW.
WE'LL TELL EVERYONE IT'S LAUNDRY DAY.
WHY??
LUCI, THIS IS PRETTY FUN. A WHOLE MORNING, JUST YOU AND ME.
GRAMMA
WE PLAYED WITH BLOCKS, WE WENT OUTSIDE, WE LISTENED TO YOUR MUSIC, WE READ THREE STORIES...
AND IT'S... 9:35.
I'M BORED NOW.
IS MAX HOME FROM PRESCHOOL?
YES. WE'RE PLAYING HIDE AND SEEK.
DON'T LOOK IN THE CLOSET!!
DON'T LOOK IN THE CLOSET!!
HE'S REALLY GOOD AT IT.

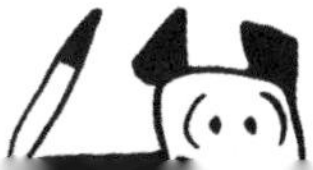

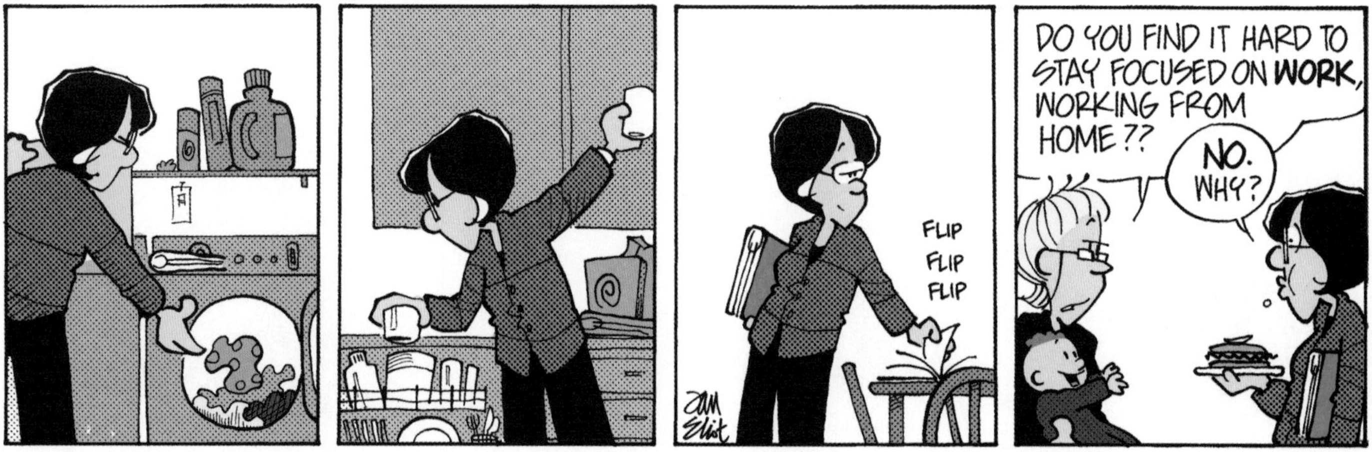
FLIP
FLIP
FLIP
DO YOU FIND IT HARD TO STAY FOCUSED ON **WORK**, WORKING FROM HOME ??
NO. WHY?

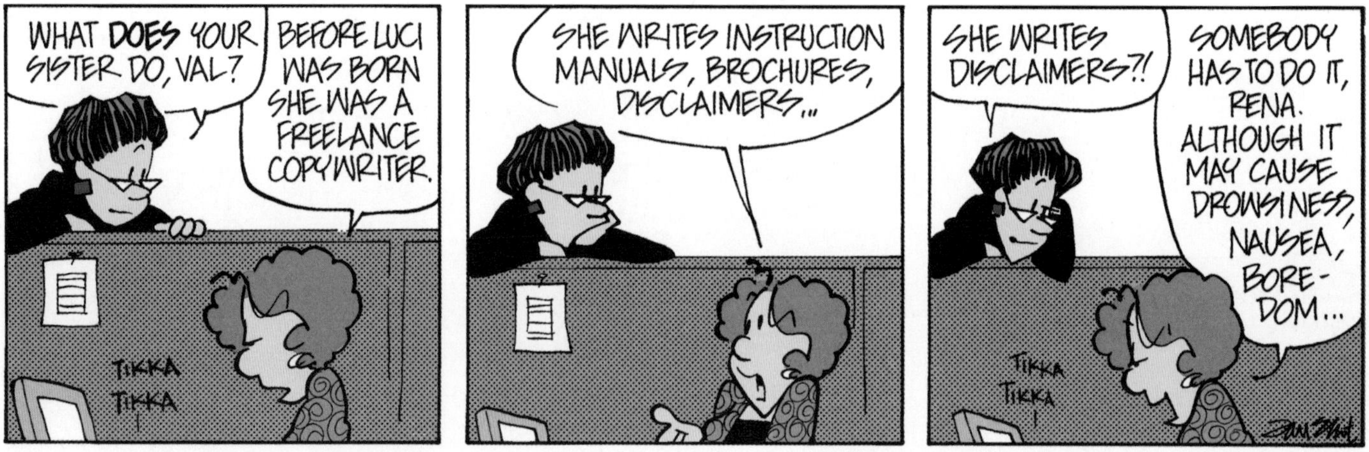
WHAT **DOES** YOUR SISTER DO, VAL?
BEFORE LUCI WAS BORN SHE WAS A FREELANCE COPYWRITER.
TIKKA
TIKKA
SHE WRITES INSTRUCTION MANUALS, BROCHURES, DISCLAIMERS...
SHE WRITES DISCLAIMERS?!
SOMEBODY HAS TO DO IT, RENA. ALTHOUGH IT MAY CAUSE DROWSINESS, NAUSEA, BORE-DOM...
TIKKA
TIKKA

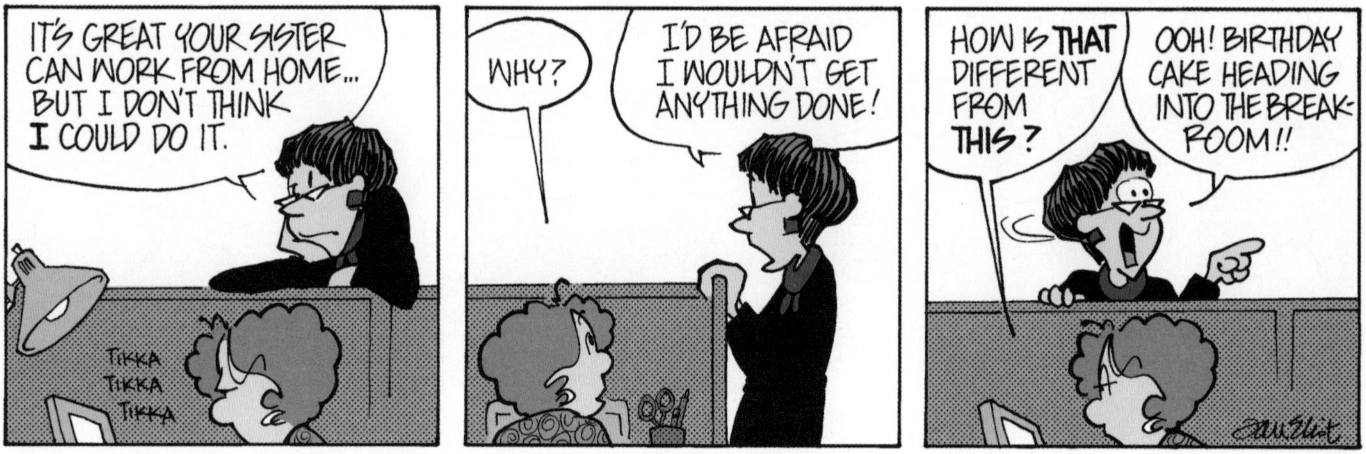
IT'S GREAT YOUR SISTER CAN WORK FROM HOME... BUT I DON'T THINK **I** COULD DO IT.
TIKKA
TIKKA
TIKKA
WHY?
I'D BE AFRAID I WOULDN'T GET ANYTHING DONE!
HOW IS **THAT** DIFFERENT FROM **THIS**?
OOH! BIRTHDAY CAKE HEADING INTO THE BREAK-ROOM!!

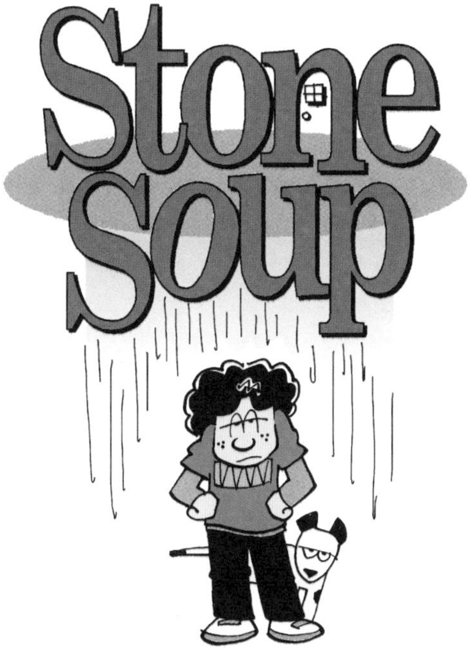
Stone Soup

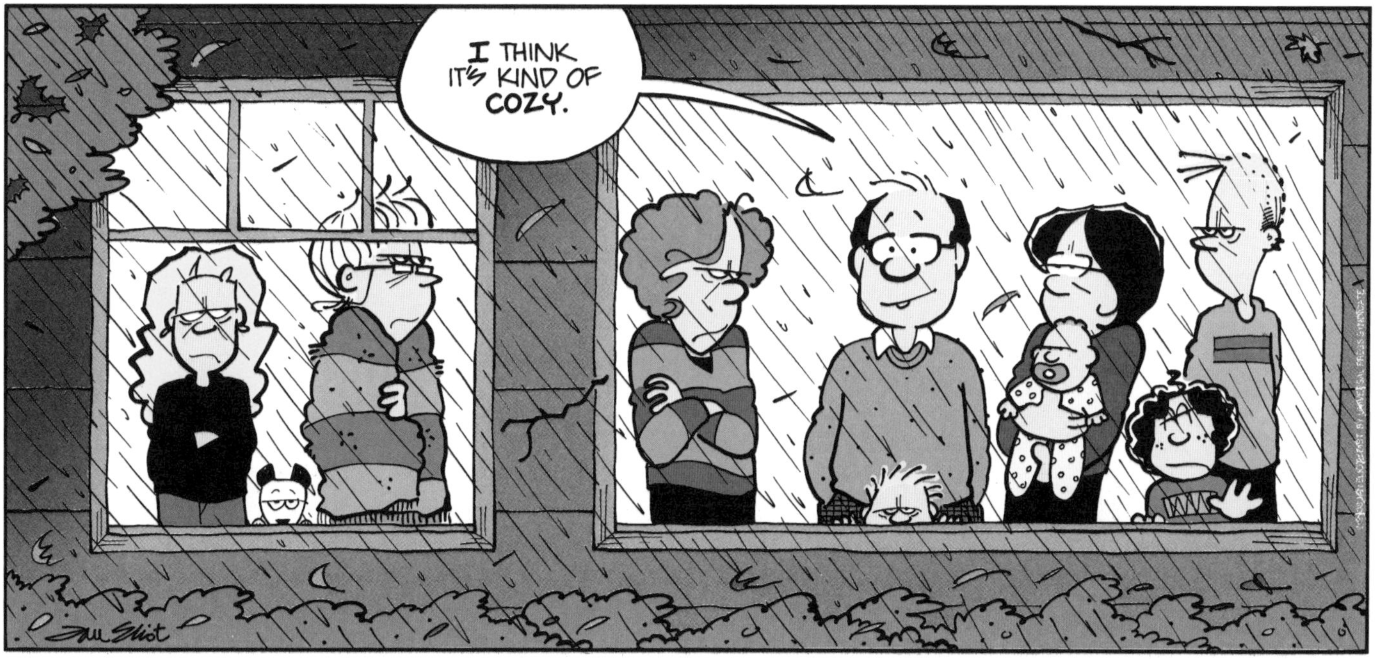
I THINK IT'S KIND OF COZY.

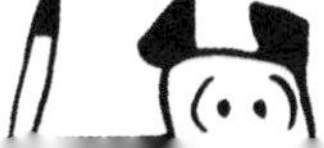

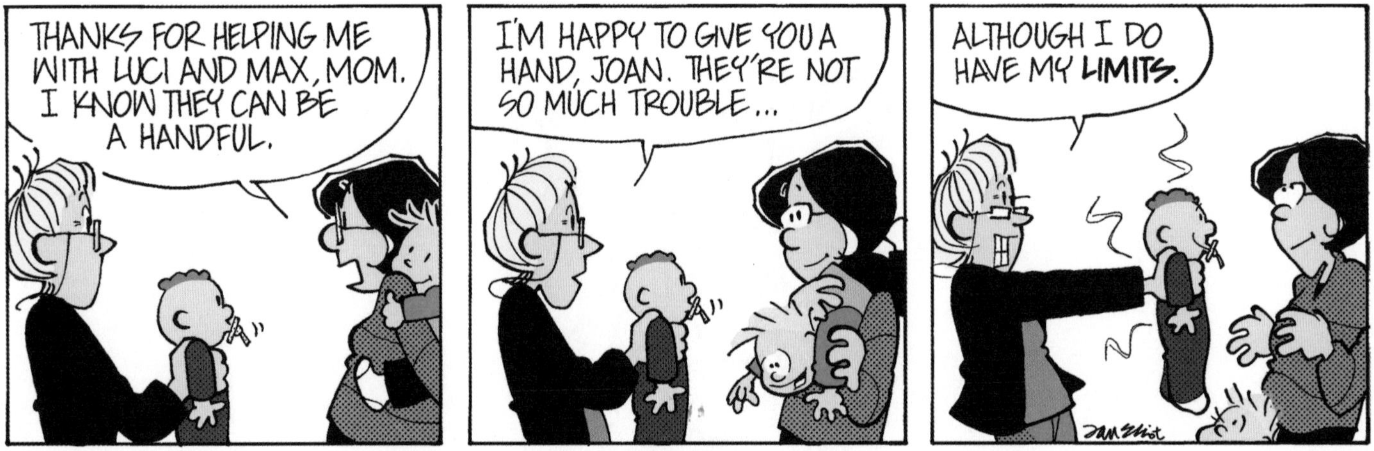
THANKS FOR HELPING ME WITH LUCI AND MAX, MOM. I KNOW THEY CAN BE A HANDFUL.
I'M HAPPY TO GIVE YOU A HAND, JOAN. THEY'RE NOT SO MUCH TROUBLE...
ALTHOUGH I DO HAVE MY **LIMITS**.

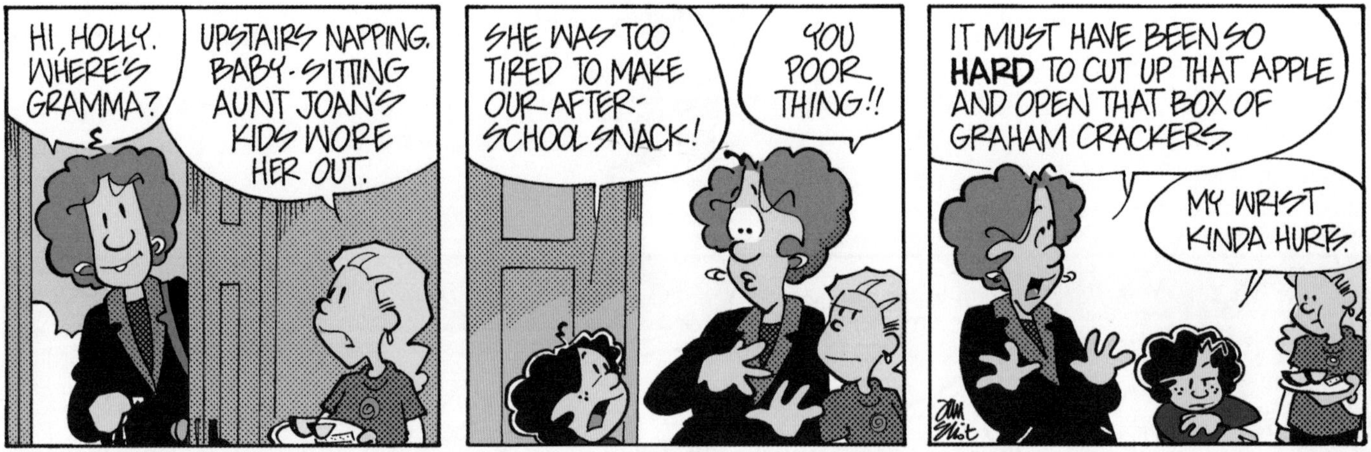
HI, HOLLY. WHERE'S GRAMMA?
UPSTAIRS NAPPING. BABY-SITTING AUNT JOAN'S KIDS WORE HER OUT.
SHE WAS TOO TIRED TO MAKE OUR AFTER-SCHOOL SNACK!
YOU POOR THING!!
IT MUST HAVE BEEN SO **HARD** TO CUT UP THAT APPLE AND OPEN THAT BOX OF GRAHAM CRACKERS.
MY WRIST KINDA HURTS.

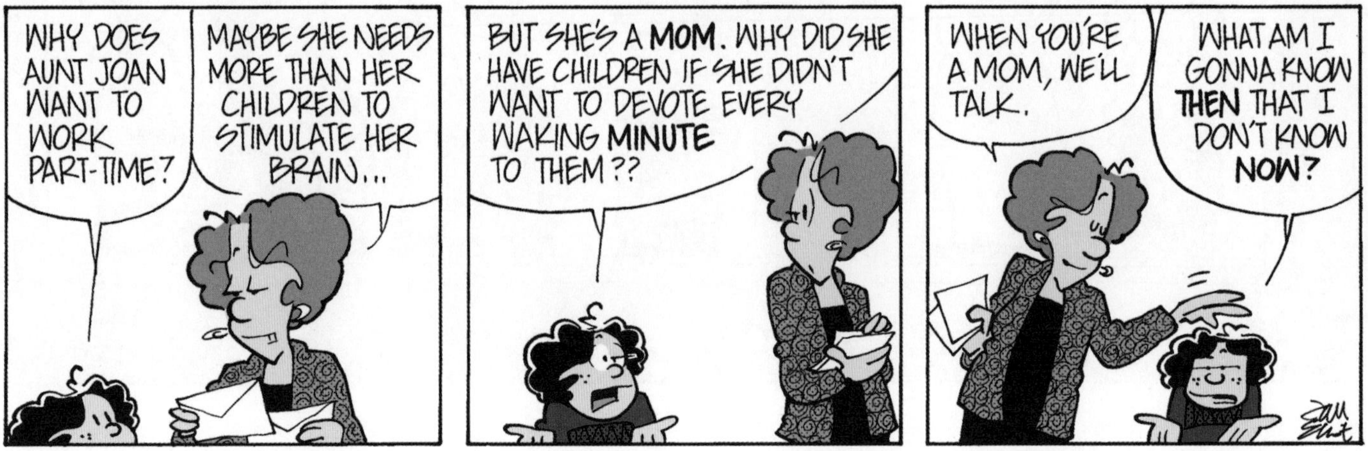
WHY DOES AUNT JOAN WANT TO WORK PART-TIME?
MAYBE SHE NEEDS MORE THAN HER CHILDREN TO STIMULATE HER BRAIN...
BUT SHE'S A **MOM**. WHY DID SHE HAVE CHILDREN IF SHE DIDN'T WANT TO DEVOTE EVERY WAKING **MINUTE** TO THEM??
WHEN YOU'RE A MOM, WE'LL TALK.
WHAT AM I GONNA KNOW **THEN** THAT I DON'T KNOW **NOW**?

Stone Soup

YOU KNOW, YOU COULD HELP OUT MORE!

IT'S NOT **HARD** TO SEE WHAT NEEDS TO BE DONE.

JUST LOOK AROUND! DISHES, LAUNDRY,... TAKE YOUR PICK.

IS ANY OF THIS EVEN **REGISTERING??**

MAYBE ... IT'S HARD TO FOCUS WHEN YOU'RE IN MY LIGHT.

IT SEEMED LIKE A GOOD IDEA AT THE TIME.

There are nine other *Stone Soup* collections, available through your favorite local or online bookstores, or at www.stonesoupcartoons.com.

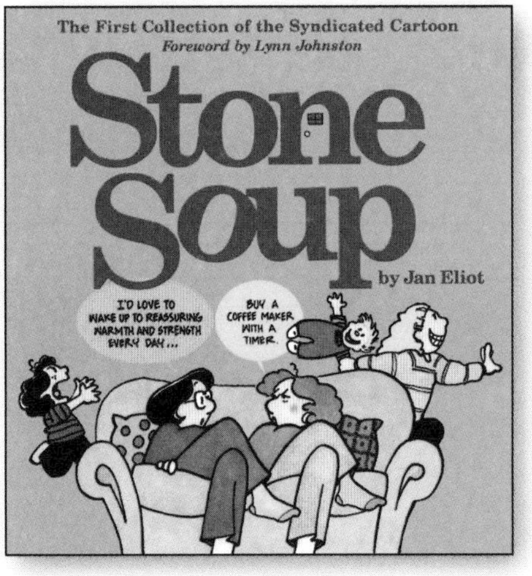
The First Collection of the Syndicated Cartoon
Foreword by Lynn Johnston
Stone Soup
by Jan Eliot
I'D LOVE TO WAKE UP TO REASSURING WARMTH AND STRENGTH EVERY DAY...
BUY A COFFEE MAKER WITH A TIMER.

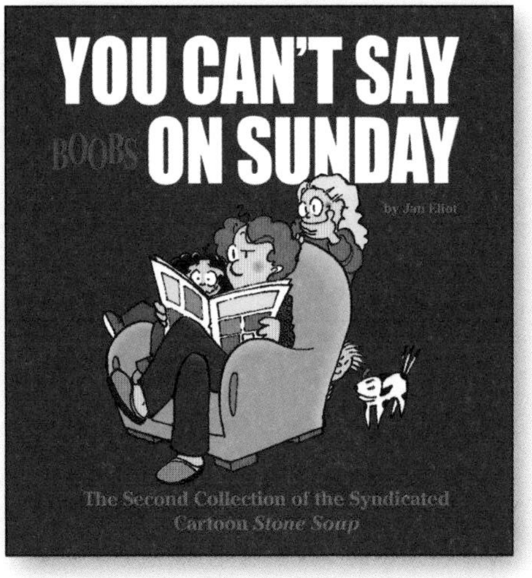
YOU CAN'T SAY
BOOBS ON SUNDAY
by Jan Eliot
The Second Collection of the Syndicated Cartoon Stone Soup

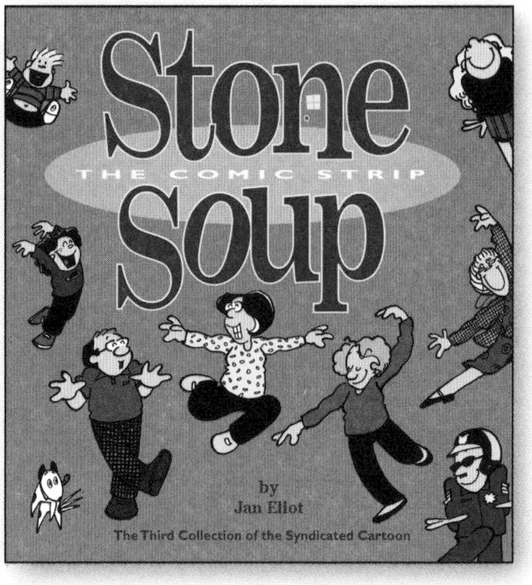
Stone
THE COMIC STRIP
Soup
by
Jan Eliot
The Third Collection of the Syndicated Cartoon

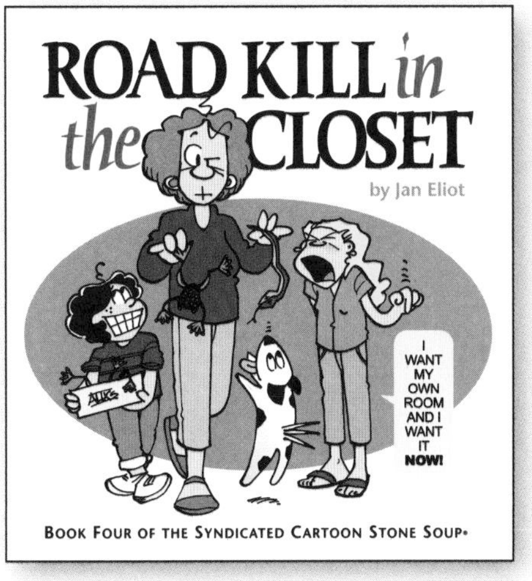
ROAD KILL in the CLOSET
by Jan Eliot
I WANT MY OWN ROOM AND I WANT IT NOW!
BOOK FOUR OF THE SYNDICATED CARTOON STONE SOUP®

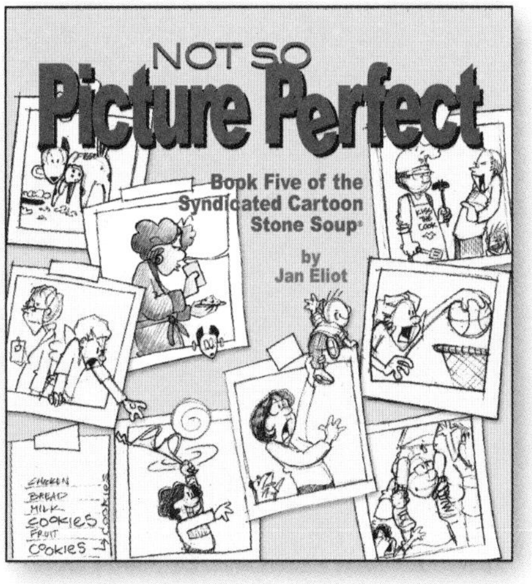
NOT SO
Picture Perfect
Book Five of the Syndicated Cartoon Stone Soup®
by
Jan Eliot
CHICKEN
BREAD
MILK
COOKIES
FRUIT
COOKIES

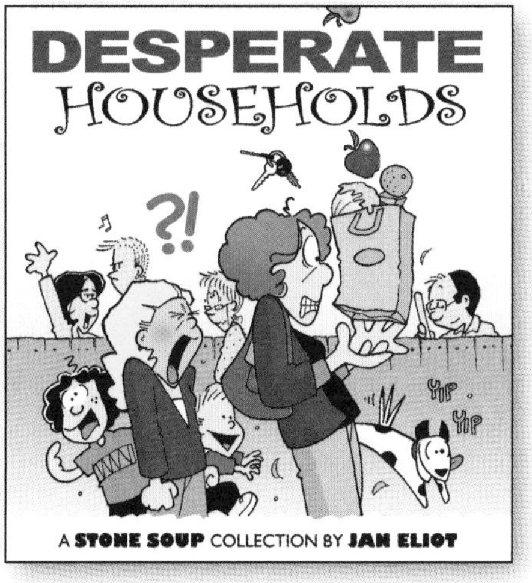
DESPERATE
HOUSEHOLDS
?!
YIP
YIP
A STONE SOUP COLLECTION BY JAN ELIOT

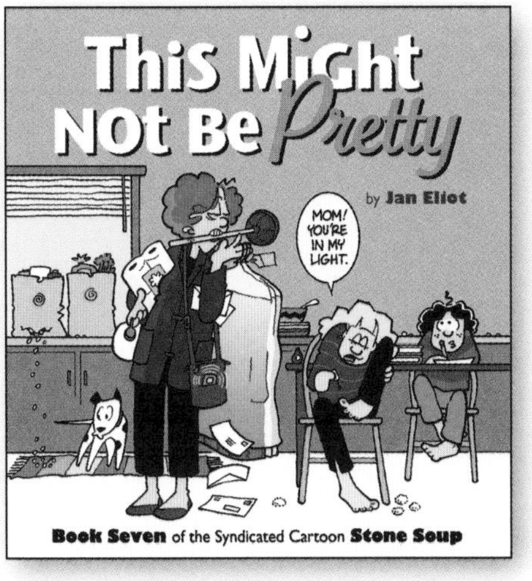
This Might
Not Be Pretty
by Jan Eliot
MOM! YOU'RE IN MY LIGHT.
Book Seven of the Syndicated Cartoon Stone Soup

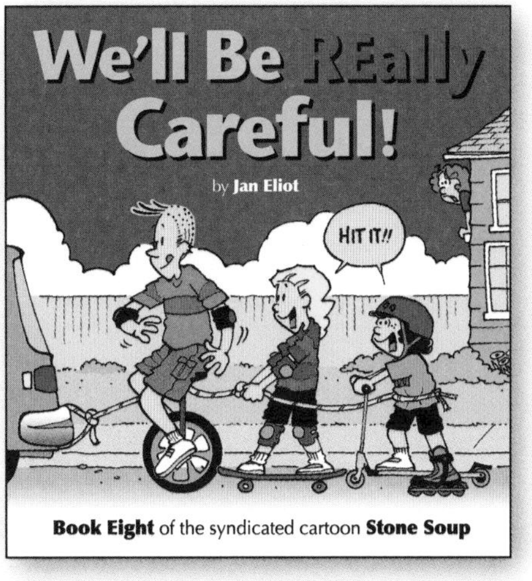
We'll Be REally
Careful!
by Jan Eliot
HIT IT!!
Book Eight of the syndicated cartoon Stone Soup

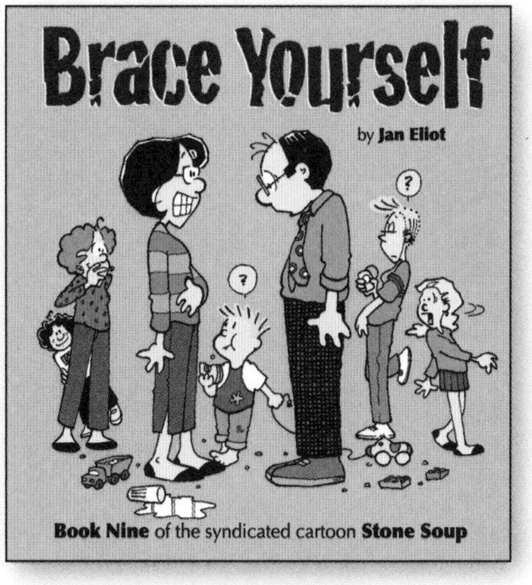
Brace Yourself
by Jan Eliot
?
?
Book Nine of the syndicated cartoon Stone Soup

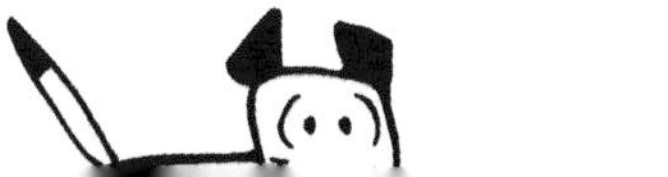